VOLUME FORTY SEVEN

Advances in
CHILD DEVELOPMENT
AND BEHAVIOR
The Role of Gender in Educational
Contexts and Outcomes

ADVANCES IN CHILD DEVELOPMENT AND BEHAVIOR

Series Editor

JANETTE B. BENSON

*Morgridge College of Education,
Department of Psychology,
University of Denver,
Denver, Colorado, USA*

VOLUME FORTY SEVEN

Advances in
CHILD DEVELOPMENT AND BEHAVIOR
The Role of Gender in Educational Contexts and Outcomes

Edited by

LYNN S. LIBEN
*Department of Psychology,
The Pennsylvania State University,
University Park, Pennsylvania, USA*

REBECCA S. BIGLER
*Department of Psychology,
University of Texas at Austin,
Austin, Texas, USA*

AMSTERDAM • BOSTON • HEIDELBERG • LONDON
NEW YORK • OXFORD • PARIS • SAN DIEGO
SAN FRANCISCO • SINGAPORE • SYDNEY • TOKYO
Academic Press is an imprint of Elsevier

Academic Press is an imprint of Elsevier
525 B Street, Suite 1800, San Diego, CA 92101-4495, USA
225 Wyman Street, Waltham, MA 02451, USA
The Boulevard, Langford Lane, Kidlington, Oxford, OX5 1GB, UK
32 Jamestown Road, London NW1 7BY, UK

First edition 2014

Copyright © 2014, Elsevier Inc. All Rights Reserved.

No part of this publication may be reproduced or transmitted in any form or by any means, electronic or mechanical, including photocopying, recording, or any information storage and retrieval system, without permission in writing from the publisher. Details on how to seek permission, further information about the Publisher's permissions policies and our arrangements with organizations such as the Copyright Clearance Center and the Copyright Licensing Agency, can be found at our website: www.elsevier.com/permissions.

This book and the individual contributions contained in it are protected under copyright by the Publisher (other than as may be noted herein).

Notices
Knowledge and best practice in this field are constantly changing. As new research and experience broaden our understanding, changes in research methods, professional practices, or medical treatment may become necessary.

Practitioners and researchers must always rely on their own experience and knowledge in evaluating and using any information, methods, compounds, or experiments described herein. In using such information or methods they should be mindful of their own safety and the safety of others, including parties for whom they have a professional responsibility.

To the fullest extent of the law, neither the Publisher nor the authors, contributors, or editors, assume any liability for any injury and/or damage to persons or property as a matter of products liability, negligence or otherwise, or from any use or operation of any methods, products, instructions, or ideas contained in the material herein.

ISBN: 978-0-12-411582-8
ISSN: 0065-2407 (Series)

For information on all Academic Press publications
visit our website at store.elsevier.com

CONTENTS

Contributors   ix
Preface   xi

1. Motivation in Educational Contexts: Does Gender Matter?   1
Ruth Butler

1. Introduction   2
2. Theoretical Frameworks: Early and Contemporary Approaches   4
3. A Question of Confidence? Gender and Perceptions of Competence and Control   8
4. Proving and Improving: Gender and Motives for Evaluation   15
5. Achievement Goals   20
6. Achievement and Social Goals, Values, and Interests   23
7. Social Influences   29
8. Conclusions   32
References   35

2. Gender-Related Academic and Occupational Interests and Goals   43
Jennifer Petersen and Janet Shibley Hyde

1. Theoretical Frameworks   45
2. Gender Similarities and Differences in Academic Ability and Dispositions   49
3. Gender Differences in Occupational Interests and Goals   55
4. Factors that may Shape Gendered Occupational Goals   61
5. Conclusions   71
References   72

3. Developmental Interventions to Address the STEM Gender Gap: Exploring Intended and Unintended Consequences   77
Lynn S. Liben and Emily F. Coyle

1. Introduction   78
2. Documenting the STEM Gender Gap   79
3. Developmental Mechanisms and a Taxonomy of STEM Intervention Goals   85
4. Illustrations of STEM Interventions   94
5. Conclusions and Recommendations   105
References   111

4. Physical Education, Sports, and Gender in Schools   117
Melinda A. Solmon

1. Introduction   117
2. Historical Overview   121
3. Curricular Issues   125
4. Gender and Motivation to be Physically Active   128
5. Fitness Testing   134
6. Social Construction of Bodily Meanings   138
7. Creating Equitable Climates in Physical Education   140
8. Education and Sport   144
9. Conclusions and Implications   146
References   147

5. Gendered-Peer Relationships in Educational Contexts   151
Carol Lynn Martin, Richard A. Fabes, and Laura D. Hanish

1. Introduction   152
2. Children's Gender Segregation   154
3. The Influence of Gendered-Peer Relationships on Children's Development   159
4. Gender Segregation in School Environments   165
5. The Role of the Child in Selecting Gendered-Peer Environments   170
6. Implications of Gender Segregation for Aggressive and Cooperative Behaviors   174
7. Conclusions and Future Directions   180
Acknowledgments   181
References   181

6. Sexism in Schools   189
Campbell Leaper and Christia Spears Brown

1. Overview of Types of Sexism   190
2. Perpetrators of Sexism   192
3. Gender Biases in School Achievement   197
4. Sexual Harassment in School   202
5. Awareness of Sexism and Coping   204
6. Reducing Sexism in Schools   209
7. Conclusions   213
References   214

7. Analysis and Evaluation of the Rationales for Single-Sex Schooling   225
Rebecca S. Bigler, Amy Roberson Hayes, and Lynn S. Liben

1. Introduction   226
2. Brief History of the Rationales for Single-Sex Schooling in the United States   226
3. Analysis and Evaluation of Contemporary Rationales for Single-Sex Schooling   228
4. Conclusions and Recommendations   252
References   254

8. Factors Affecting Academic Achievement Among Sexual Minority and Gender-Variant Youth   261
V. Paul Poteat, Jillian R. Scheer, and Ethan H. Mereish

1. Introduction   262
2. Theoretical Models for Understanding Academic Disparities   264
3. Evidence of Sexual Orientation-Based Academic Disparities   267
4. Processes and Consequences of Victimization   269
5. Additional Influences on Student Outcomes   276
6. Programming and Policy   280
7. Conclusions   293
References   294

9. Framing Black Boys: Parent, Teacher, and Student Narratives of the Academic Lives of Black Boys   301
Stephanie J. Rowley, Latisha Ross, Fantasy T. Lozada, Amber Williams, Adrian Gale, and Beth Kurtz-Costes

1. Introduction   302
2. The Peril and Promise of Black Boys   303
3. Black Boys: A Social Problem   311
4. Black Boys: Aggressive and Scary, Never Victims, Never Scared   314
5. Black Boys: Unteachable and Undeserving   315
6. Academic Identification   317
7. Cool-Pose Theory   318
8. Conclusions   323
References   327

10. Creating Developmentally Auspicious School Environments for African American Boys — 333
Oscar A. Barbarin, Lisa Chinn, and Yamanda F. Wright

1. Overview	334
2. Challenges in Educating African American Boys	334
3. Practices to Create Developmentally Auspicious School Environments	345
4. Single-Sex Schools: A Means of Rescuing African American Boys?	353
5. Conclusions and Future Directions	356
References	359

Author Index — *367*
Subject Index — *387*
Contents of Previous Volumes — *407*

CONTRIBUTORS

Oscar A. Barbarin
Department of Psychology, Tulane University, New Orleans, Louisiana, USA

Rebecca S. Bigler
Department of Psychology, University of Texas at Austin, Austin, Texas, USA

Christia Spears Brown
Department of Psychology, University of Kentucky, Lexington, Kentucky, USA

Ruth Butler
School of Education, Hebrew University of Jerusalem, Mt. Scopus, Jerusalem, Israel

Lisa Chinn
Department of Psychology, Tulane University, New Orleans, Louisiana, USA

Emily F. Coyle
Department of Psychology, The Pennsylvania State University, University Park, Pennsylvania, USA

Richard A. Fabes
Program in Family and Human Development, T. Denny Sanford School of Social and Family Dynamics, Arizona State University, Tempe, Arizona, USA

Adrian Gale
Department of Psychology, University of Michigan, Ann Arbor, Michigan, USA

Laura D. Hanish
Program in Family and Human Development, T. Denny Sanford School of Social and Family Dynamics, Arizona State University, Tempe, Arizona, USA

Amy Roberson Hayes
Department of Psychology, University of Texas at Austin, Austin, Texas, USA

Janet Shibley Hyde
Department of Psychology, University of Wisconsin, Madison, Wisconsin, USA

Beth Kurtz-Costes
Department of Psychology, University of North Carolina, Chapel Hill, North Carolina, USA

Campbell Leaper
Department of Psychology, University of California, Santa Cruz, California, USA

Lynn S. Liben
Department of Psychology, The Pennsylvania State University, University Park, Pennsylvania, USA

Fantasy T. Lozada
Department of Psychology, University of Michigan, Ann Arbor, Michigan, USA

Carol Lynn Martin
Program in Family and Human Development, T. Denny Sanford School of Social and Family Dynamics, Arizona State University, Tempe, Arizona, USA

Ethan H. Mereish
Department of Counseling, Developmental, and Educational Psychology, Boston College, Chestnut Hill, Massachusetts, USA

Jennifer Petersen
Department of Educational Foundations, University of Wisconsin, Whitewater, Wisconsin, USA

V. Paul Poteat
Department of Counseling, Developmental, and Educational Psychology, Boston College, Chestnut Hill, Massachusetts, USA

Latisha Ross
Department of Psychology, University of Michigan, Ann Arbor, Michigan, USA

Stephanie J. Rowley
Department of Psychology, University of Michigan, Ann Arbor, Michigan, USA

Jillian R. Scheer
Department of Counseling, Developmental, and Educational Psychology, Boston College, Chestnut Hill, Massachusetts, USA

Melinda A. Solmon
School of Kinesiology, Louisiana State University, Baton Rouge, Louisiana, USA

Amber Williams
Department of Psychology, University of Michigan, Ann Arbor, Michigan, USA

Yamanda F. Wright
Department of Psychology, University of Texas at Austin, Austin, Texas, USA

PREFACE

Educational accomplishments vary dramatically among individuals and profoundly affect lives by facilitating or constraining access to positive outcomes. Educational achievement is linked, for example, to later physical health, mental health, career options, income, and life satisfaction. Identifying the factors that influence educational experiences and outcomes is therefore of great interest in developmental science. Importantly, the characteristics that individuals bring to educational settings (e.g., their economic, religious, and cultural backgrounds) affect their experiences. Among the most powerful of these characteristics is gender. Gender shapes youths' understanding and experience of education across the globe and across history. Consider this quote:

> Women are larger consumers and better distributors of knowledge than men. They read more books, and get more satisfaction out of intellectual pursuits than men. Put boys and girls together in school and college, and if you are foolish enough to give them their relative rank, and to offer them prizes, the girls will win much more than their proportion. Indeed, many coeducational institutions have been forced to put up some sort of protective barrier in order to give the poor boys half a chance (p. 202).

Widespread media attention to girls' and women's recent educational successes or, conversely, boys' and men's recent struggles might lead one to assume this passage was written by a contemporary observer of the U.S. educational system. The quote comes instead from William DeWitt Hyde, former President of Bowdoin College, in a 1906 book entitled *The College Man and the College Woman* (Boston: Houghton Mifflin) that detailed his observations of gender differences in relation to education.

The more than 100 years since the publication of W. Hyde's book have witnessed both remarkable similarities and differences in the ways that gender has been relevant for education. The current volume was designed to assemble papers that discuss important contemporary issues at the intersection of gender and education. Collectively, the chapters address the gender-education nexus in academic, occupational, social, and athletic domains from childhood through adulthood.

The volume begins with an examination of one of the most important foundations of academic success: motivation. Specifically, Butler (Chapter 1) examines historical and contemporary models of achievement motivation. After reviewing the literature on youth's strategies of academic self-evaluation and self-regulation, she argues that—at the group level—boys develop a motivational orientation focused on proving their skills, whereas girls develop a motivational orientation focused on improving their skills. Her insightful analyses of the costs and benefits of both approaches shed needed light on the possible causes of current gender gaps in achievement.

Next, Petersen and Hyde (Chapter 2) examine the processes involved in the creation of a U.S. workforce characterized by high levels of gender segregation. The authors review evidence for the roles of sex-differentiated abilities and interests, gender stereotypes, and gender discrimination in shaping occupational goals. They pay special attention to the role of social cognitions (e.g., individuals' expectancies and values) in shaping youths' decisions.

Gender differentiation of academic and occupational interests is also addressed in the contribution by Liben and Coyle (Chapter 3), but with a specialized focus on interventions directed to science, technology, engineering, and math (STEM). The authors highlight historical and contemporary data on women's participation in STEM and then review intervention mechanisms implied by various theories of gender development. They offer a taxonomy of intervention goals and use it to organize a review of illustrative interventions designed to reduce the STEM gender gap.

Moving to a different—yet also gender-differentiated—domain of achievement, Solmon (Chapter 4) examines girls' and boys' interest and involvement in sport and physical activities. She presents compelling evidence that the lower participation of girls in these activities harms their well-being and derives from pedagogical practices that privilege boys. Solmon makes insightful recommendations for improving the experiences of both girls and boys in physical education with the goal of promoting life-long physical health.

Continuing the focus on gendered processes in arenas that extend beyond the learning of academic content, Martin, Fabes, and Hanish (Chapter 5) examine the causes and consequences of gender segregation in children's peer relationships. Their chapter draws attention to ways in which educators (often unknowingly) undermine versus facilitate warm, respectful, and supportive cross-gender relationships that, respectively, thereby diminish versus enhance the cohesiveness of classroom communities.

Leaper and Brown (Chapter 6) also focus on gender and relationships, describing how youths' educational experiences may be negatively affected by gender stereotyping, prejudice, and discrimination on the part of parents, teachers, and peers. Their chapter presents information about an understudied form of gender bias—sexual harassment within educational settings—and argues for the importance of providing youth with strategies for challenging and coping with sexism and sexual harassment.

Single-sex schooling—sometimes presented as a solution to the problems created by gender stereotyping, prejudice, and discrimination in schools—is examined by Bigler, Hayes, and Liben (Chapter 7). They analyze and evaluate each of five major rationales that have been given for the controversial (and increasingly common) use of gender segregation in public schools. They conclude that evidence fails to demonstrate that the single-sex structure *per se* yields better social, emotional, or academic outcomes, but note that some educational practices employed in such schools may be profitably implemented in coeducational contexts.

One area that needs more attention in coeducational settings concerns sexual minority and gender-variant youth. As Poteat, Scheer, and Mereish (Chapter 8) describe, experiences of victimization in school settings are common among lesbian, gay, bisexual, transgender (LGBT) and gender nonconforming youth. The authors posit pathways through which such experiences negatively impact individuals' learning processes that, in turn, affect their academic and occupational interests, goals, and outcomes. The authors point to resources and strategies available to educators and community members who seek to improve educational outcomes among sexual minority and gender-variant youth.

Another student group that has received attention for comparatively poor outcomes within the U.S. educational system is African American boys. Rowley and her colleagues (Chapter 9) acknowledge that Black boys' academic underperformance represents an urgent educational crisis, but they also argue that the pervasiveness of a narrative of failure is itself harmful. In particular, this narrative undermines parents' and teachers' academic expectations and simultaneously undercuts Black boys' own academic motivations and goals. The authors call for the development of counter-narratives that instead focus on African American boys' academic talents and successes.

In a related chapter, Barbarin, Chinn, and Wright (Chapter 10) address the unique barriers to academic success faced by African American boys. They outline many real and serious obstacles that these boys face in their lives both in and out of school. The authors then provide specific recommendations for educational reforms designed to support African American boys, including the provision of African American male (i.e., in-group) mentors and the establishment of positive student–teacher relationships. They suggest that such reforms may be readily implemented in single-sex schools, but note that such practices are likely to benefit students in other school settings as well, irrespective of race and gender.

In sum, this volume covers a wide range of ways in which gender has a powerful influence on individuals' education-related expectancies, interests, aptitudes, and outcomes. Throughout the volume, authors have focused not only on how empirical findings help to test and extend theoretical work on gender and education, but also on how empirical work can inform pedagogical and curricular changes aimed at increasing gender fairness, justice, and equality. Such reforms should help youth overcome the gender-, sexuality-, and race-related constraints that now operate both within and beyond educational settings.

Any volume reaches print thanks to the collective efforts of many people, and this volume is no exception. We thus close our preface by expressing our deep thanks to the many individuals who helped to make this project a reality. We begin by thanking Janette Benson for identifying the topic of gender as ripe for a thematic volume in the series she edits, for inviting us to serve as guest editors, and for supporting our proposal to focus the volume on education-related topics. Second, we are grateful to the chapter authors for their strong commitments and contributions to this research area in general, and for their willingness to write chapters for this volume in particular. They were a pleasure to collaborate with throughout the process, and their contributions will continue to push the field forward in years to come. Third, we thank the Elsevier staff with whom we have worked along the way. Although there are too many individuals to name them all, we wish to single out for special thanks Sarah Lay, Zoe Kruze, and Radhakrishnan Lakshmanan who have been particularly efficient and responsive in so many ways.

During the final stages of the production of this book, the field lost one of its earliest and most creative, productive, and foresighted contributors to the study of gender development—Sandra Bem. Among the many things that were remarkable about Sandy were her excellent theoretical and empirical scholarship and her dogged attention to what that theory and research implied about children's development in everyday settings of home, school, and community. She and her family have been models of resisting the societal gender constraints that figure so prominently in many of the chapters of this volume. We miss her as a friend, a research colleague, and as a model of integrating scholarship and practice, and dedicate this volume to her memory.

LYNN S. LIBEN
University Park, Pennsylvania, USA

REBECCA S. BIGLER
Austin, Texas, USA

CHAPTER ONE

Motivation in Educational Contexts: Does Gender Matter?

Ruth Butler[1]

School of Education, Hebrew University of Jerusalem, Mt. Scopus, Jerusalem, Israel
[1]Corresponding author: e-mail address: ruth.butler@mail.huji.ac.il

Contents

1. Introduction — 2
2. Theoretical Frameworks: Early and Contemporary Approaches — 4
   - 2.1 Beginnings — 4
   - 2.2 Expectancy-Value Theory — 6
   - 2.3 Attribution Theory — 7
   - 2.4 Achievement Goal Theory — 7
3. A Question of Confidence? Gender and Perceptions of Competence and Control — 8
   - 3.1 Perceptions of Competence — 8
   - 3.2 Do Sex Differences in Perceived Competence Change with Age? — 11
   - 3.3 Perceptions of Causality and Control — 12
4. Proving and Improving: Gender and Motives for Evaluation — 15
   - 4.1 Approaches to Evaluation — 15
   - 4.2 Development of Proving and Improving Approaches to Self-Evaluation — 16
5. Achievement Goals — 20
   - 5.1 Gender and Achievement Goals — 20
   - 5.2 Gender and Achievement Goals in Context — 21
6. Achievement and Social Goals, Values, and Interests — 23
   - 6.1 Gender and Relationships — 23
   - 6.2 Good Girls, Brainy Boys: Performing Academically and Performing Gender — 24
   - 6.3 Interests, Values, and Identity — 27
7. Social Influences — 29
   - 7.1 Parents — 29
   - 7.2 Teachers — 30
8. Conclusions — 32
   - 8.1 Improving, Proving, and Academic Motivation Among Boys and Girls — 32
   - 8.2 Implications for Theory and Research — 33
   - 8.3 Implications for Education — 34
References — 35

The Role of Gender in Educational Contexts and Outcomes (L. S. Liben & R. S. Bigler, Eds.)
Advances in Child Development and Behavior (J. B. Benson, Series Ed.), Vol. 47
ISSN 0065-2407 http://dx.doi.org/10.1016/bs.acdb.2014.05.001

© 2014 Elsevier Inc.
All rights reserved.

Abstract

Girls and women now outperform boys and men on many indices of academic achievement. Gender differences in motivation may underlie these trends. In this chapter, I review and integrate research on gender differences in self-evaluation, self-regulation, and achievement goals. I argue for the existence of gendered tendencies "to prove" versus "to try and to improve," whereby males tend to orient to demonstrating and defending their abilities, and females to working hard and addressing deficiencies. I discuss how these motivations develop within social and educational contexts of learning, and intersect with gendered patterns of socialization, values, and behaviors in other arenas, especially relational ones. Recurring themes include the costs and benefits of differential emphases on competition and self-promotion versus affiliation and consideration of others in the family, peer group, and classroom. I conclude with some recommendations for creating classroom environments that might promote optimal motivation among all students, regardless of gender.

1. INTRODUCTION

For me, as for many women who went to college in the 1970s, discovering gender was a formative and transformative experience. Feminist analyses provided us with a new way of understanding ourselves and the world that had a profound influence on the ways we lived, or at least tried to live our lives, on our career choices, on our relationships, and also on how we understood and did theory and research. The following decades brought exciting advances in understanding gender and more generally in conceptualizing the intersections of the personal and social in human psychology. But from being an important focus also of theory and research on motivation, gender has again become a somewhat neglected topic (albeit with some notable exceptions). I continue to be surprised by the number of manuscripts I come across—published papers, submissions, grant proposals—in which it does not seem to have occurred to the authors that gender might be relevant. They did not address gender in the literature review, did not conduct even a preliminary examination of possible gender effects, and at most provided a mention when describing the sample (e.g., 52% female).

One possibility is that gender no longer matters, in the sense of meaningfully impacting motivation and motivational outcomes in educational contexts, at least in the Western populations that still make up most of the samples in published studies. Another is that the study of gender is no longer intellectually engaging, because we already understand how and why it impacts motivation and achievement. So, this is a good time to ask whether gender matters for the academic motivation of females, males, or both, as a prelude to introducing the central theme of this chapter. Girls and women score higher on graded achievement from elementary school through college, are less likely to drop out of school, and are now more likely than boys to continue to further education (e.g., American Association of University Women Educational Foundation, 1998; Snyder & Dillow, 2011). Despite changes in social attitudes men continue to achieve more at work than do women, and not only in science, technology, engineering, and mathematics (STEM) fields. To take just two academic examples, men wrote 80% of the books reviewed in the New York Review of Books in 2010 (http://www.vidaweb.org/the-count-2010). In the same year, men made up 75% of the faculty at the University of Chicago, about the same as was true in 1892 (88%; https://provost.uchicago.edu/initiatives/academicwomensreport.shtml).

In this chapter, I ask how motivation contributes to differential patterns of engagement and achievement at different stages. I propose that there are gendered tendencies "to prove" versus "to try and to improve." That is, I propose that males tend to be more oriented to demonstrating and defending their abilities, and females tend to be more oriented to working hard and to identifying and addressing deficiencies. I examine the extent to which this notion can serve to organize and interpret research on gender influences on motivation in educational settings, paying particular attention to strategies of academic self-evaluation and self-regulation, and to the costs and benefits of both proving and improving approaches. Thus, throughout, rather than focusing on one or the other sex (traditionally females, but increasingly males, an interesting shift in itself), I consider how core constructs of "proving" and "improving," of competence and values impact the self-views, task engagement, self-regulation, achievement, and aspirations of both females and males. I also discuss influences on gendered motivational tendencies and strategies, focusing on how these develop within the social and educational contexts of learning and achievement. Recurring themes include motivational influences of emphases on competition and self-promotion versus affiliation and consideration of others in the family, peer group, and classroom on males and females. I also discuss how gender intersects with other categories of identity and social membership, and with gendered patterns of socialization, values, and behaviors in other arenas, especially relational ones to shape achievement motivation and behavior. I conclude with some implications for educational practice and policy.

Some clarifications before I begin. As befits a volume on gender and education, I focus on achievement motivation, the kind of motivation most studied in educational settings. In this, as in other areas, gender influences can be expressed in several ways. There might be differences in the mean level of a construct (e.g., academic self-concept), in the distribution of a variable, or in the associations among variables (e.g., between self-concept and persistence). Some words of caution are in order. First, returning to my earlier point, in many potentially relevant studies, especially in recent years, authors did not report tests for sex differences. In others, sex was entered as a control, a strategy that does not provide information about gender similarities and differences in associations among variables. Second, variance within each sex is invariably larger than differences between the sexes; mean sex differences tend to be small and not always significant. Thus, there is a real risk of exaggerating gender differences and losing sight of no less meaningful gender similarities (Hyde, 2005; Petersen & Hyde, 2014 [Chapter 2 of this volume]). Even small differences in theoretically related variables can have cumulative and reciprocal effects that yield meaningful and influential gendered patterns or motivational styles, however. Finally, any analysis in terms of gendered tendencies raises the specter of essentialist claims regarding innate differences between the sexes. This is not my view. Rather, I shall discuss throughout how boys and girls construct and maintain motivational beliefs and motivated achievement strategies within the cultural milieu, contexts, and interactions of their lives.

2. THEORETICAL FRAMEWORKS: EARLY AND CONTEMPORARY APPROACHES

2.1. Beginnings

The study of achievement motivation began with the pioneering work of McClelland and Atkinson, developed for present purposes in two main stages. First, in a major conceptual and empirical endeavor McClelland, Atkinson, and their colleagues defined and explored the intensity of the need to achieve as a dimension of personality, or individual differences (McClelland, Atkinson, Clark, & Lowell, 1953). Influenced by prevailing drive theories, they extrapolated from learning theories to conceptualize need achievement as a kind of learned drive, acquired to a greater or lesser extent during early socialization in the family. Extrapolating from psychoanalysis, they developed a projective measure that assessed need achievement according to the achievement imagery in stories people wrote about pictures that presented men and women in various ambiguous situations. Second, Atkinson (1957) posited a second motive to avoid failure, expressed in test anxiety. He also extended the theoretical model to include values and expectancies. Atkinson conceptualized value in terms of affect, which depends on task difficulty. People will experience more pride when they succeed on difficult tasks and more negative emotion when they fail on easy ones. The expectancy component recognized that resultant motivation depends not just on the intensity of motives and the value of success but also on the subjective probability of success.

McClelland and his colleagues famously, or notoriously, based their book exclusively on research with men. This is often cited as a classic example of male bias in psychology: male psychologists who equate "human" with "male," develop theories that they test mainly on men, and respond to any aberrant results with women, such as those reported by Veroff, Wilcox, and Atkinson (1953), by continuing to study men. A close reading of this early paper shows a more nuanced picture, however. Unusually for the time, the authors recognized the importance of developing two sets of pictures, one with male and one with female protagonists. The "aberrant" finding was that female high school and college students, unlike males, did not provide more achievement themes in an achievement-arousing than in a neutral condition. Women who wrote about female pictures produced hardly any achievement imagery. But the same was true of men. The most interesting finding was that women who wrote stories about male pictures produced the most achievement imagery. Discussion focused, as it might well do still today, on gendered roles, role models, expectations, and achievement opportunities. The authors concluded that rather than simply expressing societal norms, women projected their own, apparently rather high, need achievement onto plausible achievement figures—and at the time this meant males but not females.

This research group was not motivated to further explore women's achievement motivation, however. The emergence of interest in achievement motivation among girls and women coincided, unsurprisingly, with second-wave feminism. Horner (1972), intrigued by indications that competitive settings undermined the performance of women but not men, ventured that competent women experience not two, but three conflicting motives in achievement settings. Like men, they can be motivated to succeed and to avoid failure, but women are also motivated to avoid success because they learn early that achievement is incompatible with femininity. Horner found that 70% of women undergraduates who wrote about Anne, who was at the top of her class in medical school, wrote negative and occasionally quite angry descriptions, as compared with fewer than 10% of men who wrote about John. Some wrote about ambitious but unattractive and socially isolated bookworms who might become successful doctors but would live to regret not having a family, others about women who dropped out of school to find fulfillment in marriage. The notion of "fear of success" as a deeply rooted uniquely female kind of motivation fell out of favor, in part because subsequent studies showed that quite a few men also wrote negative stories about a successful man (Hoffman, 1974). The insight that aspiring to succeed can have costs when achievement runs counter to social constructions of not only female but also male opportunities and identities continues to resonate, however.

2.2. Expectancy-Value Theory

Contemporary theoretical approaches to achievement motivation in educational settings all draw on these early beginnings, but in different ways. Eccles' Expectancy-Value (E-V) framework (Eccles (Parsons) et al., 1983) posits that students will invest more in an academic domain when they both expect to succeed and value achievement. In keeping with the cognitive revolution, Eccles and colleagues emphasized students' perceptions of their competencies and values. Thus, rather than deep-rooted, semi-conscious drives or motives, E-V researchers assess students' reports of their interest (intrinsic value), desire to succeed (attainment value), and perceptions that success is important for future plans (utility value). They also consider costs. Investing in an academic domain might leave little time for other activities, have negative consequences for social relationships or status, or conflict with other, for example, family goals.

Students form self-views via processes of social learning, on the basis of their academic outcomes and beliefs and the perceptions and communications of parents, teachers, and the cultural milieu, including gender roles and expectations. Studies have confirmed the motivational role of expectancies and values (for reviews, Eccles, 2009; Petersen & Hyde, 2014 [Chapter 2 of this volume]; Valentine, DuBois, & Cooper, 2004). Academic self-concepts predict school achievement and educational choices after controlling for prior achievement. The value of success makes an additional contribution. Thus, any gender differences in expectancies or values will have important consequences for the motivation and achievement of boys and girls. Importantly, Eccles and her colleagues developed the E-V model explicitly to address the influence of possible gender differences in expectancies and values on educational and career choices, and especially on the underrepresentation of women in STEM fields (see also Leaper & Brown, 2014 [Chapter 6 of this volume] and Liben & Coyle, 2014 [Chapter 3 of this volume]). This approach continues to guide much of the research on gender and academic motivation.

2.3. Attribution Theory

Weiner's attribution theory of achievement motivation also accords pride of place to cognitions, in this case to perceptions of the causes of achievement outcomes. Early approaches emphasized the role of the locus of control, namely, the degree to which students believe that their outcomes are due to internal factors such as their capacities and investment, or to external factors such as the teacher or luck, in determining expectancy and continuing motivation (Rotter, 1966). Influenced by Atkinson's distinction between expectancy and values, Weiner (1986) developed a 2×2 framework whereby any cause could be defined not only as internal or external but also as stable or unstable. He reasoned that expectancy depends mainly on the latter dimension. Attributing an academic outcome to ability, an internal and stable cause will lead to higher expectancy that the outcome will recur than attribution to effort, an internal but instable cause. Attribution to relatively stable external causes such as task difficulty or the teacher will influence expectancy more than will attributions to luck, which might change for better or worse. The locus of control influences value, such that students experience more positive emotion when they succeed and more negative emotion when they fail if they attribute an outcome to an internal than to an external cause. As we shall see, research generated by this approach has shown quite coherent sex differences in achievement attributions.

2.4. Achievement Goal Theory

In contrast with both E-V and attribution approaches, achievement goal theory focuses on the kind of motivation that operates in achievement settings. The emphasis on the role of cognitions is similar, however. Achievement goal theory focuses on students' constructions of the meaning of success, and thus of the goals they strive to achieve. In a direct critique of McClelland and Atkinson, who in his view defined need achievement mainly as a drive to succeed more than others, Nicholls (1989) proposed that there is more than one way of defining success. Initially, theorists distinguished between ego or performance goals that orient students to *demonstrate competence* by showing superior or masking inferior ability versus task or learning goals that orient students to define success as learning, and to strive to *develop competence* by acquiring worthwhile skills and understandings (Dweck, 1986; Nicholls, 1989). Although the terms ego versus learning goals best capture the difference between strivings to prove versus improve competence emphasized in this chapter, so as not to confuse readers familiar with this literature, I shall use the more common "performance" and "mastery" labels. Influenced in part by Atkinson's distinction between motives to achieve and to avoid failure, some researchers subsequently proposed that strivings to prove superior ability and strivings to avoid failure and the demonstration of poor ability reflect distinct performance-approach versus performance-avoidance goals (e.g., Harackiewicz, Barron, Pintrich, Elliot, & Thrush, 2002).

Mastery and performance goals constitute distinct motivational systems that are associated with qualitatively different antecedents, processes, and outcomes (for a review, Butler, 2000). In present terms, mastery goals orient students to try and to improve—to attribute outcomes to effort, to define and evaluate competence relative to task demands or prior outcomes, to construe difficulty as diagnostic of the need for further learning, and to respond by increasing effort, trying different strategies, and seeking help and information that can support learning. Performance goals orient students to prove—to define and evaluate competence relative to others, to attribute outcomes to ability, to construe setbacks as diagnostic of low ability, and to avoid exposing inadequate ability by asking for help. Debates continue whether these rather negative processes are associated only with performance-avoidance or also with performance-approach goals. Both kinds of performance goals, however, are maladaptive when students do poorly, whereas mastery goals are more likely to orient students to maintain motivation and effort even if they are not at the top of the class (Butler, 2000).

In keeping with their social-constructivist approach, achievement goal theorists posit that students construct goals in large part in response to instructional emphases on the importance of learning and progress or of demonstrating superior levels of performance and achievement. Despite evidence that girls tend more to mastery and boys to performance goals, researchers in this tradition rarely focus on the far-reaching implications for understanding gender and motivation in educational settings.

3. A QUESTION OF CONFIDENCE? GENDER AND PERCEPTIONS OF COMPETENCE AND CONTROL

3.1. Perceptions of Competence

Men tend to convey more confidence than women in performance-oriented settings. Even when minimally prepared, men believe they can "wing it" and get through successfully. But, no matter how thoroughly prepared women are, they feel unprepared.

> *Successful males are sure they can obtain beneficial results, while successful females continue to express doubts about their capabilities. I find this frustrating, because the accomplished women are as proficient as accomplished males.*
>
> **Craver (2012)**

This observation by a law professor accords well with the bulk of the research on students' beliefs about their competence. On average, males score higher than females on measures of general self-esteem (Kling, Hyde, Showers, & Buswell, 1999), academic self-concept (Stetsenko, Little, Gordeeva, Grasshof, & Oettingen, 2000), and perceived intelligence (Steinmayr & Spinath, 2009). Studies of domain-specific academic self-concepts show a more nuanced picture of robust, albeit typically small sex-typed differences. Most have focused on math, in large part due to concerns about the underrepresentation of women in STEM fields, but many have examined language arts, both for purposes of comparison and because of concerns about boys' relatively poorer achievement in these subjects. Boys have more positive self-concepts in math and science; differences favoring girls in reading and language arts emerge in about Grade 3 (e.g., Jacobs, Lanza, Osgood, Eccles, & Wigfield, 2002; Wilkins, 2004). Sex differences in math were larger among gifted than non-gifted students (Preckel, Goetz, Pekrun, & Kleine, 2008). Research on academic self-efficacy, defined by Bandura as "beliefs in one's capabilities to organize and execute the courses of action required to produce given attainments" (Bandura, 1997, p. 3) has yielded similar patterns (Meece, Glienke, & Burg, 2006).

Given that students construct perceptions of competence in large part on the basis of prior outcomes, might domain-specific sex differences in self-concepts simply reflect differential abilities and achievements of boys and girls? Debates about possible biological differences in verbal and especially math abilities rage on and are addressed in other chapters in this volume (see Bigler, Hayes, & Liben, 2014 [Chapter 7 of this volume], Liben & Coyle, 2014 [Chapter 3 of this volume]; Petersen & Hyde, 2014 [Chapter 2 of this volume]). For present purposes, however, in elementary school girls receive higher grades in all subjects. Differences favoring girls in language are marked throughout the school years; on average girls do better than boys in secondary school also in math and science (American Association of University Women Educational Foundation, 1998).

Thus, early sex differences in math self-concepts cannot be attributed to differences in achievement. In studies in which researchers specifically examined self-evaluative bias, boys showed more positive bias in math than did girls. Negative bias, whereby perceived competence was actually lower than would be expected in the basis of achievement, was more prevalent among girls than boys (Dupeyrat, Escribe, Huet, & Regner, 2011; Kurman, 2004). Similarly, males overestimated and females underestimated their numerical, spatial, and general intelligence (Steinmayr & Spinath, 2009). These patterns have been linked to culturally transmitted gender roles and expectations that orient students to be both more confident and more motivated to succeed in what are perceived as gender-appropriate domains. Overall, sex-typed differences in self-concepts are more marked when students and parents endorse traditional gender attitudes and in Western countries that are less gender egalitarian (Eccles, Jacobs, & Harold, 1990; Nagy et al., 2010). Explicit endorsement of math as a male domain has decreased in recent years, but studies have shown the continuing existence of implicit stereotypes that male = male among children, adolescents, and adults; stronger implicit stereotypes predicted lower math self-concepts and achievement among women, while associations among men were on the opposite direction (Cvencek, Meltzoff, & Greenwald, 2011; Nosek, Banaji, & Greenwald, 2002).

In stereotypically feminine academic domains, girls did not show more positive and boys did not show more negative bias, however (Kurman, 2004). Controlling for the higher achievement of girls eliminated sex differences in perceived competence and self-efficacy in language (Pajares & Valiante, 1999). Given that on average boys learn to read later than girls, evidence that sex differences in reading self-concept emerge only in about Grade 3 suggests that initially boys show more positive bias also in this presumably feminine domain. Indeed in kindergarten, boys rated themselves as more competent readers than did girls; boys overestimated and girls underestimated their competence (Frey & Ruble, 1987).

School curricula typically assign more time to reading-related than to other activities in the early grades, so it seems likely that reading well is initially as much or maybe more about being a successful student than about gender roles. In the early grades, children did not have sex-typed perceptions of verbal and math abilities (Heyman & Legare, 2004). In a representative study (Jacobs et al., 2002), initially boys and girls did not differ in the degree to which they valued doing well in language; children of both sexes valued reading more than math. At older ages, boys valued success in language-related subjects less than did girls, but girls valued success in math and science as highly as did boys at all ages. Over time, students increasingly valued domains in which they were more confident and devalued domains in which their self-concept was lower. Adjusting the perceived value of success in line with expectancy is a strategy for maintaining positive self-views. The influence of perceived ability on changes in the valuing of both math and English appears more marked among boys than girls (Jacobs et al., 2002).

3.2. Do Sex Differences in Perceived Competence Change with Age?

Researchers have raised competing hypotheses about whether sex differences will increase or decrease with age (e.g., Jacobs et al., 2002). According to gender intensification theory (Hill & Lynch, 1983), internal and external pressures to conform to gender roles and expectations increase, especially after the transition to adolescence. In this case, sex-typed differences in self-appraisals should also increase, especially during secondary school, as girls become more negative about male-stereotyped domains (e.g., math) and boys about stereotypically female domains (e.g., language). The gender convergence hypothesis (Jacobs et al., 2002) predicts that sex differences will decrease because boys begin school with more inflated self-views. Given that reality constrains positive illusions, boys should subsequently lower their self-concepts more than girls in alignment with their actual achievements. But girls tend to quite realistic and boys to overestimate their capacities in valued domains throughout the school years. In this case, one can propose a third, gender stability hypothesis. The difference favoring boys in math self-concept will be stable because boys will continue to show inflated perceptions. Beginning in middle childhood, the difference favoring girls in language arts will also be stable, because boys are less prone to positive bias in this less valued domain, and girls perform better. Overall, studies support this third hypothesis (e.g., Marsh & Yeung, 1998; Nagy et al., 2010).

So, yes, gender still matters. Beliefs about male and female abilities in the sciences versus the humanities influence corresponding self-concepts, but they do not tell the whole story. Rather, a remarkably consistent pattern evident already in the early school years is for males to self-aggrandize especially when they value a domain. Self-enhancement varies in keeping with individual, cultural, and contextual emphases on the importance of demonstrating superior worth and ability (Kitayama, Markus, Matsumoto, & Norasakkunkit, 1997). Boys might value and thus self-aggrandize in STEM more than in the humanities not only because they are typed as masculine but also because of widespread beliefs that they require and reflect higher intelligence. Indeed, when perceived competence was assessed for verbal IQ, rather than for language-related school subjects, adolescent boys did not rate their ability lower than did girls (Steinmayr & Spinath, 2009). In present terms, boys seem more motivated to construct favorable views of their abilities, or to proving that they are competent, whereas girls tend to be more realistic, modest, and on occasion self-denigrating. Similar patterns emerge also from research on students' perceptions of the determinants of academic outcomes.

3.3. Perceptions of Causality and Control

Research generated by Weiner's framework has confirmed the importance of distinguishing between attributions to internal versus external causes and to stable, typically uncontrollable factors, such as ability (or gender) versus unstable, typically more controllable factors, such as effort, motivation, or learning strategies (for a review, Weiner, 1986). As is the case for self-concepts, students make causal inferences in part logically and realistically, based on prior outcomes and information in the immediate environment. Students who do poorly on a test are more likely to attribute their grade to chronic low ability rather than to inadequate preparation, difficult questions, or poor instruction if they consistently fail in school than if they generally succeed, if most of their classmates did better, or if they revised thoroughly. But studies have also confirmed a pervasive motivated bias whereby people accept more responsibility for success than for failure in the service of maintaining positive self-views (Campbell & Sedikides, 1999).

In an early study with 10-year-olds, Nicholls (1975) identified a suggestive pattern of sex differences. Children worked on problems in either a success or a failure condition. Girls attributed failure more to poor ability than did boys and attributed success less to high ability. Girls were more likely to attribute failure than success to ability, while boys showed the opposite pattern. Boys attributed failure to bad luck more than did girls. In terms of attribution theory, girls showed a low-expectancy and boys a high-expectancy pattern. Indeed, boys maintained higher expectancies after failure than did girls. Nicholls concluded that boys and girls showed contrasting self-serving versus self-denigrating biases that both reflect and reinforce sex differences in perceived competence. Results from a meta-analytic review of experimental studies with college students confirmed greater self-serving attribution bias both among high versus low self-esteem individuals and among men than women (Campbell & Sedikides, 1999).

Attributions for classroom outcomes show more similarities than differences between the sexes, presumably because students have more experience and information to draw on. For example, in keeping with cultural norms and school messages, students tend to prioritize effort. Some fairly consistent, albeit typically small, sex differences have emerged, however, again mainly for math and science. Beginning in elementary school and continuing through college, among both general and gifted samples, females rated ability as a less important determinant of success and a more important determinant of failure than did males and rated external factors as less important, especially for negative outcomes. Females tended to rate effort, especially sustained application, as a more important determinant of success; males were more likely than females to attribute failure to a combination of poor preparation, lack of interest, and external causes (e.g., Beyer, 1999; Cramer & Oshima, 1992; Ryckman & Peckham, 1987; Stipek & Gralinski, 1991).

Interpretations have typically emphasized the maladaptive consequences of attributing unsatisfactory outcomes to ability and the adaptive consequences of favoring unstable causes such as effort instead. For example, Dweck theorized that girls are more likely than boys to respond to difficulty with helpless decrements in confidence, persistence, and performance (e.g., Dweck, Davidson, Nelson, & Enna, 1978). However, selectively favoring not only external factors but also effort as a cause of failure more than success can be a defensive strategy to maintain self-worth by avoiding inferences of low ability. In this case, students may not try harder in the future because doing poorly despite high effort is clear evidence of low ability. Males are more inclined than females to construe effort as a double-edged sword, whereby the benefits of trying hard are counter-balanced by beliefs that high effort implies low ability and detracts from the value of success (Covington & Omelich, 1979). Prioritizing effort as a cause of both positive and negative outcomes, as is more typical of girls, should spur students to continue to work hard rather than resting on their laurels when they do well, and maintain or even increase effort when they are doing poorly, in part to compensate for their perceived inadequate ability.

In contrast with Dweck's proposal, girls invest more sustained effort in their studies and try harder to master difficult material than do boys, according to both teachers' and students' reports (for an overview, Duckworth & Seligman, 2006). Boys are more likely than girls to self-handicap by withdrawing effort when they fear or anticipate a poor academic outcome (Urdan & Midgley, 2001). McCrea and colleagues have showed that gender differences in self-handicapping reflected differences not only in defensive attribution bias but also in beliefs about the inherent value of effort versus ability (Hirt & McCrea, 2009). Women agreed more than men that they aspire to try hard as possible and pride themselves on being hard workers, that they admire effortful application in others, and that they disapprove of people who do not try hard. Men agreed more than women that they value ability over effort. Gender-differentiated perceptions of the relative value of ability and effort partially mediated sex differences in academic self-handicapping. Koestner, Zuckerman, and Koestner (1989) provided direct evidence that younger girls and boys responded differently to effort and ability cues. Praise for ability after success enhanced, whereas praise for effort undermined, perceived competence, performance, and intrinsic motivation among boys. The opposite pattern was true among girls. The most negative patterns were shown by boys praised for effort.

If boys are more ambivalent than girls about the value and virtue of effort, one can wonder about the effectiveness of interventions designed to enhance motivation by encouraging attributions of classroom outcomes to effort. Indeed, attribution retraining enhanced perceived academic competence, persistence, and performance among girls in elementary school (Craske, 1985) and in a secondary school chemistry course (Ziegler & Stoeger, 2004) but had no effects on boys. These findings are suggestive, but one must be cautious about generalizing because it is not clear whether in other studies that showed positive effects of attribution retraining in mixed samples researchers did not report effects by gender because they did not conduct them or because preliminary analyses showed no sex differences.

To summarize, research on perceptions of control converges with and extends that on perceptions of competence. The tendency of boys to take more responsibility for success than for failure is adaptive for maintaining confidence and self-worth, but may actually undermine continuing persistence and achievement, especially when they do poorly. Taken together with their less biased and confident self-appraisals, the attribution style more typical of girls suggests that they are indeed less inclined to "wing it" and more inclined to believe that they always need to try hard and that there is always room for improvement. The tendency of girls to take more responsibility for academic outcomes and to discount the role of ability in success should also render them more vulnerable to self-doubts and anxiety, however. Indeed, girls worry more about schoolwork than do boys (Pomerantz, Altermatt, & Saxon, 2002). This combination of lower confidence, greater anxiety, and beliefs that success depends on considerable investment may be particularly critical in influencing girls to set their sights lower than need be when making educational and career choices in secondary school and young adulthood. Clance and Imes (1978) suggested that it might also render high-achieving females vulnerable to the "imposter phenomenon"—the belief that one is less bright than one appears and will eventually be found out.

The research reviewed so far implies that boys and girls tend to use and interpret the informational environment for rather different purposes and in different ways. In the following sections, I discuss approaches to evaluation and achievement that might be related to the overconfidence of boys and to the lesser confidence and greater investment of girls.

4. PROVING AND IMPROVING: GENDER AND MOTIVES FOR EVALUATION

4.1. Approaches to Evaluation

Over 30 years ago, Lenney (1977) reviewed the extant literature and concluded that women were more likely to lower their evaluations and expectancies after receiving negative feedback than men, especially in settings that invite competition and social comparison. In a later review, Roberts (1991) reached the same conclusion. For instance, Roberts and Nolen-Hoeksema (1994) found that, although women expressed somewhat more positive initial ratings of their ability to give a persuasive, effective, and intelligent speech than men, they were significantly more likely than men to lower their appraisals when confronted with a critical peer remark about their performance. Roberts theorized that men and women approach evaluative feedback differently. Men treat evaluative settings as competitive arenas that call on them to prove and stand by their capacities and self-views, and thus to discount others' evaluations, especially if these are negative. Women are more inclined to approach such situations as opportunities to gain information about their abilities and thus treat evaluative feedback as more diagnostic.

More generally, gendered patterns of competence and control and approaches to evaluation are reminiscent of those associated with self-enhancement versus self-improvement motives for self-evaluation. When motivated primarily to maintain self-esteem (self-enhancement), individuals are prone to positive bias, prefer favorable over diagnostic but unfavorable information, and use various self-protective strategies, including attribution biases, to avoid, refute, or discount negative feedback (Crocker & Park, 2004). When motivated primarily to improve, they are interested in information relevant both to acquiring skills and understandings and to accurate self-appraisal, because one cannot know whether or how to improve without a clear sense of current performance and capacities (Butler, 2000). In this case, women might be more inclined to treat evaluative settings as opportunities not only for learning about, but also for improving their capacities.

Taking critical evaluations seriously enables one to identify and address deficiencies but carries the risk of losing self-confidence, devaluing one's capacities, and experiencing anxiety in evaluative settings such as tests. Conversely, prioritizing self-esteem carries the risk of failing to embrace and benefit from learning opportunities, including potentially useful evaluative information. A study by Mandel (2010) neatly illustrated these costs and benefits. College students rated their thoughts and emotions after they received negative feedback on their performance on an unfamiliar and challenging verbal task presented as a test of "creative intelligence." Men scored higher than women on hostile emotions and self-protective thoughts aimed at denying, discounting, or refuting the negative feedback (e.g., "I am thinking that the test is not a valid measure of creative intelligence"), whereas women scored higher on anxious emotions and self-denigrating cognitions (e.g., "I am thinking about my poor creative intelligence"). Before working on the task, men rated their "creative intelligence" higher than did women. Women rated the feedback as more diagnostic than did men. As a result, although participants of both sexes rated their performance fairly negatively, only women significantly lowered their evaluations of their general creative intelligence. However, women scored higher on self-improvement cognitions (e.g., "I am thinking about different ways to solve the problems") and spent more time than men reading information that presented examples of effective problem-solving strategies.

4.2. Development of Proving and Improving Approaches to Self-Evaluation

Gendered approaches to evaluation appear to develop well before the college years. By middle childhood (when children can respond reliably to self-report surveys) and continuing through college, girls reported basing their academic self-efficacy beliefs on social feedback from parents, teachers, and peers far more than did boys. Boys based their self-efficacy almost entirely on their past attainments and perceived ability (for a review, Usher & Pajares, 2008). Usher and Pajares interpreted these results as evidence that boys develop more internal, autonomous standards for self-evaluation than girls. This is an oversimplification, however, because from an early age boys tend to be very responsive to another kind of social information—social comparison.

In a current project, we are asking children between the ages of four and nine to give an example of something they are good at, and succeed in, and something that they are not good at, and do not succeed in (Butler, 2012a).

For each, we ask them how they know. By age five, more girls than boys spontaneously referred to social feedback (my teacher, parent, peers say I'm good or not good at the activity); more boys than girls cited social comparison ("I run faster than Adam"). Beginning at ages six to seven, boys, but not girls, showed an increasing preference for upward over downward social comparisons; they were more likely to say that they know they are good at something because they do better than others than they were to say that they are not good at something because they do worse (see Figure 1). Approaches that posit a universal tendency to self-enhance vis-à-vis valued domains and standards (Sedikides, Gaertner, & Toguchi, 2003) might imply that girls will show a bias toward valued positive over negative social feedback. If young girls attend to both positive and critical social feedback, they should not show positive bias, however. The frequencies in Figure 2 show that girls were equally likely to cite social feedback as their source of knowledge about low and high competence. There was a weak tendency among the older boys to refer to positive more than negative feedback.

There is other evidence that young boys are more interested in social comparison and that sex differences in self-appraisals and strategies are made rather than born. Some years ago I asked children between the ages of four and eight to rate their performance on a tracing task after we showed them the work of another child who had traced either more or less of the path (Butler, 1998a). I also asked children why they evaluated their performance as they did. Among even the preschoolers, more boys than girls cited the social standard. Beginning in kindergarten, boys were more likely than girls to give a social comparison reason if they did better rather than worse than

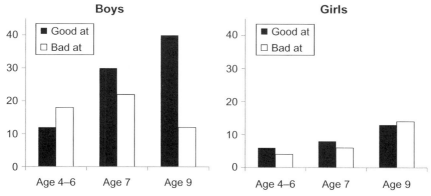

Figure 1 Standards and strategies for inferring high and low competence: Social comparison.

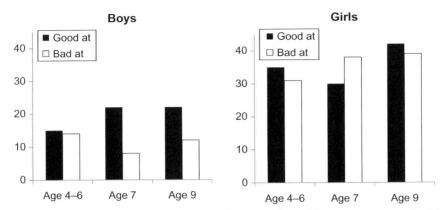

Figure 2 Standards and strategies for inferring high and low competence: Social feedback.

the other child or to refer to the social standard in a self-serving manner, for example, by saying that they did better than the superior other, "because his line is crooked." Boys rated their performance higher than did girls; they also expressed more optimistic expectancies about their future performance. In an observational study of KI to Grade 4 classrooms, Frey and Ruble (1987) found that boys made more self-congratulatory and fewer self-critical spontaneous comments than girls; boys were also more likely than girls to denigrate and less likely to praise peers' work. Ruble, Eisenberg, and Higgins (1994) found that boys were more prone to self-other bias; given the same performance outcome, boys rated themselves more favorably and the other child less favorably than did girls.

Young children rarely cite progress as a standard for self-appraisal (Frey & Ruble, 1987), possibly because the understanding that comparison information is diagnostic for self-appraisal develops later for temporal than for social comparisons (Butler, 1998a). In another study, children at ages four to nine rated their performance and explained their rating in one of two conditions (Butler, 2012a). In the normative success-temporal failure (NS-TF) condition, they saw that they had traced more of the path than a peer, but less than on an earlier attempt. In the normative failure-temporal success (NF-TS) condition, they did worse than another child, but better than before. Looking first at the results for girls in Figure 3, as one would expect on developmental grounds, the number of girls who explicitly compared current with prior performance increased with age; older (but not younger) girls attended more to the temporal than the social standard. Importantly, girls were equally likely to

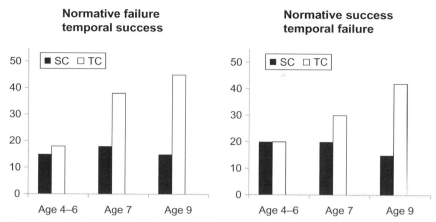

Figure 3 Developmental trends in social versus temporal comparison among girls.

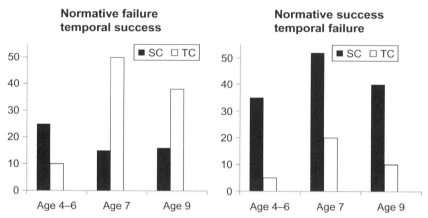

Figure 4 Developmental trends in social versus temporal comparison among boys.

base performance-appraisal on temporal comparison when they had done better than when they had done worse than before and were equally likely to cite an upward as a downward social comparison. The results for boys presented in Figure 4 were very different. Again, the youngest children attended mainly to the social standard in both conditions. By Grade 1, boys were far more likely to cite the more favorable standard and to make a gratifying downward social comparison in the NS-TF condition and a gratifying downward temporal comparison in the NF-TS condition. As a result, the sex difference favoring boys in performance-appraisal increased with age.

These results provide further confirmation of the early development of male proving. They also suggest that with age girls become increasingly interested in whether they are learning and improving. In another new study in our lab, middle school students worked on problems in which the aim was to pour a certain quantity from other jars to a target jar in as few moves as possible. Scores depended on the quality of the strategy, so it was possible to improve during the session. Students could choose whether to receive their overall percentile score, their scores on each problem in order of presentation, or no information. They also rated the degree to which normative and temporal information were each useful for evaluating their performance. As expected, girls rated temporal information as more diagnostic than normative information, whereas boys rated normative information as more diagnostic. Girls were more likely than boys to ask for their scores on problems over time, and were far less likely to choose to receive no information. Thus, by early adolescence girls were clearly more oriented to evaluating whether they had learned and improved. Furthermore, information-seeking was moderated dramatically by math self-concept among boys but not girls. Among boys who thought that they were good at math, most (70%) chose to receive their percentile score and none preferred to receive no information. In contrast, among boys who thought that they were not good at math, few (20%) chose to receive their percentile score and 40% preferred to receive no information.

So from an early age, boys and girls tend to be guided by different self-evaluative motives that orient them to different evaluative strategies and inferences. Motives for self-enhancement, veridical self-assessment, and self-improvement are themselves motivated, however, by what people are trying to achieve in a given situation, and in the classroom by their achievement goals for schoolwork (Butler, 2000).

5. ACHIEVEMENT GOALS
5.1. Gender and Achievement Goals

Much research on motivation in educational settings has been guided by the simple proposal that students' motivational beliefs, strategies, and outcomes depend importantly on their constructions of the goals or purposes of schoolwork, on the kind of success they value, and thus on what they want to achieve. If boys are more oriented to proving and girls to improving, are they also differentially inclined to corresponding performance-approach and mastery goals? Researchers did not always test for sex differences. When they did, however, girls usually endorsed mastery goals more than did boys and boys scored higher on performance-approach goals (e.g., Dupeyrat et al., 2011; Marsh, Craven, Hinkley, & Debus, 2003; Meece & Holt, 1993). Recall that because women score higher on test anxiety, Atkinson inferred that they are more motivated to avoid failure. Studies have not shown a consistent sex difference in performance-avoidance goals, however.

Thus, boys tend to be oriented to proving and girls to learning and improving in both their achievement-related judgments and strategies and the goals that they pursue in the classroom. Achievement goals and gender have similar influences on motivational beliefs and achievement-related strategies. Presenting an activity as an opportunity to develop competence (mastery goal condition) evoked motives for both self-improvement and veridical self-assessment. Presenting the task as a test of some valued ability (performance goal condition) evoked self-enhancement motivation and self-serving information-seeking biases (Butler, 2000). Competitive settings, which promote performance goals, increased self-serving bias (Campbell & Sedikides, 1999).

Similar parallels have emerged for other strategies of academic coping and defense. For example, mastery goals and contexts orient students to ask for needed help with schoolwork because they evoke positive perceptions of help seeking as an adaptive learning strategy. Performance goals and contexts invite constructions of help seeking as a threatening admission of inadequate ability and orient students to avoid overt bids for help and increase the likelihood that they will cheat instead (Butler, 2006). From elementary school through college, more girls seek help when they encounter difficulty with their schoolwork, while more boys cheat (Butler, 1998b; Newstead, Franklin-Stokes, & Armstead, 1996; Ryan, Gheen, & Midgley, 1998). Self-handicapping, is more common among students who prioritize performance over mastery goals (Urdan & Midgley, 2001); as I have already noted, boys self-handicap more than do girls.

5.2. Gender and Achievement Goals in Context

Teachers create a mastery goal structure or learning context when they emphasize meaningful learning, treat errors as learning opportunities, and consider effort and progress when evaluating students. They create a performance goal structure when they stress correct answers, assign frequent tests, and encourage competition and social comparison by grouping students by ability, grading students relative to one another, and show preferential treatment of high-achieving students. Because students in the same class do not necessarily experience the same educational context, researchers emphasize students' perceptions of the classroom goal structure as the main determinant of their motivational beliefs and responses. Perceived mastery goal structure promotes mastery goals for learning and positive kinds of academic and social engagement—deep learning strategies, satisfaction with schooling, and cooperative relationships with peers and teachers (for a review, Rolland, 2012). Perceived performance goal structure is associated with performance goals and in some studies with negative kinds of student engagement, including anxiety, disruptive behavior, and dissatisfaction with schooling and relationships. Overall, associations tend to be weaker than for perceived mastery emphases. One reasonable but rarely examined possibility is that performance-oriented classrooms, like personal performance goals, have negative effects on low but not necessarily high achievers. Solmon, 2014 [Chapter 4 of this volume] provides a discussion of performance orientation and related motivational topics within the realm of physical education.

Another possibility is that null or weak main effects might be due to interactions with gender. Specifically, boys may respond more positively to performance-oriented and girls to mastery-oriented learning contexts because these match their motivational approaches. In support, males enjoy competing and often perform better in competitive settings, in part because they tend to overestimate their chances of winning. Females prefer to cooperate and are more prone to show discomfort, anxiety, and performance decrements when competing (for a review, Croson & Gneezy, 2009). Individual differences in mastery and performance goals seem to influence motivational beliefs, strategies, and consequences in similar ways among boys and girls, however (Koul, Roy, & Lerdpornkulrat, 2012; Nolen, 1988). Mastery and performance goal conditions overrode gendered self-evaluative motives, strategies, and judgments, orienting boys to behave more like girls in mastery goal conditions, orienting girls to behave more like boys in performance goal conditions, and orienting both to show more positive patterns of motivation and self-regulation in the former (Butler, 2000). Researchers who examined effects of perceived classroom goal emphases typically did not test for main or interaction effects involving gender, but this may be the case for perceived classroom goal emphases as well (e.g., Koul et al., 2012).

These findings are a salutary reminder of gender similarities, of the benefits of mastery goals and contexts for both boys and girls, and importantly, of the malleability of motivational approaches. Boys and girls might tend to perceive the classroom environment differently, however. Students perceive the classroom goal structure in part through the lens of their own achievement goals. If boys and girls tend to construe evaluative settings as competitive arenas and learning opportunities, respectively, this might be the case for the classroom as well. In a study in 70 middle school classes in Israel, I found that boys agreed more than girls that teachers created a performance goal structure whereas girls agreed more than boys that teachers created a mastery goal structure (Butler, 2012b). Intrigued, I conducted a literature search to determine whether this was the case in other studies and countries. Researchers rarely reported tests for sex differences. In all the few exceptions, boys scored higher on perceived performance goal structure than girls, although tendencies for girls to score higher on perceived mastery goal structure than boys were not significant.

It is possible that any differences are not only in the eyes of the beholders. In a later section, I shall consider indications that teachers interact more with boys in ways that convey the importance of demonstrating superior ability and more with girls in ways that convey the importance of trying and improving. In all events, it is clearly important if girls and boys tend to experience the classroom context somewhat differently. For instance, if boys tend to perceive the classroom as more competitive, this should exacerbate their tendencies to performance goals and proving modes of self-appraisal and self-regulation. Although this may energize high-achieving boys, it may render low-achieving boys even more prone to defensively withdrawing effort, disengaging from schooling, and seeking other arenas in which they can prove themselves.

6. ACHIEVEMENT AND SOCIAL GOALS, VALUES, AND INTERESTS

6.1. Gender and Relationships

Classrooms are not only achievement but also social arenas, in which achievement and social roles, identities, motivations, goals, strategies, and behaviors, are necessarily intertwined. There are clear parallels between "proving" and "improving" orientations to self-appraisal and achievement and gendered interpersonal goals, styles, and behaviors. From an early age girls tend to display more empathic concern, interpersonal responsibility, compliance, and desire to please, whereas boys tend to be more competitive, more inclined to boast, and less amenable to adult influence (Maccoby, 1998). Biological differences may play some role but so do early social interactions (see Martin, Fabes, & Hanish, 2014 [Chapter 5 of this volume]). Parents tend to socialize children in ways that place more emphasis on the development of autonomy and agency in boys and of affiliation and consideration for others in girls

(Ruble, Martin, & Berenbaum, 2006). Gender-differentiated activities are potent arenas of gender socialization because they invite and develop different behaviors and interactions. Young boys tend to engage in competitive games with several playmates, activities that invite social comparison, and strivings for social dominance (Rose & Rudolph, 2006). Young girls, in contrast, tend to engage in socio-dramatic play, an activity that invites coordination and cooperation with others (see Martin et al., 2014 [Chapter 5 of this volume]).

In their analysis of same-sex peer groups, Maltz and Borker (1982) distinguished between the competitive, adversarial orientation of boys who speak to assert themselves and to maintain an audience, and the collaborative, affiliative orientation of girls who speak to "create and maintain relationships of closeness and equality" (p. 207). When conflicts arise, boys tend to act single-mindedly to prevail and achieve their goals, and girls to consider partners' goals as well and thus to negotiate and compromise (Sheldon, 1993). Later on, boys, more than girls, endorse "proving" kinds of social demonstration and social dominance goals to influence peers, to belong to high-status groups, to promote their own interests, and to present themselves in a positive light. Girls, more than boys, endorse intimacy and "improving" social development goals to create close and mutually supportive friendships, to resolve conflicts, to avoid hurting others, and to improve their relationships (for a review, Rose & Rudolph, 2006). During joint problem-solving, boys were more likely to denigrate and girls to try to teach less competent others (McCloskey, 1996). Boys are concerned mainly to prove themselves in interactions with boys, while girls are oriented to attending to and affiliating with both peers and adults (Maccoby, 1998). Because adult and peer norms regarding desirable social behaviors tend to correspond for girls but often conflict for boys, one route to peer approval for boys (but not girls) is to oppose adults. Boys in different cultures were more likely than girls to be swayed by peer than by adult norms and disapproval (Bronfenbrenner, 1970).

Gendered interpersonal goals and interactions develop before school entry. They likely play an important role in orienting boys and girls toward proving or improving approaches to the self and to achievement, and then in maintaining these approaches. In the following section, I consider how gender roles and social goals meet motivational goals, beliefs, and strategies in the classroom.

6.2. Good Girls, Brainy Boys: Performing Academically and Performing Gender

In many ways, female approaches to schooling and relationships match teachers' images of the ideal student; girls care more than boys about pleasing teachers, are more compliant and less disruptive, are more responsive to feedback and criticism, and try harder (for an overview, Kenney-Benson, Pomerantz, Ryan, & Patrick, 2006). But studies continue to show that it can be difficult for girls "to perform academically and to perform as feminine" (Walkerdine, 1989, p. 277), even prior to adolescence. A group of gifted girls in Grades 3–6 talked to Bell (1989) about the costs of performing academically in terms of violating feminine roles and relational goals. They were concerned about hurting other students' feelings and seeming boastful if they expressed pride in their accomplishments, and about being seen as aggressive if they asked or answered too many questions in class. In an ethnographic study of 10- to 11-year-olds in the UK 20 years later, Renold (2001a) documented how high-achieving girls negotiated student and relational goals by downplaying their achievement, which is clearly marked in British schools by ability-grouping and assignments that range in difficulty in clearly designated Levels. One girl, who was at Level 6, insisted that she was at Level 2. Another girl, described by peers in a group interview as excelling, admitted after considerable prompting that she was "quite" good. These observations accord with experimental research showing that concerns about femininity and relationships led women (but not men) to self-denigrate more in public than in private, and more in interaction with a less than a more successful other (Heatherington et al., 1993).

Even at this quite young age, girls in Renold's study expressed concerns that peers might like them less if they were in the top rather than in middle ability groups. During group work, boys ignored or denigrated the contributions of bright girls. Similarly, German adolescents in selective high schools rated a girl described as excelling in physics as more masculine, less feminine, and less liked than a girl described as excelling in music (Kessels, 2005). Girls who excelled in physics perceived themselves as less liked by boys than girls who excelled in music. Thus despite critiques of "fear of success" as a distinctly female kind of motivation, high-achieving girls may still experience conflicts between strivings for academic excellence and social acceptance.

Although high academic achievement is sometimes viewed as unfeminine, school is often analyzed, paradoxically, as a feminine arena. Brophy (1985) proposed that boys see schooling as feminine not just because most teachers are women, but because demands to behave, comply, and defer do not fit the culturally prescribed male gender role and peer norms. High-achieving boys in the classes studied by Renold (2001b) were ridiculed and marginalized by other boys as sissies and squares, but for being studious and well-behaved, rather than clever. A common strategy was for bright boys to "prove" their masculinity by becoming experts in sports trivia or subverting authority by challenging the teacher and making other kids laugh. Bright boys bragged about their accomplishments and less able boys reported getting higher grades than they did.

Jackson (2002) interviewed adolescent boys in England about what it means to be a "lad," British parlance for "one of the guys." Being a lad meant acting male by playing soccer, having a laugh in class, provoking teachers, and importantly not acting female, which for them meant not only talking about clothes, but also studying and worrying about schoolwork. Most of the boys wanted to do well in school, however, not just as a path to further education or better jobs, but also because it was important to them to present as clever, especially before other boys. Many gave explicit examples of strategies to protect and enhance academic self-worth. Typically, they downplayed their effort, but not their achievements. They denied revising not only after a poor but also a good test grade, because, as one boy put it, "that would make me sound brainier 'cause I already knew it and I didn't have to revise" (p. 595). In keeping with results from quantitative research, boys described self-handicapping before tests in hard subjects. Continuing the theme that "lads" avoid the appearance of effort, but not of ability, none talked about potential costs of success for their identities as lads or their social status. When asked if they discuss grades with friends, they typically said that they boasted about high grades and kept low ones to themselves.

Jackson concluded that "laddish" norms and behaviors protect self-worth from threats to masculinity and, perhaps more importantly, to competence. Pretending one has not worked or actually withdrawing effort while trumpeting one's achievements enabled boys to present themselves as male, because connotations of effeminacy were reserved for boys who were hardworking and well-behaved, rather than "brainy." No less important, these strategies enabled attributions of poor performance to low effort and attributions of success to effortless achievement, the hallmark of true ability for these boys and for students who pursue performance goals. So for boys, the conflict seems to be less between masculinity and excelling academically and more between masculinity and studying and deferring.

One implication is that male peers are a greater impediment to boys' academic engagement than any feminization of schooling. Boys dominate classroom environments and interactions (for a review, Beaman, Wheldall, & Kemp, 2006), to the possible detriment of students of both sexes. For instance, Lavy and Schlosser (2011) found that the achievement of both girls and boys increased with the number of girls in the class. Moreover, this was due to the effect of gender composition on the classroom environment. As the number of girls in a class increased, students of both sexes reported more enjoyment, better relationships with teachers and peers, fewer disruptive student behaviors, and less peer aggression. Teachers reported less fatigue in classes with more girls. The authors concluded that the feminizing influence of girls directly benefitted boys and teachers, while the benefit to girls derived simply from the fact that more girls in a class necessarily meant fewer boys.

6.3. Interests, Values, and Identity

In contrast with the generally small differences in other motivational variables, studies of young children's interests continue to show marked sex differences that correspond with sex-typed differences in early play and toy preferences. In a representative study, Alexander, Johnson, Leibham, and Kelley (2008) found that far more 4- to 5-year-old boys than girls had a strong and sustained interest in construction and in domains relevant to the acquisition of categories and concepts. More girls than boys had a sustained interest in socio-dramatic play and in arts and crafts. Sex differences in interest in "things" versus "people," in realistic versus social and artistic domains, and STEM versus language-related subjects continue from school through adulthood (e.g., Frenzel, Goetz, Pekrun, & Watt, 2010; Su, Rounds, & Armstrong, 2009; Wigfield et al., 1997). Effect sizes vary with the generality of interests; they are larger for measures of interest in people versus things and smaller for most academic subjects (see Petersen & Hyde, 2014 [Chapter 2 of this volume]).

Given the early divergence of interests, some researchers are now proposing that biological predispositions to different interests, possibly as a result of prenatal hormones, might drive sex differences in educational and vocational motivations and choices (Valla & Ceci, 2011). However, even Lytton and Romney (1991), who concluded that overall parents do not treat sons and daughters differently, noted that they encourage sex-typed activities in young children, and respond more negatively to cross-sex preferences among boys than girls. In addition, already by age three children are very motivated to work out what it means to be a boy or a girl and actively avoid cross-sex activities (Ruble et al., 2006). Early interests and skills can be precursors of subsequent academic interests, orienting boys to realistic and girls to expressive domains. When students are interested in a topic, they tend to process it more deeply and understand it better, are more likely to generate novel ideas, to engage in the topic outside class and to develop expertise and a sustained personal interest (Hidi & Renninger, 2006). Thus, interests promote competence and competence development enhances interest. Adolescents begin to integrate interests, for example, in math versus language into their general sense of identity. They also begin to consolidate higher order motives, or values. In studies of some 70,000 adolescents, college students, and adults in close to 70 countries, Schwartz and Rubel-Lifschitz (2009) found that females scored higher than males on altruistic values whereas males scored higher than females on self-enhancement values (proving superior achievement and exerting power).

Interests and values play a central role in educational choices of advanced courses in high school and majors in college, and in choices of subsequent jobs and careers (see Liben & Coyle, 2014 [Chapter 3 of this volume]). In keeping with their tendency to self-enhancing, proving values and motives, males typically aspire to high-status, well-paying jobs that involve working with things and systems, and offer opportunities for promotion and the exertion of power and influence over others. In keeping with their favoring of altruistic, affiliation, and self-improvement values and motives, women prefer jobs that offer opportunities to work alongside rather than above others, to help people, to make a contribution to society, to develop skills and knowledge, and to balance career and family; these values gravitate against choice of STEM fields (see Chapter 7).

Importantly, sex differences in interest in masculine versus feminine occupations develop early and remain fairly stable (Weisgram, Bigler, & Liben, 2010). By early childhood, boys expressed more negative attitudes toward feminine occupations than did girls toward male ones. During adolescence, boys tend to become more single-mindedly committed to a limited number of typically masculine values and domains, while girls develop more flexible identities that incorporate both masculine and feminine traits and interests (Eccles, 2009). A recent study by Wang, Eccles, and Kenny (2013) showed that this might be the case for abilities as well. More 12th grade girls than boys with high ability in math also had high verbal ability, possibly because girls invest in developing skills in all school subjects. Subsequently, men are less likely than women to choose majors and careers in fields traditionally associated with the other sex. Contributing personal factors include ideological beliefs about gender equality and personal beliefs about gender typicality and self-efficacy in traditional versus nontraditional domains (Leaper & Van, 2008). Thus, social pressures and personal beliefs and values constrain the choices of males as well as females (see Petersen & Hyde, 2014 [Chapter 2 of this volume]).

7. SOCIAL INFLUENCES

I have referred throughout to ways in which gendered motivational approaches are constructed within cultural milieus, families, peer groups, and classrooms. I now turn to a more systematic discussion of the role of parents and teachers. Socio-cultural differences in the socialization of boys and girls in different ethnic groups might moderate sex differences in motivational beliefs and outcomes but space constraints preclude discussion here. Barbarin, Chinn, and Wright (2014) [Chapter 10 of this volume] and Rowley et al. (2014) [Chapter 9 of this volume] provide excellent reviews of academic motivation and achievement at the intersection of gender, race, and class within the United States.

7.1. Parents

Most attention has been paid to parents' beliefs about gender roles and the sex-typed abilities of their own sons and daughters. Results are not surprising, but also not trivial (e.g., Bleeker & Jacobs, 2004; Chhin, Bleeker, & Jacobs, 2008; Eccles et al., 1990). To the extent that parents have sex-typed beliefs, they believe that sons are more talented in math and attribute the math success of sons more to ability and of daughters to hard work and good study habits. Parental perceptions of their children's competence in math predicted both parental expectancies for their children's educational and career achievement and their children's perceived competence, course selection, and occupational choices, even after controlling for students' actual achievements. Frome and Eccles (1998) reported that parents perceived girls to be more competent than boys in English; again parental perceptions significantly predicted adolescents' perceived competence. However, in keeping with the research on students' self-concepts, mothers overestimated the math competence of sons, but evaluated the English competence of children of both sexes quite realistically. Similarly, parents overestimated the intelligence of sons and underestimated that of daughters (Steinmayr & Spinath, 2009).

These differential perceptions suggest that even today, even in Western countries, parents tend to have higher and more positively biased expectations for boys than for girls (see Leaper & Brown, 2014 [Chapter 6 of this volume]). Results of a recent intervention program designed to increase adolescents' enrollment in STEM courses by promoting maternal perceptions of their utility value for their children are consistent with this analysis (Rozek, Hyde, Svolbords, Hulleman, & Harackiewicz, accepted for publication). The intervention had no effect on high-achieving boys (who were already taking many STEM courses), increased course-taking among high-achieving girls and low-achieving boys (suggesting that these students had previously received less parental encouragement), and actually decreased course-taking among low-achieving girls. Apparently, mothers of low achievers were more inclined to believe that their sons than their daughters had the requisite ability.

If parents are especially invested in maintaining favorable beliefs about their sons' academic abilities, even in the face of disconfirming evidence such as their actual achievements, one can venture that they play a role in orienting boys to believing in and proving their abilities. In support, Friedel, Cortina, Turner, and Midgley (2007) reported that boys perceived not only teachers but also parents as placing greater emphasis on performance goals than did girls. I cannot evaluate how general a phenomenon this is because other studies of perceived parental goal emphases did not look at sex differences. Conversely, if parents perceive daughters more than sons as succeeding because of effort and application, they likely also convey to girls more than boys the importance of investing effort in schoolwork. Evidence suggests that parents monitor the academic progress of girls more closely than that of boys, criticize young girls more than boys for poor performance on an achievement task, and give girls more unsolicited help than boys (for an overview, Kenney-Benson et al., 2006). Such behaviors serve as low ability cues that convey the need for greater compensatory effort. Tendencies to socialize girls more than boys to be attentive to, compliant with, and considerate of others may also orient girls to be humble about their abilities, to try hard in school to please rather than disappoint adults, and to worry about their schoolwork.

7.2. Teachers

Overall, teachers seem to evaluate the academic competence of both boys and girls more realistically than parents (Madon et al., 1998). But teachers may convey the relative importance of effort versus ability and of improving versus proving in other ways. An early study showed striking differences in teacher communications (Dweck et al., 1978). Teachers were more likely to praise boys for the intellectual quality of their work, and girls for their conduct or neatness, but criticized boys mainly for conduct and girls for performance. Thus, teachers conveyed both that girls are less able and that "positive evaluation is less indicative of ability for girls than for boys, and negative evaluation is less indicative of ability for boys" (p. 274). In support, Parsons, Kaczala, and

Meece (1982) found that the frequency of teacher praise was positively correlated with student ratings of both teacher expectancies and their own ability for boys, but not for girls. The tendency for boys to more selective than girls in attending to positive more than to negative evaluative feedback should increase the impact of such differential communications.

Subsequent studies have confirmed that teachers tend to interact differently with boys and girls (see Beaman et al., 2006; Leaper & Brown, 2014 [Chapter 6 of this volume]). They pay more attention to boys, across different cohorts, ethnicities, and social classes. Teachers give boys more negative attention in the form of reprimands about their conduct, but also direct more high-level questions to boys than girls and give boys more academic feedback. In large part, these differential responses are due to the different behaviors of boys and girls. Boys dominate classroom interactions both because they are more disruptive and less compliant than girls, especially if they are low achievers, and because they are more likely to call out answers to questions directed to the whole class, especially if they are high achievers. Thus, teachers tend to encourage able boys more than girls to demonstrate their knowledge and abilities. In contrast, teachers tend to engage in escalating cycles of negative interactions with low-achieving boys that may contribute to deepening their academic disaffection and alienation. These patterns might also mean that they create a more performance-oriented climate for boys than for girls.

Overall, teachers' interactions with girls are less stimulating, but more pleasant and harmonious than their interactions with boys. Teachers typically perceive girls as more attentive, conscientious, cooperative, teachable, hard-working, and persistent in trying to overcome difficulty than boys (e.g., Beaman et al., 2006; Mullola et al., 2012). Girls in turn have more positive perceptions of the school environment and a greater sense of belonging in school than boys. An implication generally overlooked in the literature concerns the presumably reciprocal influences of student tendencies and teacher responses on the self-regulation of boys and girls. To do well in school, students need to pay attention in class even when the material or teacher is boring, read questions carefully before answering them, and do their homework even when TV and Facebook beckon. Girls score higher than boys on effortful control in early childhood and on conscientiousness and self-discipline at later ages (Duckworth & Seligman, 2006). As a result, they tend to be less dependent on teacher control, leading teachers to pay them less attention and thus to reinforce continuing self-discipline to a greater extent among girls than boys.

8. CONCLUSIONS

8.1. Improving, Proving, and Academic Motivation Among Boys and Girls

There is still so much I want and need to learn. Every sentence I write raises questions that send me back to the literature. How can I submit a manuscript until I'm sure I've understood the full complexity and have something new and worthwhile to say?

S, a gifted (female) postdoc

Gender still matters, for the academic motivation of both females and males. Studies guided by different theoretical frameworks that assessed different motivational constructs among diverse cohorts, populations, and age-groups show patterns of typically small but consistent sex differences that by and large can be conceptualized in terms of coherent gendered motivational approaches "to prove" versus "to try and to improve." These approaches emerge very early and continue through college; studies converge in showing striking similarities among children, adolescents, and young adults. Considering the role of the socialization and development of competitive versus affiliation social goals and interaction styles has proven helpful in accounting for both the early emergence and the persistence of gendered motivational approaches.

Thinking in terms of gendered approaches to "trying and improving" and "proving" can shed light on the apparent paradox I mentioned in my opening comments that girls do better in school but men achieve more in later life. There is consensus among researchers, parents, and teachers that girls show more adaptive patterns of motivation in school than do boys. Girls' motivational strengths go hand in hand with their vulnerabilities, however. As girls learn to attend to the needs and evaluations of others and to be conscientious and hardworking in school, they also learn to question their abilities and downplay their accomplishments. Tendencies to favor veridical and self-improving motives, judgments, and strategies enable girls to learn from negative performance outcomes and evaluations, but render them vulnerable to self-doubts and anxiety. The relational goals that orient girls to please, affiliate with, and accommodate others help them assimilate school demands, but also orient them to avoid presenting as too clever. During the school years, girls' strengths tend to prevail. Although female motivational vulnerabilities do not intensify markedly during adolescence, the pipeline starts to leak in secondary school when girls are called on to make decisions. Discussion has focused mainly on avoidance of STEM domains and careers. But the reflections of the postdoc, who did not pursue the academic career in psychology to which she was eminently suited, well illustrate how believing that there is always room for improvement and caring too much what others say or write may exacerbate self-doubts and impede women's achievement in other fields as well.

What are the consequences of male proving for boys' academic motivation? One clear conclusion is that they differ substantially for high- versus low-achieving boys. Boys who excel reap the benefits because they are able to prove themselves in school. Their positive illusions are not extreme and presumably do not require much protection. Even in socially diverse schools, the route to peer acceptance for high-achieving boys generally lies more in hiding effort and performing as masculine than in downplaying their ability or avoiding success. These boys' self-confidence, together with the greater early interest of boys in realistic domains and continuing social pressures and gender expectations, prepare them to aspire to prove themselves in prestigious, demanding, and remunerative careers. However, I have also discussed the attendant risks of failing to learn and benefit from difficulties and performance evaluation, even among bright boys. For low or even some average achievers, male proving has many costs and apparently no benefits for their academic motivation and achievement in later life. In their case, concerns about boys' academic disaffection, alienation, poor motivation, and low achievement are fully justified.

8.2. Implications for Theory and Research

My discussion of gendered motivational approaches is intended to complement, integrate, and extend other theoretical perspectives. Returning to my opening complaints about incipient gender-blindness, E-V theory is exempt. This approach continues to generate an impressive body of empirical research that increasingly considers the influence of socio-cultural beliefs, practices, and affordances on the gender-typed motivational beliefs and choices of both boys and girls, not only in STEM but also in other domains. The focus on sex-typed domains may disguise more general gendered motivational tendencies, however, such as those discussed in this chapter. Achievement goal theory has confirmed the importance of considering not only the value of success but also the kind of success students strive to achieve. My own grounding in this approach pointed me in the direction of male proving and female improving, but readers cannot fail to notice my frustration that researchers in this tradition so often ignore gender. As a result, we still know little, for example, as to whether and how gender might moderate the effects of performance goals and contexts among low versus high achievers. In my discussion of attributions and self-evaluative motives, I often had to rely on relatively early studies because recent ones did not consider gender. Thus, it is possible that some of the trends I identified might have changed, in keeping with changes in social attitudes and affordances. I have focused on gender and motivation in the West, simply because there is not yet enough relevant research in other countries. Few studies of academic motivation in Eastern cultures have compared boys and girls. It is suggestive, however, that although students in collectivistic cultures self-enhance less in agentic and achievement domains than do their counterparts in the West, women self-enhanced less than males also in Japan (Kitayama et al., 1997). Last, but not least, thinking about gender led to many insights about motivation in the past and can, I believe, continue to do so in the future.

8.3. Implications for Education

Evidence that girls and boys tend to develop different motivational approaches suggests two contrasting kinds of educational recommendations. One would be to fit the learning environment to the motivational styles of boys and girls via the establishment of single-sex frameworks. Single-sex frameworks are discussed extensively in other chapters of this volume (Bigler et al., 2014 [Chapter 7 of this volume]; Barbarin et al., 2014 [Chapter 10 of this volume]). Here, I shall just note that there are some grounds for proposing that these might benefit girls by building on their motivational strengths and mitigating their vulnerabilities. In contrast, the evidence reviewed here implies that all-boy classes will reinforce tendencies to pursue performance over mastery goals, to value ability over effort, and to respond to difficulty with attempts to protect and salvage self-esteem, rather than by trying harder. Thus, they should exacerbate boys' motivational vulnerabilities and undermine rather than sustain their academic confidence, especially if they are low achievers.

The other, in my view preferable, approach would be to learn from the respective benefits and costs of each style to adapt the learning environment to promote optimal motivation among students, regardless of gender. One possibility would be to capitalize on evidence that mastery goals evoke positive patterns of motivation, self-regulation, and learning among both boys and girls by encouraging teachers to create mastery rather performance-oriented school and classroom environments. Classrooms that value learning and progress might be very effective in enabling even less able boys to experience a sense of success, self-worth, and belonging in school. But might such classrooms lead high-achieving boys to lose some of their drive and edge? And might girls not benefit from opportunities to more confidently embrace and learn from a measure of intellectual competition? One direction could be raise awareness of the advantages and disadvantages of each motivational approach through explicit classroom discussions. Incorporating practices of critical argumentation and joint problem-solving (e.g., Muller Mirza & Perret-Clermont, 2009) into mastery-oriented classrooms might then be a fruitful way for students to put their insights into practice. Learning to present and defend a reasoned idea or solution while considering other students' arguments and contributions can mitigate boys' tendencies to adversarial discourse, balance girls' tendencies to accommodate and affiliate, and promote meaningful learning among both. Most generally, sex differences are constructed and thus best modified in social interactions (Maccoby, 1998). Coeducational classes can be fruitful arenas to confront sex-typed beliefs about academic abilities and interests, to equip girls to confidently take their place in a co-sex world and boys to embrace effortful accomplishment, emerge from the confines of their peer group and accept girls as equal participants in learning and life.

REFERENCES

Alexander, J. M., Johnson, K. E., Leibham, M. E., & Kelley, K. (2008). The development of conceptual interests in young children. *Cognitive Development, 23*, 324–334.

American Association of University Women Educational Foundation. (1998). *Gender gaps: Where schools still fail our children.* Washington, DC: American Association of University Women Educational Foundation.

Atkinson, J. W. (1957). Motivational determinants of risk-taking behavior. *Psychological Review, 64,* 359–372.

Barbarin, O. A., Chinn, L., & Wright, Y. F. (2014). Creating developmentally auspicious school environments for African American boys. In L. S. Liben & R. S. Bigler (Vol. Eds.) *The role of gender in educational contexts and outcomes.* In J. B. Benson (Series Ed.), *Advances in child development and behavior: Vol. 47* (pp. 333–365). London: Elsevier.

Bandura, A. (1997). *Self-efficacy: The exercise of control.* New York, USA: W H Freeman/Times Books/Henry Holt & Co.

Beaman, R., Wheldall, K., & Kemp, C. (2006). Differential teacher attention to boys and girls in the classroom. *Educational Review, 58,* 339–366.

Bell, L. A. (1989). Something's wrong here and it's not me: Challenging the dilemmas that block girls' success. *Journal for the Education of the Gifted, 12,* 118–130.

Beyer, S. (1999). Gender differences in causal attributions by college students of performance on course examinations. *Current Psychology, 17,* 346–358.

Bigler, R.S., Hayes, A. R., & Liben, L. S. (2014). Analysis and evaluation of the rationales for single-sex schooling. In L. S. Liben & R. S. Bigler (Vol. Eds.) *The role of gender in educational contexts and outcomes*. In J. B. Benson (Series Ed.), *Advances in child development and behavior: Vol. 47* (pp. 225–260). London: Elsevier.

Bleeker, M. M., & Jacobs, J. E. (2004). Achievement in math and science: Do mothers' beliefs matter 12 years later? *Journal of Educational Psychology, 96*, 97–109.

Bronfenbrenner, U. (1970). Reaction to social pressure from adults versus peers among Soviet day school and boarding school pupils in the perspective of an American sample. *Journal of Personality and Social Psychology, 15*, 179–189.

Brophy, J. (1985). Male and female teacher-student interaction. In L. C. Wilkinson, & C. B. Marrett (Eds.), *Gender influences in classroom interaction* (pp. 115–142). Orlando, FL: Academic Press.

Butler, R. (1998a). Age trends in the use of social and temporal comparison for self-evaluation: Examination of a novel developmental hypothesis. *Child Development, 69*, 1054–1073.

Butler, R. (1998b). Determinants of help-seeking: Relations between perceived reasons for classroom help-avoidance and help-seeking behaviors in an experimental context. *Journal of Educational Psychology, 90*, 630–643.

Butler, R. (2000). What learners want to know: The role of achievement goals in shaping information-seeking, performance and interest. In C. Sansone, & J. Harackiewicz (Eds.), *Intrinsic and extrinsic motivation: The search for optimal motivation and performance* (pp. 161–194). New York: Academic Press.

Butler, R. (2006). An achievement goal perspective on student help seeking and teacher help giving in the classroom: Theory, research, and educational implications. In S. Karabenick, & R. Newman (Eds.), *Help seeking in academic settings: Goals, groups and contexts* (pp. 17–34). New York: Erlbaum.

Butler, R. (2012a). Proving and improving: Gender and the development of self-evaluative strategies and biases. In *Gender Development Research Conference, San Francisco*.

Butler, R. (2012b). Striving to connect: Extending an achievement goal approach to teacher motivation to include relational goals for teaching. *Journal of Educational Psychology, 104*, 726–742.

Campbell, W. K., & Sedikides, C. (1999). Self-threat magnifies the self-serving bias: A meta-analytic integration. *Review of General Psychology, 3*, 23–43.

Chhin, C. S., Bleeker, M. M., & Jacobs, J. E. (2008). Gender-typed occupational choices: The long-term impact of parents' beliefs and expectations. In H. M. G. Watt, & J. S. Eccles (Eds.), *Gender and occupational outcomes: Longitudinal assessments of individual, social, and cultural influences* (pp. 215–234). Washington, DC, USA: American Psychological Association.

Clance, P., & Imes, S. A. (1978). The imposter phenomenon in high achieving women: Dynamics and therapeutic intervention. *Psychotherapy: Theory, Research and Practice, 15*, 241–247.

Covington, M. V., & Omelich, C. L. (1979). Effort: The double-edged sword in school achievement. *Journal of Educational Psychology, 71*, 169–182.

Cramer, J., & Oshima, T. C. (1992). Do gifted females attribute their math performance differently than other students? *Journal for the Education of the Gifted, 16*, 18–35.

Craske, M. L. (1985). Improving persistence through observational learning and attribution retraining. *British Journal of Educational Psychology, 55*, 138–147.

Craver, C. B. (2012). The impact of gender on bargaining interactions. From http://www.negotiations.com/articles/gender-interaction/.

Crocker, J., & Park, L. E. (2004). The costly pursuit of self-esteem. *Psychological Bulletin, 130*, 392–414.

Croson, R., & Gneezy, U. (2009). Gender differences in preferences. *Journal of Economic Literature, 47*, 448–474.

Cvencek, A., Meltzoff, A. N., & Greenwald, A. G. (2011). Math-gender stereotypes in elementary school children. *Child Development, 82*, 766–779.

Duckworth, A. L., & Seligman, M. E. P. (2006). Self-discipline gives girls the edge: Gender in self-discipline, grades, and achievement test scores. *Journal of Educational Psychology, 98*, 198–208.

Dupeyrat, C., Escribe, C., Huet, N., & Regner, I. (2011). Positive biases in self-assessment of mathematics competence, achievement goals, and mathematics performance. *International Journal of Educational Research, 50*, 241–250.

Dweck, C. S. (1986). Motivational processes affecting learning. *American Psychologist, 41*, 1040–1048.

Dweck, C. S., Davidson, W., Nelson, S., & Enna, B. (1978). Sex differences in learned helplessness: II. The contingencies of evaluative feedback in the classroom and III. An experimental analysis. *Developmental Psychology, 14*, 268–276.

Eccles, J. S. (2009). Who am I and what am I going to do with my life? Personal and collective identities as motivators of action. *Educational Psychologist, 44*, 78–89.

Eccles (Parsons), J., Adler, T. F., Futterman, R., Goff, S. B., Kaczala, C. M., Meece, J. L., et al. (1983). Expectations, values and academic behaviors. In J. T. Spence (Ed.), *Perspectives on achievement and achievement motivation* (pp. 75–146). San Francisco: W. H. Freeman.

Eccles, J. S., Jacobs, J. E., & Harold, R. D. (1990). Gender role stereotypes, expectancy effects, and parents' socialization of gender differences. *Journal of Social Issues, 46*, 183–201.

Frenzel, A. C., Goetz, T., Pekrun, R., & Watt, H. M. G. (2010). Development of mathematics interest in adolescence: Influences of gender, family, and school context. *Journal of Research on Adolescence, 20*, 507–537.

Frey, K. S., & Ruble, D. N. (1987). What children say about classroom performance: Sex and grade differences in perceived competence. *Child Development, 58*, 1066–1078.

Friedel, J. M., Cortina, K. S., Turner, J. C., & Midgley, C. (2007). Achievement goals, efficacy beliefs and coping strategies in mathematics: The roles of perceived parent and teacher goal emphases. *Contemporary Educational Psychology, 32*, 434–458.

Frome, P. M., & Eccles, J. S. (1998). Parents' influence on children's achievement-related perceptions. *Journal of Personality and Social Psychology, 74*, 435–452.

Harackiewicz, J. M., Barron, K. E., Pintrich, P. K., Elliot, A. J., & Thrush, T. M. (2002). Revision of achievement goal theory: Necessary and illuminating. *Journal of Educational Psychology, 94*, 638–645.

Heatherington, L., Daubman, K. A., Bates, C., Ahn, A., Brown, H., & Preston, C. (1993). Two investigations of "female modesty" in achievement situations. *Sex Roles, 29*, 739–754.

Heyman, G. D., & Legare, C. H. (2004). Children's beliefs about gender differences in the academic and social domains. *Sex Roles, 50*, 227–239.

Hidi, S., & Renninger, K. A. (2006). The four-phase model of interest development. *Educational Psychologist, 41*, 111–127.

Hill, J. P., & Lynch, M. E. (1983). The intensification of gender-related role expectations during early adolescence. In J. Brooks-Gunn, & A. C. Petersen (Eds.), *Girls at puberty* (pp. 201–228). New York: Plenum.

Hirt, E. R., & McCrea, S. M. (2009). Man smart, woman smarter? Getting to the root of gender differences in self-handicapping. *Social and Personality Psychology Compass, 3*, 260–274.

Hoffman, L. W. (1974). Fear of success in males and females: 1965 and 1971. *Journal of Consulting and Clinical Psychology, 42*, 353–358.

Horner, M. S. (1972). Toward an understanding of achievement-related conflicts in women. *Journal of Social Issues, 28*, 157–175.

Hyde, J. (2005). The gender similarities hypothesis. *American Psychologist, 60*, 581–592.

Jackson, C. (2002). "Laddishness" as a self-worth protection strategy. *Gender and Education, 14*, 37–51.

Jacobs, J. E., Lanza, S., Osgood, D. W., Eccles, J. S., & Wigfield, A. (2002). Changes in children's self competence and values: Gender and domain differences across grades one through twelve. *Child Development, 73*, 509–527.

Kenney-Benson, G. A., Pomerantz, E. M., Ryan, A. M., & Patrick, H. (2006). Sex differences in math performance: The role of children's approach to schoolwork. *Developmental Psychology, 42*, 11–26.

Kessels, U. (2005). Fitting into the stereotype: How gender-stereotyped perceptions of prototypic peers relate to liking for school subjects. *European Journal of Psychology of Education, 20*, 309–323.

Kitayama, S., Markus, H. R., Matsumoto, H., & Norasakkunkit, V. (1997). Individual and collective processes in the construction of the self: Self-enhancement in the United States and self-criticism in Japan. *Journal of Personality and Social Psychology, 72*, 1245–1267.

Kling, K. C., Hyde, J. S., Showers, C. J., & Buswell, B. N. (1999). Gender differences in self-esteem: A meta-analysis. *Psychological Bulletin, 125*, 470–500.

Koestner, R., Zuckerman, M., & Koestner, J. (1989). Attributional focus of praise and children's intrinsic motivation: The moderating role of gender. *Personality and Social Psychology Bulletin, 15*, 61–72.

Koul, R., Roy, L., & Lerdpornkulrat, T. (2012). Motivational goal orientation, perceptions of biology and physics classroom learning environments, and gender. *Learning Environments Research, 15*, 217–229.

Kurman, J. (2004). Gender, self-enhancement, and self-regulation of learning behaviors in junior high school. *Sex Roles, 50*, 725–735.

Lavy, V., & Schlosser, A. (2011). Mechanisms and impacts of gender peer effects at school. *American Economic Journal: Applied Economics, 3*, 1–33.

Leaper, C., & Brown, C. S. (2014). Sexism in schools. In L. S. Liben & R. S. Bigler (Vol. Eds.) *The role of gender in educational contexts and outcomes.* In J. B. Benson (Series Ed.), *Advances in child development and behavior: Vol. 47* (pp. 189–223). London: Elsevier.

Leaper, C., & Van, S. R. (2008). Masculinity ideology, covert sexism, and perceived gender typicality in relation to young men's academic motivation and choices in college. *Psychology of Men & Masculinity, 9*, 139–153.

Lenney, E. (1977). Women's self-confidence in achievement settings. *Psychological Bulletin, 84*, 1–13.

Liben, L. S., & Coyle. E. F. (2014). Developmental interventions to address the STEM gender gap: Exploring intended and unintended consequences. In L. S. Liben & R. S. Bigler (Vol. Eds.) *The role of gender in educational contexts and outcomes.* In J. B. Benson (Series Ed.), *Advances in child development and behavior: Vol. 47* (pp. 77–116). London: Elsevier.

Lytton, H., & Romney, D. M. (1991). Parents' differential socialization of boys and girls: A meta-analysis. *Psychological Bulletin, 109*, 267–296.

Maccoby, E. E. (1998). *The two sexes: Growing up apart, coming together.* Cambridge, MA: Harvard University Press.

Madon, S., Jussim, L., Keiper, S., Eccles, J., Smith, A., & Palumbo, P. (1998). The accuracy and power of sex, social class, and ethnic stereotypes: A naturalistic study in person perception. *Personality and Social Psychology Bulletin, 24*, 1304–1318.

Maltz, D. N., & Borker, R. A. (1982). A cultural approach to male-female miscommunication. In J. J. Gumperz (Ed.), *Language and social identity* (pp. 195–216). Cambridge, England: Cambridge University Press.

Mandel, O. (2010). *Responses to failure and self-presentation: When gender and achievement goals meet.* Unpublished doctoral dissertation. Jerusalem, Israel: Hebrew University.

Marsh, H., Craven, R., Hinkley, J. W., & Debus, R. L. (2003). Evaluation of the big two-factor theory of academic motivation orientations: An evaluation of jingle-jangle fallacies. *Multivariate Behavioral Research, 38*, 189–224.

Marsh, H. W., & Yeung, A. S. (1998). Longitudinal structural models of academic self-concept and achievement: Gender differences in the development of math and English constructs. *American Educational Research Journal, 35*, 705–738.

Martin, C. L., Fabes, R. A., & Hanish, L. D. (2014). Gendered-peer relationships in educational contexts. In L. S. Liben & R. S. Bigler (Vol. Eds.) *The role of gender in educational contexts and outcomes*. In J. B. Benson (Series Ed.), *Advances in child development and behavior: Vol. 47* (pp. 151–187). London: Elsevier.

McClelland, D. C., Atkinson, J. W., Clark, R. A., & Lowell, E. L. (1953). *The achievement motive*. East Norwalk, CT, USA: Appleton-Century-Crofts.

McCloskey, L. A. (1996). Gender and the expression of status in children's mixed-age conversations. *Journal of Applied Developmental Psychology, 17,* 117–133.

Meece, J. L., Glienke, B. B., & Burg, S. (2006). Gender and motivation. *Journal of School Psychology, 44,* 351–373.

Meece, J. L., & Holt, K. (1993). A pattern analysis of students' achievement goals. *Journal of Educational Psychology, 85,* 582–590.

Muller Mirza, N., & Perret-Clermont, A. (Eds.). (2009). *Argumentation and education*. Dordrecht: Springer.

Mullola, S., Ravaja, N., Lipsanen, J., Alatupa, S., Hintsanen, M., Jokela, M., et al. (2012). Gender differences in teachers' perceptions of students' temperament, educational competence, and teachability. *British Journal of Educational Psychology, 82,* 185–206.

Nagy, G., Watt, H. M. G., Eccles, J. S., Trautwein, U., Lüdtke, O., & Baumert, J. (2010). The development of students' mathematics self-concept in relation to gender: Different countries, different trajectories? *Journal of Research on Adolescence, 20,* 482–506.

Newstead, S. E., Franklin-Stokes, A., & Armstead, P. (1996). Individual differences in student cheating. *Journal of Educational Psychology, 88,* 229–241.

Nicholls, J. G. (1975). Causal attributions and other achievement-related cognitions: Effects of task outcome, attainment value, and sex. *Journal of Personality and Social Psychology, 31,* 379–389.

Nicholls, J. G. (1989). *The competitive ethos and democratic education*. Cambridge: Harvard University Press.

Nolen, S. B. (1988). Reasons for studying: Motivational orientations and study strategies. *Cognition and Instruction, 5,* 269–287.

Nosek, B., Banaji, M., & Greenwald, A. (2002). Math=male, me=female, therefore math not equal me. *Journal of Personality and Social Psychology, 83,* 44–59.

Pajares, F., & Valiante, G. (1999). Grade level and gender differences in the writing self-beliefs of middle school students. *Contemporary Educational Psychology, 24,* 390–405.

Parsons, J. E., Kaczala, C. M., & Meece, J. L. (1982). Socialization of achievement attitudes and beliefs: Classroom influences. *Child Development, 53,* 322–339.

Petersen, J., & Hyde, J. S. (2014). Gender-related academic and occupational interests and goals. In L. S. Liben & R. S. Bigler (Vol. Eds.) *The role of gender in educational contexts and outcomes*. In J. B. Benson (Series Ed.), *Advances in child development and behavior: Vol. 47* (pp. 43–76). London: Elsevier.

Pomerantz, E., Altermatt, E. R., & Saxon, J. L. (2002). Making the grade but feeling distressed: Gender differences in academic performance and internal distress. *Journal of Educational Psychology, 94,* 396–404.

Preckel, F., Goetz, T., Pekrun, R., & Kleine, M. (2008). Gender differences in gifted and average-ability students: Comparing girls' and boys' achievement, self-concept, interest, and motivation in mathematics. *Gifted Child Quarterly, 52,* 146–159.

Renold, E. (2001a). 'Square-girls', femininity and the negotiation of academic success in the primary school. *British Educational Research Journal, 27,* 577–587.

Renold, E. (2001b). Learning the 'hard' way: Boys, hegemonic masculinity and the negotiation of learner identities in the primary school. *British Journal of Sociology of Education, 22,* 39–385.

Roberts, T. (1991). Gender and the influence of evaluations on self-assessments in achievement settings. *Psychological Bulletin, 109*, 297–308.

Roberts, T. A., & Nolen-Hoeksema, S. (1994). Gender comparisons in responsiveness to others' evaluations in achievement settings. *Psychology of Women Quarterly, 18*, 221–240.

Rolland, R. G. (2012). Synthesizing the evidence on classroom goal structures in middle and secondary schools: A meta-analysis and narrative review. *Review of Educational Research, 82*, 396–435.

Rose, A. J., & Rudolph, K. D. (2006). A review of sex differences in peer relationship processes: Potential trade-offs for the emotional and behavioral development of girls and boys. *Psychological Bulletin, 132*, 98–131.

Rotter, J. B. (1966). Generalized expectancies for internal versus external control of reinforcement. *Psychological Monographs, 80*, 1–28.

Rowley, S. J., Ross, L., Lozada, F., Williams, A., Gale, A., & Kurtz-Costes, B. (2014). Framing black boys: Parent, teacher, and student narratives of the academic lives of black boys. In L. S. Liben & R. S. Bigler (Vol. Eds.) *The role of gender in educational contexts and outcomes*. In J. B. Benson (Series Ed.), *Advances in child development and behavior: Vol. 47* (pp. 301–332). London: Elsevier.

Rozek, C. S., Hyde, J. S., Svoboda, R. C., Hulleman, C. S., & Harackiewicz, J. M. (accepted). Gender differences in the effects of a utility-value intervention to help parents motivate adolescents in mathematics and science. *Journal of Educational Psychology*.

Ruble, D. N., Eisenberg, R., & Higgins, E. T. (1994). Developmental changes in achievement evaluation: Motivational implications of self-other differences. *Child Development, 65*, 1091–1106.

Ruble, D. N., Martin, C. L., & Berenbaum, S. A. (2006). Gender development. In N. Eisenberg, W. Damon, & R. M. Lerner (Eds.), *Handbook of child psychology: Vol. 3, social, emotional, and personality development* (pp. 858–932) (6th ed.). Hoboken, NJ, USA: John Wiley & Sons.

Ryan, A. M., Gheen, M. H., & Midgley, C. (1998). Why do some students avoid asking for help? An examination of the interplay among students' academic efficacy, teachers' social–emotional role, and the classroom goal structure. *Journal of Educational Psychology, 90*, 528–535.

Ryckman, D. B., & Peckham, P. (1987). Gender differences in attributions for success and failure situations across subject areas. *Journal of Educational Research, 81*, 120–125.

Schwartz, S. H., & Rubel-Lifschitz, T. (2009). Cross-national variation in the size of sex differences in values: Effects of gender equality. *Journal of Personality and Social Psychology, 97*, 171–185.

Sedikides, C., Gaertner, L., & Toguchi, Y. (2003). Pancultural self-enhancement. *Journal of Personality and Social Psychology, 84*, 60–79.

Sheldon, A. (1993). Pickle fights: Gendered talk in preschool disputes. In D. Tannen (Ed.), *Oxford studies in sociolinguistics. Gender and conversational interaction* (pp. 83–109). New York, NY, US: Oxford University Press.

Snyder, T. D., & Dillow, S. A. (2011). *Digest of education statistics 2010*. Washington, DC: National Center for Education Statistics, U.S. Department of Education.

Solmon, M. A. (2014). Physical education, sports, and gender in schools. In L. S. Liben & R. S. Bigler (Vol. Eds.) *The role of gender in educational contexts and outcomes*. In J. B. Benson (Series Ed.), *Advances in child development and behavior: Vol. 47* (pp. 117–150). London: Elsevier.

Steinmayr, R., & Spinath, B. (2009). What explains boys' stronger confidence in their intelligence? *Sex Roles, 61*, 736–749.

Stetsenko, A., Little, T. D., Gordeeva, T., Grasshof, M., & Oettingen, G. (2000). Gender effects in children's beliefs about school performance: A cross-cultural study. *Child Development, 71*, 517–527.

Stipek, D. J., & Gralinski, J. H. (1991). Gender differences in children's achievement-related beliefs and emotional responses to success and failure in mathematics. *Journal of Educational Psychology, 83*, 361–371.

Su, R., Rounds, J., & Armstrong, P. I. (2009). Men and things, women and people: A meta-analysis of sex differences in interests. *Psychological Bulletin, 135*, 859–884.

Urdan, T., & Midgley, C. (2001). Academic self-handicapping: What we know, what more there is to learn. *Educational Psychology Review, 13*, 115–138.

Usher, E. L., & Pajares, F. (2008). Sources of self-efficacy in school: Critical review of the literature and future directions. *Review of Educational Research, 78*, 751–796.

Valentine, J. C., DuBois, D. L., & Cooper, H. (2004). The relation between self- beliefs and academic achievement: A meta-analytic review. *Educational Psychologist, 39*, 111–133.

Valla, J., & Ceci, S. J. (2011). Can sex differences in science be tied to the long reach of prenatal hormones? Brain organization theory, digit ratio (2D/4D), and sex differences in preferences and cognition. *Perspectives on Psychological Science, 6*, 134–146.

Veroff, J., Wilcox, S., & Atkinson, J. W. (1953). The achievement motive in high school and college age women. *Journal of Abnormal and Social Psychology, 48*, 108–119.

Walkerdine, V. (1989). *Counting girls out*. London, UK: Virago.

Wang, M. T., Eccles, J. S., & Kenny, S. (2013). Not lack of ability but more choice: Individual and gender differences in choice of careers in science, technology, engineering, and mathematics. *Psychological Science, 24*, 770–775.

Weiner, B. (1986). An attributional theory of achievement motivation and emotion. *Psychological Review, 92*, 548–573.

Weisgram, E. S., Bigler, R., & Liben, L. S. (2010). Gender, values, and occupational interests among children, adolescents, and adults. *Child Development, 81*, 778–796.

Wigfield, A., Eccles, J. S., Yoon, K. S., Harold, R. D., Arbreton, A. J. A., Freedman-Doan, C., et al. (1997). Change in children's competence beliefs and subjective task values across the elementary school years: A 3-year study. *Journal of Educational Psychology, 89*, 451–469.

Wilkins, J. L. M. (2004). Mathematics and science concept: An international investigation. *Journal of Experimental Education, 72*, 331–346.

Ziegler, A., & Stoeger, H. (2004). Evaluation of an attributional retraining (modeling technique) to reduce gender differences in chemistry instruction. *High Ability Studies, 15*, 63–83.

CHAPTER TWO

Gender-Related Academic and Occupational Interests and Goals

Jennifer Petersen[*,1], Janet Shibley Hyde[†]

[*]Department of Educational Foundations, University of Wisconsin, Whitewater, Wisconsin, USA
[†]Department of Psychology, University of Wisconsin, Madison, Wisconsin, USA
[1]Corresponding author: e-mail address: petersej@uww.edu

Contents

1. Theoretical Frameworks — 45
   1.1 Expectancy-Value Theory — 45
   1.2 Stereotype Threat Theory — 46
   1.3 Sociocultural Theory — 48
   1.4 The Gender Similarities Hypothesis — 48
2. Gender Similarities and Differences in Academic Ability and Dispositions — 49
   2.1 Mathematical Performance — 50
   2.2 Spatial Performance — 51
   2.3 Verbal Skills — 51
   2.4 Communication — 52
   2.5 Helping Behavior — 53
   2.6 Leadership — 54
   2.7 Self-Esteem and Self-Concept — 55
3. Gender Differences in Occupational Interests and Goals — 55
   3.1 Interests — 56
   3.2 Expectancy for Success — 57
   3.3 Utility Value — 58
   3.4 Job Attribute Preferences — 59
4. Factors that may Shape Gendered Occupational Goals — 61
   4.1 Parental Expectations — 61
   4.2 Stereotypes and Discrimination — 63
   4.3 Work–Family Balance — 66
   4.4 Developmental Trends — 67
   4.5 Training, Practice, and Interventions — 69
   4.6 Cultural Differences — 70
5. Conclusions — 71
References — 72

Abstract

This chapter reviews the theories and empirical evidence concerning whether gender differences in academic and occupational goals and interests exist, and if so, why those differences may be present. Expectancy-value theory, stereotype threat, sociocultural theory, and the gender similarities hypothesis lay the theoretical framework for this chapter. Following a brief review of these theories, we describe the evidence for gender differences in academic ability and occupational interests and goals, using meta-analytic reviews wherever possible. Although there are few gender differences in academic ability, some gender differences in occupational goals and interests persist, particularly in science and mathematics. These gender differences may be due to parental or cultural expectations, changes in developmental trends, stereotypes and discrimination, or gendered-expectations to achieve work–family balance. Overall, the pathways to adult occupations are complex, involving many factors that affect occupational goals, interests, and self-concept.

In the United States and many other Western nations, most adult occupations are highly gender segregated. For example, in 2009 in the United States, only 1.3% of airline pilots were women, as were 1.6% of carpenters and 3.7% of telephone installers; yet women were 95.0% of childcare workers, 96.6% of dental hygienists, and 92.0% of registered nurses (Bureau of Labor Statistics, 2011). This gender segregation is important for many reasons, including the concern that it perpetuates gender stereotypes and is the major source of the gender wage gap (Ridgeway, 2011). Gender segregation in the workplace may also influence men and women to select careers based on the gender composition of the workplace rather than on interests or skills (Weisgram, Bigler, & Liben, 2010).

Many factors have been hypothesized to contribute to the underrepresentation of women in many occupations, including sex discrimination, gender stereotypes, and gender differences in abilities or interests (e.g., Ceci & Williams, 2011; Moss-Racusin, Dovidio, Brescoll, Graham, & Handelsman, 2012; Su, Rounds, & Armstrong, 2009). Here, we focus on the processes involved in gender development that lead most adults to occupy gender-typical occupations. We ask questions such as the following: Are there gender differences in academic abilities or in interests that contribute to the gender segregation of adult occupations? Are these gender differences modifiable? First, however, we consider psychological theories that are relevant to understanding of psychological gender differences, especially gender differences in academic and occupational outcomes.

1. THEORETICAL FRAMEWORKS

We begin by reviewing theories relevant to questions of gender differences and gender segregation, specifically, expectancy-value theory, stereotype threat theory, sociocultural theory, and the gender similarities hypothesis.

1.1. Expectancy-Value Theory

As formulated by Eccles and colleagues, expectancy-value theory holds that achievement-related choices—such as deciding to major in engineering with the goal of becoming a civil engineer—are governed by a variety of factors (Eccles, 1994; Eccles (Parsons) et al., 1983; Meece, Eccles-Parson, et al., 1982). The details of this theory are beyond the scope of this chapter, but Figure 1 provides additional information about the proposed factors that lead students to occupational and educational decisions. In particular, these factors may be divided into two categories: expectancy for success and subjective task value. Expectancy of success refers to the individual's expectation that he or she can succeed at the challenging task, such as majoring in

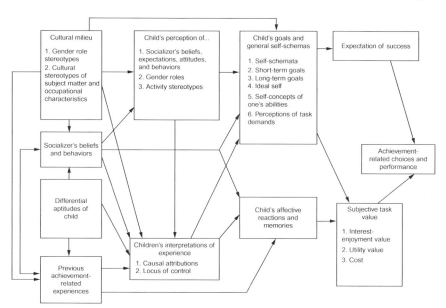

Figure 1 Eccles and colleagues' (1983) expectancy-value model of academic and occupational choices.

engineering. Expectations for success develop over childhood and adolescence (see Butler, 2014 [Chapter 1 of this volume]) and are shaped by factors such as self-concept of abilities (e.g. "I am good at math so I can succeed in engineering"), gender stereotypes (e.g. "I am a girl and engineering is for men"), the beliefs of socializers such as parents (e.g. "my daughter is good at math and thus engineering would be a good field for her"), and previous achievement-related experiences (e.g. "I scored in the 99th percentile on my state's standardized math test").

Subjective task value involves several aspects, including interest (intrinsic value) and utility value, which refers to a person's perception of the usefulness of the task either currently or in the future (Meece et al., 1982). For example, if a student wants to become a civil engineer, undertaking an engineering major has very high utility value for her. Interest, utility value, and self-concept of ability tend to correlate with each other. That is, people who have a positive math self-concept also tend to be interested in math and to see it as useful.

Expectancy-value theory is a developmental theory, incorporating factors such as the development of self-concept and the influence of socializers such as parents and teachers. Moreover, it recognizes the importance of the cultural milieu—such as cultural gender stereotypes and the easily observed gender segregation of adult occupations—in shaping adolescents' and adults' occupational choices. In later sections, we will review specific research that derives from the theory.

1.2. Stereotype Threat Theory

Stereotype threat refers to a phenomenon in which people feel that they are personally at risk of confirming a negative stereotype about their group, which interferes with their performance (Steele, 1997; Steele & Aronson, 1995). The original research dealt with racial stereotypes and, specifically, the stereotype that African Americans are intellectually inferior. In one typical experiment, Steele administered a test of verbal intelligence to highly talented Black and White students at Stanford. Half the students were randomly assigned to a condition in which they were told that the test they were about to take was diagnostic of intelligence. The remaining students were told the test was not diagnostic of intelligence. The Black students who believed that the test measured intelligence (the threat condition) performed worse than the Black students who believed that it did not, whereas White students' performance was unaffected by the instructions.

Research soon followed demonstrating that stereotype threat also occurs with gender stereotypes, in particular, the stereotype that women are bad at math (Brown & Josephs, 1999; Inzlicht & Schmader, 2012; Quinn & Spencer, 2001; Schmader, Johns, & Forbes, 2008). Stereotype threat is also discussed in detail by Leaper and Brown (2014) [Chapter 6 of this volume]. In one experiment, male and female college students with equivalent math backgrounds were randomly assigned to one of two conditions (Spencer, Steele, & Quinn, 1999). In the threat condition, they were told that the math test they were about to take had shown gender differences in the past. In the other condition, they were told that the test was gender fair. Among those who were told that the test was gender fair, there were no gender differences in performance, whereas in the threat condition, women had significantly lower scores than men did.

It appears that stereotype threat impairs performance because of several factors: (1) a physiological stress response that impairs processing in the prefrontal cortex; (2) increased active monitoring of performance; and (3) efforts to suppress negative thoughts and emotions (Schmader et al., 2008). All of these combine to reduce executive functioning, which is crucial for performance on academic tasks, especially challenging ones.

Stereotype threat effects have been examined among children, especially for girls and mathematics (e.g., Ganley et al., 2013). The findings tend to be inconsistent, probably because stereotype threat effects are found only under certain conditions. In particular, the person has to be identified with the domain in question, in this case, mathematics. Moreover, the test needs to be introduced as being indicative of a person's ability, and the test must be difficult. Gender stereotype threat effects might not be expected at younger ages because certain concepts have not yet developed. Aronson and Good (2003) argued that, for stereotype threat to occur for girls, they must (1) be aware of the content of gender stereotypes, (2) understand both the personal and societal implications of gender stereotypes, (3) have a well-developed concept of gender identity, and (4) have a firm concept of academic ability. Aronson and Good concluded that all of these are present by about ages 11 to 12, that is, at the beginning of middle school. More research is needed to test Aronson and Good's hypotheses and determine exactly when, in development, stereotype threat begins to occur.

Certainly, there is ample evidence of gender stereotype threat in the area of mathematics for college women, that is, precisely the people who are choosing to pursue or not careers in math-intensive, male-typical fields such as physics and engineering. Stereotype threat, therefore, may contribute to the dearth of women in these fields. As discussed in a later section, interventions have been developed to counteract stereotype threat effects.

1.3. Sociocultural Theory

Sociocultural theory, also called social structural theory or social role theory, was proposed by Eagly and Wood (1999). According to this view, a society's division of labor by gender drives all other gender differences in behavior. That is, for example, women's greater nurturance is a result of, rather than the cause of, their assignment to caring for children. Psychological gender differences result from individuals' adaptations to the particular roles to which they are assigned as well as the roles that are proscribed. Biological differences between males and females are important because they are magnified by culture. Men's greater size and strength, historically, led them to pursue activities such as warfare, which gave them greater status, power, and wealth than women. Once in those roles, men's behavior became more dominant and women's behavior accommodated by becoming more subordinate. Women's biological capacity for bearing children and breastfeeding led them to care for children, which in turn led them to develop nurturance and relationship skills.

This line of theorizing led Eagly and Wood to predict that the greater the gender difference in status and roles in a culture, the greater the psychological gender differences would be. That is, there should be a positive correlation between the amount of gender inequality in countries and the magnitude of psychological gender differences in those countries. Using cross-national data, Else-Quest, Hyde, and Linn (2010) tested these predictions for gender differences in math performance. Using two international data sets, the Trends in International Mathematics and Science Study and the Programme for International Student Assessment (PISA), they found that, across nations, the size of the gender gap in math performance of 15-year-olds was correlated with nations' gender equity in school enrollment, women's share of research jobs, and women's representation in parliament. In short, nations with more gender equality have smaller gender gaps in math performance.

Sociocultural theory was proposed by social psychologists and has received little attention by developmentalists, with the exception of the study of adolescents and math performance described above. However, research reviewed by Leaper and Brown (2014) [Chapter 6 of this volume] has examined the development of some of the psychological constructs that are key to the theory, such as the development of children's understanding of sexism.

1.4. The Gender Similarities Hypothesis

The gender similarities hypothesis, proposed by Hyde (2005), states that males and females are similar on most, but not all, psychological variables.

Based on a meta-analysis of 46 meta-analyses of psychological gender differences, 30% of effect sizes were trivial in magnitude (d between 0 and 0.10) and an additional 48% were small (0.10–0.35). Gender similarities were found for self-esteem, math performance, self-disclosure, and reading comprehension. Exceptions were found for some aspects of motor performance such as throwing distance, some measures of sexuality like the prevalence of masturbation, and physical aggression, all of which showed moderate or large gender differences.

Some gender meta-analyses have taken a developmental approach, computing effect sizes at different ages. When available, these findings are reviewed in later sections of this chapter. Hyde (2005) noted that the magnitude of gender differences varies considerably across age for some measures.

The gender similarities hypothesis has profound implications for research on gender development. Much gender development research aims at explaining why, in development, large gender differences are present by adolescence or adulthood. The gender similarities hypothesis holds that many gender similarities are found in adulthood, even in domains such as math performance. In short, in many areas there may be no gender difference to explain. This approach encourages researchers to balance emphasis on gender differences with emphasis on gender similarities.

In the context of the gender similarities hypothesis, the gender segregation of most adult occupations is striking. This observation encourages researchers to consider influences outside the individual, such as cultural sexism and stereotypes, as part of the explanation for the gender segregation of adult occupations.

2. GENDER SIMILARITIES AND DIFFERENCES IN ACADEMIC ABILITY AND DISPOSITIONS

The self-perceived ability to succeed at a career is one of the leading factors in choosing an occupation (Bandura, Barbaranelli, Caprara, & Pastoreli, 2001; Eccles, 1994). Young people often ask themselves about their skills and talents before choosing a career. Will I succeed in a career that involves math? Would I like a career that requires leadership responsibility? The answers to these questions may vary by gender. Therefore, examining gender differences in academic and dispositional outcomes is essential for understanding gender differences in occupational interests, goals, and performance.

As much as possible, the data here are reported using meta-analyses because they rely on multiple studies rather than using a single source, and they report the magnitude of gender differences (Hedges & Nowell, 1995). In a meta-analysis, the magnitude of the gender difference is measured with an effect size, d, which measures the standardized difference between males and females on some construct. In this chapter, negative effect sizes indicate that girls or women scored higher on the measure, whereas positive effect sizes indicate that boys or men scored higher. Cohen (1988) developed criteria to help interpret the magnitude of effect sizes. According to these criteria, $d=0.20$ is a small effect, $d=0.50$ is a medium effect, and $d=0.80$ is a large effect. Effect sizes smaller than 0.10 are so small that they are considered trivial (Hyde, 2005).

2.1. Mathematical Performance

Science, technology, engineering, and math (STEM) are particularly important when it comes to occupational choices because they are among the fastest growing fields in the world. In particular, the areas of technology and engineering are advancing very quickly and there is high demand for workers to fill these jobs (Freeman & Aspray, 1999). Because people with these career skills are in such high demand and require a great deal of specialization, these careers are often given a high level of prestige and an accompanying high salary (National Association of Colleges and Employers, 2013). However, a gender gap remains in many STEM fields; women are underrepresented (e.g., Eccles, 1994). Girls and women who are not trained in math and science are doing themselves a disservice by not keeping up with the growing trends in technology and eliminating themselves from the pool of applicants available for these prestigious careers. If the gender gap in STEM careers continues, then men are likely to hold more prestigious jobs and earn more, and occupational gender stereotypes will be perpetuated.

Despite the stereotype that boys are more successful than girls at math, recent evidence suggests that gender differences in math performance are trivial. In a meta-analysis using U.S. state assessments of children's math ability, data represented the testing of several million students across the country (Hyde, Lindberg, Linn, Ellis, & Williams, 2008). Effect sizes were very small indicating no gender difference at any grade level. This meta-analysis also looked at gender differences in complex problem solving using data from the National Assessment of Educational Progress. At grade 12, the average effect size was $d=0.07$, indicating that girls and boys did not differ in solving complex mathematical problems. Complex problem-solving skills are especially important for science and technology careers.

In another meta-analysis, Lindberg and colleagues synthesized data from 242 studies appearing between 1990 and 2007, representing the testing of 1.2 million people (Lindberg, Hyde, Petersen, & Linn, 2010). Overall, the gender difference in overall math performance was trivial ($d=0.05$), and the gender difference in complex problem solving was small ($d=0.16$).

These studies combined suggest minimal gender differences in mathematics performance, at least in the United States. Although gender differences continue to exist in STEM occupations, those differences are unlikely to be due to gender differences in math ability or performance.

2.2. Spatial Performance

Potential gender differences in spatial ability have often been discussed as an explanation for girls' underrepresentation in STEM careers. Spatial abilities are assessed in a variety of ways. One way is three-dimensional (3D) mental rotation, which requires the test taker to mentally rotate an object in three dimensions and then identify what the object would look like after rotation. 3D mental rotation is necessary in many STEM occupations, especially engineering.

According to an early meta-analysis, the gender difference in 3D mental rotation is large, favoring males, $d=0.73$ (Linn & Petersen, 1985). In a later meta-analysis, the gender difference was moderately sized, $d=0.56$ (Voyer, Voyer, & Bryden, 1995). However, the studies that were reviewed often used tests with time limits, which examine speed as much as ability. Therefore, gender differences on these tests may be due to tight time limits rather than differences in 3D mental rotation ability. One meta-analysis found that with shorter time limits, the gender difference in mental rotation was large ($d=1.03$), whereas in tests with no time limits the effect size was only moderate ($d=0.51$) (Voyer, 2011; see also Maeda & Yoon, 2013).

Overall, then, there is a moderate gender difference favoring males in 3D mental rotation. However, gender differences in spatial skills training such as video games may explain this difference, as discussed later in this chapter.

2.3. Verbal Skills

All occupations require some degree of verbal and communication skills. From writing briefings and reports to communicating with colleagues, workers who are skilled with words are more likely to be successful employees. Traditional gender stereotypes suggest that women are more adept than men at verbal and communication skills, but meta-analytic research suggests that these gender differences may be smaller than popular opinion might suggest.

Overall, gender differences in verbal skills are small, favoring females, $d=-0.11$ (Hyde & Linn, 1988). However, when different types of verbal ability are examined, the results appear more complex. In the same meta-analysis, trivial gender differences were found for vocabulary ($d=-0.02$), reading comprehension ($d=-0.03$), and essay writing ($d=-0.09$). The largest effect was for verbal fluency, $d=-0.33$.

Hedges and Nowell (1995) conducted a meta-analysis of gender differences in reading comprehension and vocabulary among adolescents. For reading comprehension, effect sizes ranged from -0.18 to $+0.002$. For vocabulary, effect sizes ranged from -0.06 to $+0.25$. Again, the differences were not large and did not consistently favor females.

International data analyzed from PISA found an effect size of $d=-0.44$ for reading achievement (Reilly, 2012). However, boys were significantly more likely to fall at the lower end of the distribution. Across all 65 participating nations, the gender difference was moderate, $d=-0.44$. In accordance with sociocultural theory (Eagly & Wood, 1999), the variability across nations was accounted for by gender equality in the participating nations.

2.4. Communication

Communication in the workplace is vital to the successful completion of group projects, collaboration, and to the harmony of the working environment. As gender integration becomes increasingly prevalent in the workplace, it is important for both men and women to communicate effectively with one another. However, stereotypes about enormous gender differences in communication, and the inability of women and men to communicate, abound. Some have even argued that women's and men's patterns of speaking are so vastly different that men and women essentially belong to different linguistic communities (Tannen, 1991) In particular, it has been said that women use more tentative speech than do men, as indicated by greater use of tag questions (e.g. "He is very tall, isn't he?") and hedge statements (e.g. "I'm not an expert, but I do like math"). These forms of speech can convey a lack of self-confidence and strength.

According to a meta-analysis of studies of tentative speech, however, the gender differences favor women, but are small for tag questions, $d=-0.23$, and for verbal hedges, $d=-0.15$ (Leaper & Robnett, 2011). Moreover, the magnitude of the gender difference depends on context. It is larger in lab studies ($d=-0.28$) than in naturalistic studies outside the lab ($d=-0.09$).

Stereotypes that suggest that women use more tentative language and are less self-confident may play a role in occupational goals and achievements. For example, in business and many other careers, it is important for employees to express self-confidence. Employers who endorse the stereotype that women are less confident than men may be less likely to hire and promote women than men. Similarly, women, conforming to stereotypes that demand interpersonal sensitivity in women (Leaper & Robnett, 2011), may engage in more tentative speech.

2.5. Helping Behavior

The "nurturer" stereotype suggests that women are more skilled than men at helping others because of their "natural role" as mother or caretaker. This stereotype may lead women to pursue careers that help others, such as nursing and teaching, and it may lead men away from such careers. Even women who do not believe this stereotype directly may be influenced by gender roles in society to aspire to careers that help others.

Eagly and Crowley (1986) (see also Eagly, 2009) conducted a meta-analysis of research on gender differences in helping behavior. Contrary to stereotypes, this meta-analysis yielded $d=0.34$, a small effect indicating that males help more. Moderator analyses indicated that some helping behaviors were more common among men, such as stopping to help a motorist with a flat tire, but that other types of helping were more common among women, such as helping a distressed child. The authors argued that women are more likely to engage in relational helping behavior and men are more likely to initiate agentic helping and prosocial behaviors that require strength because they are consistent with social gender roles.

Helping others may take on a variety of forms and different forms of helping may be associated with the male or female role (Weisgram et al., 2010). For example, helping careers such as police officer or firefighter, which involve danger, are stereotyped as male professions, whereas careers that help more vulnerable populations, such as nurses or social workers, are more likely to be associated with women. These cultural stereotypes may limit career opportunities for men and women. It is also important to remember that many careers that may not initially appear to involve helping may help others indirectly. Civil engineering is one example. A person who designs a bridge or a sewer system is providing major help to others, albeit the help is indirect.

One explanation for women's underrepresentation in STEM careers is the lack of communal goals associated with the STEM disciplines (Diekman, Brown, Johnston, & Cark, 2010). Indeed, adults who value communal goals such as helping others were more likely to pursue female-stereotyped careers and were less likely to pursue STEM careers, even when controlling for math–science experience and self-efficacy. Communal goal orientation also mediated the association between gender and STEM careers, suggesting that women's lack of interest in STEM careers may result from the perceived lack of opportunity to help others in STEM careers. Although participants reported that they perceived STEM careers to impede their communal goals, the STEM disciplines do a great deal to help others. Emphasizing the communal goals in the STEM fields, such as the need for collaborative work and indirect helping influences on society, may redirect girls and women to the STEM fields (Weisgram & Bigler, 2006).

2.6. Leadership

Leadership skills are crucial in many occupations, particularly more prestigious careers, such as those requiring managerial responsibilities. Stereotypes that men have more natural leadership ability than women do may prevent women from being hired to leadership positions or may prevent them from being promoted to a higher rank.

A meta-analysis examined data on gender and the effectiveness of leaders (Eagly, Karau, & Makhijani, 1995). Overall, the gender difference in leadership effectiveness was trivial, $d=-0.02$. Moderator analyses indicated that male leaders were somewhat more effective in positions that were consistent with the male role, and female leaders were more effective in positions consistent with the female role.

A separate question is whether women and men differ in their leadership styles. Generally, there are three forms of leadership styles. (1) A transformational leader serves as a positive role model by gaining the trust of the followers. (2) A transactional leader administers rewards for good behaviors and punishments or corrections for undesirable behavior. (3) The laissez-faire leader is neglectful and uninvolved. For transformational leadership, $d=-0.10$, that is, a trivial difference (Eagly, Johannesen-Schmidt, & van Engen, 2003). For transactional leadership, women had a slight edge in reward-based approaches, although the difference is small, $d=-0.13$, whereas men were more inclined to wait until problems crop up and then address them, $d=0.27$. Men were also somewhat more likely than women to engage in laissez-faire leadership, although the difference is small $d=0.16$. Overall, the gender differences for leadership effectiveness and style are small despite gender stereotypes to the contrary.

2.7. Self-Esteem and Self-Concept

The popular media suggest that a lack of self-esteem is a serious problem for girls and women, and that by comparison boys do not have problems with self-esteem. If girls and women lack self-esteem, they may be less likely to pursue training in competitive fields such as science and engineering and thus will be less likely to apply for prestigious jobs.

A meta-analysis examining gender differences in self-esteem found a small overall gender difference favoring boys and men ($d=0.21$) (Kling, Hyde, Showers, & Buswell, 1999). The effect size increased from 0.16 in elementary school to 0.23 in middle school and 0.33 in high school, but then declined to 0.18 among college students and 0.10 among adults between the ages of 23 and 59. The effect size was not large in any age group, and it decreased among adults. An analysis by ethnicity for United States samples showed that the magnitude of the gender difference was larger for whites ($d=0.20$) than it was for blacks ($d=-0.04$). Sociocultural explanations may help explain gender differences in self-esteem in addition to explaining why gender differences vary across ethnic groups.

In terms of career aspirations, it may be more valuable to look at gender differences in self-esteem in specific areas rather than global self-esteem. For example, boys and girls may have high self-esteem in different areas, which may ultimately drive gender differences in career aspirations. A different meta-analysis examined studies that had measured domain-specific self-esteem or self-concept (Gentile et al., 2009). Males scored higher than females on physical appearance ($d=0.35$), athletic ($d=0.41$), and self-satisfaction ($d=0.33$) self-esteem, whereas females scored higher on behavioral conduct ($d=-0.17$) and moral-ethical self-esteem ($d=-0.38$). For all other domains, gender similarities were found; effect sizes were close to 0 for academic, social, and family self-esteem. Men and women may be more likely to choose careers consistent with their self-concept. For example, men may be more likely to pursue careers in athletics, whereas women may be more comfortable in careers requiring high standards of behavioral and moral conduct.

3. GENDER DIFFERENCES IN OCCUPATIONAL INTERESTS AND GOALS

As indicated in Section 2, gender similarities prevail in academic ability and many job-relevant traits. Any small gender differences in ability are unlikely to have a major impact on gendered career aspirations. Therefore, many occupational researchers have chosen to focus their energy instead on gender differences in occupational interests and goals.

3.1. Interests

Su et al. (2009) conducted a meta-analysis on gender differences in vocational interests. The authors summarized their global findings as "Men and Things, Women and People." That is, women were more interested in working with people, whereas men were more interested in working with things ($d=0.93$). For example, men preferred careers in realistic ($d=0.84$) and investigative fields ($d=0.26$), whereas women were more interested in artistic ($d=-0.35$), social ($d=-0.68$), and conventional careers ($d=-0.33$). Although gender differences in interests in math ($d=0.34$) and science ($d=0.36$) slightly favored males, the gender difference in engineering interest was quite large ($d=1.11$). Consistent with these findings, research indicates that women who endorse altruistic goals were less likely to pursue careers in math and science (Weisgram et al., 2010). However, women who viewed math and science as having altruistic goals were more likely to pursue careers in those areas.

Despite evidence that gender differences in occupational interest may exist, rigid stereotypes about gender differences in interest may limit boys' and girls' career aspirations and may even lead to discrimination in the workplace. It is important to remember that there are many counter-examples of the "Men and Things, Women and People" dimension. For example, the world of business and politics, typically male-dominated fields, require a great deal of person-to-person interaction, whereas dental hygienists and librarians are female-dominated careers that require the employee to work with things. In addition, the gender differences in this meta-analysis were generally small, indicating great overlap in the distributions of scores for males and females. By implication, there are many individuals who are interested in counter-stereotypical careers. Assuming that girls are not interested in engineering, for example, or that boys are not interested in teaching, may limit career aspirations and may lead to sex discrimination in the workplace.

It is also important to recognize that these gender differences in interests are not innate or immutable. Gender differences in interest among high school students, for example, are most likely the result of years of gender socialization that shape girls toward nurturance and people-oriented interests, and boys toward athletics and mechanical toys such as trucks.

Because of the gender gap in some STEM careers, a great deal of research has focused on gender differences in interest in mathematics. If girls are less interested in math or less likely to feel competent in math, then they may be less likely to choose STEM careers. Generally, girls do show more negative attitudes toward math and less interest in math than boys do (Eccles, 1994), but these interests are likely more influenced by socialization factors than lack of ability (Hyde et al., 2008).

3.2. Expectancy for Success

Bandura suggested that children's career aspirations are based largely on their expectancy for success (Bandura et al., 2001). He suggested that children's occupational aspirations are based on their occupational efficacy in that domain. Some evidence supports this view. For example, boys were more likely than girls to report high self-efficacy in traditionally male careers were, but both boys and girls reported high self-efficacy for traditionally female job skills (Fulcher, 2011). Perhaps boys and girls feel that stereotypical female job skills are easier than stereotypical male job skills.

According to a meta-analysis, 15-year-olds in the United States show gender differences in math self-confidence ($d=0.27$) and math anxiety ($d=-0.23$) that are larger than the gender difference in actual performance. Girls are more likely than boys to underestimate their math ability even when objective math scores show no gender difference (Eccles et al., 1983). Girls who have higher levels of self-efficacy and self-perceived math ability are more likely to pursue careers in math and science (Eccles, 1994).

Developing math self-efficacy is particularly important for high school students who have options for which math courses they will take, because these decisions may have long-term consequences for the careers available to those students. Math courses, in particular, may act as a gateway to STEM careers (Sells, 1980). Students who have little confidence in their math ability may choose not to take higher level math courses, which are often prerequisites for achieving prestigious STEM careers. Indeed, research suggests that students who had low math grades at the start of high school had low career aspirations and those aspirations decreased significantly across high school. Students who had high math grades at the beginning of high school had higher career aspirations and those aspirations increased throughout high school (Shapka, Domene, & Keating, 2008).

Girls who have low expectancy for success in math may take fewer math courses, thus limiting themselves from taking higher level math and science courses that require math as a prerequisite (Ma & Johnson, 2008; Sells, 1980). In particular, girls who do not take calculus are limiting themselves, because calculus is frequently required for students pursuing college majors in STEM. Students who take higher level math courses tend to have higher career aspirations regardless of their gender (Ma & Johnson, 2008).

3.3. Utility Value

In addition to interest and expectancy for success, students must also believe that a task is valuable, particularly that the task is useful to them or others, in order to pursue a career in that field. Students who do not see utility value in a task are likely to under-perform and to show little interest in the task (Hulleman, Godes, Hendricks, & Harackiewicz, 2010). Students who saw the utility value of math were more likely to enroll in more mathematics courses (Wigfield, 1994). Similarly, math utility value predicted the number of mathematics courses taken in high school, controlling for the effect of objective and self-perceived math ability (Updegraff, Eccles, Barber, & O'Brien, 1996). In samples of Canadian and Australian students, utility value predicted aspirations for careers in math, even though self-concept and interest in math did not (Watt et al., 2012). Gender differences in utility values may predict gender differences in occupational goals. Students who do not see the value in math are unlikely to pursue a STEM career.

Some evidence suggests that individuals' perceptions of the utility value of mathematics or science can be increased. In one experimental study, utility value was manipulated in a college math classroom by asking students in the experimental group to write a brief essay about how a new math technique was relevant to their lives (Hulleman, et al., 2010). In the control condition, students were asked to write an essay describing the new math technique. Following the intervention students in the experimental group reported more utility value, more interest in math, and higher grades in comparison to the control group, regardless of gender. This effect was particularly evident among students who previously performed poorly in the class.

This study suggests that the importance of a task can be highlighted by allowing students the time to focus on how it might be personally useful to them. Research suggests that girls do not value math as much as boys do and that this lack of utility value in math is associated with reduced achievement in math (Eccles (Parsons) et al., 1983; Watt, 2004). Lower utility value in math is also associated with taking fewer math classes (Eccles (Parsons) et al., 1983). Highlighting the utility value of math and STEM occupations may open additional career opportunities for young people, especially girls.

3.4. Job Attribute Preferences

A meta-analysis examined gender differences in job attribute preferences such as the potential for high earnings, good work hours, challenges, leadership opportunities, and so on (Konrad, Ritchie, Lieb, & Corrigall, 2000). The authors suggested that, according to gender stereotypes, men would prefer financial incentives and leadership opportunities in their careers, whereas women would prefer jobs that allow for flexibility and nurturance. Of the 40 preferences, 33 exhibited significant effect sizes. For example, men were slightly more likely than women to report that earnings ($d=0.12$) and leadership opportunities ($d=0.14$) were important, whereas women were more likely to prefer working with people ($d=-0.35$) and having opportunities to help others ($d=-0.36$). Some of the job preferences were contrary to gender stereotypes. For example, women were slightly more likely than men to prefer some stereotypically masculine roles such as a feeling of accomplishment ($d=-0.14$) and good benefits ($d=-0.09$). In general, gender differences were smaller for masculine job attributes, but were larger for feminine job attributes. Other research also indicates that women endorse both masculine and feminine job attributes, wanting both a high salary and family flexibility, for example, whereas men endorse only masculine job attributes (Weisgram et al., 2010).

Although the majority of job attribute preferences showed significant differences, the differences were generally small (Konrad et al., 2000). The authors noted that the small gender differences may be due to few studies including homemakers in their sample. Female homemakers are likely to hold highly traditional gender-role beliefs and traditional job attribute preferences, but they were missing from the samples.

Evidence suggests that, over time, women have become increasingly free to adopt masculine characteristics, but that men have not been eager to adopt feminine characteristics. For example, a meta-analysis showed that women in the early 1990s reported more masculine characteristics on the Bem sex-role inventory than women in the 1970s, but that there was little change in reported femininity for men (Twenge, 1997). This meta-analysis indicated that job attributes traditionally associated with masculine careers became more important to women between the 1970s and 1980s, but became less important from 1980 to 1990. Traditionally feminine job attributes followed a similar trend (Konrad et al., 2000). Perhaps some changes from the feminist movement in the 1970s have leveled off.

Research suggests that children, teens, and adults all associate stereotypically male professions with masculine values such as money and power (Weisgram et al., 2010; Weisgram, Dinella, & Fulcher, 2011). Female stereotyped careers were associated with family values. Job attribute preferences then predicted whether students were interested in female or male-stereotyped careers (Weisgram et al., 2010). For example, participants who endorsed power as an important job attribute were significantly more likely to pick a male-dominated career and significantly less likely to pursue a female-dominated career.

In an experimental manipulation, children, teens, and adults were asked to rate how interested they were in a novel job (Weisgram et al., 2010). Although the novel job remained the same, the gender of the employees and the gender-stereotyped properties of the job were manipulated. Participants were significantly more likely to show interest in a job that included employees of their own gender than an identical job with workers of the other gender. In other words, gender composition of the occupation alone was a significant factor in job preferences even with all other characteristics held equal. Interestingly, participants assumed particular job affordances based on the sex of the workers in the novel job. For example, participants viewed a job as having family flexibility if women (but not men) were described as the typical employee for the job.

The connection between job attribute preferences and traditionally male- and female-dominated careers is more complex than it may seem. For example, jobs that are traditionally associated with male job preferences may attract more men to those careers. As more men are hired for these careers, the more likely it is that women will avoid them because they are perceived as male-dominated. Furthermore, careers that are perceived as male-dominated are likewise perceived as having more job affordances attractive to men. The same complexities are evident in female-dominated careers. Thus, there is a circular association between job affordance and whether a particular career is male- or female-dominated. It may be that gender segregation stems from the affordances that a career offers, or it may be that the gender composition of a particular occupation leads to gendered-stereotypes about the job itself. This complex association makes it increasingly difficult to reduce gender segregation in the workplace and to increase representation of women in male-dominated careers and men in female-dominated careers (Weisgram et al., 2011).

4. FACTORS THAT MAY SHAPE GENDERED OCCUPATIONAL GOALS

Although there are some gender differences in occupational goals and interests, a myriad of other external factors may explain gender differences in occupational pursuits. Socializing forces teach very young children that boys and girls are different and that some careers are more appropriate for one gender than another. Despite the fact that these external factors come in a variety of forms throughout the lifespan, the gender-socializing messages are the same, and they can have a substantial impact on shaping individuals' occupational goals and interests.

4.1. Parental Expectations

Parents are one of the greatest socializing forces in a child's life and their messages about gender roles and stereotypes contribute to a child's expectancy for success in particular careers and motivation to pursue those careers (Eccles (Parsons), Adler, & Kaczala, 1982). Prior research suggests that parents influence their child's occupational aspirations by influencing their academic values and beliefs (Eccles (Parsons) et al., 1982; Fulcher, 2011; Jodl, Michael, Malanchuk, Eccles, & Sameroff, 2003).

The values and beliefs that parents convey to their children may be rooted in gender stereotypes. In particular, the stereotype that boys and men are more proficient in math than girls and women are endorsed by many parents (Eccles, Freedman-Doan, Frome, Jacobs, & Yoons, 2000). Even when there was no gender difference in objective test scores, parents who held gender stereotypic beliefs about math performance overestimated their son's math ability while underestimating their daughter's math ability (Eccles et al., 2000). Over time these parental perceptions began to influence the child's own opinions of her math ability, her likelihood to take math courses in the future, and ultimately her occupational aspirations (Eccles et al., 2000). Similarly, subtle forms of parental stereotypes may be evidenced in the domain of science. When parents talk with their children about science, parents are more likely to use complex explanations with their sons than with their daughters (Tenenbaum & Leaper, 2003). This provides increasing support and encouragement to boys and helps to explain why boys might be more interested than girls in math and science careers.

Parents may convey these subtle stereotypes through the attributions they give for their child's success in math (see Butler, 2014 [Chapter 1 of this volume]). Parents often attribute their daughter's success in math to hard work and their son's successes to natural ability (Raty, Vanska, Kasanen, & Karkkainen, 2002; Yee & Eccles, 1988). Parents also reported that their daughters would need to work harder in math classes than their sons, regardless of the fact that boys and girls reported working equally hard in math class and those reports were corroborated by their teachers (Raty et al., 2002; Yee & Eccles, 1988). Mothers are more likely to intrude on their daughters' math homework than on their sons', subtly conveying the message that girls are not as good as boys at math (Lindberg, Hyde, & Hirsch, 2008).

Parental expectations may influence their children's educational choices and ultimately their career decisions. In one study, mother's gender-role attitudes when her child was 12 years old predicted the likelihood that her child would choose a traditionally feminine career when she was 20. Mothers with more traditional attitudes were associated with a greater likelihood for daughters to choose female-typed careers and a lesser likelihood that sons would choose female-typed careers (Chhin, Bleeker, & Jacobs, 2008). In contrast, parents who convey nontraditional gendered messages are more likely to have children who report a high degree of self-efficacy in gender nontraditional skills and those children are more likely to report nontraditional careers (Fulcher, 2011).

New research suggests that parents who are given educational material may increase their adolescent's interest in math (Harackiewicz, Rozek, Hulleman, & Hyde, 2012). In an experimental manipulation, some parents were given two brochures and access to a website that highlighted the utility value of math and science courses. Compared to control families who were not given the brochures, students in the experimental group took more math and science classes in their last 2 years of high school.

Parents may also influence their children's career choices by acting as role models. For example, preschool children whose parents held traditional gender roles in the household were more likely to engage in gender-stereotyped behavior (Fulcher, Sutfin, & Patterson, 2008). Conversely, children whose parents had more egalitarian household roles were more likely to endorse less gender-stereotyped careers. Children may look to their parents to understand gender roles and use the parents' gendered behavior as a model for imitation. Children may also look to their same-gender parent's occupation when choosing a career goal. For example, mothers who work outside the home are more likely to have daughters who aspire to prestigious occupations (Goldberg, Prause, Lucas-Thompson, & Himsel, 2008). However, other research suggests that parents' attitudes, rather than parental behaviors, are associated with children's gender-stereotyped beliefs and gendered career aspirations (Fulcher, 2011).

It should also be noted that career beliefs and interests are characterized by bidirectional influence between parent and child. Children who express interest in particular careers may receive encouragement and guidance from their parents regardless of whether those career aspirations are gender-typed. Adolescents who have more traditional gender-role beliefs are more likely to choose gender-typed careers, which may then be encouraged by their parents (Chhin et al., 2008). It should also be noted that a third variable, the child's ability, may influence both the child and the parents to maintain careers goals consistent with that skill, regardless of whether that skill and career are gender traditional or nontraditional.

4.2. Stereotypes and Discrimination

Recent evidence confirms that bias against women job candidates continues to exist in the sciences (Moss-Racusin et al., 2012). This gender discrimination, in addition to stereotypes conveyed by parents and teachers (see Leaper & Brown, 2014 [Chapter 6 of this volume]), may discourage students from pursuing gender-atypical careers (Beilock, Gunderson, Ramirez, & Levine, 2010).

Self-efficacy is a powerful motivating tool in choosing an occupation (Bandura et al., 2001). Students who do not feel a sense of self-efficacy in a particular domain are likely to avoid careers in that domain. Despite small and nonsignificant gender differences in math ability (Hyde, 2005), girls continue to report lower levels of math self-efficacy (Else-Quest et al., 2010). As noted earlier, gender stereotypes and stereotype threat are likely to contribute to these lower levels of self-efficacy, regardless of actual performance.

Because of the stereotype that men are better than women at math, many women may feel anxiety about doing math. This math anxiety can be increasingly problematic if the subject of the anxiety is a math teacher. Because the majority of elementary educators are women (Beilock et al., 2010). Female elementary teachers frequently are charged with the responsibility of teaching math, a stereotypically male domain. Evidence suggests that female elementary teachers who have high math anxiety may convey gender stereotypes about math to their students (Beilock et al., 2010). Although there was no association between teacher math anxiety and math performance at the beginning of the year, by the end of the year, girls who had a female teacher with math anxiety were more likely to endorse gender stereotypes about math and show poor math performance than their peers. Although it may be the case that teachers with high math anxiety are simply not as good at teaching math, the results indicated that only female students' math performance was affected, indicating that gender stereotypes are at play. This study is an example of how factors that discourage girls in math are often more subtle than outright discrimination. For example, teachers in this study did not directly treat their male and female students differently, yet students picked up on subtle gender stereotypes in their environment.

Ceci and Williams (2011) argued that sex discrimination is no longer present and that women's underrepresentation in the sciences is due to gender differences in interest and family focus. The authors cited the lack of gender differences in journal acceptance rates and in the hiring process to support their view that gender discrimination does not exist. They argued that a focus on discrimination prevents researchers from looking for the real issues underlying women's underrepresentation in science. Although we agree that it is important to consider all factors that may contribute to gender differences in occupational choices, it is impossible to deny that sex discrimination continues to exist in the sciences and in other male-dominated careers. Sex discrimination in the workplace is likely to be more subtle than journal acceptance rates and hiring procedures. Instead, women may feel discrimination such as not being asked to collaborate on a new study or being left out of workplace conversations that may lead to a policy decision (Committee on gender differences in the careers of science, engineering, and mathematics faculty, 2010). Overt sexism is typically not tolerated in most work environments, yet subtle forms of discrimination based on gender stereotypes abound, especially in male-dominated fields. Indeed, women in male-dominated fields reported experiencing high levels of gender discrimination (Settles, Cortina, Buchanan, & Miner, 2013) and female graduate students in the sciences also reported that women were more likely than men to be the target of gender discrimination in their field (Hayes & Bigler, 2013). Interestingly, women who valued power and altruism in their careers were more likely to perceive gender discrimination than were women who valued family. Perhaps gender discrimination targets the most ambitious women who strive for nontraditional gendered careers. Men and women may see these powerful women as a threat.

Perhaps the strongest recent evidence of continued sex discrimination in the sciences comes from a high-profile study by Moss-Racusin and colleagues (2012). In this double-blind, experimental study, science faculty at research-intensive universities received an application, labeled as being from either a male or female student, for a lab manager position. The applications were otherwise identical. Science faculty rated the male applicant as significantly more competent and hireable than the female applicant, and suggested a higher starting salary for the man. These expressions of bias did not differ as a function of the gender of the faculty rater. Given studies such as this, it is difficult to justify arguments that sex discrimination in the sciences no longer exists.

In a similar vein, *Nature* magazine, the most prestigious scientific journal in the United Kingdom, has admitted to massive sex bias in matters such as the choice of reviewers (Editors, 2013). Only 14% of reviewers of submitted articles in 2011 were women, and, of researchers chosen for the honor of being profiled in the journal, only 18% were women. The editors vowed to change these practices, and by 2013, 40% of the profiled scientists were women; however, only 13% of reviewers were women (Editors, 2013). Some of these sex-biased practices are doubtless nonconscious and therefore somewhat resistant to change.

Subtle forms of sexist discrimination are akin to subtle racism in the workplace. Although overt racism and sexism are not tolerated, discrimination continues to exist in less obvious ways. Research with African American children indicates that children who were aware of racial discrimination in the workplace were less likely to pursue high-status occupations (Hughes, 2010). However, after students attended a bias-resistance workshop, their occupational aspirations improved as a result of improved perceived occupational outcomes. Perhaps, a similar study conducted with girls in STEM occupations would indicate that bias-resistance training could improve girls' career aspirations in STEM careers.

Research suggests that there is hope for reducing gender occupational stereotypes among youth and increasing interest in gender-atypical careers (Pahlke, Bigler, & Green, 2010). In an experimental study, students were taught a historical lesson that either (a) focused on biographical information about a woman who succeeded in a male-dominated career or (b) identical information that also included information about gender discrimination (Pahlke et al., 2010). Following the lessons, both boys and girls who were taught about gender discrimination were more aware of gender discrimination than the control group and were more likely to perceive gender discrimination even 6 months later. Interestingly, however, students in both conditions were more likely to report egalitarian occupational beliefs 6 months after the lesson. That is, learning about women succeeding in male-dominated careers reduced gendered occupational beliefs regardless of whether gender discrimination was mentioned. Students from both conditions also reported being interested in a wider variety of careers after the lesson regardless of gendered expectation. Therefore, hearing anecdotal evidence about individuals in counter-stereotypical occupations may benefit both boys and girls to hold more egalitarian occupational beliefs and to open themselves up to different careers that may defy gender stereotypes.

4.3. Work–Family Balance

Even today the gendered social structure expects women to be the primary caretaker of children regardless of their work responsibilities. Therefore, for many women, occupational choice is contingent on the perceived ability to balance work and family obligations. In the contemporary United States, cultural beliefs hold that women should be characterized by family devotion, regardless of their employment status (Blair-Loy, 2003). Female-dominated occupations such as teaching may be perceived as being more flexible and thus offering more accommodations for family life, whereas careers in math and science may be perceived as more rigid. Female college students who placed a high priority on family life were less academically oriented in general than their female peers, and they were specifically less likely to pursue a career in math and science (Ware & Lee, 1988). Other research suggests that women who changed their career aspirations from the math and science domain to something else were more likely to desire a family-flexible job and had less interest in physical science than women who continued to have career aspirations in math and science (Frome, Alfeld, Eccles, & Barber, 2006).

Women may choose careers that are less ambitious or have less upward mobility if they anticipate that they will leave work to raise children. Although the United States Family and Medical Leave Act allows both men and women to take an equal amount of time from work to attend to family responsibilities such as the birth of a child, women are much more likely than men to take advantage of their employer's family leave policy (Hyde, Essex, Clark, Klein, & Byrd, 1996). The Family Leave policy in the United States provides a minimum of 12 weeks of unpaid family leave, but zero days of paid leave, although paid sick leave and personal leave may be used (Hyde et al., 1996). This policy is restrictive for parents and others with family obligations in comparison to policies in other developed countries such as Germany, which offers up to 14 months of paid leave (Spiess & Wrohlick, 2008).

Women who desire to continue working after they have had children may desire jobs with greater flexibility. Therefore, they may choose careers that allow them to work less than 40 hours a week so that they may spend more time raising their children. Women are more likely than men to be employed part-time (United States Census, 2012). Working part-time gives women greater flexibility to attend to family matters, but is inconsistent with pursuing an ambitious career in the sciences.

Men may also be thinking about their families as they choose future careers, even if they do not value work flexibility. For example, men, particularly those high in masculinity, may choose a career with a high salary with the intention of being the family breadwinner (Weisgram et al., 2011). Men may see their family role as providing financial opportunities for their children's mother to stay home with the children or as an opportunity to provide money to pay for high-quality child care.

Although many people continue to struggle with balancing work and family, a number of incentives have made it easier for women to find a balance. First, affirmative action and equal employment opportunity programs have provided women increased access to high-level jobs. Second, high-quality child care and well-educated early childhood professionals provide an opportunity for parents to work with fewer concern about their child's welfare. Finally, some employers have provided assistance to parents who struggle with the work–family balance, such as opportunities to work from home or on-site child care. Although these incentives are not provided universally and many parents may struggle to afford high-quality child care, increased availability of these programs and increased awareness of work–family struggles have provided many additional opportunities for parents in the workplace.

4.4. Developmental Trends

Occupational choices and aspirations typically change across development as youth gain an increasing sense of self- and gendered-expectations. Gender schema theory suggests that children form a schema for gender at a very early age and that the gender schema becomes increasingly complex as children develop (Bem, 1981).

Preschool children often have unrealistic expectation for their careers, yet those fantasy careers are typically based on gender stereotypes. For example, young boys often aspire to become professional athletes or take on careers that require bravery and strength such as firefighter or police officer. Young girls often aspire to careers that require grace such as ballerina or helping careers such as veterinarian or teacher. When children reach school age, gender becomes the most powerful predictor of occupational aspirations (Teig & Susskind, 2008).

When students reach early adolescence they often report that multiple values are important to them in their future career, even if those values are incongruent. For example, young teens reported that they wanted a job that helps others, pays well, provides power and responsibility, and allows them time with their family, even though very few careers might actually provide all of these goals (Weisgram et al., 2010). As teens grow older and become more realistic, they report fewer goals to be "very important." They seem to recognize that sacrifices and compromises must be made in careers and therefore goals must be prioritized. For example, college students recognized that having a high salary or a job with a lot of power might not allow them to have as much time with their family (Weisgram et al., 2011).

The meta-analysis on gender differences in job attribute preferences found that gender differences among elementary school children were small (Konrad et al., 2000). Although elementary school boys were more likely to prefer a job that included power ($d=0.28$), there were small gender differences in preferences for earnings ($d=0.14$) and trivial differences in helping others ($d=-0.08$). Junior high and high school students showed greater gender differences in job attribute preferences than did elementary school students. For example, high school boys were slightly more likely than girls to prefer higher earning ($d=0.20$) and girls were more likely than boys to prefer jobs that included helping others ($d=-0.45$). Undergraduate students reported even more gender-stereotyped job attribute preferences than high school students, but gender differences among college students decreased when students were matched by major.

Women's representation in STEM careers has often been called a "leaky pipeline" because girls' interest and self-efficacy in STEM declines with age (Alper, 1993). Whereas young girls often enjoy math and science and earn high grades in these subjects, they become less interested in science courses in high school (Miller, Blessing, & Schwartz, 2007). Perhaps girls are more likely to perceive gender discrimination in advanced math and science courses (Hayes & Bigler, 2013), or years of gender stereotyping and stereotype threat wear on girls who were once interested in science and math. Perhaps women become more aware of their occupational goals and see STEM careers as incongruent with their goals for family life or altruism (Diekman et al., 2010).

4.5. Training, Practice, and Interventions

Despite the fact that most gender differences in intellectual and academic skills are small (Hyde, 2005), many people continue to attribute gender differences to differences in natural ability. However, it is important to remember that gender-socializing forces often provide one gender with more practice or training than they do for another gender. For example, although educational opportunities are generally equal for men and women in developed countries, the same is not always true in developing nations. For example, girls in many rural areas of the world are afforded educational opportunities that are inferior to those offered to boys, and parents who can afford to send only one child to school frequently give preference to their sons (Tinker, 1990). As a result, many women in these communities do not have the opportunity to work at better-paying jobs.

Gender differences in training may also be prevalent around the world even in developed nations. For example, many researchers note that there is no formal spatial training in the schools. Due to socializing factors, boys are likely to receive a disproportionate amount of informal spatial training in the form of sports and video games. Such informal training may have an effect on mental 3D rotation (Newcombe, Mathason, & Terlecki, 2002; Uttal et al., 2013). In one experiment, college students were given 10 hours of training on an action video game (Feng, 2007). Both women and men who were given this training improved their performance on a mental rotation test. The women improved more than the men, and women in the experimental group performed as well as men in the control group. On average, boys in the United States spend about twice as much time playing video games as do girls (Rideout, Foehr, & Roberts, 2010). This gender difference represents a sizable discrepancy in spatial training.

Formal training in spatial skills may also increase mental rotation ability for women and increase their retention in fields such as engineering. (These and other training programs are also discussed by Liben and Coyle, 2014 [Chapter 3 of this volume]). When multimedia software that provides training in mental rotation was implemented in college engineering classrooms, the retention of women in the engineering majors increased from 47% to 77% (Gerson, Sorby, Wysocki, & Baartmans, 2001).

Interventions have also been designed to deal with the problem of stereotype threat for women. Miyake et al. (2010) used a values-affirmation technique to close the gender gap in performance in a college physics class. In the values-affirmation condition, students wrote about their most important values, whereas control-group students wrote about their least important values and why they might be important to other people. The idea is that, when students affirm their core values in a threatening environment (for women, a physics class is presumed to be threatening because of stereotype threat), they affirm their own sense of personal integrity and worth, which provides them with psychological resources to cope with the situation. Results indicated that, whereas in the control condition men performed significantly better than women on exams in the physics class, in the values-affirmation condition, women performed as well as men.

Another intervention strategy involved simply teaching women about stereotype threat and math performance (Johns, Schmader, & Martens, 2005). In the condition in which women received the teaching intervention, they performed as well as men.

Overall, then, a number of interventions are available to close gender gaps in performance in mathematics and the sciences. What we do not yet know is whether these interventions can ultimately increase the representation of women in STEM careers.

4.6. Cultural Differences

As suggested by sociocultural theory, individuals' choices of gender-typed careers are influenced by the gender stereotypes and discrimination in a particular culture. Historical shifts in gender equality are an excellent example of society's role in shaping gender differences in occupations (Kessler-Harris, 2003). World Wars I and II provided opportunities for many American and European women to gain employment outside of the home as young men left for war. Although many women returned to working in the home after the war, the understanding that women were capable workers, even for physically demanding jobs, was established (Kessler-Harris, 2003). From the 1950s to the 1980s there was a dramatic change in women's representation in the working world (Kessler-Harris, 2003). As more women went to work and held increasingly prestigious jobs, the gender gap in pay decreased and occupational opportunities for both men and women increased.

Despite increasing opportunities for women in the workplace, gender gaps in pay continue to exist in all industrialized nations around the world (Ridgeway, 2011) even though the size of the gap varies internationally. In the United States the pay gap is roughly 23%, larger than many other industrialized countries such as Italy (4.9%), Sweden (17%), and the United Kingdom (21%) (European Commission, 2011). The size of the pay gap may be due to a variety of sociocultural forces, including gender differences in job prestige, gender differences in full-time workers, and gender discrimination.

Turkey is an interesting country in that gender-role beliefs and expectations are currently changing to become more egalitarian. Although many Turks still hold traditional gender stereotypes, more opportunities are becoming available to women across the country (Tatli, Ozbilgin, & Kusku, 2008). In fact, the proportion of Turkish women in science, engineering, and technology is high in comparison to the United States and most of Europe. Although the number of Turkish women in engineering is increasing, stereotypes and prejudices against women in engineering remain prominent. Therefore, the "critical mass" hypothesis, which suggests that increasing the number of women in male-dominated careers will decrease gender stereotypes in those careers, is not supported in Turkey. Changing attitudes and beliefs about women on the societal level is essential for reducing gender stereotypes in the workplace.

5. CONCLUSIONS

In this chapter, we have reviewed research on gender differences and similarities in academic and occupational skills, interests, and goals, basing our conclusions on meta-analyses whenever possible. Although substantial gender differences are found for some relevant variables, gender similarities are found for many others. The pathways to adult occupations are complex, involving many factors that come into play over time (Eccles, 1994). Certainly socializers, such as parents and schools, play a role in nudging youth toward gender-stereotyped occupations. Sex discrimination persists, although perhaps in a subtler form than a generation ago. At the same time, children's differential skills and their emerging domain-specific self-concepts play a role as well. Several strategies for interventions that promote interest and self-confidence in counter-stereotyped directions have been developed and show much promise for the future.

REFERENCES

Alper, J. (1993). The pipeline is leaking women all the way along. *Science, 260,* 409–412.

Aronson, J., & Good, C. (2003). The development and consequences of stereotype vulnerability in adolescents. In F. Pajares, & T. Urdan (Eds.), *Academic motivation of adolescents. Vol 2. Adolescence and education* (pp. 229–330). Greenwich, CT: Information Age.

Bandura, A., Barbaranelli, C., Caprara, G. V., & Pastoreli, C. (2001). Self-efficacy beliefs and shapers of children's aspirations and career trajectories. *Child Development, 72,* 187–206.

Beilock, S. L., Gunderson, E. A., Ramirez, G., & Levine, S. C. (2010). Female teachers' math anxiety affects girls math achievement. *Proceedings of the National Academy of Science, 107,* 1860–1863.

Bem, S. L. (1981). Gender schema theory: A cognitive account of sex typing. *Psychological Review, 88,* 354–364.

Blair-Loy, M. (2003). *Competing devotions: Career and family among women executives.* Cambridge, MA: Harvard University Press.

Brown, R. P., & Josephs, R. A. (1999). A burden of proof: Stereotype relevance and gender differences in math performance. *Journal of Personality and Social Psychology, 76,* 246–257.

Bureau of Labor Statistics. (2011). *Women at work.* www.bls.gov/cps.

Butler, R. (2014). Motivation in educational contexts: Does gender matter? In L. S. Liben & R. S. Bigler (Vol. Eds.), *The role of gender in educational contexts and outcomes.* In J. B. Benson (Series Ed.), *Advances in child development and behavior: Vol. 47* (pp. 1–41). London: Elsevier.

Ceci, S. J., & Williams, W. M. (2011). Understanding current causes of women's underrepresentation in science. *Proceedings of the National Academy of Science, 108,* 3157–3162.

Chhin, C. S., Bleeker, M. M., & Jacobs, J. E. (2008). Gender-typed occupational choices: The long-term impact of parents' beliefs and expectations. In H. Watt, & J. Eccles (Eds.), *Gender and occupational outcomes* (pp. 215–234). Washington, DC: American Psychological Association.

Cohen, J. (1988). *Statistical power analysis for the behavioral sciences* (2nd ed.). Hillsdale, NJ: Erlbaum.

Committee on gender differences in the careers of science, engineering, and mathematics faculty. (2010). *Gender differences at critical transitions in the careers of science, engineering, and mathematics faculty.* Washington, DC: The National Academic Press. http://www.nap.edu/catalog.php?record_id=12062.

Diekman, A., Brown, E., Johnston, A., & Cark, E. (2010). Seeking congruity between goals and roles: A new look at why women opt out of science, technology, engineering, and math careers. *Psychological Science, 21,* 1051–1057.

Eagly, A. H. (2009). The his and hers of prosocial behavior: An examination of the social psychology of gender. *American Psychologist, 64,* 644–658.

Eagly, A. H., & Crowley, M. (1986). Gender and helping behavior: A meta-analytic review of the social psychological literature. *Psychological Bulletin, 100,* 283–308.

Eagly, A. H., Johannesen-Schmidt, M. C., & van Engen, M. L. (2003). Transformational, transactional, and laissez-faire leadership styles: A meta-analysis comparing women and men. *Psychological Bulletin, 129,* 569–591.

Eagly, A. H., Karau, S., & Makhijani, M. (1995). Gender and the effectiveness of leaders: A meta-analysis. *Psychological Bulletin, 117,* 125–145.

Eagly, A. H., & Wood, W. (1999). The origins of sex differences in human behavior: Evolved dispositions versus social roles. *American Psychologist, 54,* 408–423.

Eccles, J. S. (1994). Understanding women's educational and occupational goals. *Psychology of Women Quarterly, 18,* 585–609.

Eccles (Parsons), J. S., Adler, T. F., Futterman, R., Goff, S. B., Kaczala, C. M., Meece, J. L., et al. (1983). Expectancies, values, and academic behavior. In J. T. Spence (Ed.), *Achievement and achievement motivation* (pp. 75–146). San Francisco: Freeman.

Eccles (Parsons), J. S., Adler, T. F., & Kaczala, C. M. (1982). Socialization of achievement attitudes and beliefs: Parental influences. *Child Development, 53*, 322–419.

Eccles, J. S., Freedman-Doan, C., Frome, P., Jacobs, J., & Yoons, K. S. (2000). Gender-roles socialization in the family: A longitudinal perspective. In T. Eckes, & H. M. Trautner (Eds.), *The developmental social psychology of gender* (pp. 333–360). Mahwah, NJ: Erlbaum.

Editors, (2013). Science for all. *Nature, 495*, 5.

Else-Quest, N. M., Hyde, J. S., & Linn, M. C. (2010). Cross-national patterns of gender differences in mathematics: A meta-analysis. *Psychological Bulletin, 136*, 103–127.

European Commission (2011). *The situation in the EU.* http://ec.europa.eu/justice/gender-equality/gender-pay-gap/situation-europe/index_en.htm.

Feng, J. (2007). Playing an action video game reduces gender differences in spatial cognition. *Psychological Science, 18*, 850–855.

Freeman, P., & Aspray, W. (1999). *The supply of information technology workers in the United States.* Washington, DC: Computing Research Foundation. http://files.eric.ed.gov/fulltext/ED459346.pdf.

Frome, P. M., Alfeld, C. J., Eccles, J. S., & Barber, B. L. (2006). Why don't they want a male-dominate job? An investigation of young women who changed their occupational aspirations. *Educational Research and Evaluation, 4*, 359–372.

Fulcher, M. (2011). Individual differences in children's occupational aspirations as a function of parental traditionality. *Sex Roles, 64*, 117–131.

Fulcher, M., Sutfin, E. L., & Patterson, C. J. (2008). Children's future occupational aspirations: Associations with parental sexual orientation, attitudes, and division of labor. *Sex Roles, 58*, 330–341.

Ganley, C. M., Mingle, L. A., Ryan, A. M., Ryan, K., Vasilyeva, M., & Perry, M. (2013). An examination of stereotype threat effects on girls' mathematics performance. *Developmental Psychology, 49*, 1886–1897.

Gentile, B., Grabe, S., Dolan-Pascoe, B., Twenge, J. M., Wells, B. E., & Maitino, A. (2009). Gender differences in domain-specific self-esteem: A meta-analysis. *Review of General Psychology, 13*, 34–45.

Gerson, H., Sorby, S. A., Wysocki, A., & Baartmans, B. J. (2001). The development and assessment of multimedia software for improving 3-D visualization skills. *Computer Applications in Engineering Education, 9*, 105–113.

Goldberg, W. A., Prause, J., Lucas-Thompson, R., & Himsel, A. (2008). Maternal employment and children's achievement in context: A meta-analysis of four decades of research. *Psychological Bulletin, 134*, 77–108.

Harackiewicz, J., Rozek, C., Hulleman, C., & Hyde, J. (2012). Helping parents to motivate adolescents in mathematics and science: An experimental test of utility value intervention. *Psychological Science, 23*, 899–906.

Hayes, A. R., & Bigler, R. S. (2013). Gender-related values, perceptions of discrimination, and mentoring in STEM graduate training. *International Journal of Gender, Science and Technology, 5*, 254–280.

Hedges, L. V., & Nowell, A. (1995). Sex differences in mental test scores, variability, and numbers of high-scoring individuals. *Science, 269*, 41–45.

Hughes, J. M. (2010). Influences of discrimination awareness on the occupational awareness of African American children. *Journal of Applied Developmental Psychology, 32*, 369–378.

Hulleman, C. S., Godes, O., Hendricks, B. L., & Harackiewicz, J. (2010). Enhancing interest and performance with a utility value intervention. *Journal of Educational Psychology, 102*, 880–895.

Hyde, J. S. (2005). The gender similarities hypothesis. *American Psychologist*, *60*, 581–592.
Hyde, J. S., Essex, M. J., Clark, R., Klein, M. H., & Byrd, J. E. (1996). Parental leave: Policy and research. *Journal of Social Issues*, *52*, 91–109.
Hyde, J. S., Lindberg, S. M., Linn, M. C., Ellis, A., & Williams, C. (2008). Gender similarities characterize math performance. *Science*, *321*, 494–495.
Hyde, J. S., & Linn, M. C. (1988). Gender differences in verbal ability: A meta-analysis. *Psychological Bulletin*, *104*, 53–69.
Inzlicht, M., & Schmader, T. (Eds.). (2012). *Stereotype threat: Theory, process, and application*. New York: Oxford University Press.
Jodl, K., Michael, A., Malanchuk, O., Eccles, J. S., & Sameroff, A. (2003). Parents' roles in shaping early adolescents occupational aspirations. *Child Development*, *72*, 1247–1266.
Johns, M., Schmader, T., & Martens, A. (2005). Knowing is half the battle: Teaching stereotype threat as a means of improving women's math performance. *Psychological Science*, *16*, 175–179.
Kessler-Harris, A. (2003). *Out to work: A history of wage earning women in the United States*. Oxford, England: Oxford University Press.
Kling, K. C., Hyde, J. S., Showers, C. J., & Buswell, B. N. (1999). Gender differences in self-esteem: A meta-analysis. *Psychological Bulletin*, *125*, 470–500.
Konrad, A. M., Ritchie, E., Lieb, P., & Corrigall, E. (2000). Sex differences and similarities in job attribute preferences: A meta-analysis. *Psychological Bulletin*, *126*, 593–641.
Leaper, C., & Brown, C. S. (2014). Sexism in schools. In L. S. Liben & R. S. Bigler (Vol. Eds.), *The role of gender in educational contexts and outcomes*. In J. B. Benson (Series Ed.), *Advances in child development and behavior: Vol. 47* (pp. 189–223). London: Elsevier.
Leaper, C., & Robnett, R. D. (2011). Women are more likely than men to use tentative language, aren't they? A meta-analysis testing for gender differences and moderators. *Psychology of Women Quarterly*, *35*, 129–142.
Liben, L. S., & Coyle, E. F. (2014). Developmental interventions to address the STEM gender gap: Exploring intended and unintended consequences. In L. S. Liben & R. S. Bigler (Vol. Eds.), *The role of gender in educational contexts and outcomes*. In J. B. Benson (Series Ed.), *Advances in child development and behavior: Vol. 47* (pp. 77–116). London: Elsevier.
Lindberg, S. M., Hyde, J. S., & Hirsch, L. M. (2008). Gender and mother-child interactions during mathematics homework: The importance of individual differences. *Merrill-Palmer Quarterly*, *54*, 232–255.
Lindberg, S. M., Hyde, J. S., Petersen, J., & Linn, M. C. (2010). New trends in gender and mathematics performance: A meta-analysis. *Psychological Bulletin*, *136*, 1123–1135.
Linn, M. C., & Petersen, A. C. (1985). Emergence and characterization of sex differences in spatial ability: A meta-analysis. *Child Development*, *56*, 1479–1498.
Ma, X., & Johnson, W. (2008). Mathematics as a critical filter: Curricular effects on gendered career choices. In H. Watt, & J. Eccles (Eds.), *Gender and occupational outcomes* (pp. 55–84). Washington, DC: American Psychological Association.
Maeda, Y., & Yoon, S. Y. (2013). A meta-analysis on gender differences in mental rotation ability measured by the purdue spatial visualization tests: Visualization of rotations (PSVT:R). *Educational Psychology Review*, *25*, 69–94.
Meece, J. L., Eccles-Parson, J., et al. (1982). Sex differences in math achievement: Toward a model of academic choice. *Psychological Bulletin*, *91*, 324–348.
Miller, P. H., Blessing, J. S., & Schwartz, S. (2007). Gender differences in high school students' views about science. *International Journal of Science Education*, *28*, 363–381.
Miyake, A., Kost-Smith, L. E., Finkelstein, N. D., Pollock, S. J., Cohen, G. L., & Ito, T. A. (2010). Reducing the gender achievement gap in college science: A classroom study of values affirmation. *Science*, *330*, 1234–1237.

Moss-Racusin, C. A., Dovidio, J. F., Brescoll, V. L., Graham, M. J., & Handelsman, J. (2012). Science faculty's subtle gender biases favor male students. *Proceedings of the National Academy of Sciences, 109,* 16474–16479.

National Association of Colleges and Employers (2013). *Salary survey: Starting salaries for new college graduate.* http://www.naceweb.org/salary-survey-data/.

Newcombe, N. S., Mathason, L., & Terlecki, M. (2002). Maximization of spatial competence: More important than finding the cause of sex differences. In A. McGillicuddy-De Lisi, & R. De Lisi (Eds.), *Biology, society, and behavior: The development of sex differences in cognition* (pp. 183–206). Westport, CT: Ablex.

Pahlke, E., Bigler, R., & Green, V. (2010). Effects of learning about historical gender discrimination on early adults' career aspirations. *Journal of Early Adolescence, 30,* 854–894.

Quinn, D. M., & Spencer, S. J. (2001). The interference of stereotype threat with women's generation of mathematical problem-solving strategies. *Journal of Social Issues, 57,* 55–72.

Raty, H., Vanska, J., Kasanen, K., & Karkkainen, R. (2002). Parents explanations of their child's performance in mathematics and reading. A replication and extension of Yee and Eccles. *Sex Roles, 46,* 121–128.

Reilly, D. (2012). Gender, culture, and sex-typed cognitive abilities. *PLoS One, 7,* e39904.

Rideout, V. J., Foehr, U. G., & Roberts, D. F. (2010). *Generation M^2: Media in the lives of 8- to 18-year-olds.* Menlo Park, CA: Kaiser Family Foundation.

Ridgeway, C. L. (2011). *Framed by gender: How gender inequality persists in the modern world.* New York: Oxford University Press.

Schmader, T., Johns, M., & Forbes, C. (2008). An integrated process model of stereotype threat effects on performance. *Psychological Review, 115,* 336–356.

Sells, L. W. (1980). Mathematics: The invisible filter. *Engineering Education, 70,* 340–341.

Settles, I. H., Cortina, L. M., Buchanan, N. T., & Miner, K. N. (2013). Derogation, discrimination, and (dis)satisfaction with jobs in science: A gendered analysis. *Psychology of Women Quarterly, 37,* 179–191.

Shapka, J. D., Domene, J. F., & Keating, D. P. (2008). Gender, mathematics achievement, and the educational and occupational aspirations of Canadian youth. In H. Watt, & J. Eccles (Eds.), *Gender and occupational outcomes* (pp. 27–54). Washington, DC: American Psychological Association.

Spencer, S. J., Steele, C. M., & Quinn, D. M. (1999). Stereotype threat and women's math performance. *Journal of Experimental Social Psychology, 35,* 4–28.

Spiess, C. K., & Wrohlick, K. (2008). The parental leave benefit reform in Germany: Costs and labour market outcomes of moving toward the Nordic model. *Popular Research and Policy Review, 27,* 575–591.

Steele, C. M. (1997). A threat in the air: How stereotypes shape intellectual identity and performance. *American Psychologist, 52,* 613–629.

Steele, C. M., & Aronson, J. (1995). Stereotype threat and the intellectual test performance of African Americans. *Journal of Personality and Social Psychology, 69,* 797–811.

Su, R., Rounds, J., & Armstrong, P. (2009). Men and things, women and people: A meta-analysis of sex differences in interests. *Psychological Bulletin, 135,* 859–884.

Tannen, D. (1991). *You just don't understand: Women and men in conversation.* New York: Ballantine.

Tatli, A., Ozbilgin, M. F., & Kusku, F. (2008). Gendered occupational outcomes from multilevel perspectives: The case of professional training and work in Turkey. In H. Watt, & J. Eccles (Eds.), *Gender and occupational outcomes* (pp. 267–298). Washington, DC: American Psychological Association.

Teig, S., & Susskind, J. E. (2008). Truck driver or nurse? The impact of gender roles and occupational status on children's occupational preferences. *Sex Roles, 58,* 848–863.

Tenenbaum, H. R., & Leaper, C. (2003). Parent–child conversations about science: The socializations of gender inequities? *Developmental Psychology, 39*, 34–47.

Tinker, I. (1990). *Persistent inequalities: Women and world development.* Oxford: Oxford University Press.

Twenge, J. M. (1997). Changes in masculine and feminine traits over time: A meta-analysis. *Sex Roles, 36*, 305–325.

United States Census (2012). *The labor force statistical abstract: Labor force, earning and employment.* http://www.census.gov/compendia/statab/cats/labor_force_employment_earnings.html.

Updegraff, K. A., Eccles, J. S., Barber, B. L., & O'Brien, K. M. (1996). Course enrollment as self-regulatory behavior: Who takes optional high school math courses? *Learning and Individual Differences, 8*, 239–259.

Uttal, D. H., Meadow, N. G., Tipton, E., Hand, L. L., Alden, A. R., et al. (2013). The malleability of spatial skills: A meta-analysis of training studies. *Psychological Bulletin, 139*, 352–402.

Voyer, D. (2011). Time limits and gender differences on paper-and-pencil tests of mental rotation: A meta-analysis. *Psychological Bulletin Review, 18*, 267–277.

Voyer, D., Voyer, S., & Bryden, M. P. (1995). Magnitude of sex differences in spatial abilities: A meta-analysis and consideration of critical variables. *Psychological Bulletin, 117*, 250–270.

Ware, N. C., & Lee, V. E. (1988). Sex differences in choice of college science majors. *American Educational Research Journal, 25*, 593–614.

Watt, H. (2004). Development of adolescent's self-perceptions, values, and task perceptions according to gender and domain in 7th and 11th grade Australian students. *Child Development, 75*, 1556–1574.

Watt, H. M. G., Shapka, J. D., Morris, Z. E., Durik, A. M., Keating, D. P., & Eccles, J. S. (2012). Gendered motivational processes affecting high school mathematics participation, educational aspirations, and career plans: A comparison of samples from Australia, Canada, and the United States. *Developmental Psychology, 48*, 1594–1611.

Weisgram, E. S., & Bigler, R. S. (2006). Girls and science careers: The role of altruistic values and attitudes about scientific tasks. *Journal of Applied Developmental Psychology, 27*, 326–348.

Weisgram, E., Bigler, R., & Liben, L. (2010). Gender, values, and occupational interests among children, adolescents, and adults. *Child Development, 81*, 778–796.

Weisgram, E., Dinella, L., & Fulcher, M. (2011). The role of masculinity/feminity, values, and occupational value affordances in shaping young men's and women's occupational choices. *Sex Roles, 65*, 243–258.

Wigfield, A. (1994). Expectancy-value theory of achievement motivation: A developmental perspective. *Educational Psychology Review, 6*, 49–78.

Yee, D. K., & Eccles, J. S. (1988). Parent perceptions and attributions for children's math achievement. *Sex Roles, 19*, 317–333.

CHAPTER THREE

Developmental Interventions to Address the STEM Gender Gap: Exploring Intended and Unintended Consequences

Lynn S. Liben[1], Emily F. Coyle

Department of Psychology, The Pennsylvania State University, University Park, Pennsylvania, USA
[1]Corresponding author: e-mail address: liben@psu.edu

Contents

1. Introduction 78
2. Documenting the STEM Gender Gap 79
3. Developmental Mechanisms and a Taxonomy of STEM Intervention Goals 85
   3.1 Intervention Mechanisms Implicated by Theories of Gender Development 85
   3.2 STEM Intervention Goals 91
4. Illustrations of STEM Interventions 94
   4.1 Remediate 94
   4.2 Revise 96
   4.3 Refocus, Recategorize, and Resist 99
5. Conclusions and Recommendations 105
   5.1 Comparison Groups 106
   5.2 STEM-Relevant Outcome Measures 107
   5.3 Measuring Unintended Outcomes 108
   5.4 Characterizing and Building on Past Interventions 109
   5.5 A Relational Perspective Revisited 110
References 111

Abstract

Women and girls in the United States continue to be underrepresented in STEM, particularly in engineering and technology fields. This gap has been attracting recent attention from those motivated to ensure that girls and women have access to a full range of personally satisfying careers as well as from those concerned with developing a rich talent pool to meet national workforce needs. This chapter is focused on interventions that have been designed to address this STEM gender gap. We begin by documenting the STEM gender gap and then review change mechanisms emerging from theories of gender development that may be harnessed in intervention efforts. In addition, we provide a taxonomy of intervention goals which we then use to organize an illustrative review of sample interventions. After commenting on some of the findings and limitations of past work, we offer suggestions for enhancing the systematic evaluation of intervention programs that include careful selection of comparison groups, a broad array of STEM outcome measures, assessment of potentially unintended consequences, and meta-analyses.

1. INTRODUCTION

From a global perspective, it is obvious that gender is linked to educational outcomes. In some societies—for example, contemporary Chad where 72% of girls marry before the age of 18 (United Nations Girls' Education Initiative, 2013)—girls are discouraged from attending or completing school, reducing their educational achievements relative to boys. Others—for example, the contemporary United States—encourage, and indeed require, equivalent educational opportunities for boys and girls. However, even in the United States (the major focus of the current chapter), girls and boys follow somewhat different educational and occupational paths. One arena in which gender distinctions are striking is STEM—science, technology, engineering, and math. As discussed in more detail later, women are especially underrepresented in the technology and engineering sectors of STEM. This gender gap has been attracting much attention at all levels, from parents concerned about their daughters' personal fulfillment and their ability to compete for and succeed in emerging and well-compensated STEM jobs, to local educators concerned about delivering equitable educational programs, and to national governmental agencies concerned about having an adequate US talent pool to meet the country's workforce needs. These concerns have spawned a wide array of intervention programs intended to reduce the STEM gender gap.

This chapter is designed to document the STEM gender gap, describe theory-identified mechanisms relevant for interventions, identify categories of intervention goals, illustrate intervention programs, and offer recommendations for designing and evaluating such programs in future work. More specifically, in Section 2, we provide descriptive data showing the continuing existence of a gender gap in STEM. In Section 3, we review key change mechanisms that emerge from theories of gender development that are relevant for interventions. Additionally, we offer a taxonomy of intervention goals. In Section 4, we provide readers with a flavor of interventions by describing sample programs that harness various developmental mechanisms and illustrate various goal types. In Section 5, we summarize key points and suggest approaches that may enhance the value of interventions and intervention research related to the STEM gender gap.

2. DOCUMENTING THE STEM GENDER GAP

STEM-related educational outcomes may be evaluated by examining various components of K–16 choices and successes including, among others, choice of electives; class performance; performance on standardized tests of achievement in STEM fields; participation and success in STEM-related academic competitions; and selection, matriculation, and retention in STEM programs in institutions of higher education. Still longer-term indices of educational outcomes may be found in individuals' selection of, and perseverance, satisfaction, and success in, STEM occupations.

Gender differences on outcome measures like these show considerable variability over historical time, specific STEM field, and phase of life. To illustrate the relevance of both historical time and field while holding age roughly constant, Figure 1 presents data on the numbers of bachelor's level

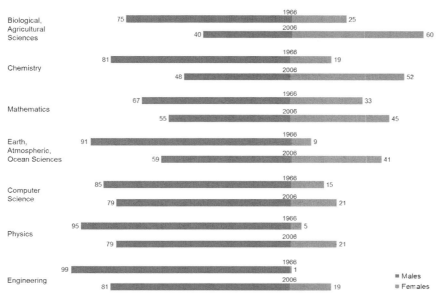

Figure 1 Bachelor's degrees in STEM awarded by sex, 1966 and 2006. *Data from NSF (2013).*

degrees awarded to men and women in various STEM fields in two specific years separated by four decades (1966 and 2006). These data show that in 1966, the percentage of men was greater than the percentage of women in every STEM field, without exception. The field with the highest percentage of women was mathematics in which women were awarded 33% of the degrees. By 2006, the picture had changed, but not entirely. Now there were two fields in which women received more degrees than men—the biological sciences and chemistry. Women were not far behind men in receipt of degrees in mathematics or Earth sciences. However, women continued to be significantly outnumbered by men in computer science, physics, and engineering.

For slightly younger students—those in high school—a snapshot of STEM gender differences is provided by data on students who took 2013 Advanced Placement (AP) tests, shown in Figure 2. Paralleling the data on bachelor's degrees, girls outnumbered boys in taking Biology AP exams. However, on all other AP tests in STEM domains, the pattern was reversed. Differences were relatively small in some fields (Calculus and Chemistry) but considerable in others (Computer Science A and all three Physics exams). Not a single girl took the Computer Science A exam in three states—Mississippi, Montana, and Wyoming (although in Wyoming, no boys took this exam either). Girls' representation in remaining states ranged between a low of 4% in Utah to a high of 29% in Tennessee (Ericson, 2014).

A STEM gender gap is found not only in proportions of girls and boys who take the AP STEM tests but also in relative performance. On nearly all these tests, boys' scores surpass girls'. For example, in 2013, passing grades

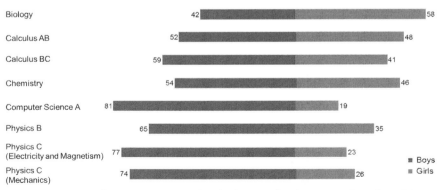

Figure 2 Percent of STEM AP exams taken by boys and girls in 2013. *Data from Ericson (2014).*

(scores of ≥3 out of 5) were received on the Calculus AB exam by 56% of girls compared to 61% of boys; on the Computer Science A exam the proportions were, respectively, 62% versus 67% (Ericson, 2014). At the same time that gender differences continue to be observed on AP examinations, however, data from other standardized achievement tests are more mixed. For example, in the field of mathematics in general, a meta-analysis by Lindberg, Hyde, Petersen, and Linn (2010) led to the conclusion that gender differences in math performance are generally trivial (see also Leaper & Brown, 2014 [Chapter 6 of this volume]; Petersen & Hyde, 2014 [Chapter 2 of this volume]).

A snapshot of longer-term STEM educational outcomes is provided by examining occupational placement and success. One simple measure is the gender distribution of the STEM workforce. Although women make up close to half (47%) of the American work force (United States Department of Labor, 2013), they are strikingly underrepresented in STEM-related jobs. In 2013, for example, the STEM workforce was only 25% female (NSF, 2013). Furthermore, women are even more dramatically underrepresented in the highly selective academic sector: Despite receiving almost half the doctoral degrees in science, women comprise only about one third of scientists employed in academic settings. As shown in Figure 3, there has been some increase in the proportion of women in this occupational segment over time, but the general picture of women's underrepresentation has remained remarkably similar over the years.

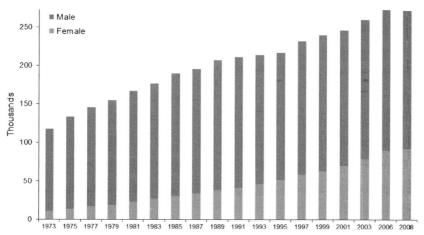

Figure 3 Men and women employed as academic scientists and engineers, all fields. *Data from NSF (2013).*

Even in areas such as psychology in which women have recently received a substantial majority of doctoral degrees (e.g., in 2010, women received 71% of psychology Ph.D.'s), women were only a slight majority (55%) of the academic workforce a few years later (NSF, 2013). In areas such as engineering in which women are already underrepresented in graduate study, they were even more dramatically underrepresented in academic employment (26% vs. 13%, respectively, for the same reporting periods, NSF, 2013). Although in part these discrepancies reflect the progression of cohorts (it takes time before higher numbers of graduates from Ph.D. programs work their way into elite employment levels), this cannot entirely account for the pattern. Even among those who enter and proceed through the science pipeline, losses over time are greater for women than men, a pattern often referred to as the leaky pipeline (Alper, 1993).

Interestingly, and despite many individuals' strongly held stereotypes about gender differences in STEM-related school achievement (particularly with respect to mathematics, see Eccles, Freedman-Doan, Frome, Jacobs, & Yoons, 2000), there are not analogous gender gaps on indices of success in STEM coursework. Indeed, beginning as early as kindergarten and persisting through college, girls receive higher grades than boys (e.g., Cornwell, Mustard, & Van Parys, 2013; Hill, Corbett, & St. Rose, 2010; Voyer & Voyer, 2014). This generalization applies to math and science courses as well as to courses in culturally feminine domains such as language arts and foreign language.

On the other hand, there is evidence for a continuing gender gap in one domain that has been identified as foundational for many STEM domains—spatial skills (Hegarty, 2014; Liben, 2006; Linn & Petersen, 1985; National Research Council, 2006; Shea, Lubinski, & Benbow, 2001; Wai, Lubinski, & Benbow, 2009). More specifically, there is a large literature demonstrating that boys and men surpass girls and women on many spatial tasks, with particularly large effect sizes on tasks that require mental rotation and the perception or use of Cartesian coordinate axes (e.g., Liben, 1991; Linn & Petersen, 1985; Voyer, Voyer, & Bryden, 1995). Recent research has shown that gender differences in mental rotation are evident even in early infancy (e.g., Moore & Johnson, 2011; Quinn & Liben, 2014). Although there is evidence that the gender gap is only moderate (rather than large) when the spatial tasks are untimed (Voyer, 2011), leading some to downplay the importance of the spatial-skills gap (e.g., see Petersen & Hyde, 2014 [Chapter 2 of this volume]), we judge that the gender difference in spatial skills remains important for STEM because some tasks require quick solutions and because facile solutions of lower-level spatial tasks leave more cognitive capacity free for higher-level cognition. Furthermore, there are multiple demonstrations that performance on spatial tasks predicts mastery of specific STEM concepts (e.g., Liben, Kastens, & Christensen, 2011; for reviews, see Hegarty, 2014; Liben, 2006; Wai et al., 2009).

There is also continued and often dramatic evidence of a gender gap in STEM-related competitions, particularly those requiring quick answers to publicly presented questions that have dichotomously correct or incorrect answers (such as the National Geographic Bee) rather than requiring extended projects explained to judges (such as the Intel Science Competition). Illustratively, in the 1993 National Geographic Bee, the proportions of boys and girls entering the contest were roughly equal (51% boys), but the representation of boys increased dramatically at each successive step of the competition: 78% of school-level winners were boys; 84% of school winners who scored high enough to qualify to compete in their state-level bee were boys; 96% of the state winners were boys; and 100% of the 10 national finalists were boys (Liben, 2002). This general pattern has continued over the decades that followed, and in the 25 years of the competition, only three of the National Champions have been girls. The gender ratios are also highly imbalanced on the International Mathematical Olympiad. For example, in the 2011, 2012, and 2013 competitions, boys were, respectively, 90%, 91%, and 90% of the contestants (International Math Olympiad, 2014). That these gender gaps cannot be explained by the competition format alone is suggested by the balanced gender pattern among both contestants and winners of the annual Scripps National Spelling Bee, a competition that is similarly high pressure (e.g., public, televised, and time-constrained). Illustratively, the percentages of boys competing in the final Scripps National Spelling Bee competition held in Washington, D.C. over the same three recent years were, respectively, 50%, 48%, and 48% (P. Kimball, personal communication, April 14, 2014).

None of the preceding observations about gender gaps in various indicators of STEM success and involvement speaks to the origins or developmental course of observed differences. This is especially important to underscore because there is a tendency for both laypersons and research scientists alike to infer that statements about gender differences necessarily imply something about cause, commonly presumed to be biological, particularly when observed differences are found during infancy. However, to the degree that one works within a relational systems approach to human development—as we do—our emphasis is on individual ↔ context relations that include "biological-physiological processes, behavioral and social relationship processes, and physical, ecological, cultural, and historical processes" (Lerner & Callina, 2013, p. 374). That is, we expect that explanations lie in multiple levels of the child (biological, behavioral, and social) and in the surrounding ecology that likewise involves multiple levels and dynamically interacting influences (Bronfenbrenner, 1977).

A relational perspective is also useful for underscoring a second important point which is that there is also no reason to suppose that observed STEM gender differences are immutable, as captured in the following additional description of a relational perspective:

> …another distinctive feature of relational developmental systems theories is the presence of (relative) plasticity in human development. Such plasticity reflects the potential for systematic change in individual ↔ context relations, a potential that derives from connections between the individual and the multiple levels of his or her changing context.
>
> **Lerner & Callina (2013, p. 373)**

Importantly, mutability is just as relevant to biology and culture as it is to individuals' cognitive and social qualities. In biology, for example, brain plasticity may be observed as one develops expertise in playing the piano or participates in a rehabilitation program following a stroke. In culture, for example, change occurs with new political parties, wars, and the passage of laws such as those that affect the shape of girls' access to education. And, of course, cognitive and social qualities change as children have experiential interactions with their physical and social worlds including those of families, schools, and communities.

All of these are relevant for STEM outcomes, and all of these are potentially open to intervention. In the remaining sections of this chapter, we focus primarily on the last of these, that is, processes and interventions that address individuals' experiences in their immediate surrounding contexts within the United States. To focus on interventions aimed at the individual level in a single geopolitical unit is not to imply that other interventions and contexts are any less important as targets of change. Consider, for example, approaches grounded in social rather than developmental psychology such as Eagly and Wood's (1999) social role theory. This theory holds that the societal assignment of roles leads individuals to adapt psychologically in ways that enable them to embrace and satisfy those roles (see also Petersen & Hyde, 2014 [Chapter 2 of this volume]). Empirical support for this position within the domain of STEM comes from research showing that differential societal constraints on men's and women's roles (i.e., societal levels of gender equity) predict gender differences in mathematics performance (Else-Quest, Hyde, & Linn, 2010; Hyde & Mertz, 2009) and science performance (Farfield & McLean, 2013). Societal-level analyses may thus also suggest potential avenues for intervention. For example, the studies just described might lead to the proposal that enhancing societal gender equity would effect a reduction in the STEM gender gap. Or, as another example, if work–family role conflict is linked to women's disproportionate tendency to exit highly prestigious and time-demanding STEM academic positions, societal interventions might include increasing the availability of day care facilities or modifying parental-leave policies rather than personological interventions that offer counseling to individual women to help them withstand internal, psychological role conflict.

3. DEVELOPMENTAL MECHANISMS AND A TAXONOMY OF STEM INTERVENTION GOALS

Our aim in this section is to offer ways of conceptualizing the variety of interventions that have (or could be) designed to reduce the gender gap in STEM engagement and success. We first draw from major theories of gender development to identify mechanisms proposed to influence girls' and women's cognitions and behaviors in the natural ecology. Such mechanisms may be harnessed by or implicated in intervention programs as well. Second, based on an examination of a wide range of intervention programs and on our conceptual analysis of their (often implicit) goals, we propose a taxonomy of goal types. Such a taxonomy may be useful for clarifying program assumptions and for suggesting outcome variables of interest.

3.1. Intervention Mechanisms Implicated by Theories of Gender Development

Within the study of gender development, three families of theories have been identified: gender essentialism, gender environmentalism, and gender constructivism (Liben & Bigler, 2002). We discuss each briefly in turn, and in the course of doing so, highlight change mechanisms that can potentially be called upon for or influential in STEM interventions. More detailed reviews of gender developmental theories and relevant research may be found in Ruble, Martin, and Berenbaum (2006), Blakemore, Berenbaum, and Liben (2009), Hines (2015), Leaper (2015), and in other contributions to this volume (see, especially, Bigler, Hayes, & Liben, 2014 [Chapter 7 of this volume]; Butler, 2014 [Chapter 1 of this volume]; Leaper & Brown,

2014 [Chapter 6 of this volume]; Martin, Fabes, & Hanish, 2014 [Chapter 5 of this volume]; Petersen & Hyde, 2014 [Chapter 2 of this volume]).

3.1.1 Gender Essentialism

The first theoretical family, gender essentialism, takes the categories of male and female as inherent, and emphasizes the far-reaching "essence" of being male or female. Essentialist approaches typically assign an important role to biological processes of the individual (e.g., Gurian, Henley, & Trueman, 2001) or of the species, including evolutionary forces on males and females (e.g., Geary & Bjorklund, 2000). It is important to note, however, that the study of biological processes does not automatically signal a gender-essentialist approach. Many who examine the role of biology in behavioral outcomes examine that role in a relational context that considers the dynamic interactions or transactions among biological and other individual- and societal-level processes (e.g., Halpern, 2012; Hines, 2015).

What characterizes gender essentialism is the deep-seated view that boys (girls) are "just like that" coupled with the position that it is largely futile (and indeed, generally undesirable) to attempt to interfere with those fundamental, natural differences. As reviewed at length elsewhere (Liben, 2014), voluminous instantiations of this position are found in historical and contemporary educational writings. Illustrative of the former is William DeWitt Hyde, an influential educator of the early twentieth century. He wrote that in both educational and occupational contexts, girls and women are intellectually "receptive" whereas boys and men are intellectually "productive," and that "This differentiation is a decree of nature, and one which it is useless for us to fight against, and highly profitable for us to recognize" (W. Hyde, 1906, p. 207). Among contemporary essentialists are Leonard Sax and Michael Gurian (e.g., Gurian et al., 2001; Sax, 2005) who have fueled the national movement for single-sex public education (see Bigler et al., 2014 [Chapter 7 of this volume]; Liben, 2014). Sax, for example, takes the position that "human nature is gendered to the core" (Weil, 2008, p. 43) and that "Boys are boys and girls are girls" (NACE, 2013). This position appears to underlie educational claims as when he suggests, for example, that: "the best way to get girls excited about quantum mechanics turns out to be quite different from the best way to get boys excited about quantum mechanics" (NACE, 2013).

Given the foundational belief that gender differences are predestined, pervasive, and acceptable, gender essentialists have no reason to postulate additional mechanisms to account for gender differentiation, nor to suggest interventions to prevent or diminish it. Thus, interventions to reduce the STEM gender gap are best served by respecting these essentialist gender differences and adjusting lesson content, pedagogy, and perhaps expectations accordingly.

3.1.2 Gender Environmentalism

As would be expected from the root term "environment" contained in the term "gender environmentalism," the emphasis in this approach is largely on forces in the external environment. Early environmentalist approaches were built on behaviorist principles that were applied to child development in general (e.g., Bijou & Baer, 1961) and to gender development in particular (e.g., Mischel, 1966). In this perspective, key mechanisms shaping children's behaviors include reinforcement and punishment. Just as rats' or pigeons' maze-running, bar-pressing, or pecking behaviors can be effectively trained and modified by selective rewards or punishments, so, too, children's gender-differentiated behaviors can be shaped. For example, a girl versus a boy who donned a princess gown could be expected to receive admiring versus disparaging comments from parents or peers, reinforcement in the former case and punishment in the latter. Furthermore, environments are powerful forces because they contain within them models whose behaviors can be observed and imitated. Extensive research within social-learning theory (SLT) supported the hypothesized importance of modeling and imitation mechanisms. Children were shown to be especially likely to observe and imitate models of their own gender (e.g., Bussey & Bandura, 1984).

Early theorists operating within SLT also acknowledged that individuals' cognitions and reasoning processes are entailed in gender development. They did not, however, choose to study them. Mischel (1966, p. 62), for example, wrote: "It is often mistakenly assumed that social-learning theories deny the existence of mediating cognitive processes. Men and women, as well as boys and girls, do think. They experience wishes, fears, and hopes; they even dream." He argued that the contrast between SLT and the more cognitive theorists such as Kohlberg (1966) was with respect to the "referents selected for the analysis of behavior. In the present formulation, discriminable antecedent events, rather than inferred intrapsychic activities, are used to predict and analyze behavior" (p. 62).

Later social-learning theorists have given more explicit attention to the role of individuals' cognitions, seen most clearly in a variant of SLT named social cognitive theory (SCT; Bandura, 1992). In a recent discussion of the SCT label, for example, Bandura and Bussey (2004) noted that ". . . the *social* portion of the title acknowledges the social origins of much human thought and action; the *cognitive* portion recognizes the influential contribution of thought processes to human motivation, affect, and action" (p. 693). One implication of this position is that although environments are thought to shape and model children's behaviors, children themselves are thought to influence which environments they encounter and how they are processed. In particular, Bussey and Bandura (1999) proposed that in addition to the imposed environment over which the child has little choice (as in the princess example given above), there are also selected and constructed environments. The former refers to the idea that children differentially place themselves in different environments (e.g., ballet vs. martial arts classes), placements that necessarily affect the environmental experiences that they have. The latter refers to the idea that children's own qualities affect the way they think about or use any given environmental input.

Relatedly, Bandura (2001) has also given increasing attention to the role of individuals' self-efficacy beliefs, arguing that one's sense of competence in a domain influences one's willingness to engage in that domain and affects what is ultimately taken away from that engagement. Whether or not these constructs blur distinctions between families of theories (see Bandura & Bussey, 2004; Bussey & Bandura, 1999, vs. Martin, Ruble, & Szkrybalo, 2002, 2004), what is most important for the purposes of the present chapter is that gender environmentalist approaches highlight the relevance of environmentally-based change mechanisms in STEM interventions. These include contingent responses to children's behaviors (e.g., adults' and peers' responses to children's STEM-related behaviors or foundational skills), provision of models who enact STEM-relevant behaviors and who are thus available to be imitated (e.g., exposing girls to women engaged in STEM activities), and the manipulation of environmental contexts (e.g., designing educational environments that will engage children in STEM-relevant activities).

3.1.3 Gender Constructivism

A constructivist approach to gender—like a constructivist approach to any aspect of social or cognitive development—assigns key explanatory power to the individual. In the case of gender development, this means that gender outcomes are not simply reflections of gender-related experiences imposed upon children by either biology or environment, but rather emerge from children's self-directed uses and interpretation of such experiences.

As suggested in Section 3.1.2, some theories that descended from learning theory also assign important roles to children's qualities in their approach to gender development. Bandura (1992) argued for three sets of factors: behavior, personal cognitions and perceptions, and the external environment. Because these factors include child-based constructs such as the child's own sense of self-efficacy, SCT can be considered a constructivist approach. However, because SCT emphasizes the role of environmental factors in generating these individuals' behaviors and cognitions, it is still somewhat distinct from more classic constructionist theories.

The quintessential example of the latter is the theory of gender development proposed by Kohlberg. This theory, too, acknowledged the role of the environment, as evidenced in Kohlberg's (1966) statement that "At any given point, the child uses … experiences of … body and … social environment to form basic sex-role concepts and values, but at any given point environmental experiences also stimulate restructuring these concepts and values" (p. 85). However, Kohlberg also emphasized child-based processes identified in Piagetian theory, suggesting, that that "Sex-role concepts and attitudes change with age in universal ways because of universal age changes in basic modes of cognitive organization" (p. 83).

Much of the empirical work of Kohlberg and his followers was directed toward cataloguing the emergence of three basic cognitive achievements related to gender: gender identity, gender stability, and full gender constancy. Although the definitions and measurement of these constructs are beyond the scope of this chapter (see Blakemore et al., 2009; Ruble & Martin, 1998), what is most important here is the basic idea that children's explicit recognition of their own gender (gender identity) is foundational for children's emerging gender-differentiated interests and behaviors. Using a hypothetical boy for his example, Kohlberg (1966) characterized the sequential process as follows: "I am a boy, therefore I want to do boy things, therefore the opportunity to do boys things (and to gain approval for doing them) is rewarding" (p. 89). Kohlberg explicitly contrasted this sequence to one that he argued captured the social-learning view: "I want rewards, I am rewarded for doing boy things, therefore I want to be a boy" (p. 89). In the former, the sequence begins from the child's gender self-categorization; in the latter, from social contingencies that ultimately lead to self-categorization. The developmental mechanisms that one would harness for STEM interventions would be somewhat different under each of these two scenarios. A focus on self-categorization as a causal mechanism would appear to imply the value of either finding ways to decrease a young girl's tendency to focus on her gender category in the first place, or, alternatively (and better-suited to a culture that generally believes in differentiated gender roles), to broaden her concept of "girl things" to include STEM-related activities and goals. A focus on social contingencies as causal mechanisms would appear to imply the value of shifting reinforcement patterns delivered from the surrounding environment. Such reinforcement patterns ultimately result in the development of the child's internalized personal cognitions, including the qualities of the child's ideal self, which in turn influence further behaviors and their impact.

Several other constructivist accounts of gender development have been proffered during the half century that followed Kohlberg's initial theory. Especially seminal was Martin and Halverson's (1981) "schematic processing model of sex typing and stereotyping in children," referred to as gender schema theory (GST). As suggested by the label, a core concept in GST is the schema, defined by Martin and Halverson as "naïve theories that guide information processing by structuring experiences, regulating behavior, and providing bases for making inferences and interpretations" (p. 1120). They illustrate the process by a girl who encounters a doll. She decides that dolls are self-relevant, then that dolls are for girls, and then, knowing that she is a girl, concludes that "dolls are for me." In turn, she approaches and interacts with the doll which leads her to become more knowledgeable about dolls. The inverse scenario occurs when she encounters a truck. Viewing the truck as for boys, she would be less likely to interact with and learn about trucks, how their motors work, and so on. In essence, then, children's internalized cultural beliefs about what is for girls versus boys (i.e., cultural gender stereotypes), coupled with self-identifications as girls or boys, drive choices and experiences to develop further knowledge and skills. For the present discussion, again what is especially important is the recognition that beliefs about what is linked to each gender (i.e., cultural gender stereotypes) are thus critical factors in the experiences that children seek out and have.

Building from this model, Liben and Bigler (2002) generated "dual-pathway models" (DPM) that made more explicit the role of individual differences in schematic gender processing. DPM highlighted individual differences in children's personal interests (particular toy and activity preferences), attitudes (differing levels of endorsement of cultural gender stereotypes for themselves and/or others), and attention to gender (labeled as *gender salience filters*—the tendency to see the world through gendered lenses). Additionally, the DPM framework also proposed that gender development proceeds along two simultaneous pathways. One—the attitudinal pathway—is similar to that proposed by Martin and Halverson (1981): Children use knowledge of what is culturally defined as for boys or girls and knowledge of their own gender to guide them to differential pursuit of masculine versus feminine activities. The other—the personal pathway—proposed that children's idiosyncratic talents or interests lead them to engage in certain activities, and that their personal engagement, in turn, affects how they view the gender-appropriateness of those activities. Children's gender beliefs and personal qualities thus influence, and are influenced by, cultural and individual gender stereotypes and behaviors.

Another theoretical model that addresses a broad range of factors like these is the expectancy-value model developed by Eccles over a quarter-century ago (e.g., see Eccles, 2014; Eccles et al., 1983). This program of research has been focused explicitly on understanding the pathways to academic success, particularly in girls and women, and is thus especially useful for identifying mechanisms that can be used in interventions to reduce the STEM gender gap. More detailed descriptions of this approach are provided by Petersen and Hyde (2014) [Chapter 2 of this volume].

Collectively, constructivist theories of gender development point to many potential avenues for STEM interventions, including efforts to modify children's, parents', teachers', peers' or others' STEM-relevant gender stereotypes about themselves or others; to minimize attention to gender divisions through changing the surrounding environment or children's vigilance about gender; to foster participation in behaviors or activities traditionally associated with the other sex; and to enhance children's beliefs about self-efficacy, values, and enjoyment related to STEM. Before turning to descriptions of sample interventions and identifying ways that various theory-derived mechanisms are entailed in them, we turn to an analysis of interventions from the perspective of program goals.

3.2. STEM Intervention Goals

In this section, we build on an earlier analysis (Liben, 2012) to offer a taxonomy of five intervention goals, all of which are designed to in some way enhance the match between (a) cognitive, personal, or perceived qualities of girls and women and (b) demands or opportunities of STEM. The first two goal types are aimed at revising the way that qualities of girls or women and qualities of STEM are matched by changing one or the other side of the equation, that is, by changing something about either girls (women) or by changing something about STEM. The third leaves each side of the equation fundamentally unchanged, but highlights existing compatibilities. The final two goal types are aimed at neutralizing beliefs about incompatibilities between traditional STEM domains and traditional qualities of girls and women. These goal types do not aim to adjust compatibility by bringing the two sides of the equation into alignment, but rather to revise *beliefs* about incompatibilities. Each is explained in turn.

The first goal type—*Remediate*—reflects the premise that girls and women are in some way inadequately prepared to learn from or fully participate or succeed in STEM educational or occupational activities. Thus, in this category of interventions the goal is to in some way to fix, correct, or overcome girls' or women's failings or lacunae. The second—*Revise*—likewise presumes a mismatch between what the STEM domain requires and what girls or women bring to the table. However, rather than trying to change girls or women, here the goal is to change either STEM or STEM instruction to make it more consistent with girls' and women's qualities. Note that in this goal type—unlike the next—STEM itself is in some way reworked.

The third—*Refocus*—presumes that there are, indeed, some mismatches or incompatibilities between STEM domains and traditionally feminine qualities but that there are, simultaneously, also matches between other pairs of qualities. The goal of this category of interventions is to focus attention away from mismatches and toward matches, thereby emphasizing existing compatibilities.

The fourth—*Recategorize*—is aimed at reducing the belief that there is an orthogonal relation between (a) members of the STEM category (i.e., people who have and pursue scientific values, habits of mind, activities, and the like) and (b) members of the FEMININE category (i.e., people who evidence culturally feminine values, interests, appearance, and the like). The fifth—*Resist*—aims to sensitize individuals (self or others) to the existence of cultural gender stereotypes, and to provide strategies that help to defuse, confront, or negate cultural stereotypes and prejudicial behaviors that erect barriers to girls' and women's participation and success in STEM.

Table 1 contains a brief summary of the five intervention goals just described; Figure 4 suggests that at least some of these alternative approaches have been noticed outside academia.

Table 1 The Five R's: Intervention Goal Types for Reducing the STEM Gender Gap

Goal Types	Definitions
Remediate (girls)	Correct or adjust some cognitive or personal quality of girls (women) judged to be both important for STEM and disproportionately underdeveloped in girls (women)
Revise (STEM)	Modify STEM (e.g., skills, methods, tasks, instructions) to render it better-matched to perceived traditional feminine cognitive or personal qualities, preferences, or epistemology
Refocus (attention)	Highlight and emphasize compatibilities between affordances or requirements of participation in STEM and traditional feminine preferences or skills
Recategorize (individuals)	Replace dichotomous, mutually exclusive categories (either STEM or FEMININE) with multiple classification possibilities (permitting assignment to both STEM and FEMININE categories simultaneously)
Resist (stereotypes)	Identify, challenge, and work to eradicate self- and other-directed beliefs, biases, and discriminatory practices concerning girls' (women's) unsuitability or incapacity for STEM

Figure 4 Cartoon illustrating two intervention goal types including *Resist* (left panel) and *Revise* (right panel). *Reproduced by permission of Zach Weinersmith, http://www.smbc-comics.com/index.php?db=comics&id=1962#comic.*

4. ILLUSTRATIONS OF STEM INTERVENTIONS

We now describe some specific intervention programs designed to reduce the STEM gender gap. Our aims are to provide readers with a sense of the kinds of activities and techniques that are employed in educational efforts, to illustrate how given interventions involve one or more theory-based mechanisms described earlier, and to demonstrate variability in program goals. We organize the discussion of interventions by using the goal taxonomy. We selected illustrative programs with an eye toward diversity in STEM domains (e.g., computer science; engineering), contexts and durations (e.g., semester-long curriculum units; day-long campus events), targeted participant qualities (e.g., cognitive spatial skills; personal self-efficacy beliefs), and grade levels (e.g., college; preschool). An illustrative, narrative review of this kind is well-suited for providing a sense of the methods, concepts, challenges, and consequences of specific programs, but it is less well-suited for evaluating the overall impact of extant interventions or for identifying the circumstances under which they are more or less effective. The latter goals are better addressed using meta-analytic approaches, a point to which we return in Section 5.

4.1. Remediate

Interventions commonly have remediation goals. Such interventions rest on the assumption that girls or women are missing some critical prerequisite for STEM engagement or success. What they are missing might be a cognitive skill, motivation to engage in or persist in STEM (perhaps failing to appreciate the potential personal value or enjoyment from participation in STEM), or a depressed sense of self-efficacy or self-competence with respect to STEM (see Butler, 2014 [Chapter 1 of this volume]). We illustrate the remediate approach by focusing primarily on interventions designed to enhance girls' and women's spatial skills. Spatial skills have been a particularly attractive target for remediation in light of strong evidence for the association between spatial skills and success in STEM fields (e.g., Hegarty, 2014; Wai et al., 2009), the persistent gender differences observed in spatial skills (e.g., Voyer et al., 1995), and analyses showing that spatial skills are open to training (e.g., Uttal et al., 2013).

One illustrative spatial intervention program was developed at Michigan Technological University in 1993 by Sorby and colleagues (Sorby & Baartmans, 1996; Veurink & Sorby, 2011). Their goal was to increase engineering students' success and to reduce attrition from the program which is a particularly problematic issue among women. In the inaugural year, students were given a mental rotation task prior to beginning their coursework in engineering graphics, and of the 96 students who scored below a minimum threshold (60% correct on the Purdue Spatial Visualization Test), 24 randomly selected students were assigned to receive spatial visualization training. The program has continued since then, although the discontinuation of random assignment to training in subsequent years (Corbett, 2011) makes it more difficult to interpret the meaning of observed changes.

The published version of the curriculum includes six modules that teach isometric drawings and coded plans, orthographic drawings, rotation of objects about a single axis, rotation of objects about two or more axes, object reflections and symmetry, and cutting planes and cross sections. Each module begins with a lecture demonstrating potential techniques for solving workbook problems, for example, using physical gestures to determine motion or dividing up problems into smaller, simpler components. After attempting to solve a workbook problem, students watch the instructor demonstrate a correct solution. They then work with computer software that demonstrates and reinforces the spatial concepts and strategies, and provides practice problems. Finally, students sketch their solutions in their workbooks, thus requiring them to translate three-dimensional solutions into two-dimensional representations. Veurink and Sorby (2011) report that students who completed the spatial skills course outperformed students who did not take the class, earning better course grades and being less likely to fail or withdraw from courses and more likely to complete their degree.

Because this intervention program was targeted for students who had already applied to and been admitted into an engineering program, and because the spatial training curriculum was specifically designed to be relevant to the engineering curriculum that followed, this research cannot speak to its potential impact on nonengineering students or on a broad range of STEM domains. A recent investigation by Miller and Halpern (2012) was designed to address these issues. They provided the same curriculum to a random sample of undergraduate students enrolled in a range of STEM majors at a highly selective liberal arts college. On average, these students' spatial skills were strong upon entry, but also on average, women's entry scores were lower than men's.

The spatial training experience was found to improve students' spatial skills pre- to posttest, even among students who had entered with high spatial skills. However, Miller and Halpern (2012) found only mixed evidence for training effects on STEM performance. Within physics, scores on a number of specific course examinations were higher among students who received the spatial training than among control students, but this advantage was not evident on a posttest measuring conceptual understanding of physics (the Force Concept Inventory). With a single exception (biology), sophomore STEM grades were unrelated to spatial training condition. Thus although it is clear from both studies that spatial skills training improved students' performance on specific tests of spatial skills, it is not yet clear whether improvement extends to generalized STEM performance and retention.

In an ongoing study (Liben, Signorella, & Sorby, 2013), the same curriculum is being used with a much younger and more diverse sample of students. Specifically, the curriculum is being given to middle-school students as part of their math classes. Outcome measures examined in students from experimental and control classes tap performance on spatial tests, STEM achievement (e.g., scores on state math and science achievement tests), STEM engagement (e.g., self-reports of their self-competence, valuing, and liking of STEM fields), and interest in future STEM careers. Although only a portion of the data have been collected to date, preliminary findings are encouraging with respect to showing a positive effect of the curriculum on specific spatial skills, but—at least as yet—they show no parallel indication of positive effects on student engagement (e.g., measures of self-efficacy, valuing, and interest).

Given that these data come from only a small subset of the sample and do not yet include all scheduled waves of testing, it is premature to draw conclusions. However, the data in hand do suggest the wisdom of assessing a broad range of outcomes in evaluations of intervention effects. It is not enough to evaluate only whether the identified prerequisites (here, spatial skills) have been remediated as intended. It is also critical to test explicitly whether improvements in the targeted construct lead to improved STEM outcomes. Additionally, it is important to assess a wide range of mechanisms discussed earlier (e.g., STEM self-efficacy, valuing, liking; STEM-relevant gender stereotypes; reinforcement patterns or modeling of teachers; and the like) to clarify why or why not a particular intervention led to improvement in STEM. This understanding is valuable for testing theoretical models such as those discussed earlier in this chapter, as well as suggesting targets for future interventions. For example, if an intervention were shown to leave student interest unchanged or even depressed, it would suggest the value of finding ways to make future interventions more fun.

4.2. Revise

A second goal-type is one that aims to bring STEM into closer alignment with girls or women by modifying STEM in some way. Given that girls and women are commonly thought to excel in and prefer language-rich activities (although differences are actually small, e.g., see Hyde, 2005), one instantiation of this general idea has been to embed STEM skills or activities in reading or storytelling activities.

An illustration of this approach is found in the domain of computer science (CS). Noting that girls and women are especially underrepresented in CS and that programming is a gateway to the field, Kelleher, Pausch, and Kiesler (2007) developed a new programming environment within a storytelling context. They began with an existing educational tool called Alice which exposes students to the principles underlying programming languages such as Java, C++, and Python as they control animations. In addition to allowing students to see graphic results immediately, Alice allows students to ignore code altogether by working entirely within the graphic interface. Kelleher et al. then created a modified version of Alice—called Storytelling Alice—that allows users to create stories in which program characters move, speak, and think across scenes.

To test of the effectiveness of Storytelling Alice, Kelleher et al. (2007) recruited middle-school girls from local Girl Scout troops to workshops. Girls were randomly assigned to work for 2¼ hours with tutorials for either Generic Alice or Storytelling Alice, building a program with their assigned tool. Girls then completed a programming quiz and survey, followed by a half-hour session during which they were given whichever version of Alice they had not already used and asked to build something with it. Finally, they were asked to share with others one of the Alice programs they had created and were invited to take home either Generic or Storytelling Alice.

Findings showed that girls learned programming equally well from either Alice environment. However, in comparison to girls who had been assigned to Generic Alice, girls given Storytelling Alice were more interested in using it again and were more likely to spend extra time using it during a brief period in which Alice remained available but there was no requirement to use it. Of those girls assigned to Storytelling Alice, almost all (90%) chose to take that version home; of those assigned to Generic Alice, only about a quarter (23%) chose their assigned version. Of particular interest is that in comparison to girls who had been assigned to Generic Alice, girls who had been assigned to Storytelling Alice spent more time actually programming (as opposed to working within the graphic interface). These data are especially important because a potential drawback of instruction with Alice (in either version) is that it allows learners to avoid working directly with code, which could potentially undermine students' later CS success.

This is a case in which the STEM pedagogy has been revised for intervention with a positive immediate outcome, although further work on long-term outcomes is needed. Additionally, it is important to consider the gender-specific rationale for this intervention. Indeed, subsequent work (Rodger et al., 2009) has suggested that boys profit from Storytelling Alice as well.

A belief about the special appeal of narrative for girls has also been a rationale underlying the design of a new construction toy recently marketed to young girls—*GoldieBlox* (Coyle & Liben, 2014; Newcomb, 2014). The toy sets include books in which the narrative leads the user to solve a variety of challenges by assembling simple machines, thus using a traditionally feminine activity—reading—to engage girls in a traditionally masculine activity—construction. For example, in the first set in the series, *GoldieBlox and the Spinning Machine*, Goldie wants to understand how the ballerina in her mother's jewelry box spins. She discovers that the ballerina is on a wheel and axle, and so she builds one. Her animal friends (included as small dolls in the toy set) want to participate in the fun and thus the story invites the child to build increasingly complex belt drives that spin, first, a single animal, then two, and finally all five animals. Although the series was developed as a commercial toy rather than as an educational intervention, it nevertheless illustrates how designers may adapt materials and curricula to make them more "girl friendly."

There have been other attempts to develop girl friendly versions of toys that are thought to be (and increasingly demonstrated to be) supportive of STEM outcomes. Experience in creating constructions from blocks, for example, has been linked to children's later mathematics performance (e.g., Casey, Kersh, & Young, 2004; Verdine et al., 2014; Wolfgang, Stannard, & Jones, 2003). Particularly popular are block sets manufactured by LEGO. Although individual LEGO blocks are not generally viewed as highly masculine (e.g., Blakemore & Centers, 2005; reported that adults' gender ratings of LEGO blocks placed them within the "neutral" category, just shy of the "moderately masculine" category), marketing research shows that traditionally 90% of LEGO construction sets have been purchased for or by boys (Allen, 2014). In 2012, the company began to market boxed sets designed explicitly for girls. In commenting on this series, a senior creative director was quoted as saying: "Unlike previous LEGO toys for girls, LEGO Friends, at its core, does not apologize for being a construction toy and delivers, for the first time, a building experience in the same scale as our classic offerings" (Gudum, quoted on Stylist.co.uk, n.d.). Interestingly, however, LEGO advertisements for girls' sets appear to say little about construction. Illustrative is the description on the website advertisement for the *Butterfly Beauty Shop* which reads:

> It's a busy day of beauty fun down at the Butterfly Beauty Shop! Emma loves this posh little salon at the center of Heartlake City! Shop for lipstick, makeup and hair accessories! Emma and all of her friends will look fabulous with bows, sunglasses, a hairbrush, mirror, lipsticks and new hair styles. Get the girls ready for any event with the salon where you can rearrange the interior! Includes Emma and Sarah mini-doll figures.
>
> *LEGO (2014)*

In general, then, both STEM educators and toy manufacturers have attempted to modify existing materials (e.g., Alice in computer science; *GoldieBlox* in a mechanical construction toy; LEGO sets in a block construction toy) in ways thought to be better-suited to girls' interests and qualities. From an educational perspective, the goal is to draw girls into activities that are salutary for STEM. What is in need of evaluation is precisely how these revised materials function and their long-term impact on STEM. For example, when girls interact with *GoldieBlox*, do they expend their energy building a belt drive to spin the characters and thereby develop mechanical understanding, or do they focus primarily on the book itself, perhaps inventing and enacting new story lines with the characters? When they interact with the *Butterfly Beauty Shop*, do they spend time building and then disassembling and renovating the structure, or do they focus largely on scenarios in which they shop for lipstick, makeup, and hair accessories? When they use Storytelling Alice, do they become sufficiently interested in programming that they move on to learning and enjoying code or do they turn their experiences into pursuing, say, careers that involve the use of already-designed software rather than into careers in which they are the *designers* of such software? Again, these and other important questions can be addressed only if evaluations examine a range of potentially relevant mechanisms and include assessments of generalized and temporally distant STEM outcomes.

4.3. Refocus, Recategorize, and Resist

Our final group of illustrative interventions represents the last three R's of goal types—refocus, recategorize, and resist. We have clustered them together in a single section for both practical and conceptual reasons. At the practical level, it is convenient to combine the discussion because interventions often represent more than one of these goal types simultaneously. At the conceptual level, it is suitable to group them together because they share the foundational assumption that it is unnecessary to change either girls (women) or STEM to make the two compatible. Rather, compatibility is presumed, and interventions are aimed at making that compatibility more apparent.

One focus of compatibility that has been targeted by STEM interventions concerns career values (Weisgram, Bigler, & Liben, 2010). Based on the premise that women, as a group, are people-oriented and altruistic (see Petersen & Hyde, 2014 [Chapter 2 of this volume]), some interventions have attempted to promote the message that science careers improve people's lives (even as they simultaneously afford other career goals). Illustrative is the campaign by the European Commission (2012) entitled *Science: It's a Girl Thing*! On the home page appears a pink rectangular block entitled "Why you'll LOVE science" in which the first graphic that appear in a sequence of images includes the following text:

You Can Really Improve People's Lives.
Getting involved in science means making a "world of difference". If you want to prevent the spread of disease, improve the quality of life for people, protect the fragile natural environment, put food into people's hands and combat poverty, then science is for you.

In keeping with our earlier comments about the importance of casting a broad net in evaluating the impact of interventions, it would be important to assess whether exposure to these materials results in girls' increased liking, pursuit, and success in STEM, as well as whether exposure affects girls' or others' more general beliefs about what girls are like and whether their qualities differ systematically from those of boys (i.e., gender stereotypes about girls or women in science and as scientists).

Although we have been unable to locate evaluations by the European Commission on the impact of this campaign, a study by Weisgram and Bigler (2006b) was explicitly designed to address the effectiveness of a career-values approach in the context of an intervention program called *Expanding Your Horizons* (EYH). EYH is publicized as "girls' gateway to science, technology, engineering and mathematics" (EYHN, 2013). Middle-school girls participate in day-long conferences, usually held on a university or college campus. The day includes workshops designed around topical projects. For example, in "Engineering Candy Bridges," girls meet an engineer, learn about civil engineering in relation to bridges, and then build bridges from candy and toothpicks. A key feature of EYH is that both scientists and attendees are female. Program descriptions on the EYH Website explicitly emphasize this demographic as in statements such as "you'll have fun along with other girls your age" and "conferences are full of enjoyable hands-on activities led by real women who have STEM jobs" (EYHN, 2013). We infer from the gender demographics as well as from the way presenters and participants are described that a major goal of EYH is to dispel the notion that being a member of the female category does not, in fact, preclude being a member of the scientist category. Thus, the goal of this intervention program appears to fall under the goal-type category we have labeled recategorize.

Weisgram and Bigler (2006b) examined the efficacy of both standard and modified versions of the EYH program. The former, as just explained, involves exposing girls to women scientists (recategorize). The second added a component to EYH that was intended to highlight compatibility between the altruistic values of girls and the altruistic affordances of science careers (refocus). To provide a test of the impact of observing and interacting with women scientist models as well as to study whether the effect would be enhanced by drawing attention to the altruism-affordance of science, Weisgram and Bigler experimentally manipulated the way that the scientists described their jobs during the EYH workshops. Some girls were randomly assigned to the standard condition. These girls heard women scientists describe and demonstrate their scientific activities as they normally would, meaning that they made no specific references to altruism. Other girls were randomly assigned to an altruism condition. These girls heard women scientists not only describe and demonstrate their jobs, but also heard them discuss how their own and other scientists' careers help people at both individual and societal levels. In addition to testing girls who had attended either the standard or altruism conditions at EYH, the researchers also tested students who did not attend EYH but were enrolled in the same schools from which the EYH participants had come. Dependent measures tapped students' science self-efficacy, the utility value and egalitarianism of science, and interest in science careers.

The data showed that—in comparison to the no-EYH comparison group—girls who attended EYH had higher science self-efficacy. There were no significant differences between the two EYH groups. The identical pattern held for utility value of science. The egalitarianism measure showed no difference between EYH versus comparison groups.

From the perspective of attracting girls into STEM careers, probably the most important question concerns whether EYH affected girls' expressed interest in science. Overall, girls who attended EYH expressed higher levels of interest than did girls in the comparison group. Contrary to expectations, girls in the altruism EYH condition reported no greater interest than did girls in the standard EYH condition. Interestingly, however, when Weisgram and Bigler (2006b) took into account not simply each girl's assigned condition, but rather whether each girl had been convinced about the altruistic value of science by the presenter, the findings did support predicted associations between values and interests. That is, compared to girls who had not internalized the message about science and altruism, those girls who had become more convinced that science fulfilled altruistic purposes showed (a) more science self-efficacy, (b) thought science was more valuable, and (c) expressed greater interest in pursuing a career in science. A similar set of findings was reported for a second study that used a pre- and posttest design.

Other interventions have also attempted to try to break down girls' beliefs about the incompatibility between femininity and science by exposing girls to models that we would label as "hyper-feminine women scientists." We use this label to denote women scientists whose physical appearance and observable behaviors display (or exaggerate) qualities that are viewed by the culture as feminine and that are viewed by ethologists (e.g., Barber, 1995) as markers of reproductive fitness (what in common parlance might be labeled more simply as "sexy"). A particularly striking example of this approach is the *Science Cheerleaders* program (Cavalier, 2014). Former National Football League and National Basketball Association cheerleaders who are currently employed in STEM fields (ranging from neuroscience to astrophysics) present cheerleading demonstrations. They cheer with slogans that tout science and deny stereotypes, as, for example, "We're bustin', we're bustin', we're bustin' down the stereotypes! Goooooo SCIENCE!"

Their stated mission is to convey the message that careers in science are accessible to everyone:

> By tapping into girls' personal interests, namely, cheerleading, and building confidence in them by sharing real, personal stories of dealing with stereotypes while excelling in science and engineering careers, the Science Cheerleaders are poised to effectively steer the estimated 3–4 million U.S. cheerleaders towards science!.
>
> *Cavalier (2014; FAQ tab)*

What is most visible in some venues (e.g., a You Tube clip from their 2010 appearance at the U.S.A. Science and Engineering Festival, Science Cheerleaders, 2014, Watch the Science Cheerleaders sidebar) is the women's physical beauty and cheerleading talent rather than their scientific engagement. However, as part of their appearances, Science Cheerleaders are also actively engaged in encouraging participation in various citizen science projects. Illustrative is their 2012 appearance at a basketball game of the Philadelphia 76ers where, in addition to presenting a halftime cheerleading show, they shot microbe-collection kits wrapped in T-shirts to fans, who were asked to collect microbes by swabbing their shoes and cell phones. Samples were later sent to Argonne National Laboratory to be sequenced and added to the Earth Microbiome Project (see Cavalier, 2014; Citizen Science tab).

Of particular interest in the current context is what children learn from exposure to the Science Cheerleaders. Do they learn that one can be both an attractive woman and scientist simultaneously? Do they come to understand that these are not mutually exclusive, binary categories but instead are dimensions along which a single person can be categorized simultaneously? Earlier research (Bigler & Liben, 1992) has already demonstrated the value of teaching children multiple classification skills to reduce their occupational gender stereotyping, although this work simultaneously demonstrated that classification training is not effective for all children. Or, might exposure to attractive women scientist cheerleaders lead girls to become interested in becoming cheerleaders rather than scientists?

Again, we have been unable to locate evaluation research by the developers of the Science Cheerleaders that addresses these questions. However, data from a recent laboratory study with preschool girls (Coyle & Liben, 2013) underscores the importance of addressing them. In this study, girls played a computer game involving various occupations, including traditionally masculine STEM careers. The model who appeared in the game was experimentally varied between participants. For some girls, the game model was a hyper-feminine character (Barbie) and for other girls the model was a more typical female character (a Playmobil figure). The data showed that neither group of girls showed significant increases in their interests in the masculine STEM jobs following the game. However, for girls who—before the game began—already had strongly traditional feminine interests, exposure to the Barbie model (but not to the Playmobil model) led them to display significantly even more-intensified traditional feminine interests by game's end. Girls who were initially less gender traditional were unaffected by either model. The clear lesson is the importance of systematically evaluating effects of intervention programs in ways that take individual differences into account and that include assessments of not only intended outcomes, but also of potentially unintended (perhaps undesirable) outcomes as well.

The final illustrative interventions we describe are ones that in some way address societal messages about gender and STEM evident in sexist comments or discriminatory practices. The first illustration of this resist goal category of interventions is another investigation by Weisgram and Bigler (2007), also conducted in the context of EYH. In this study, girls attended the EYH science workshops described earlier, but a randomly assigned experimental group also attended an additional session about gender discrimination in scientific fields. The discrimination session was taught by psychology graduate students who explained what gender discrimination is, how it affects women in science today, and how it affected four accomplished female scientists in history (Rosalind Franklin, Cecilia Payne-Gaposchkin, Lise Meitner, and Emily Roebling).

Not surprisingly, girls who received this additional training perceived more discrimination against women in science than did girls who participated in only the standard EYH program. As hypothesized from various theories of gender development and attribution theories, girls who participated in the discrimination program showed an increase in their own sense of science self-efficacy and in the utility value of science. Neither of these changes occurred in girls who attended only the standard EYH program. Interestingly, although girls in the standard EYH condition showed a significant *decrease* in egalitarian attitudes toward science (a finding that had also been reported by Weisgram & Bigler, 2006a), girls in the experimental condition showed no such effect. This was thus another apparently positive outcome of the added discrimination programming.

Importantly, however, in neither condition did girls' own interest in science increase significantly from pre- to posttest assessments, thus failing to replicate a finding reported earlier (Weisgram & Bigler, 2006b; described above). However, Weisgram and Bigler's use of the identical, reliable measure of STEM interest in several experimental studies allows some clear conclusions. For girls who received the standard EYH lessons in different years (Weisgram & Bigler, 2006b, 2007), posttest levels of STEM interest were similar and relatively low: They fell between "a little bit" and "somewhat" (scale points 2 and 3, respectively, with $Ms = 2.32$ and 2.37). For girls who received EYH lessons that had been enhanced by the addition of information about altruism (Weisgram & Bigler, 2006b) or discrimination (Weisgram & Bigler, 2007), posttest levels of STEM interest were in this same narrow range: $Ms = 2.31$ and 2.41. Overall, then, the findings from these intervention studies suggest that even when program manipulations show impact on some measures, their impact on girls' own STEM career interests is at best small.

Another potential means of encouraging resistance to societal gender stereotypes about STEM careers is to teach children directly that gender is irrelevant to entering and succeeding in these careers. Although not directed specifically and uniquely at STEM careers, a study by Bigler and Liben (1990) employed this intervention approach with elementary school children in an attempt to reduce occupational gender stereotypes in general. Children were first assessed for their gender attitudes. Based on their scores, experimental and control groups were formed so that they would have approximately equal numbers of girls and boys and roughly similar levels of gender stereotyping. Each day for a week, children received classroom lessons about two jobs (one culturally masculine and one feminine). In the control group, children were taught about what people in each of the ten jobs did. In the experimental group, children were taught about necessary job interests and skills, and about the irrelevance of gender. For example, they were taught that to become a firefighter a person must like to fight fires and learn to drive fire trucks, but that their gender was irrelevant. In the course of group lessons, children were asked questions such as: "Ann loves to build things and knows how to drive a bulldozer. Could Ann be a construction worker?" When necessary, children were corrected, reminded of the rules, and asked another practice question.

As expected from constructivist theories of gender development, some children had difficultly learning the lessons or even remembering premises. In responding to the construction worker question posed above, for example, one child responded that Ann could not be a construction work "because Ann is a girl" and another responded yes, "because he [sic] followed the rules." After the week's lessons were completed, children were assessed for their occupational gender stereotypes. Children who had entered the study with high occupational gender stereotypes showed reduction in those stereotypes only if they had been in the experimental group. This finding held both when children were asked questions about jobs that had been covered during the class lessons, as well as about other culturally stereotyped jobs that had not been discussed during the week, suggesting that lessons generalized effectively. Although the experimental group showed reduced gender stereotyping compared to a control group, children's own occupational aspirations did not differ across conditions, echoing the EYH work discussed above.

5. CONCLUSIONS AND RECOMMENDATIONS

The material discussed in this chapter demonstrates that even as gender gaps have disappeared or reversed in many STEM domains, they have remained persistent and striking in others. Irrespective of what factors may have initiated and sustained a STEM gender gap, its existence is troublesome for a society that strives to provide every citizen with access to a full range of potential human outcomes and that wishes to maximize its talent pool for meeting practical needs and for advancing human knowledge. The focus of our chapter has been on ways to conceptualize and evaluate interventions designed to reduce this STEM gender gap.

The illustrative interventions we have discussed (as well as others we have examined but not described) are uniformly well-intentioned. As developmental scientists, we find it encouraging that programs universally draw so heavily on change mechanisms identified in theories and empirical research on gender development. We would, however, urge interventionists to be more systematic in articulating theoretical foundations of their programs. This should not only help make findings more valuable for academic scholarship; it should also increase the likelihood that interventions will be programmatic, generalizable, and informative.

What is more problematic, however, is that many interventions are conducted with little attention to systematic evaluation. In some cases, there is no formal program evaluation at all, and success is claimed on the basis of anecdotal accounts about students' enjoyment or subsequent involvement in STEM activities. In other cases, data are reported from systematic assessments, but these data are often limited in important ways. Below we consider some issues that should be addressed, including the need for greater attention to comparison groups, the value of including a broad range of STEM outcome measures, and the importance of testing for unintended as well as intended effects. We end by suggesting next steps for clarifying the extant intervention literature.

5.1. Comparison Groups

One limitation of prior work is that even in cases in which program developers report positive pre- to posttest changes, they often do so without examining whether the changes differ significantly from those that might have occurred without the intervention. Absent findings from a no-treatment comparison group, observed increments might be attributable to other factors such as practice effects or the passage of time. These threats are particularly problematic when interventions include repeated waves of testing distributed over semesters or years.

Even when comparison groups are included, experimental and control samples often differ in important ways. Participation in many STEM programs is determined by self-selection or by parent or teacher referrals, both likely to privilege involvement of students who have atypically strong STEM interests and skills as well as other academically advantageous qualities. Program directors may be unable or unwilling to assign students randomly to intervention versus control groups or to use waitlist control group designs. Even when these are impractical, it may be possible to draw comparison groups from other settings in which students are similar to intervention participants along important dimensions (e.g., with respect to socioeconomic status, general intelligence, prior STEM coursework). Some of the illustrative interventions described in the previous section have successfully designed their evaluations in just this way. With appropriate assessment data, effects of group differences can be handled statistically. Without any comparison group, however, it is difficult to reach any conclusions at all about program effectiveness.

5.2. STEM-Relevant Outcome Measures

Apart from arguing for increased attention to which samples of students are sampled and compared, we also urge more attention to the selection of STEM outcome measures. First, and most obviously, it is important to measure constructs that are explicitly targeted by a given intervention program. If, for example, an intervention is aimed at increasing interest or success in engineering by enhancing students' spatial skills or science self-efficacy, outcome measures would need to address, respectively, spatial performance and self-efficacy.

Second, it is critical to include explicit, ecologically valid measures of STEM achievement and participation. One cannot simply assume that an increase in component skills or motivations—even those that have been convincingly demonstrated to predict STEM success—will necessarily translate into increasing girls' interest in, engagement in, and sustained participation in STEM. For example, although spatial skills may indeed be entailed in STEM success, improving a girl's spatial skills through an intervention may be ineffective for STEM because the skill improvement cannot compensate for an experiential deficiency that has built up from years of avoiding spatially demanding activities. Or, involving girls in intriguing, hands-on STEM activities may well increase girls' enjoyment of STEM, but this increased enjoyment may be ineffective, not because girls are uninterested in STEM or feel ill-equipped to handle it, but rather because they like one or more of their many other well-developed interests better (see Riegle-Crumb, King, Grodsky, & Muller, 2012). If the goal is truly to close the STEM gender gap, testing the impact of interventions on STEM itself is essential.

Third, for many purposes, it is important to examine STEM outcomes not only immediately following the intervention, but also long after the program has ended. If the goal is to change the gender distributions of the STEM workforce discussed in the beginning of this chapter, it would be important to collect data on later career choices and persistence. If the goal is to enhance engagement in and enjoyment of STEM more broadly, it would be important to find ways to assess behaviors indicative of such outcomes, for example, monitoring later attendance at science museums or engaging in scientifically sound citizen behaviors. Although such recommendations are unfortunately difficult to implement for practical reasons (particularly when interventions are targeted for children rather than for college students), we believe that there is value in explicitly identifying long-term goals of this kind, and then at least attempting to identify more immediate indices of later outcomes. For example, some prediction of later career choices might be gleaned from proximal course selections; some prediction of later science-based citizenship might be gleaned from tracking participants' pre- versus postintervention recycling behaviors. It may also be possible to develop creative, brief behavioral measures at the close of interventions that could capture participants' willingness and ability to solve challenges that entail material covered during the intervention experience.

5.3. Measuring Unintended Outcomes

In medicine it is well understood that testing a new drug requires not only evaluating the drug's efficacy in curing or diminishing an unwanted disease or condition, but also requires due diligence in searching for potential deleterious side effects. We urge the equivalent due diligence when evaluating the consequences of gender-targeted STEM interventions. What are the consequences of setting up special STEM programs exclusively for girls, apart from their intended consequences on STEM outcomes? Do programs with remediation and revision goals send messages to parents, teachers, and peers that girls are ill-equipped to handle science as usually taught? In other words, might such programs promote or reinforce gender stereotypes in the society more broadly? If gender stereotypes are exaggerated, what might the effects be on parents', teachers', and peers' behaviors as they in interact with girls? Might girls' own gender schemata be modified, and if so, what might this mean for gender-schematic behaviors, information processing, and stereotype threat?

As discussed in more detail in relation to single-sex education (Bigler et al., 2014 [Chapter 7 of this volume]), there is already compelling evidence that attention to gender distinctions in classrooms (e.g., teachers' labeling children as boys and girls or lining up boys and girls in sequence to go to lunch or recess) increases children's gender stereotypes and biases, and reduces their willingness to play with children of the other sex (Bigler, 1995; Hilliard & Liben, 2010). Might gender-targeted STEM interventions have similar consequences? Might such outcomes later reduce girls' collaborative interactions with male scientists? Likewise, consider the study discussed earlier in which preschool girls played a game about jobs enacted by either Barbie or a Playmobil character (Coyle & Liben, 2013). In this study, those girls who were already highly feminine and randomly assigned to the Barbie version of the game failed to show increased interest in the masculine jobs after the game, but they did show significantly increased attraction to traditionally feminine activities. In parallel, might girls exposed to hyper-feminine Science Cheerleaders end up drawn to cheerleading rather than science?

The goal of posing these questions and including these illustrative empirical findings is not to argue that existing data demonstrate that unintended, undesired consequences of STEM interventions outweigh intended, desired ones. Rather, it is to argue for the need to routinely test for possible undesirable consequences of STEM interventions as well as for desirable ones. As with testing new medicines, monitoring both kinds of outcomes is critical for judging the risk-benefit ratio. Results may be used to help guide iterative revisions of treatment protocols that ultimately reduce risks and maximize benefits.

5.4. Characterizing and Building on Past Interventions

Our final suggestion concerning future work returns to and extends our earlier acknowledgment about the limitations of an illustrative, narrative review. Illustrative reviews are essentially anecdotal scholarship. Authors have control over which illustrations are included and what aspects of the illustrative work are discussed. They are under no obligation to provide systematic data for the basis on which they selected their illustrations, nor the extent to which their selections are, or are not, representative of the full corpus of similar studies. In a sense, any individual study can be viewed similarly: Each is a study in a particular time, at a particular place, with a particular sample, using particular measures and particular statistical analyses that allow probabilistic but not definitive conclusions. These points lead to two overarching recommendations about next steps for work on STEM interventions.

One is the need for additional empirical work. Some of this work should undoubtedly involve new, innovative STEM intervention programs. But importantly, some of this work should replicate and extend previous efforts. There is growing recognition in the scientific community of the importance of replications, both direct—attempting to reproduce reported results by repeating the original procedures as closely as possible—and conceptual—attempting to reproduce the original findings about a concept, phenomenon, or hypothesis, but via the use of different paradigms or methods (e.g., see Spellman, 2012). There is also growing awareness in developmental science of the need to document the temporal, geopolitical, and demographic contexts in which data are collected, and of the need to work toward collecting data that are more fully reflective of both group and individual diversity (e.g., see Garcia Coll, 2013). Both replications and extensions are needed to further scholarship and practice related to STEM interventions.

The second recommendation concerns the need for taking more systematic stock of the corpus of extant work. As argued in a growing series of publications addressed to distinguishing real versus mythical gender differences in cognitive skills or educational outcomes (e.g., Hyde, 2005; Pahlke, Hyde, & Allison, 2014; Petersen & Hyde, 2014 [Chapter 2 of this volume], Signorella, Hayes, & Li, 2013; Voyer & Voyer, 2014), a powerful means of integrating and weighting often inconsistent findings across studies is meta-analysis. Although as discussed earlier, many individual STEM intervention evaluations described in the literature are not well-controlled studies and provide little usable quantitative data. However, there is a sufficiently large and diverse corpus of work to support a meta-analysis, an effort that is now underway (Coyle, Cundiff, & Liben, in preparation). Others' integrative efforts will be valuable for the field as well.

5.5. A Relational Perspective Revisited

We close by returning to our earlier comment that this chapter has focused exclusively on interventions targeted to individuals. Given our relational perspective that presumes the contributions of, and dynamic interactions among, multiple components of the individual ↔ context nexus, we would not want to leave readers with the impression that we believe that interventions directed at individuals can singlehandedly ameliorate the STEM gender gap. Even if such interventions have great success in preparing all girls to develop necessary foundational cognitive skills and in exciting them to be interested and engaged by STEM, the gap will persist if discrimination and sexism remain in the workplace. For both individual and societal good it is therefore essential that scholars and educators examine and ameliorate barriers that continue to constrain girls' and women's pursuit of, and success in STEM.

REFERENCES

Allen, C. (2014). *How LEGO earned the wrath of the 'gender-neutral toys' crowd.* Los Angeles: Op-Ed LA Times. http://articles.latimes.com/2014/feb/28/opinion/la-oe-allen-lego-gender-neutral-toys-20140228.

Alper, J. (1993). The pipeline is leaking women all the way along. *Science, 260,* 409–411.

Bandura, A. (1992). Social cognitive theory. In R. Vasta (Ed.), *Six theories of child development: Revised formulations and current issues* (pp. 1–60). Bristol, PA: Jessica Kingsley.

Bandura, A. (2001). Social cognitive theory: An agentic perspective. *Annual Review of Psychology, 52,* 1–26.

Bandura, A., & Bussey, K. (2004). On broadening the cognitive, motivational, and sociostructural scope of theorizing about gender development and functioning: Comment on Martin, Ruble, and Szkrybalo (2002). *Psychological Bulletin, 130,* 691–701.

Barber, N. (1995). The evolutionary psychology of physical attractiveness: Sexual selection and human morphology. *Ethology and Sociobiology, 16,* 395–424.

Bigler, R. S. (1995). The role of classification skill in moderating environmental influences on children's gender stereotyping: A study of the functional use of gender in the classroom. *Child Development, 66,* 1072–1087.

Bigler, R. S., Hayes, A. R., & Liben, L. S. (2014). Analysis and evaluation of the rationales for single-sex schooling. In L. S. Liben & R. S. Bigler (Vol. Eds.), *The role of gender in educational contexts and outcomes.* In J. B. Benson (Series Ed.), *Advances in child development and behavior: Vol. 47* (pp. 225–260). London: Elsevier.

Bigler, R. S., & Liben, L. S. (1990). The role of attitudes and interventions in gender-schematic processing. *Child Development, 61,* 1440–1452.

Bigler, R. S., & Liben, L. S. (1992). Cognitive mechanisms in children's gender stereotyping: Theoretical and educational implications of a cognitive-based intervention. *Child Development, 63,* 1351–1363.

Bijou, S. W., & Baer, D. M. (1961). *Child development: A systematic and empirical theory,* (Vol. 1). East Norwalk, CT: Appleton-Century-Crofts.

Blakemore, J. E. O., Berenbaum, S. A., & Liben, L. S. (2009). *Gender development.* New York: Psychology Press.

Blakemore, J. E. O., & Centers, R. E. (2005). Characteristics of boys' and girls' toys. *Sex Roles, 53,* 619–633.

Bronfenbrenner, U. (1977). Toward an experimental ecology of human development. *American Psychologist, 32,* 513–531.

Bussey, K., & Bandura, A. (1984). Influence of gender constancy and social power on sex-linked modeling. *Journal of Personality and Social Psychology, 47,* 1292–1302.

Bussey, K., & Bandura, A. (1999). Social cognitive theory of gender development and differentiation. *Psychological Review, 106,* 676–713.

Butler, R. (2014). Motivation in educational contexts: Does gender matter? In L. S. Liben & R. S. Bigler (Vol. Eds.), *The role of gender in educational contexts and outcomes*. In J. B. Benson (Series Ed.), *Advances in child development and behavior: Vol. 47* (pp. 1–41). London: Elsevier.

Casey, B., Kersh, J. E., & Young, J. M. (2004). Storytelling sagas: An effective medium for teaching early childhood mathematics. *Early Childhood Research Quarterly, 19*, 167–172.

Cavalier, D. (2014). *Science cheerleader*. www.sciencecheerleader.com.

Corbett, C. (2011). *Spatial-skills training can improve STEM retention*. Washington DC: AAUW Education. http://www.aauw.org/2011/09/29/spatial-skills-training-can-improve-stem-retention/.

Cornwell, C., Mustard, D. B., & Van Parys, J. (2013). Noncognitive skills and the gender disparities in test scores and teacher assessments: Evidence from primary school. *Journal of Human Resources, 48*, 236–264.

Coyle, E. F., & Liben, L. S. (2013). *Attracting girls to STEM: Personal gender salience moderates the outcome of an occupational game*. Poster presented at the biennial meetings of the Society for Research in Child Development, Seattle, WA.

Coyle, E. F., & Liben, L. S. (2014). *The earliest STEM learning: The influences of parents and gender-based marketing on preschoolers' play with a construction toy*. Poster presented at the International Gender and STEM Conference, Berlin.

Coyle, E. F., Cundiff, J., & Liben, L. S. (in preparation). Closing the gender gap in STEM: A meta-analysis of interventions to increase girls' and women's STEM participation.

Eagly, A. H., & Wood, W. (1999). The origins of sex differences in human behavior: Evolved dispositions versus social roles. *American Psychologist, 54*, 408–423.

Eccles, J. S. (2014). Gender and achievement choices. In C. Wainryb, & H. E. Recchia (Eds.), *Talking about right and wrong: Parent-child conversations as contexts for moral development* (pp. 19–34). Cambridge: Cambridge University Press.

Eccles, J. S., Adler, T. F., Futterman, R., Goff, S. B., Kaczala, C. M., Meece, J., et al. (1983). Expectancies, values, and academic behaviors. In J. T. Spence (Ed.), *Achievement and achievement motives* (pp. 75–146). San Francisco: Freeman.

Eccles, J. S., Freedman-Doan, C., Frome, P., Jacobs, J., & Yoons, K. S. (2000). Gender-role socialization in the family: A longitudinal approach. In T. Eckes, & H. M. Trautner (Eds.), *The developmental social psychology of gender* (pp. 333–360). Mahwah, NJ: Erlbaum.

Else-Quest, N. M., Hyde, J. S., & Linn, M. C. (2010). Cross-national patterns of gender differences in mathematics: A meta-analysis. *Psychological Bulletin, 136*, 103–127.

Ericson, B. (2014). *AP data for the United States*. tp://home.cc.gatech.edu/ice-gt/321.

European Commission (2012). *Science: It's a girl thing!*. http://science-girl-thing.eu/en/about-this-site.

Expanding Your Horizons Network. (2013). *Come to an EYH conference: What happens at an EYH conference*. http://www.eyhn.org/.

Farfield, H., & McLean, A. (2013). *Girls lead in science exam, but not in the United States*. http://www.nytimes.com/interactive/2013/02/04/science/girls-lead-in-science-exam-but-not-in-the-united-states.html?_r=1&.

Garcia Coll, C. (2013). *Child Development welcomes new editor Cynthia Garcia Coll: Cynthia Garcia Coll's editorial statement*. Hoboken, NJ: Wiley. http://onlinelibrary.wiley.com/journal/10.1111/%28ISSN%291467-8624/homepage/call_for_editor_in_chief.htm.

Geary, D. C., & Bjorklund, D. F. (2000). Evolutionary developmental psychology. *Child Development, 71*, 57–65.

Gurian, M., Henley, P., & Trueman, T. (2001). *Boys and girls learn differently: A guide for teachers and parents*. San Francisco: Jossy-Bass.

Halpern, D. F. (2012). *Sex differences in cognitive abilities* (4th ed.). New York: Psychology Press.

Hegarty, M. (2014). Spatial thinking in undergraduate science education. *Spatial Cognition and Computation, 14*, 142–167.

Hill, C., Corbett, C., & St. Rose, A. (2010). *Why so few? Women in science, technology, engineering, and mathematics.* Washington, DC: AAUW.

Hilliard, L. J., & Liben, L. S. (2010). Differing levels of gender salience in preschool classrooms: Effects on children's gender attitudes and intergroup bias. *Child Development, 81*, 1787–1798.

Hines, M. (2015). Gendered development. In M. E. Lamb (Ed.), *Handbook of child psychology and developmental science, Vol. 3* (7th ed.). Hoboken, NJ: Wiley, in press.

Hyde, J. S. (2005). The gender similarities hypothesis. *American Psychologist, 60*, 581.

Hyde, J. S., & Mertz, J. E. (2009). Gender, culture, and mathematics performance. *Proceedings of the National Academy of Sciences of the United States of America, 106*, 8801–8807.

Hyde, W. D. (1906). *The college man and the college woman.* Boston: Houghton Mifflin.

International Mathematical Olympiad. (2014). http://www.imo-official.org/.

Kelleher, C., Pausch, R., & Kiesler, S. (2007). Storytelling Alice motivates middle school girls to learn computer programming. In *Proceedings of the SIGCHI Conference on Human Factors in Computing Systems* (pp. 1455–1464).

Kohlberg, L. (1966). A cognitive developmental analysis of children's sex role concepts and attitudes. In E. E. Maccoby (Ed.), *The development of sex differences* (pp. 82–172). Stanford, CA: Stanford University Press.

Leaper, C. (2015). Gender and social-cognitive development. In L. S. Liben, & U. Müller (Eds.), *Handbook of child psychology and developmental science, Vol. 2* (7th ed.). Hoboken, NJ: Wiley, in press.

Leaper, C., & Brown, C. S. (2014). Sexism in schools. In L. S. Liben, & R. S. Bigler (Vol. Eds.), *The role of gender in educational contexts and outcomes.* In J. B. Benson (Series Ed.), *Advances in child development and behavior: Vol. 47* (pp. 189–223). London: Elsevier.

LEGO (2014). *LEGO Friends Butterfly Beauty Shop.* http://shop.lego.com/en-US/Butterfly-Beauty-Shop-3187.

Lerner, R. M., & Callina, K. S. (2013). Relational developmental systems theories and the ecological validity of experimental designs. *Human Development, 56*, 372–380.

Liben, L. S. (1991). The Piagetian water-level task: Looking beneath the surface. In R. Vasta (Ed.), *Annals of child development: Vol. 8.* (pp. 81–143). London: Jessica Kingsley Publishers.

Liben, L. S. (2002). The drama of sex differences in academic achievement: And the show goes on. *Issues in Education, 8*, 65–75.

Liben, L. S. (2006). Education for spatial thinking. In K. A. Renninger, & I. E. Sigel (Eds.), *Handbook of child psychology: Vol. 4.* (pp. 197–247). Hoboken, NJ: Wiley.

Liben, L. S. (2012). *Making STEM girly or making girls STEMy? Rationales and ramifications.* Paper presented at the Gender Development Research Conference, San Francisco, CA.

Liben, L. S. (2014). Probability values and human values in evaluating single-sex education. Invited commentary, *Sex Roles*, under review.

Liben, L. S., & Bigler, R. (2002). The developmental course of gender differentiation: Conceptualizing, measuring, and evaluating constructs and pathways. *Monographs of the Society for Research in Child Development, 67*.

Liben, L. S., Kastens, K. A., & Christensen, A. E. (2011). Spatial foundations of science education: The illustrative case of instruction on introductory geological concepts. *Cognition and Instruction, 29*, 45–87.

Liben, L. S., Signorella, M. L., & Sorby, S. (2013). *The impact of a spatial skills curriculum in middle school: Cognitive and social-cognitive outcomes in spatial and STEM domains.* Symposium presented at the biennial meetings of the Society for Research in Child Development, Seattle, WA.

Lindberg, S. M., Hyde, J. S., Petersen, J. L., & Linn, M. C. (2010). New trends in gender and mathematics performance: A meta-analysis. *Psychological Bulletin, 136*, 1123–1135.

Linn, M. C., & Petersen, A. C. (1985). Emergence and characterization of sex differences in spatial ability: A meta-analysis. *Child Development, 56*, 1479–1498.

Martin, C. L., Fabes, R. A., & Hanish, L. D. (2014). Gendered peer relationships in educational contexts. In L. S. Liben, & R. S. Bigler (Vol. Eds.), *The role of gender in educational contexts and outcomes*. In J. B. Benson (Series Ed.), *Advances in child development and behavior: Vol. 47* (pp. 151–188). London: Elsevier.

Martin, C. L., & Halverson, C. F. (1981). A schematic processing model of sex typing and stereotyping in children. *Child Development, 42*, 1119–1134.

Martin, C. L., Ruble, D. N., & Szkrybalo, J. (2002). Cognitive theories of early gender development. *Psychological Bulletin, 128*, 903–933.

Martin, C. L., Ruble, D. N., & Szkrybalo, J. (2004). Recognizing the centrality of gender identity and stereotype knowledge in gender development and moving toward theoretical integration: Reply to Bandura and Bussey (2004). *Psychological Bulletin, 130*, 702–710.

Miller, D. I., & Halpern, D. F. (2012). Can spatial training improve long-term outcomes for gifted stem undergraduates? *Learning and Individual Differences, 26*, 141–152.

Mischel, W. (1966). A social-learning view of sex differences in behavior. In E. E. Maccoby (Ed.), *The development of sex differences* (pp. 56–81). Stanford, CA: Stanford University Press.

Moore, D. S., & Johnson, S. P. (2011). Mental rotation of dynamic, three-dimensional stimuli by 3-month-old infants. *Infancy, 16*, 435–445.

National Association for Choice in Education. (2013). http://www.4schoolchoice.org/.

National Research Council (2006). *Learning to think spatially: GIS as a support system in the K-12 curriculum*. Washington, DC: National Academy Press.

National Science Foundation. (2013). Women, minorities, and persons with disabilities in science and engineering. Special Reports. http://www.nsf.gov/statistics/wmpd/2013/start.cfm?CFID=14614984&CFTOKEN=56461309&jsessionid=f0306d628c00285dc6a71c511a3461f5b7a7.

Newcomb, T. (January 27, 2014). *Targeting the toy aisle to lure young girls into engineering*. Engineering News-Record. New York: McGraw-Hill. http://enr.construction.com/people/awards/2014/0127-targeting-the-toy-aisle-to-get-young-girls-into-engineering.asp.

Pahlke, E., Hyde, J. S., & Allison, C. M. (2014). The effects of single-sex compared with coeducational schooling on students' performance and attitudes: A meta-analysis. *Psychological Bulletin, 140*, 1072.

Petersen, J., & Hyde, J. S. (2014). Gender-related academic and occupational interests and goals. In L. S. Liben, & R. S. Bigler (Vol. Eds.), *The role of gender in educational contexts and outcomes*. In J. B. Benson (Series Ed.), *Advances in child development and behavior: Vol. 47* (pp. 43–76). London: Elsevier.

Quinn, P. C., & Liben, L. S. (2014). A sex difference in mental rotation in infants: Convergent evidence. *Infancy, 19*, 103–116.

Riegle-Crumb, C., King, B., Grodsky, E., & Muller, C. (2012). The more things change, the more they stay the same? Prior achievement fails to explain gender inequality in entry into STEM College majors over time. *American Educational Research Journal, 49*, 1048–1073.

Rodger, S. H., Hayes, J., Lezin, G., Qin, H., Nelson, D., Tucker, R., et al. (2009). Engaging middle school teachers and students with Alice in a diverse set of subjects. *ACM SIGCSE Bulletin, 41*, 271–275.

Ruble, D. N., & Martin, C. L. (1998). Gender development. In N. Eisenberg (Ed.), *Handbook of child psychology: Vol. 3.* (pp. 933–1016). New York: Wiley.

Ruble, D. N., Martin, C. L., & Berenbaum, S. A. (2006). Gender development. In N. Eisenberg (Ed.), *Handbook of child psychology: Vol. 3.* (pp. 858–932) (6th ed.). Hoboken, NJ: John Wiley & Sons, Inc.

Sax, L. (2005). *Why gender matters*. New York: Doubleday.
Shea, D. L., Lubinski, D., & Benbow, C. P. (2001). Importance of assessing spatial ability in intellectually talented young adolescents: A 20-year longitudinal study. *Journal of Educational Psychology, 93*, 604.
Signorella, M. L., Hayes, A. R., & Li, Y. (2013). A meta-analytic critique of Mael et al'.s (2005) review of single-sex schooling. *Sex Roles, 69*, 423–441.
Sorby, S. A., & Baartmans, B. J. (1996). A course for the development of 3-D spatial visualization skills. *Engineering Design Graphics Journal, 60*, 13–20.
Spellman, B. A. (2012). Introduction to the special section on research practices. *Perspectives on Psychological Science, 7*, 655–656.
Stylist.co.uk. (n.d.). LEGO launches 'girl-friendly' range: Toymakers woo girls with LEGO Friends. http://www.stylist.co.uk/life/lego-launches-girl-friendly-range-191211#image-rotator-5.
United Nations Girls' Education Initiative. (2013). Information by country: Chad. http://www.ungei.org/infobycountry/chad.html.
United States Department of Labor (2013). *Latest annual data*. http://www.dol.gov/wb/stats/recentfacts.htm.
Uttal, D. H., Meadow, N. G., Tipton, E., Hand, L. L., Alden, A. R., Warren, C., et al. (2013). The malleability of spatial skills: A meta-analysis of training studies. *Psychological Bulletin, 139*, 352–402.
Verdine, B. N., Golinkoff, R. M., Hirsh-Pasek, K., Newcombe, N. S., Filipowicz, A. T., & Chang, A. (2014). Deconstructing building blocks: Preschoolers' spatial assembly performance relates to early mathematical skills. *Child Development, 85*, 1062–1076.
Veurink, N. L., & Sorby, S. A. (2011). Raising the bar? Longitudinal study to determine which students would benefit most from spatial training. *Proceedings of the Annual Conference of the American Society for Engineering Education, Vancouver, BC*.
Voyer, D. (2011). Time limits and gender differences on paper-and-pencil tests of mental rotation: A meta-analysis. *Psychonomic Bulletin & Review, 18*, 267–277.
Voyer, D., & Voyer, S. D. (2014). Gender differences in scholastic achievement: A meta-analysis. *Psychological Bulletin, 140*, 1174–1204.
Voyer, D., Voyer, S. D., & Bryden, M. P. (1995). Magnitude of sex differences in spatial abilities: A meta-analysis and consideration of critical variables. *Psychological Bulletin, 117*, 250–270.
Wai, J., Lubinski, D., & Benbow, C. P. (2009). Spatial ability for STEM domains: Aligning over 50 years of cumulative psychological knowledge solidifies its importance. *Journal of Educational Psychology, 101*, 817–835.
Weil, E. (2008). Teaching boys and girls separately. *New York Times Magazine*. http://www.nytimes.com/2008/03/02/magazine/02sex3-t.html.
Weisgram, E. S., & Bigler, R. S. (2006a). Girls and science careers: The role of altruistic values and attitudes about scientific tasks. *Journal of Applied Developmental Psychology, 27*, 326–348.
Weisgram, E. S., & Bigler, R. S. (2006b). The role of attitudes and intervention in high school girls' interest in computer science. *Journal of Women and Minorities in Science and Engineering, 12*, 325–336.
Weisgram, E. S., & Bigler, R. S. (2007). Effects of learning about gender discrimination on adolescent girls' attitudes toward and interest in science. *Psychology of Women Quarterly, 31*, 262–269.
Weisgram, E. S., Bigler, R. S., & Liben, L. S. (2010). Gender, values, and occupational interests among children, adolescents, and adults. *Child Development, 81*, 778–796.
Wolfgang, C., Stannard, L., & Jones, I. (2003). Advanced constructional play with LEGOs among preschoolers as a predictor of later school achievement in mathematics. *Early Child Development and Care, 173*, 467–475.

CHAPTER FOUR

Physical Education, Sports, and Gender in Schools

Melinda A. Solmon[1]
School of Kinesiology, Louisiana State University, Baton Rouge, Louisiana, USA
[1]Corresponding author: e-mail address: msolmo1@lsu.edu

Contents

1. Introduction 117
2. Historical Overview 121
3. Curricular Issues 125
4. Gender and Motivation to be Physically Active 128
5. Fitness Testing 134
6. Social Construction of Bodily Meanings 138
7. Creating Equitable Climates in Physical Education 140
8. Education and Sport 144
9. Conclusions and Implications 146
References 147

Abstract

> The benefits associated with engaging in regular physical activity are well documented, but a large segment of the population is not sufficiently active. School physical education and sport programs are identified as important components in efforts to promote physical activity. Girls are less active than boys, and there is evidence that physical education programs are not effectively meeting their needs. The focus of this chapter is to examine gender as a construct in the domains of physical education and sport, clarifying the reasons girls tend to be less active and less involved in physical education. Following an historical overview, curricular issues and motivational aspects are considered. Implications are focused on ways that educators can provide positive experiences for all students in physical education and sport that will encourage them to adopt and maintain healthy active lifestyles and enhance their quality of life across the life span.

1. INTRODUCTION

The benefits of a physically active lifestyle are well documented. Individuals who engage in recommended levels of physical activity have decreased risk of cardiovascular disease, type II diabetes, and certain kinds of cancer, as well as improved mental health. Additionally, those who engage in a physically active lifestyle are likely to live longer than those who do not and to report a higher quality of life as they age. A majority of the United States population is insufficiently active and that translates to negative, long-term implications related to health care costs and mortality rates that can be attributed directly to inactive lifestyles. A related issue associated with physical inactivity is a rise in the incidence of overweight and obesity in all segments of the population. National reports detailing the problems associated with inactivity reveal that certain segments of U.S. society are at a disproportionate risk to be inactive. Girls are less active than boys, ethnic populations tend to be less physically active than Whites, and children of lower socioeconomic status are less likely to be physically active than children in higher income families (U.S. Department of Health and Human Services (USDHHS), 1996, 2000). With specific regard to school-aged children, they are not as active as they should be and, furthermore, tend to decrease their physical activity as they age (USDHHS, 1996, 2000). The decrease for girls is more pronounced than for boys. This is of particular consequence given that activity patterns tend to track from childhood into adulthood (Janz, Dawson, & Mahoney, 2000). That is, children who are physically active are likely to remain active across the life span, whereas those who are inactive are unlikely to make decisions to become active.

Physical activity is an umbrella term that has been traditionally defined as "any bodily movement produced by skeletal muscle that results in caloric expenditure" (Caspersen, 1989, p. 424). It is generally agreed that a behavioral component is also inherent in physical activity, meaning that typical conceptualizations of physical activity include activity that is a voluntary choice (Freedson & Miller, 2000). School physical education and sports programs are consistently identified in government reports and by national organizations as important components in efforts to promote physical activity with the goal of addressing public health concerns. Educators and public health officials recognize the need to provide opportunities for school students to develop the skills and dispositions that will increase the likelihood that children adopt and maintain physically active lifestyles. Given that females are consistently less active than males at all ages, addressing gender inequities related to physical activity is an important concern. It has been suggested that girls' perceptions of physical education classes, and the negative experiences they have, may be an important factor in their low levels of physical activity (Cairney et al., 2012).

In addition to the role that physical education and sports should play in promoting physical activity and public health, there are other domains in which they affect schools and society. Social development and academic function are areas in which physical education and sport have the potential to have a powerful influence on children's development and their overall well-being. Socialization is generally characterized as a process through which individuals acquire information about acceptable and unacceptable behaviors and responses, including developing social, cognitive, and physical skills (Solmon & Lee, 2008). Schools are recognized as a major influence on the socialization of children, and students' experiences in physical education, on playgrounds, and on sports fields provide boundless opportunities to learn expectations and roles related to gender, culture, and race. Interactions that occur in physical activity settings are public, as motor skill performance is by its very nature open to observation by significant others. A complex interrelationship exists among perceived physical competence, social status, and self-esteem that affects social development and ultimately educational outcomes. For example, elementary school–aged children associate physical competence with high status among peers, and as they age, children place more value on sport activities (Wigfield & Eccles, 1992).

Relevant to academic performance, recent evidence supports the conclusion that children who are physically active (Donnelly & Lambourne, 2011) and physically fit (Chomitz et al., 2009) perform better academically than those who are not. Faced with diminishing resources, coupled with the national focus on high stakes testing and teacher accountability related to student learning outcomes, many states and school districts have taken steps to decrease instructional time allocated for physical education and opportunities to be physically active. Physical education is typically not included as a content area in educational accountability systems, which has served to further marginalize it as a school subject. Recent studies show, however, that increasing time in core academic subjects at the expense of encouraging children to be physically active does not produce academic gains, and in fact, may be detrimental. Considering the prominent role that physical education and sport play in educational contexts with regard to pertinent issues surrounding health status, social development, and academic function, and in light of the fact that girls are less active than boys, the importance of considering gender issues in physical education and sport as they relate to educational outcomes is clear.

Although physical education is often closely linked to the domain of sport, and they certainly share many commonalities, in many ways the two areas are distinct. Physical education is a school subject, at least in most states, that is required of all students for at least a portion of the school years. According to the National Association for Sport and Physical Education (NASPE), "The ultimate purpose of any physical education program is to help children develop the skills, knowledge and desire to enjoy a lifetime of physical activity" (NASPE, 2008, p. 4). Sport programs, on the other hand, are not required of all students and participation is generally voluntary. A variety of sport programs are available in schools ranging from interscholastic varsity athletic programs that are focused on elite competition to intramural sport programs primarily designed to promote physical activity opportunities for a broad range of children.

The focus of this chapter is to examine gender as a construct in the domains of physical education and sport with the goal of generating strategies that have the potential to improve educational outcomes for girls and boys. I begin with a brief historical overview of physical activity, physical education, and sport to provide a context for the current status of programs, issues that permeate this area, and opportunities that currently exist. This historical background provides the basis for the examination of curricular issues in physical education emanating from the historical division of girls and boys in the physical domain that affect the quality of educational experiences for all students. Next, motivational aspects of physical education and sport are considered. I provide an argument that value and competence beliefs are critical issues with regard to motivation to be physically active and that the social construction of gender for girls and boys has far reaching implications that affect decisions about being active. Findings from two areas of research, physical fitness testing and the social construction of bodily meanings, which are especially problematic in light of gender concerns, are then discussed. A summary of research on how teachers can structure climates to promote equity and engagement for all students is presented, followed by consideration of how sport is intertwined with gender issues and can function in educational settings either to promote child development or to privilege elite skillful students, many of whom are male, at the expense of the mainstream. This chapter concludes with implications that are supported by research evidence concerning ways that educators can work to provide positive experiences for all students in physical education and sport that will encourage youth to adopt and maintain healthy active lifestyles and enhance their quality of life across the life span.

2. HISTORICAL OVERVIEW

Issues of equity and social justice are especially complex in the realm of physical activity. Historically, the development of physical ability through physical activity was viewed as essential to the evolution of a more perfect race (Azzarito, Munro, & Solmon, 2004). The institutionalization of playgrounds and physical education in schools in the early twentieth century was grounded in the belief that opportunities for physical activity were essential for normal development. What was considered to be normal development, however, was vastly different for men and women. Physical education and sport for men was focused on the goal of developing physical abilities needed to support society through labor and statesmanship, while the goal for activities for women was to prepare for motherhood. This delineation of responsibilities between men and women was viewed as biologically determined. Girls' physical abilities were viewed as naturally inferior to boys'. It was assumed that because of biological differences between sexes that activity for girls should be limited and differentiated from activities for boys. Athletic competitions were promoted for boys to develop power, strength, and speed, while girls' activities were relegated to moderate forms of exercise emphasizing grace and beauty. It was even suggested that "over-educating" girls could interfere with their physical and sexual development. According to Azzarito et al. (2004), female participation in physical activity and play was promoted in political and social discourses so that girls could attain perfect womanhood in preparation for child bearing and motherhood.

Beliefs reflecting a view of binary opposition rooted in the physical inferiority of females served to limit opportunities for girls and women in sport and guided curricular models for girls in schools for the first three-fourths of the twentieth century (see also Bigler, Hayes, & Liben, 2014 [Chapter 7 of this volume]). A sporting ideology embracing the notion that engaging in physical pursuits was a mechanism to develop character and improve conduct drove the development of interscholastic and intercollegiate sport beginning in the latter part of nineteenth century (Phillips & Roper, 2006). These were initially exclusively male activities. Programs expanded over the years, growing into a major industry, generating massive revenues through ticket sales, media coverage, merchandising, and marketing. This endeavor was heavily gendered. Competitive sport for women was opposed by both male administrators and female physical educators, and women were encouraged to become involved in less competitive intramural sports. The opposition to women's involvement in competitive sport was entrenched in the perception that idealized femininity would be in peril in the masculine nature of interscholastic sport.

In the U.S., the passage of Title IX of the Education Amendments in 1972 precipitated far reaching consequences that have evolved over the past four decades. The fundamental premise of Title IX and its reauthorizations that have been implemented is that individuals cannot be excluded on the basis of gender from participation in any educational program or activity that receives federal financial assistance, so all educational contexts were affected. Physical education and sport, however, are most likely the two settings that were the most profoundly affected and have received the most notoriety.

Prior to Title IX, virtually all physical education classes were single-sex classes, even when physical education was provided at the elementary school level, when there is no reason other than different experiences that boys and girls would be expected to perform differently on physical tasks. Physical education for girls was taught by female teachers and instruction centered around recreational games, sports, and activities that were deemed appropriate for females. In contrast, physical education for boys was generally taught by males who also coached varsity sports, and the curriculum for them consisted mainly of whatever sport was in season at the time. Physical education departments at colleges and universities were also segregated by gender. Men's departments had higher status and women's departments were typically a subcomponent subsumed in men's departments. Lecture classes in the physical education major were often coeducational, but male professors were generally given preference to teach the content courses, while female professors were relegated to teaching lower level courses and activity courses for women. Across all school levels, males were given priority for facilities and scheduling. In colleges and high schools that had more than one gymnasium, the men's gymnasium was the newer and larger one, while the older, smaller, and outdated facilities were the "women's gym."

With the implementation of Title IX, separate programs were no longer the standard for physical education, and the interpretation of the regulations was that single-sex physical education classes would become a thing of the past. School districts, to comply with the law, mandated coeducational classes but did not provide guidelines or professional development for teachers to facilitate the transition. Teachers and students were thrust into situations that they were not prepared to handle. Men, trained in men's physical education programs steeped in competitive sport, were expected to teach girls who had been taught by women in programs focused on activities deemed appropriate for girls. Conversely, women who had been prepared to teach physical education for girls suddenly had boys, who had been involved in programs focused on masculine activities and sports, to contend with in their classes (Ennis, 1998). Meeting with resistance from both students and teachers, many districts found creative ways to comply with the regulations on a minimal level but to continue to segregate physical education classes in reality. One approach was to allow students to select activities, but to offer choices that virtually guaranteed that girls would opt for one class and boys for another (i.e., football or aerobic dance). The implementation of Title IX and the problems that accompanied mandating coeducational classes affected curricular issues and instruction. The work of Ennis (1996, 1998, 1999) supports the conclusion that in some ways, this has been detrimental to the quality of physical education for girls.

The effect of Title IX on sports was more dramatic. Chances for girls to be involved in sports began to become available slowly during the mid-twentieth century, but few opportunities were available for girls to become involved in athletic competition. Girls who were interested in sports often were relegated to either intramural competition on a recreational level or had to pursue opportunities outside of school systems such as privately funded teams organized within the framework of the American Athletic Union (AAU). Basketball provides an example of the contrast between boys' and girls' sports. Although schools in certain areas of the country did have interscholastic competition for girls in basketball, the rules for girls were altered to protect girls from being overly taxed by the demands of the game. While boys played full court basketball, running the length of the court, and playing offense and defense, girls played one of several variations of those rules which generally limited them to playing on only a portion of the court (offense or defense). The rationale was either that girls lacked the physical stamina to play the full game or that the demands of playing the full court could result in damage to their health, especially relevant to their ability to reproduce. Girls' sports were only supported to the degree that they did not impinge on the programs for boys.

The implementation of Title IX produced a dramatic increase in the opportunities for girls in athletics. According to the regulations, school administrators were no longer allowed to privilege males and provide financial support and scheduling preferences for facilities at the expense of opportunities for girls. Since 1972 when Title IX was enacted, athletic participation has increased 904% at the high school level and 456% in colleges (Kennedy, 2010). The increases in opportunities for girls and women have been dramatic, but this shift generated controversy and there has been considerable opposition on many fronts. Much of the progress in women's sports has been the result of legal challenges and government activity, rather than an ethical commitment to provide opportunities for girls and women in sport.

Ironically, sport is an area in which African Americans have made great strides since the Civil Rights Act of 1964. Certainly, racial bias continues to exist on many levels in sport, but according to Reyna (2011), "sports have helped give African Americans a voice in American society...American interest in sports has promoted racial equality and multiculturalism" (p. 248). With respect to gender equality, however, rather than leading the way for social justice, sport has been an arena in which obvious gender inequality and discrimination against girls continued long after the Civil Rights Act. Seemingly, sport has been the last bastion of male superiority and privilege. Although the passage of Title IX of the Education Amendments in 1972 resulted in a tremendous increase in opportunities for girls in sport, there has been a lack of enforcement of the laws and regulations over the years and opportunities and support for girls' involvement in sport continues to lag far behind those for boys (Kennedy, 2010). Pickett, Dawkins, and Braddock (2012) concur that opportunities for girls have increased dramatically, but additionally provide evidence that not only has gender equity not been achieved in sport, but also that African American females have not benefitted as much as White females.

The strides that have been made in women's sports since the passage of Title IX demonstrate how important policies and regulations are in the administration and implementation of educational programs. The examination of what has occurred historically in educational settings with regard to physical education and sport as it relates to gender provides an example of how social culture and politically driven policies worked to constrain opportunities for girls, as well as how advocates for social justice and equity can change the status so that girls can be granted opportunities that were considered to be inherent rights for boys. Although progress has been made with regard for opportunities for girls in physical education and sport, there is concern about the viability of physical education as a content area (Solmon & Garn, 2014). Time allocated for physical activity in schools including physical education and recess continues to decline in the face of limited resources and focus on high stakes testing. State requirements for physical education are continually at risk and many states allow for substitutions and online programs to meet the limited requirements they maintain. Physical education in general struggles to be relevant in educational contexts. The argument can be made that the decline of physical education programs likely has a more detrimental effect on girls and children of lower socioeconomic status than on boys and affluent children. Boys are socialized to be involved in active play and sporting activities, and their families are generally more supportive of their involvement in sport programs. Children of higher socioeconomic status are also more likely to have opportunities to develop motor skills and be physically active via access to private lessons and after school sport programs. It is of critical importance that viable physical education programs be maintained so that all children have access to educational experiences that will enable them to learn how to be physically active. Offering a physical education curriculum that meets the needs of a diverse student population is the cornerstone of maintaining that viability.

3. CURRICULAR ISSUES

The curriculum in core academic subjects such as math is generally straightforward. Although there may be debates on the best progressions, appropriate grade level standards, or the most effective pedagogies, there are not extensive debates concerning what knowledge should be taught or what learning outcomes students should achieve. For content areas included in high stakes testing, the specific content to be mastered is, for the most part, clarified by what is measured on the test. That is not the case for physical education, and the content that should comprise school-based physical education has been the subject of extensive discussion in the literature (Siedentop, 2002; Ward, 2013). National standards have been established by NASPE (2004), the leading professional organization for physical education, and many states have established benchmarks and standards using the NASPE standards as a guideline. In many cases, however, there is not a strong administrative interest in assuring that the established standards are addressed. Often individual teachers are free to implement curricular models of their choice and have the freedom to make decisions about the nature of the content they deliver to their students. This is confounded by the fact that physical education has generally been overlooked in teacher accountability and student assessment programs, so principals and other school administrators have not been compelled to provide administrative support or supervision for physical education programs (Solmon & Garn, 2014).

Curricular models at the elementary school level generally focus on the development of basic motor skills and incorporate games and activities that reinforce skill development. As students enter middle and high school, the focus moves toward organized games and a sport based curriculum. Most physical education teacher preparation programs encourage their graduates to employ curricular models that focus on educational activities to develop knowledge, dispositions, and skills that are necessary to adopt and maintain a healthy active lifestyle across the life span. The reality, however, is that many secondary school programs still adhere to what is referred as a multi-activity model (Ennis, 1999). This approach is characterized by short units that include minimal time for instruction, fails to include educational sequences across lessons and units, and do not focus on using skills and strategies in game play. Units are often only 3–4 weeks in duration. Rules and a few basic skills are introduced during the first few lessons, and the remainder of the unit is spent in game play that is often dominated by highly skilled players, usually males.

In her analysis of teachers' perspectives of the implementation of Title IX and coeducational physical education classes, Ennis (1998) reports that incorporating boys and girls into the same classes ultimately resulted in the maintenance of the boys' sport-oriented curriculum rooted in this multi-activity model, while many activities that had been traditionally been part of the girls' programs, such as individual sports, gymnastics, and dance disappeared from the curriculum. It seems that curricular change driven by Title IX, in reality, simply eliminated what had been activities geared for girls and incorporated girls into the male-dominant sports oriented curriculum. Using the analogy of canaries in the coal mine, Ennis (2000) warns that disengaged students in physical education classes provide a warning about practices in physical education classes that are ineffective at best, and often times negative and harmful. According to Ennis (1996), many students have negative experiences in sport-based classes, in which competition is the focus and superior athletes are allowed to dominant game play. She argues:

> Physical education programs that do not provide all students with interesting, meaningful, and intrinsically rewarding opportunities to participate skillfully in games and sport are discriminatory and limit access not only to the joys of participation, but also to many personally and socially rewarding and satisfying ways to gain the health-related benefits of physical activity (p. 455).

Those who are discriminated against in competitive sport-based programs in physical education classes are primarily students of low skill and/or those who lack the requisite experiences to be successful in competitive game play.

Girls in particular have less than satisfactory experiences when team sports are taught using this model (Ennis, 1999). Boys are characterized as more motivated and assumptions of male superiority and female inferiority are often perpetuated (Satina, Solmon, Cothran, Loftus, & Stockin-Davidson, 1998). As Ennis (1996) points out, curricular models that focus on educational aspects rather than competitive game play can be implemented so that sport can become a positive experience for all students, but competitive sport-based models that have been dominant in school physical education do not address the needs of many students, and curricular reform is needed to address that concern.

More recent studies suggest that current secondary curricula continue to be problematic. Using a feminist poststructuralist framework, Azzarito, Solmon, and Harrison (2006) explored high school girls' participation in physical education. From this perspective, rather than being viewed as oppressed, marginalized, and passive, girls can be perceived as active agents who are able to make choices concerning their engagement in physical education classes. The girls in their study identified gender barriers related to curricular choice. So, too, did the teachers, who felt that they had to select activities such as playing basketball games that boys dominated to accommodate them and to keep them from causing difficulties. The girls felt the boys had more real choices. They acknowledged that the girls often declined to participate, but the teachers did not take steps to encourage them. When curricular choices were more equitable, and the classes were instructional units such as tennis and badminton, the girls were more involved in class and expressed the belief that boys and girls could learn these activities together. Fagrell, Larsson, and Redelius (2012) used a case study approach to examine how competitive games in physical education place girls and boys in different subject positions. They argue that girls underperform and that this is not merely reflective of problems in the gym, but rather of problems in society.

Many scholars have argued that systemic change is needed to transform sport-based curricula into programs that educate children to adopt and maintain physically active lifestyles (Azzarito & Solmon, 2005). Ennis (1999, 2000, 2006) makes a strong case for the important role that quality physical education should play in educational contexts and offers an array of curricular alternatives that can be employed to address the issue of relevance. These include theme-based approaches and a focus on health-related fitness and life time activities. At the heart of those alternatives is the issue of student interest and motivation. Motivation to be physically active declines as children progress through school. Many students are not interested in, or motivated by, traditional sport-based models. In the next section, issues that underlie the decline in motivation and strategies that can be employed to address this concern are examined.

4. GENDER AND MOTIVATION TO BE PHYSICALLY ACTIVE

Although motivation is often cited as a central concern in our society, it is in some respects a vague and poorly understood concept, especially in schools and sport settings. According to Roberts (2012), the preponderance of motivational theories and associated definitions make a clear definition of this complex construct very difficult to conceptualize. He contends that motivational theorists often fail to consider other perspectives, drawing only from their own work to guide efforts to clarify motivational constructs. He concludes that most contemporary theorists agree that motivation is a *process* surrounding goal-directed behavior that involves the initiation, direction, magnitude, perseverance, and quality of actions. Motivation is a cognitive construct that underlies decisions that individuals make in achievement settings (Solmon, 2003). Motivation cannot be measured directly, but instead we make inferences concerning whether students are motivated by observing what they do. Actions that reflect motivated behavior are a willingness to engage, to exert effort, to persist in the face of difficulty, and to choose to work at a challenging level (see Butler, 2014 [Chapter 1 of this volume], for a detailed description of academic motivation).

There are volumes of research in educational settings that address motivation in education and sport settings from a multitude of theoretical perspectives. Although there may be many prerequisites for motivation unearthed from various theories, there are two conditions that seem to consistently underlie most of these frameworks. A strong argument can be made across major theories that, in order for individuals to be motivated to engage in an activity, they must associate some level of value or importance to the task and believe that they can achieve some measure of success. This is the basic premise of expectancy-value model of achievement choices (Wigfield & Eccles, 1992) and is a thread that runs through myriad motivational theories as well (see Petersen & Hyde, 2014 [Chapter 2 of this volume]). This framework has been used extensively in the literature to explore motivational and social factors that influence career aspirations, course selections, persistence on challenging tasks, and willingness to exert effort across a variety of settings including physical education and sport (Eccles, 2005). The development of this model was driven by the quest to understand gender differences in patterns of achievement. Research efforts guided by this framework have yielded considerable insight regarding the reasons that girls make different choices concerning their academic pursuits, and it serves as an excellent organizing structure for considering gender issues in physical education and sport.

Perceptions of value. It is unlikely that individuals will be motivated to exert effort or actively engage in a task or activity if they do not associate some type of value to that endeavor. Four aspects of task values are outlined by Wigfield and Eccles (1992): (a) attainment value or the importance of doing well on a task; (b) utility value which is how the task relates to future goals; (c) perceived cost, or the negative aspects of the activity such as the amount of effort required or what has to be given up to engage in the task; and (d) intrinsic value, which is defined as the enjoyment derived from the activity itself. Intrinsic value is perhaps the most influential dimension of value, and the one that it is most desirable to foster. We might choose to engage in activities that will help us attain something, or that we find useful or important in an immediate setting. However, when we find value in an activity as an end in itself, for enjoyment and personal satisfaction, we are especially likely to exert effort and to persist in that particular activity. Intrinsic value relates strongly to interest and enjoyment. Intrinsic motivation is associated with exerting effort and demonstrating persistence in physical education classes (Ferrer-Caja & Weiss, 2000). Chen (2001) has investigated the construct of interest in physical education settings, which is related to intrinsic value. He reports students are more likely to engage in activities that are novel, challenging, and that generate enjoyment. He advocates making tasks in physical education interesting, linking motivation to the curriculum. He points out that curricular decisions should also consider the socioeconomic and cultural environment.

Value is an especially important concern in secondary physical education classes (Cothran & Ennis, 1997; Ennis, 1996; Solmon, 2006). A consistent finding in the themes across these studies is that high school students reported they see no value in the physical education curriculum and that they do not understand why physical education classes are required. This is especially true for many girls, and one factor in their dissatisfaction relates to the curricular issues discussed above. In many secondary physical education programs, the curriculum is centered on sports that are traditionally male oriented and are of little interest to many girls. Every curricular area has to convince students that they are teaching knowledge of worth. In some cases, it is clear that knowledge is essential (i.e., reading and math are essential life skills), but in physical education, it is hard to make the case that flag football or basketball are essential skills for a successful career. The case for the value of content in physical education is much easier to make when the focus of the content is on developing skills and knowledge needed to maintain an active healthy lifestyle.

Azzarito et al.'s (2006) study provides some insight concerning the issue of value of physical education for high school girls. In contrast to other studies that portrayed girls as disengaged and disenfranchised, the girls interviewed in this study reported that they enjoyed and valued physical activity. They made decisions, however, to engage in certain activities and avoid others through their negotiations of gender relations. Their physical education classes were characterized as a contested terrain in which the girls viewed their choices to be limited as compared to their male peers. Girls are often portrayed as a "problem" in physical education research because of they are described as disengaged. Through the poststructuralist lens presented in this study, it is suggested that the problem in physical education classes is the curricular choices rather than the girls.

Ability beliefs. Elliot and Dweck (2005) contend that competence is the conceptual core of motivation. They observe that, whether we are conscious of it or not, much of our everyday behavior is guided by the notion of demonstrating competence or avoiding incompetence. It is recognized that, in general, competence infers the condition or quality of demonstrating high ability, of being effective, or of being successful. When individuals do not believe that they can experience some level of success in an activity, or demonstrate some level of competence, they are unlikely to choose to engage in an activity, or to persist in an activity when they experience difficulty, even if they see value in the activity (see also Butler, 2014 [Chapter 1 of this volume]). Competence can be evaluated in a variety of ways. Competence can be judged according to a standard of mastery or a criterion inherent in a task (running a mile in a specified time), referencing competence relative to exceeding prior personal performance (running a mile faster than before), or by comparing one's performance to that of significant others (whether an individual can run as fast or faster than their peers). The manner in which one defines competence, that is, whether it is self-referenced and based on personal improvement or externally referenced in comparison to the performance of others, is a determining factor in how competence beliefs can act to enhance or constrain decisions to engage in an activity.

Competence is a basic psychological need that affects cognition and behavior across gender and culture (Elliot & Dweck, 2005). Feelings of competence affect emotions and feelings of well-being. Physical competence is associated with high status among peers during the elementary school years (Wigfield & Eccles, 1992) and that link between competence beliefs and social status can have an effect on self-esteem in the long run. Perceptions of, or beliefs about, competence are closely related to actual or measured competence and are considered to be an essential facet of actual competence (Markus, Cross, & Wurf, 1990). Beliefs about ability are as important, or maybe even more important, than actual ability (Solmon & Lee, 2008).

Young children are unable to differentiate between ability and effort. Rather, they equate effort with high ability and, as long as they are trying hard, typically have high perceptions of competence (Nicholls, 1989). As they age, they learn to distinguish effort from ability and to compare their performance to others. Their perceptions of competence tend to decline, becoming more realistic and more closely associated with their actual ability. Higher perceptions of competence in physical activity are consistently associated with higher levels of enjoyment, more positive affect, and higher levels of participation in physical activity (Cairney et al., 2012). There are many factors that affect perceptions of competence, and past experiences in a specific or similar domain are inarguably a very powerful influence.

Gender and competence in physical activity. Especially in the physical domain, gender is often a significant issue that has far reaching effects on perceptions of competence that can in turn affect motivation to engage in physical education, physical activity, and sport. Boys consistently report higher perceptions of physical and athletic competence and report higher levels of enjoyment of and participation in physical activity than girls (Cairney et al., 2012; Sabiston & Crocker, 2008). Researchers in physical education have investigated gender differences in motor skill performance and have explored explanations for differences that exist. Young boys generally outperform young girls on many motor tasks and the gap between girls' and boys' performance increases with age (Smoll & Schutz, 1990; Thomas & French, 1985). After puberty, differences in performance can be attributed to some degree to size and strength advantages for males, but motor skill differences are evident far earlier than is to be expected based on biological differences.

Although individual differences in motor ability have a strong influence on both children's decisions to engage in physical activity and the level of success they experience, Solmon and Lee (2008) argued that social and environmental influences affect the opportunities children have and the quality of their experiences in physical activity. Historically, sport and many forms of vigorous activity have been an exclusively male domain. There have been many changes over the years associated with more equitable opportunities for women in sport and physical activity, but many traditional gender roles are reinforced in schools, society, and the media. The socially constructed conceptions of masculinity and femininity (Vygotsky, 1978) can act to discourage girls' participation in physical education, sport, and physical activity in general. Feminine-typed tasks are typically associated with the attributes of graceful movement qualities, while masculine-typed tasks are generally those requiring strength, power, and competitiveness.

Gender stereotypes are often learned early in life and are reinforced in families, schools, communities, media, and society. Markus' (1977) characterization of self-schemata provides a framework to understand how socially constructed definitions of masculinity and femininity can enhance or constrain involvement in physical activity. Self-schemata are cognitive structures that are developed to explain a behavior in a specific domain. These self-perceptions are based on prior experiences and information in the environment. Individuals define possible selves based on what they believe they can become, what they would like to become, or what they are want to avoid becoming (Markus et al., 1990). The possible self represents the scope of behaviors that individuals believe are available to them. Possible selves are influenced by stereotypical beliefs, including those based on gender, race, and social class, as well as influential individuals such as role models, teachers, coaches, family members, and peers. If girls are socialized to believe that physical activities are not consistent with the self-schemata they have developed, they are at risk for lower perceptions of competence and are unlikely to pursue activities that are not encompassed within their possible selves.

Researchers in physical education have, over the years, identified activities according to sex type. Team sport activities such as football, basketball, and soccer are routinely deemed to be masculine, whereas rhythmic-type activities such as dance and gymnastics are considered to be feminine (Clifton & Gill, 1994). While there are some changes evident in society about appropriate physical activity choices for males and females, there are still many activities that are considered masculine or feminine. A large sample of first, third, and fifth graders characterized activities according to the appropriateness of participation by boys and girls (Lee, Fredenburg, Belcher, & Cleveland, 1999). Football, soccer, and basketball were labeled more appropriate for boys, while cheerleading, dance, and gymnastics were viewed as more suitable for girls. Activities including jogging, roller skating, tennis, volleyball, and softball were routinely characterized as appropriate for both boys and girls.

Given that the physical education curriculum is often focused on team sport activities that have been traditionally male dominated, the consistently lower perceptions of competence in the physical domain are not unexpected and can be explained through the framework of the possible self. When girls do not view activities as appropriate for them, or within the scope of the possible self, then they are at risk not only for lower perceptions of competence but also to be unable to see any value in the activity. Generally, boys report higher levels of perceived competence in the activities designated as better suited for males, while girls have higher perceptions of competence than boys on feminine activities (Lee et al., 1999).

Gender stereotypes and the associated expectations also affect decisions to be involved in sport. Even though opportunities for girls to be involved in sport have dramatically increased since the enactment of Title IX, girls in some social settings may experience a gender role conflict if they choose to participate in a sport that has been stereotyped as a male activity. A girl who experiences role conflict may choose to challenge societal conceptions of what is acceptable and ignore expectations, especially if social support is available. Alternatively, she may choose to give up and select activities deemed more appropriate for females. Despite the progress made over the past four decades in opportunities for girls in sport, many girls are still not encouraged to participate in a large range of vigorous physical activities.

There is evidence that the decline in motivation to be physically active for girls begins early in their school years. As early as the fourth grade, girls report lower expectations for success and intentions to take physical education when given a choice than boys their age and as compared to younger children (Xiang, McBride, Guan, & Solmon, 2003). A recent study by Cairney et al. (2012) demonstrates how important it is to address concerns about girls' low perceived competence in physical education. In their longitudinal investigation, they tracked fourth graders over a 2-year period. Overall, boys had higher levels of perceived athletic competence and reported higher levels of enjoyment than girls, but the analysis revealed two important interactions. Boys' enjoyment remained constant over the 2-year period, but girls' declined, so the gap between enjoyment levels increased. Of perhaps greater consequence, the study revealed that girls who had high levels of perceived athletic competence reported high levels of enjoyment in their physical education classes, and their enjoyment increased over time. Boys who had low perceived athletic competence reported lower levels of enjoyment than those with higher perceptions, but their levels of enjoyment remained constant over time. Taken together, the findings of this study suggest that girls with low perceived competence are a special concern and demonstrate that when perceptions of competence are high, girls enjoy physical activity.

To optimize opportunities for girls in physical education and sport programs so that girls will be more inclined to be physically active, the issues of value and ability beliefs must be addressed. Current programs as they are situated in society and culture tend to foster stereotypical attitudes that nurture higher perceptions of competence for boys than for girls. Furthermore, girls are at greater risk for than boys for failing to see value in sport and physical activities. It is critical that programs be structured to promote girls' beliefs that physical activity is appropriate for them and that they can be successful. A comprehensive effort is needed in physical education, sport opportunities, and the school culture in general to create contexts in which girls can overcome the biases inherent in current curricular approaches that have often served to alienate them. A thread that runs through the discussion of curriculum, value, and perceptions of ability is that physical education and sport have generally been structured in ways that tend to privilege males. An examination of fitness testing in schools provides an illustration of how practices in physical education can serve to reinforce conceptions of fitness that reflect dominant gender discourses.

5. FITNESS TESTING

Physical fitness testing has been used as a form of assessment in physical education classes in the United States since 1957 (Freedson, Cureton, & Heath, 2000). Particularly for children and youth who are not athletically inclined, skillful, and/or highly fit, the most vivid memories of physical education are often related to fitness testing. It has been common practice over many years for physical education teachers to administer a test of physical fitness at the beginning and end of the school year. In some cases, this test administration is mandated by district or state policy. Proponents of fitness testing contend that it serves to increase children's motivation to be physically active, but others argue that there is not sufficient evidence to support the notion that fitness testing motivates children (Harris & Cale, 2006). Although there are beneficial educational outcomes when fitness testing is administered effectively by teachers, anecdotal stories of humiliation and ridicule associated with poor performance on test items appear frequently in the literature.

The focus on physical fitness testing in schools received a major impetus when President Eisenhower was informed that children in the United States performed poorly on the Kraus–Weber minimum fitness test in comparison to European children (Domangue & Solmon, 2012). Military personnel also expressed concerns about the subpar fitness levels of military recruits, fearful that the United States would not be prepared to staff the armed forces in the event of a war (Domangue & Solmon, 2009). So policies were developed to address this concern, including the establishment of the President's Council for Physical Fitness and Sport (PCPFS). Early versions of tests administered in schools included items that were geared toward motor fitness and athletic performance. More recent iterations of tests have evolved from a focus on performance-based factors such as speed and agility to an emphasis on health-related fitness components (Baumgartner, Jackson, Mahar, & Rowe, 2007). To some degree, however, performance on test items, particularly when administered in schools, is influenced by genetic ability. Although many scholars advise against this practice, some school districts mandate that fitness scores be used as a measure of teacher effectiveness in their accountability systems (Solmon & Garn, 2014). This is problematic on many levels, in that teachers could feel pressured to optimize test results to avoid being penalized for poor performance, given that they are the individuals responsible for observing and evaluating performance and reporting scores.

Although a variety of tests are available, the two that are most prominently in use today are the President's Challenge Physical Fitness Awards Program (PCPFAP) and FITNESSGRAM® (Domangue & Solmon, 2010). Age group norms for boys and girls from 6 to 17 years have been established for the PCPFAP, and students are awarded the Presidential Award for exceeding the 85th percentile on all five items included in test battery. Students who exceed the 50th percentile on each item receive the National Award. FITNESSGRAM® is a criterion-referenced test which establishes age and gender standards for the healthy fitness zone for the components that are assessed. Rather than striving to meet a standard indicative of elite performance, participants are encouraged to work toward achieving a standard that reflects a level of health enhancing fitness.

Examination of both sets of standards (see Baumgartner et al. (2007) for standards) reveals that the benchmarks communicate strong and contrasting messages to girls and boys. For example, in the PCPFAP pull-ups are one option for the assessment of upper arm strength. For 6-year-old boys and girls, the standard for the Presidential Award in pull-ups is two. Benchmarks for boys steadily increase across the age span until the standard at 17 years for the Presidential Award is 13 pull-ups. In contrast, the Presidential Award benchmark for girls remains at either two or three pull-ups until the age of 15, when it drops to one. The mile run is the measure of aerobic capacity in the PCPFAP for 10–17 year olds. The standard for the Presidential Award for boys at the age of 10 is 7:57 min, while the criterion for girls is 9:19 min, even though no gender differences should be expected based on biological factors at this age. Expectations for boys for continually reflect faster mile times from ages 10 to 17, while standards for girls reflect only slightly faster times until the age of 14, when the benchmarks for the Presidential Award actually become slower for the older age groups. The message for boys is that their upper arm strength and running speed should increase as they grow, while the expectation communicated to girls is that they are not expected to develop strength and that their ability to mile run decreases as they age.

It can be argued that the norms are based on scores from a large, representative sample and thus that they accurately reflect the age group norms, but norms developed in other domains are not segregated by gender based on normative performance. If standards for boys' and girls' achievement differed in academic domains included in high stakes testing programs, parents would likely express concerns that, for example, their daughters were held accountable to lower expectations in math and science. That reinforces the argument that we should carefully consider the implications of gender-differentiated standards on fitness testing and explore ways that fitness testing can be used effectively. FITNESSGRAM® identifies criterion rather than normative standards, and criterion-referenced standards for healthy fitness awards are also included in the PCPFAP. The criterion-referenced standards in both tests also consistently communicate lower standards for girls, although the divergence between standards for boys and girls is not as marked as the normative tests. The one exception to this pattern is the benchmark for flexibility; girls are expected to outperform boys on both batteries.

In a series of studies, Domangue and Solmon (2010, 2012) investigated motivational and gendered aspects of physical fitness testing by comparing students who received either the presidential or national award to those who did not. Students who received awards were more task-oriented, reported higher levels of perceived competence, effort, and enjoyment, and were more likely to indicate future intentions to engage in fitness activities. Seemingly, fitness testing using normative standards served to foster motivational levels for children who were fit, while discouraging those who were not fit and in need of support that would encourage and enable them to become more engaged in fitness activities. It was encouraging to note in this study that gender differences in motivational constructs did not emerge. The proportion of girls and boys who received awards did not differ, so it seemed that when girls received positive feedback about their performance they maintained higher levels of perceived competence that foster motivation. A follow-up study (Domangue, 2009) comparing norm referenced and criterion-based tests supports the conclusion that a criterion-based approach fosters higher perceptions of competence, enjoyment, and intentions to engage in fitness activities.

Using a qualitative approach to explore the gendered nature of children's perceptions of fitness testing and the disparities in the expectations for girls and boys, Domangue and Solmon (2012) interviewed a group of fifth grade students who had recently completed the PCPFS. The participants' responses clearly indicated that, despite the changes that have occurred in the post-Title IX era, gendered notions of physical activity permeate children's understandings of fitness testing. When asked to explain why boys were expected to run faster and complete more pull-ups than girls, both girls and boys made attributions to experience more than natural ability or biological differences. Children explained the differing expectations in terms of experiences and preferred activities, expressing the belief that boys were stronger and faster than girls because they exercise more and play outside more while girls prefer less active pursuits, such as shopping. The influence of pop culture and media was also evident in their responses, in that they cited examples from television programs and advertisements portraying males as stronger and more active than females.

Other findings indicated that children recognized that some girls were able to outperform some boys and recognized that the differential standards could discourage girls from exerting effort (Domangue & Solmon, 2012). They also pointed out that, when boys were outperformed by girls, the differential standards contributed to a stigma of inferiority associated with being beaten by a girl.

Consistent with findings in the Satina et al. (1998) study, when girls performed well, their performance was validated in terms of male standards, or by being "as good as the boys." This perspective reinforces the view of binary opposition and female inferiority that dominated schools and society prior to the implementation of Title IX. Domangue and Solmon (2012) conclude that the normative context of fitness testing reinforces notions of male superiority and gendered constructions of the body. The gendered discourse that surrounds fitness testing contributes to the gendered nature of social construction of bodily meanings that can affect girls' decisions about being physically active.

6. SOCIAL CONSTRUCTION OF BODILY MEANINGS

Girls' and boys' experiences in physical education and sport, within the larger context of schools and societies, act to influence the ways that they think about their bodies. Discourses are ways of thinking and producing meanings that are situated in cultural and historical contexts. Dominant discourses around gender dichotomies of masculinity and femininity are entrenched in many physical activity practices in schools, influencing the social construction of identities (Azzarito & Solmon, 2006b). Many girls experience conflict related to femininity, physicality, and physical activity (Hills, 2006). The study of the body has emerged over the past two decades as a central element in academic discourses in the field of education. Researchers in physical education have explored ways that media and marketing images influence students' perceptions of their bodies, the development of their physicality, and ultimately their decisions concerning participating in physical activity (Azzarito & Solmon, 2006a). In sport, Daniels' work investigating media representations of female athletes is relevant to the discussion of social construction of bodily meanings. She provides evidence that sexualized images of female athletes elicit objectified appraisals from both boys (Daniels & Wartena, 2011) and girls (Daniels, 2012), whereas performance-based images reinforced perceptions of physical competence. Images that are sexualized may attract attention for girls in sport and physical activity but it does not seem to be the type of attention that promotes equity and respect. It is not possible in the framework of this chapter to provide an extensive overview of the literature in this area. Readers are referred to the work of Azzarito and her colleagues (Azzarito & Kirk, 2013; Azzarito & Solmon, 2005) for an in depth analysis of this issue.

From a poststructuralist perspective, the human body is viewed as a site of conflicting social, political, and economic forces that function to normalize the process of constructing personal identities (Azzarito & Solmon, 2006b). Appearance, size, shape, and muscularity are factors that are interwoven in gendered discourses around bodily meanings (Azzarito & Solmon, 2006a). Consistent with the historically accepted notions of gender, power, strength, competitiveness, muscularity, and aggressiveness are qualities associated with masculinity, whereas slenderness and grace are qualities associated with femininity. Girls may resist masculinizing physical activities in sport-focused physical education classes, reflecting a form of disembodiment of the self (Azzarito et al., 2006). The same can be true for boys who are unskilled or overweight, but the sense of disembodiment can be more problematic for girls. Their sense of physicality can be limited by social construction of the female body as slim and small, and less skilled and powerful than males. Conversely, males experience their physicality through masculinizing practices and are encouraged to participate in a broad range of sport and physical activities (Azzarito & Solmon, 2006a).

There is evidence that socially constructed bodily meanings influence decisions to engage in physical activity. Azzarito and Solmon (2006b) examined high school students' physical activity participation in relation to their racial and gendered construction of bodily meanings around five discourses: (a) muscularity, skill, and power; (b) appearance and size; (c) prior experience and ability; (d) fun and sociability; and (e) academics. Students who reported higher levels of participation in physical education rated bodily meanings as more important than those who were less active. Boys rated muscularity, skill and power, appearance and size, and academics as more influential than girls and were more engaged in their physical education classes. Girls reported lower levels of participation than boys, and their responses suggested that they viewed physical education as irrelevant to achieving a desired body shape or size.

In a subsequent study, Azzarito and Solmon (2009) explored how ratings of discursive constructs, defined as parents', physical education teachers', and young peoples' own discourses around the body and the relevance of physical activity, differed by gender and whether discursive constructs were related to physical activity choice. Skillfulness was rated as a more important discursive construct by boys than girls. In contrast, the gendered body was a more important construct for girls than boys. Girls' responses also reflected a lack of value and importance of physical activity, as compared to the boys' responses. Discursive constructs influenced students' selections of favorite activities. Students who rated the gendered body as an important construct were more likely to select feminine than masculine activities. Those students who favored gender neutral and traditionally masculine activities rated support and encouragement from influences outside of physical education, such as parents, as important.

Using images from fitness and sports magazines, Azzarito and Solmon (2006a) investigated how high school students' body narratives related to their engagement in physical education and their physical activity choices. Students' narratives reflected both sites of compliance to dominant gendered discourses as well as sites of resistance to existing practice. Narratives of comfortable and "bad bodies" conformed to dominant discourses and conceived of physical education practice as a technology for achieving the ideal feminine (slender) and masculine (muscular) body. Boys were characterized as more comfortable in their narratives, which reflected male ideals. Few girls were characterized as comfortable, and they were girls whose narratives reproduced discourses of femininity related to flexibility and a lack of muscularity. Narratives characterized as "bad bodies" were those of students who had internalized gendered ideals and were dissatisfied with their physiques. Some students, mostly girls, rejected dominant-gendered discourses and presented narratives of borderland bodies. These narratives reflected resistance to the gendered norms of slim feminine and muscular masculine bodies and instead embraced notions of skillfulness and muscularity for girls, graceful movement for boys, and acceptance of a range of shapes and sizes. Boys were more likely to present comfortable narratives, while girls' narratives tended to be characterized as bad or borderland bodies. These results demonstrate that it is important for physical education teachers to present a broad range of alternatives so that girls and boys can construct meanings about the body that are not confined to conceptions of masculine and feminine ideals, enabling them to construct positive and personally meaningful physicalities that foster confidence needed to actively engage in physical activities.

7. CREATING EQUITABLE CLIMATES IN PHYSICAL EDUCATION

The goal of quality physical education programs is to help all children learn skills and develop dispositions that will enable them to enjoy physical activity across the life span. Children whose parents engage in and value physical activity are at an advantage and are more likely to be physically active. Some children are athletically skilled and seem naturally inclined to participate in physical activity. A large proportion of children, however, do not have these advantages and consequently are at risk for high levels of physical inactivity that can result in negative health outcomes, low self-esteem, and lower quality of life. Girls, as well as children who lack athletic ability and/or are overweight, are of particular concern. It is easy for teachers and coaches to engage students who enjoy physical activity and sport and are already motivated to be active. It is a far greater challenge to meet the needs of children who are not in that category. There is clear evidence that a traditional multi-activity curricular model centered around male-dominated sports has served to alienate groups of students, including girls, children who lack experience and skill, children who are overweight, and girls and boys who do not conform to the socially accepted male and female ideals (Azzarito et al., 2006; Ennis, 1996, 1998, 1999, 2000; Satina et al., 1998).

It is inarguable that families, media images, and community settings outside of schools are influential socializing agents with regard to gender and physical activity, but there is evidence that teachers' practices can also have an influential effect on whether students are motivated to engage in physical activity (Satina et al., 1998). Good teachers across academic domains have a clear understanding of the knowledge and skills they want their students to learn and communicate that message in clear and deliberate ways. In addition to the content knowledge that teachers intend for their students to master, teachers also communicate other messages through their actions, including attitudes, values, norms, and expectations for students that often mirror socially constructed notions of gender and other stereotypical views related to race and social economic status. These implicit messages that teachers send through their interactions in the classroom are often referred to as a hidden curriculum (Solmon & Lee, 2008).

Several studies in physical education demonstrate that girls and boys can receive very different messages from their teachers, and those messages, even though they may be unintentional, can serve to constrain girls' engagement in physical activity (Ronholt, 2002; Satina et al., 1998; Solmon & Carter, 1995). A common thread across these studies is that teachers often communicate lower expectations for success to girls than to boys (see Leaper & Brown, 2014 [Chapter 6 of this volume]). An exemplary elementary physical education teacher in the Solmon and Carter (1995) study used gender for grouping, and in that process unintentionally communicated to children that girls and boys are suited for different kinds of tasks and activities. She paired boys and girls with the intention of promoting equity, but tended to praise the boys for their skill in the activities while recognizing girls for their compliant behavior and following the rules. Her actions were reflected in the children's perceptions, in that boys thought the teacher wanted them to learn to throw, catch, and run, while girls thought the teacher wanted them to learn to follow the rules. This ultimately communicated lower expectations for success in physical activity to girls. A more recent study by Ronholt (2002) mirrors these findings with regard to images of running that the teacher communicated. For boys, running was competitive and the teacher communicated high expectations. Consequently, boys linked their identities to their performance and success in running. Girls, however, connected running to health and fitness and their identities were not rooted in the running performance. The teacher communicated lower expectations, and performance was of less consequence. Conversely, when teachers make a concerted effort to structure a learning environment that is inclusive and promotes respect for all individuals, these values are reflected in the perspectives of their students (Satina et al., 1998).

The importance of competence beliefs in motivation to engage in any activity has been clearly established (Elliot & Dweck, 2005). When teachers, whether intentionally or inadvertently, communicate differing expectations for girls and boys it is likely that the motivational consequences will be detrimental. Positive ability beliefs are requisite for active involvement in an activity, and it is imperative that teachers communicate to all students the belief that, if they are willing to exert effort, they will be able to demonstrate competence in an activity. To accomplish this, teachers must structure activities at an appropriate level of difficulty, designing tasks that enable students to learn skills and develop their abilities.

Confounding this issue is the inclusion of highly competitive activities in physical education classes, in which the range of individual ability and experiences is often very broad and performance is, by nature, observable and public. When success is measured in normative terms, in comparison with the performance of more skilled and experienced peers, then competence beliefs can easily be threatened. Measuring success in terms of personal improvement and mastery criteria rather than solely on competitive outcomes makes it possible for all students to demonstrate a level of competence and to feel a sense of success when they have improved. There is a compelling body of evidence that a mastery motivational climate, in which the emphasis is on learning a task, working at a challenging level, attributing success to effort, and demonstrating personal improvement, is preferable for students in physical education (Solmon, 2003). Highly skilled students fare well in performance climates, in which the emphasis is on demonstrating competence by outperforming others, but that emphasis alienates a significant proportion of students. Highly skilled students also fare well in a mastery climate, and competition can be used in that context effectively to promote effort and engage all students in ways that promote positive ability beliefs and confidence.

A central issue in providing an equitable climate is reconceptualizing curriculum from a traditional sport-based model toward a focus on activities that enhance health-related fitness and are culturally meaningful to a wide range of students (Azzarito & Solmon, 2005). Girls in the study by Azzarito et al. (2006) indicated that they value physical activity and that they would engage in their physical education classes if the environment was more equitable for them.

Rather than trying to force or entice girls to engage in activities that are unfairly biased for boys, they recommend supporting efforts to confront barriers girls encounter and facilitating efforts to negotiate gender relations. This can be realized by moving beyond traditional sports to provide alternative activities that can promote development of physicality that is not limited by gendered discourse. Likewise, Hills (2006) advocates for inclusive practices that recognize girls' interests and preferences and for the creation of space for critical inquiry.

In their exploration of performing identities in physical education, Azzarito and Katzew (2010) provide an example of the use of critical inquiry to understand young people's experiences as they resist and negotiate their identities in a physical education context. In their year-long ethnographic study, they employed a photo-elicitation technique using pictures from health, sport, and fitness magazines. Creating what they termed a "cultural inventory" of "performing bodies" (p. 28), they explored high school girls' and boys' narratives about the body and the self. Researchers used pictures to explore participants' perceptions of the messages that were expressed in the pictures, sharing stories about what the pictures portrayed and relating that to personal experience. The school site for the study was purposively selected because the teachers in their study had made a commitment to promote gender equity. Both girls and boys were empowered by an approach that reconceptualized identity as fluid and created safe spaces for students to develop identities that were not constrained by gendered norms. Conversations revolving around the portrayal of males and females in diverse activities and with a variety of body sizes and types helped participants to conceptualize a broader range of possibilities for males and females in sport and physical activity. Students' narratives at times reflected a biological discourse of difference, such as boys are powerful, muscular, and competitive and girls are graceful. There were, however, contradictions in those narratives acknowledging that girls can be muscular and skillful and that boys can be masculine in activities other than competitive sport, reflecting realizations that masculinity and femininity are not binary constructs but instead are overlapping social constructions. Their study demonstrates that there is hope that physical education classes can facilitate social change by becoming more equitable and, furthermore, that critical conversations can help to unsettle a dichotomous view of gender to create more flexible gender boundaries that can, in turn, promote physicality and physical activity for both girls and boys.

8. EDUCATION AND SPORT

The role of sport in education and society has become increasingly controversial in many respects. Numerous scandals related to both interscholastic and professional sports have garnered extensive coverage in media outlets involving major sport figures and educational institutions. Historically, sport evolved in society and educational programs as a means to develop character and to provide an outlet for naturally aggressive and competitive males (Phillips & Roper, 2006). Sport was associated with developing not only physicality but also as an arena to learn lessons about life, leadership, and perseverance. Initially, sport was an exclusively a male domain and females were largely relegated to recreational games and graceful pursuits. From those origins, sport has expanded dramatically over the past century, not only to include females but also to become a major influence in our society. Although opportunities for girls in sport have risen dramatically in the post-Title IX era, they continue to lag behind those for boys (Kennedy, 2010; Pickett et al., 2012) and they receive much less media attention.

As opportunities for girls to be involved in intercollegiate sports have increased, there has not been a corresponding increase in opportunities for women in coaching and other leadership positions in athletic administration. When Title IX was enacted in 1972, more than 90% of women's college teams were coached by women and more than 90% of women's athletic programs were led by a female administrator (Acosta & Carpenter, 2012). In 2012, the number of women's teams coached by women had shrunk to 42.9%. Women hold only 35.8% of jobs in athletic administration and only 20.3% of schools have female athletic directors. It is of interest to note that only 10% of division I schools have female athletic directors, and the largest proportion of female directors is found in division III schools. As resource allocations have increased for women's sports, coaching positions are more attractive and men now hold the majority of head coaching positions for women's teams. Databases are not available concerning the gender of coaches in secondary schools, but it reasonable to expect that, as girls' athletics have gained prominence, a similar trend of increasing numbers of male coaches is evident. Acosta and Carpenter suggest that male administrators seem more likely to hire male coaches and that it is problematic that fewer opportunities for leadership are available to women. It is important that girls see women in leadership roles in all domains and that is especially true in sport.

Sport has evolved into a major business, not only in colleges and universities but also in secondary schools (Conn, 2012). Financial issues related to athletic competition confounds issues that surround sport and schools on multiple levels. One is the use of tax dollars to support athletic programs, ultimately resulting in decreased resources for academic programs. A few high profile athletic programs at large universities are self-supporting but those are rare. There is a positive economic impact for schools and surrounding communities related to revenue generated through events and merchandizing, and often it seems that athletics receives a disproportionate share of attention.

In his commentary, Conn (2012) argues that it is not just the diversion of financial resources from educational programs to athletics that is problematic. He contends that the trend toward professionalization that has permeated college and high school athletics detracts from educational pursuits, as athletes are required to spend vast amounts of time in practice, game planning, and off season training. Rather than focusing on schooling, many athletes, and their parents, focus on athletic pursuits as potential careers at the expense of their academic progress. For many of those, however, attaining a college scholarship and/or pursuing a career as a professional athlete is not realistic, and their time might be better spent on their academic studies.

Although the role of sport in schools and society is a topic of consequence, of greater concern relative to this chapter is consideration of the school children who do not have the opportunity to play on teams during their school years. As schools have become larger to accommodate growing student populations, and the professionalism that Conn (2012) refers to continues to creep down to lower and lower age levels, the proportion of children who have the option to be involved in interscholastic programs has decreased. Interscholastic sports, particularly at large schools, can be elitist, involving only those who are athletically gifted and/or have parents who support their development through experiences outside of schools. An unfortunate consequence of this is that limited numbers of students are involved in athletic programs in roles other than spectators.

9. CONCLUSIONS AND IMPLICATIONS

If schools are to realize their potential to increase physical activity levels for girls, as well as other groups of children who are at risk for high levels of physical inactivity, through physical education and sport programs, it is clear that changes are needed. Several implications are supported based on the arguments and evidence presented in this chapter that have the potential to work toward that goal. First, the issue of value of physical education classes must be addressed. Boys and students who are highly skilled and physically active often value the sport-focused models that tend to dominate secondary physical education programs, but they can pursue those opportunities in competitive sport programs. They are already interested and motivated, and they would most likely also be interested and motivated if the curricular focus was broadened to include a variety of fitness activities, games and life time sports that would in all probability be more appealing to students who are disengaged in and alienated by current programs. Offering curricula that are culturally meaningful and relevant to their lives is an important first step to address the needs of girls, students who have not had opportunities to develop sport skills, and students who are overweight, that is, the students who need physical education the most. Focusing on educational aspects of health-related fitness is one approach that has potential to meet those needs. It is also clear that gendered notions of what is masculine and feminine must be broadened so that both boys and girls see that a wide range of activities fit their bodily meanings. Azzarito and Katzew (2010) and Ennis (1999, 2000) identify other approaches that have great potential. To accomplish this will require a commitment to social justice and equity on the part of teachers.

It is of critical importance to address issues related to competence and expectations for success. It is essential for teachers and other school personnel to communicate high expectations for success to all students, and to structure the curriculum and learning activities in ways that students believe that they can succeed at the tasks with effort and that they see the activities as appropriate and meaningful. Lastly, highly competitive athletics should be left to elite athletes, while physical education programs focus on inclusive, educational activities. Physical activity should be promoted throughout the school day including intramural sport programs and fitness activities that provide children of all skill levels opportunities to experience the joys of movement.

REFERENCES

Acosta, R. V. & Carpenter, L. J. (2012). Women in intercollegiate sport: A longitudinal study—A thirty five year update 1977–2012. Retrieved http://acostacarpenter.org/AcostaCarpenter2012.pdf

Azzarito, L., & Katzew, A. (2010). Performing identities in physical education: (En)gendering fluid selves. *Research Quarterly for Exercise and Sport, 81*, 25–37.

Azzarito, L., & Kirk, D. (Eds.). (2013). *Pedagogies, physical culture, and visual methods.* New York: Routledge.

Azzarito, L., Munro, P., & Solmon, M. A. (2004). Unsettling the body: The institutionalization of physical activity at the turn of the 20th century. *Quest, 56*, 377–396.

Azzarito, L., & Solmon, M. A. (2005). A reconceptualization of physical education: The intersection of race, gender, and social class. *Sport, Education, and Society, 10*, 25–47.

Azzarito, L., & Solmon, M. A. (2006a). A feminist poststructuralist view on student bodies in physical education: Sites of compliance, resistance, and transformation. *Journal of Teaching in Physical Education, 25*, 200–225.

Azzarito, L., & Solmon, M. A. (2006b). A poststructural analysis of high school students' gendered and racialized bodily meanings. *Journal of Teaching in Physical Education, 25*, 75–98.

Azzarito, L., & Solmon, M. A. (2009). An investigation of students' embodied discourses in physical education: A gender project. *Journal of Teaching in Physical Education, 28*, 173–191.

Azzarito, L., Solmon, M. A., & Harrison, L. (2006). "···If I had a choice, I would." A feminist post-structuralist perspective on girls in physical education classes. *Research Quarterly for Exercise and Sport, 77*, 222–239.

Baumgartner, T. A., Jackson, A. S., Mahar, M. T., & Rowe, D. A. (2007). *Measurement for evaluation in physical education and exercise science.* New York: McGraw Hill.

Bigler, R. S., Hayes, A. R., & Liben, L. S. (2014). Analysis and evaluation of the rationales for single-sex schooling. In L. S. Liben, & R. S. Bigler (Vol. Eds.), *The role of gender in educational contexts and outcomes.* In J. B. Benson (Series Ed.), *Advances in child development and behavior: Vol. 47* (pp. 225–260). London: Elsevier.

Butler, R. (2014). Motivation in educational contexts: Does gender matter? In L. S. Liben, & R. S. Bigler (Vol. Eds.), *The role of gender in educational contexts and outcomes.* In J. B. Benson (Series Ed.), *Advances in child development and behavior: Vol. 47* (pp. 1–41). London: Elsevier.

Cairney, J., Kwan, M. Y., Velizen, S., Jay, J., Bray, S. R., & Faught, B. E. (2012). Gender, perceived competence and the enjoyment of physical education in children: A longitudinal examination. *International Journal of Behavioral Nutrition and Physical Activity, 9*, 26–33.

Caspersen, C. J. (1989). Physical activity epidemiology: Concepts, methods and applications to exercise science. *Exercise and Sports Sciences Reviews, 17*, 423–473.

Chen, A. (2001). A theoretical conceptualization for motivation research in physical education: An integrated perspective. *Quest, 53*, 59–76.

Chomitz, V. R., Slining, M. M., McGowan, R. J., Mitchell, S. E., Dawson, G. F., & Hacker, K. A. (2009). Is there a relationship between physical fitness and academic achievement? Positive results from public school children in the northeastern United States. *Journal of School Health, 79*, 30–37.

Clifton, R., & Gill, D. (1994). Gender differences in self-confidence on a feminine-typed task. *Journal of Sport & Exercise Psychology, 16*, 150–162.

Conn, S. (2012). *In college classrooms, the problem is high-school athletics.* Washington, D.C: The Chronicle of Higher Education, April 15. http://chronicle.com/article/In-College-Classrooms-the/131550/.

Cothran, D. J., & Ennis, C. D. (1997). Students and teachers' perceptions of conflict and power. *Teaching and Teacher Education, 13*, 541–553.

Daniels, E. A. (2012). Sexy versus strong: What girls and women think of female athletes. *Journal of Applied Developmental Psychology, 33*, 79–90.

Daniels, E. A., & Wartena, H. (2011). Athlete or sex symbol: What boys think of media representations of female athletes. *Sex Roles, 65*, 566–579.

Domangue, E. (2009). *A critical examination into motivation and gender in youth physical fitness testing*. Unpublished doctoral dissertation, Louisiana State University.

Domangue, E. A., & Solmon, M. A. (2009). A feminist poststructuralist examination into the President's Challenge Physical Fitness Test Awards Program. *Gender and Education, 21*, 583–600.

Domangue, E. A., & Solmon, M. A. (2010). Motivational responses to fitness testing by award status and gender. *Research Quarterly for Exercise and Sport, 81*, 310–318.

Domangue, E. A., & Solmon, M. A. (2012). Fitness testing: How do students make sense of the gender disparities? *Sport, Education and Society, 17*, 207–224.

Donnelly, J. E., & Lambourne, K. (2011). Classroom-based physical activity, cognition, and academic achievement. *Preventive Medicine, 52*, S36–S42.

Eccles, J. S. (2005). Subjective task value and the Eccles et al. model of achievement-related choices. In A. J. Elliot, & C. S. Dweck (Eds.), *Handbook of competence and motivation* (pp. 105–121). New York: Guilford Press.

Elliot, A. J., & Dweck, C. S. (2005). Competence and motivation: Competence as the core of achievement. In A. J. Elliot, & C. S. Dweck (Eds.), *Handbook of competence and motivation* (pp. 3–12). New York: Guilford Press.

Ennis, C. D. (1996). Students' experiences in sport-based physical education: [More than] apologies are necessary. *Quest, 48*, 453–456.

Ennis, C. D. (1998). The context of a culturally unresponsive curriculum: Constructing ethnicity and gender with a contested terrain. *Teaching and Teacher Education, 14*, 749–760.

Ennis, C. D. (1999). Creating a culturally relevant curriculum for disengaged girls. *Sport, Education, and Society, 4*, 31–49.

Ennis, C. D. (2000). Canaries in the coal mine: Responding to disengaged students using theme-based curricula. *Quest, 52*, 119–130.

Ennis, C. D. (2006). Curriculum: Forming and reshaping the vision of physical education in a high need, low demand world of schools. *Quest, 58*, 41–59.

Fagrell, G., Larsson, H., & Redelius, K. (2012). The game within the game: Girls underperforming position in physical education. *Gender and Education, 24*, 101–118.

Ferrer-Caja, E., & Weiss, M. R. (2000). Predictors of intrinsic motivation among adolescent students in physical education. *Research Quarterly for Exercise and Sport, 71*, 267–279.

Freedson, P. S., Cureton, K. J., & Heath, G. W. (2000). Status of field-based testing in children and youth. *American Journal of Preventive Medicine, 31*, s77–s85.

Freedson, P. S., & Miller, K. (2000). Objective monitoring of physical activity using motion sensors and heart rate. *Research Quarterly for Exercise and Sport, 71*, S21–S29.

Harris, J., & Cale, L. (2006). A review of children's fitness testing. *European Physical Education Review, 12*, 201–225.

Hills, L. A. (2006). Playing the field(s): An exploration of change, conformity and conflict in girls' understandings of gendered physicality in physical education. *Gender and Education, 18*, 539–556.

Janz, K. F., Dawson, J. D., & Mahoney, L. T. (2000). Tracking physical fitness and physical activity from childhood to adolescence: The Muscatine study. *Medicine & Science in Sports & Exercise, 32*, 1250–1257.

Kennedy, C. L. (2010). A new frontier for women's sports (beyond Title IX). *Gender Issues, 27*, 78–90.

Leaper, C., & Brown, C. S. (2014). Sexism in schools. In L. S. Liben, & R. S. Bigler (Vol. Eds.), *The role of gender in educational contexts and outcomes*. In J. B. Benson (Series Ed.), *Advances in child development and behavior: Vol. 47* (pp. 189–223). London: Elsevier.

Lee, A., Fredenburg, K., Belcher, D., & Cleveland, N. (1999). Gender differences in children's conceptions of competence and motivation in physical education. *Sport, Education and Society*, *4*, 161–174.

Markus, H. (1977). Self-schemata and processing information about the self. *Journal of Personality and Social Psychology*, *35*, 63–78.

Markus, H., Cross, S., & Wurf, E., Jr. (1990). The role of the self-system in competence. In R. J. Sternberg, & J. Kolligan, Jr., (Eds.), *Competence considered* (pp. 205–225). New Haven, CT: Yale University Press.

National Association for Sport and Physical Education (NASPE). (2004). *Moving into the future: National standards for physical education* (2nd ed.). Reston, VA: Author.

National Association for Sport and Physical Education (NASPE). (2008). *Comprehensive school physical activity programs*. Reston, VA: Author.

Nicholls, J. G. (1989). *The competitive ethos and democratic education*. Cambridge, MA: Harvard University Press.

Petersen, J., & Hyde, J. S. (2014). Gender-related academic and occupational interests and goals. In L. S. Liben, & R. S. Bigler (Vol. Eds.), *The role of gender in educational contexts and outcomes*. In J. B. Benson (Series Ed.), *Advances in child development and behavior: Vol. 47* (pp. 43–76). London: Elsevier.

Phillips, M. G., & Roper, A. P. (2006). History of physical education. In D. Kirk, D. Macdonald, & M. O'Sullivan (Eds.), *Handbook of physical education* (pp. 123–140). London: Sage.

Pickett, M. W., Dawkins, M. P., & Braddock, J. H. (2012). Race and gender equity in sports: Have White and African American females benefited equally from Title IX? *American Behavioral Scientist*, *56*, 1581–1603.

Reyna, A., III. (2011). An introduction to the Arthur Miller dialogue on "Sports, media and race: The impact on America". *Texas Review of Entertainment & Sports Law*, *12*, 239–249.

Roberts, G. C. (2012). Motivation in sport and exercise from an achievement goal theory perspective: After 30 years, where are we? In G. C. Roberts, & D. C. Treasure (Eds.), *Advances in motivation in sport and exercise* (pp. 5–58). Champaign, IL: Human Kinetics.

Ronholt, H. (2002). "It's only the sissies...": Analysis of teaching and learning process in physical education: A contribution to the hidden curriculum. *Sport, Education, and Society*, *3*, 181–200.

Sabiston, C., & Crocker, P. R. E. (2008). Exploring self-perceptions and social influences as correlates of adolescent leisure-time physical activity. *Journal of Sport & Exercise Psychology*, *30*, 3–22.

Satina, B., Solmon, M. A., Cothran, D. J., Loftus, S. J., & Stockin-Davidson, K. (1998). Patriarchal consciousness: Middle school students' and teachers' perspectives of motivational practices. *Sport, Education, and Society*, *2*, 181–200.

Siedentop, D. (2002). Content knowledge for physical education. *Journal of Teaching in Physical Education*, *21*, 368–377.

Smoll, F. L., & Schutz, R. W. (1990). Quantifying gender differences in physical performance: A developmental perspective. *Developmental Psychology*, *26*, 360–369.

Solmon, M. (2003). Student issues in physical education classes: Attitude, cognition, and motivation. In S. J. Silverman, & C. D. Ennis (Eds.), *Student learning in physical education: Applying research to enhance instruction* (pp. 147–163) (2nd ed.). Champaign, IL: Human Kinetics.

Solmon, M. A. (2006). Goal theory in physical education classes: Examining goal profiles to understand achievement motivation. *International Journal of Sport and Exercise Psychology*, *4*, 325–346.

Solmon, M. A., & Carter, J. A. (1995). Kindergarten and first grade students' perceptions of physical education in one teacher's classes. *Elementary School Journal*, *95*, 355–365.

Solmon, M. A., & Garn, A. C. (2014). Effective teaching in physical education: Using transportation metaphors to assess our status and drive our future. *Research Quarterly for Exercise and Sport, 85,* 20–26.

Solmon, M. A., & Lee, A. M. (2008). Research on social issues in elementary school physical education. *Elementary School Journal, 108,* 229–240.

Thomas, J. R., & French, K. (1985). Gender differences across age in motor performance: A meta-analysis. *Psychological Bulletin, 98,* 260–282.

U.S. Department of Health and Human Services. (1996). *Physical activity and health: A report of the surgeon general.* Atlanta: Centers for Disease Control and Prevention.

U.S. Department of Health and Human Services. (2000). *Healthy people 2010 (Conference Ed., in Two Vols.).* Washington, DC: U.S. Government Printing Office.

Vygotsky, L. S. (1978). *Mind in society: The development of higher psychological processes.* Cambridge: Harvard University Press.

Ward, P. (2013). The role of content knowledge in physical education. *Research Quarterly for Exercise and Sport, 48,* 431–440.

Wigfield, A., & Eccles, J. S. (1992). The development of achievement task values: A theoretical analysis. *Development Review, 12,* 256–310.

Xiang, P., McBride, R., Guan, J., & Solmon, M. A. (2003). Children's motivation in elementary physical education: An expectancy-value model of achievement choice. *Research Quarterly for Exercise and Sport, 74,* 25–35.

CHAPTER FIVE

Gendered-Peer Relationships in Educational Contexts

Carol Lynn Martin[1], Richard A. Fabes, Laura D. Hanish

Program in Family and Human Development, T. Denny Sanford School of Social and Family Dynamics, Arizona State University, Tempe, Arizona, USA
[1]Corresponding author: e-mail address: Carol.Martin@asu.edu

Contents

1. Introduction — 152
2. Children's Gender Segregation — 154
   2.1 Why Do Children Segregate by Gender? — 155
3. The Influence of Gendered-Peer Relationships on Children's Development — 159
   3.1 What Do Children Learn in Gender-Segregated Peer Groups? — 160
   3.2 Binary and Gradient Views of Gender Segregation — 161
4. Gender Segregation in School Environments — 165
   4.1 School Contexts and Teachers' Promotion of Gender Segregation — 166
   4.2 Gender-Segregated Schooling — 167
   4.3 Consequences of Gender-Segregated Schooling — 168
5. The Role of the Child in Selecting Gendered-Peer Environments — 170
   5.1 Children's Affective Attitudes — 171
   5.2 Children's Gender-Related Relationship Efficacy — 173
6. Implications of Gender Segregation for Aggressive and Cooperative Behaviors — 174
   6.1 Same- and Other-Sex Aggression — 175
   6.2 Benefits of Interacting with Other-Sex Peers on Aggressive and Competent Behaviors — 177
   6.3 Importance of Enhancing Gender Integrated Interactions at School — 179
7. Conclusions and Future Directions — 180
Acknowledgments — 181
References — 181

Abstract

The goals of this chapter are to discuss the theories and evidence concerning the roles of gendered-peer interactions and relationships in children's lives at school. We begin by discussing the tendency of boys and girls to separate into same-sex peer groups and consider the theories and evidence concerning how gender segregation occurs and how peers influence children's learning and development. We then turn to the important and understudied question of why some children have more exposure to same-sex peers than others. We consider factors that contribute to variability in children's experiences with gender segregation such as the types of schools children attend and the kinds of classroom experiences they have with teachers. Finally, we review new evidence concerning the cognitive and affective factors that illustrate that children are actively involved in constructing the social world that surrounds them.

1. INTRODUCTION

Considering children's lives at school, most of us envision children sitting at desks learning about history or biology, doing science experiments, or working to solve math problems. However, the reality is that school involves much more than solving academic challenges. Because schools bring together large numbers of similarly-aged children, they provide a provocative setting in which children face social challenges and rewards as they learn to negotiate and interact with peers. Grant (1985, as cited by Maccoby, 1998) noticed that peer interactions "constituted a quasi-autonomous component of classroom life not directly regulated (and sometimes not even fully observable) by teachers" (p. 70). Peer interactions and relationships may be largely unregulated, but they have enormous impact on whether students feel comfortable in school, are engaged in learning, and are successful in school (Betts, Rotenberg, Trueman, & Stiller, 2011; Ladd, 1990; Ladd & Coleman, 1997; Ladd, Kochenderfer, & Coleman, 1996; Ryan, 2001; Wentzel & Caldwell, 1997). However, peer relationships at school have received relatively little attention in school-related research.

Peer interactions at school may be either structured or unstructured. Because children's peer interactions in school are often child-initiated, they frequently occur during unstructured times, such as on the playground, in the lunchroom, or passing in the hallways. At other times, however, peer interactions are teacher-initiated, such as when teachers assign children to sit near particular peers in the classroom or place them into cooperative learning groups. Peer interactions may also be structured by the learning environment, for instance, by the policies of the schools that children attend. Regardless of whether peer interactions are child-initiated or structured within the educational system, the social interactions that occur among peers at school are strongly influenced by gender and these gendered-peer interactions and relationships at school have important consequences for children's social and academic functioning[1].

The goals of this chapter are to discuss the theories and evidence concerning the roles of gendered-peer interactions and relationships in children's lives at school. We begin with a description of the ubiquity and strength of gender segregation—the tendency of boys and girls to separate into same-sex peer groups—and consider the theories and evidence concerning how gender segregation occurs. We then discuss how the sex of peers may influence children's learning and development. After making the case that children's experiences in gender-segregated peer groups at school affect students' lives, we return to a further exploration of the important and understudied question of why some children have more exposure to same-sex peers than others. We consider several sources that relate to variability in children's experiences with gender segregation. The types of schools parents select for their children is one such source—if children attend gender-segregated schools or classes, their exposure to same-sex peers is high. However, even within mixed-sex schools, children vary in exposure to same-sex peers. Teachers' practices in the classroom can minimize or exaggerate gender segregation. In addition, to further explore variability in exposure, we review new evidence concerning the cognitive and affective factors that illustrate that children are actively involved in constructing the social world that surrounds them.

We next consider the role of gender in the dark side of peer relationships—aggression and victimization. Most research on aggression and victimization has focused on the predictors and consequences of these behaviors without considering the gendered nature of bullying and victimization. We explore the question of whether spending time with other-sex peers creates tensions in peer relationships. Finally, we review evidence and speculate on the importance and long-term consequences of children having exposure to and experiences with both girls and boys during school.

---

[1] A note about terminology. Although both "sex" and "gender" are terms commonly used to describe the social categories that include women/girls and men/boys, we also made a few distinctions in using these terms. First, we used "gender" when referring to "gender segregation" since that is most commonly used in the developmental science. Second, we also used "gender" to describe the theories about how children learn to use these social categories and when we intended to encompass the full range of effects that might include those associated with sex, gender-typed behavior/activities/interests/expression, sexual orientation, etc. Finally, we used the common convention of using "sex" when describing differences between the sexes and when referring to children's peers.

2. CHILDREN'S GENDER SEGREGATION

The tendency of children to segregate into same-sex peer groups is an almost universal feature of children's social play (Carter, 1987). Beginning around 30–36 months of age, children begin to show a strong preference for playing with peers of the same sex and this preference increases across childhood (Mehta & Strough, 2009). Given the ubiquity of gender segregation, it is not surprising that one of the most salient features of children's peer experiences at school (or elsewhere) is their tendency to spend time with same-sex peers. In some cases, gender segregation is enforced or encouraged by the school environment, for instance, in gender-segregated schools or classes, or in mixed-sex classes where teachers use practices that promote gender segregation. Classrooms that are segregated by gender, or teacher practices that segregate children (e.g., lining boys and girls separately, seating boys and girls separately, etc.) make the category of sex more salient, and this heightened salience promotes biased and gender-stereotyped perceptions and behaviors and increases children's tendencies to avoid other-sex children in free play (Hilliard & Liben, 2010).

The sex of peers that children spend time with (either by choice or school structure) has important ramifications on development, and these socialization experiences are different for girls and boys (Harris, 1995; Leaper, 1994; Maccoby, 1994, 1998). Maccoby (Maccoby, 1990, 1998; Maccoby & Jacklin, 1987) theorized that, due to the large amount of time that young children spend socializing with children of the same gender, same-sex peer contexts create two distinctive cultures for boys and girls, thus leading to qualitatively different impacts on their development. Experiences gained within boys' and girls' groups foster different behavioral norms and interaction styles, and, over time, these interactions may promote the development of different school-related skills, attitudes, motives, interests, and aspirations (Leaper, 1994; Maccoby, 1998). As such, same-sex peer groups represent a potentially powerful context for socialization (Serbin, Moller, Gulko, Powlishta, & Colburne, 1994), including school and academic socialization.

Despite its ubiquity, it is clear from empirical research that there is significant variability in how much exposure children have to same-sex peers (Maccoby & Jacklin, 1987). Importantly, these differences in exposure to same-sex peers relate to children's outcomes. Early research and theorizing assumed a threshold approach to influence, meaning that after having spent a certain amount of time with same-sex peers, children gained gender-related experiences and further exposure did not add incrementally to the effects of the threshold level of exposure. More recently, evidence and theorizing suggest a social dosage model, in which children with more exposure show more socialization from same-sex peers than do children with less exposure (Martin & Fabes, 2001).

2.1. Why Do Children Segregate by Gender?

Social psychological research has demonstrated that children show preferences for members of their own groups across many domains, including gender, race, nationality, and even novel groups (Bigler & Liben, 2006), and these preferences are considered normative by children (Diesendruck, Goldfein-Elbaz, Rhodes, Gelman, & Neumark, 2013; Martin, Fabes, Evans, & Wyman, 1999). Furthermore, there is social pressure to act in accord with one's group: children who do not conform to the social norms of the in-group are judged more harshly than children who do, and this is especially true for older children as compared to younger children (Abrams, Rutland, Cameron, & Marques, 2003). These group-based pressures certainly contribute to gender segregation but also specific theories have been put forth to explain why children prefer same-sex peers.

Several broad explanations have been offered to account for gender segregation (Martin, Fabes, & Hanish, 2011; Mehta & Strough, 2009). Some of the more recent explanations focus on the importance of children using the social categories of gender, whereas most of the historically popular explanations have focused on indirect causation, meaning that they invoke distal or indirect causes. For instance, evolutionary theorists suggest a distal cause, namely that children prepare for gender-typed adult roles through gender-segregated play early in life (Geary & Bjorklund, 2000; Pellegrini, 2004). Another common explanation involves indirect causation by arguing that children experience gender segregation because of sharing similar or compatible play styles with same-sex peers. Given the focus of recent research on the topic, we focus on shared interests and children's use of social categories as explanations of gender segregation.

2.1.1 Shared Interests and Compatibility

Theories that highlight the role of common interests and compatibility focus on the idea that gender segregation is a by-product of children's preferences to play with certain toys and activities. Children who share interests, activities, or compatible play styles are presumed to come into contact with like-minded peers, most likely same-sex peers, resulting in gender segregation (Baines & Blatchford, 2009; La Freniere, Strayer, & Gauthier, 1984; Moller & Serbin, 1996; Serbin et al., 1994). For instance, behavioral similarity would include young boys being drawn to interacting with other boys through shared interest in transportation toys and girls being drawn to interacting with girls through shared interest in playing house. Surprisingly, little research has tested these ideas (Serbin et al., 1994) and the extant evidence has been mixed (Hoffman & Powlishta, 2001) although a recent study found some support for shared interests drawing children together (Martin et al., 2013).

2.1.2 Social Cognitions About Gender

One area that has received little attention until recently is the idea that children's expectations about peers, that is, the *expected* similarity that children believe they share with same-sex peers contributes to gender segregation (Barbu, Le-Maner-Idrissi, & Jouanjean, 2000; Powlishta, 1995). This idea begins with children recognizing and acting upon the knowledge that some peers belong to the same social category as they do (McPherson, Smith-Lovin, & Cook, 2001). For instance, children may be biased in favor of in-group members as theories of social identity and intergroup relations suggest (Arthur, Bigler, Liben, Gelman, & Ruble, 2008; Bigler & Liben, 2006; Tajfel & Turner, 1979; Turner, Hogg, Oakes, Reicher, & Wetherell, 1987). Once children recognize who belongs to each gender category, according to gender schema theory, they are motivated to learn about the category of gender (especially their own gender), and they strive for consistency between their gender cognitions and behavior (Martin & Halverson, 1981). For instance, children want to be like their own gender group members, which leads them to choose to interact with same-sex peers (Martin, 1994). Empirical evidence supports this claim: a number of studies have demonstrated that children report that they would prefer to interact with even unfamiliar same-sex peers (Lobel, Gewirtz, Pras, Schoeshine-Rokach, & Ginton, 1999; Martin, 1989; Zucker, Wilson-Smith, Kurita, & Stern, 1995). Consistent with these approaches and with gender schema theory, we agree that the in-group versus out-group features associated with gender provide the initial and most basic form of expected similarity (Martin, 2000; Martin & Halverson, 1981), but we also believe that children abstract information about similarities and draw strong conclusions based on their beliefs about shared similarity within gender. That is, beyond simple category similarity, we argue that children develop global "gender theories" about same-sex peers—that they like the same activities and believe they are similar in other ways—and that is these theories that largely drive the appeal of same-sex playmates (Martin, 2000). These theories are also likely grounded in children's beliefs that there are "essences" that define social categories (Gelman & Taylor, 2000). The appeal of social cognitive gender theories is that they provide proximal explanations of gender segregation based on children's knowledge of peers' sex and the expectancies they hold about members of each sex.

2.1.3 An Expanded Explanation for Gender Segregation

The idea that children develop gender-based expectancies or theories was the basis for a newly proposed model for gender segregation (Martin, Fabes, Hanish, Leonard, & Dinella, 2011). In this comprehensive model, called the "Cognitive–Behavioral Similarity Model," both experienced and expected similarity are offered as explanations of gender segregation (see Figure 1). Children are assumed to hold expectancies about sharing similarities with same-sex peers but also they are assumed to be drawn to other children with similar interests, regardless of gender. Support for the model was found in that gender cognitions about perceived similarity related to partner choices for both preschool and kindergarten girls and boys and accounted for a significant amount of the variance in observed play partners even after behavioral similarity was included in the regression analyses.

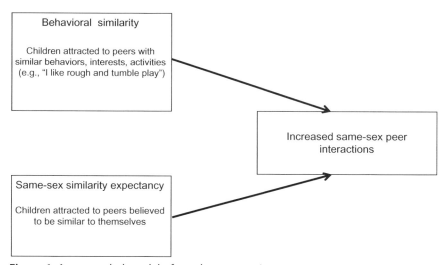

Figure 1 An expanded model of gender segregation.

Specifically, boys were found to prefer interacting with boys the more they liked rough-and-tumble play (behavioral similarity), but the degree to which they felt more similar to boys versus girls was also predictive even after accounting for their play-style preference. For girls, play-style preferences did not predict interacting with female peers (neither rough or tumble play or lack of interest in this) but the degree to which they perceived more similarity to girls relative to boys did predict their preferences for female peers as interactional partners.

2.1.4 Exploring Children's Gender-Based Peer Selection Using Social Networks Analyses

Additional support consistent with the idea that children's gender theories about peers influence their playmate choices comes from a study designed to explore how children select playmates and then how time spent with those playmates influences their gender-typed behavior (Martin et al., 2013). Most traditional analytic approaches do not provide ways to distinguish between how individuals select interactional partners and the potential influence that those partners have on one another. Furthermore, the data required to do this must be longitudinal. One new approach that has proved effective in separately assessing the effects of selection and influence in longitudinal data is a social network analytic method called SIENA—a stochastic actor-based models for network dynamics program (Snijders, 2001; Snijders, van de Bunt, & Steglich, 2010). We used SIENA to explore selection and influence effects in 292 preschool-age children based on observational data collected over a school year. From these observations, we were able to ascertain exactly which peers children interacted with, and then how they changed to become more or less similar to their friends over time.

Gender was found to have powerful effects, both directly and indirectly. We found that children selected playmates who were of the same sex and who had similar levels of gender-typed activities. These findings provide support that children select peer partners based on both expecting and experiencing similarities with same-sex peers. In-depth explorations of the contributors to gender segregation showed that the largest contributor was selection of peers based on their sex (57%), and much less was due to activity-based selection (13%) (see Figure 2). Although this study did not directly assess children's social cognitions about same- and other-sex peers, the large contribution of sex of peers to selection processes leaves open the possibility that either social category similarity or children's beliefs about those social categories greatly influences who they select as playmates.

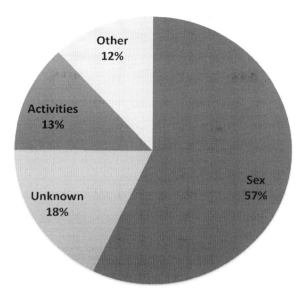

Figure 2 Decomposition of the factors accounting for gender segregation.

Given the recent empirical studies, it is evident that theories about gender segregation need to recognize that both experienced behavioral similarity and expected similarity are needed to more fully understand why children find same-sex peers more interesting and compatible than other-sex peers. Additionally, finding that so much of the variance in gender segregation is based simply on sex of peers strongly suggests that further research is needed to explore why the social categories of gender matter so much to children. This finding suggests that children hold strong beliefs and affective reactions related to same- and other-sex peers. Those beliefs and feelings may contribute to the individual variation that is apparent in gender segregation. After we consider how peers exert influence on children, we return to the discussion and review of recent studies that explore contributions to individual differences in gender segregation.

3. THE INFLUENCE OF GENDERED-PEER RELATIONSHIPS ON CHILDREN'S DEVELOPMENT

It has long been acknowledged that peers have both positive and negative influences on children's and adolescents' development (Berndt & Keefe, 1995; Brechwald & Prinstein, 2011; Dishion, Spracklen, Andrews, & Patterson, 1996; Rubin, Bukowski, & Parker, 2006). A rich history of research has been conducted on this topic, especially concerning the role of peers as socializers of adolescents' negative behaviors, such as smoking, delinquency, and drug use, and this focus is understandable given the implications of these behaviors for well-being (for review, see Brechwald & Prinstein, 2011). Much less research has been conducted on peer influences in younger children, presumably because most often researchers considered that peers were less able to influence younger children. Over the past decade or two, that picture has changed. We now know that even young children are influenced by their peers and that this influence may be positive (Fabes, Hanish, Martin, Moss, & Reesing, 2012) or negative (Hanish, Martin, Fabes, Leonard, & Herzog, 2005). Furthermore, more attention has been focused on peer influences within a school setting such that it is clear that attitudes toward school and academic success are influenced by peers (Berndt & Keefe, 1995; Kindermann, 1993).

A significant and still-evolving topic is the role of gender in peer influence. Given the large amounts of time spent with same-sex peers, the experiences that children have in these same-sex peer groups likely have a major impact on their development (Harris, 1995; Leaper, 1994; Maccoby, 1988, 1998). Although there is much speculation about the importance of the different peer subcultures of girls and boys, evidence supporting the links between early same-sex peer experiences and behavior has been limited (albeit supportive). The research that is needed to answer questions about gendered-peer effects on behavior is difficult to conduct, largely due to the need for direct observations of children's behavior and due to the difficulties of analyzing complex relationship data. Nonetheless, there is compelling evidence that peer interactions influence children's behavior in several domains (Fabes, Hanish, Martin, Reesing, & Moss, 2012; Martin & Fabes, 2001).

Two issues are at the forefront of understanding gendered-peer influence. One issue concerns the content of what children learn from same- versus other-sex peers or from mixed-sex groups of peers. The second issue concerns the amount of exposure to peers that is required for children to be influenced by them. Thus far, most of the theorizing and evidence concerns what children learn from same-sex peers and how much interaction is required to learn from same-sex peers.

3.1. What Do Children Learn in Gender-Segregated Peer Groups?

Theorizing about what children learn from peers has involved the reasonable assumption that powerful socializing effects of same-sex peers result from the ubiquity of gender-segregated groups. Given that boys and girls behave differently (especially in groups) (Maccoby, 1991) and appear to encourage different skills and interaction styles (Leaper, 1994; Rose & Rudolph, 2006), it is not surprising that theorists assume that socialization occurs in these groups, with boys and girls essentially growing up in different cultures. As a result, children would be expected to learn culture-specific norms, behaviors, and styles of interaction of their group, which in turn would make them increasingly comfortable in same-sex peer groups (Leaper, 1994; Maccoby, 1994, 1998). This is thought to create a gender-segregation cycle (Fabes, Martin, Hanish, Galligan, & Pahlke, 2013) in which same-sex behaviors, attitudes, and cognitions become socialized as children spend time with same-sex peers, increasing their comfort with and influence over same-sex peers, which in turn promotes in children stronger preferences for same-sex peers in the future.

Because same-sex experiences are common in school settings, we can envision an expansion of the gender-segregation cycle, one that includes longer-term outcomes in the school setting (see Figure 3). Specifically, as children become increasingly comfortable with same-sex peers and have more positive attitudes about same-sex peers than about other-sex peers, they may balk at working with other-sex peers and create a context for poor interactions in mixed-sex groups. In turn, this could influence teachers' willingness to assign children to work in mixed-sex work groups. As children have fewer mixed-sex experiences within their classrooms, the likelihood of changing attitudes toward other-sex peers may become even more challenging, adding further impetus to maintaining or increasing same-sex experiences in the class. Although some of these ideas are speculative, the long-term consequences of high levels of exposure to same-sex peers and low levels of exposure to other-sex peers or to mixed-sex groups may be a poor and unsupportive classroom climate (since half the children may not interact much or know much about one another), reduced effectiveness of group interactions and problem solving, and lowered academic success for children.

3.2. Binary and Gradient Views of Gender Segregation

The second issue concerns how gender segregation influences children. Specifically, we address how much time children need to have with same-sex peers to be socialized by them. Some controversy has surrounded this issue of how gender-segregated peer interactions and relationships

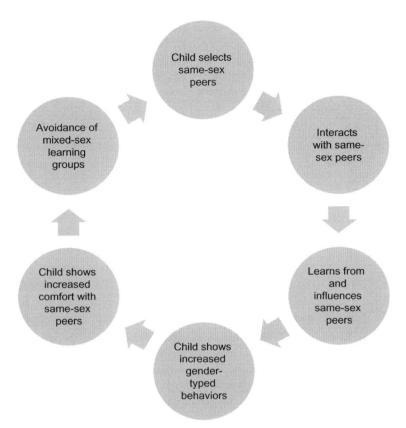

Figure 3 The gender-segregation cycle in a school context.

influence children. Early theorizing was based on the idea that a low-level exposure was all that was needed to learn from same-sex peers but later research suggested that the variations in children's exposure also contributed to peer socialization.

The leading conceptual view concerning how playing with girls or playing with boys influences children's development has been a *binary view* of socialization (Maccoby, 1998). Based on her early research on children's same-sex play-partner choices and the seeming instability in these choices, Maccoby (1998) proposed the idea that each sex is socialized by same-sex peers and only a low threshold of exposure is needed to learn the interaction patterns and behaviors associated with one's own-sex group. To illustrate, the threshold idea would suggest that most girls will learn about "girl culture" because of much of their social time with girls, and whether they spend 80% or only 30% of their time with girls, they will be socialized in similar ways. It follows that the socialization experiences children have with same-sex peers would be relatively uniform across all members of the group. This view can be interpreted as deemphasizing individual differences and emphasizing the binary nature of the groups—differences between the sexes. According to such a view, only a relatively small amount of exposure to one's same-sex peer group is considered necessary for children to learn the norms and styles of one's own-sex group.

Although the binary perspective accurately reflected the available data from earlier research (Maccoby & Jacklin, 1987), the sample upon which it was based was relatively small. Furthermore, the observations of the children used to assess play-partner choices were constrained to occur over a few days, which may not have been long enough to discern stable individual differences. In a more recent study that included a larger sample of children and obtained observations over months instead of days, individual differences became much more evident, causing Martin and Fabes (2001) to modify Maccoby's conclusions about the influence of gendered peers. Rather than emphasizing a binary or threshold perspective, we proposed that some threshold is likely to be evident for influence to occur (that is, there are binary effects), but even more importantly, the "social dosage" of same-sex peers that children are exposed to will influence their socialization experiences. Martin and Fabes (2001) found that boys who played more frequently with boys during the fall term of preschool were observed in the spring term showing higher levels of activity, rough-and-tumble play, playing apart from adults, and gender-typed play (e.g., activities, etc.). In contrast, girls who played more with other girls during the fall term of preschool were observed in the spring term showing higher levels of playing near adults and gender-typed play. Additionally, in the social network study described above (Martin et al., 2013), we found that not only did children select same-sex playmates, but also they were influenced over time to become more like their friends in their gender-typed interests and activities. These studies support a *gradient view* and reflect the idea that the more exposure a child has to same-sex peers, the more the child will be socialization by these experiences. Thus, in addition to binary effects, *gradient effects*—individual differences in same-sex peer exposure—need to be considered.

To depict the binary and gradient perspectives on influence, we used data from a longitudinal study of early school readiness. These data were based on observations taken during the fall semester for 308 Head Start children (over 3 years in 3 separate cohorts from 18 classrooms; 163 boys;

$M_{age}=51.73$ months at start of fall). Repeated 10-s observations ($M=131$ per child) of the children during their free play were conducted (Martin et al., 2013). During these observations, every time a child was observed playing with a peer, the sex of the peer was recorded. The proportions of social interactions that each child had with male and female peers were then calculated based on each child's total number of social interactions observed (to account for differences due to absences and availability).

For both boys and girls, over 85% of their observed interactions involved playing with same-sex peers. This strong tendency of children to play with same-sex peers reflects gender segregation and supports the view that children tend to grow in separate peer cultures—boys playing with boys and girls playing with girls. Moreover, these data support a "two worlds" conceptualization of gender socialization and reflects the binary view discussed above.

In Figure 4, we graphically represent the results of the observational data as an index of the relative proportion of time children were observed to spend playing with girls minus the proportion of time they were observed to play with boys. Positive scores reflect more time spent playing with girls and negative scores reflect more time spent playing with boys. A score of zero reflects a balance of the two. These data are presented in a histogram in which every child's data point is plotted within the histogram. Boys are color coded as white and girls are color coded as black.

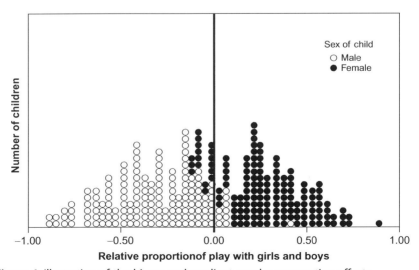

Figure 4 Illustration of the binary and gradient gender-segregation effects.

Inspection of Figure 4 provides evidence for both the binary and gradient views. If one looks to the right and left of the dark vertical line drawn at zero on the horizontal axis, it is clear that the dominant color to the right of the line is black and the dominant color to the left of the line is white. Although there are some outliers, these are essentially nonoverlapping distributions for boys and girls. Thus, the division on either side of the drawn line reflects the binary nature of the separate gender worlds/cultures of boys' and girls' peer preferences and interactions.

Importantly, however, Figure 4 also depicts the gradient view. If one looks to the right or left of the drawn line, it is also clear that there is variability in the degree to which boys and girls play with same-sex peers. This variability is considerable and findings from several studies suggest that it is meaningful and predictive (Fabes, Martin, Hanish, Anders, & Madden-Derdich, 2003; Martin & Fabes, 2001). Thus, the degree to which children spend time in same-sex groups matters and the effects of this exposure is "dosage-dependent."

In summary, gender segregation is a pervasive and powerful social phenomenon. Children learn about the "culture" of their gender group from spending time with same-sex peers: that is, they learn how members of their sex communicate, they activities they like, and the ways they behave. Importantly, there appears to be a cycle or feedback loop in that as children learn about same-sex culture, their comfort with same-sex peers increases, and their tendencies to seek out others of their same sex also increase. This gender-segregation cycle leads to increased divisions and separation between girls and boys and may lead to disharmony in and out of the classroom. However, the degree to which children are impacted by their gendered peers depends greatly on their level of exposure to same-sex peers. As noted in Figure 4, although almost all children show same-sex peer preferences, there is significant variation in this across children and this variation is impactful. Children vary in exposure to same-sex environments for many reasons, but gender-segregated effects can be greatly enhanced by structural features of schools. We now turn to a discussion of this controversial element of children's schooling.

4. GENDER SEGREGATION IN SCHOOL ENVIRONMENTS

The theories and research discussed thus far have emphasized a broad understanding of gender segregation. In this section, we review two topics: how school contexts and teachers promote or hinder gender segregation in their classes and the provocative topic of gender-segregated schools and classes. These environments structure and can institutionalize the segregation of boys and girls and provide further evidence of power of gendered-peer socialization. For this reason, it is important to critically examine what is known about the consequences associated with these structured approaches to gender segregation.

4.1. School Contexts and Teachers' Promotion of Gender Segregation

When left to their own, children tend to show same-sex peer preferences, but these preferences also can be shaped by the environments they are in, by the feedback their receive for their preferences, and by practices that teachers use to promote or hinder gender segregation. For instance, especially for younger children, teachers often structure the play areas in the classroom, which may promote increased gender segregation as boys and girls might be drawn to different tables/areas. In one of the earliest studies of how teachers influence interactions of children in the classroom, Serbin and colleagues conducted an experiment in which they asked teachers to make a point of verbally acknowledging when children interacted with other-sex peers (Serbin, Tonick, & Sternglanz, 1977). The results showed that simple acknowledgments increased the likelihood of cross-sex play, but when these rewards were ended, cross-sex play reverted to the original levels seen before the study had begun. Nonetheless, these findings provide the first experimental evidence that teachers' behavior can have dramatic impact on children's peer preferences.

In a more recent study, Hilliard and Liben (2010) tested the hypothesis that teachers would impact peer preferences by their making gender salient in the classroom (e.g., separating classroom activities according to gender, lining up children by gender) (also see Bigler, 1995). In preschool classrooms, teachers either made gender salient or not for a 2-week period. Children in the high gender salience classrooms showed stronger stereotypes, less positive ratings of other-sex children, and were observed having fewer interactions with other-sex peers compared to children in the low salience classrooms. These results are significant because they demonstrate that teachers play an important role in gender segregation: when teachers make gender salient in their classes, it has a pervasive and powerful influence on children's classroom behavior (Bigler, 1995).

To better understand the role of teachers on children's peer preferences, it is important to explore how frequently they make gender salient in their classes and how often they engage in practices that might promote gender integration rather than segregation. Some studies report that teachers frequently use gender labels in their classes (Lloyd & Duveen, 1992). In a more recent study of over 500 Pre-K, second, and fifth grades teachers, teachers reported using moderate levels of practices that draw attention to gender and that they seldom used practices that promoted gender integration (Farago, Kornienko, Martin, Granger, & Santos, 2014, under review). Furthermore, holding strong stereotypes about gender differences was related to teachers' use of gender in the classroom, suggesting that their practices are directly influenced by the beliefs they hold about girls and boys.

School contexts play important roles in how children think about and interact with their peers. Teachers and other educators need to be mindful of using gender terms when talking to students and to recognize how easily children detect the functional use of gender in classes so these practices can be minimized or avoided. Practices that promote gender integration also should be beneficial for undermining or at least not exacerbating children's stereotypes and behavior.

4.2. Gender-Segregated Schooling

Nowhere is the issue of gender-segregated peer relationships in educational contexts more salient than in the current controversy surrounding gender-segregated public schooling (Halpern et al., 2011, 2012). Although private gender-segregated schools have been available to parents and students for some time, public gender-segregated classes and schools are relatively new. In 2006, the U.S. Congress made changes to the No Child Left Behind Act that eased restrictions on gender-segregated education in public schools and approved federal funding for innovative education programs, including gender-segregated programs within existing coeducational schools. Public school officials across the country have responded by increasingly implementing gender-segregated educational programs. By some accounts, there are now more than 1000 schools in the United States experimenting with gender-segregated schooling (Klein, 2012). Moreover, a growing industry has developed around gender-segregated education driven by those who promote and market a gender-essentialist view that boys and girls differ so fundamentally in brain functioning, competitiveness, activity level, cognitive processing, etc., that they cannot effectively be taught in the same classroom (Gurian, Henley, & Trueman, 2001; Sax, 2005). Gender-segregated classrooms have also been hailed as a way to help address the distractions that the other sex presents, as well as an innovative way to address the crisis related to boys not succeeding in U.S. schools (Kafer, 2007). Additionally, some feminists have touted gender-segregated classrooms as a way to reduce genderism in coeducational classrooms and increase interest and performance in academic subjects that are not stereotypical for one's sex (Bigler & Eliot, 2011). A detailed analysis and evaluation of the varied rationales for public single-sex schooling is provided by Bigler, Hayes, and Liben (2014) [Chapter 7 of this volume].

4.3. Consequences of Gender-Segregated Schooling

The scientific evidence, however, does not support this growing movement. In fact, every major review has concluded that gender-segregated K-12 schooling is not superior to coeducational schooling (Bigler et al., 2014 [Chapter 7 of this volume]; Halpern et al., 2011; Pahlke, Hyde, & Mertz, 2013). After accounting for differences in the qualities of the children who attend gender-segregated schools, the resources and novelty of gender-segregated programs, and methodological and analytical problems, the positive outcomes of gender-segregated schooling disappear (Bigler et al., 2014 [Chapter 7 of this volume]; Halpern et al., 2011; Hayes, Pahlke, & Bigler, 2011; Jackson, 2012). Moreover, in a large-scale study of first-graders, multilevel analyses revealed that *both* boys and girls performed better in reading, had greater self-control and interpersonal skills, and had lower internalizing problems when there was a higher percentage of girls in the classroom (Pahlke, Cooper, & Fabes, 2013). Given the growing concern related to the relatively lower levels of educational performance and achievement by American boys, educational decisions that segregate boys and girls in classrooms are a source of concern.

Proponents of gender-segregated schooling also view such schooling as a means to address sex differences in learning and behavior (Chadwell, 2010; James, 2007, 2009). To the contrary however, reviews of neuroscience and the available data directly contradict such claims and reveal that these claims are based on faulty science and promote stereotyped and essentialist view of males and females (Eliot, 2013; Halpern et al., 2011). In fact, evidence suggests that gender segregation actually increases sex differences rather than reducing and addressing them, and this is the case even if it occurs within coed settings. For example, Galligan, Fabes, Martin, and Hanish (2011) examined sex differences in the play qualities of young girls and boys when playing in gender-integrated versus gender-segregated contexts. In general, the findings revealed that sex differences in children's behaviors were found primarily when children were playing with same-sex rather than with other-sex peers. Boys, for instance, were found to be more aggressive than girls but only when they were playing with other boys. When girls and boys played in gender-integrated playgroups, no sex differences in aggression were found. Moreover, gender-typed activity play (e.g., girls playing with feminine toys and boys playing with masculine toys) was greater in gender-segregated than gender-integrated playgroups. Although these data did not directly compare gender-segregated versus gender-integrated schooling and were conducted within coeducational settings, the findings support the notion that sex differences tend to be accentuated in gender-segregated interactions (Maccoby, 1998) and raise doubts about the claims that gender-segregated schooling can reduce sex differences in learning and behavior.

Moreover, gender-segregated contexts and preferences appear to be related to increases in sexism, rather than the decreases proposed by advocated of gender-segregated schooling. In a recent study, the association between gender-segregated peer preferences and sexism in adolescents was examined (Keener, Mehta, & Strough, 2013). A complex pattern was found but generally speaking, sexism was associated with increased gender-segregated preferences. For example, for boys, the stronger their gender-segregated peer preferences, the greater were their scores on a scale measuring Antagonism Toward Women's Demands. For girls, the stronger their gender-segregated peer preferences, the more likely they were to deny that discrimination against women continues to exist. Such findings suggest that gender segregation is related to sexism toward women and raises doubts that gender-segregated schooling is a way to address such prejudice. In fact, it is by bringing boys and girls together—rather than separating them—that sexist attitudes may be reduced (see Bigler et al., 2014 [Chapter 7 of this volume]; Leaper & Brown, 2014 [Chapter 6 of this volume]). Meta-analytic research confirms a highly robust negative correlation between contact and prejudice (Pettigrew & Tropp, 2006), and such findings are directly relevant to gender-segregated schooling where boys and girls are separated from each other.

The fact that these studies find such effects of gender segregation in coeducational settings suggests that any context that increases the salience of gender magnifies differences between and stereotypes about girls and boys (Fabes, Martin, Hanish, Galligan, & Pahlke, 2013). Thus, we are especially likely to see such effects in schools that institutionally segregate boys and girls, particularly when one considers the dosage effects found in the Martin and Fabes (2001) study. Importantly, the limited evidence suggests that this is the case for gender-segregated schooling. For example, Fabes and colleagues (Fabes, Pahlke, Martin, & Hanish, 2013) found that being in gender-segregated classes was related to junior high school students' greater gender-stereotypic beliefs. Boys and girls who were enrolled in gender-segregated classes showed a 14% increase in the odds of responding in a stereotypic manner for each gender-segregated class a student took. Thus, for example, if a student was enrolled in the maximum of eight gender-segregated classes, there was a 112% increase of the odds of responding in a stereotypic manner relative to a student enrolled in only coeducational classes. Because initial levels of gender-stereotypic beliefs were controlled, the findings suggest that gender-segregated classes increased later stereotypic beliefs and that the *more* time spent in gender-segregated classes, the *more* stereotyped students became beyond their initial tendencies to respond stereotypically in the fall (i.e., supporting a gradient view). That this happened in a relatively short period of time (from fall to spring) highlights the potency of sex segregation and parallels findings about the power of peer socialization of gender typing with younger children (Martin & Fabes, 2001). These results add to the growing body of evidence raising concerns about educational policy decisions related to the use of gender-segregated classrooms and suggest that gender-segregated schooling is not an answer to any of the problems or issues faced in contemporary educational settings. (The use of single-sex schools to address the unique educational challenges faced by African American boys is addressed by Barbarin, Chinn, & Wright, 2014 [Chapter 10 of this volume]). In fact, as noted in a study of principals of coeducational and gender-segregated schools (Fabes, Pahlke, Galligan, & Borders, 2014), although some problems or issues were perceived to be addressed by gender-segregated programs, other problems and issues were perceived to arise. The comments we received from principals add further evidence to the conclusion that separating boys and girls in schools is not a panacea for any problems facing the education of our children and youth and may simply trade one set of perceived problems for another.

5. THE ROLE OF THE CHILD IN SELECTING GENDERED-PEER ENVIRONMENTS

In addition to structured impositions of gender-segregated classes or schools, and teachers who promote gender segregation in their classes by their assignments, seating, and use of gender to manage the classroom (Hilliard & Liben, 2010), children also play a role in selecting with whom they spend time in school through their expectancies about same- and other-sex peers as we discussed above. Because of the potential for social cognitive and affective factors to explain how gender segregation occurs and to explain how different children vary in their exposure to same-sex peers, we have focused our recent research on exploring these factors. The overarching goal is to advance our knowledge of children's active role in gender segregation. In this section, we review several studies that we have done to explore both cognitive and affective attitudes in explaining variations in children's exposure to same-sex and other-sex peers.

5.1. Children's Affective Attitudes

Even by preschool, children report feeling more positively about same-sex peers (Yee & Brown, 1994), and these reactions continue throughout the time they are in school (Heyman, 2001). At a group level, these affective reactions to same- and other-sex peers may fuel gender segregation by either causing children to approach same-sex peers because they like them more than other-sex peers, or they may avoid other-sex peers because they dislike them, or they may experience both the pull toward same-sex peers and the avoidance of other-sex peers. A related idea is that children might fear being teased for interacting with other-sex peers, and this could be based on norm violations (Abrams, Rutland, Cameron, & Ferrell, 2007) or might include heterosexual teasing ("he's your boyfriend") (Maccoby, 1998). At an individual level, children who show more positive affect toward same-sex peers or more negative affect toward other-sex peers would be more likely to spend time with children of their own gender, thereby increasing the group level of gender segregation.

Previous research on children's affective reactions to peers has been limited and has often confounded liking of own-sex peers with disliking of other-sex peers; that is, scales have been used in which the response options do not separate these two affective reactions (e.g., Powlishta, 1995; Yee & Brown, 1994). For instance, if a girl indicates that she likes other girls more than boys, she could mean that she like girls a lot and boys less so, which would indicate an in-group positivity bias. Or, she could mean that she likes girls and dislike boys, which would indicate an in-group positivity bias and derogation of the out-group. Until recently, confounding of these has left an important question unanswered: whether gender segregation reflects children's dislike of other-sex peers.

In recent research (Zosuls et al., 2011), we addressed this question in a sample of 98 fifth-grade children. An important methodological feature of the study was the use of separate positivity and negativity scales (on a 1-to-3 point scale). Both girls and boys showed high levels of liking for same-sex peers (2.71 and 2.60, respectively), and these liking scores were significantly higher than liking for other-sex peers (1.75 and 1.74, respectively). Interestingly, children did not give significantly higher negative affective ratings to other-sex peers ($M_{girls}=1.29$, $M_{boys}=0.81$) than to own-sex peers ($M_{girls}=1.14$, $M_{boys}=0.73$), although girls gave higher negative affective ratings than did boys to peers of both genders. For both girls and boys, the negative responses were relatively low on the scale, suggesting that there is little negativity toward peers of either gender. To further explore whether liking might influence gender segregation, we (Zosuls et al., 2011) tested whether positive affective attitudes toward one's own sex were related to holding more positive expectancies about interactions with same-sex peers, and these relations were supported for both sexes. Interestingly, children with positive affective attitudes toward the other sex also showed more positive expectancies about other-sex peers. Negative affective attitudes negatively predicted expectancies about same- and other-sex peers but accounted for less of the variance than did positive attitudes.

In this study, we also explored whether teasing or discomfort with the other sex related to expectancies about inclusion in other-sex groups and found that these two measures were negatively correlated, and the same was true for the negative relation between teasing and discomfort with one's own group and feelings of inclusion to same-sex groups. These findings suggest that feelings of discomfort or fear of teasing may play some role in gender segregation but that the same feelings relate to same-sex interactions.

Overall, when children hold positive feelings toward a group, they may be more likely to develop positive expectancies about interacting with members of that group, which should lead to increased interactions. Negative feelings appear to play less of a role in pushing children away from the other sex (also see Bukowski, Gauze, Hoza, & Newcomb, 1993; Sippola, Bukowski, & Noll, 1997). Although children's gender-related attitudes are not very negative, these attitudes are consequential and related to their reported expectancies about peers. Thus, a source of variability in children's gender-based relationships is their affective attitudes toward members of same- and other-sex peers, with positive affective attitudes appearing to play a stronger role than negative affective attitudes. An implication of these findings is that children may also develop positive feelings toward the out-group, which should enhance their potential for other-sex interactions, while possibly not affecting their level of interaction with same-sex peers. Further studies of these individual differences should be conducted to better understand how affective attitudes contribute to children's peer preferences and gender segregation.

5.2. Children's Gender-Related Relationship Efficacy

Recently, we introduced a new gender-related construct that we believe is a key component in understanding children's gender segregation and variations in gendered-peer preferences (Zosuls, Field, Martin, Andrews, & England, 2014). The new construct is called gender-based relationship efficacy (GBRE), which refers to beliefs about one's abilities to relate to own- and other-sex peers; this includes understanding, communicating with, and engaging in activities with peers. Based on the idea that self-perceptions of social competence are sensitive to the gender-related context of social interactions, we proposed that efficacy in relationships must be assessed separately for own- and other-sex peers. If children spend much of their time in gender-segregated groups, for instance, they are likely to develop more comfort and knowledge about the interactions styles of same-sex peers, and that may lead to greater efficacy with them but may not contribute to developing efficacy with other-sex peers. For this reason, we developed GBRE-Own (gender) and GBRE-Other (gender) as separate scales and have conducted several studies using these scales.

In the first set of studies conducted with GBRE scales, we conducted a factor analyses on data from both fourth graders ($n=403$) and seventh and eighth graders ($n=453$) and confirmed that the scales were distinguishable. More importantly, children at all ages felt higher efficacy in interacting with own-sex peers than with other-sex peers. Furthermore, in a second study, we found that the gender-based efficacy measures were predictive of children's beliefs and social behavior, and these patterns were gender sensitive. Specifically, in a sample of fourth-grade children, higher GBRE-Own positively related to feeling included by *own-sex* peers ($r=0.47$, $p<0.001$) and to having *own-sex* friendships ($r=0.37$, $p<0.001$) but did not relate to other-sex inclusion or friendships. Higher scores on GBRE-Other were also related to feeling included by *other-sex* peers ($r=0.63$, $p<0.001$) and to having *other-sex* friendships ($r=0.53$, $p<0.001$) but did not predict inclusion or friendship with own-sex peers. That is, the findings suggest that using more nuanced and specific gender-based efficacy measures was necessary to detect patterns of beliefs and relationships with each sex.

These results suggest that children who feel efficacious for own- and/or other-sex peer relationships are more likely to expect to be included by those peers and to make friends with them. That is, one source of variation in gender segregation and preference for same-sex peers revolves around social cognitive beliefs about feeling efficacious in those relationships. Children who feel more efficacious with same-sex peers will likely spend more time with in gender-segregated groups, thereby further increasing their feelings of efficacy and comfort with same-sex peers. However, children may also develop a sense of efficacy with other-sex peers, increasing their preferences for interactions with them, and conversely, as children spend more time with other-sex peers, they are likely to improve their sense of relationship efficacy with the other gender.

Children play an active role in constructing their gendered or nongendered social worlds. Many children develop strong positive feelings about their own gender, feel more efficacious with them, and may find the appeal of same-sex interactions to be strong because of feeling more comfortable and knowledgeable about the norms and culture of that group. Such feelings may contribute to children's interest in pursuing sex-typed academic and occupational interests (see Butler, 2014 [Chapter 1 of this volume]; Liben & Coyle, 2014 [Chapter 3 of this volume]; Petersen & Hyde, 2014 [Chapter 2 of this volume]). Other children may develop strong positive feelings about both sexes, feel efficacious with both sexes, and find themselves feeling comfortable and knowledgeable about both gendered cultures of childhood. These individual variations are significant in that determine the nature of children's gendered or less gendered-peer socialization contexts and effects of those contexts. Moreover, these variations also contribute to the quality of peer interactions, a topic we now turn to.

6. IMPLICATIONS OF GENDER SEGREGATION FOR AGGRESSIVE AND COOPERATIVE BEHAVIORS

Because gender-segregated interactions provide children with greater comfort and experience with same-sex peers, and because children hold gendered attitudes and beliefs that they will prefer interacting with same-sex peers, one might hypothesize that this translates to behavioral features of their peer interactions. In other words, perhaps spending time with members of the other sex creates tensions or conflicts that result in increased aggression, whereas spending time with members of the same sex creates social harmony. In particular, the potential for aversive and victimizing interactions among and between girls and boys is a concern and we now consider the role that gender–peer interactions might play in these.

6.1. Same- and Other-Sex Aggression

A number of observational studies of preschoolers have considered whether rates of same- and other-sex aggression differ (Crick et al., 2006; DiDonato et al., 2012; Hanish, Sallquist, DiDonato, Fabes, & Martin, 2012; Ostrov, 2006; Ostrov & Keating, 2004; Pellegrini, Long, Roseth, Bohn, & Van Ryzin, 2007; Pellegrini, Roseth, et al., 2007). These studies provide no evidence that other-sex aggression occurs more frequently than same-sex aggression. Instead, they suggest that, if anything, same-sex aggression is somewhat more likely than other-sex aggression. For instance, Pellegrini, Roseth, and colleagues (2007) reported that same-sex aggression occurred more frequently than other-sex aggression for both girls and boys. Crick et al. (2006) found that girls were more likely to direct relational aggression to other girls and that boys were more likely to direct physical aggression to other boys. But, there was no same-sex preference for boys' use of relational aggression or for girls' use of physical aggression—boys directed relational aggression to male and female peers at similar rates and girls directed physical aggression to male and female peers at similar rates.

In another study, Ostrov (2006) reported a same-sex preference for girls' use of relational aggression, boys' use of relational aggression, and boys' use of physical aggression, but not for girls' use of physical aggression. However, in each of these studies, the extent of gender segregation was not controlled. This raises the possibility that the apparent preference for aggressing against same-sex peers is simply due to availability of targets and the fact that children tend to spend more time around same-sex peers than around other-sex peers. Once the sex of peers was taken into account, the same-sex bias for aggression among preschoolers was weaker. Yet, there is still no evidence for an other-sex bias in the targeting of young children's aggression. For instance, Ostrov and Keating (2004) covaried time spent with male and female peers and found that preschool boys and girls were similar in directing relational and verbal aggression to both male and female peers, but they differed in that boys directed more physical aggression to male than to female peers, whereas girls directed physical aggression to males and females equally. Similarly, Hanish et al. (2012) reported that rates of same- and other-sex aggression were similar once time spent with male and female peers was controlled.

Based on the findings from young children, it appears that interacting with same-sex peers does not necessarily lead to more social harmony, nor does interacting with other-sex peers lead to social discord. Are these conclusions also warranted for older children and adolescents? Fewer studies are available examining the gendered targeting of aggression at older ages. One study revealed that boys were more likely to direct aggression to other boys than they were to direct aggression to girls across the transition to middle school (Pellegrini & Long, 2002). Yet, in several other studies, findings suggested that same- and other-sex aggression occur at similar rates. When other-sex aggression was reported among young adolescents, it tended to be greater for boys' aggression toward girls than for girls' aggression toward boys (Berger & Rodkin, 2009; Olweus, 1993; Veenstra et al., 2007).

Taken together, the studies cited above provide no evidence that other-sex aggression is more common than same-sex aggression, suggesting instead that rates of same- and other-sex aggression are relatively similar (or possibly with a slight preference for same-sex aggression). Nevertheless, there is evidence to suggest that the reasons underlying why aggression occurs depend on whether the aggression is directed to same- or other-sex peers. Why might this be? According to sexual selection theory, same-sex aggression is stimulated by intrasexual competition for status or resources (Geary, Byrd-Craven, Hoard, Vigil, & Numtee, 2003; Hawley, Little, & Card, 2007; Pellegrini, 2008). There is evidence to support this assumption in that indicators of social or interpersonal dominance (or attempts at dominance) are predictive of same-sex aggression. For instance, Hanish et al. (2012) observed preschoolers' peer interactions and coded the behaviors that directly preceded an aggressive response by a same- or other-sex peer. Dominance-related behaviors, such as those that involved attempts for control via aggression or commands, were predictive of both girls' and boys' same-sex aggression. Additionally, in a study of peer-nominated adolescent aggressor–victim dyads, Rodkin and Berger (2008) found that that aggressors were more popular (i.e., more socially dominant) than their same-sex victims. Yet, dominance-related factors appear to be less strongly related to the occurrence of other-sex aggression. In the Hanish et al. study, dominance-related factors accounted for less of the variance in other-sex aggression than in same-sex aggression, this was particularly true for girls' aggression toward boys. In the Rodkin and Berger study, dyads in which girls were aggressive to boys were not studied. But, there was no evidence that boys who aggressed against girls were more popular than their female victims. In fact, the reverse was true; in this case, the female victims were more popular than the male aggressors. These findings hint that there are variations in the correlates and predictors of same- and other-sex aggression that need to be considered, and future research is needed to continue to address this issue.

6.2. Benefits of Interacting with Other-Sex Peers on Aggressive and Competent Behaviors

The studies cited above addressed questions of similarities and differences in same- and other-sex aggression. In another line of research, we see evidence to suggest that interactions with other-sex peers actually have the potential to minimize the likelihood of aggressive, harassing, and exclusionary behaviors. For instance, evidence suggests that, in early childhood, mixed-sex play, or play in which children interact with both boys and girls simultaneously, is related to more harmonious and less harmful peer interactions. For instance, one study of young children showed that those with other-sex friends were more sociable and more likely to express positive affect in the classroom than those without other-sex friends (Howes, 1988). Relatedly, another study of young children showed that playing in mixed-sex groups was related to lower rates of being victimized by peers, particularly for those young children who are most at risk for victimization (Andrews, Hanish, Fabes, & Martin, 2014). Research on adolescents supports a similar conclusion—when gender-integrated interactions within a school were relatively more frequent, overall levels of aggression were diminished (Faris & Felmee, 2011).

Findings from a quasi-experimental study with preschoolers support the same interpretation (Martin et al., 2012). The quasi-experimental study involved a test of the "Buddy-Up" component of the Sanford Harmony Program—a peer relationship intervention program (www.sanfordharmonyprogram.org) (and see below for more information). The overarching goal of the Sanford Harmony Program is to provide teachers with the tools and resources to build positive, supportive relationships among girls and boys in their classrooms. Preschool teachers in the "Buddy-Up" intervention condition "buddied up" girls and boys each week by assigning them to dyads with an other-sex peer. "Buddy" dyads participated in everyday collaborative activities several times over the course of the week (e.g., contributing jointly to a drawing, blowing bubbles together, tossing balls to one another). "Buddies" were rotated each week to allow students the opportunity to interact with multiple other-sex peers. Teachers in the control condition conducted the classroom as usual. Controlling for initial levels, analyses of teachers' ratings of children's behaviors at outcome revealed significant decreases in aggression toward both male and female peers, less exclusion of both male and female peers, and less gender-related harassment for children who had been buddied with other-sex peers as compared to those in the control condition. Thus, spending time with other-sex peers appears to lead to positive social outcomes.

The degree to which children feel comfortable with classmates in school is a known factor in their academic performance and engagement in learning (Ladd & Coleman, 1997). Interestingly, little attention has been paid to whether children's gender-related peer experiences relate to their comfort in the classroom. Just as one could hypothesize that aggression and negative feelings would result from children crossing gender lines, it is equally plausible that children who have more experiences with other-sex peers and who have more feelings of efficacy in dealing with other-sex peers might have a stronger sense of classroom community than do other children. Another possibility is that because children spend so much time in gender-segregated groups, their sense of classroom community is determined by their efficacy with same-sex peers and that other-sex peers play little or no role in feeling comfortable in school. To explore these ideas, we conducted analyses of how several gender-specific social cognitive constructs relate to comfort in school. In the same study that provided data about GBRE, we collected data from children in second and fourth grades ($n=409$) in which we asked them to report on their relationships with same- and other-sex peers. We also assessed their sense of classroom community. A positive sense of classroom community was related to many of the social cognitive factors. High own-sex relationship efficacy, high other-sex relationship efficacy, stronger inclusion expectancies for own-sex peers, and stronger inclusion expectancies for other-sex peers related to higher levels of classroom community (all $ps<0.001$). We also considered the nature of children's experiences with same- and other-sex peers by exploring their perceived stressors associated with each sex. Not surprisingly, reporting fewer stressors related to own- and other-sex interactions also related to having a higher sense of classroom community. Therefore, even if children spent more time with same-sex peers, their feelings of comfort in school were related to the experiences they had and the beliefs they held about both same- and other-sex peers.

Rather than creating a stage upon which aggression is encouraged to erupt, the set of findings cited above indicates that when children have interactions with other-sex peers, these interactions appear to provide some protection from aggression and promote a greater sense of classroom community. Furthermore, we propose a broad range of benefits for having gender-diverse peer experiences. Specifically, as children gain greater comfort and experience with other-sex peers, their social skills and competencies for playing and working with a wide array of peers increase, thereby benefitting interactions with both male and female peers. Few studies have examined this directly. However, there is some empirical support for our proposition. For instance, playing with the other sex peers, whether in other-sex (with other-sex peers only) or mixed-sex (with both same- and other-sex peers) configurations, provides children with unique opportunities that are less available when playing alone or with same-sex peers. During other- and mixed-sex play, for example, children are more likely to engage in gender neutral or cross-gender activities (Fabes, Martin, Hanish, Anders, et al., 2003), thereby expanding their opportunities to learn new skills. Moreover, other- and mixed-sex interactions tend to occur in closer proximity to teachers than do same-sex interactions, resulting in increased opportunities for adult support and guidance (Fabes, Martin, & Hanish, 2003; Goble, Martin, Hanish, & Fabes, 2012). Such opportunities can be beneficial for children. In support of this idea, DiDonato et al. (2012) found that preschool girls' flexibility in gendered interactional styles, as indicated by their ability to engage with both male and female peers and in both masculine-typed and feminine-typed activities, was negatively correlated with aggression and positively correlated with social competence, positive emotion, and adaptability.

6.3. Importance of Enhancing Gender Integrated Interactions at School

As we have discussed, gender influences a wide array of aspects of children's social lives, including with whom children spend their time, the attitudes, beliefs, and expectancies that they hold about interacting with same- and other-sex peers, and the nature and quality of their interactions with same- and other-sex peers. From an educational perspective, variations in girls' and boys' same- and other-sex relationships are meaningful because the nature and quality of children's peer interactions impact the overall classroom climate, student's engagement and participation in learning activities, and achievement. When peer interactions are positive and supportive such that they promote social bonds, learning is enhanced; when they are harmful, exclusionary and socially distancing, learning is diminished (Wilson, Karimpour, & Rodkin, 2011). For these reasons, it is important that efforts be made to build strong, positive relationships among girls and boys at school.

The Sanford Harmony Program is a school-based, teacher-led curriculum for the early childhood and elementary grades that does just that. The proximal goal of the Sanford Harmony Program is to support the development of healthy relationship skills and positive interactions among girls and boys at school (Martin et al., 2012). Unique features of the Sanford

Harmony Program include relationship-building lessons to support children's skill development and simple suggestions for providing children with practice opportunities to develop positive peer interactions that can be easily integrated into the existing curriculum. We previously reported on our initial test of the "Buddy-Up" component of the Sanford Harmony Program. Here, we report on an initial test of the efficacy of the relationship-building lessons and demonstrate their relevance to fifth graders' overall classroom experience. In this quasi-experimental study, teachers in the intervention classrooms provided a series of relationship-building lessons to children over a 5-month period. Lessons covered a range of topics that are relevant to building understanding, respect, and support within and across sexes. These topics consist of diversity and inclusiveness, stereotyping and critical thinking, communication, building positive peer relationships, and problem solving. Lessons involved opportunities to learn and practice relationship-building skills via engaging games and activities. Students in the intervention classrooms, relative to students in the control classrooms, reported greater classroom climate and connection to school at posttest (controlling for initial levels). Moreover, this effect was mediated by an increase in positive peer interactions in intervention classrooms. Classroom climate is central to engagement and participation in school and a precursor to learning and achievement (Wilson et al., 2011). The results of this study highlight the benefits of building a strong social environment among girls and boys.

7. CONCLUSIONS AND FUTURE DIRECTIONS

The social ecology for children at school is full of challenges. These challenges include negotiating the different social cultures of girls and boys, learning the norms that are inherent in these cultures, and in some cases breaking free of any restraints associated with the these norms. School is gendered for children, and the gendered nature of schooling is due to both the imposed structuring of gender relations, such as when classes or schools are constrained to be for only one sex, and children's own choices of play partners. Children tend to select playmates that they believe are the same as they are, enjoy the same activities, or have the same behavioral styles as they do. Selecting and spending time with same-sex peers increase the likelihood of future choices being influenced by the sex of peers. In this way, a gender-segregation cycle develops. More time spent in these gender-segregated interactions leads to the potential for more peer influence to occur. Recent advancements in knowledge about peer influence suggest that the social dosage of same-sex peers relates to how much socialization is likely to occur. For that reason, new studies have begun to focus more attention on the social cognitive and affective factors that direct children toward same-sex interactions, and on the factors that might also draw children toward other-sex peers.

The influence of peers extends to both positive and negative behaviors, and questions have arisen about how gendered-peer groups might promote or minimize aggression and cooperative behaviors among children. Several intriguing studies provide support for the contention that gender-segregated peer interactions may be less beneficial for development than having more diverse peer experiences in which children learn about, become comfortable with, and enjoy interacting with members of both sexes. The data suggest that efforts to institutionalize or structure gender-segregated interactions and schools make gender salient, increase gender-stereotyped behavior and attitudes, and contribute to problematic interactions and behaviors between girls and boys. Future research studies need to be devoted to exploring how to enhance and promote a wider range of peer experiences to enrich children's time at school, at home, and in their future lives.

ACKNOWLEDGMENTS

Several of the research studies that are discussed in this chapter were supported in part by funds provided by the T. Denny Sanford School of Social and Family Dynamics as part of the Lives of Girls and Boys Research Enterprise (http://livesofgirlsandboys.org/). The Sanford Harmony Program (http://sanfordharmonyprogram.org/) was supported by funds from T. Denny Sanford. We thank the teachers, parents, and children who have been involved in our research and in the Sanford Harmony Program. We also thank the graduate and undergraduate students who have worked on the research and on the Sanford Harmony Program.

REFERENCES

Abrams, D., Rutland, A., Cameron, L., & Ferrell, J. (2007). Older but wilier: In-group accountability and the development of subjective group dynamics. *Developmental Psychology, 43*, 134–148.

Abrams, D., Rutland, A., Cameron, L., & Marques, J. M. (2003). The development of subjective group dynamics: When in-group bias gets specific. *British Journal of Developmental Psychology, 21*, 155–176.

Andrews, N. C. Z., Hanish, L. D., Fabes, R. A., & Martin, C. L. (2014). With whom and where you play: Preschoolers' social context predicts peer victimization. *Social Development, 23*(2), 357–375.

Arthur, A. E., Bigler, R. S., Liben, L. S., Gelman, S. A., & Ruble, D. N. (2008). Gender stereotyping and prejudice: A developmental intergroup perspective. In S. Levy, & M. Killen (Eds.), *Intergroup attitudes and relations in childhood through adulthood* (pp. 66–86). New York: Oxford University Press.

Baines, E., & Blatchford, P. (2009). Sex differences in the structure and stability of children's playground social networks and their overlap with friendship relations. *British Journal of Developmental Psychology, 27*, 743–760.

Barbarin, O. A., Chinn, L., & Wright, Y. F. (2014). Creating developmentally auspiciousschool environments for African American boys. In L. S. Liben, & R. S. Bigler (Vol. Eds.), *The role of gender in educational contexts and outcomes*. In J. B. Benson (Series Ed.), *Advances in child development and behavior: Vol. 47* (pp. 333–365). London: Elsevier.

Barbu, S., Le-Maner-Idrissi, G., & Jouanjean, A. (2000). The emergence of gender segregation: Towards an integrative perspective. *Current Psychology Letters: Behavior, Brain, and Cognition, 3*, 7–18.

Berger, C., & Rodkin, P. C. (2009). Male and female victims of male bullies: Social status differences by gender and informant source. *Sex Roles, 61*, 72–84.

Berndt, T. J., & Keefe, K. (1995). Friends' influence on adolescents' adjustment to school. *Child Development, 66*, 1312–1329.

Betts, L. R., Rotenberg, K. J., Trueman, M., & Stiller, J. (2011). Examining the components of children's peer liking as antecedents of school adjustment. *British Journal of Developmental Psychology, 30*, 303–325.

Bigler, R. S. (1995). The role of classification skill in moderating environmental effects on children's gender stereotyping: A study of the functional use of gender in the classroom. *Child Development, 66*, 1072–1087.

Bigler, R. S., & Eliot, L. (2011). The feminist case against single-sex schools. *Slate*. Retrieved from Slate website: http://www.slate.com/articles/double_x/doublex/2011/10/the_single_sex_school_myth_an_overwhelming_body_of_research_show.2.html.

Bigler, R. S., Hayes, A. R., & Liben L. S. (2014). Analysis and evaluation of the rationales for single-sex schooling. In L. S. Liben, & R. S. Bigler (Vol. Eds.), *The role of gender in educational contexts and outcomes*. In J. B. Benson (Series Ed.), *Advances in child development and behavior: Vol. 47* (pp. 225–260). London: Elsevier.

Bigler, R. S., & Liben, L. S. (2006). A developmental intergroup theory of social stereotypes and prejudice. In R. V. Kail (Ed.), *Advances in child development and behavior: Vol. 34*. (pp. 39–89). San Diego: Elsevier.

Brechwald, W. A., & Prinstein, M. J. (2011). Beyond homophily: A decade of advances in understanding peer influence processes. *Journal of Research on Adolescence, 21*, 166–179.

Bukowski, W. M., Gauze, C., Hoza, B., & Newcomb, A. F. (1993). Differences and consistency between same-sex and other-sex peer relationships during early adolescence. *Developmental Psychology, 29*, 255–263.

Butler, R. (2014). Motivation in educational contexts: Does gender matter? In L. S. Liben, & R. S. Bigler (Vol. Eds.), *The role of gender in educational contexts and outcomes*. In J. B. Benson (Series Ed.), *Advances in child development and behavior: Vol. 47* (pp. 1–41). London: Elsevier.

Carter, D. B. (1987). The roles of peers in sex role socialization. In D. B. Carter (Ed.), *Current conception of sex roles and sex typing* (pp. 101–121). New York: Praeger.

Chadwell, D. W. (2010). *A gendered choice: Designing and implementing single-sex programs and schools*. Thousand Oaks, CA: Corwin.

Crick, N. R., Ostrov, J. M., Burr, J. E., Cullerton-Sen, C., Jansen-Yeh, E., & Ralston, P. (2006). A longitudinal study of relational and physical aggression in preschool. *Journal of Applied Developmental Psychology, 27*, 254–268.

DiDonato, M. D., Martin, C. L., Hessler, E. E., Amazeen, P. G., Hanish, L. D., & Fabes, R. A. (2012). Gender consistency and flexibility: Using dynamics to understand the relation between gender and adjustment. *Nonlinear dynamics, Psychology, and Life Sciences, 16*, 159–184.

Diesendruck, G., Goldfein-Elbaz, R., Rhodes, M., Gelman, S. A., & Neumark, N. (2013). Cross-cultural differences in children's beliefs about the objectivity of social categories. *Child Development, 84*, 1906–1917.

Dishion, T. J., Spracklen, K. M., Andrews, D. W., & Patterson, G. R. (1996). Deviancy training in male adolescent friendships. *Behavior Therapy, 27*, 373–390.

Eliot, L. (2013). Single-sex education and the brain. *Sex Roles, 69*, 363–381.

Fabes, R. A., Hanish, L. D., Martin, C. L., Moss, A., & Reesing, A. (2012). The effects of young children's affiliations with prosocial peers on subsequent emotionality in peer interactions. *British Journal of Developmental Psychology, 30*, 569–585.

Fabes, R. A., Hanish, L. D., Martin, C. L., Reesing, A., & Moss, A. (2012). The effects of young children's affiliations with prosocial peers on subsequent emotionality in social interactions. *British Journal of Developmental Psychology, 30*, 569–585.

Fabes, R. A., Martin, C. L., & Hanish, L. D. (2003). Young children's play qualities in same-, other-, and mixed-sex peer groups. *Child Development, 74*, 921–932.

Fabes, R. A., Martin, C. L., Hanish, L. D., Anders, Mary C., & Madden-Derdich, Debra A. (2003). Early school competence: The roles of sex-segregated play and effortful control. *Developmental Psychology, 39*(5), 848–858.

Fabes, R. A., Martin, C. L., Hanish, L. D., Galligan, K., & Pahlke, E. (2013). Gender segregated schooling: A problem disguised as a solution. *Educational Policy, 26*, 1–17.

Fabes, R. A., Pahlke, E., Martin, C. L., & Hanish, L. D. (2013). Gender-segregated schooling and gender stereotyping. *Educational Studies, 39*, 315–319.

Fabes, R. A., Pahlke, E., Galligan, K., & Borders, A. (2014). U.S. Principals' attitudes about and experiences with single-sex schooling. Manuscript submitted for publication.

Farago, F., Kornienko, O., Martin, C. L., Granger, K. L., & Santos, C. E. (2014). *Teachers' gender-role attitudes, gender stereotypes, and gendered classroom practices*. Arizona State University, Tempe, Arizona.

Faris, R., & Felmee, D. (2011). Status struggles: Network centrality and gender segregation in same- and cross-gender aggression. *American Sociological Review, 76*, 48–73.

Galligan, K. M., Fabes, R. A., Martin, C. L., & Hanish, L. D. (2011). *Gender differences in young children's play qualities in gender-segregated and gender-integrated peer interactions*. Paper presented at the biennial meeting of the Society for Research in Child Development, Montreal, Quebec, Canada.

Geary, D. C., & Bjorklund, D. F. (2000). Evolutionary developmental psychology. *Child Development, 71*, 57–65.

Geary, D. C., Byrd-Craven, J., Hoard, M. K., Vigil, J., & Numtee, C. (2003). Evolution and development of boys' social behavior. *Developmental Review, 23*, 444–470.

Gelman, S. A., & Taylor, M. G. (2000). Gender essentialism in cognitive development. In P. H. Miller, & E. Kofsky Scholnick (Eds.), *Toward a feminist developmental psychology* (pp. 169–190). Florence, KY: Taylor & Frances.

Goble, P., Martin, C. L., Hanish, L. D., & Fabes, R. A. (2012). Children's gender-typed activity choices across social contexts. *Sex Roles, 67*, 435–451.

Gurian, M., Henley, P., & Trueman, T. (2001). *Boys and girls learn differently!: A guide for teachers and parents*. New York, NY: Jossey-Bass.

Halpern, D. F., Eliot, L., Bigler, R. S., Fabes, R. A., Hanish, L. D., Hyde, J., et al. (2011). The pseudoscience of single-sex schooling. *Science, 333*, 1706–1707.

Halpern, D. F., Eliot, L., Bigler, R. S., Fabes, R. A., Hanish, L. D., Hyde, J., et al. (2012). Response: The pseudoscience of single-sex schooling. *Science, 335*, 166–168.

Hanish, L. D., Martin, C. L., Fabes, R. A., Leonard, S., & Herzog, M. (2005). Exposure to externalizing peers in early childhood: Homophily and peer contagion processes. *Journal of Abnormal Child Psychology, 33*(3), 267–281.

Hanish, L. D., Sallquist, J., DiDonato, M., Fabes, R. A., & Martin, C. L. (2012). Aggression by whom–aggression toward whom: Behavioral predictors of same- and other-gender aggression in early childhood. *Developmental Psychology, 48*, 1450–1462.

Harris, J. R. (1995). Where is the child's environment? A group socialization theory of development. *Psychological Review, 102*, 458–489.

Hawley, P. H., Little, T. D., & Card, N. A. (2007). The allure of a mean friend: Relationship quality and processes of aggressive adolescents with prosocial skills. *International Journal of Behavioral Development, 31*, 170–180.

Hayes, A. R., Pahlke, E., & Bigler, R. S. (2011). The efficacy of single-sex education: Testing for selection and peer quality effects. *Sex Roles, 65*, 693–703.

Heyman, G. D. (2001). Children's interpretation of ambiguous behavior: Evidence for a "boys are bad" bias. *Social Development, 10*, 230–247.

Hilliard, L. J., & Liben, L. S. (2010). Differing levels of gender salience in preschool classrooms: Effects on children's gender attitudes and intergroup bias. *Child Development, 81*, 1787–1798.

Hoffman, M. L., & Powlishta, K. K. (2001). Gender segregation in childhood: A test of the interaction style theory. *Journal of Genetic Psychology, 162*(3), 298–313.

Howes, C. (1988). Same- and cross-sex friends: implications for interaction and social skills. *Early Childhood Research Quarterly, 3*, 21–37.

Jackson, C. K. (2012). Single-sex schools, student achievement, and course selection: Evidence from rule-based student assignments in Trinidad and Tobago. *Journal of Public Economics, 96*(1–2), 173–187.

James, A. N. (2007). *Teaching the male brain: How boys think, feel, and learn in school*. Thousand Oaks, CA: Corwin.

James, A. N. (2009). *Teaching the female brain: How girls learn science and math*. Thousand Oaks, CA: Corwin.

Kafer, K. (2007). *Taking the boy crisis in education seriously: How school choice can boost achievement among boys and girls* (Position Paper No. 604). Washington, DC: Independent Women's Forum. Retrieved from www.iwf.org/files/49ba4dcb1f95dacf6d20aa721e429c88.pdf.

Keener, E., Mehta, C., & Strough, J. (2013). Should educators and parents encourage other-gender interactions? Gender segregation and sexism. *Gender and Education, 25*, 818–833.

Kindermann, T. A. (1993). Natural peer groups as contexts for individual development: The case of children's motivation in school. *Developmental Psychology, 29*, 970–977.

Klein, S. (2012). *State of public school sex segregation in the United States 2007–2010*. Retrieved from http://feminist.org/education/pdfs/sex_segregation_study_part1.pdf.

Ladd, G. W. (1990). Having friends, keeping friends, making friends, and being liked by peers in the classroom: Predictors of children's early school adjustment? *Child Development, 61*, 1081–1100.

Ladd, G. W., & Coleman, C. C. (1997). Children's classroom peer relationships and early school attitudes: Concurrent and longitudinal associations. *Early Education and Development*, (8), 51–66.

Ladd, G. W., Kochenderfer, B. J., & Coleman, C. C. (1996). Friendship quality as a predictor of young children's early school adjustment. *Child Development, 67*, 1103–1118.

La Freniere, P., Strayer, F. F., & Gauthier, R. (1984). The emergence of same-sex affiliative preferences among preschool peers: A developmental/ethological perspective. *Child Development, 55*, 1958–1965.

Leaper, C. (1994). Exploring the consequences of gender segregation on social relationships. In C. Leaper (Ed.), *Childhood gender segregation: causes and consequences* (pp. 67–86). San Francisco: Jossey-Bass.

Leaper, C., & Brown, C. S. (2014). Sexism in schools. In L. S. Liben, & R. S. Bigler (Vol. Eds.), *The role of gender in educational contexts and outcomes*. In J. B. Benson (Series Ed.), *Advances in child development and behavior: Vol. 47* (pp. 189–223). London: Elsevier.

Liben, L. S., & Coyle, E. F. (2014). Developmental interventions to address the STEM gender gap: Exploring intended and unintended consequences. In L. S. Liben, & R. S. Bigler (Vol. Eds.), *The role of gender in educational contexts and outcomes*.

In J. B. Benson (Series Ed.), *Advances in child development and behavior: Vol. 47* (pp. 77–116). London: Elsevier.

Lloyd, B., & Duveen, G. (1992). *Gender identities and education: the impact of starting school.* New York: St. Martin's Press.

Lobel, T. E., Gewirtz, J., Pras, R., Schoeshine-Rokach, M., & Ginton, R. (1999). Preadolescents' social judgments: The relationship between self-endorsements of traits and gender-related judgments of female peers. *Sex Roles, 40*(5/6), 483–498.

Maccoby, E. E. (1988). Gender as a social category. *Developmental Psychology, 24*(6), 755–765.

Maccoby, E. E. (1990). Gender and relationships: A developmental account. *American Psychologist, 45*(4), 513–520.

Maccoby, E. E. (1991). Gender and relationships: A reprise. *American Psychologist, 46*(5), 538–539.

Maccoby, E. E. (1994). Commentary: gender segregation in childhood. In C. Leaper (Ed.), *Childhood gender segregation: causes and consequences: Vol. 65.* (pp. 87–97). San Francisco: Jossey-Bass.

Maccoby, E. E. (1998). *The two sexes: Growing up apart, coming together.* Cambridge, MA: Belknap Press.

Maccoby, E. E., & Jacklin, C. N. (1987). Gender segregation in childhood. In W. R. Hayne (Ed.), *Advances in child development and behavior: Vol. 20.* (pp. 239–287). Orlando, FL: Academic Press, Inc.

Martin, C. L. (1989). Children's use of gender-related information in making social judgments. *Developmental Psychology, 25*(1), 80–88.

Martin, C. L. (1994). Cognitive influences on the development and maintenance of gender segregation. In C. Leaper (Ed.), *Childhood gender segregation: Causes and consequences. New directions for child development, No. 65* (pp. 35–51). San Francisco, CA: Jossey-Bass Inc, Publishers.

Martin, C. L. (2000). Cognitive theories of gender development. In T. Eckes, & H. M. Trautner (Eds.), *The developmental social psychology of gender* (pp. 91–121). Mahwah, NJ: Erlbaum.

Martin, C. L., & Fabes, R. A. (2001). The stability and consequences of young children's same-sex peer interactions. *Developmental Psychology, 37,* 431–446.

Martin, C. L., Fabes, R. A., Evans, S. M., & Wyman, H. (1999). Social cognition on the playground: children's beliefs about playing with girls versus boys and their relations to sex segregated play. *Journal of Social and Personal Relationships, 16,* 751–771.

Martin, C. L., Fabes, R. A., & Hanish, L. D. (2011). Gender and temperament in young children's social play. In A. D. Pellegrini (Ed.), *Handbook of play* (pp. 14–230). Oxford: Oxford University Press.

Martin, C. L., Fabes, R. A., Hanish, L. D., Leonard, S., & Dinella, L. (2011). Experienced and expected similarity to same-gender peers: Moving toward a comprehensive model of gender segregation. *Sex Roles, 65,* 826–842.

Martin, C. L., Fabes, R. A., Hanish, L., Updegraff, K., Miller, C., Gaertner, B., et al. (2012). *The Sanford Harmony Program: Program description and preliminary findings.* Paper presented at the Gender Development Research Conference, San Francisco, CA.

Martin, C. L., & Halverson, C. F. (1981). A schematic processing model of sex typing and stereotyping in children. *Child Development, 52,* 1119–1134.

Martin, C. L., Kornienko, O., Schaefer, D. R., Hanish, L. D., Fabes, R. A., & Goble, P. M. (2013). The role of sex of peers and gender-typed activities in young children's peer affiliative networks: A longitudinal analysis of selection and influence. *Child Development, 84,* 921–937.

McPherson, M., Smith-Lovin, L., & Cook, J. M. (2001). Birds of a feather: Homophily in social networks. *Annual Review of Sociology, 27,* 415–444.

Mehta, C. M., & Strough, J. (2009). Sex segregation in friendships and normative contexts across the life span. *Developmental Review, 29,* 201–220.

Moller, L. C., & Serbin, L. A. (1996). Antecedents of toddler gender segregation: Cognitive consonance, gender-typed toy preferences and behavioral compatibility. *Sex Roles, 35,* 445–460.

Olweus, D. (1993). *Bullying at school.* Oxford: Blackwell.

Ostrov, J. M. (2006). Deception and subtypes of aggression during early childhood. *Journal of Experimental Child Psychology, 93,* 322–336.

Ostrov, J. M., & Keating, C. F. (2004). Gender differences in preschool aggression during free play and structured interactions: An observational study. *Social Development, 13,* 255–277.

Pahlke, E., Cooper, C. E., & Fabes, R. A. (2013). Classroom sex composition and first-grade school outcomes: The role of classroom behavior. *Social Science Research, 42,* 1650–1658.

Pahlke, E., Hyde, J. S., & Mertz, J. E. (2013). The effects of single-sex compared with coeducational schooling on mathematics and science achievement: Data from Korea. *Journal of Educational Psychology, 105*(2), 444–452.

Pellegrini, A. D. (2004). Sexual segregation in childhood: Review of evidence for two hypotheses. *Animal Behavior, 68,* 435–443.

Pellegrini, A. D. (2008). The roles of aggressive and affiliative behaviors in resources control: A behavioral ecological perspective. *Developmental Review, 28,* 461–487.

Pellegrini, A. D., & Long, J. D. (2002). A longitudinal study of bullying, dominance, and victimization during the transition from primary school through secondary school. *British Journal of Developmental Psychology, 20,* 259–280.

Pellegrini, A. D., Long, J. D., Roseth, C. J., Bohn, C. M., & Van Ryzin, M. (2007). A short-term longitudinal study of preschoolers' *(Homo sapiens)* sex segregation: The role of physical activity, sex, and time. *Journal of Comparative Psychology, 121*(3), 282–289.

Pellegrini, A. D., Roseth, C. J., Mliner, S., Bohn, C. M., Van Ryzin, M., Vance, N., et al. (2007). Social dominance in preschool classrooms. *Journal of Comparative Psychology, 121,* 54–64.

Petersen, J., & Hyde, J. S. (2014). Gender-related academic and occupational interests and goals. In L. S. Liben, & R. S. Bigler (Vol. Eds.), *The role of gender in educational contexts and outcomes.* In J. B. Benson (Series Ed.), *Advances in child development and behavior: Vol. 47* (pp. 43–76). London: Elsevier.

Pettigrew, T. F., & Tropp, L. R. (2006). A meta-analytic test of intergroup contact theory. *Journal of Personality and Social Psychology, 90,* 751–783.

Powlishta, K. K. (1995). Intergroup process in childhood: Social categorization and sex role development. *Developmental Psychology, 31,* 781–788.

Rodkin, P. C., & Berger, C. (2008). Who bullies whom? Social status asymmetries by victim gender. *International Journal of Behavioral Development, 32,* 473–485.

Rose, A. J., & Rudolph, K. D. (2006). A review of sex differences in peer relationship processes: Potential trade-offs for the emotional and behavioral development of girls and boys. *Psychological Bulletin, 132,* 98–131.

Rubin, K. H., Bukowski, W. M., & Parker, J. G. (2006). Peer interactions, relationships, and groups. In N. Eisenberg (Ed.), *Handbook of child psychology: Vol. 3.* (pp. 517–645). New York: Wiley.

Ryan, A. M. (2001). The peer group as a context for the development of young adolescent motivation and achievement. *Child Development, 72,* 1135–1150.

Sax, L. (2005). *Why gender matters: What parents and teachers need to know about the emerging science of sex differences.* New York, NY: Doubleday.

Serbin, L. A., Moller, L. C., Gulko, J., Powlishta, K. K., & Colburne, K. A. (1994). The emergence of gender segregation in toddler playgroups. In C. Leaper (Ed.), *Childhood gender segregation: Causes and consequences. New directions for child development, No. 65* (pp. 7–17). San Francisco, CA: Jossey-Bass Inc, Publishers.

Serbin, L. A., Tonick, I. J., & Sternglanz, S. H. (1977). Shaping cooperative cross-sex play. *Child Development, 48,* 924–929.

Sippola, L. K., Bukowski, W. M., & Noll, R. B. (1997). Dimensions of liking and disliking underlying the same-sex preference in childhood and early adolescence. *Merrill Palmer Quarterly, 43,* 591–609.

Snijders, T. A. B. (2001). The statistical evaluation of social network dynamics. In M. Sobel, & M. Becker (Eds.), *Sociological methodology* (pp. 361–395). Boston/London: Basil Blackwell.

Snijders, T. A. B., van de Bunt, G., & Steglich, C. E. G. (2010). Introduction to stochastic actor-based models for network dynamics. *Social Networks, 32*(1), 44–60.

Tajfel, H., & Turner, J. C. (1979). An integrative theory of intergroup conflict. In W. G. Austin, & S. Worchel (Eds.), *The social psychology of intergroup relations.* Brooks/Cole: Monterey, CA.

Turner, J. C., Hogg, M. A., Oakes, P. J., Reicher, S. D., & Wetherell, M. S. (1987). *Rediscovering the social group: A self-categorization theory.* Oxford, England: Basil Blackwell.

Veenstra, R., Lindenberg, S., Zijlstra, B. J. H., De Winter, A. F., Verhulst, F. C., & Ormel, J. (2007). The dyadic nature of bullying and victimization: Testing a dual-perspective theory. *Child Development, 78,* 1843–1854.

Wentzel, K. R., & Caldwell, K. (1997). Friendships, peer acceptance, and group membership: Relations to academic achievement in middle school. *Child Development, 68,* 1198–1209.

Wilson, T., Karimpour, R., & Rodkin, P. C. (2011). African American and European American students' peer groups during early adolescence: Structure, status, and academic achievement. *Journal of Early Adolescence, 31,* 74–98.

Yee, M., & Brown, R. (1994). The development of gender differentiation in young children. *British Journal of Social Psychology, 33,* 183–196.

Zosuls, K. M., Martin, C. L., Ruble, D. N., Miller, C., Gaertner, B. M., & England, D. E. (2011). "It's not that we hate you": Understanding children's gender attitudes and expectancies about peer relationships. *British Journal of Developmental Psychology, 29,* 288–304.

Zosuls, K. M., Field, R. D., Martin, C. L., Andrews, N. C. Z., & England, D. E. (2014). Gender-based relationship efficacy: Children's self-perceptions in intergroup contexts. *Child Development, 85,* 1663–1676.

Zucker, K. J., Wilson-Smith, D. N., Kurita, J. A., & Stern, A. (1995). Children's appraisals of sex-typed behavior in their peers. *Sex Roles, 33*(11–12), 703–725.

CHAPTER SIX

Sexism in Schools

Campbell Leaper[*,1], Christia Spears Brown[†]
[*]Department of Psychology, University of California, Santa Cruz, California, USA
[†]Department of Psychology, University of Kentucky, Lexington, Kentucky, USA
[1]Corresponding author: e-mail address: cam@ucsc.edu

Contents

1. Overview of Types of Sexism	190
2. Perpetrators of Sexism	192
2.1 Teachers	193
2.2 Peers	194
2.3 Parents	195
2.4 Media	196
3. Gender Biases in School Achievement	197
3.1 Biases Against Girls in STEM	197
3.2 Biases Against Girls in Sports	200
3.3 Biases Against Boys in School Achievement	201
4. Sexual Harassment in School	202
4.1 Prevalence of Sexual Harassment in School Settings	203
4.2 Consequences of Sexual Harassment	204
5. Awareness of Sexism and Coping	204
5.1 Awareness of Sexism	205
5.2 Coping with Sexism	208
6. Reducing Sexism in Schools	209
6.1 Single-Gender Versus Coeducational Schools' Debate	210
6.2 Interventions	211
6.3 School Climate	213
7. Conclusions	213
References	214

Abstract

Sexism is gender-based prejudice or discrimination. As with other forms of prejudice and discrimination, it functions to maintain status and power differences between groups in society. One manifestation of sexism involves prejudice and discrimination against girls and women who seek to achieve in prestigious fields traditionally associated with males. Another manifestation of sexism, however, occurs when pressures are placed on boys and men to conform to traditional conceptions of masculinity. Over the last two decades, an increasing number of developmental and educational psychologists have become concerned about sexism directed toward children and adolescents in school contexts. Our chapter reviews the research on this topic. After providing an overview of different processes related to sexism, we examine how it is manifested in school contexts. Sexism is seen through gender-stereotyped biases against girls and boys in academic and athletic achievement. Also, it occurs through sexual harassment in social interactions. We also address factors related to children's awareness of sexism and coping responses to sexism. Finally, we consider possible ways to reduce sexism and foster effective coping in schools.

1. OVERVIEW OF TYPES OF SEXISM

The constructs known as stereotypes, attitudes, prejudice, and discrimination are interrelated. The term stereotypes refers to particular attributes believed to characterize a group (e.g., "Girls play with dolls"). The term attitudes refers to the positive or negative emotional associations between particular attributes and groups. More specifically, a proscriptive attitude refers to an attribute that the perceiver believes a group should exhibit (e.g., "Girls should play with dolls"); whereas a prescriptive attitude refers to an attribute that the perceiver considers that members of a group should avoid (e.g., "Boys should not play with dolls"). Prejudice occurs when the perceiver evaluates other persons based on their own stereotypes and attitudes (e.g., negative perception of boys who play with dolls). Discrimination is the behavioral expression of prejudice (e.g., bullying a boy who plays with dolls). When prejudice and discrimination are based on a person's gender, it constitutes sexism. Analogous bias against sexual minorities is known as heterosexism.

There are two distinct, but related, types of sexism. According to Glick and Fiske's (1996) ambivalent sexism model, gender-based prejudice is ambivalent because there are asymmetries in status and power between men and women, yet there is male–female interdependence within families and heterosexual relationships. In the model, sexism can include both hostile and benevolent types. Hostile sexism refers to negative attitudes toward individuals who violate traditional gender stereotypes. For example, as in the previous example, teasing a boy who plays with dolls is an expression of hostile sexism. In contrast, benevolent sexism includes protective paternalism (i.e., belief that men must protect women) and complementary gender differentiation (i.e., belief that women and men are different and complement one another). For example, classrooms that teach boys and girls very differently based on presumed gender differences often express benevolent sexism. Although benevolent sexism is often more attractive to women and men than hostile sexism, both reinforce traditional gender roles and status imbalances.

Researchers studying social cognition, based on a dual-process model of cognition, have illustrated that stereotypes, attitudes, and prejudices can operate at both conscious (or explicit) and unconscious (or implicit) levels (e.g., Greenwald et al., 2002). Conscious or explicit stereotyped attitudes are reflected in the views that individuals deliberately express to others. For example, a child might observe a boy playing with a doll and state, "Only girls can play with dolls." Unconscious or implicit stereotyped attitudes are seen when individuals respond automatically in situations based on conditioned semantic and emotional associations to particular social categories. These automatic responses sometimes differ from the conscious or explicit beliefs that children and adults hold (Greenwald et al., 2002).

Two kinds of sexism occurring in school contexts are addressed in this chapter. First, gender biases are sometimes reflected in differential expectations for girls and boys in overall school success, particular academic subjects, or athletics. These biases can affect children's developing beliefs, motives, and abilities. Second, sexual harassment is another form of sexism that affects many students in schools. It refers to inappropriate or hostile sexual behaviors that occur in face-to-face interactions (e.g., sexual teasing, unwanted touching) or through the use of online social media. With both types of sexism, children's achievement and well-being can be affected both directly and indirectly. Direct influences occur when institutions, adults, and peers encourage or discourage particular behaviors based on children's gender. Indirect influences occur when children internalize gender-stereotyped expectations and thereby avoid practicing particular behaviors or achieving in particular domains they see as contrary to their gender ideology.

Sexism is sometimes experienced differently based on the individual's ethnicity or race. As explicated in feminist standpoint theory, ethnicity/race intersect with gender in complicated ways (Basow & Rubin, 1999; Stewart & McDermott, 2004). Barbarin, Chinn, and Wright (2014) [Chapter 10 of this volume] and Rowley et al. (2014) [Chapter 9 of this volume] address this complexity by highlighting the unique experiences of African American boys within and outside of school contexts. This intersection can impact sexism within schools in at least three related ways. One issue is that children from different ethnic/racial groups may be differentially knowledgeable about and sensitive to sexism. In some situations, both boys and girls from minority ethnic/racial groups (such as African Americans, Latino/a Americans, and Asian Americans) are more sensitive to all forms of discrimination and therefore are more likely than White European American children to recognize sexism (see Kane, 2000). However, at times, the opposite trend seems to occur; that is, gender bias is most salient to White European American children because gender is their primary social identity (Brown, Alabi, Huynh, & Masten, 2011; Turner & Brown, 2007).

A second issue related to ethnicity/race is that gender is sometimes constructed differently in certain cultural contexts. For example, gender-typing pressures tend to be more traditional among Latino children compared to White European American children (e.g., Azmitia & Brown, 2000). Furthermore, among adolescents, many Latinas have distinct conceptions of feminism, in which they combine cultural ideals of *marianismo* (e.g., Hurtado, 2003) with notions of gender equality (Manago, Brown, & Leaper, 2009). In contrast, gender typing tends to be less traditional among African American children than among European American children (see Kane, 2000).

Finally, ethnicity and race are associated with their own academic stigmas and achievement gaps. For example, throughout elementary school, Latino students perform worse on average in math and reading, and are more likely to perform below grade level, than their European American counterparts (e.g., Lee & Bowen, 2006). These types of ethnic achievement gaps can exacerbate or mitigate gender-based achievement gaps (e.g., gender gaps in math achievement are highest for European American students and nonexistent among African American students; McGraw, Lubienski, & Strutchens, 2006). Thus, any discussion of sexism within schools should acknowledge that sexism occurs within a particular ethnic/racial context and does not impact all children in the same way.

2. PERPETRATORS OF SEXISM

Sexism can be perpetuated in schools directly and indirectly. Within the classroom, teachers can express implicit and explicit sexist attitudes and show differential treatment of boys and girls (e.g., Tiedemann, 2000). Within hallways and other public spaces in schools, peers can perpetrate sexism by harassing and rejecting the target of their gender bias. Sexism can also be perpetuated in schools indirectly. Parents are influential in shaping the academic attitudes that children bring to school (e.g., Frome & Eccles, 1998; Herbert & Stipek, 2005). Popular media consumed by most children is also a powerful source of sexism through its pervasive reinforcement of gender stereotypes (Signorielli, 2012).

2.1. Teachers

Once children begin school, teachers may perpetuate sexism in various ways. Studies from the 1990s found that some teachers hold sexist attitudes about children's abilities and interests. Some teachers, for example, were more likely to perceive boys than girls as logical, competitive, liking math, independent in math, and needing math and were more likely to attribute boys' success in math to ability but attribute girls' success to effort (Fennema, Peterson, Carpenter, & Lubinski, 1990; Jackson & Leffingwell, 1999; Li, 1999; Tiedemann, 2000). These implicit and explicit biases can affect teacher's expectations for their students, and research has consistently shown that expectations about students' abilities can be self-fulfilling (Jussim & Harber, 2005).

The same era of research revealed that, in some studies, teachers treated boys and girls differently in the classroom, such as favoring boys over girls when calling on students, asking students to explain their answers, and giving repeated explanations in science and math classes (AAUW, 1992; Jackson & Leffingwell, 1999). When girls did get attention, it could be contradictory: They may have received criticism for the content of work completed, yet praise for the neatness and timeliness of the work (AAUW, 1992). Perhaps because of this differential treatment, teachers' gender stereotypes are reflected in students' gender stereotypes (Keller, 2001).

More recent research has shown that many teachers try to be egalitarian in their explicit beliefs (Garrahy, 2001; Jones & Myhill, 2004). Teachers often rate boys and girls similarly on math competencies, which is consistent with boys' and girls' actual performance (Helwig, Anderson, & Tindal, 2001; Herbert & Stipek, 2005). Researchers have observed patterns that are opposite to those seen in earlier studies; that is, some teachers now evaluate girls higher than boys in math competence when they are aware of students' gender—but not when they are blind to students' gender (Lavy, 2008). Conversely, some teachers perceive boys as more likely to be underachievers and troublemakers compared to girls (Jones & Myhill, 2004); this difference is particularly pronounced for African American boys and girls (Wood, Kaplan, & McLoyd, 2007). Yet, even when teachers perceive gender similarities in overall academic competence, they often assume that boys and girls have different learning styles and interests (Skelton et al., 2009).

Current research focuses on how teachers' implicit gender biases may influence children within the classroom. An example of a how implicit sexism can affect children is the finding that female teachers' own math anxiety is associated with an increase in girls endorsing the stereotype that "boys are good at math and girls are good at reading" (Beilock, Gunderson, Ramirez, & Levine, 2010).

This in turn is associated with girls' lower math performance (Beilock et al., 2010). Although the exact mechanism of influence is unclear, some female teachers may model these stereotypes through their own nonverbal behavior (see Lane, 2012; Petersen & Hyde, 2014 [Chapter 2 of this volume]).

2.2. Peers

Peers can also be sources of sexism at school for children and adolescents. Although peer-directed sexism can be important across all school years, the impact of peers is particularly influential during middle school (Brown & Larson, 2009). Most frequently, peers express sexism through perpetrating sexual harassment toward classmates and through rejecting or teasing gender-atypical classmates.

As will be described below, peers are the most frequent perpetrators of sexual harassment (Fineran & Bennett, 1999). Furthermore, because sexual harassment typically occurs in public (often in school hallways and classrooms; Harris Interactive, 2001; Timmerman, 2005), peers have the opportunity to reinforce and regulate these behaviors. Indeed, adolescents indicate that sexual harassment is both implicitly condoned and explicitly encouraged by peers. About 54% of adolescents admit to perpetrating sexual harassment against a peer (Harris Interactive, 2001). Of those students, a majority stated that they sexually harassed a peer because "a lot of people do it" (reported by 39% of perpetrators) or "their friends encouraged them" (reported by 24% of perpetrators; Harris Interactive, 2001). Peer norms about the acceptability of sexual harassment are a strong predictor of an individual's own sexually harassing behavior (Jewell & Brown, 2013).

In addition to perpetrating and condoning sexual harassment, peers also perpetrate sexism by teasing other classmates who do not conform to gender norms. Research on group norms indicates that children who do not meet the norms or fit the stereotypes of the group can be bullied, mocked, or ostracized by group members (Abrams, Rutland, Cameron, & Ferrell, 2007). Peers frequently harass and ostracize boys and girls who are deemed atypical for their gender (Jewell & Brown 2014; Russell, Kosciw, Horn, & Saewyc, 2010; Smith & Leaper 2006; Young & Sweeting, 2004). Conversely, highly gender-typical children have the most positive peer relations, being rated as the most liked and the most popular (Egan & Perry, 2001; Jewell & Brown, 2014; Lobel, Bempechat, Gewirtz, Shoken-Topaz, & Bashe, 1993; Rose, Glick, & Smith, 2011). This form of sexism is condoned, with adolescents reporting that it is more acceptable to exclude or tease a gender-atypical peer than a gender-typical peer (Horn, 2008).

There is asymmetry, however, in that boys are more likely than girls to experience negative peer sanctions for low levels of gender typicality. Although peers make negative comments to girls when they engage in traditionally male activities such as athletics and mathematics (Leaper & Brown, 2008), boys who appear feminine or have poor athletic abilities face even harsher repercussions from their peers (Lee & Troop-Gordon, 2011; Pascoe, 2007). Poteat, Scheer, and Mereish (2014) [Chapter 8 of this volume] provide a detailed account of the frequency and consequences of the victimization of gender non-conforming and sexual minority youth.

2.3. Parents

Although a discussion of the myriad ways that parents shape children's gendered behavior is beyond the scope of this chapter, parents can influence children's academic lives through their own implicit and explicit sexism, thus becoming an indirect means by which sexism occurs in school (Gunderson, Ramirez, Levine, & Beilock, 2012). Like teachers, some parents show implicit sexist attitudes about their children's academic abilities. In some studies, parents perceived both science and math to be more important for boys than for girls; they perceived boys to be more competent in science and math than girls; and they expected higher science and math performance from boys than from girls (Andre, Whigham, Hendrickson, & Chambers, 1999; Eccles, Freedman-Doan, Frome, Jacobs, & Yoon, 2000). Parents assumed girls are as not interested in computer science as sons (Sáinz, Pálmen, & García-Cuesta, 2012). Furthermore, in one older study, parents attributed boys' math success to ability, but they attributed girls' math success to effort (Yee & Eccles, 1988).

Parents' stereotypes, assumptions, and expectations can influence their beliefs about their children's abilities and interests, which in turn affect children's self-perceptions and performance (Gunderson et al., 2012; Jacobs, Chhin, & Shaver, 2005). Research has consistently shown that parents' expectations and beliefs about math (particularly when they align with gender stereotypes) can impact children's math attitudes and aptitudes (Yee & Eccles, 1988). Parental expectations, and the resulting encouragement and support behaviors, can be more important than any actual academic experiences. For example, Greek parents' expectations and encouragement about computer science were stronger predictors than children's own computer-based activities in predicting children's computer self-efficacy (Vekiri & Chronaki, 2008). Beyond that, parents have been shown to steer children's occupational choices in stereotypical directions (Chhin, Bleeker, & Jacobs, 2008; Whiston & Keller, 2004).

Parents' gender biases regarding academic achievement may also include the differential treatment of daughters and sons (Gunderson et al., 2012). Studies conducted in the United States observed that parents of sons discussed math and science concepts more frequently and in more detail with their children than parents of daughters. For example, parents of preschoolers at a science museum were three times more likely to explain science exhibits to sons than to daughters (Crowley, Callanan, Tenenbaum, & Allen, 2001). Another study observed that when parents were assigned to teach their 10-year-old child about a physics phenomenon, fathers were more likely to use teaching talk (e.g., by asking for causal explanations and using conceptual descriptions) with sons than with daughters (Tenenbaum & Leaper, 2003). Still another investigation noted that mother–son conversations included three times more talk about numbers and quantities than did mother–daughter conversations (Chang, Sandhofer, & Brown, 2011). These patterns of differential treatment can privilege boys with relatively more background knowledge and comfort in math and science; in turn, these experiences help to strengthen boys' self-efficacy and interest in these academic domains.

2.4. Media

Sexism has been documented in nearly all forms of children's media. Media, by presenting sexist images and narratives, perpetuates common gender stereotypes that are then applied to children within schools. This perpetuation of stereotypes can justify and reinforce sexism at school. For example, analyses of popular children's television programs show that boys are portrayed as answering more questions, telling others what to do more often, and showing more ingenuity than girls (Aubrey & Harrison, 2004). These stereotypes of boys as more assertive than girls are then reinforced by the differential treatment of boys shown by teachers. Video games typically portray boys as aggressive and girls as sexually objectified (Dill & Thill, 2007). These stereotypes of aggressive boys and sexual girls further justify sexual harassment by boys directed at girls.

Sexist portrayals of boys and girls also infiltrate educational media. In elementary school textbooks, females possess some masculine characteristics (such as assertiveness), but males rarely possess feminine characteristics (such as empathy; Evans & Davies, 2000). This trend is also evident in books prevalent in school libraries. Even among award-winning children's books considered to be nonsexist, boys rarely have feminine-stereotyped traits or occupations (Diekman & Murnen, 2004). Girls' underrepresentation and the gender-stereotypical portrayal of occupations in children's book continue in the new millennium (Hamilton, Anderson, Broaddus, & Young, 2006).

3. GENDER BIASES IN SCHOOL ACHIEVEMENT

Sexism affects both boys and girls in school. Girls are stereotypically assumed to be less competent than boys in subjects related to science, technology, engineering, and mathematics (STEM). Girls are also assumed to be less athletically competent than boys (see Solmon, 2014 [Chapter 4 of this volume]). Boys, however, are stereotypically assumed to perform worse than girls in their overall school achievement. On the basis of these negative stereotypes, boys and girls can be the target of sexism during academic classes and sports participation. In this section, we outline the differences between boys and girls in STEM subjects, athletic participation, and overall school achievement and describe the ways in gender biases partially explain the gender differences in these domains.

3.1. Biases Against Girls in STEM

Students' achievement in subjects related to STEM is considered important for economic success in today's increasingly technological world (Zakaria, 2011). Accordingly, policymakers and researchers have been concerned with the gender gap in some STEM fields. Compared to 57% of all bachelor's degrees recently going to women in the United States, only 43% of mathematics degrees, 20% of physics degrees, 16% of computer and information sciences, and 18% of engineering went to women (National Center for Education Statistics [NCES], 2013). The association between gender and bachelor's degrees in these fields varies somewhat across the world, however (UNESCO, 2010). Also, the gender gap in all of these fields has narrowed over the last four decades within the United States (National Science Foundation [NSF], 2013). Finally, women are not underrepresented in all STEM fields. In the United States, 58% of bachelor's degrees in the biological and biomedical sciences recently went to women (NSF, 2013).

Average gender differences in achievement in mathematics and some science subjects emerge during adolescence (see Petersen & Hyde, 2014, [Chapter 2 of this volume] for a review). The STEM-related subject that has garnered the most interest is mathematics. Based on a recent meta-analysis of data collected across the world (Lindberg, Hyde, Petersen, & Linn, 2010), no significant average gender differences in mathematics test performance were indicated during elementary school and middle school; however, there was a significant but small difference favoring boys in high school and college. The slight advantage seen among boys in high school parallels a trend whereby girls tend to decrease their interest in mathematics between middle school and high school (Hill, Corbett, & St. Rose, 2010).

As far as other STEM-related subjects, there is cross-national evidence that boys scored significantly higher on average than girls on the TIMMS high school physics test (TIMMS International Study Center, 2000). Also, significantly higher averages for boys than for girls were indicated on the AP Physics and the AP Computer Science exams (Hill et al., 2010). Despite the slight average advantage for boys over girls in standardized test performances, girls actually attained higher average grades in American high school math and science courses (Hill et al., 2010; NCES, 2013).

Developmental scientists recognize that multiple factors contribute to gender-related variations in achievement (see Leaper, 2013). There is strong evidence, however, that gender biases are among these influences. Studies suggest that many children stereotype males as better than females in many STEM-related fields or they view STEM fields as male domains. For example, this pattern has been indicated for mathematics (e.g., Muzzatti & Agnoli, 2007; Steffens, Jelenec, & Noack, 2010), physics (e.g., Andre et al., 1999; Kessels, 2005), and computer science (e.g., Mercier, Barron, & O'Connor, 2006).

A few studies have begun to examine both implicit and explicit stereotyping in children. In these investigations, some children who did not explicitly endorse gender stereotypes about math showed evidence of implicit gender stereotypes (Cvencek, Meltzoff, & Greenwald, 2011; Del Río & Strasser, 2013; Steffens et al., 2010). These findings are notable because implicit attitudes may have an impact on self-concepts and performance (e.g., Nosek et al., 2009; Steffens & Jelenec, 2011). Nosek and colleagues (2009) examined nation-level variations in gender-science implicit stereotypes and eighth graders' achievement in science and mathematics. Across the 34 countries sampled, the implicit stereotyping of science as male was strongly related to national gender differences in eighth graders' performances in science ($\beta=0.56$) and mathematics ($\beta=0.52$).

Girls' internalization of gender stereotypes may affect achievement in STEM-related subjects. When interest and the perceived value of particular subjects have been assessed, researchers commonly observed girls tended to rate mathematics, physical science, and computers and technology lower than did boys (e.g., Chow, Eccles, & Salmela-Aro, 2012; Dickhäuser & Stiensmeier-Pelster, 2003; Else-Quest, Hyde, & Linn, 2010; Kessels, 2005; Riegle-Crumb, Farkas, & Muller, 2006). As several studies have documented, the perceived value of a domain generally predicts subsequent achievement (see Eccles & Wigfield, 2002).

The impact of negative gender stereotypes on performance has also been illustrated in research on stereotype threat. When a social identity is threatened, it can lead to heightened arousal that disrupts working memory and can impair controlled cognitive processing (Krendl, Richeson, Kelley, & Heatherton, 2008). As a result, performance in assessment settings can suffer. According to a recent meta-analysis testing for stereotype threat effects on female math performance (Picho, Rodriguez, & Finnie, 2013), there was a small overall effect size for high school students ($d=0.30$) indicating girls' math performance significantly declined during stereotype threat conditions. Other studies find it is possible to counteract stereotype threat. For example, it is sometimes possible to boost a person's performance when a positive stereotype about a self-relevant social identity is made salient (Ambady, Shih, Kim, & Pittinksy, 2001). Furthermore, stereotype threat effects can be subverted if the person uses strategies such as self-affirmation or focusing on an alternative social identity (Shapiro & Williams, 2012).

Girls learn about negative gender stereotypes through their interactions with parents, teachers, and peers. According to one survey study in the United States, half of adolescent girls between 13 and 18 years reported hearing disparaging statements about girls in math, science, or computers from these sources (Leaper & Brown, 2008). The most commonly cited perpetrators were male peers (32%), which were followed by female peers (22%), teachers/coaches (23%), fathers (15%), and mothers (12%). The likelihood of these reports increased with age. In a subsequent analysis of this data (Brown & Leaper, 2010), it was found that girls' experiences hearing these sexist comments were negatively related to their ability beliefs and interests in math and science (even after controlling for grades and family backgrounds).

Some parents hold gender-stereotypical views about math and science that may not reflect their children's actual achievement. When this occurs, girls' motivation and performance may suffer. One longitudinal study found that these negative stereotypes in mothers predicted subsequent declines in daughters' self-concepts and motivation in math and science (e.g., Bleeker &

Jacobs, 2004). Another investigation observed that parental gender stereotyping of math was related to higher levels of intrusive parental support during homework and lower math ability beliefs in daughters (Bhanot & Jovanovic, 2005). Conversely, other studies suggest ways that some parents may provide more encouraging behaviors to sons than to daughters regarding their achievement in STEM-related subjects (e.g., Simpkins, Davis-Kean, & Eccles, 2005; Tenenbaum & Leaper, 2003; Tenenbaum, Snow, Roach, & Kurland, 2005).

In summary, negative gender stereotypes persist about girls in some STEM fields. These stereotypes may lead some parents and teachers to underestimate girls' potential. Discrimination may occur through the relatively greater provision of encouragement to boys than to girls for achievement in STEM subjects. Moreover, it may also involve overtly discouraging comments about girls' capacities to do well in these areas. Evidence suggests many girls internalize these biases, decreasing their achievement within STEM fields.

3.2. Biases Against Girls in Sports

One of the most dramatic gender-related changes in achievement seen in the United States (and many other countries) has been the tenfold increase in girls' participation in high school sports since the 1972 enactment of Title IX of the U.S. Civil Rights Act. At the time, participation in high school sports was approximately 4% for girls and 50% for boys; today, it is approximately 40% for girls and remains 50% for boys (Women's Sports Foundation, 2009).

Despite this change, many children continue to stereotype sports as a male domain (e.g., Cockburn & Clarke, 2002; Rowley, Kutz-Costes, Mistry, & Feagans, 2007; Shakib, 2003). Also, certain sports tend to be viewed as appropriate for "boys only" (e.g., football, wrestling) or for "girls only" (e.g., cheerleading, ballet) (Schmalz, Kerstetter, & Anderson, 2008). Furthermore, some girls may find athleticism conflicts with their peers' norms for femininity and heterosexuality (Cockburn & Clarke, 2002; Shakib, 2003). Hence, in some social settings, girls may experience pressures to drop out of sports. According to one survey study in the United States, three-fourths of adolescent girls between 13 and 18 years reported hearing disparaging statements about girls in sports (Leaper & Brown, 2008). The most commonly cited perpetrators were male peers (54%), which were followed by female peers (38%), teachers/coaches (28%), fathers (30%), and mothers (25%). The likelihood of these reports increased with age.

Even if most girls are not being actively discouraged to participate in sports, many of them may not be getting the same degree of support that boys experience. Studies suggest that peer popularity is more strongly tied to athletic participation among boys than among girls (e.g., Shakib, Veliz, Dunbar, & Sabo, 2011). Also, some parents are more likely to expect athletic achievement in sons than in daughters and therefore may express more enthusiasm for their son's sports involvement. In turn, parents' expectations of success generally tend to predict children's actual achievement (e.g., Fredricks & Eccles, 2002).

Finally, the sports culture can be a context in which sexist and heterosexist attitudes are reinforced in boys. In many schools, teammates and coaches use misogynistic and antigay comments to enforce conformity and pressure achievement in players (Messner, 1998). Furthermore, tolerance for aggression on the field or court may generalize whereby some athletes view aggressive behavior as legitimate for solving problems outside of the sport (Conroy, Silva, Newcomer, Walker, & Johnson, 2001). In some cases, this may extend to an increased risk among some male athletes for sexual violence (Forbes, Adams-Curtis, Pakalka, & White, 2006).

3.3. Biases Against Boys in School Achievement

Compared to girls, boys are more likely to get lower grades and are more likely to drop out of high school in most industrialized countries (UNESCO, 2010). (In many nonindustrialized countries, the opposite trend is seen, whereby school access may be limited primarily or solely to boys.) The specific subjects with the largest gender gap in achievement favoring girls include reading, writing, and the arts (Eurydice Network, 2010; NCES, 2013). The gender gap in academic achievement extends into college. Among all bachelor's degrees recently awarded in the United States, only 43% went to men (NCES, 2013); a similar gender gap in college degrees is seen in most OECD countries (OECD, 2013). Within the United States, the gender gap in academic achievement is wider for African Americans and Latino/as youths than for White European Americans or Asian Americans (NCES, 2013). Research suggests that sexism and adherence to traditional notions of masculinity may partly account for these gender gaps.

Sexism functions to maintain traditional status and power relations between men and women in society. One manifestation of sexism involves discrimination against girls and women who seek to achieve in prestigious fields traditionally associated with males (e.g., STEM fields and sports). Another manifestation of sexism, however, occurs when pressures are placed on boys and men to conform to traditional conceptions of masculinity. For example, boys who are not viewed as tough or athletic are commonly teased (Jewell & Brown, 2014).

Traditional masculinity can undermine some boys' academic achievement. In some communities, doing well in school is viewed as a violation of masculine norms (Kessels & Steinmayr, 2013; Legewie & DiPrete, 2012). For example, boys who are concerned with appearing tough may be reluctant to seek help or to comply with teachers' authority (e.g., Kiefer & Ryan, 2008; Santos, Galligan, Pahlke, & Fabes, 2013). In addition, specific subjects—such as reading or the arts—may be viewed as being especially feminine (e.g., Plante, Théorêt, & Favreau, 2009; Rowley et al., 2007). Thus, boys who do well in school or who like feminine-stereotyped subjects may be teased by their male peers (e.g., Sherriff, 2007; Van de Gaer, Pustjens, Van Damme, & De Munter, 2006). Furthermore, these pressures may be more common among youths from lower-income or some ethnic minority backgrounds (Fuller-Rowell & Doan, 2010).

Endorsement of traditional masculinity ideology may undermine some boys' academic achievement and lead them to resist teachers' authority. However, some teachers and school administrators may exaggerate the extent and the degree that these patterns occur among boys. Teachers may form generalized expectations that girls are better than boys at school (e.g., Jones & Myhill, 2004). Boys may infer these sentiments about teachers' expectations (e.g., Hartley & Sutton, 2013). Also, boys in general—but especially African American and Latino boys—are subject to disproportionate rates of disciplinary action for school misbehavior (Barbarin et al., 2014 [Chapter 10 of this volume]; Losen, 2011; Rowley et al., 2014 [Chapter 9 of this volume]).

4. SEXUAL HARASSMENT IN SCHOOL

Sexual harassment includes sexually disparaging comments, unwanted sexual interest, unwanted touching, and sexual coercion. It can involve physical aggression (e.g., unwanted touching, sexual coercion) or verbal aggression (e.g., unwelcome sexual comments, homophobic insults). Also, it can be expressed directly in face-to-face interactions or via electronic messages sent to the victim; or sexual harassment can be expressed indirectly behind the target's back (e.g., spreading sexual rumors). The prevalence and the consequences of sexual harassment in school are reviewed below.

4.1. Prevalence of Sexual Harassment in School Settings

Sexual harassment is a common experience for girls and boys in many countries around the world (see Leaper & Robnett, 2011 for a review). For example, the American Association of University Women (AAUW, 2011) conducted a study of sexual harassment in the United States based on a nationally representative sample of students in grades 7–11. Across all grades, 56% of girls and 40% of boys reported experiences with sexual harassment. The gender gap in sexual harassment increased with age; among 12th graders, 62% of girls and 32% of boys reported having experienced sexual harassment. When specific types of sexual harassment were examined across all grade levels, girls were twice as likely as boys to report being targets of unwelcome sexual comments/jokes (46% of girls vs. 22% of boys). Girls and boys reported experiencing antigay or anti-lesbian insults at similar rates (18% of girls vs. 19% of boys). Given the importance of electronic media in many youths' lives, it is also pertinent to note that 36% of girls and 24% of boys experienced online sexual harassment through text messages, e-mail, or Web postings.

The AAUW survey also asked students to identify the gender of the perpetrators and to evaluate the attributes most likely associated with the targets of sexual harassment. In general, boys were more likely than girls to be perpetrators of sexual harassment. Among the students experiencing sexual harassment, 66% identified boys, 19% identified girls, and 11% identified a combination of boys and girls as the perpetrators. The attributes associated with students viewed as most likely to be sexually harassed reflected characteristics associated with sexual attractiveness or traditional gender roles. The qualities attributed to girls who were most likely to be sexually harassed included being physically developed (58%), very pretty (41%), not pretty or not very feminine (32%), or overweight (30%). The attributes associated with boys considered most likely to be sexually harassed included being not athletic or not very masculine (37%), overweight (30%), or good looking (11%).

Other surveys point to similar patterns as those reported in the AAUW survey, although the incidences of sexual harassment vary somewhat (Chiodo, Wolfe, Croosk, Hughes, & Jaffe, 2009; Lacasse, Purdy, & Mendelson, 2003; Leaper & Brown, 2008; Pepler et al., 2006; Petersen & Hyde, 2009; Wei & Chen, 2012). In some studies, higher rates of peer sexual harassment were indicated for boys than for girls (Petersen & Hyde, 2009; Wei & Chen, 2012), which may be related to higher rates of same-gender harassment among boys than among girls. Studies further suggest sexual harassment may be especially likely for sexual-minority youths (i.e., lesbian, gay, bisexual, transgender, and intersex; e.g., Williams, Connolly, Pepler, & Craig, 2005). Also, higher rates of sexual harassment may occur for students in lower than in higher income neighborhoods (AAUW, 2011). The AAUW survey did not find evidence that ethnic or racial background moderated the incidence of sexual harassment (AAUW, 2011).

4.2. Consequences of Sexual Harassment

Besides being somewhat more liable to be targets of sexual harassment, girls are more likely than boys to be negatively affected by sexual harassment (AAUW, 2011; Fineran & Bolen, 2006). Sexual harassment also tends to have a more negative impact on sexual-minority boys than on heterosexual boys (Kosciw, Greytak, Diaz, & Bartkiewicz, 2010). Negative reactions to sexual harassment include internalizing symptoms (e.g., anxiety, depression) and decline in academic performance (see AAUW, 2011; Leaper & Robnett, 2011; Poteat et al., 2014 [Chapter 8 of this volume]). For example, in the AAUW survey, some of the most commonly reported reactions to sexual harassment included not wanting to go to school (37% of girls and 25% of boys), finding it difficult to study (24% of girls and 24% of boys), staying home from school (14% of girls and 9% of boys), and stopping doing an activity or sport (9% of girls and 5% of boys). A longitudinal study of Canadian youths (Chiodo et al., 2009) found that sexual harassment victimization during the 9th grade predicted higher incidences during the 11th grade of feeling unsafe in school, emotional distress, substance abuse, and victimization by peers and dating partners. Experiences with sexual harassment also appear related to increased body image concerns among girls (Chiodo et al., 2009; Lindberg, Grabe, & Hyde, 2007). Thus, repeated experiences with sexual harassment can have negative consequences on girls' and boys' socioemotional adjustment and academic achievement.

5. AWARENESS OF SEXISM AND COPING

In addition to research focusing on the impacts of sexism within schools, research also examines children's perceptions of sexism at the individual level, their developing awareness of sexism in general, and their coping responses when sexism is encountered. Perceiving sexism can be a complex phenomenon. There are some instances when a child or an adolescent may be the target of sexism but is unaware of it. For example, a girl can hear a discouraging comment about her math abilities, but she may attribute it to her individual poor performance rather than a gender-based stereotype. There are other instances when the child is the target of sexism and perceives it as bias. A high-achieving boy may be teased for not seeming tough, but he can recognize the teasing is based on a stereotype of how boys are supposed to act. Each situation may differentially impact the child.

At the individual level, perceiving sexism can be associated with negative psychological outcomes, such as greater stress, lower global self-esteem, more emotional problems, and more behavioral problems (e.g., DuBois, Burk-Braxton, Swenson, Tevendale, & Hardesty, 2002). Simultaneously, there can also positive consequences of perceiving individual sexism. After receiving personal negative feedback, individuals can attribute the feedback to gender bias as opposed to their own competency, thus maintaining a positive sense of self-efficacy (Brown, Bigler, & Chu, 2010). At the broader group level, knowledge of sexism can help members of a group attribute underrepresentation to gender bias instead of innate group traits. Girls, for example, can attribute the lack of female U.S. Presidents to institutional sexism instead of women being incompetent leaders (Bigler, Arthur, Hughes, & Patterson, 2008). Knowledge of historical sexism regarding math and science careers has been shown to motivate girls to combat future discrimination (Pahlke, Bigler, & Green, 2010). Knowledge of sexism can also help individuals be more accepting of gender nonconforming peers, to challenge sexist comments by their peers, and to view media (and all other environmental inputs) through a "sexism" filter that prevents such messages from reinforcing personal gender stereotyping and prejudice (Pahlke, Bigler, & Martin, 2014).

Most importantly, when children are aware of sexism and can perceive it in any given situation, they then have the opportunity to cope with it. In the following section, we first describe children's developing awareness of sexism and then describe ways in which children cope with sexism when it does occur.

5.1. Awareness of Sexism

To be generally aware of sexism, children must first have knowledge of gender stereotypes and gender inequalities. Evidence suggests that children are aware of gender stereotypes early in childhood, well before they enter elementary school (see Halim & Ruble, 2010). As children get older, their knowledge of gender inequalities increases. Liben, Bigler, and Krogh (2001) found that, by middle childhood, children were aware of the greater status (e.g., greater income) associated with the jobs performed by men compared to jobs performed by women, even when the jobs are fictional and thus not based on actual job characteristics. By the start of elementary school, the majority of children were aware that no woman has ever been president of the United States, although this knowledge became more common across the elementary school years (Bigler et al., 2008). A little more than one-quarter of children (with slightly higher rates among girls than among boys) spontaneously attributed the historical lack of female presidents to discrimination (e.g., "People like voting for boys more than girls."). One quarter of children agreed with the statement that it is *currently* against the law for a woman to be president (a form of institutional sexism) and half believed that individual voters would be discriminatory (Bigler et al., 2008). As children enter adolescence, they become more aware of societal levels of gender inequality. Yet, although women still make 70 cents for every dollar paid to men and are underrepresented in the upper echelon of corporations, children are more likely to perceive status inequalities in politics than in the business world (Neff, Cooper, & Woodruff, 2007).

Beyond knowledge of sexism in general, children can also recognize gender discrimination in their own lives by middle childhood. In surveys about school gender bias given to students in fourth through eighth grade (Brown et al., 2011), girls typically reported that boys receive preferential treatment in athletics (e.g., "The P.E. teacher always thinks boys will be faster"); in contrast, boys reported that girls are given preferential treatment within the classroom (e.g., "When a girl does something wrong, the teacher never gets her in trouble; a boy does the same thing, and he always gets in trouble").

Although children and adolescents are generally aware of sexism and capable of perceiving discrimination (see Brown & Bigler, 2005), individuals perceive themselves to be the target of discrimination rather infrequently (Crosby, 1984; Taylor, Wright, Moghaddam, & Lalonde, 1990). As reported above, although approximately 50% of adolescent girls reported that they had experienced gender discrimination within academic or athletic domains, most girls reported it happening only once or twice within the last year. Interestingly, such low frequencies are common in studies of perception of racial and ethnic discrimination as well (e.g., Benner & Graham, 2011; Brody et al., 2006; Greene, Way, & Pahl, 2006). The adoption of conservative standards for labeling negative treatment as gender discrimination or sexism may be due to the psychological costs associated with perceiving oneself to be the target of discrimination (Quinn, Roese, Pennington, & Olson, 1999).

To date, most research on children's perceptions of sexism involves retrospective self-reports of their past experiences with discrimination. Although such studies are important, they provide little information about *when* and *why* some but not other individuals perceive themselves to be targets of discrimination. Furthermore, it begs the question of whether children are actually only infrequently subject to discriminatory treatment on the basis of gender or whether individual and developmental factors affect children's tendency to perceive experiences as discriminatory. To answer these questions, experimental studies are required in which the feedback and the context are tightly controlled. Two experimental studies have examined children's perceptions of individual sexism. In one study, elementary school children were read stories in which a teacher treated a boy and a girl differently from one another. When children were told that the teacher had a history of favoring one gender over the other, children were more likely to attribute the teacher's behavior to discrimination than more benign reasons, and this attribution was more frequent among children in upper than in lower elementary school (Brown & Bigler, 2004). However, when children were given no information about the teacher's past choices or were told the teacher had a history of fairness, they were more likely to blame the child's lack of effort or ability for the negative treatment. A slightly different pattern emerged in a separate experimental study in which children were given negative feedback about their own performance in a presumed art contest (i.e., they were told they lost an art contest; Brown et al., 2010). Of the very few children who perceived personal discrimination (8 of 108 children), they *only* perceived their own negative feedback to be due to gender discrimination when they were told (a) the contest judges were of the other gender, (b) the contest judges picked other-gender winners in previous years, and (c) the contest judges picked other-gender winners this year. Despite all of the experimental "clues" suggesting gender discrimination at work and despite children's awareness of sexism in general, very few children perceived themselves to the target of gender discrimination. These findings suggest that surveys of children and adolescents' experience with sexism are likely to yield underestimates of the frequency of these experiences.

Beyond children's tendency to perceive gender discrimination in certain contexts more than others, developmental models of children and adolescents' perceptions of discrimination posit that awareness of sexism is influenced by the child's cognitive development, situational variables, gender attitudes, and gender (Brown & Bigler, 2005). For example, within any given situation, children with more advanced social perspective-taking abilities and classification skills, and children who can better compare their outcomes with others, will be more likely to perceive sexism than children with less advanced cognitive abilities. Furthermore, evidence suggests that children perceive sexism more readily when it is directed toward others or toward a group than when directed at themselves (Brown & Bigler, 2004; Brown et al., 2010), and when they perceive available social supports (Leaper & Brown, 2008). Children's gender attitudes are also associated with their awareness of sexism. Adolescent girls were more likely to recognize gender discrimination when they held gender-egalitarian attitudes (Brown & Bigler, 2004; Leaper & Brown, 2008) or reported having learned about feminism (Leaper & Brown, 2008). Finally, girls are more likely to perceive sexism than boys during middle childhood and adolescence; this pattern may reflect girls' greater awareness of their lower social status relative to males (e.g., Brown & Bigler, 2004; Brown et al., 2011, 2010; DuBois et al., 2002). When youths perceive sexism, the ways in which they cope with the experience are important in influencing the outcome.

5.2. Coping with Sexism

According to Lazarus and Folkman's (1984) model of stress and coping, effective coping to any stressful situation, including experiencing sexism, depends on the person's cognitive appraisal of the stressful event, and the subsequent type of behavioral coping strategy used. There are two broad types of coping strategies used in response to sexism, and the type of strategy used is partially based on the individual's appraisal of the costs and benefits of each behavioral response. A general distinction is often made between approach (or engagement) and avoidant (or disengagement) coping strategies (Compas, Connor-Smith, Saltzman, Thomsen, & Wadsworth, 2001; Lazarus, 1999; Lazarus & Folkman, 1984; Magley, 2002). *Approach strategies* are oriented toward addressing the threat. These might include confronting the source of the stress (e.g., confronting someone about sexist behavior) or seeking social support (e.g., talking to someone about what happened). People may seek others to gain emotional reassurance, to clarify their understanding of the situation, or to get advice. In contrast, *avoidance strategies* are oriented away from the threat such as downplaying or ignoring the event. In general, research indicates that approach strategies are more effective than avoidant strategies in reducing stress in adolescents (Compas et al., 2001) and adults (Lazarus, 1999). In response to sexism, approach strategies can empower the individual, reduce stress, and increase motivation; whereas avoidance strategies can lead to a sense of helplessness and diminish motivation (e.g., Miller & Major, 2000; Swim & Thomas, 2006).

Recent research has highlighted the relevance of the stress and coping model to adolescent girls and women's experiences with sexism (e.g., Ayres, Friedman, & Leaper, 2009; Cortina & Wasti, 2005; Kaiser & Miller, 2004). For example, Kaiser and Miller (2004) found that women's cognitive appraisals predicted their likelihood of confrontational responses to recent experiences with sexism. Researchers have found that adolescent girls and young women who perceive social support were more likely to use approach coping strategies than girls without social support (Holahan, Valentiner, & Moos, 1995; Moradi & Funderburk, 2006). Feeling supported from friends or parents (particularly mothers) may bolster girls' confidence to use approach coping strategies when sexism occurs (Leaper, Brown, & Ayres, 2013). This could include either confronting perpetrators of sexism or seeking others for advice and emotional support (e.g., Cortina & Wasti, 2005).

Having a meaningful social identity, particularly one that is empowering in the face of sexism, also seems to be important in helping individuals cope with sexism. Some evidence, for example, suggests that having a feminist identification helps girls (and women) cope with gender discrimination (e.g., Ayres et al., 2009; Leaper & Arias, 2011). This parallels research on ethnic identity, which finds that having a positive ethnic identity helps buffer against the negative effects of ethnic discrimination (e.g., Umaña-Taylor & Updegraff, 2007).

6. REDUCING SEXISM IN SCHOOLS

Because of the important social, emotional, and academic consequences of sexism from peers and teachers, numerous attempts have been made to reduce gender biases in school. Some attempts involve experimental interventions directed at changing children's behaviors and attitudes. Some attempts involve changing the school itself: either the school climate or the school infrastructure. In this section, we outline ways that sexism can potentially be reduced within schools, beginning with changes to the gender composition of the schools and then discussing interventions that have been implemented within existing schools.

6.1. Single-Gender Versus Coeducational Schools' Debate

One approach to reduce sexism within schools has been to segregate schools, or at least classes within schools, on the basis of gender (see Bigler, Hayes, & Liben, 2014 [Chapter 7 of this volume]). Instituting single-gender public education is possible because of changes to educational policy enacted after No Child Left Behind Act was passed in 2001 and the U.S. Department of Education (DOE) issued new regulations in 2006. Since then, more than 1000 school districts in 46 states have instituted some degree of single-sex public education (although the exact numbers are difficult to determine; Klein & Sesma, 2011).

Proponents of single-gender schools argue that segregated education reduces sexism in schools in two ways. First, several influential proponents of single-gender education argue that there are important, innate sex differences between boys' and girls' brain structure (e.g., differences in size of corpus collosum), hormones, and physiology (Gurian, 2001; Sax, 2005). Because of these supposed differences, they argue that boys and girls have different learning styles and interests, and teaching boys and girls similarly constitutes a form of bias. For example, Gurian (2001) argues that girls are not as capable as boys of abstract thought, instead needing to "have things conceptualized in usable, everyday language, replete with concrete details" (p. 46). Thus, according to this argument, it is unfair to teach girls' abstract concepts in the same way that boys are taught. Supporters of this approach also argue that boys and girls have innately different interests, and to be equitable, schools should tailor education toward those interests. For example, some schools are using hunting analogies in lessons for boys and dishwashing analogies for girls (Weil, 2008).

The second reason that some schools implement single-gender education is based on the argument that, regardless of biological and neurological differences, the current coeducational schools are overly feminine and fail to meet the needs of boys, especially ethnic minority boys (see Barbarin et al., 2014 [Chapter 10 of this volume]), thus contributing to the behavioral problems of boys (e.g., Whitmire, 2010). They cite evidence that boys are twice as likely as girls to be suspended and more than twice as likely to be diagnosed with Attention Deficit-Hyperactivity Disorder (Rao & Seaton, 2009). They also argue that girls are overly inhibited around boys, largely because of boys' domination of teacher attention and girls' concerns with being attractive to boys (see Salomone, 2006).

There are many critics of single-gender education. Critics of single-gender education argue that educational segregation by gender is, by definition, a form of gender bias (Halpern et al., 2011). Critics point to research indicating that gender segregation in education actually fosters and increases gender stereotypes (Fabes, Pahlke, Martin, & Hanish, 2013). Recent research shows that randomly assigning children to one single-gender class led to a 14% increase in the odds of believing that "boys are better than girls at math" and "girls are better than boys at language arts." Children who were randomly assigned to eight single-gender classes were 112% more likely to become gender-stereotypic (Fabes et al., 2013). Additional negative consequences of gender segregation are outlined by Martin, Fabes, & Hanish (2014) [Chapter 5 of this volume].

Neuroscientists also point out that there are, in fact, very few innate differences in brain structures, hormones, and physiology (Eliot, 2009). They argue that there are small differences at birth that become larger as children are increasingly socialized in gender-stereotypical ways (Eliot, 2009). Thus, basing educational policy on sex differences that do not exist is misguided (Halpern et al., 2011).

Several meta-analyses have examined whether single-gender education is educationally beneficial compared to coeducational education. Shortly before issuing regulations for the implementation of single-gender education, the U.S. Department of Education (2005) found that there were no conclusive educational advantages to single-gender education. After taking into account various moderators (e.g., participants' socioeconomic status, methodological factors), the results of two additional meta-analyses indicated no meaningful differences in educational outcomes when comparing single-gender versus coeducational schooling (Pahlke, Hyde, & Allison, 2014; Signorella, Hayes, & Li, 2013). Because there seem to be important disadvantages of single-gender education (i.e., increased gender stereotypes), and no educational advantages (Pahlke et al., 2014; Signorella et al., 2013; U.S. Department of Education, 2005), critics of single-gender education argue that segregating by gender is not the solution for reducing sexism within schools (see Bigler et al., 2014 [Chapter 7 of this volume]).

6.2. Interventions

Other approaches to reducing sexism within schools have taken a more direct approach to countering the bias that occurs. Some approaches teach children to confront sexism they encounter; some approaches help children attribute negative feedback to discrimination when it is appropriate; and other approaches try to reduce the impact of sexism on children's academic outcomes.

First, some interventions have taught individuals to confront instances of bias that they witness. Research has shown that teaching people to publically confront instances of prejudice can reduce the biases of those who witness the confrontation (Czopp, Monteith, & Mark, 2006). This has been shown to be particularly influential when the confrontation comes from an individual who is not the target of bias but rather from a bystander (Rasinski & Czopp, 2010). Extending this research (which was focused on ethnic bias) to instances of gender bias, some studies have examined whether confronting sexism reduces the sexist attitudes of those who witness the confrontation. Within the classroom, teachers are important individuals to train to confront sexism. Teachers who confront sexism in the classroom, because of their special authority within the class, are particularly able to model a gender-fair norm (Pornpitakpan, 2004). In one study, students saw videotaped vignettes in which a student made a sexist comment about girls not being good at math (Boysen, 2013). The teacher in the video either confronted the offending student or ignored the comment. College students who watched the teacher confront the sexist student showed reduced sexist attitudes after watching the confrontation (Boysen, 2013). Importantly, in a follow-up study, students showed a similar reduction in sexist attitudes after watching a peer confront a sexist student (Boysen, 2013).

Fewer interventions have tried to teach children how to confront, and thus reduce, sexism. In one effective example, Lamb, Bigler, Liben, and Green (2009) taught elementary school children to respond to sexist comments they heard from peers. Most of the comments that peers said to one another involved teasing a gender-atypical student. The researchers taught children to use funny retorts (e.g., "You can't say 'Girls can't play'") or direct rebuttals to the sexist comments. They found that the training intervention, particularly when children practiced the responses using role-playing, was effective in increasing children's confrontation of sexist comments (similar results were replicated in Pahlke et al., 2014). Indeed, using retorts in response to sexism seemed to spread over time to the other experimental groups. Large-scale bystander intervention studies (e.g., the Green Dot program in which college students are taught to speak out and report instances of violence against women) have also been effective in increasing confrontations against sexism (Coker et al., 2011).

Other approaches have suggested that it is beneficial for children to recognize sexism when they encounter it, thus making it possible to attribute their negative feedback to external (rather than internal) causes and recognize it as unfair. To test this premise, the effects of learning about gender discrimination on American adolescent girls' science motivation were tested in an experiment (Weisgram & Bigler, 2007). Girls participated in a program aimed at increasing interest in science, with the experimental group additionally receiving lessons about gender-based occupational discrimination. Girls in the experimental group showed increased self-efficacy and value about science after learning about gender discrimination compared to the control group (who did not learn about discrimination). Additional research has shown that learning about past discrimination inspires girls to battle future discrimination (Pahlke et al., 2010). These studies suggest that one way to reduce the impact of sexism is to directly teach about sexism.

6.3. School Climate

Because bystander inventions and confronting sexism when it is encountered seem to be an important step in reducing sexism within schools, approaches that alter the entire school climate are likely to be the most effective in reducing sexism. In other words, it is likely that school-wide programs that make sexism unacceptable, and make it normative to confront sexism, will show the greatest reduction in sexism. These broad-based interventions have been shown to be effective in reducing bullying at schools (O'Moore & Minton, 2005; Salmivalli, Kaukiainen, & Voeten, 2005). The goal of these approaches is to change the climate so that peers are intolerant to bullying. Research has shown that the greater and more widespread the implementation, the larger the effects. For example, schools were most effective in reducing bullying when they implemented a school-wide policy against bullying; when teachers were educated about bullying; and when teachers worked with their entire classroom using role-playing and establishing anti-bullying rules (Salmivalli et al., 2005).

Sexual harassment perpetration seems to be largely influenced by school climate (Attar-Schwartz, 2009). For example, Ormerod, Collinsworth, and Perry (2008) examined the impact of sexual harassment on high school students. School climate moderated the impact of sexual harassment on both girls and boys. When the school climate was tolerant of sexual harassment, the impacts on self-esteem, body image, psychological distress, school withdrawal, and perceptions of school safety were worse.

7. CONCLUSIONS

As we have reviewed in our chapter, sexism in schools can undermine the academic achievement and social adjustment of girls and boys. Sexism outside of school can also affect children's behavior and motivation in the classroom. The perpetrators of sexism may include teachers, parents, peers, and media. In these contexts, children may experience gender-stereotyped biases regarding the kinds of achievements that are viewed desirable or inappropriate for girls and boys. Some of the biases that we reviewed include negative stereotypes about girls and women in many STEM fields and athletics. We also noted how traditional notions of masculinity can undermine boys' overall academic achievement. Furthermore, surveys indicate that most girls and boys experience sexual harassment in schools. In addition to the negative impact on their socioemotional adjustment, sexual harassment can reduce students' academic motivation. Next, we addressed factors related to students' awareness of sexism in schools as well as effective coping strategies that can bolster students' resilience in the face of sexist events. Finally, we considered some of the strategies that have been examined for reducing gender bias and sexism in schools. In contrast to some who have advocated single-gender schools as a means to improve boys' and girls' academic success, comprehensive reviews of the research literature do not point to meaningful difference between single-gender and coeducational schooling in relation to student outcomes. Other strategies, such as teaching about gender bias, promoting proactive coping in children, and fostering an egalitarian school climate, may be more promising ways to increase the success of both girls and boys in our schools.

REFERENCES

Abrams, D., Rutland, A., Cameron, L., & Ferrell, J. (2007). Older but wilier: In-group accountability and the development of subjective group dynamics. *Developmental Psychology, 43*, 134–148.

Ambady, N., Shih, M., Kim, A., & Pittinksy, T. L. (2001). Stereotype susceptibility in children: Effects of identity activation on quantitative performance. *Psychological Science, 12*, 385–390.

American Association of University Women (AAUW). (1992). *How schools shortchange girls.* Washington, DC: Author.

American Association of University Women (AAUW). (2011). *Crossing the line: Sexual harassment at school.* Washington, DC: Author.

Andre, T., Whigham, M., Hendrickson, A., & Chambers, S. (1999). Competency beliefs, positive affect, and gender stereotypes of elementary students and their parents about science versus other school subjects. *Journal of Research in Science Teaching, 36*, 719–747.

Attar-Schwartz, S. (2009). Peer sexual harassment victimization at school: The roles of student characteristics, cultural affiliation, and school factors. *The American Journal of Orthopsychiatry, 79*, 407–420.

Aubrey, J., & Harrison, K. (2004). The gender-role content of children's favorite television programs and its links to their gender-related perceptions. *Media Psychology, 6*, 111–146.

Ayres, M. M., Friedman, C. K., & Leaper, C. (2009). Individual and situational factors related to young women's likelihood of confronting sexism in their everyday lives. *Sex Roles, 61*, 449–460.

Azmitia, A., & Brown, J. R. (2000). Latino immigrant parents' beliefs about the "path of life" of their adolescent children. In J. M. Contreras, K. A. Kerns, & A. M. Neal-Barnett (Eds.), *Latino children and families in the United States* (pp. 77–106). Westport, CT: Praeger Press.

Barbarin, O. A., Chinn, L., & Wright, Y. F. (2014). Creating developmentally auspicious school environments for African American boys. In L. S. Liben & R. S. Bigler (Vol. Eds.), *The role of gender in educational contexts and outcomes*. In J. B. Benson (Series Ed.), *Advances in child development and behavior: Vol. 47* (pp. 333–365). London: Elsevier.

Basow, S., & Rubin, L. (1999). Gender influences on adolescent development. In N. Johnson, M. C. Roberts, & J. Worrell (Eds.), *Beyond appearance: A new look at adolescent girls* (pp. 25–52). Washington, DC: American Psychological Association.

Beilock, S. L., Gunderson, E. A., Ramirez, G., & Levine, S. C. (2010). Female teachers' math anxiety affects girls' math achievement. *Proceedings of the National Academy of Sciences of the United States of America, 107*, 1860–1863.

Benner, A. D., & Graham, S. (2011). Latino adolescents' experiences of discrimination across the first 2 years of high school: Correlates and influences on educational outcomes. *Child Development, 82*, 508–519.

Bhanot, R., & Jovanovic, J. (2005). Do parents' academic gender stereotypes influence whether they intrude on their children's homework? *Sex Roles, 52*, 597–607.

Bigler, R. S., Arthur, A. E., Hughes, J. M., & Patterson, M. M. (2008). The politics of race and gender: Children's perceptions of discrimination and the U.S. presidency. *Analyses of Social Issues and Public Policy: ASAP, 8*(1), 83–112.

Bigler, R. S., Hayes, A. R., & Liben, L. S. (2014). Analysis and evaluation of the rationales for single-sex schooling. In L. S. Liben & R. S. Bigler (Vol. Eds.), *The role of gender in educational contexts and outcomes*. In J. B. Benson (Series Ed.), *Advances in child development and behavior: Vol. 47* (pp. 225–260). London: Elsevier.

Bleeker, M. M., & Jacobs, J. E. (2004). Achievement in math and science: Do mothers' beliefs matter 12 years later? *Journal of Educational Psychology, 96*, 97–109.

Boysen, G. A. (2013). Confronting math stereotypes in the classroom: Its effect on female college students' sexism and perceptions of confronters. *Sex Roles, 69*, 297–307.

Brody, G. H., Chen, Y. F., Murry, V. M., Ge, X., Simons, R. L., Gibbons, F. X., et al. (2006). Perceived discrimination and the adjustment of African American youths: A five-year longitudinal analysis with contextual moderation effects. *Child Development, 77*, 1170–1189.

Brown, C. S., Alabi, B. O., Huynh, V. W., & Masten, C. L. (2011). Ethnicity and gender in late childhood and early adolescence: Group identity and awareness of bias. *Developmental Psychology, 47*, 463–471.

Brown, C. S., & Bigler, R. S. (2004). Children's perceptions of gender discrimination. *Developmental Psychology, 40*, 714–726.

Brown, C. S., & Bigler, R. S. (2005). Children's perceptions of discrimination: A developmental model. *Child Development, 76*, 533–553.

Brown, C., Bigler, R. S., & Chu, H. (2010). An experimental study of the correlates and consequences of perceiving oneself to be the target of gender discrimination. *Journal of Experimental Child Psychology, 107*, 100–117.

Brown, B. B., & Larson, J. (2009). Peer relationships in adolescence. In R. M. Lerner & L. Steinberg (Eds.), *Handbook of adolescent psychology* (pp. 74–103) (3rd ed.). Hoboken, NJ: John Wiley & Sons Inc.

Brown, C. S., & Leaper, C. (2010). Latina and European American girls' experiences with academic sexism and their self-concepts in mathematics and science during adolescence. *Sex Roles, 63*, 860–870.

Chang, A., Sandhofer, C. M., & Brown, C. S. (2011). Gender biases in early number exposure to preschool-aged children. *Journal of Language and Social Psychology, 30*, 440–450.

Chhin, C. S., Bleeker, M. M., & Jacobs, J. E. (2008). Gender-typed occupational choices: The long-term impact of parents' beliefs and expectations. In Helen M. G. Watt, &

Jacquelynne S. Eccles (Eds.), *Gender and occupational outcomes: Longitudinal assessments of individual, social, and cultural influences* (pp. 215–234). Washington, DC: American Psychological Association.

Chiodo, D., Wolfe, D. A., Croosk, C., Hughes, R., & Jaffe, P. (2009). Impact of sexual harassment victimization by peers on subsequent adolescent victimization and adjustment: A longitudinal study. *Journal of Adolescent Health, 45*, 246–252.

Chow, A., Eccles, J. S., & Salmela-Aro, K. (2012). Task value profiles across subjects and aspirations to physical and IT-related sciences in the United States and Finland. *Developmental Psychology, 48*, 1612–1628.

Cockburn, C., & Clarke, G. (2002). "Everybody's looking at you!" Girls negotiating the "femininity deficit" they incur in physical education. *Women's Studies International Forum, 25*, 651–665.

Coker, A. L., Cook-Craig, P. G., Williams, C. M., Fisher, B. S., Clear, E. R., Garcia, L. S., et al. (2011). Evaluation of Green Dot: An active bystander intervention to reduce sexual violence on college campuses. *Violence Against Women, 17*, 777–796.

Compas, B. E., Connor-Smith, J. K., Saltzman, H., Thomsen, A. H., & Wadsworth, M. E. (2001). Coping with stress during childhood and adolescence: Problems, progress, and potential in theory and research. *Psychological Bulletin, 127*, 87–127.

Conroy, D. E., Silva, J. M., Newcomer, R. R., Walker, B. W., & Johnson, M. S. (2001). Personal and participatory socializers of the perceived legitimacy of aggressive behavior in sport. *Aggressive Behavior, 27*, 405–418.

Cortina, L. M., & Wasti, S. A. (2005). Profiles in coping: Responses to sexual harassment across persons, organizations, and cultures. *Journal of Applied Psychology, 90*, 182–192.

Crosby, F. (1984). The denial of personal discrimination. *American Behavioral Scientist, 27*, 371–386.

Crowley, K., Callanan, M. A., Tenenbaum, H. R., & Allen, E. (2001). Parents explain more often to boys than to girls during shared scientific thinking. *Psychological Science, 12*, 258–261.

Cvencek, D., Meltzoff, A. N., & Greenwald, A. G. (2011). Math–gender stereotypes in elementary school children. *Child Development, 82*, 766–779.

Czopp, A. M., Monteith, M. J., & Mark, A. Y. (2006). Standing up for a change: Reducing bias through interpersonal confrontation. *Journal of Personality and Social Psychology, 90*, 784.

Del Río, M. F., & Strasser, K. (2013). Preschool children's beliefs about gender differences in academic skills. *Sex Roles, 68*, 231–238.

Dickhäuser, O., & Stiensmeier-Pelster, J. (2003). Gender differences in the choice of computer courses: Applying an expectancy-value model. *Social Psychology of Education, 6*, 173–189.

Diekman, A. B., & Murnen, S. K. (2004). Learning to be little women and little men: The inequitable gender equality of nonsexist children's literature. *Sex Roles, 50*, 373–385.

Dill, K. E., & Thill, K. P. (2007). Video game characters and the socialization of gender roles: Young people's perceptions mirror sexist media depictions. *Sex Roles, 57*, 851–864.

DuBois, D. L., Burk-Braxton, C., Swenson, L. P., Tevendale, H. D., & Hardesty, J. L. (2002). Race and gender influences on adjustment in early adolescence: Investigation of an integrative model. *Child Development, 73*, 1573–1592.

Eccles, J. S., Freedman-Doan, C., Frome, P., Jacobs, J., & Yoon, K. S. (2000). Gender-role socialization in the family: A longitudinal approach. In T. Eckes, & H. M. Trautner (Eds.), *The developmental social psychology of gender* (pp. 333–360). Mahwah, NJ: Erlbaum.

Eccles, J. S., & Wigfield, A. (2002). Motivational beliefs, values, and goals. *Annual Review of Psychology, 53*, 109–132.

Egan, S., & Perry, D. (2001). Gender identity: A multidimensional analysis with implications for psychosocial adjustment. *Developmental Psychology, 37*, 451–463.

Eliot, L. (2009). *Pink brain, blue brain*. Boston: Houghton Mifflin Harcourt.
Else-Quest, N., Hyde, J., & Linn, M. C. (2010). Cross-national patterns of gender differences in mathematics: A meta-analysis. *Psychological Bulletin, 136*, 103–127.
Eurydice Network (2010). *Gender differences in educational outcomes: Study on the measures taken and the current situation in Europe*. Brussels: EACEA P9 Eurydice.
Evans, L., & Davies, K. (2000). No sissy boys here: A content analysis of the representation of masculinity in elementary school reading textbooks. *Sex Roles, 42*, 255–270.
Fabes, R. A., Pahlke, E., Martin, C. L., & Hanish, L. D. (2013). Gender-segregated schooling and gender stereotyping. *Educational Studies, 39*, 315–319.
Fennema, E., Peterson, P. L., Carpenter, T. P., & Lubinski, C. A. (1990). Teachers' attributions and beliefs about girls, boys, and mathematics. *Educational Studies in Mathematics, 21*, 55–69.
Fineran, S., & Bennett, L. (1999). Gender and power issues of peer sexual harassment among teenagers. *Journal of Interpersonal Violence, 14*, 626–641.
Fineran, S., & Bolen, R. M. (2006). Risk factors for peer sexual harassment in schools. *Journal of Interpersonal Violence, 21*, 1169–1190.
Forbes, G. B., Adams-Curtis, L. E., Pakalka, A. H., & White, K. B. (2006). Dating aggression, sexual coercion, and aggression-supporting attitudes among college men as a function of participation in aggressive high school sports. *Violence Against Women, 12*, 441–455.
Fredricks, J. A., & Eccles, J. S. (2002). Children's competence and value beliefs from childhood through adolescence: Growth trajectories in two male-sex-typed domains. *Developmental Psychology, 38*, 519–533.
Frome, P., & Eccles, J. (1998). Parents' influence on children's achievement-related perceptions. *Journal of Personality and Social Psychology, 74*, 435–452.
Fuller-Rowell, T. E., & Doan, S. N. (2010). The social costs of academic success across ethnic groups. *Child Development, 81*, 1696–1713.
Garrahy, D. A. (2001). Three third-grade teachers' gender-related beliefs and behavior. *The Elementary School Journal, 102*, 81–94.
Glick, P., & Fiske, S. T. (1996). The ambivalent sexism inventory: Differentiating hostile and benevolent sexism. *Journal of Personality and Social Psychology, 70*, 491.
Greene, M. L., Way, N., & Pahl, K. (2006). Trajectories of perceived adult and peer discrimination among Black, Latino, and Asian American adolescents: Patterns and psychological correlates. *Developmental Psychology, 42*, 218.
Greenwald, A. G., Banaji, M. R., Rudman, L. A., Farnham, S. D., Nosek, B. A., & Mellott, D. S. (2002). A unified theory of implicit attitudes, stereotypes, self-esteem, and self-concept. *Psychological Review, 109*, 3–25.
Gunderson, E. A., Ramirez, G., Levine, S. C., & Beilock, S. L. (2012). The role of parents and teachers in the development of gender-related math attitudes. *Sex Roles, 66*, 153–166.
Gurian, M. (2001). *Boys and girls learn differently!*. San Francisco, CA: Jossey-Bass.
Halim, M. L., & Ruble, D. (2010). Gender identity and stereotyping in early and middle childhood. In J. C. Chrisler, & D. R. McCreary (Eds.), *Handbook of gender research in psychology* (pp. 495–525). New York: Springer.
Halpern, D. F., Eliot, L., Bigler, R. S., Fabes, R. A., Hanish, L. D., Hyde, J., et al. (2011). The pseudoscience of single-sex schooling. *Science, 333*(6050), 1706–1707.
Hamilton, M. C., Anderson, D., Broaddus, M., & Young, K. (2006). Gender stereotyping and under-representation of female characters in 200 popular children's picture books: A twenty-first century update. *Sex Roles, 55*, 757–765.
Harris Interactive (2001). *Hostile hallways: Bullying, teasing, and sexual harassment in school*. Washington, DC: American Association of University Women Educational Foundation.
Hartley, B. L., & Sutton, R. M. (2013). A stereotype threat account of boys' academic underachievement. *Child Development, 84*, 1716–1733.

Helwig, R., Anderson, L., & Tindal, G. (2001). Influence of elementary student gender on teachers' perceptions of mathematics achievement. *The Journal of Educational Research, 95,* 93–102.

Herbert, J., & Stipek, D. (2005). The emergence of gender differences in children's perceptions of their academic competence. *Journal of Applied Developmental Psychology, 26,* 276–295.

Hill, C., Corbett, C., & St. Rose, A. (2010). *Why so few? Women in science, technology, engineering, and mathematics.* Washington, DC: AAUW.

Holahan, C. J., Valentiner, D. P., & Moos, R. H. (1995). Parental support, coping strategies, and psychological adjustment: An integrative model with late adolescents. *Journal of Youth and Adolescence, 24,* 633–648.

Horn, S. S. (2008). The multifaceted nature of sexual prejudice: How adolescents reason about sexual orientation and sexual prejudice. In S. R. Levi & M. Killen (Eds.), *Intergroup attitudes and relations in childhood through adulthood* (pp. 173–188). New York, NY: Oxford University Press.

Hurtado, A. (2003). *Voicing Chicana feminisms: Young women speak out on sexuality and identity.* New York: New York University Press.

Jackson, C. D., & Leffingwell, R. J. (1999). The role of instructions in creating math anxiety in students from kindergarten through college. *The Mathematics Teacher, 92,* 583–586.

Jacobs, J. E., Chhin, C. S., & Shaver, K. (2005). Longitudinal links between perceptions of adolescence and the social beliefs of adolescents: Are parents' stereotypes related to beliefs held about and by their children? *Journal of Youth and Adolescence, 34,* 61–72.

Jewell, J. A., & Brown, C. S. (2013). Sexting, catcalls, and butt slaps: How gender stereotypes and perceived group norms predict sexualized behavior. *Sex Roles, 69,* 594–604.

Jewell, J. A., & Brown, C. S. (2014). Relations among gender typicality, peer relations, and mental health during early adolescence. *Social Development, 23,* 137–156.

Jones, S., & Myhill, D. (2004). 'Troublesome boys' and 'compliant girls': Gender identity and perceptions of achievement and underachievement. *British Journal of Sociology of Education, 25,* 547–561.

Jussim, L., & Harber, K. D. (2005). Teacher expectations and self-fulfilling prophecies: Knowns and unknowns, resolved and unresolved controversies. *Personality and Social Psychology Review, 9,* 131–155.

Kaiser, C. R., & Miller, C. T. (2004). A stress and coping perspective on confronting abstract sexism. *Psychology of Women Quarterly, 28,* 168–178.

Kane, E. (2000). Racial and ethnic variations in gender-related attitudes. *Annual Review of Sociology, 26,* 419–439.

Keller, C. (2001). Effect of teachers' stereotyping on students' stereotyping of mathematics as a male domain. *The Journal of Social Psychology, 141,* 165–173.

Kessels, U. (2005). Fitting into the stereotype: How gender-stereotyped perceptions of prototypic peers relate to liking for school subjects. *European Journal of Psychology of Education, 20,* 309–323.

Kessels, U., & Steinmayr, R. (2013). Macho-man in school: Toward the role of gender role self-concepts and help seeking in school performance. *Learning and Educational Differences, 23,* 234–240.

Kiefer, S. M., & Ryan, A. M. (2008). Striving for social dominance over peers: The implications for academic adjustment during early adolescence. *Journal of Educational Psychology, 100,* 417–428.

Klein, S., & Sesma. E. (2011). *What are we learning from the 2006–7 Office for Civil Rights Survey question about public schools with single-sex academic classes? An exploratory study.* Arlington, VA: Feminist Majority Foundation.

Kosciw, J. G., Greytak, E. A., Diaz, E. M., & Bartkiewicz, M. J. (2010). *The 2009 national school climate survey: The experiences of lesbian, gay, bisexual, and transgender youth in our nation's schools.* New York, NY: GLSEN.

Krendl, A. C., Richeson, J. A., Kelley, W. M., & Heatherton, T. F. (2008). The negative consequences of threat: A functional magnetic resonance imaging investigation of the neural mechanisms underlying women's underperformance in math. *Psychological Science, 19*, 168–175.

Lacasse, A., Purdy, K. T., & Mendelson, M. J. (2003). The mixed company they keep: Potentially offensive sexual behaviors among adolescents. *International Journal of Behavioral Development, 27*, 532–540.

Lamb, L. M., Bigler, R. S., Liben, L. S., & Green, V. A. (2009). Teaching children to confront peers' sexist remarks: Implications for theories of gender development and educational practice. *Sex Roles, 61*, 361–382.

Lane, K. A. (2012). Being narrow while being broad: The importance of construct specificity and theoretical generality. *Sex Roles, 66*, 167–174.

Lavy, V. (2008). Do gender stereotypes reduce girls' or boys' human capital outcomes? Evidence from a natural experiment. *Journal of Public Economics, 92*, 2083–2105.

Lazarus, R. S. (1999). *Stress and emotion: A new synthesis*. New York: Springer.

Lazarus, R. S., & Folkman, S. (1984). *Stress, appraisal, and coping*. New York: Springer.

Leaper, C. (2013). Gender development during childhood. In P. D. Zelazo (Ed.), *Oxford handbook of developmental psychology: Vol. 2* (pp. 327–377). New York: Oxford University Press.

Leaper, C., & Arias, D. M. (2011). College women's feminist identity: A multidimensional analysis with implications for coping with sexism. *Sex Roles, 64*, 475–490.

Leaper, C., & Brown, C. S. (2008). Perceived experiences with sexism among adolescent girls. *Child Development, 79*, 685–704.

Leaper, C., Brown, C. S., & Ayres, M. M. (2013). Adolescent girls' cognitive appraisals of coping responses to sexual harassment. *Psychology in the Schools, 50*, 969–986.

Leaper, C., & Robnett, R. D. (2011). Sexism. In J. R. Levesque (Ed.), *Encyclopedia of adolescence* (pp. 2641–2648). New York: Springer.

Lee, J. S., & Bowen, N. K. (2006). Parent involvement, cultural capital, and the achievement gap among elementary school children. *American Educational Research Journal, 43*, 193–218.

Lee, E., & Troop-Gordon, W. (2011). Peer processes and gender role development: Changes in gender atypicality related to negative peer treatment and children's friendships. *Sex Roles, 64*, 90–102.

Legewie, J., & DiPrete, T. A. (2012). School context and the gender gap in educational achievement. *American Sociological Review, 77*, 463–485.

Li, Q. (1999). Teachers' beliefs and gender differences in mathematics: A review. *Educational Research, 41*, 63–76.

Liben, L. S., Bigler, R. S., & Krogh, H. R. (2001). Pink and blue collar jobs: Children's judgments of job status and job aspirations in relation to sex of worker. *Journal of Experimental Child Psychology, 79*, 346–363.

Lindberg, S. M., Grabe, S., & Hyde, J. S. (2007). Gender, pubertal development, and peer sexual harassment predict objectified body consciousness in early adolescence. *Journal of Research on Adolescence, 17*, 723–742.

Lindberg, S. M., Hyde, J. S., Petersen, J. L., & Linn, M. C. (2010). New trends in gender and mathematics performance: A meta-analysis. *Psychological Bulletin, 136*, 1123–1135.

Lobel, T. E., Bempechat, J., Gewirtz, J. C., Shoken-Topaz, T., & Bashe, E. (1993). The role of gender-related information and self-endorsement of traits in preadolescents' inferences and judgments. *Child Development, 64*, 1285–1294.

Losen, D. J. (2011). *Discipline policies, successful schools, and racial justice*. Boulder, CO: National Education Policy Center. Retrieved from http://nepc.colorado.edu/publication/discipline-policies.

Magley, V. J. (2002). Coping with sexual harassment: Reconceptualizing women's resistance. *Journal of Personality and Social Psychology, 83*, 930–946.

Manago, A., Brown, C., & Leaper, C. (2009). Feminist identity among Latina adolescents. *Journal of Adolescent Research, 24*, 750–776.

Martin, C. L., Fabes, R. A., & Hanish, L. D. (2014). Gendered-peer relationships in educational contexts. In L. S. Liben & R. S. Bigler (Vol. Eds.), *The role of gender in educational contexts and outcomes.* In J. B. Benson (Series Ed.), *Advances in child development and behavior: Vol. 47* (pp. 151–187). London: Elsevier.

McGraw, R., Lubienski, S. T., & Strutchens, M. E. (2006). A closer look at gender in NAEP mathematics achievement and affect data: Intersections with achievement, race/ethnicity, and socioeconomic status. *Journal for Research in Mathematics Education, 37*, 129–150.

Mercier, E. M., Barron, B., & O'Connor, K. M. (2006). Images of self and others as computer users: The role of gender and experience. *Journal of Computer Assisted Learning, 22*, 335–348.

Messner, M. A. (1998). Boyhood, organized sports, and the construction of masculinities. In M. A. Messner (Ed.), *Men's lives* (pp. 109–121). Boston, MA: Allyn & Bacon.

Miller, C. T., & Major, B. (2000). Coping with stigma and prejudice. In T. F. Heatherton, R. E. Kleck, M. R. Hebl, & J. G. Hull (Eds.), *The social psychology of stigma* (pp. 243–272). New York: Guilford.

Moradi, B., & Funderburk, J. R. (2006). Roles of perceived sexist events and perceived social support in the mental health of women seeking counseling. *Journal of Counseling Psychology, 53*, 464–473.

Muzzatti, B., & Agnoli, F. (2007). Gender and mathematics: Attitudes and stereotype threat susceptibility in Italian children. *Developmental Psychology, 43*, 747–759.

National Center for Education Statistics. (2013). *The condition of education.* Washington, DC: U.S. Department of Education. Retrieved from http://nces.ed.gov/pubsearch.

National Science Foundation (2013). *Women, minorities, and persons with disabilities in science and engineering.* Washington, DC: National Science Foundation. Retrieved from http://www.nsf.gov/statistics/wmpd/.

Neff, K. D., Cooper, C. E., & Woodruff, A. L. (2007). Children's and adolescents' developing perceptions of gender inequality. *Social Development, 16*, 682–699.

Nosek, B. A., Smyth, F. L., Sriram, N., Lindner, N. M., Devos, T., Ayala, A., et al. (2009). National differences in gender–science stereotypes predict national sex differences in science and math achievement. *Proceedings of the National Academy of Sciences of the United States of America, 106*, 10593–10597.

OECD (2013). *Education at a glance 2013: OECD indicators.* Author: OECD Publishing. Retrieved from http://dx.doi.org/10.1787/eag-2013-en.

O'Moore, A., & Minton, S. (2005). Evaluation of the effectiveness of an anti-bullying programme in primary schools. *Aggressive Behavior, 31*, 609–622.

Ormerod, A. J., Collinsworth, L. L., & Perry, L. A. (2008). Critical climate: Relations among sexual harassment, climate, and outcomes for high school girls and boys. *Psychology of Women Quarterly, 32*, 113–125.

Pahlke, E., Bigler, R. S., & Green, V. A. (2010). Effects of learning about historical gender discrimination on early adolescents' occupational judgments and aspirations. *The Journal of Early Adolescence, 30*(6), 854–894.

Pahlke, E., Bigler, R. S., & Martin, C. L. (2014). Can fostering children's ability to challenge sexism improve critical analysis, internalization, and enactment of inclusive, egalitarian peer relationships? *Journal of Social Issues, 70*, 113–131.

Pahlke, E., Hyde, J. S., & Allison, C. M. (2014). The effects of single-sex compared to coeducational schooling on students' performance and attitudes: A meta-analyses. *Psychological Bulletin.* Advance online publication http://dx.doi.org/10.1037/a0035740.

Pascoe, C. J. (2007). *Dude, you're a fag: Masculinity and sexuality in high school.* Berkeley: University of California Press.

Pepler, D. J., Craig, W. M., Connolly, J. A., Yuile, A., McMaster, L., & Jiang, D. (2006). A developmental perspective on bullying. *Aggressive Behavior, 32*, 376–384.

Petersen, J. L., & Hyde, J. S. (2009). A longitudinal investigation of peer sexual harassment victimization in adolescence. *Journal of Adolescence, 32*, 1173–1188.

Petersen, J., & Hyde, J. S. (2014). Gender-related academic and occupational interests and goals. In L. S. Liben & R. S. Bigler (Vol. Eds.), *The role of gender in educational contexts and outcomes*. In J. B. Benson (Series Ed.), *Advances in child development and behavior: Vol. 47* (pp. 43–76). London: Elsevier.

Picho, K., Rodriguez, A., & Finnie, L. (2013). Exploring the moderating role of context on the mathematics performance of females under stereotype threat: A meta-analysis. *Journal of Social Psychology, 153*, 299–333.

Plante, I., Théorêt, M., & Favreau, O. E. (2009). Student gender stereotypes: Contrasting the perceived maleness and femaleness of mathematics and language. *Educational Psychology, 29*, 385–405.

Pornpitakpan, C. (2004). The persuasiveness of source credibility: A critical review of five decades' evidence. *Journal of Applied Social Psychology, 34*, 243–281.

Poteat, V. P., Scheer, J. R., & Mereish, E. H. (2014). Factors affecting academic achievement among sexual minority and gender-variant youth. In L. S. Liben & R. S. Bigler (Vol. Eds.), *The role of gender in educational contexts and outcomes*. In J. B. Benson (Series Ed.), *Advances in child development and behavior: Vol. 47* (pp. 261–300). London: Elsevier.

Quinn, K. A., Roese, N. J., Pennington, G. L., & Olson, J. M. (1999). The personal/group discrimination discrepancy: The role of informational complexity. *Personality and Social Psychology Bulletin, 25*, 1430–1440.

Rao, A., & Seaton, M. (2009). *The way of boys*. New York, NY: HarperCollins.

Rasinski, H. M., & Czopp, A. M. (2010). The effect of target status on witnesses' reactions to confrontations of bias. *Basic and Applied Social Psychology, 32*, 8–16.

Riegle-Crumb, C., Farkas, G., & Muller, C. (2006). The role of gender and friendship in advanced course taking. *Sociology of Education, 79*, 1017–1045.

Rose, A. J., Glick, G. C., & Smith, R. L. (2011). Popularity and gender: The two cultures of boys and girls. In A. H. N. Cillessen, D. Schwartz, & L. Mayeux (Eds.), *Popularity in the peer system* (pp. 79–102). New York, NY: Guilford Press.

Rowley, S. J., Kutz-Costes, B., Mistry, R., & Feagans, L. (2007). Social status and a predictor of race and gender stereotypes in late childhood and early adolescence. *Social Development, 16*, 150–168.

Rowley, S. J., Ross, L., Lozada, F., Williams, A., Gale, A., & Kurtz-Costes, B. (2014). Framing black boys: Parent, teacher, and student narratives of the academic lives of black boys. In L. S. Liben & R. S. Bigler (Vol. Eds.), *The role of gender in educational contexts and outcomes*. In J. B. Benson (Series Ed.), *Advances in child development and behavior: Vol. 47* (pp. 301–332). London: Elsevier.

Russell, S., Kosciw, J., Horn, S., & Saewyc, E. (2010). Safe schools policy for LGBTQ students. *Social Policy Report, 24*, 1–25.

Sáinz, M., Pálmen, R., & García-Cuesta, S. (2012). Parental and secondary school teachers' perceptions of ICT professionals, gender differences and their role in the choice of studies. *Sex Roles, 66*, 235–249.

Salmivalli, C., Kaukiainen, A., & Voeten, M. (2005). Anti-bullying intervention: Implementation and outcome. *British Journal of Educational Psychology, 75*, 465–487.

Salomone, R. C. (2006). Single-sex programs: Resolving the research conundrum. *Teachers College Record, 108*, 778–802.

Santos, C. E., Galligan, K., Pahlke, E., & Fabes, R. A. (2013). *American Journal of Orthopsychiatry, 83*, 252–264.

Sax, L. (2005). *Why gender matters: What parents and teachers need to know about the emerging science of sex differences*. New York, NY: Doubleday.

Schmalz, D. L., Kerstetter, D. L., & Anderson, D. M. (2008). Stigma consciousness as a predictor of children's participation in recreational vs. competitive sports. *Journal of Sport Behavior, 31*, 276–297.

Shakib, S. (2003). Female basketball participation. *American Behavioral Scientist, 46*, 1405–1422.

Shakib, S., Veliz, P., Dunbar, M. D., & Sabo, D. (2011). Athletics as a source for social status among youth: Examining variation by gender, race/ethnicity, and socioeconomic status. *Sociology of Sport Journal, 28*, 303–328.

Shapiro, J. R., & Williams, A. M. (2012). The role of stereotype threats in undermining girls' and women's performance and interest in STEM fields. *Sex Roles, 66*, 175–183.

Sherriff, N. (2007). Peer group cultures and social identity: An integrated approach to understanding masculinities. *British Educational Research Journal, 33*, 349–370.

Signorella, M. L., Hayes, A. R., & Li, Y. (2013). A meta-analytic critique of Mael et al.'s (2005) review of single-sex schooling. *Sex Roles, 69*, 423–441.

Signorielli, N. (2012). Television's gender-role images and contribution to stereotyping: Past, present and future. In D. G. Singer & J. L. Singer (Eds.), *Handbook of children and the media* (pp. 321–339) (2nd ed.). Thousand Oaks, CA: Sage.

Simpkins, S. D., Davis-Kean, P., & Eccles, J. S. (2005). Parents' socializing behavior and children's participation in math, science, and computer out-of-school activities. *Applied Developmental Science, 9*, 14–30.

Skelton, C. C., Carrington, B. B., Francis, B. B., Hutchings, M. M., Read, B. B., & Hall, I. I. (2009). Gender 'matters' in the primary classroom: Pupils' and teachers' perspectives. *British Educational Research Journal, 35*, 187–204.

Smith, T. E., & Leaper, C. (2006). Self-perceived gender typicality and the peer context during adolescence. *Journal of Research on Adolescence, 16*, 91–103.

Solmon, M. A. (2014). Physical education, sports, and gender in schools. In L. S. Liben & R. S. Bigler (Vol. Eds.), *The role of gender in educational contexts and outcomes*. In J. B. Benson (Series Ed.), *Advances in child development and behavior: Vol. 47* (pp. 117–150). London: Elsevier.

Steffens, M. C., & Jelenec, P. (2011). Separating implicit gender stereotypes regarding math and language: Implicit ability stereotypes are self-serving for boys and men, but not for girls and women. *Sex Roles, 64*, 324–335.

Steffens, M. C., Jelenec, P., & Noack, P. (2010). On the leaky math pipeline: Comparing implicit math-gender stereotypes and math withdrawal in female and male children and adolescents. *Journal of Educational Psychology, 102*, 947–963.

Stewart, A., & McDermott, C. (2004). Gender in psychology. *Annual Review of Psychology, 55*, 519–544.

Swim, J. K., & Thomas, M. A. (2006). Responding to everyday discrimination: A synthesis of research on goal-directed, self-regulatory coping behaviors. In S. Levin, & C. VanLaar (Eds.), *Stigma and group inequality: Social psychological perspectives* (pp. 105–126). Mahwah, NY: Lawrence Erlbaum Associates.

Taylor, D. M., Wright, S. C., Moghaddam, F. M., & Lalonde, R. N. (1990). The personal/group discrimination discrepancy: Perceiving my group, but not myself, to be a target for discrimination. *Personality and Social Psychology Bulletin, 16*, 254–262.

Tenenbaum, H. R., & Leaper, C. (2003). Parent-child conversations about science: The socialization of gender inequities? *Journal of Applied Developmental Psychology, 26*, 1–19.

Tenenbaum, H. R., Snow, C. E., Roach, K. A., & Kurland, B. (2005). Talking and reading science: Longitudinal data on sex differences in mother-child conversations in low-income families. *Developmental Psychology, 39*, 34–47.

Tiedemann, J. (2000). Parents' gender stereotypes and teachers' beliefs as predictors of children's concept of their mathematical ability in elementary school. *Journal of Educational Psychology, 92*, 144–151.

Timmerman, G. (2005). A comparison between girls' and boys' experiences of unwanted sexual behaviour in secondary schools. *Educational Research, 47,* 291–306.

TIMSS International Study Center. (2000). *TIMSS physics achievement comparison study.* Boston, MA: Author.

Turner, K. L., & Brown, C. S. (2007). The centrality of gender and ethnic identities across individuals and contexts. *Social Development, 16,* 700–719.

U.S. Department of Education, Office of Planning, Evaluation, and Policy Development, Policy and Program Studies Service. (2005). *Single-sex versus secondary schooling: A systematic review.* Washington, DC: U.S. Government Printing Office.

Umaña-Taylor, A. J., & Updegraff, K. A. (2007). Latino adolescents' mental health: Exploring the interrelations among discrimination, ethnic identity, cultural orientation, self-esteem, and depressive symptoms. *Journal of Adolescence, 30,* 549–567.

UNESCO. (2010). *Global education Digest 2010: Comparing education statistics across the world.* Montreal, Quebec: Author.

Van de Gaer, E., Pustjens, H., Van Damme, J., & De Munter, A. (2006). The gender gap in language achievement: The role of school-related attitudes of class groups. *Sex Roles, 55,* 397–408.

Vekiri, I., & Chronaki, A. (2008). Gender issues in technology use: Perceived social support, computer self-efficacy and value beliefs, and computer use beyond school. *Computers & Education, 51,* 1392–1404.

Wei, H., & Chen, J. (2012). Factors associated with peer sexual harassment victimization among Taiwanese adolescents. *Sex Roles, 66,* 66–78.

Weil, E. (2008, March 2). Teaching boys and girls separately. *New York Times Magazine.*

Weisgram, E. S., & Bigler, R. S. (2007). Effects of learning about gender discrimination on adolescent girls' attitudes toward and interest in science. *Psychology of Women Quarterly, 31,* 262–269.

Whiston, S. C., & Keller, B. K. (2004). The influences of the family of origin on career development: A review and analysis. *The Counseling Psychologist, 32,* 493–568.

Whitmire, R. (2010). *Why boys fail: Saving our sons from an educational system that's leaving them behind.* New York, NY: AMACOM.

Williams, T., Connolly, J., Pepler, D., & Craig, W. (2005). Peer victimization, social support, and psychosocial adjustment of sexual minority adolescents. *Journal of Youth and Adolescence, 34*(5), 471–482.

Women's Sports Foundation. (2009). *Women's sports and fitness facts and statistics.* Retrieved from http://www.womenssportsfoundation.org/home/research/.

Wood, D., Kaplan, R., & McLoyd, V. C. (2007). Gender differences in the educational expectations of urban, low-income African American youth: The role of parents and the school. *Journal of Youth and Adolescence, 36,* 417–427.

Yee, D. K., & Eccles, J. S. (1988). Parent perceptions and attributions for children's math achievement. *Sex Roles, 19,* 317–333.

Young, R., & Sweeting, H. (2004). Adolescent bullying, relationships, psychological well-being, and gender-atypical behavior: A gender diagnosticity approach. *Sex Roles, 50,* 525–537.

Zakaria, F. (2011). *The post-American world: Release 2.0.* New York, NY: W. W. Norton.

CHAPTER SEVEN

Analysis and Evaluation of the Rationales for Single-Sex Schooling[‡]

Rebecca S. Bigler[1,*], Amy Roberson Hayes[*], Lynn S. Liben[†]
[*]Department of Psychology, University of Texas at Austin, Austin, Texas, USA
[†]Department of Psychology, The Pennsylvania State University, University Park, Pennsylvania, USA
[1]Corresponding author: e-mail address: rebeccabigler28@gmail.com

Contents

1. Introduction	226
2. Brief History of the Rationales for Single-Sex Schooling in the United States	226
3. Analysis and Evaluation of Contemporary Rationales for Single-Sex Schooling	228
3.1 Rationale #1: It Works for All Students for Unspecified Reasons	229
3.2 Rationale #2: It Works for Some Students for Unspecified Reasons	233
3.3 Rationale #3: It Works by Capitalizing on Gender Differences	235
3.4 Rationale #4: It Works by Reducing Sexism	241
3.5 Rationale #5: It Works by Reducing Attention to Gender	247
4. Conclusions and Recommendations	252
References	254

Abstract

Amendments passed as part of the No Child Left Behind Act in 2006 made some forms of single-sex (SS) public education legal in the United States. Proponents offer a host of arguments in favor of such schooling. This chapter identifies and evaluates five broad rationales for SS schooling. We conclude that empirical evidence fails to support proponents' claims but nonetheless suggests ways in which to improve coeducation. Specifically, we (a) show that the purported benefits of SS schooling arise from factors confounded with, but not causally linked to, single-sex composition; (b) challenge claims that biological sex is an effective marker of differences relevant to instruction; (c) argue that sexism on the part of teachers and peers persists in SS contexts; and (d) critique the notion that gender *per se* "disappears" in SS contexts. We also address societal implications of the use of sex-segregated education and conclude that factors found to be beneficial for students should be implemented within coeducational schools.

[‡]This chapter represents a fully collaborative effort; order of authorship was determined alphabetically.

1. INTRODUCTION

Public single-sex (SS) schools and classrooms in the United States have become increasingly common in the past decade (Klein & Sesma, 2010; National Association for Single Sex Public Education, 2011). Although official governmental numbers are unavailable, data from the Office of Civil rights indicate that the number of public SS schools in the United States grew from a mere handful in 2000 to more than 600 by 2010. In addition, several thousand public coeducational (CE) schools offer SS academic classes (Klein & Sesma, 2010). As the number of public SS programs has increased, so too have the scope and divisiveness of the debate surrounding the purpose and efficacy of this educational practice (Bigler & Signorella, 2011; Chadwell, 2010a, 2010b; Halpern et al., 2011; Sax, 2011; Signorella & Bigler, 2013).

The creation of SS programming is typically costly in both time and money because it requires at least some separate physical spaces and schedules for male and female students (Signorella & Bigler, 2013). For this reason alone it is vital that decisions to implement SS programs be based on sound rationales. Our current chapter is therefore designed to catalogue and evaluate the major rationales that have been given by proponents of SS schooling. We hope that this approach will contribute to a better understanding of the conflicting patterns of findings and conclusions in the literature on SS versus CE schooling (see also Liben, 2014).

Our chapter is divided into three sections. In Section 2, we briefly review the history of rationales for SS schooling in the United States. In Section 3, we present our analysis and evaluation of proponents' rationales for SS schooling, organized by the causal mechanisms that have been hypothesized to link the sex-composition of classrooms to student outcomes. In Section 4, we summarize our analyses and describe policy implications that arise from our evaluation of proponents' claims' regarding SS education in the United States.

2. BRIEF HISTORY OF THE RATIONALES FOR SINGLE-SEX SCHOOLING IN THE UNITED STATES

Rationales for SS schooling vary across U.S. history and are described in detail elsewhere (see Liben, 2014; Spielhagen, 2008); we review major shifts in reasoning here. In the early history of the United States (i.e., the

1600s and 1700s), primary and secondary education was conducted almost entirely within SS environments (Hansot & Tyack, 1988), largely within schools that were exclusively for boys. The rationale for excluding girls was that educating women was a poor investment, tantamount to a waste of time and effort. The schooling laws of the mid-1600s established Latin "grammar" schools (selective schools that prepared students for a university education) and common schools, with the goal of preserving the spiritual and intellectual standards of the colony. There was no reason to include girls in such schools because they could play no role in the ministry, attend a college, nor participate in government. Thus, the great majority of schools did not accept girls (Monaghan, 1988).

Coeducation became increasingly common during the 1800s, largely in response to religious and financial rationales. Religious institutions pressed for literacy education for both girls and boys, in part because women were increasingly entrusted with the moral regulation of behavior and thus it was important that women themselves engage in religious training (e.g., reading the Bible; see Conway, 1974). Religious institutions typically viewed sex-segregated settings as optimal for such training (see Cooper, 2008, for a history of SS parochial schools in the United States). The more powerful rationale for CE schools was financial. Most regions of the country were sparsely populated and could not afford to support separate schools for boys and girls. By 1918, all states had passed mandatory education laws, forcing the creation of many small schools that housed male and female students (Gray, 1973). By the early twentieth century, most American children attended CE schools (Tyack & Hansot, 1990).

Although financial pressure produced CE institutions, belief in innate sex differences led to new gender-specific curricula (see Liben, 2014). Girls were taught traditionally feminine skills including sewing, cooking, and typing. Boys were instructed in industrial arts, bookkeeping, and commercial geography. These different courses reflected the rationale that schooling prepared individuals to participate in a labor market that was characterized by sharp gender divisions. Even during the early 1970s, girls and boys were routinely separated for some of their classes on a daily basis.

During the 1970s, the second-wave feminist movement influenced public opinion about the nature and size of sex differences. Many feminists argued that the sexes were more similar than had been supposed and pressure mounted for CE schools, as well as equal opportunities and treatment within schools (DeBare, 2004; Klein & Sesma, 2010). Although gender equity became an increasing basis for CE and gender-fair schooling, it was a law passed in 1972 that become the most powerful rationale for such schooling. Title IX of the Education Amendments stipulated that, "No person in the United States shall, on the basis of sex, be excluded from participation in, be denied the benefits of, or be subjected to discrimination under any education program or activity receiving federal financial assistance." (20 U.S.C. § 1681 (a)) (Education Amendments, 1972). The ruling led to the near extinction of public SS schools in the United States.

In 2006, Congress amended the original 1972 Title IX regulations as part of the No Child Left Behind Act (NCLBA), easing extant restrictions on sex-segregated education. Specifically, the act approved federal funding for innovative education programs, including SS schools and SS programs within CE schools (which we hereafter refer to collectively as SS schooling), with the proviso that districts conduct self-evaluations of their SS classes at least every 2 years and ensure that a "substantial relationship" exists between the SS nature of the classes and achievement of the schools' educational objectives, see F.R. § 106.34(b)(1) (U.S. Department of Education, 2006). Even before these amendments were adopted, however, interest in public SS education in the United States had been on the rise (Klein & Sesma, 2010; Thompson & Underleider, 2004). What types of rationales fueled the contemporary reimplementation SS education? And does the pool of available evidence support these rationales?

3. ANALYSIS AND EVALUATION OF CONTEMPORARY RATIONALES FOR SINGLE-SEX SCHOOLING

Proponents of SS schooling have used a wide range of rationales when arguing that SS contexts yield superior outcomes to CE contexts. We have organized these rationales into five categories of argument. The first two rationales do not directly identify a mechanism by which SS schooling is said to be effective, but instead simply assert that SS schooling is effective for youth (rationale #1) or subsets of youth (rationale #2) on the basis of purportedly observed student outcomes. The remaining three rationales identify explicit mechanisms. Rationale #3 begins from claims about sex differences in boys' and girls' qualities (e.g., differences in maturation rates) that are taken to imply the need for different pedagogical approaches. Rationale #4 begins from claims that SS schooling reduces teachers' and peers' gender biases and thereby reduces students' experience of sexism. Finally, rationale #5 begins from the claim that SS schooling diminishes the psychological salience of gender in the classroom, and, as a consequence, reduces a host of gender-related phenomena that are educationally counterproductive (e.g., sexual distraction, self-stereotyping).

3.1. Rationale #1: It Works for All Students for Unspecified Reasons

Schools looking for ways to increase student motivation and academic achievement ought to consider offering single-gender classrooms as one highly effective change that can address students' needs.

Chadwell (2010b)

Some proponents of SS schooling claim that such contexts produce advantages for academic achievement for reasons that are as yet unidentified or unidentifiable. That is, these proponents base their rationales for SS schooling on the notion that there is empirical evidence of a benefit of such educational contexts even though the exact mechanisms via which such benefits are derived are unknown. In essence, this rationale is simply the argument that SS education "works."

There are indeed individual studies that report advantages for SS over CE education (e.g., Marsh, 1991), but there are also individual studies showing the reverse (e.g., advantage for CE over SS schooling, Garcia, 1998). Clearly, it is imperative to go beyond reports of individual studies and instead to examine the literature broadly. To date, four major reviews of the SS education literature have been conducted. The first was a 1998 report by the American Association of University Women (AAUW; Morse, 1998) that reviewed the research and practice of SS education. The authors concluded that there is no credible evidence that SS education is more effective than CE education at improving academic, social, and emotional outcomes for either boys or girls. They acknowledged, however, that the term "single-sex education" covers many different types of schools and programs and thus that it is difficult to make a generalization about its efficacy (Morse, 1998). A few years later, in 2005, the American Institutes for Research prepared an extensive and systematic review of the literature on SS education, including studies of its effects on academic and social-emotional outcomes (Mael, Alonso, Gibson, Rogers, & Smith, 2005). This later review reported a slightly greater number of studies demonstrating positive effects of SS than CE schooling, although almost as many studies reported mixed or no differences.

Meta-analyses of the literature provide more informative data. In 2013, Signorella et al. provided a detailed critique of the methods and analyses used in the widely influential Mael et al. (2005) report. They reanalyzed the Mael et al. (2005) data, including 40 studies, using meta-analysis and found: (1) preexisting differences between students enrolled in SS and CE schools; (2) small to nonexistent benefits of SS schooling; and (3) associations between the degree to which SS schooling was confounded with other advantageous variables (e.g., high SES), on the one hand, and the size of the effect of SS schooling, on the other; so, for example, SS schools that served higher rather than SES populations showed better outcomes. Still more recently, Pahlke, Hyde, and Allison (2014) published a major meta-analysis of the literature on SS schooling. Their analysis, which included 184 studies that tested 1.6 million students, examined effect sizes separately for studies that did and did not attempt to control for preexisting differences between students assigned to SS versus CE settings. Modest advantages associated with SS schooling were found in studies that had not controlled for confounding variables (e.g., family SES), whereas only small to trivial effects were found in studies that controlled for confounding variables. In both controlled and uncontrolled studies, effects varied across dependent measures.

Given these reviews of the literature, what can be concluded? The meta-analytic (Pahlke et al., 2014; Signorella, Hayes, & Li, 2013) reviews of the SS schooling literature make clear that students who enroll in SS and CE educational contexts differ prior to their enrollment in these contexts and in ways that lead to superior outcomes for those attending SS schools. Understanding the factors that affect students' selection into school contexts is vital, therefore, to interpreting data on outcomes.

3.1.1 Confounds Associated with Selection into SS and CE Contexts

Two types of selection effects operate to affect outcomes associated with SS schooling. The first type of selection effect stems from student (or family) actions: those students who elect to attend SS schools may differ systematically from those students who do not elect to attend SS schools (i.e., student-driven selection effects). The second type of selection effect stems from school actions: those applicants who are selected by school administrators to attend SS schools may differ systematically from those applicants who are not selected (i.e., school-driven selection effects). Evidence suggests two primary bases for selection effects stemming from students and schools: socioeconomic background and prior academic achievement (Pahlke et al., 2014; Signorella et al., 2013).

3.1.2 Students' Socioeconomic Background

> Rich parents send their daughters to all-female schools; why shouldn't the daughters of the poor enjoy similar advantages?
>
> ***Kaminer (April 1998)***

Studies have shown that there are indeed preexisting differences among the family backgrounds of students who elect to attend SS schools versus those who attend CE schools (Mael, 1998). Compared to students who attend CE schools, students who attend SS schools typically have parents with more years of education and higher incomes (Smithers & Robinson, 1995). Students' socioeconomic background (SES) is important because of the strong associations between SES and a host of academic-related characteristics and outcomes, including discipline records, grades, and standardized test scores (Bradley & Corwyn, 2002). In an era in which even public schools rely on private fund-raising to supplement their budgets, the affluence of a school's parent body is also typically associated with the affluence of the school and the resulting availability of special programming (tutoring, clubs, enrichment opportunities, etc.). Perhaps for this reason, school-level SES, in addition to child-level SES, is a powerful predictor of academic achievement (Bradley & Corwyn, 2002). No studies of SS schooling to our knowledge make use of samples of SS and CE students who are matched for SES. Results of studies that employ SES as a control variable in comparisons of students of SS and CE schools typically show that this variable eliminates what otherwise appear to be effects of SS education on achievement (Daly & Shuttleworth, 1997; Harker & Nash, 1997; Lee & Marks, 1990; Lee, Marks, & Byrd, 1994; Marsh, 1991; Signorella et al., 2013).

In addition to accounting for the superior outcomes of SS versus CE samples, SES appears to predict achievement within SS contexts. Patterson and Pahlke (2011) examined predictors of achievement within a public SS middle school. Consistent with studies within CE settings, family SES predicted achievement, with children from higher SES backgrounds showing higher achievement levels. In sum, SES is an important factor that affects student achievement and that, because of its confounding link to school-type enrollment, has led to a spurious appearance of SS schooling benefits.

3.1.3 Students' Academic Motivation and Aptitude

> This choice [to attend a single-sex school] is about the rejection of antiacademic values that predominates in our culture and school.
>
> **Riordan (2002, pp. 19–20)**

Students' academic motivation and scholastic aptitude appear to underlie both student-driven and school-driven selection effects. With respect to student-driven selection effects, Riordan et al. (2008) and Riordan (2002) have argued that the choice to move from a CE school to a SS school is inherently proacademic, and thus students who enroll in SS schools are initially more accomplished and academically motivated than their peers at CE schools. Additionally, because SS schools typically employ some form of selective admissions processes, students with lower levels of academic achievement are less likely to apply and fulfill the application requirements than students with higher levels of academic achievement. With respect to school-driven selection effects, most public and private SS schools retain control of student admission and dismissal. In contrast, standard public schools must accept all students within a particular geographic boundary and are unable to terminate students on the basis of their academic performance. Like public charter and magnet schools, public SS schools typically accept students from across their district, and thus admission to these schools is competitive.

Given the presence of student- and school-driven selection biases, it is possible that any positive academic outcomes associated with SS schools are attributable to these schools systematically enrolling and retaining academically more qualified students. Consistent with this possibility are findings from a study of a public SS middle school in Texas by Hayes, Pahlke, and Bigler (2011). They compared earlier standardized test scores of girls who were later accepted into the school versus those who were later rejected from the school. They found that—in the year before any of the girls had begun to attend the SS school—girls who were later accepted into the SS school had significantly higher standardized test scores than those girls who were later rejected for admission. This was true despite the school's claim that admission had been determined by a lottery. Thus, the finding that later standardized test scores were higher in girls who attended the SS school than in girls who had attended regular CE public schools would be more parsimoniously attributed to the fact that those in the former group were higher achievers in the first place. When the researchers substituted a comparison sample of students who attended a CE school with a comparably selective admissions process (specifically, students from a public school magnet program), the apparent advantage of SS schooling on later standardized achievement scores evaporated. Thus, we argue that—regardless of the gender of the student body—schools that employ selective admissions procedures that allow them to enroll and retain a highly a motivated and achievement-oriented student body will show higher rates of academic success than will schools that do not employ such selection criteria.

3.2. Rationale #2: It Works for Some Students for Unspecified Reasons

No one is arguing that single-sex education is the best option for every student. But it is preferable for some students...
Hutchison & Mikulski (2012)

One of the most common rationales for SS schooling in recent years is based on the idea that children vary in their responses to both SS and CE contexts and, as a consequence, which context is best varies across children, albeit again for reasons that are largely unknown. Below, we discuss two broad subtypes of students that are hypothesized to thrive within SS educational contexts by some proponents of SS schooling: first, girls and second, children of color, who are struggling or underperforming academically (and hence are "at risk") within CE settings.

3.2.1 At-Risk Girls

As soon as [my daughter] hit middle school, I've watched with my heart breaking how her quiet, intelligent, sensitive, confident nature is being eroded by boys picking on her.
A parent quoted by Chadwell (2010a, p. 1)

Proponents of SS schools have argued that many girls fail to thrive in CE contexts, often as a result of their tendency to be passive, diffident, quiet, and cooperative (rather than assertive, confident, loud, and competitive) in the classroom, leading boys to dominate them and undermine their self-concepts (Chadwell, 2010a, 2010b; Salomone, 2006; Sax, 2005). Indeed, students' conceptions of the self are both a cause and consequence of academic and social behavior (Liu, Kaplan, & Risser, 1992). For example, students with higher academic self-esteem are more highly motivated and persevere longer at academic tasks than their peers with lower self-esteem (Wigfield & Eccles, 2000). In addition, there are well-documented sex differences in children's academic motivations and self-conceptions (see Butler, 2014 [Chapter 1 of this volume]). However, research on the relation between SS schooling and the broad range of variables related to self-concept (global self-esteem, locus of control, domain-specific self-esteem) is mixed (Mael et al., 2005). Pahlke et al.'s (2014) meta-analyses showed no significant effect of SS versus CE schooling on girls' self-concepts. Furthermore, it seems unlikely that the removal of boys from the classroom serves as an effective long-term solution to the challenges that girls who are passive, diffident, quiet, and cooperative may face when interacting with boys. It seems more likely that intervention strategies that focus on creating classroom climates that provide peer support for all students would be more cost effective than segregating schools and classrooms by gender.

Alternatively, some proponents of SS schooling have argued that girls who are perceived as gender atypical and thus at risk of social rejection are more successful within SS than CE environments. Gender atypical children are indeed sometimes socially rejected and bullied, and such treatment is associated with poor mental health outcomes (Egan & Perry, 2001; Smith & Leaper, 2006). There is, however, very little empirical research addressing whether children's gender typicality interacts with gender composition to affect student outcomes. Most studies that have examined gender typicality have used atypical interests as an outcome—rather than a predictor—of effects of SS versus CE school contexts. In sum, there is little evidence that SS schools attract or protect gender atypical children. Instead, school contexts (regardless of gender composition) that support children with a range of gender expression are likely to promote their school achievement (see Leaper & Brown, 2014 [Chapter 6 of this volume]).

3.2.2 At-Risk Students of Color

In the case of Foley Intermediate School, installing [gender] segregated classes was a reaction to the poor performance of the school's minority male students on standardized tests.

Goudreau (2010)

SS education is used with increasing frequency in low-income districts to address the underperformance of African American and Latino students, especially boys (see Barbarin, Chinn, & Wright, 2014 [Chapter 10 of this volume]). Indeed, many of the public SS schools that have garnered attention in the US specifically recruit and are geared toward African American and Latino youth (see Barbarin et al., 2014 [Chapter 10 of this volume], for description of one such school). Proponents of such academies laud these schools' attention to issues that affect African American and Latino youth and the fact that these new public schools provide much-needed resources to youth who are otherwise commonly placed in underfunded, understaffed, low-performing schools. The Eagle Academy for Young Men in the Bronx, NY, for example, boasts impressive graduation and college attendance rates of its students compared to peer schools in the area (Barbarin et al., 2014 [Chapter 10 of this volume]). Importantly, however, this public school differs from other neighborhood schools not only in its gender composition but also in other characteristics including its quantity of academic instruction (extended school days and Saturday school), in its involvement of ingroup mentors (African American male community members participate in school activities), and in its disciplinary policies and practices.

As Barbarin et al. (2014) [Chapter 10 of this volume] note, there is no empirical evidence for the effectiveness of SS versus CE schooling among African American and Latino youth when studies control for student- and school-based selection effects. Critics of such schools worry about the emphasis these schools place on gender rather than race. Goodkind (2013) argued that, by creating SS schools that serve low-income boys and girls of color, educators "blame educational failures in schools serving low-income youth of color on lack of attention to gender differences in learning rather than poverty and racism" (p. 400). It is likely that the successes of SS schools such as the Eagle Academy are due to the same selection biases described in the previous section, rather than to mechanisms specifically related to their gender composition. Additionally, the factors that differentiate such schools from other community schools are likely to improve performance of students of both genders. Extended school days and years, for example, are strongly correlated with student achievement among both boys and girls (Patal, Cooper, & Allen, 2010). In sum, it is difficult to isolate the causal mechanisms related to the much-publicized success of these students because so many factors are confounded with the gender composition of the school.

3.3. Rationale #3: It Works by Capitalizing on Gender Differences

In each of the [single-sex] schools just mentioned, teachers received training from NASSPE in practical gender-specific classroom strategies...
National Association for Single Sex Public Education [NASSPE] Website

A third broad set of rationales for SS schooling posits that boys and girls differ in cognitive capabilities and proclivities that underlie learning, and that SS schooling capitalizes on such difference to produce superior outcomes. These sex differences are said to be evident in (a) maturation, (b) aptitudes, (c) disruptive behavior, (d) participatory style, and (e) interests. In each case, proponents argue that SS education is beneficial because it allows teachers to tailor educational practices to the sex-differentiated qualities and needs of children.

3.3.1 Sex Differences in Maturation

Recent research has demonstrated profound differences in the trajectories of brain development. In some brain regions, boys lag behind girls by as much as four years, on average, with no overlap between the trajectories of girls and boys.
Sax (2007)

Some proponents of SS schools have argued that boys show a slower rate of maturation of cognitive skills than girls and thus they lack many of the cognitive skills that girls of the same age typically have acquired (Gurian, Henley, & Trueman, 2001; Sax, 2005). The slower maturation of cognitive skills is hypothesized to interact with gender composition of schools such that academic motivation and achievement are undermined among boys in CE—but not SS—schools. Neuroimaging research has shown that the peak of girls' brain development (roughly 11-years-old) occurs 1–2 years earlier than boys' peak of development (Lenroot et al., 2007). Although this means that age-matched peers may be at slightly different cognitive developmental levels, as Basow (2010) explains, the implications for classroom instructive are unclear. Proponents of SS classes argue that this difference in cognitive maturity is linked to behaviors that affect classroom management strategies. Gurian et al. (2001) argued, "More impulsive and thus less mature than the female brain, the male brain gets a boy into far more trouble in class and in school. The kind of discipline that works for girls...does not work so well for many boys" (p. 61). Behavioral problems, which are discussed below, constitute only one consequence of cognitive immaturity, however. Boys have been hypothesized to lag behind in a host of other skills (e.g., reading ability). Thus, SS schooling advocates argue that separating the sexes will allow teachers to structure classrooms around girls' and boys' different levels of cognitive maturity.

It is true that schools are typically organized around inferred cognitive maturity, as evidenced by the reliance of chronological age as the major criterion for assigning children to school grades in the United States. It is the case, however, that there are vast variations in children's cognitive and emotional abilities and skills within even very narrow age and maturation levels, and within each sex. Thus, it appears that teachers would be best served by adopting one of two strategies: (1) employing instructional practices that are effective among pupils with diverse levels of cognitive and emotional maturity or (2) assessing students on the basis of specific skills and abilities (e.g., emotion regulation) and assigning them to classes on the basis of these assessments (i.e., maturational tracking). Using biological sex as a proxy for general cognitive maturation may be less controversial than using explicit tests of cognitive maturity, but is also less likely to be efficient for reducing the skill variation within classrooms. Tracking of any kind also reduces the advantages that accrue from collaborative learning environments that allow students to benefit (as learners and teachers) when they interact with peers who have different intellectual strengths and experiences (Braddock & Slavin, 1993). Thus, although it is pedagogically demanding of teachers, the use of multiple pedagogical strategies to reach a wide range of maturational levels within a single classroom is likely to be the most effective approach for improving outcomes of diverse students.

Pahlke et al.'s (2014) meta-analysis also provided some data relevant to claims about cognitive maturation and educational outcomes. They found small academic advantages associated with SS schooling for boys during elementary school, but the reverse (academic advantages associated with CE schooling) during middle school. Given that boys—at the group level—lag behind girls in cognitive maturation through adolescence, these data are inconsistent with the hypothesis that boys' slower maturation leads them to benefit from SS schooling.

3.3.2 Sex Differences in Aptitudes

Lessons for boys should focus less on language and more on graphs, charts, and manipulatives.

Gurian et al. (2001, p. 101)

Some proponents of SS education claim that such settings benefit students when teachers have been trained in pedagogical methods that are tailored to the "natural strengths" of girls and boys (Chadwell, 2010; Gurian et al., 2001; Sax, 2005). As the above quote illustrates, Sax and Gurian, both proponents of SS education, advocate lessons that for girls are tailored to superior verbal skills, and that for boys, de-emphasize verbal instruction and instead "focus on graphs, charts, and manipulatives" (Gurian et al., 2001, pp. 101). Implicit in this argument (and often made explicit, see Liben, 2014) is the assumption of gender differences in both innate skills and learning styles that, in turn, necessitate gender-specific pedagogies.

Parallel to our arguments about cognitive maturation, research also suggests that there are large within-sex differences, and small between-sex differences, in most academic skills (mathematical computation, scientific reasoning, writing; see Petersen & Hyde, 2014 [Chapter 2 of this volume]). Furthermore, the notion that students differ in "learning styles" has been discredited by researchers in both education and psychology (Pashler, McDaniel, Rohrer, & Bjork, 2009). Although most educators agree that students' motivation to tackle new skills can be bolstered by invoking well-developed skills and interests (Hidi & Renninger, 2004; Jones & Nimmo, 1994), it is also important that students are exposed to new interests and practice skills that are under-developed. Thus, both boys and girls are likely to benefit from lessons that focus on teaching literacy, mathematical, spatial, emotional, and interpersonal skills via varied types of activities.

There is also evidence that boys' and girls' academic outcomes may be harmed by teachers' gender-differentiated instructional styles. A study by Pahlke et al. (2013) addressed the relation between the gender make-up of the classroom and teacher pedagogy. Using a nationally representative sample of kindergarten classrooms, the researchers found that classes with a higher percentage of female students were associated with higher levels of reading and math achievement by the end of kindergarten. Importantly, classroom gender composition was associated with the level of phonics instruction, widely recognized as the most effective form of reading instruction (Ehri, Nunes, Stahl, & Willows, 2001). Teachers with a higher percentage of girls in their classrooms spent more time in phonics instruction than their colleagues, raising the possibility that boys would have benefited had teachers used the same (i.e., phonics) instruction in all classrooms.

3.3.3 Sex Differences in Disruptive Behavior

Boys were getting suspended for the most ridiculous things in the world—a boy would burp, or he'd pass gas...

Wright, quoted by Weil (2008)

Some proponents of SS schooling have argued that sex differences in disruptive classroom behavior are mitigated in SS schools. Research indicates that boys—as a group—have more attentional and self-regulatory problems than girls (Else-Quest, Hyde, Goldsmith, & Van Hulle, 2006; Matthews, Ponitz, & Morrison, 2009) and, perhaps as a result, they have higher rates of disciplinary problems than girls (Downey & Vogt Yuan, 2005; Schaefer, 2004). These disruptions take up teachers' instructional time and take attention away from well-behaved students (Brophy & Good, 1974). As discussed in more detail by Liben (2014), economists' analyses have also led to the conclusion that classrooms with higher proportions of boys result in greater classroom disruption which, in turn, lead to reduced cognitive outcomes (Lavy & Schlosser, 2011). It is statistically likely, therefore, that all-girls schools would have fewer instances of these behavioral disruptions than CE schools. The absence of these disruptions could affect girls' achievement by allowing more time for instruction (Lavy & Schlosser, 2011; Pahlke et al., 2013).

Two types of problems arise, however, from using SS schooling as a solution to the problem of sex differences in behavior problems. First, not all boys have attention and behavioral problems; nor are all girls free from such problems. Like sex differences in most domains, there is more overlap than disparity (Hyde, 2005). Thus, the reliance on biological sex for sorting students does not guarantee all-girls classroom will be free from disruptions, and conversely, subjects boys without behavioral issues to classrooms with distracting peers.

Second, boys' classrooms would have higher—rather than lower—concentrations of students with discipline problems. How then would disruptions within all-boys classrooms be reduced to levels below CE classrooms? Two types of discipline policies for all-boys settings have been proposed. One proposal is for teachers to relax their behavioral standards, by, for example, not requiring young boys to sit still and be quiet (Gurian et al., 2001; Sax, 2005). The alternative proposal is to stiffen disciplinary standards significantly, with significant punishment (including suspension) for misdeeds (e.g., military school models). Importantly, either type of classroom management could be implemented within CE classrooms, thereby affecting boys' behavior. Indeed, many CE schools have implemented the relaxed standards, making use, for example, of exercise balls as chairs for those students who request them, thereby eliminating the demand that all students be sedentary while at their desks.

3.3.4 Sex Differences in Participatory Style

> 'When they're outdoing the boys, they kind of wade back,' said Arnette Crocker, principal of the Bronx Young Women's Leadership School, 'but in a single-sex environment, they speak up as much as they want.'
>
> *Hulette (2007)*

Some proponents of SS schooling have argued that such contexts are beneficial because teachers in these classrooms are able to tailor instructional activities to the participatory styles of male and female students. Scholarly attention to participatory style has focused primarily on assertive versus passive roles in the classroom. There is some evidence that boys are more assertive in their participation style within classrooms than are girls

(Basow, 2010). Salomone (2006) states, boys are "monopolizing the linguistic space" in the classroom, leaving girls no opportunity to speak up (p. 790). Jovanovic and King (1998) observed classes of fifth through eighth grade students in a performance-based science classroom. They found that female and male students began the year with similar achievement and participation levels, but that the classroom dynamic dramatically changed over the course of the academic year. Boys assumed more of the active leading and manipulating roles in the classroom, whereas girls assumed more passive, assisting roles. Additionally, girls' self-perceptions of science ability significantly decreased over the course of the year, whereas boys' self-perceptions of science ability remained steady. Thus, it is possible that girls in SS schools may outperform their peers in CE schools because their more assertive peers (i.e., male students) have been removed from their classrooms.

There are several reasons to suspect, however, that girls are not strongly disadvantaged by whatever style of engagement that they adopt in the classroom. Girls outperform boys on tests of academic learning in schools around the globe (Voyer & Voyer, 2014) and, in the United States, throughout grades K to 12 (see Butler, 2014 [Chapter 1 of this volume]; Petersen & Hyde, 2014 [Chapter 2 of this volume]). Furthermore, SS schooling might be thought to be especially protective in math and science courses because of the importance of active, hands on (e.g., lab-based) learning. Contrary to this notion, however, Pahlke et al.'s (2014) meta-analyses failed to find advantages of SS schooling for math and science achievement among those studies that controlled for preexisting student differences. Finally, when problems of male domination of materials or conversation arise within classrooms or small groups, several solutions are possible. The permanent removal of one gender from the classroom or school is likely to be the most dramatic and costly. Alternatives include pedagogical strategies for increasing the inclusiveness of participation in classroom activities, such as teaching children assertive and effective strategies for joining conversations and groups, providing incentives for students who interact effectively with others (e.g., rewarding those who share materials; see Boekaerts & Corno, 2005), and introducing coping strategies for dealing with sexism (see Leaper & Brown, 2014 [Chapter 6 of this volume]; Liben & Coyle, 2014 [Chapter 3 of this volume]).

3.3.5 Sex Differences in Interests

School is taught 'by soft-spoken women who bore' boys.
Sax, quoted by Weil (2008)

Some proponents of SS education argue that part of its efficacy lies in providing students with both teachers and subject matter that interest them (Chadwell, 2010a, 2010b). According to this argument, boys benefit from teachers who are loud, assertive, active, strong, and adventurous, whereas girl benefit from teachers who are soft-spoken, nurturing, patient, and timid. The implicit assumption in this argument is that SS schools positively affect boys' academic performance because such settings attract a higher percentage of teachers, usually males, who have masculine sex-typed traits, and vice versa for all-girls schools. We could locate no research that examined whether boys' achievement was higher in classrooms with masculine sex-typed rather than feminine sex-typed teachers. However, extant research indicates that teacher gender has no effect on the achievement, motivation, or engagement of either male or female students (Carrington, Tymss, & Merrell, 2008; Martin & Marsh, 2005).

Another manner in which gender differences in students' interest may affect educational outcomes concerns the content of curricula. Teachers might, for example, assign reading materials featuring male or female main characters, or traditionally masculine versus feminine activities, such as "Treasure Island" by Robert Louis Stevenson (1883) versus "Rebecca of Sunnybrook Farm" by Kate Douglas Wiggin (1903), respectively. It is well established that, given the choice between two sex-typed activities, children—at the group level—will select the items that are consistent with the cultural stereotype of their gender (see Blakemore, Berenbaum, & Liben, 2009). Although it is true that teachers in all-boys schools might opt to adopt curricular materials with strongly masculine context (and vice versa for teachers at all-girls schools), such a procedure would not allow for within-gender variations in interests. Furthermore, it seems possible to give students within CE classrooms the freedom to engage with books, toys, and activities that vary along a continuum from traditionally masculine to feminine. Finally, the goal of education is construed by some theorists as expanding individuals' knowledge and appreciation within diverse domains. Thus, providing support and scaffolding for engagement with non- and cross-sextyped materials is likely to be beneficial (see Liben, 2014; Liben & Coyle, 2014 [Chapter 3 of this volume]; Martin, Fabes, & Hanish, 2014 [Chapter 5 of this volume]).

3.4. Rationale #4: It Works by Reducing Sexism

A fourth rationale for SS schooling suggests that such contexts provide a solution to the problems of teachers' and peers' sexism within CE contexts.

This rationale includes the more specific arguments that SS eliminates gender bias in teachers' (a) division of attention, (b) styles of interaction, and (c) expectations, and reduces or eliminates peers' (d) sexist comments and (e) sexual harassment.

3.4.1 Teacher Attention

I was so concerned about that group of boys, so worried they would act out, I didn't pay much attention to the rest of the class.
A teacher, quoted in Sadker, Sadker, & Zittleman (2009, p. 85)

Some proponents of SS schooling claim that, in CE settings, teachers attend differentially to boys and girls in ways that disadvantage girls. This problem is precluded in SS settings by the exclusion of one gender. Educational research from the 1970s and 1980s reported that boys receive both more positive and more negative attention from teachers than do girls (French & French, 1984). Leinhardt, Seewald, and Engel (1979) examined teachers' interactions with girls and boys and tested whether these interactions contributed to sex differences in reading and mathematics abilities. They observed that second-grade math teachers spent more time instructing and managing boys than girls in their classes. Although there were no differences in mathematics abilities at the beginning of the study, there were significant differences in mathematics achievement scores and tests of general cognitive ability by the end of the year that favored boys. Similarly, Lee et al. (1994) examined teachers' interactions with students in both SS and CE schools and found that, in CE settings, boys sought out and received the majority of attention from teachers. Other studies show that disruptive boys disproportionately receive teachers' attention (Beaman, Wheldall, & Kemp, 2006; Lavy & Schlosser, 2011). Thus, some educators argue that dividing boys and girls into separate classes eliminates the problem of gender-differentiated amounts of teacher attention.

Does SS education necessarily address the problem of teacher attention when it is present in CE schools? Teachers have limited attentional capacities and thus, as long as class size remains constant, the overall amount of attention available to students remains constant (Lazear, 2001). Additionally, more disruptive children will garner more attention than less disruptive children even within SS classrooms. Importantly, gender biases in teacher attention can be removed without sex segregation of students. Simple interventions with teachers in CE classrooms have been shown to impact teachers' attention to students (Sadker & Sadker, 1986; Sadker et al., 2009). Sadker and Sadker (1986) designed and implemented an extensive, multi-day intervention with elementary school teachers aimed at eliminating bias in the amount and type of interaction with their male and female students. As part of the intervention, the Sadkers videotaped short segments of individual teachers' classroom interactions, and then showed the tapes to the teachers and pointed out the instances in which they called on boys and girls. Follow-up comparisons between the teachers who completed the training and those who did not showed that the trained teachers called on male and female students at rates equal to the gender distribution of their class, whereas the control teachers did not. Additionally, the trained teachers had significantly higher levels of interaction with students overall than did control teachers. Several similar interventions with teachers have shown comparable effects on the gender distribution of teacher attention (Biklen & Pollard, 1993; Lundeberg, 1997). Thus, there is no reason to believe that creation of SS contexts is necessary for correcting imbalances in teachers' distribution of attention to boys and girls in their classrooms.

3.4.2 Teacher–Student Interaction

When boys are praised, it is most often for the intellectual quality of their ideas. Girls are twice as likely to be praised for following the rules of form. 'I love your margins' or 'What perfect handwriting' are the messages.

Sadker et al. (2009)

Some proponents of SS schooling claim that, in CE settings, teachers interact differentially with boys and girls and that this gender-biased behavior is eliminated within SS settings. Research indicates that teachers reinforce (praise, reward) male and female students for different types of behaviors and these differential reinforcement patterns undermine students' academic development (Beaman et al., 2006). For example, Dweck, Davidson, Nelson, and Enna (1978) observed teacher–student interactions in classes of fourth- and fifth-graders. Boys were more likely to receive praise for intellectual competence than girls; conversely, girls were more likely than boys to receive feedback that attributed their failure to intellectual ability (see Butler, 2014 [Chapter 1 of this volume], for a review of teachers' feedback to boys and girls). Advocates of SS education claim that SS schools benefit girls and boys by increasing teachers' appropriate and effective use of reinforcement in the classroom.

It remains unclear, however, whether SS contexts are necessarily linked to reductions in gender stereotypic feedback to students. For example, Lee et al. (1994) observed teachers in all-girls, all-boys, and CE secondary classrooms. In each classroom, they recorded varied forms of sexist behavior. Overall, incidence of teacher sexism did not vary across classroom type. Other work has also reported that teachers in SS classrooms engage in sexist practices. Glaser (2011) observed two SS classes, one all-girls and one all-boys class, taught by the same teacher at a CE middle school. He found that, although the average grades in the two classes were not different, there were significantly more instances of argumentation and discursive teaching in all-boys than all-girls classes. Boys were exposed to more than triple the instances of conceptual argumentation over the period of a year than were girls. The teacher posed more open-ended questions—and was more likely to challenge students' responses—in the all-boys class than in the all-girls class. Thus, it seems preferable to address the problem of gender-differentiated teacher-student interactions by implementing classroom interventions that educate teachers about gender biases that affect student-teacher interactions rather than by separating students into SS environments (Sadker & Sadker, 1986).

3.4.3 Teacher Expectations

To expect a second grade boy to stay still in his chair all day at school is not only unproductive, it's detrimental to his learning potential.
Duncan & Schmidt (2009, p. 24)

It is possible that SS schools benefit girls and boys by altering teachers' expectations of the academic and social abilities of each group. For example, it is possible that teachers in SS settings expect higher academic performance from their students than do teachers in CE settings. Or—as the quote illustrates—teachers in SS settings may expect lower compliance with conventional classrooms rules (sitting in desks, raising one's hand, using indoor voices) than do their colleagues in CE settings.

Research suggests that teachers' expectations do, indeed, often differ for male versus female students (see Leaper & Brown, 2014 [Chapter 6 of this volume], for a review). Fennema, Peterson, Carpenter, and Lubinski (1990) found that first grade teachers were more likely to nominate males than females as their most successful math students, regardless of students' achievement test scores. Furthermore, the researchers found that teachers had more accurate knowledge of girls' than boys' math abilities, largely because they were more likely to overestimate boys' than girls' academic abilities. Using a nationally representative sample, Riegle-Crumb and Humphries (2012) confirmed that, overall, U.S. teachers believe that mathematics is easier for boys than girls, even among boys and girls in advanced high school math classes with identical grades and standardized test scores.

Although teacher expectations are often linked to school achievement, we could locate no empirical work that compared teachers' expectations of girls (or boys) within SS and CE classrooms. Because gender biases with respect to ability are pervasive among adults, it is unclear how SS classes or schools would eliminate teachers' gender biases. As was true of gender biases in teacher attention, it seems likely that gender equity training for teachers is necessary for the creation of gender-fair classrooms.

3.4.4 Peer Gender Stereotyping

Girl: 'I wore a dress once and it was disgusting. I hate dresses.' Boy: 'If you're a girl, you have to wear dresses sometimes. That's how people know you're a girl.'
Discussion between kindergarten students, quoted in Kowalski & Kanitkar (2003)

Some proponents of SS schooling argue that children endorse gender stereotypes that interfere with academic achievement, especially girls' achievement in stereotypically masculine fields (e.g., science, math) and boys' achievement within stereotypically feminine fields (e.g., poetry, art; see Salomone, 2006). A good deal of research indicates that men and boys personally endorse cultural gender stereotypes to a greater degree than women and girls (Signorella, Bigler, & Liben, 1993). Thus, it is possible that educational environments that do not include males are more accepting of girls who express interest in counter-stereotypic domains, including math and science. The absence of potentially sexist male peers would then be a mechanism that could affect girls' academic interests, motivation, and self-efficacy. However, girls also engage in gender bullying and other behaviors that police the gender norms and behaviors of their own gender group (Craig, Pepler, Connolly, & Henderson, 2001; O'Brien, 2011). Therefore, the act of removing boys from an educational setting does not guarantee the removal of all sexist peers from the class. Additionally, it is not the case that all boys endorse gender stereotypes or harass girls who excel in counter-stereotypic domains (Signorella, 1987). In both of these examples, the presence or absence of one gender is not the mechanism that leads to gender stereotyping among peers; rather, it is the presence of sexist peers, be they male or female, that leads to the negative outcomes associated with gender stereotyping (see Leaper & Brown, 2014 [Chapter 6 of this volume]; Poteat, Scheer, & Mereish, 2014 [Chapter 8 of this volume], for reviews). Thus, the use of interventions designed to reduce sexism in the classroom (e.g., Lamb, Bigler, Liben, & Green, 2009) is likely to be more effective than gender segregation for eliminating children's exposure to sexist comments by peers.

3.4.5 Peer Sexual Harassment

In our school a girl was pinched on the derriere by two boys and verbally harassed. When she reported the incident to the principal, she was told that her dress was inappropriate and that she had asked for it.

A teacher, quoted in Sadker et al. (2009)

Some proponents of SS education argue that SS schools and classes may reduce the incidence of sexual harassment, defined as unwanted sexual behaviors and sexist comments (see AAUW, 2001; Leaper & Brown, 2014 [Chapter 6 of this volume]), experienced by girls at school. Many girls report having experienced sexual harassment, especially during adolescence (AAUW, 2001; McMaster et al., 2002). Using a sample of 600 adolescent girls, Leaper and Brown (2008) found that 90% of the girls had experienced some form of sexual harassment at least once. The most frequently cited form of harassment was unwanted or inappropriate romantic attention, most frequently directed at them by male peers. Thus, it is possible that single-sex settings eliminate much of the sexual harassment experienced by girls at schools simply as a consequence of eliminating the main source of the harassment.

Leaper and Brown did not, however, ask girls about harassment and unwanted sexual attention from teachers, coaches, or female peers. Girls report experiencing romantic attention and unwanted physical contact from these sources as well (Ormerod, Collinsworth, & Perry, 2008; Timmerman, 2003). Indeed, any claim that SS schools completely eliminate girls' experiences with sexual harassment assumes heteronormativity among peers. Same-sex sexual harassment also occurs in schools; research has shown that both boys and girls who are sexually harassed by same-sex peers felt more threatened and upset than those harassed by peers of the other sex (Fineran, 2002). Furthermore, the legal definition of sexual harassment has been expanded to include harassment due to sexual orientation, and there is little reason to assume that this kind of sexual harassment would be reduced among students in SS classes (Mayes, 2001). Although sexual harassment is an oft-cited justification for the creation of all-girls classes, boys experience sexual harassment from peers as well (AAUW, 2001; Hand & Sanchez, 2000; Ormerod et al., 2008).

Sexual harassment, whether from peers or teachers, has detrimental effects for girls and boys in educational contexts. Incidence of sexual harassment has been linked to low self-esteem (Goldstein, Malanchuk, Davis-Kean, & Eccles, 2007), poor body image (Goldstein et al., 2007), and elevated risk of abusive relationships (Leaper & Anderson, 1997). Thus, any educational environment that could reduce the incidence of sexual harassment perpetrated against children of either sex would have beneficial effects. Unfortunately, however, no research on SS education has specifically addressed the issue of sexual harassment. Furthermore, the ideal solution to sexual harassment is to prevent its occurrence and to teach youth how to respond to it appropriately both within and outside of school, rather than to shield them temporarily from victimization within school contexts alone. Thus, the incorporation of educational programming that creates and practices respectful, appropriate interpersonal behavior within CE settings would appear to be a more effective long-term solution to the reduction of sexual harassment than the creation of temporary SS environments.

3.5. Rationale #5: It Works by Reducing Attention to Gender

Proponents of SS schools have claimed that removing one gender from school contexts causes gender *per se* to recede in psychological salience and importance. As consequence of this presumed reduction in gender salience, three gender-related problems subsequently recede as well: sexual distraction, peer rejection, and self-stereotyping.

3.5.1 Gender Salience

How is our campus different from others? The Girls' School of Austin is a remarkably gender-free environment.
The Girls' School Website, www.thegirlsschool.org

Some proponents of SS schools argue that such schools benefit girls and boys by decreasing the psychological salience of gender and, in turn, gender stereotypes and gender-based stereotype threat. So, for example, girls should perform better in physics classes if there is little in the environment to remind them that they are girls, and boys should perform better in reading classes if there is little to remind them that they are boys.

Consistent with this notion, Kessels and Hannover (2008) found that girls in SS physics classes had less activation of gender-related self-knowledge than girls in CE physics classes. That is, the girls in SS classrooms endorsed feminine trait adjectives as less descriptive of themselves than girls in the CE classes. The researchers argued that the mechanism underlying these results is accessibility of gender-related knowledge: "We conclude that girls will develop a positive self-concept of ability in physics to the extent that 'incongruent' feminine self-knowledge is inaccessible and 'congruent' masculine self-knowledge is accessible during lessons" (p. 284).

Other work, however, indicates that the mere absence of one gender from the classroom does not necessarily render gender-related knowledge inaccessible. Even for girls and women of high ability in math, simply being reminded of negative stereotypes of girls and women can induce the threat of confirming the negative stereotype and thereby undermine their academic performance (Steele, 1997). Importantly, stereotype threat can undermine women's performance and affect their sense of self even within classrooms that contain no men and indeed, even when no other people are present at all (Pronin, Steele, & Ross, 2004).

Additionally, it is possible that SS environments lessen attention to gender through a reduction in teachers' labeling and using of gender categories. In their developmental intergroup theory, Bigler and Liben (2006) theorize that making a characteristic of a person salient through explicit labeling and use of that characteristic affects children's stereotyping of and prejudice towards members of groups defined by that characteristic. Consistent with this notion, empirical work indicates gender labeling enhances gender stereotyping and prejudice (Bigler, 1995; Bigler & Liben, 2006; Hilliard & Liben, 2010). Gender categories are frequently invoked in many CE classrooms (Bigler, 2005). It is possible that teachers in SS classrooms label gender less often their colleagues in CE classrooms because only one gender is present. However, to our knowledge, no research has examined explicitly the frequency with which teachers in SS classes label gender. Anecdotal evidence suggests, however, that gender labeling occurs in SS environments. For some children, the name of their school includes a gender label (e.g., Ann Richards School for Young Women Leaders, 2011); other children are routinely addressed by gendered nouns ("Good morning, ladies"). As noted earlier, the most cost- and time-effective solution to the labeling issue would be ban the routine use of gender labels by teachers, as some CE schools have done (e.g., Swedish schools, Hebblethwaite, 2011).

An additional research literature that may shed light on the role of gender salience in stereotyping and prejudice concerns racial attitudes. The salience of race is likely to be low among White students within all-White classrooms and African Americans within all-African American classrooms, conditions that are common within racial segregated schools and that sometimes occurs as a result of tracking within racially diverse schools (see Rowley et al., 2014 [Chapter 9 of this volume]). But does race really go unnoticed among White and African American students that attend racially segregated classrooms or schools? The answer is "no." White students who leave their AP classes and enter hallways with peers of color who are instructed in separate classes have been shown to endorse more racially biased attitudes and show more racially biased peer relations than do White students who attend integrated classes (Khmelkov & Hallinan, 1999). The same is true at the school level; students who attend racially segregated schools are more racially biased than those who attend racially integrated schools (Killen, Margie, & Sinno, 2006).

3.5.2 Sexual Distraction

> *The best grade level to start a single-gender classroom is at the middle school. This is when girls notice boys and boys notice girls.*
>
> ***Ferrara (2010)***

Some proponents of SS schools have argued that such settings act as a buffer against the negative consequences of heterosexual attraction (see Chadwell, 2010; Gurian et al., 2001; Sax, 2005). Youth who attend SS schools have restricted access to other-gender individuals during much of their day, and thus might be expected to engage in fewer heterosexual romantic relationships than their peers at CE schools. Empirical research by Bruce and Sanders (2001), however, suggests otherwise. They found that students at SS secondary schools had an equivalent number of heterosexual relationships as did students at CE secondary schools.

Another form of distraction that may be related to heterosexual interest is a concern about appearance. For example, it is possible that girls in SS schools place less emphasis on their appearance at school than girls in CE schools because they are free from the male gaze. Of course, SS classes within CE schools would not be expected to reduce girls' appearance-focused concerns because of the continued presence of males in many settings (e.g., hallways, lunchroom). Again, however, there is little support for this hypothesis in the empirical literature. For example, Dyer and Tiggemann (1996) reported more instances of disordered eating and body dissatisfaction among girls in SS schools than CE schools. Furthermore, to the extent that girls internalize cultural messages about the importance of sexual attractiveness to males, such views are likely to guide their behavior—and shape judgments of other girls' and women's appearance—even in the absence of males. That is, girls may focus on their appearance to the detriment of their schoolwork in response to pressure their female friends and their own self-standards. We elaborate on this notion in the section on "self-stereotyping" below.

Importantly, the desire to remove the consequences of adolescent romantic relationships by separating males and females is a heteronormative (and untenable) assumption on the part of policy makers. Some accounts of sex-segregated schooling in England and the U.S. portray same-sex romantic attractions as common and highly salient. Graves (1957) wrote, "In English preparatory and public schools romance is necessarily homosexual...For every one born homosexual, at least ten permanent pseudo-homosexuals are made by the public school system" (p. 19). Whether students' attractions are toward same- or other-sex individuals, learning to manage sexual feelings and negotiate sexual relationships is a developmental necessity. We argue that eliminating one gender from educational contexts is an ineffective strategy for facilitating such skills.

3.5.3 Peer Rejection

'It's where you can be comfortable,' she said, 'because you have girls around you who understand you.'

A female student, quoted by Hulette (2007)

Some proponents of SS schools argue that such settings are beneficial because they increase rates of friendship and decrease rates of peer rejection in the classroom. Gender is an important determinant of the type and quality of peer interaction (see Martin et al., 2014 [Chapter 5 of this volume], for a review). Several studies have demonstrated that children and adolescents are more comfortable interacting with same- than other-gender peers (Benenson, Markovits, Thompson, & Wrangham, 2011; Lundy, Field, McBride, Field, & Largie, 1998). Greater comfort with same-gender peers extends to academic and school settings (Strough & Covatto, 2002; Strough & Meegan, 2001). Peer acceptance predicts children's academic performance in schools, beginning as early as kindergarten (Ladd, Kochenderfer, & Coleman, 1997). Furthermore, Patterson and Pahlke (2011) found that interest in having more female friends was positively related to happiness and retention within an all-girls school.

It is also clear, however, that students in both CE and SS schools are bullied by same-sex peers. For example, girls are frequently the perpetrators of bullying toward other girls (Benenson et al., 2011; Besag, 2006). Thus, it is unlikely that removing one gender from educational settings eliminates peer rejection and maltreatment (Craig et al., 2001). Furthermore, there are consequences of peer homophily for children's behavior over time. Martin and Fabes (2004) found that young children who spend large amounts of time in

SS groups become increasingly sex-typed over time. For example, preschool girls who socialize predominately with same-sex rather than other-sex children adopt increasingly feminine styles of play, and are more likely to avoid boys, over time. As Liben (2014) argued, contexts that serve to increase gender differentiation in children's traits, interests, and skills are likely to be viewed by proponents of SS schools as—at worst—neutral. In contrast, contexts that serve to increase gender differentiation are likely to be viewed as negative by proponents of CE education (like us) who value the development of broad, flexible skills and interests that enable boys and girls to interact with diverse individuals (e.g., competitive, cooperative) in diverse contexts (e.g., home, work).

3.5.4 Self-Stereotyping

> *I hide my good grades so my boyfriend doesn't get insulted.*
> **A ninth grade girl, quoted in Sadker et al. (2009)**

Some proponents of SS schooling argue that such settings free youth from self-imposed constraints on their gender-role behaviors (Salomone, 2006). Research suggests that children engage in sex-typed behavior as a result of how they are treated by others (e.g., peers' comments, addressed earlier) and by their own self-imposed sanctions. Several studies have addressed the presence of conflicting gendered expectations for girls attending SS institutions. Although many all-girls schools have the explicit mission of increasing girls' interest and performance in counter-stereotypical domains such as math and science, the girls at these schools sometimes report feeling a 'hidden curriculum' that promotes traditionally feminine traits (Mensinger, 2000). A qualitative study by Brody et al. (1998) showed that girls are often aware of this hypocrisy at the school level, feeling pressure to achieve "female empowerment" as well as fulfillment through marriage and family. A study by Tiggemann (2001) found that higher academic motivation predicted endorsement of thinner ideal body types among girls at SS but not at CE schools, suggesting that girls at SS schools include "thinness" in their schema of overall success. Mensinger (2001) argued that conflicting messages about womanhood and femininity could contribute to the development of negative body image and eating disorders in SS schools. This kind of conflict was apparent in a study by Lee et al. (1994) in which the researchers found feminism and sexism present simultaneously within a single-sex classroom. These data suggest a potential negative consequence of SS education, particularly all-girls environments; when the student population is restricted to only one gender, gendered norms may become especially salient and self-socialization pressures may increase. We argue that the most effective means to reduce children's and adolescents' tendency to constrain their own activities and interests to those that are stereotypical of their gender is to confront the problem explicitly via intervention programming. CE schools can (and should) build climates that support children's engagement in gender nontraditional activities (e.g., Lamb et al., 2009).

4. CONCLUSIONS AND RECOMMENDATIONS

There is considerable disagreement in the United States over the efficacy of SS schooling. In this chapter, we have provided a critical analysis of the rationales given for SS schooling by its proponents. We argued that rationales for SS schooling can be sorted into five categories and evaluated using evidence pertaining to each. We began by noting that some proponents argue that SS is effective, albeit for reasons that have not yet been identified. We provided evidence that selection effects produce apparent advantages to SS schooling that are misleading. The use of indices of student academic motivation and aptitude as a basis for assignment to schools and classes has long been used in many parts of the world (as in Germany's education system). Many educational observers have noted that the United States has moved in a similar direction, often under a guise that distracts attention from the use of such markers (e.g., charter schools). We do not take a stand on such policies here, but note that "tracking" should be subject to scrutiny and that SS schooling has, in some instances, made use of selection biases. Because SS schooling is a "choice" (and to be consistent with legal regulations must remain one), it is likely to lure higher achieving youth (and education-invested parents) away from standard CE classrooms, further weakening those original classrooms (Hayes et al., 2011).

Second, we addressed the argument that SS schools are beneficial to specific subsets of students. This argument appears to be gaining strength among SS proponents, as evidenced by the National Association for the Advancement of Single-Sex Public Education (NASSPE) being renamed the "National Association for Choice in Education" (NACE, 2011; www.4schoolchoice.org). The organization advocates for the availability of SS education as a choice for parents: "Some kids do better in coed; some do better in single-gender. We don't blindly promote single-gender education for all students; we promote *choice* for all families" [emphasis in original] (NACE, 2011). Importantly, the association's website does not identify which students are expected to do better in each type of environment, nor does it offer parents any information to help guide their choice. An argument that SS schools are a better choice than CE schools for some students is unpersuasive in the absence of evidence about which types of students fall into the "some" category and in the absence of information about ways that specific traits might operate to make those unidentified children especially responsive.

A third set of rationales for SS schooling concerns the use of gender-specific pedagogy, tailored to match sex differences in children's skills and abilities. Because research clearly shows large within-sex, but relatively small between-sex differences in cognitive and affective skills (Hyde, 2005), we argue that the use of biological sex as marker of academically related skills and interests is inaccurate and inefficient.

Fourth, although numerous problems with CE schools have been correctly identified, the answer is not to eliminate one gender from the setting. Instead, the answer is to transport to CE settings those educationally valuable methods that have been demonstrated to be effective in other (including SS) school contexts. For example, Hubbard and Datnow (2005) found that teachers within California's public SS schools spent substantial time talking with their students about safe sex, pregnancy, and healthy heterosexual relationships. They argued that, "the absence of students of the opposite sex made it possible to have candid conversations that were essential to students' well-being" (p. 124). There is, however, no reason to presume that similar conversations would be any less effective within CE schools. We suggest that this particular example points to a general problem with interpreting the effects of SS environments. That is, some educators and policy makers appear to be quick to presume that when a SS school shows some positive outcome, the explanation lies in its SS structure rather than in any one of the many other factors that distinguish the SS school from the CE schools to which it is compared. We urge therefore that researchers investigate programs that have been identified as successful within SS settings, and import and test the viability of these programs in CE settings. Such an approach would permit one to distinguish between effects of program content and effects (if any) of the gender composition of the school in which such content is delivered.

The final set of rationales for SS schooling argues that SS schools reduce gender salience and, consequently, reduce negative consequences of such salience (e.g., stereotype threat, appearance-focused behavior, peer exclusion). Based on the available evidence from SS contexts, however, it does not appear that such schools actually accomplish these salience-related goals.

The bulk of extant literature suggests that integration and the avoidance of routine labeling of groups reduce social stereotyping and prejudice in CE settings.

In summary, we conclude that the rationales offered by proponents of SS schooling are insufficient to justify the time and expense of converting CE schools and programs to SS ones. Instead, we argue for strengthening the commitment to gender-fair education within CE settings through teacher training and through effective intervention programs that address both academic and social development goals. Such approaches are likely to produce the greatest dividends in school achievement, mental health outcomes, and interpersonal relationships among the diverse population of students who attend U.S. schools and among the adult citizens they will later become.

REFERENCES

American Association of University Women. (2001). *Hostile hallways: Bullying, teasing, and sexual harassment in school*. Washington, D.C.: American Association of University Women.

Ann Richards School for Young Women Leaders. Wellness Program. (2011). Retrieved from Ann Richards School for Young Women Leaders Website http://www.annrichardsschool.org/studentlife/wellness.php Accessed June 24, 2011.

Barbarin, O. A., Chinn, L., & Wright, Y. F. (2014). Creating developmentally auspicious school environments for African American boys. In L. S. Liben & R. S. Bigler (Vol. Eds.) *The role of gender in educational contexts and outcomes*. In J. B. Benson (Series Ed.), *Advances in child development and behavior: Vol. 47* (pp. 333–365). London: Elsevier.

Basow, S. A. (2010). Gender in the classroom. In J. C. Chrisler, & D. R. McCreary (Eds.), *Handbook of gender research in psychology: Volume 1: Gender research in general and experimental psychology* (pp. 277–295). New York: Springer.

Beaman, R., Wheldall, K., & Kemp, C. (2006). Differential teacher attention to boys and girls in the classroom. *Educational Review, 58*, 339–366.

Benenson, J. F., Markovits, H., Thompson, M. E., & Wrangham, R. W. (2011). Under threat of social exclusion, females exclude more than males. *Psychological Science, 22*, 538–544.

Besag, V. E. (2006). Bullying among girls: Friends or foes? *School Psychology International, 27*, 535–551.

Bigler, R. S. (1995). The role of classification skill in moderating environmental influences on children's gender stereotyping: A study of the functional use of gender in the classroom. *Child Development, 66*, 1072–1087.

Bigler, R. S. (2005). Good morning boys and girls. *Teaching Tolerance Magazine, 28*, 22–23.

Bigler, R. S., & Liben, L. S. (2006). A developmental intergroup theory of social stereotypes and prejudice. In R. V. Kail (Ed.), *Advances in child development and behavior*, Vol. 34. (pp. 39–89). San Diego: Elsevier.

Bigler, R. S., & Signorella, M. L. (2011). Single-sex education: New perspectives and evidence on a continuing controversy. *Sex Roles, 65*, 659–669.

Biklen, S. K., & Pollard, D. (Eds.). (1993). *Gender and education. Nintety-second yearbook of the National Society for the Study of Education*. Chicago: National Society for the Study of Education.

Blakemore, J. E. O., Berenbaum, S. A., & Liben, L. S. (2009). *Gender development.* New York: Taylor & Francis.

Boekaerts, M., & Corno, L. (2005). Self-regulation in the classroom: A perspective on assessment and intervention. *Applied Psychology, 54,* 199–231.

Braddock, J. H., & Slavin, R. E. (1993). Why ability grouping must end: Achieving excellence and equity in American education. *Journal of Intergroup Relations, 20,* 51–64.

Bradley, R. H., & Corwyn, R. F. (2002). Socioeconomic status and child development. *Annual Review of Psychology, 53,* 371–399.

Brody, C., Fuller, K., Gosetti, P., Moscato, S., Nagel, N., Pace, G., et al. (1998). *Gender and the culture of schools.* Paper presented at the Annual Meeting of the American Educational Research Association, San Diego, CA.

Brophy, J., & Good, T. (1974). *Teacher-student relationships: Causes and consequences.* New York: Holt, Rinehart & Winston.

Bruce, N. W., & Sanders, K. A. (2001). Incidence and duration of romantic attraction in students progressing from secondary to tertiary education. *Journal of Biosocial Science, 33,* 173–184.

Butler, R. (2014). Motivation in educational contexts: Does gender matter? In L. S. Liben & R. S. Bigler (Vol. Eds.) *The role of gender in educational contexts and outcomes.* In J. B. Benson (Series Ed.), *Advances in child development and behavior: Vol. 47* (pp. 1–41). London: Elsevier.

Carrington, B., Tymss, P., & Merrell, C. (2008). Role models, school improvement and the 'gender gap'—Do men bring out the best in boys and women the best in girls? *British Educational Research Journal, 34,* 315–327.

Chadwell, D. (2010a). *A gendered choice: Designing and implementing single-sex programs and schools.* Thousand Oaks, CA: Corwin.

Chadwell, D. (2010b). *Single-gender classes can respond to the needs of boys and girls. ASCD Express.* Retrieved from: http://www.ascd.org/ascd-express/vol5/512-newvoices.aspx.

Conway, J. K. (1974). Reinterpreting women's education. *History of Education Quarterly, 14,* 1–12.

Cooper, B. S. (2008). Single sex parochial schools: Why or why not. In F. Spielhagen (Ed.), *Debating single-sex education: Separate and equal?.* Lanham, MD: Rowman & Littlefield Education.

Craig, W. M., Pepler, D., Connolly, J., & Henderson, K. (2001). Developmental context of peer harassment in early adolescence: The role of puberty and the peer group. In J. Juvonen, & S. Graham (Eds.), *Peer harassment in school: The plight of the vulnerable and victimized* (pp. 242–261). New York: Guildford Press.

Daly, P., & Shuttleworth, I. (1997). Determinants of public examination entry and attainment in mathematics: Evidence on gender and gender-type of school from the 1980s and 1990s in Northern Ireland. *Evaluation and Research in Education, 11,* 91–101.

DeBare, I. (2004). *Where girls come first: The rise, fall, and surprising revival of girls' schools.* New York: Penguin.

Downey, D. B., & Vogt Yuan, A. S. (2005). Sex differences in school performance during high school: Puzzling patterns and possible explanations. *Sociological Quarterly, 46,* 299–321.

Duncan, A., & Schmidt, A. (2009). Building sisterhood and brotherhood in gender-specific classrooms. *Advances in Gender and Education, 1,* 24–25.

Dweck, C. S., Davidson, W., Nelson, S., & Enna, B. (1978). Sex differences in learned helplessness: II. The contingencies of evaluative feedback in the classroom and III. An experimental analysis. *Developmental Psychology, 14,* 268–276.

Dyer, G., & Tiggeman, M. (1996). The effect of school environment on body concerns in adolescent women. *Sex Roles, 34,* 127–138.

Egan, S. K., & Perry, D. G. (2001). Gender identity: A multidimensional analysis with implications for psychosocial adjustment. *Developmental Psychology, 37,* 451–463.

Education Amendments of 1972. (1972). 20 U.S.C. 1681 (Title IX).

Ehri, L. C., Nunes, S. R., Stahl, S. A., & Willows, D. M. (2001). Systematic phonics instruction helps students learn to read: Evidence from the national reading panel's meta-analysis. *Review of Educational Research*, 71, 393–447.

Else-Quest, N. M., Hyde, J., Goldsmith, H. H., & Van Hulle, C. A. (2006). Gender differences in temperament: A meta-analysis. *Psychological Bulletin*, 132, 33–72.

Fennema, E., Peterson, P. L., Carpenter, T. P., & Lubinski, C. A. (1990). Teachers' attributions and beliefs about girls, boys, and mathematics. *Educational Studies in Mathematics*, 21, 55–69.

Ferrara, M. M. (2010). A chat with a passenger about single-gender learning. *Advances in Gender and Education*, 2, 34–38.

Fineran, S. (2002). Sexual harassment between same-sex peers: Intersection of mental health, homophobia, and sexual violence in schools. *Social Work*, 47, 65–74.

French, J., & French, P. (1984). Gender imbalance in the primary classroom: An interactional account. *Educational Research*, 26, 127–136.

Garcia, D. M. (1998). *Single-sex vs. coeducational public schooling for girls: A high school comparison study*. Unpublished doctoral dissertation, New York: Columbia University.

Glaser, H. M. (2011). Arguing separate but equal: A study of argumentation in public single-sex science classes in the United States. *International Journal of Gender, Science, and Technology*, 3, 71–92.

Goldstein, S. E., Malanchuk, O., Davis-Kean, P. E., & Eccles, J. S. (2007). Risk factors of sexual harassment by peers: A longitudinal investigation of African American and European American adolescents. *Journal of Research on Adolescence*, 17, 285–300.

Goodkind, S. (2013). Single-sex public education for low-income youth of color: A critical theoretical review. *Sex Roles*, 69, 393–402.

Goudreau, J. (2010). *The new segregation battle: Boy vs. girl*. Forbes. Retrieved from http://www.forbes.com/2010/05/20/public-schools-education-single-sex-classrooms-forbes-woman-leadership-test-scores.html.

Graves, R. (1957). *Good-bye to all that*. Garden City, NY: Doubleday.

Gray, V. (1973). Innovation in the states: A diffusion study. *American Political Science Review*, 67, 1174–1185.

Gurian, M., Henley, P., & Trueman, T. (2001). *Boys and girls learn differently!*. San Francisco, CA: Jossey-Bass.

Halpern, D. F., Elliot, L., Bigler, R. S., Fabes, R. A., Hanish, L. D., Hyde, J., et al. (2011). The pseudoscience of single-sex schooling. *Science*, 333, 1706–1707.

Hand, J. Z., & Sanchez, L. (2000). Badgering or bantering? Gender differences in experience of, and reactions to, sexual harassment among U.S. high school students. *Gender and Society*, 14, 718–746.

Hansot, E., & Tyack, D. (1988). Gender in American schools: Thinking institutionally. *Journal of Women in Culture and Society*, 13, 741–760.

Harker, R., & Nash, R. (1997). *School type and the education of girls: Co-ed or girls only?* Paper presented at the annual meeting of the American Educational Research Association, Chicago, IL.

Hayes, A. R., Pahlke, E. E., & Bigler, R. S. (2011). The efficacy of single-sex education: Testing for selection and peer quality effects. *Sex Roles*, 65, 693–703.

Hebblethwaite, C. (2011). Sweden's 'gender-neutral' pre-school. BBC News. www.bbc.co.uk.

Hidi, S., & Renninger, K. A. (2004). Interest, a motivational variable that combines affective and cognitive functioning. In D. Y. Dai, & R. J. Sternberg (Eds.), *Motivation, emotion, and cognition: Integrative perspectives on intellectual functioning and development* (pp. 89–115). Mahwah, NJ: Erlbaum.

Hilliard, L. J., & Liben, L. S. (2010). Differing levels of gender salience in preschool classrooms: Effects on children's gender attitudes and intergroup bias. *Child Development*, 81, 1787–1798.

Hubbard, L., & Datnow, A. (2005). Do single-sex schools improve the education of low-income and minority students? An investigation of California's Public Single-gender academies. *Anthropology and Education Quarterly, 36*, 115–131.

Hulette, E. (2007). Single-sex schools and minority achievement: The young women's leadership school brings girl power to Bronx student. *The Columbia Journalist.* Retrieved from http://cjarchives.jrn.columbia.edu/.

Hutchison, K. B., & Mikulski, B. (2012, October 16). A right to choose single-sex education. *The Wall Street Journal.* Retrieved from http://online.wsj.com.

Hyde, J. S. (2005). The gender similarities hypothesis. *American Psychologist, 60*, 581–592.

Jones, E., & Nimmo, J. (1994). *Emergent curriculum.* Washington, D.C.: NAEYC.

Jovanovic, J., & King, S. S. (1998). Boys and girls in the performance-based science classroom: Who's doing the performing? *American Educational Research Journal, 35*, 477–496.

Kaminer, W. (1998, April 1). The trouble with single-sex schools. *The Atlantic.* Retrieved from http://www.theatlantic.com.

Khmelkov, V. T., & Hallinan, M. T. (1999). Organizational effects on race relations in schools. *Journal of Social Issues, 55*, 627–645.

Kessels, U., & Hannover, B. (2008). When being a girl matters less: Accessibility of gender-related self-knowledge in single-sex and co-educational classes and its impact on students' physics-related self-concept of ability. *British Journal of Educational Psychology, 78*, 273–289.

Killen, M., Margie, N. G., & Sinno, S. (2006). Morality in the context of intergroup relationships. In M. Killen, & J. Smetana (Eds.), *Handbook of moral development* (pp. 155–183). Mahwah, NJ: Erlbaum.

Klein, S., & Sesma, E. (2010). *What are we learning from the 2006–7 office for civil rights survey question about public schools with single-sex academic classes? Preliminary report.* Arlington, VA: Feminist Majority Foundation.

Kowalski, K., & Kanitkar, K. (2003). Ethnicity and gender in the kindergarten classroom: A naturalistic study. In *Poster presented at the meeting of the Society for Research in Child Development, Tampa, FL.*

Ladd, G. W., Kochenderfer, B. J., & Coleman, C. C. (1997). Classroom peer acceptance, friendship, and victimization: Distinct relational systems that contribute uniquely to children's school adjustment? *Child Development, 68*, 1181–1197.

Lamb, L., Bigler, R. S., Liben, L. S., & Green, V. A. (2009). Teaching children to confront peers' sexist remarks: Implications for theories of gender development and educational practice. *Sex Roles: A Journal of Research, 61*, 361–382.

Lavy, V., & Schlosser, A. (2011). Mechanisms and impacts of gender peer effects at school. *American Economic Journal: Applied Economics, 3*, 1–33.

Lazear, E. P. (2001). Educational production. *The Quarterly Journal of Economics, 116*, 777–803.

Leaper, C., & Anderson, K. J. (1997). Gender development and heterosexual romantic relationships during adolescence. *New Directions for Child and Adolescent Development, 1997*(78), 85–103.

Leaper, C., & Brown, C. S. (2008). Perceived experiences with sexism among adolescent girls. *Child Development, 79*, 685–704.

Leaper, C., & Brown, C. S. (2014). Sexism in schools. In L. S. Liben & R. S. Bigler (Vol. Eds.) *The role of gender in educational contexts and outcomes.* In J. B. Benson (Series Ed.), *Advances in child development and behavior: Vol. 47* (pp. 189–223). London: Elsevier.

Lee, V. E., & Marks, H. M. (1990). Sustained effects of the single-sex secondary school experience on attitudes, behaviors, and values in college. *Journal of Educational Psychology, 82*, 578–592.

Lee, V. E., Marks, H. M., & Byrd, T. (1994). Sexism in single-sex and co-educational independent secondary school classrooms. *Sociology of Education, 67*, 92–120.

Leinhardt, G., Seewald, A. M., & Engel, M. (1979). Learning what's taught: Sex differences in instruction. *Journal of Educational Psychology, 71*, 432–439.

Lenroot, R. K., Gogtay, N., Greenstein, D. K., Wells, E. M., Wallace, G. L., Clasen, L. S., et al. (2007). Sexual dimorphism of brain developmental trajectories during childhood and adolescence. *NeuroImage, 36*, 1065–1073.

Liben, L. S. (2014). Probability values and human values in evaluating single-sex education. Invited commentary, *Sex Roles*, under review.

Liben, L. S., & Coyle. E. F. (2014). Developmental interventions to address the STEM gender gap: Exploring intended and unintended consequences. In L. S. Liben & R. S. Bigler (Vol. Eds.) *The role of gender in educational contexts and outcomes*. In J. B. Benson (Series Ed.), *Advances in child development and behavior: Vol. 47* (pp. 77–116). London: Elsevier.

Liu, X., Kaplan, H. B., & Risser, W. (1992). Decomposing the reciprocal relationships between academic achievement and general self-esteem. *Youth & Society, 24*, 123–148.

Lundeberg, M. A. (1997). You guys are overreacting: Teaching prospective teachers about subtle gender bias. *Journal of Teacher Education, 48*, 55–61.

Lundy, B., Field, T., McBride, C., Field, T., & Largie, S. (1998). Same-sex and opposite-sex best friend interactions among high-school juniors and seniors. *Adolescence, 33*, 279–289.

Mael, F. A. (1998). Single-sex and coeducational schooling: Relationships to socioemotional and academic development. *Review of Educational Research, 68*, 101–129.

Mael, F., Alonso, A., Gibson, D., Rogers, K., & Smith, M. (2005). *Single-sex versus coeducational schooling: A systematic review*. Washington, D. C.: American Institutes for Research, Prepared for the U.S. Department of Education.

Marsh, H. W. (1991). Public, catholic single-sex and catholic coeducational high schools: Their effect on achievement, affect, and behaviors. *American Journal of Education, 99*, 320–356.

Martin, C. L., & Fabes, R. A. (2004). The stability and consequences of young children's same-sex peer interactions. *Developmental Psychology, 37*, 431–446.

Martin, C. L., Fabes, R. A., & Hanish, L. D. (2014). Gendered-peer relationships in educational contexts. In L. S. Liben & R. S. Bigler (Vol. Eds.) *The role of gender in educational contexts and outcomes*. In J. B. Benson (Series Ed.), *Advances in child development and behavior: Vol. 47* (pp. 151–187). London: Elsevier.

Martin, A., & Marsh, H. (2005). Motivating boys and motivating girls: Does teacher gender really make a difference? *Australian Journal of Education, 49*, 320–334.

Matthews, J. S., Ponitz, C. C., & Morrison, F. J. (2009). Early gender differences in self-regulation and academic achievement. *Journal of Educational Psychology, 3*, 689–704.

Mayes, T. A. (2001). Confronting same-sex, student-to-student sexual harassment: recommendations for educators and policy makers. *Fordham Urban Law Journal, 29*, 641–682.

McMaster, L. E., Connolly, J., Pepler, D., & Craig, W. M. (2002). Peer to peer sexual harassment in early adolescence: A developmental perspective. *Development and Psychopathology, 14*, 91–105.

Mensinger, J. L. (2000). *An exploration of gender role attitudes and disordered eating in adolescent females attending single sex and coeducational school environments*. Unpublished master's thesis, City University of New York.

Mensinger, J. (2001). Conflicting gender role prescriptions and disordered eating in single-sex and coeducational school environments. *Gender and Education, 13*, 417–429.

Monaghan, E. J. (1988). Literacy instruction and gender in Colonial New England. *American Quarterly, 40*, 18–41.

Morse, S. (1998). *Separated by sex: A critical look at single-sex education for girls*. Washington, DC: American Association of University Women Educational Foundation.

National Association for Choice in Education, NACE. (2011). Retrieved from http://www.4schoolchoice.org/.

O'Brien, C. (2011). Young people's comparisons of cross-gender and same-gender bullying in British secondary schools. *Educational Research, 53*, 257–301.

Ormerod, A. J., Collinsworth, L. L., & Perry, L. A. (2008). Critical climate: Relations among sexual harassment climate and outcomes for high school girls and boys. *Psychology of Women Quarterly, 32*, 113–125.

Pahlke, E., Cooper, C. E., & Fabes, R. A. (2013). Classroom sex composition and first-grade school outcomes: The role of classroom behavior. *Social Science Research, 42*, 1650–1658.

Pahlke, E., Hyde, J. S., & Allison, C. M. (2014, February 3). The effects of single-sex compared with coeducational schooling on students' performance and attitudes: A meta-analysis. *Psychological Bulletin*. Advance online publication. http://dx.doi.org/10.1037/a0035740.

Pashler, H., McDaniel, M., Rohrer, D., & Bjork, R. (2009). Learning styles: Concepts and evidence. *Psychological Science in the Public Interest, 3*, 105–119.

Patal, E. A., Cooper, H., & Allen, A. B. (2010). Extending the school day or school year: A systematic review of research (1985–2009). *Review of Educational Research, 80*, 401–436.

Patterson, M. M., & Pahlke, E. E. (2011). Student characteristics associated with girls' success in a single-sex school. *Sex Roles, 65*, 737–750.

Petersen, J., & Hyde, J. S. (2014). Gender-related academic and occupational interests and goals. In L. S. Liben & R. S. Bigler (Vol. Eds.) *The role of gender in educational contexts and outcomes*. In J. B. Benson (Series Ed.), *Advances in child development and behavior: Vol. 47* (pp. 43–76). London: Elsevier.

Poteat, V. P., Scheer, J. R., & Mereish, E. H. (2014). Factors affecting academic achievement among sexual minority and gender-variant youth. In L. S. Liben & R. S. Bigler (Vol. Eds.) *The role of gender in educational contexts and outcomes*. In J. B. Benson (Series Ed.), *Advances in child development and behavior: Vol. 47* (pp. 261–300). London: Elsevier.

Pronin, E., Steele, C. M., & Ross, L. (2004). Identity bifurcation in response to stereotype threat: Women and mathematics. *Journal of Experimental Social Psychology, 40*, 152–168.

Riegle-Crumb, C., & Humphries, M. (2012). Exploring bias in math teachers' perceptions of students' ability by gender and race/ethnicity. *Gender & Society, 26*, 290–322.

Riordan, C. (2002). What do we know about the effects of single-sex schools in the private sector? Implications for public schools. In A. Datnow, & L. Hubbard (Eds.), *Gender in policy and practice: Perspectives on single-sex and coeducational schooling* (pp. 10–30). New York: Routledge Falmer.

Riordan, C., Faddis, B. J., Beam, M., Seager, A., Tanney, A., DiBiase, R., et al. (2008). *Early implementation of public single-sex schools: Perceptions and characteristics*. Portland: RMC Research Corporation, Prepared for the U.S. Department of Education.

Rowley, S. J., Ross, L., Lozada, F., Williams, A., Gale, A., & Kurtz-Costes, B. (2014). Framing black boys: Parent, teacher, and student narratives of the academic lives of black boys. In L. S. Liben & R. S. Bigler (Vol. Eds.) *The role of gender in educational contexts and outcomes*. In J. B. Benson (Series Ed.), *Advances in child development and behavior: Vol. 47* (pp. 301–332). London: Elsevier.

Single-Sex Schools. (2011). National Association for Single-Sex Public Education. http://www.singlesexschools.org/schools-schools.htm Accessed April 9, 2009.

Sadker, M., & Sadker, D. (1986). Sexism in the classroom: From grade school to graduate school. *Phi Delta Kappan, 67*, 512–515.

Sadker, D., Sadker, M., & Zittleman, K. R. (2009). *Still failing at fairness: How gender bias cheats girls and boys in school and what we can do about it*. New York: Simon & Schuster.

Salomone, R. C. (2006). Single-sex programs: Resolving the research conundrum. *Teachers College Record, 4*, 778–802.

Sax, L. (2005). *Why gender matters*. New York: Doubleday.

Sax, L. (2007). *Boys adrift: The five factors driving the growing epidemic of unmotivated boys and underachieving young men*. New York: Basic Books.

Sax, L. (2011). *Know your child*. Online editorial in the New York Times. http://www.nytimes.com/roomfordebate/2011/10/17/single-sex-schools-separate-but-equal/know-whats-best-for-your-child.

Schaefer, B. (2004). A demographic survey of learning behaviors among American students. *School Psychology Review, 33*, 481–497.

Signorella, M. L. (1987). Gender schemata: Individual differences and context effects. In L. S. Liben, & M. L. Signorella (Eds.), *Children's gender schemata: 38. New directions for child development* (pp. 89–105). San Francisco: Jossey-Bass.

Signorella, M. L., & Bigler, R. S. (2013). Single-sex schooling: Bridging science and school boards in educational policy. *Sex Roles, 69*, 349–355.

Signorella, M. L., Bigler, R. S., & Liben, L. S. (1993). Developmental differences in children's gender schemata about others: A meta-analytic review. *Developmental Review, 13*, 147–183.

Signorella, M. L., Hayes, A. R., & Li, Y. (2013). A meta-analytic critique of Mael et al.'s (2005) review of single-sex schooling. *Sex Roles, 69*, 423–441.

Smith, T. E., & Leaper, C. (2006). Self-perceived gender typicality and the peer context during adolescence. *Journal of Research on Adolescence, 16*, 91–104.

Smithers, A., & Robinson, P. (1995). *Coeducational and single-sex schooling*. Manchester: Centre for Education and Employment Research.

Spielhagen, F. R. (2008). *Debating single-sex education: Separate and equal?*. Lanham, MD: Rowman & Littlefield Education.

Steele, C. M. (1997). A threat in the air: How stereotypes shape intellectual identity and performance. *American Psychologist, 52*, 613–629.

Stevenson, R. L. (1883). *Treasure Island*. London, England: Cassell and Co.

Strough, J., & Covatto, A. M. (2002). Context and age differences in same- and other-gender peer preferences. *Social Development, 11*, 346–361.

Strough, J., & Meegan, S. P. (2001). Friendship and gender differences in task and social interpretations of peer collaborative problem solving. *Social Development, 10*, 1–22.

Thompson, T., & Underleider, C. (2004). *Single sex schooling: Final Report*. Toronto, Ontario, Canada: Council of Ministers of Education, Canada. http://www.cmec.ca/Publications/Lists/Publications/Attachments/61/singlegender.en.pdf.

Tiggemann, M. (2001). Effect of gender composition of school on body concerns in adolescent women. *International Journal of Eating Disorders, 29*, 239–243.

Timmerman, G. (2003). Sexual harassment of adolescents perpetrated by teachers and by peers: An exploration of the dynamics of power, culture, and gender in secondary schools. *Sex Roles, 48*, 231–244.

Tyack, D., & Hansot, E. (1990). *Learning together: A history of coeducation in American public schools*. New Haven, CT: Yale University Press.

U.S. Department of Education. (2006). 34 C.F.R. § 106.34(b)(1).

Voyer, D., & Voyer, S. D. (2014). Gender differences in scholastic achievement: A meta-analysis. *Psychological Bulletin*. Advance online, publication, http://dx.doi.org/10.1037/a0036620.

Weil, E. (2008). *Teaching boys and girls separately*. New York Times.

Wigfield, A., & Eccles, J. S. (2000). Expectancy-value theory of achievement motivation. *Contemporary Educational Psychology, 25*, 68–81.

Wiggin, K. D. (1903). *Rebecca of Sunnybrook Farm*. New York: Grosset & Dunlap.

CHAPTER EIGHT

Factors Affecting Academic Achievement Among Sexual Minority and Gender-Variant Youth

V. Paul Poteat[1], Jillian R. Scheer, Ethan H. Mereish

Department of Counseling, Developmental, and Educational Psychology, Boston College, Chestnut Hill, Massachusetts, USA
[1]Corresponding author: e-mail address: PoteatP@bc.edu

Contents

1. Introduction	262
2. Theoretical Models for Understanding Academic Disparities	264
2.1 The Sexual Minority Stress Model	265
2.2 Social Cognitive Career Theory	265
3. Evidence of Sexual Orientation-Based Academic Disparities	267
4. Processes and Consequences of Victimization	269
4.1 Homophobic Victimization and Academic Disparities	269
4.2 Processes by Which Victimization Affects Learning and Academic Performance	272
4.3 Diminished Mental and Physical Health	272
4.4 School Avoidance	273
4.5 Substance Use as an Externalizing Coping Strategy	274
4.6 Chronic Vigilance	275
5. Additional Influences on Student Outcomes	276
5.1 The Timing and Onset of Victimization as a Risk Factor	276
5.2 Exclusionary Discipline as a Disruptive Process	278
5.3 Unique Stressors Among Transgender Youth	279
6. Programming and Policy	280
6.1 Promoting Academic Resilience in the Face of Victimization	280
6.2 Peer, Parent, and General Adult Support	281
6.3 The Role of Gay–Straight Alliances	283
6.4 Broader Extracurricular Opportunities	285
6.5 School-Wide Policies and Academic Programs	287
6.6 Anti-discrimination Policies	287
6.7 Inclusive Curriculum	289
7. Conclusions	293
References	294

Abstract

Experiences of victimization among sexual minority youth (e.g., lesbian, gay, bisexual, transgender; LGBT) and gender-variant youth remain pronounced in many schools. Although much work has shown the connection between homophobic bullying and mental and physical health, there has been limited attention to how victimization impedes learning, academic achievement, and other school-related outcomes for these youth. In this chapter, we propose several pathways through which victimization leads to academic disparities among sexual minority and gender-variant youth, with attention to its effects on individual learning processes (e.g., motivation, concentration, self-efficacy, and other cognitive stressors) as well as broader psychological and social processes (e.g., mental health, school avoidance, harmful coping strategies, exclusionary discipline). We also consider protective factors (e.g., social support, Gay–Straight Alliances, extracurricular involvement, nondiscrimination policies, inclusive curriculum) that could promote resilience and suggest potential mechanisms by which they may operate. In doing so, we aim to stimulate ideas for an advancement of research in this area.

1. INTRODUCTION

Schools are a critical setting for many aspects of youth development, ranging from academic to social development (Eccles & Roeser, 2011; Larson, Hansen, & Moneta, 2006). Nevertheless, many youth continue to experience hostility, rejection, and victimization in this context and perceive their schools as unsafe and unwelcoming (Cook, Williams, Guerra, Kim, & Sadek, 2010). These experiences carry serious physical and mental health consequences, impede learning processes, and act as barriers to academic achievement for these youth (Gini & Pozzoli, 2009; Nakamoto & Schwartz, 2010; Reijntjes, Kamphuis, Prinzie, & Telch, 2010; van Lier et al., 2012).

Experiences of victimization among sexual minority youth (e.g., lesbian, gay, bisexual, transgender; LGBT) remain particularly pronounced in many schools. In fact, several recent meta-analyses show that sexual minority youth experience higher rates of school-based victimization than heterosexual youth and that this constitutes a sizable difference (Katz-Wise & Hyde, 2012; Toomey & Russell, 2013b). Further, there is robust support for strong associations between homophobic victimization, discrimination, and a range of mental health, physical health, and academic concerns (Friedman, Koeske, Silvestre, Korr, & Sites, 2006; Hershberger & D'Augelli, 1995; Huebner, Rebchook, & Kegeles, 2004; Poteat, Mereish, DiGiovanni, & Koenig, 2011; Russell, Sinclair, Poteat, & Koenig, 2012).

Similarly, youth experience victimization on the basis of their gender identity or expression, particularly for behaviors that violate rigidly prescribed masculinity or femininity norms (Aspenlieder, Buchanan, McDougall, & Sippola, 2009; D'Augelli, Grossman, & Starks, 2006; Pascoe, 2007; Phoenix, Frosh, & Pattman, 2003; Toomey, McGuire, & Russell, 2012; Toomey, Ryan, Diaz, Card, & Russell, 2010). It is important to note that sexual orientation and gender identity and expression are not synonymous. Both sexual minority and heterosexual youth vary in the extent to which they express behaviors traditionally labeled as masculine or feminine, and thus both may experience victimization when they violate gender norms (Friedman et al., 2006; Pascoe, 2007; Phoenix et al., 2003). At the same time, due to their shared experiences of discrimination, transgender youth often have been grouped with lesbian, gay, and bisexual youth when researchers make broader comparisons between sexual minorities and heterosexuals. Nevertheless, it is important to note that transgender youth (as well as gender-variant youth more broadly) may identify as heterosexual or as lesbian, gay, or bisexual. Because most of the research we review in this chapter has not distinguished between transgender youth who identify as lesbian, gay, or bisexual, and those who identify as heterosexual, for the purpose of this chapter we refer broadly to the sexual minority youth community to include transgender youth. As with victimization based on sexual orientation, victimization based on gender expression is associated with elevated health and academic concerns (Grossman & D'Augelli, 2006; Toomey et al., 2010). Thus, both forms of bias-based victimization affect school and academic outcomes.

Research on sexual minority and gender-variant youth has focused heavily on their experiences of victimization and other stressors specifically within the school context. Taking into consideration this focus on school-based experiences, it is surprising that there has been rather limited direct attention to various academic and career development concerns faced by many of these youth. Nevertheless, some extant findings do indicate sexual orientation-based academic disparities in several areas such as enrollment in advanced courses, earned grades, and risk of school dropout (Aragon, Poteat, & Espelage, 2014; Pearson, Muller, & Wilkinson, 2007; Poteat et al., 2011; Russell, Seif, & Truong, 2001). Undeniably, continued attention to mental and physical health disparities is critical. A number of comprehensive reviews on the health disparities faced by sexual minorities emphasize the continued need for this research (e.g., Graham, Bradford, de Vries, & Garofalo, 2011). At the same time, it is important for researchers to extend their focus on sexual minority and gender-variant youth to include issues related to learning, academic performance, and career development. These educational and career issues are fundamentally interconnected with mental and physical health issues. It is clear from the general psychological literature, for example, that mental health concerns predict academic and other school-related concerns; furthermore, the effects of victimization on academic outcomes are partly mediated through their negative effects on mental health (DeRosier & Mercer, 2009; Juvonen, Nishina, & Graham, 2000; Kochenderfer & Ladd, 1996). Given the limited attention to academic issues among sexual minority and gender-variant youth, we seek to highlight current issues in this area and suggest new avenues for research.

We have several primary aims for this chapter. First, we bridge concepts from multiple theories, including minority stress theory and theories of learning and career development, to provide a framework on which to base research on academic disparities faced by sexual minority and gender-variant youth. Second, we synthesize findings on the existence of sexual orientation-based academic disparities. Third, we consider the role of victimization and other stressors in shaping the school-based experiences of sexual minority and gender-variant youth. We offer several suggestions for how these barriers may operate in combination to predict school and academic outcomes among sexual minority and gender-variant youth. Although we emphasize the role of victimization and the school context, we acknowledge that victimization is only one of many stressors experienced by sexual minority and gender-variant youth and that school is one of multiple contexts in which it is experienced. Fourth, we consider factors that moderate and attenuate the effects of victimization and other disruptive processes that impede learning and academic performance. Finally, we discuss relevant programming and policy issues at a broader systems level. As part of this discussion, we suggest several pathways by which they may improve the school-based experiences and academic achievement of sexual minority and gender-variant youth.

2. THEORETICAL MODELS FOR UNDERSTANDING ACADEMIC DISPARITIES

In this section, we review two major theories that we apply throughout this chapter as frameworks for understanding academic disparities faced by sexual minority and gender-variant youth. Both models suggest various pathways through which disparities may arise for these youth. The minority stress model (Meyer, 2003) has been widely used to explain sexual orientation-based disparities related to mental and physical health, but it has been used markedly less when considering academic disparities. In comparison, social cognitive career theory (SCCT; Lent, Brown, & Hackett, 1994, 2000) focuses directly on individual and social processes that influence learning and career development. SCCT has been applied in some limited cases to identify barriers to career development among sexual minority adults, but with little attention to sexual minority youth. In combination, however, these two theories provide a strong framework to identify processes that could contribute to sexual orientation-based academic disparities.

2.1. The Sexual Minority Stress Model

The minority stress model (Meyer, 2003) offers one framework to understand sexual orientation-based disparities in school and academic outcomes. The minority stress model posits that sexual minorities face unique and hostile stressors (e.g., homophobic victimization) related to their sexual minority identity; consequently, these stressors have negative effects on their health (Meyer, 2003). Although the model was originally conceptualized for sexual minorities, it can be applied similarly to gender-variant individuals. The model outlines distal and proximal stressors that are unique and chronic for minority populations. Distal stressors may constitute experiences such as discrimination, while proximal stressors represent more internally based processes such as internalized homonegativity (Meyer, 2003). Although the model has received much empirical support, its focus has been on mental and physical health outcomes with little attention to academic outcomes. We believe, however, that the model offers a useful lens to conceptualize sexual minority and gender-variant youths' school experiences and academic outcomes.

2.2. Social Cognitive Career Theory

As a complement to the minority stress model, we utilize SCCT (Lent et al., 1994, 2000) to frame our discussion of sexual minority and gender-variant youths' experiences in the school and academic domain. Although SCCT focuses on career development, we consider educational and academic experiences to be part of and contributing to this long-term process. Of note, much of SCCT is grounded in Bandura's work on social learning theory and self-efficacy (Bandura, 1977).

SCCT proposes that individuals' personal attributes (e.g., sexual orientation) and their context (e.g., environmental conditions and events) influence their learning experiences (Lent et al., 1994, 2000). For instance, and as we later note, contextual factors such as unwelcoming school climates and victimization can exert a sizeable negative effect on the learning experiences of sexual minority and gender-variant youth. In turn, these learning experiences influence individuals' self-efficacy, interests, outcome expectations, and personal goals. Self-efficacy refers to confidence in one's abilities (e.g., to perform well in a course or graduate from high school). Self-efficacy can be influenced by personal accomplishments (e.g., prior academic performance), vicarious learning (e.g., observing teachers model ways to solve a problem), persuasion (e.g., receiving positive reinforcement from teachers), and physiological states (e.g., physical health). Self-efficacy is important because it can summarily influence individuals' continued interest in an area (e.g., continued interest in science, sports, music). Both self-efficacy and interest are related to individuals' outcome expectations (i.e., beliefs about what will result from one's behavior and performance). Outcome expectations, in turn, shape individuals' personal goals and aspirations. Butler (2014) [Chapter 1 of this volume] and Petersen and Hyde (2014) [Chapter 2 of this volume] provide accounts of these processes in the development of gender-differentiated academic motivation and achievement. As an example related to sexual minority youth, a lesbian adolescent's intent to remain in high school may be shaped by her expectations of continued victimization, level of encouragement from teachers to stay in school, and from her past academic success.

In addition to the set of factors above, SCCT emphasizes that personal and contextual factors can affect learning and career development (Lent et al., 2000). These components are critical, considering the unique barriers faced by sexual minority and gender-variant youth that disrupt their learning and impede their academic performance. For instance, distal and proximal stressors outlined by the minority stress model may act as barriers and negatively affect the learning process outlined by SCCT. One study among sexual minority college students, for example, found that discrimination was associated negatively with career development (Schneider & Dimito, 2010). Ultimately, we suspect that chronic victimization experienced by sexual minority and gender-variant youth may influence academic performance through its negative effects on self-efficacy, outcome expectations, and other related pathways.

Overall, sexual minority and gender-variant youth face unique barriers to achieving their academic and career goals. The minority stress model and SCCT provide useful frameworks to consider the complex processes that lead to academic disparities. In the sections that follow, we apply these frameworks to highlight potential pathways that should be tested empirically in order to address the academic needs of sexual minority and gender-variant youth.

3. EVIDENCE OF SEXUAL ORIENTATION-BASED ACADEMIC DISPARITIES

There is a sizable literature base on the achievement gap and educational disparities faced by minority youth populations, particularly racial and ethnic minority youth (Cohen, Garcia, Apfel, & Master, 2006; Ladson-Billings, 2006; Lee, 2002; Rothstein, 2004). Comprehensive reviews have highlighted issues such as inequitable and limited access to educational resources, the discrepant quality of education provided, concerns related to academic assessment and testing, and differential treatment by educators that contribute to race- and ethnicity-based academic disparities. Nevertheless, studies have systematically overlooked and failed to consider the academic needs of sexual minority youth and potential sexual orientation-based academic disparities. Furthermore, educational policies have failed to address issues of school accountability to ensure the academic success of these youth. In this section, we review the limited findings on school and academic concerns among sexual minority youth, as well as concerns related to their future academic intentions and career aspirations.

Basic disparities between sexual minority and heterosexual youth have been documented across multiple school-related and academic indices. School safety and belonging have been among the most extensively examined of these indices. Many sexual minority youth perceive their schools as unsafe and unwelcoming, and their perceptions of safety and belonging are lower compared to heterosexual youth (Bochenek & Brown, 2001; Eisenberg & Resnick, 2006; Murdock & Bolch, 2005; Poteat et al., 2011; Toomey et al., 2012). Several crucial components of school safety and belonging have been considered as part of this research, such as the availability of a supportive adult, feelings of isolation or disconnection, attachment to teachers or peers, and perceptions of the school as a welcoming environment. As we later note, school belonging is especially important to consider based on its association with victimization and academic outcomes.

Other studies have given attention to disparities related to course grades and GPA. For example, some findings have noted that, on average, sexual minority youth report poorer grades than heterosexual youth (Poteat et al., 2011). When considering gender differences, however, other findings suggest that this applies primarily to gay and bisexual males rather than to lesbian or bisexual females (Pearson et al., 2007). Still other findings have indicated that GPA differences are more pronounced for male and female bisexual youth than they are for same-sex-only attracted youth (Russell et al., 2001). Thus, although grade disparities appear evident, there remains ambiguity as to which groups of sexual minority youth they most apply.

Studies also have considered differences between heterosexual and sexual minority youth in the courses they take in high school. Some findings have shown that sexual minority males are less likely to take advanced math and science courses than heterosexual males, and that sexual minority females are less likely to take advanced science courses than heterosexual females (Pearson et al., 2007). These course-related differences may explain why some sexual minority youth maintain a relatively strong GPA, despite their frequent victimization. These findings are concerning for several reasons. Advanced courses are critical for competitive college acceptance and as part of preparation for the rigor of college-level courses. As such, even though sexual minority youth may perform well in their classes, taking fewer rigorous classes places them at a competitive disadvantage for longer-term academic opportunities. Disadvantages may be evident in areas such as admittance to highly competitive universities, securing academic merit scholarships, or fulfilling prerequisite courses for certain college majors. Research is needed to consider these potential disparities.

These course-related disparities also may carry implications for longer-term career development. There continues to be substantial growth and career opportunities in STEM-related fields (i.e., science, technology, engineering, and mathematics). Following the SCCT model, however, sexual minority youth who take fewer courses in these areas may feel lower self-efficacy to perform well in these areas; subsequently, their lower self-efficacy may lead them to express less interest in pursuing STEM-related careers. Of importance, we suspect that sexual orientation-based differences in course enrollment are not simply a reflection of different interests between sexual minority and heterosexual youth. We later note how victimization may operate as a barrier to taking and excelling in advanced courses. These emerging findings underscore the need for research to consider not only immediate sexual orientation-based academic disparities, but also whether these disparities extend beyond secondary education and are compounded over time.

Adding to the concerns noted above, heterosexual and sexual minority youth differ in their projected future academic intentions. One study found that sexual minority youth were more than twice as likely as heterosexual youth to report that they would not complete high school, and they were significantly less likely to report intentions to go to a 4-year college (Aragon et al., 2014). There is little disagreement that a college degree is now a minimal standard for many careers. Thus, sexual minority youth who do not complete high school or who do not pursue a full college degree may face more limited career options after high school.

As research continues to advance in this area, researchers also must give greater consideration to diversity within the sexual minority youth community. Academic disparities may be even more evident when considering the intersection of sexual orientation with other social identities. Whereas some studies have considered gender differences (e.g., Pearson et al., 2007; Russell et al., 2001), other forms of diversity also should be included. Given the notable education disparities faced by youth of color (Barbarin, Chinn, & Wright, 2014 [Chapter 10 of this volume]; Ladson-Billings, 2006; Lee, 2002; Rowley et al., 2014 [Chapter 9 of this volume]), combined with findings that sexual minorities of color can experience unique stressors from White sexual minorities (Meyer, Dietrich, & Schwartz, 2008; Rosario, Schrimshaw, Hunter, & Gwadz, 2002), academic disparities may be especially pronounced for sexual minority youth of color. Similarly, there is a dearth of research on transgender youth in relation to academic outcomes. Yet, they face many of the same barriers as LGB youth, as well as other unique barriers (Grossman & D'Augelli, 2006; Mallon & DeCrescenzo, 2006; McGuire, Anderson, Toomey, & Russell, 2010). Attention to variability within the sexual minority youth community is important as part of larger efforts to ensure that adequate resources are provided to these youth and that these resources are tailored to meet the needs of specific populations within this community.

4. PROCESSES AND CONSEQUENCES OF VICTIMIZATION
4.1. Homophobic Victimization and Academic Disparities

Among the distal stressors outlined in minority stress theory (Meyer, 2003), homophobic victimization represents a prominent one faced by sexual minority youth. Name-calling, rumor-spreading, teasing, and assault are among the most common forms of victimization experienced by these youth (Kosciw, Diaz, & Greytak, 2008; Rivers, 2001). Of concern, findings from multiple data sources over several decades show little evidence of a decrease in the large proportion of sexual minority youth who face this form of victimization (Hershberger & D'Augelli, 1995; Kosciw, Greytak, & Diaz, 2009; Rivers, 2001). A few longitudinal and retrospective findings indicate that many sexual minority youth experience chronic and prolonged victimization (Rivers, 2001; Rosario et al., 2002). For example, sexual minority adults have reported retrospectively that their victimization at school often was ongoing (Rivers, 2001). Prospective longitudinal studies also indicate this relative stability. Sexual minority youth who experience higher levels of gay-related stress than other youth continue to report higher levels than other youth over a 12-month period (Rosario et al., 2002). As we will note, such persistent victimization stands to have a substantial negative effect on academic performance.

Our knowledge of victimization based on gender expression has grown with recent research. Gender-variant behavior is associated with victimization for heterosexual and sexual minority youth (Aspenlieder et al., 2009; D'Augelli et al., 2006; Pascoe, 2007; Young & Sweeting, 2004). Other studies among sexual minority youth note the association between victimization based on gender expression and mental health concerns (Friedman et al., 2006; Toomey et al., 2012). Based on retrospective reports from sexual minority adults, higher levels of recalled victimization based on gender expression during adolescence predicted their current life satisfaction (Toomey et al., 2012) and adult gay men's current suicidality (Friedman et al., 2006). There remains little attention, however, to academic disparities faced by gender-variant youth.

Several meta-analyses provide a characterization of the victimization faced by sexual minority youth. One meta-analysis found that sexual minority youth reported higher levels of multiple forms of victimization than heterosexual youth, with small to moderate effect sizes (Katz-Wise & Hyde, 2012). Some of these differences were slightly higher for males than females. Another meta-analysis specific to school-based victimization came to similar conclusions and deemed the overall magnitude of sexual orientation-based differences to be moderate (Toomey & Russell, 2013b). Furthermore, there was some evidence that the disparity was greater for males than females.

Some scholars have argued that sexual prejudice and discrimination have dissipated among youth and that the serious health risks faced by sexual minority youth have been exaggerated or no longer apply to many of these youth (McCormack, 2012; Savin-Williams, 2005). The empirical evidence, however, is largely unsupportive of or runs counter to these claims. At best, the prevailing evidence suggests that this counter-argument applies to a small subsample of sexual minority youth. This is not to diminish the case that many sexual minority youth are resilient in the face of discrimination and that others demonstrate healthy development in physical, psychological, social, and academic domains. Nevertheless, a large number of sexual minority youth continue to experience chronic victimization and related hardships in each of these domains. As such, the nature and prevalence of these concerns cannot be minimized.

Although studies offer firm evidence that sexual minority youth report higher rates of victimization than heterosexual youth, it is important to note that heterosexual youth also are called homophobic epithets and experience victimization that is homophobic (Pascoe, 2007; Phoenix et al., 2003; Plummer, 2001; Poteat & Espelage, 2007; Poteat, Scheer, DiGiovanni, & Mereish, 2014). Notably, homophobic victimization is associated with psychosocial and academic concerns for heterosexual youth in a similar manner as for sexual minority youth (Poteat & Espelage, 2007; Poteat, Scheer, et al., 2014). Homophobic victimization among heterosexual youth has been explained based on several factors. Because of the societal stigmatization of sexual minorities, referring to a student as a sexual minority in a disparaging manner, regardless of whether the student identifies as such, symbolically places that student in a subordinate position. Also, using homophobic epithets is one means by which aggressive students intensify bullying behavior, irrespective of the targeted individual's actual or perceived sexual orientation (Plummer, 2001; Thurlow, 2001). Finally, these epithets are used to enforce gender-normative behavior and punish gender-transgressive behavior, particularly among boys (Pascoe, 2007; Phoenix et al., 2003; Plummer, 2001). This latter dynamic highlights some of the overlap between homophobic victimization and victimization based on gender-variant behavior.

Congruent with assertions that homophobic bias intensifies aggressive acts, the associations between homophobic victimization and academic concerns are greater in size than for general victimization (e.g., victimization that students do not perceive to be based on their sexual orientation). Specific to school and academic outcomes, Russell and colleagues (2012) found that students who experienced general victimization were 1.32 times as likely as nonvictimized youth to report that their grades were mostly C's or below and they were 1.79 times as likely to report truancy. This disparity was greater for youth who had experienced homophobic victimization: they were 1.52 times as likely as nonvictimized youth to report that their grades were mostly C's or below and 2.52 times as likely to report truancy. This study was unable to differentiate heterosexual and sexual minority youth, yet past research suggests that sexual minority youth experience more homophobic victimization than heterosexual youth (Katz-Wise & Hyde, 2012; Poteat et al., 2011; Toomey & Russell, 2013b). Homophobic victimization may result in these heightened detrimental effects for sexual minority youth because it directly denigrates their marginalized social identity. Consequently, it may not simply be that sexual minority youth experience more frequent victimization than heterosexual youth, but that the victimization they experience (i.e., homophobic victimization) is also more severe.

Chronic victimization among sexual minority youth may partly explain how sexual orientation-based academic disparities arise. Although short-term stressors (e.g., a brief illness) may impede learning or affect academic performance temporarily, students may be able to improve without a lasting consequence. Chronic victimization, however, jeopardizes students' learning and performance across multiple assignments and tests. Moreover, because later educational material often builds on earlier material, the effects of chronic homophobic victimization on academic performance may be compounded over time for sexual minority youth. It may be much more difficult for these youth to recover academically, which ultimately may affect their final grades. Over an even greater time period, this may limit their opportunities to enroll in advanced courses. Ultimately, chronic victimization could partly account for findings that sexual minority youth enroll in fewer advanced math or science courses than heterosexual youth (Pearson et al., 2007), a possibility in need of empirical examination.

4.2. Processes by Which Victimization Affects Learning and Academic Performance

Victimization operates in combination with other factors in ways that lead to poorer educational outcomes among sexual minority than heterosexual youth. Although most of this research has been conducted among sexual minority youth, we believe it is also relevant for gender-variant youth (either sexual minority or heterosexual). In this section, we review the connections between victimization and other psychological and social factors that shape the experiences of these youth. In addition, we point to several potential mechanisms by which these factors could lead to poor learning and academic outcomes.

4.3. Diminished Mental and Physical Health

A number of studies have focused on the mediating role of mental health in accounting for the association between victimization and academic outcomes. Specifically, victimization predicts diminished mental health, which in turn predicts elevated school and academic concerns such as truancy, poorer grades, and risk for school dropout (Juvonen et al., 2000). There is evidence that this also applies to sexual minority youth (Poteat et al., 2011).

There are several potential reasons for why mental health concerns resulting from victimization have a central role in predicting academic outcomes for sexual minority and gender-variant youth. In addition to the direct disruptive effect of victimization on learning (Boulton, Trueman, & Murray, 2008), mental health concerns such as depression can further impede learning processes. These learning processes can include concentration, motivation to learn the material, active participation and engagement in the learning process, and the ability to retain and recall information (Buhs & Ladd, 2001). Mental health concerns also may lead youth to miss days from school (Egger, Costello, & Angold, 2003), which further disrupts the learning process. Given that sexual minority and gender-variant youth experience more frequent victimization than heterosexual and gender-typical youth (Katz-Wise & Hyde, 2012), that homophobic victimization is more severe than general victimization (Russell et al., 2012), and that many sexual minority and gender-variant youth have fewer support outlets than heterosexual youth (Goodenow, Szalacha, & Westheimer, 2006; Ryan, Huebner, Diaz, & Sanchez, 2009), it is perhaps unsurprising that mental health concerns have a major role in accounting for academic concerns among sexual minority and gender-variant youth.

In a similar manner, physical health concerns also may impede learning and academic performance among sexual minority and gender-variant youth. There is robust support for the association between victimization and physical health concerns (Gini & Pozzoli, 2009; Nishina, Juvonen, & Witkow, 2005), and there is additional evidence that physical health concerns are even higher among sexual minorities than heterosexuals (Cochran, Mays, Alegria, Ortega, & Takeuchi, 2007; Sandfort, Bakker, Schellevis, & Vanwesenbeeck, 2006). Physical health impairments may disrupt learning through its effects on impaired concentration or forcing students to miss classes (e.g., for doctor appointments, pain management, complications arising from the primary health concern). These findings highlight the need to consider not only mental health concerns but also physical health concerns that contribute to sexual orientation-based academic disparities.

4.4. School Avoidance

Certain protective strategies used by sexual minority and gender-variant youth to avoid victimization also carry risks connected to their academic performance. For instance, some sexual minority youth report school avoidance and absenteeism out of serious safety concerns (Goodenow et al., 2006; Poteat et al., 2011). Often, these youth must contend with immediate safety needs that supersede their ability to focus on academic tasks and goals. Several factors contribute to sexual minority and gender-variant youth engaging in school avoidance as a protective strategy. A number of sexual minority youth report that teachers often fail to intervene when students make homophobic comments or use homophobic epithets (Elze, 2003). Similarly, documents from lawsuits filed by sexual minority and gender-variant youth against their school systems have shown that these youth often were blamed for their victimization, were at times viewed as instigators of these experiences, and faced added discrimination from adults and authority figures at school (Cianciotto & Cahill, 2012). In the absence of support or protection from adults at school, sexual minority and gender-variant youth may view school avoidance as one of few ways to protect themselves, despite its consequences in other areas (e.g., learning and academic performance).

School avoidance may negatively affect academic outcomes through several pathways. Repeated truancy presents a barrier to sexual minority and gender-variant students' access to course material and participation in class-based learning activities. Also, it isolates them from other teachers and peers who may be in a position to provide academic support. In relation to this latter issue, help avoidance may be a particular concern for sexual minority and gender-variant youth. Help avoidance is a significant barrier to learning and academic achievement in general (Butler, 1998; Ryan, Patrick, & Shim, 2005). For sexual minority and gender-variant youth in particular, some may avoid help seeking because they anticipate being treated in a biased manner or fear rejection from their teachers on the basis of their sexual orientation or gender expression. Some youth also may hesitate to access help from teachers who have failed to intervene during instances of homophobic harassment (Elze, 2003). This underscores the need to work with teachers on ways to serve as allies for sexual minority and gender-variant youth, and to foster stronger teacher-student connections with these youth in ways that could promote both their well-being and academic achievement.

4.5. Substance Use as an Externalizing Coping Strategy

Some sexual minority and gender-variant youth use other strategies to cope with victimization that place their academic performance at risk. Studies have documented the connection between victimization and substance use among sexual minority youth (Bontempo & D'Augelli, 2002; Marshal et al., 2008). Some sexual minority youth use substances to cope with chronic victimization because other support structures are not accessible (Rosario, Schrimshaw, & Hunter, 2011). Nevertheless, this form of coping carries negative implications for school and academic outcomes. As with diminished mental and physical health, substance use can inhibit learning processes such as concentration, motivation, and information retention and recall (Bryant, Schulenberg, O'Malley, Bachman, & Johnston, 2003). Thus, although some sexual minority and gender-variant youth may experience internalizing concerns (e.g., depression or anxiety) and others may experience externalizing concerns (e.g., truancy or substance use), these two types of coping responses may operate through similar pathways to undermine academic achievement.

4.6. Chronic Vigilance

The minority stress model (Meyer, 2003) suggests several other internal processes by which homophobic victimization may disrupt the learning and academic performance of sexual minority and gender-variant youth. As noted in the model, distal stressors (e.g., discrimination) can contribute to other proximal stress processes. One such stressor is heightened and chronic vigilance to guard against potential discrimination and rejection (Meyer, 2003). Vigilance is an especially relevant factor when considering issues related to learning and academic performance. Heightened vigilance to ensure physical safety likely comes at the expense of time and energy available to engage in other actions (e.g., studying) that serve to promote higher-order academic needs.

The effects of vigilance on academic achievement may become more pronounced as sexual minority and gender-variant youth progress through school. As students take more advanced classes, learning the material requires a substantially greater cognitive load (e.g., it requires a higher level of abstract reasoning, problem-solving, simultaneous consideration of multiple pieces of information; Sweller, 1988; van Merriënboer & Sweller, 2005). Thus, students must invest a much greater amount of working memory to attend to, process, retain, and eventually reproduce the information taught in these courses. Many sexual minority and gender-variant youth must contend with chronic vigilance in the face of perpetual discrimination. This additional cognitive demand is likely to reduce their capacity to master the material in these courses.

There has been virtually no attention to the role of vigilance in relation to learning and academic performance among sexual minority and gender-variant youth. This factor could have a significant role in explaining academic concerns among these youth, over and above effects tied to internalizing or externalizing concerns. Indeed, this process could partly explain the basic finding that sexual minority youth tend to enroll in less advanced math and science courses than their heterosexual peers (Pearson et al., 2007). Sexual minority and gender-variant youth may enroll in less demanding courses based on their anticipation of poor performance due to these added distal (e.g., homophobic victimization) and proximal (e.g., chronic vigilance) stressors.

5. ADDITIONAL INFLUENCES ON STUDENT OUTCOMES
5.1. The Timing and Onset of Victimization as a Risk Factor

The time period during which sexual minority and gender-variant youth begin to experience victimization is important to consider. Heterosexual and sexual minority youth have reported that homophobic victimization often began in elementary school (Kosciw et al., 2008; Plummer, 2001). Findings also suggest that the school climate for sexual minority youth is especially hostile during middle school compared to high school. In one large study of heterosexual youth in grades 7–12, over 40% of students in grade 7 strongly agreed or agreed with the statement that they could "never stay friends with someone who told me that he or she was gay or lesbian," while 45% of students in grade 7 strongly agreed or agreed with the statement that they would "rather attend a school where there are no gay or lesbian students" (Poteat, Espelage, & Koenig, 2009). The proportion of students who endorsed these items steadily decreased over corresponding grade levels. Nevertheless, students' support for such blatant rejection of sexual minority youth presents a stark representation of the climate in which many sexual minority youth must attempt to learn at such formative developmental periods.

These patterns of victimization and rejection should be considered as they overlap with the coming out process for sexual minority youth. Younger generations of sexual minorities are coming out at earlier ages than older generations (Floyd & Bakeman, 2006; Grov, Bimbi, Nanín, & Parsons, 2006). Some findings have placed the average age of coming out among contemporary sexual minority youth as between 14 and 15 or between 16 and 17 years of age (Floyd & Bakeman, 2006; Grov et al., 2006). These averages are distinct from those of older generations of sexual minorities, whose general age range of coming out was from 24 to 27 years of age (Grov et al., 2006). In other words, whereas older generations of sexual minorities tended to come out well after completing their secondary education (or even higher education for those who were able to attend college), contemporary youth now come out, on average, during high school. As an average, this suggests that other sexual minority youth come out even earlier. This represents a critical issue for psychologists and educators when these trends are paired with findings that prejudice against sexual minorities is at its highest among younger age groups (Horn, 2006; Poteat & Anderson, 2012). As sexual minority youth begin to come out at earlier ages, they also face a heightened potential for peer rejection. This underscores the need for schools to ensure the safety of these youth, to provide them with supportive resources, and to address the broader school climate.

These co-occurring processes (i.e., emergence of homophobic victimization, developmental trajectories of prejudice, and the coming out process) intersect with educational processes and academic expectations at these same points in time. Discrimination and hostility toward sexual minority youth peak at a time when academic expectations are becoming more demanding (e.g., during the transition from middle school to high school) and when students are being considered for placement in advanced courses. Thus, although Pearson and colleagues (2007) found that sexual minority youth were less likely than heterosexual youth to have taken advanced math and science courses in high school, it seems possible that sexual orientation-based academic disparities emerge earlier than high school. If so, they may partly result from the co-occurring stressors noted above that sexual minority and gender-variant youth contend with in their early school-based experiences. The immediate effects of early victimization on academic performance may lead to prolonged academic consequences for sexual minority and gender-variant youth. Again applying the SCCT model (Lent et al., 1994), poorer grades could lead these youth to face restricted course options in the future, lower their academic self-efficacy, and lead them to foreclose on pursuing their interests in certain careers. To our knowledge, longitudinal research has not yet addressed these issues. It is critical for research to test whether sexual orientation-based academic disparities in high school are a product not only of immediate circumstances (e.g., current victimization) but also of a prolonged history of discrimination and an extensive sequence of negative academic outcomes. This information would carry significant implications for interventions to counter these disparities.

5.2. Exclusionary Discipline as a Disruptive Process

There has been a recent emergence of attention to exclusionary discipline and its effects among sexual minority and gender-variant youth. Although it has been studied only recently among this youth population, exclusionary discipline has been studied extensively among other minority youth populations. Exclusionary forms of discipline, ranging from school office referrals, to suspensions, to incarceration, are directed disproportionately toward racial minority youth (for reviews, see Gregory, Skiba, & Noguera, 2010; Wallace, Goodkind, Wallace, & Bachman, 2008). Furthermore, these youth are more likely to face harsher sanctions than White youth who report similar infractions (Piquero, 2008; Skiba, Michael, Nardo, & Peterson, 2002). Based on the empirical data, researchers have argued persuasively that there may be a strong connection between discipline bias and the achievement gap among racial minority youth (Gregory et al., 2010). These forms of exclusionary discipline can be disruptive to the learning process and may be linked to a number of academic risks such as school dropout (Ekstrom, Goertz, Pollack, & Rock, 1986). Causes, consequences, and solutions to the problem of racial biases in the use of exclusionary discipline are addressed by Barbarin et al. (2014) [Chapter 10 of this volume] and Rowley et al. (2014) [Chapter 9 of this volume].

Building on this established literature base, there is initial evidence that sexual minority youth experience exclusionary discipline at higher rates than heterosexual youth. Himmelstein and Brückner (2011) found that non-heterosexual youth were more likely than heterosexual youth to report juvenile arrests and convictions. In addition, we have found that sexual minority youth were more likely to have been suspended from school and to have been involved in the juvenile justice or prison system than heterosexual youth (Poteat, Scheer, & Chong, under review). These experiences have the potential to act as significant barriers to learning and academic performance for sexual minority youth.

It is important to identify factors that contribute to the existence of these discipline disparities. In our recent work (Poteat et al., under review), we used the minority stress model (Meyer, 2003) as a framework to demonstrate that victimization is again a key factor that contributes to these disparities. Specifically, we built on the well-established connection between victimization and externalizing behaviors (e.g., substance use, truancy; Goodenow et al., 2006; Rosario et al., 2011) to show that these factors predicted increased risk for suspension and juvenile justice system involvement. This extended link may have been evident because, as minors, some of the very ways in which sexual minority youth cope with discrimination are punishable infractions. Moreover, we found evidence suggestive of bias against sexual minority youth in the disciplinary process: these externalizing behaviors were stronger predictors of suspension and juvenile justice system involvement for sexual minority youth than heterosexual youth.

To our knowledge, research has not yet examined how exclusionary discipline leads to poorer academic outcomes among sexual minority and gender-variant youth. We suspect, however, that exclusionary discipline creates significant academic hardships for these youth. Indeed, the model we have proposed is itself a cascade of stressors experienced by these youth, extended to include exclusionary discipline. In this sense, many sexual minority and gender-variant youth who experience exclusionary discipline also are coping with other stressors that place them at risk for academic concerns. Furthermore, sexual minority and gender-variant youth who are temporarily restricted from attending school may be even less likely to return (i.e., more likely to drop out) compared to heterosexual and gender-typical youth. This possibility should be explored, as there are several circumstances that could contribute to such an increased risk. Sexual minority youth, more than heterosexual youth, already may perceive their school to be a hostile and unsupportive environment in which they feel disconnected from adults and peers. In short, there is a pressing need for research and intervention work to address the issue of exclusionary discipline among sexual minority youth while also attending to the underlying causes (e.g., mental health concerns, safety concerns) that place these youth at greater risk.

5.3. Unique Stressors Among Transgender Youth

Up to this point, we have focused our discussion on sexual minority youth, broadly considered to include lesbian, gay, bisexual, and transgender youth. However, most of the research on sexual minorities either has not included transgender youth participants or these youth were significantly underrepresented. Nevertheless, transgender youth experience many of the same stressors we have reviewed earlier. Some transgender youth are victimized at school because they are perceived to be gay or lesbian and they may also experience victimization for their gender expression or violation of rigid gender norms (Grossman & D'Augelli, 2006; Mallon & DeCrescenzo, 2006; McGuire et al., 2010). There is some evidence that suggests transgender youth face even greater victimization than their lesbian, gay, and bisexual peers (McGuire et al., 2010). Like other sexual minority youth, transgender youth report heightened health and academic risks as a consequence of victimization (e.g., depression, suicidality, truancy, lack of safety, risk of school dropout; Garofalo, Deleon, Osmer, Doll, & Harper, 2006; McGuire et al., 2010; Rosenberg, 2002). In effect, these discriminatory experiences could impede learning and academic performance for transgender youth in the same way as for other sexual minority youth.

At the same time, it is important to highlight several unique stressors faced by transgender youth within the school context and the implications of these stressors for learning and academic performance. Some of these additional stressors include school resistance to referring to transgender youth by their affirmed gender (i.e., the gender with which they personally identify) and preventing them from using the bathroom and locker room of their affirmed gender or playing on the sports team of their affirmed gender (Barron & Bradford, 2007; McGuire et al., 2010). Transgender youth also may face increased discrimination throughout their transition process (e.g., as they begin to express their affirmed gender in the way they dress, make legal changes to their name and sex designation, undergo hormone therapy or medical procedures). These additional forms of resistance and discrimination are likely to act as barriers to learning and academic performance through many of the pathways we have described. For instance, school resistance and lack of safety may lead to increased absenteeism, diminished health, heightened vigilance, and isolation among transgender youth (Garofalo et al., 2006; Grossman & D'Augelli, 2006; Rosenberg, 2002), all of which may impede learning and academic progress. It is important to highlight these needs because few schools receive adequate training for working with transgender youth. Although some schools may receive training and service learning opportunities that focus on lesbian, gay, and bisexual issues, these trainings rarely provide sufficient time to review and discuss the specific needs of transgender youth and ways to meet their needs. In essence, the lack of attention to transgender youth is a major limitation in the field that extends not only to issues of academic disparities but to disparities in general. As such, greater inclusion of transgender youth is a necessity in order for research on sexual minority and gender-variant youth to make continued advances.

6. PROGRAMMING AND POLICY

6.1. Promoting Academic Resilience in the Face of Victimization

As research continues to identify the various pathways by which victimization disrupts and impedes learning and academic performance among sexual minority and gender-variant youth, it is equally important to identify factors that attenuate and buffer against such negative effects. There has been a growing interest in understanding resilience among sexual minority and gender-variant youth and factors that promote their healthy development. Positive youth development models provide a framework for this expansion (Damon, 2004; Larson, 2000). These models highlight that youth possess inner strengths that interact with assets in their environments to promote healthy development. In addition, these models point to various approaches that facilitate this process such as capitalizing on youth strengths, empowering youth, placing them in leadership positions, and providing opportunities to develop skills. These models also point to the need for supportive adults throughout this process. Intellectual development and academic excellence is a major domain of positive youth development, yet it has been less studied than psychological health among sexual minority and gender-variant youth. Using the positive youth development framework, we consider several relevant factors at the individual and systems level that may attenuate the effects of victimization on academic outcomes and that may promote resilience among sexual minority and gender-variant youth.

6.2. Peer, Parent, and General Adult Support

Much research on buffers against the negative effects of victimization has focused on the effects of peer, parent, or general adult support. Although sexual minority and gender-variant youth often have less access to support from these individuals due to discrimination or rejection (D'Augelli, Hershberger, & Pilkington, 1998; Ryan et al., 2009), the support that they do receive can be crucial in fostering their resilience. This has been considered primarily in relation to mental health outcomes, yet these same sources (e.g., peers, parents, or other adults) also can provide support relevant for academic achievement and career development.

There are several ways in which support operates to promote resilience. There has been consistent evidence that peer, parent, and adult support are directly associated with psychological well-being for sexual minority and gender-variant youth (Doty, Willoughby, Lindahl, & Malik, 2010; Eisenberg & Resnick, 2006; Hershberger & D'Augelli, 1995; Murdock & Bolch, 2005). These direct associations suggest that social support promotes overall health and well-being among these youth. In contrast, there has been mixed evidence for whether support from these sources attenuates the effects specifically tied to victimization. The attenuating effects have been weak or nonsignificant when considering general support from parents or peers

(Murdock & Bolch, 2005; Poteat et al., 2011), but they have been significant when considering sexual orientation-specific support (Doty et al., 2010). There are several reasons why parent support may be an inconsistent buffer of victimization effects among sexual minority youth. Many of these youth face or fear parental rejection of their sexual orientation (D'Augelli et al., 1998; Ryan et al., 2009). Therefore, they may hesitate to approach their parents for support when they are victimized, particularly if the victimization is homophobic and they are not yet out to their parents. This same concern and hesitance may apply to accessing support from peers, teachers, and other adults. Youth who are not out to these individuals may fear inadvertent disclosure or discovery of their sexual orientation in the process of help seeking. This may be perceived as an additional stressor when youth are unsure of whether these individuals would be affirming of their sexual orientation. This issue might suggest why sexual orientation-specific support has more consistent moderating effects. This specific kind of support conveys affirmation and may lead youth to feel safer in their help seeking behavior from these individuals.

We raise several issues that warrant further consideration in how peer, parent, and adult support are tied to academic outcomes for sexual minority and gender-variant youth. Notably, most of the research on how support promotes resilience among these youth has considered its moderating effects on the association between victimization and mental health outcomes. Indeed, it is likely that the primary intent of the support that sexual minority and gender-variant youth seek and receive is meant to ensure their safety and promote their psychological health, as this is a fundamental need for these youth. To what extent should we expect support to moderate the effects of victimization on academic outcomes? Most studies in this area have assessed support in terms of emotional and social support (e.g., caring, acceptance, warmth, encouragement), which are closely tied to mental health. As we have noted, diminished mental health mediates the association between victimization and academic outcomes (Juvonen et al., 2000). Therefore, social support may promote academic resilience in an indirect manner. Specifically, it may do so by attenuating the effects of victimization on mental health concerns, which in turn affect academic outcomes (Poteat et al., 2011). As such, the effects of victimization on academic performance through diminished mental health may apply more strongly for sexual minority and gender-variant youth who receive less social support. At the same time, other forms of support (e.g., instrumental or informational support such as tutoring) may have direct ties to academic performance for sexual minority and gender-variant youth. These forms of support have been understudied and should be considered in future research.

Our limited knowledge of how to promote academic excellence among sexual minority and gender-variant youth underscores the need for researchers to consider more expansive resilience-based models that incorporate academic outcomes. For example, public single-sex schooling has become more common in the U.S. in response to proponents claims that such settings reduce gender-related bullying and sexual harassment, and thereby promote achievement (see Bigler, Hayes, & Liben, 2014 [Chapter 7 of this volume]). Some critics are skeptical that such settings are associated with positive academic outcomes among sexual minorities and gender-variant youth, yet little empirical work on the topic exits. This call for attention to academic outcomes is not to detract attention from the serious and immediate safety needs of sexual minority and gender-variant youth in schools or to suggest a diversion of resources. Rather, it is meant to add to this scope of work to ensure that, in the face of such adversity, sexual minority and gender-variant youth also receive adequate support to meet their academic needs and to work toward their long-term career aspirations. These goals are crucial for promoting a more comprehensive sense of long-term well-being and resilience for these youth.

6.3. The Role of Gay–Straight Alliances

Structures at the systems level also may promote academic resilience among sexual minority and gender-variant youth. Some work has focused on the effects of Gay–Straight Alliances (GSAs). GSAs have a strong foundation in positive youth development models. They are meant to be youth-led and adult-supported groups that provide a setting for gender-variant, sexual minority, and heterosexual youth to receive emotional and social support, to socialize, and to lead advocacy efforts that address discrimination and inequality in the school and community (Griffin, Lee, Waugh, & Beyer, 2004; Russell, Muraco, Subramaniam, & Laub, 2009). GSAs have a strong potential to promote resilience among a large number of youth because they are directly situated within schools and are showing expansive growth across the country (GLSEN, 2012; GSA Network, 2013).

The presence of GSAs in schools has been linked to a number of academic and health-related indices. For example, sexual minority youth in schools with GSAs report more welcoming climates for diversity, greater perceived safety, less truancy, lower suicidality, less frequent engagement in risky sexual behavior, and lower substance use than those in schools without GSAs (Goodenow et al., 2006; Poteat, Sinclair, DiGiovanni, Koenig, & Russell, 2013; Szalacha, 2003; Walls, Kane, & Wisneski, 2010). It appears that GSAs have the potential to promote resilience across a broad range of factors. Researchers have referred to the dual purpose of GSAs to provide support to their members and to address broader systems of inequality to explain these patterns.

These GSA-related findings are encouraging, yet several issues should be considered in relation to how GSAs promote resilience in academic domains. As stated, one of the primary intentions of GSAs is to provide emotional and social support to members. This is distinct from the provision of academic support. In fact, most of the research on GSA-related effects has focused on indices of psychological and behavioral health and social well-being. Fewer studies have examined purely academic outcomes in relation to GSA membership, and their findings have been mixed. For example, while some studies have found that students who attend schools with GSAs report higher GPAs (Walls et al., 2010), the magnitude of this difference was not large. Other studies have failed to identify GPA differences based on GSA presence when controlling for other school characteristics (e.g., school size or socioeconomic status; Poteat, Sinclair, et al., 2013). Although it is powerful to see that GSAs may promote resilience, it would be unfair and unreasonable to expect GSAs to serve as an all-encompassing panacea in promoting resilience across all domains of youth development. They should not be expected to serve as the sole source or primary mechanism of change for either psychosocial or academic resilience (Poteat, Sinclair, et al., 2013). Rather, it would be optimal and perhaps necessary for GSAs to operate in conjunction with other programs and groups within the school (e.g., guidance offices, administrators and teachers, other student groups) to address large-scale concerns such as prejudice and discrimination.

Although the primary emphasis of GSAs may not be to provide direct academic support or enhancement to their members, GSAs are nonetheless in a position to advocate for programs, policies, or other efforts that could improve the educational experience for sexual minority and gender-variant students. This could be considered as part of the advocacy-based nature of GSAs. For instance, GSAs may petition for policies and programs such as inclusive curricula (e.g., course-based material that is representative of sexual minority and gender-variant individuals). We later discuss how these materials could enrich the learning process and academic performance for sexual minority and gender-variant youth. Because many GSAs seek to engage in advocacy efforts that benefit the entire school and not only immediate club members (Griffin et al., 2004), these actions could result in positive outcomes for the general student population. Thus, even sexual minority and gender-variant youth who are not members of GSAs may derive benefits from their actions.

6.4. Broader Extracurricular Opportunities

More broadly than GSAs, many youth participate in a range of school-based extracurricular activities and groups (e.g., sports or clubs) as a part of their educational experience. These settings also can promote resilience and healthy youth development (Fredricks, 2012). Participating in extracurricular activities is associated with higher GPAs and school completion rates (Darling, 2005; Eccles & Barber, 1999; Feldman & Matjasko, 2005) and higher self-esteem (Blomfield & Barber, 2009). Extracurricular participation also has been linked to greater interpersonal competence, school engagement, sense of belonging, and educational aspirations (Denault & Poulin, 2009; Marsh & Kleitman, 2002).

There are several explanations for the academic benefits derived through extracurricular involvement. Structured activities promote physical safety, supportive relationships, positive social norms, and self-efficacy (Eccles & Gootman, 2002). Participation in extracurricular activities increases school connectedness, self-worth, and sense of school belonging (Libbey, 2004). In essence, extracurricular sports and clubs are positioned to promote healthy development in many of the same domains around which sexual minority and gender-variant youth experience greater hardships due to victimization and marginalization in schools.

Despite the benefits of extracurricular involvement, discrimination is evident in these contexts for many sexual minority and gender-variant youth. Organized sports can be particularly hostile environments in which hegemonic masculinity and sexual prejudice are pervasive (Gill, Morrow, Collins, Lucey, & Schultz, 2010). These unwelcoming and unsafe climates may discourage or explicitly prevent sexual minority and gender-variant youth from participating in these activities (Gill et al., 2010; Mishna, Newman, Daley, & Solomon, 2009). Ultimately, social exclusion and homophobic climates within certain extracurricular groups deprive many sexual minority and gender-variant youth of the benefits of participating in them.

Males who are involved in sports are socialized to conform to a restricted masculine and heterosexual identity; those who deviate from these norms often face ridicule, harassment, or physical violence (Gill et al., 2010; Messner, 1992). Furthermore, males who wish to participate in stereotypically female-oriented activities, such as cheerleading, often are victimized based on their perceived sexual orientation (Barron & Bradford, 2007). Sexual minority males who are involved in sports often feel pressured to conceal their sexual orientation out of fear of reprisal or rejection (Griffin, 1993). Although sexual minority males involved in sports may avoid being targets of discrimination because peers are less likely to suspect them to be gay or bisexual, this carries a substantial psychological and social cost of hiding their identity and facing exposure to prejudice and homophobic behavior from peers and adult figures (Griffin, 1993).

Sexual minority females also face barriers and challenges to sports participation, although they differ in some ways from those faced by males. (Barriers to physical activity and sport participation faced by girls in K–12 education are reviewed by Solmon, 2014 [Chapter 4 of this volume].) For instance, males who participate in sports are validated for their heightened displays of masculinity, yet females often feel pressured to compensate with heightened femininity to offset their engagement in stereotypically masculine behavior (Griffin, 1993; Stoelting, 2011). Consequently, whereas males who participate in sports may be less likely to be considered gay or bisexual, females who participate in sports may be more likely to be considered lesbian or bisexual (Gill et al., 2010). At the same time, it is unclear whether homophobic expressions and pressure to conform to feminine norms arise from within the setting (e.g., from teammates or coaches) as they do for males, or whether they originate from outside the setting (e.g., from other students within the school). In general, little research has explored the experiences of sexual minority youth athletes or whether experiences differ for male and female youth athletes due to gender differences in sexual prejudice and its intersection with traditional gender norms. Nevertheless, attention to these issues would be quite valuable for efforts to develop tailored programming to counter sexual prejudice and sexism in these settings within which sexual minority youth may face the greatest hostility.

Adding to these concerns, some school policies perpetuate the marginalization of transgender youth. Participation in some clubs, particularly sports teams, is sometimes restricted by one's biological sex (Barron & Bradford, 2007). For example, transgender females may not be allowed to participate in women's sports teams. As with most other areas of research, however, there has been a severe lack of attention to the experiences of transgender youth in these contexts. As schools begin to address issues related to gender identity and expression, however, there has been a growing awareness that this constitutes a priority area within research, practice, and policy work.

Although sexual minority and gender-variant youth face barriers and resistance to their involvement in sports and clubs, recent research suggests that these outlets may promote overall well-being and positive academic outcomes for those who are involved in them (Toomey & Russell, 2013a). If barriers to extracurricular involvement can be diminished, these settings could be a major source of support and may promote healthy social and academic development for sexual minority and gender-variant youth. Thus, researchers should give much greater attention to how school-based extracurricular involvement may foster social relationships, improve mental health, and promote academic achievement among sexual minority and gender-variant youth.

6.5. School-Wide Policies and Academic Programs

We have used the school context as a setting for our discussion of various individual psychological and proximal social factors that contribute to variability in the learning experiences and academic outcomes of sexual minority and gender-variant youth. In addition, it is important to consider even broader school characteristics that have the potential to affect the academic outcomes of these youth. There has been growing attention to variability among sexual minority youth as a function of the policies and programs that exist at their schools (Chesir-Teran & Hughes, 2009; Hatzenbuehler & Keyes, 2013; O'Shaughnessy, Russell, Heck, Calhoun, & Laub, 2004; Szalacha, 2003). In this section, we extend our focus to this systems level and suggest how several school-wide policy and programming efforts may promote resilience among these youth.

6.6. Anti-discrimination Policies

Passage of enumerated anti-bullying and anti-discrimination school policies is a prominent issue that continues to undergo contentious debate in many states and at the federal level. Although nearly all states and the District of Columbia have passed some form of anti-bullying legislation, at present only a small percentage of these states have passed enumerated policies that extend explicit protection to students based on their actual or perceived sexual orientation or gender identity and expression (Russell, Kosciw, Horn, & Saewyc, 2010). Arguments in support of these policies have emphasized the need to ensure safe environments for students from social groups that historically have faced disproportionately higher rates of victimization (Jacob, 2013; Russell et al., 2010). In this sense, enumerated policies are not limited to sexual orientation and gender identity or expression; many include other protected categories such as disability, race, religion, or sex. Yet, sexual orientation and gender identity and expression often are the most contested categories of those included in these policies (Horn, Szalacha, & Drill, 2008; Russell et al., 2010).

Although there has been marked resistance to these inclusive policies, emerging empirical findings suggest that such policies contribute to greater safety for youth in these schools. In the state of Oregon, lesbian and gay high school students in counties where a larger number of districts had adopted enumerated policies reported fewer suicide attempts than those in counties where fewer districts had adopted these policies (Hatzenbuehler & Keyes, 2013). Data from students across the state of California also suggest that sexual minority youth who attend schools with enumerated protective policies report greater perceptions of safety than youth in schools without these policies (O'Shaughnessy et al., 2004). Finally, reports from the Gay, Lesbian, and Straight Education Network (GLSEN) that draw from their school climate survey of youth also suggest that sexual minority and gender-variant students in states with enumerated policies report hearing fewer homophobic epithets at school and observe more consistent staff intervention during these instances (Kosciw et al., 2008).

Although these policies appear to serve their intended purpose, sexual minority and gender-variant youth in schools with these policies continue to face some level of discrimination. Researchers and policies advocates have thus pointed to issues in how these policies are applied. For instance, there is a need to address how these policies are implemented, the extent to which they are consistently enforced, and the extent to which students understand the procedures for reporting discrimination (Hansen, 2007; Russell et al., 2010).

As researchers consider issues related to policy implementation, they also must consider the underlying mechanisms by which these policies promote safety and well-being for sexual minority and gender-variant youth. Some scholars have proposed that enumerated policies provide a clear indication to students and adults that sexual minority and gender-variant youth must be protected (Russell et al., 2010). This formal recognition may empower youth to report instances of discrimination. It may also encourage adults to be more responsive to these instances, addressing concerns from students who have reported that teachers often do not intervene during instances of homophobic behavior (Elze, 2003). Such policies may also lead teachers to perceive and experience administrative support for their efforts to challenge sexist and homophobic behavior in their classrooms. Empirical research has not yet tested these mechanisms.

It is also important to consider the effects of these protective policies on academic outcomes and to identify how these policies operate to promote learning and academic success. Although these policies exist at the broader systems level, they may exert a significant influence on individual students' experiences that are relevant to learning and academic performance. For instance, if these policies prompt adults to intervene more consistently when homophobic behavior occurs, this may eventually lead to more welcoming school climates and to less frequent victimization of sexual minority and gender-variant youth. In turn, this may lead these youth to attend school more consistently due to lowered safety concerns, and they may experience less vigilance, less engagement in harmful externalizing coping strategies, and improved psychological health. Also, youth may feel more welcomed to approach teachers for emotional and academic support. Each of these outcomes ultimately may create more optimal conditions for learning, opportunities to take part in extracurricular activities for further enrichment, and the necessary support to excel academically.

6.7. Inclusive Curriculum

Course material and discussions on sexual orientation-related diversity issues are limited or absent in many classrooms (Lipkin, 1999; Rogers & Mosley, 2006; Wills, 2001). As a complement to enumerated nondiscrimination policies, an inclusive curriculum has the potential to promote positive learning experiences for sexual minority and gender-variant youth. In this case, an inclusive curriculum would represent the integration of sexual orientation and gender diversity topics and the representation of sexual minority and transgender individuals within the standard curriculum. As examples, this could involve the inclusion of the sexual minority civil rights movement in history courses, acknowledging that certain pioneers in many fields (e.g., the arts and sciences) identified as lesbian, gay, bisexual, or transgender, or ensuring that word problems in math assignments are not strictly heteronormative (e.g., only referring to opposite-sex couples or "nuclear" families).

There are a number of sources that provide inclusive lesson plans appropriate for different grade levels and course subjects (e.g., GLSEN; www.glsen.org). In addition, extensive materials are available to supplement the standard curriculum (e.g., Welcoming Schools from the Human Rights Campaign, www.welcomingschools.org; films with accompanying curricula on family diversity, gender identity and expression, and bias-based harassment from Groundspark, www.groundspark.org). In this section, we review some of the initial research related to inclusive curricula and suggest various pathways by which inclusive curricula could promote positive developmental outcomes, including those related to academic achievement.

There are some limited findings that an inclusive school curriculum is associated with greater perceptions of safety among students in those schools. One report found that students who attended schools that included sexual minority issues in the curriculum reported greater perceptions of safety than students in schools where this material was absent (Russell, Kostroski, McGuire, Laub, & Manke, 2006). Similarly, students in schools with an inclusive curriculum report greater perceptions of positive diversity climates at their schools (Szalacha, 2003). The data from GLSEN suggest a similar pattern; students who reported learning about sexual minority issues in their schools reported less victimization and greater perceptions of safety than their peers who did not report such learning opportunities (Kosciw et al., 2008). These findings point to the value and importance of an inclusive curriculum as it relates to the fundamental safety concerns of youth. Given that heterosexual and sexual minority youth can experience homophobic victimization and victimization for gender-variant behavior (Pascoe, 2007; Phoenix et al., 2003; Plummer, 2001; Poteat & Espelage, 2007), an inclusive curriculum that promotes respect for these forms of diversity stands to benefit all youth along indices of psychological and social well-being. Nevertheless, there is a dearth of research on whether such curricula have effects on academic outcomes.

Before we proceed to outline the various pathways through which inclusive curricula may promote academic performance, we would first argue that students' knowledge of diverse groups is itself a necessary and legitimate area of academic competence. Students must be aware of how their own attitudes, beliefs, and behaviors are situated within a diverse society; they must have knowledge and an understanding of the diverse views and experiences of others; and they must be able to relate and work successfully with their peers in increasingly diverse schools and workforces (Gurin, Dey, Hurtado, & Gurin, 2002). In this way, an inclusive curriculum is directly connected to meeting these needs and this facet of academic competence.

We suspect that an inclusive curriculum promotes positive learning experiences and greater overall academic performance for sexual minority and gender-variant youth through several pathways. First, an inclusive curriculum serves to destigmatize sexual minority and gender-variant youth. It also presents opportunities for learning and dialogue about stereotypes and about the experiences of sexual minority and gender-variant individuals. Destigmatization efforts carry important implications for all students. Sexual minority youth experience invisibility within heteronormative school systems (Black, Fedewa, & Gonzalez, 2012; Chesir-Teran & Hughes, 2009). Thus, it is imperative that they begin to find themselves equally represented and valued. In addition, it is important for heterosexual youth to learn about sexual minorities as a diverse group in society. Furthermore, it is important for all youth to see that their schools recognize and value sexual minority and gender-variant youth as a part of the school community.

Research on intergroup contact also may help to explain how an inclusive curriculum leads to decreased bias against sexual minority and gender-variant individuals. There is strong support for the association between direct contact with sexual minorities (e.g., through friendships or family connections) and lower sexual prejudice (Heinze & Horn, 2009; Smith, Axelton, & Saucier, 2009). (Empirical support for a parallel association between direct contact with other-gender peers and lower gender prejudice is reviewed by Martin, Fabes, and Hanish, 2014 [Chapter 5 of this volume].) In addition to direct contact, researchers have given attention to the influence of extended contact (Crisp & Turner, 2009). Extended contact can range from knowing that another friend has sexual minority or gender-variant friends to simply imagining interactions with a sexual minority or gender-variant individual. The material and discussions that are embedded within inclusive curricula may provide opportunities for these types of extended contact. For instance, even in the absence of "out" sexual minority youth in the classroom, students may learn that another classmate has sexual minority friends, or students may begin to consider what it would be like to interact with sexual minority peers.

Inclusive curricula also may promote safer and more welcoming schools for sexual minority and gender-variant youth. Some youth may come to reconsider their language and actions that contribute to hostile climates for sexual minority and gender-variant youth and this may lead to decreased discriminatory behavior against these youth. Additionally, as sexual minority and gender-variant youth begin to see themselves represented and acknowledged by teachers and administrators in respectful ways, they may feel a greater sense of support and school belonging. In effect, these processes may partly explain the extant findings that sexual minority youth in schools with inclusive curricula report greater safety and positive climates (Kosciw et al., 2008; Russell et al., 2006; Szalacha, 2003).

Through destigmatization, direct or extended contact opportunities, and efforts to promote more respectful and welcoming climates, inclusive curricula ultimately may promote better academic outcomes for sexual minority and gender-variant youth. We expect this connection because under these circumstances, sexual minority and gender-variant youth are likely to face fewer affective, cognitive, and social stressors that impede many of the learning processes that we have discussed (e.g., high vigilance, concentration difficulties, school avoidance). Furthermore, because a number of heterosexual youth face homophobic victimization or victimization based on gender-variant behavior (Pascoe, 2007; Phoenix et al., 2003; Plummer, 2001; Poteat & Espelage, 2007), inclusive curricula also could benefit their ability to learn and perform at their maximum potential.

The effects of inclusive curricula on academic outcomes also may operate through pathways that directly represent individual learning processes. Sexual minority and gender-variant youth who see themselves represented in course material may connect with the material in more meaningful ways. Educators have noted the value of connecting with and relating to course material for students from other marginalized groups (Barbarin et al., 2014 [Chapter 10 of this volume]; Lee & Buxton, 2008; Matthews & Smith, 1994; Rowley et al., 2014 [Chapter 9 of this volume]). These youth also may feel a greater sense of self-efficacy in contributing to class discussions because they can more easily relate to the material. In addition, inclusive curricula across multiple course subjects may lead sexual minority and gender-variant youth to consider careers in fields that they may have initially considered inaccessible. In addition, sexual minority and gender-variant youth may feel more motivated to learn the material, may express greater interest in the subject, and may engage in the overall learning process more actively (e.g., through class participation, homework completion). All of these processes fit well within the SCCT model (Lent et al., 1994), in which learning experiences (e.g., exposure to inclusive curricula) predict self-efficacy and outcome expectations (e.g., confidence in contributing to discussions, anticipating good performance), which in turn predict interests and ensuing actions (e.g., studying, completing homework, reading more about the subject) that ultimately lead to performance outcomes (e.g., higher grades, working toward a career in that area). Thus, in addition to addressing broader social contextual concerns (e.g., improving intergroup relations, fostering more welcoming school climates), inclusive curricula may promote the academic performance of sexual minority and gender-variant youth through these more individual-based learning processes.

7. CONCLUSIONS

The discrimination that sexual minority and gender-variant youth experience affects many interrelated areas of their lives, ranging from their psychological, to social, to academic development. Consequently, sexual orientation-based and gender identity or expression-based disparities constitute major areas of research across many disciplines in the social sciences. In this chapter, we have focused on school and academic concerns faced by sexual minority and gender-variant youth, while considering how these concerns are connected to concerns in other domains. Our aim was to highlight the current state of research in this area and to stimulate a significant expansion of research by highlighting current limitations and issues that have not yet been addressed. In doing so, we have drawn from theories such as minority stress theory (Meyer, 2003), SCCT (Lent et al., 1994), and positive youth development (Damon, 2004) to propose several processes by which multiple factors could contribute to academic disparities, as well as processes that could promote academic resilience. These processes, as well as others, should be formally examined and tested in future research. In addition, there is a substantial need for research to evaluate the immediate and long-term effectiveness of prevention and intervention programs and the effectiveness of school policies in promoting the well-being of sexual minority and gender-variant youth. These evaluations should include attention to how such efforts enrich the learning experiences of these youth, promote their academic excellence, and provide opportunities for long-term career development.

These future directions represent an ambitious undertaking at the intersection of research, policy, and practice across multiple disciplines. This work necessitates a continued long-term commitment to address the array of factors at the individual and systems level that affect the learning and academic growth of sexual minority and gender-variant youth. Such work also requires awareness of the substantial diversity among these youth and attention to their unique needs and experiences. Ultimately, these advances stand to have a significant and long-lasting impact on the development of sexual minority and gender-variant youth well beyond their years of formal schooling and education.

REFERENCES

Aragon, S. R., Poteat, V. P., & Espelage, D. L. (2014). The influence of peer victimization on educational outcomes for LGBTQ and non-LGBTQ high school students. *Journal of Lesbian, Gay, Bisexual, Transgender Youth, 11*, 1–19.

Aspenlieder, L., Buchanan, C. M., McDougall, P., & Sippola, L. K. (2009). Gender nonconformity and peer victimization in pre- and early adolescence. *European Journal of Developmental Science, 3*, 3–16.

Bandura, A. (1977). *Social learning theory*. New York: General Learning Press.

Barbarin, O. A., Chinn, L., & Wright, Y. F. (2014). Creating developmentally auspicious school environments for African American boys. In L. S. Liben & R. S. Bigler (Vol. Eds.) *The role of gender in educational contexts and outcomes*. In J. B. Benson (Series Ed.), *Advances in child development and behavior: Vol. 47* (pp. 333–365). London: Elsevier.

Barron, M., & Bradford, S. (2007). Corporeal controls: Violence, bodies, and young gay men's identities. *Youth & Society, 39*, 232–261.

Bigler, R. S., Hayes, A. R., & Liben, L. S. (2014). Analysis and evaluation of the rationales for single-sex schooling. In L. S. Liben & R. S. Bigler (Vol. Eds.) *The role of gender in educational contexts and outcomes*. In J. B. Benson (Series Ed.), *Advances in child development and behavior: Vol. 47* (pp. 225–260). London: Elsevier.

Black, W. W., Fedewa, A. L., & Gonzalez, K. A. (2012). Effects of 'safe school' programs and policies on the social climate for sexual-minority youth: A review of the literature. *Journal of Lesbian, Gay, Bisexual, Transgender Youth, 9*, 321–339.

Blomfield, C. J., & Barber, B. L. (2009). Performing on the stage, the field, or both? Australian adolescent extracurricular activity participation and self-concept. *Journal of Adolescence, 32*, 733–739.

Bochenek, M., & Brown, A. W. (2001). *Hatred in the hallways: Violence and discrimination against lesbian, gay, bisexual, and transgender students in U.S. schools*. New York: Human Rights Watch.

Bontempo, D. E., & D'Augelli, A. R. (2002). Effects of at-school victimization and sexual orientation on lesbian, gay, or bisexual youths' health risk behavior. *Journal of Adolescent Health, 30*, 364–374.

Boulton, M., Trueman, M., & Murray, L. (2008). Associations between peer victimization, fear of future victimization, and disrupted concentration on classwork among junior school pupils. *British Journal of Educational Psychology, 78*, 473–489.

Bryant, A. L., Schulenberg, J. E., O'Malley, P. M., Bachman, J. G., & Johnston, L. D. (2003). How academic achievement, attitudes, and behaviors relate to the course of substance use during adolescence: A 6-year, multiwave national longitudinal study. *Journal of Research on Adolescence, 13*, 361–397.

Buhs, E. S., & Ladd, G. W. (2001). Peer rejection as antecedent of young children's school adjustment: An examination of mediating processes. *Developmental Psychology, 37*, 550–560.

Butler, R. (1998). Determinants of help seeking: Relations between perceived reasons for classroom help-avoidance and help-seeking behaviors in an experimental context. *Journal of Educational Psychology, 90*, 630–643.

Butler, R. (2014). Motivation in educational contexts: Does gender matter? In L. S. Liben & R. S. Bigler (Vol. Eds.), *The role of gender in educational contexts and outcomes*. In J. B. Benson (Series Ed.), *Advances in child development and behavior: Vol. 47* (pp. 1–41). London: Elsevier.

Chesir-Teran, D., & Hughes, D. (2009). Heterosexism in high school and victimization among lesbian, gay, bisexual, and questioning students. *Journal of Youth and Adolescence, 38*, 963–975.

Cianciotto, J., & Cahill, S. (2012). *LGBT youth in America's schools*. Ann Arbor: University of Michigan Press.

Cochran, S. D., Mays, V. M., Alegria, M., Ortega, A. N., & Takeuchi, D. (2007). Mental health and substance use disorders among Latino and Asian American lesbian, gay, and bisexual adults. *Journal of Consulting and Clinical Psychology, 75*, 785–794.

Cohen, G. L., Garcia, J., Apfel, N., & Master, A. (2006). Reducing the racial achievement gap: A social-psychological intervention. *Science, 313*, 1307–1310.

Cook, C. R., Williams, K. R., Guerra, N. G., Kim, T. E., & Sadek, S. (2010). Predictors of bullying and victimization in childhood and adolescence: A meta-analytic investigation. *School Psychology Quarterly, 25*, 65–83.

Crisp, R. J., & Turner, R. N. (2009). Can imagined interactions produce positive perceptions? Reducing prejudice through simulated social contact. *American Psychologist, 64*, 231–240.

Damon, W. (2004). What is positive youth development? *Annals of the American Academy of Political and Social Science, 591*, 13–24.

Darling, N. (2005). Participation in extracurricular activities and adolescent adjustment: Cross-sectional and longitudinal findings. *Journal of Youth and Adolescence, 34*, 493–505.

D'Augelli, A. R., Grossman, A. H., & Starks, M. T. (2006). Childhood gender atypicality, victimization, and PTSD among lesbian, gay, and bisexual youth. *Journal of Interpersonal Violence, 21*, 1462–1482.

D'Augelli, A. R., Hershberger, S. L., & Pilkington, N. W. (1998). Lesbian, gay, and bisexual youth and their families: Disclosure of sexual orientation and its consequences. *American Journal of Orthopsychiatry, 68*, 361–371.

Denault, A. S., & Poulin, F. (2009). Predictors of adolescent participation in organized activities: A five-year longitudinal study. *Journal of Research on Adolescence, 19*, 287–311.

DeRosier, M. E., & Mercer, S. H. (2009). Perceived behavioral atypicality as a predictor of social rejection and peer victimization: Implications for emotional adjustment and academic achievement. *Psychology in the Schools, 46*, 375–387.

Doty, N. D., Willoughby, B. L. B., Lindahl, K. M., & Malik, N. M. (2010). Sexuality related social support among lesbian, gay, and bisexual youth. *Journal of Youth and Adolescence, 39*, 1134–1147.

Eccles, J. S., & Barber, B. L. (1999). Student council, volunteering, basketball, or marching band: What kind of extracurricular involvement matters? *Journal of Adolescent Research, 14*, 10–43.

Eccles, J. S., & Gootman, J. A. (2002). *Community programs to promote youth development*. Washington, DC: National Academies Press.

Eccles, J. S., & Roeser, R. W. (2011). School and community influences on human development. In M. H. Bornstein, & M. E. Lamb (Eds.), *Developmental sciences: An advanced textbook* (pp. 571–644) (6th ed.). New York: Psychology Press.

Egger, H. L., Costello, E. J., & Angold, A. (2003). School refusal and psychiatric disorders: A community study. *Journal of the American Academy of Child & Adolescent Psychiatry, 42*, 797–807.

Eisenberg, M. E., & Resnick, M. D. (2006). Suicidality among gay, lesbian, and bisexual youth: The role of protective factors. *Journal of Adolescent Health, 39*, 662–668.

Ekstrom, R. B., Goertz, M. E., Pollack, J. M., & Rock, D. A. (1986). Who drops out of high school and why? Findings from a national study. *Teachers College Record, 87*, 356–373.

Elze, D. E. (2003). Gay, lesbian, and bisexual youths' perceptions of their high school environments and comfort in school. *Children & Schools, 25*, 225–239.

Feldman, A. F., & Matjasko, J. L. (2005). The role of school-based extracurricular activities in adolescent development: A comprehensive review and future directions. *Review of Educational Research, 75*, 159–210.

Floyd, F. J., & Bakeman, R. (2006). Coming-out across the life course: Implications of age and historical context. *Archives of Sexual Behavior, 35*, 287–296.

Fredricks, J. A. (2012). Extracurricular participation and academic outcomes: Testing the over-scheduling hypothesis. *Journal of Youth and Adolescence, 41*, 295–306.

Friedman, M. S., Koeske, G. F., Silvestre, A. J., Korr, W. S., & Sites, E. W. (2006). The impact of gender-role nonconforming behavior, bullying, and social support on suicidality among gay male youth. *Journal of Adolescent Health, 38*, 621–623.

Garofalo, R., Deleon, J., Osmer, E., Doll, M., & Harper, G. W. (2006). Overlooked, misunderstood and at-risk: Exploring the lives and HIV risk of ethnic minority male-to-female transgender youth. *Journal of Adolescent Health, 38*, 230–236.

Gill, D. L., Morrow, R. G., Collins, K. E., Lucey, A. B., & Schultz, A. M. (2010). Perceived climate in physical activity settings. *Journal of Homosexuality, 57*, 895–913.

Gini, G., & Pozzoli, T. (2009). Association between bullying and psychosomatic problems: A meta-analysis. *Pediatrics, 123*, 1059–1065.

Gay, Lesbian, and Straight Education Network (GLSEN). (2012). About gay-straight alliances. Retrieved from http://www.glsen.org.

Goodenow, C., Szalacha, L., & Westheimer, K. (2006). School support groups, other school factors, and the safety of sexual minority adolescents. *Psychology in the Schools, 43*, 573–589.

Graham, R., Bradford, J., de Vries, B., & Garofalo, R. (2011). *The health of lesbian, gay, bisexual, and transgender people: Building a foundation for better understanding.* Washington, DC: Institute of Medicine.

Gregory, A., Skiba, R. J., & Noguera, P. A. (2010). The achievement gap and the discipline gap two sides of the same coin? *Educational Researcher, 39*, 59–68.

Griffin, P. (1993). Homophobia in sport: Addressing the needs of lesbian and gay high school athletes. *The High School Journal, 77*, 80–87.

Griffin, P., Lee, C., Waugh, J., & Beyer, C. (2004). Describing roles that gay-straight alliances play in schools: From individual support to school change. *Journal of Gay & Lesbian Issues in Education, 1*, 7–22.

Grossman, A. H., & D'Augelli, A. R. (2006). Transgender youth: Invisible and vulnerable. *Journal of Homosexuality, 51*, 111–128.

Grov, C., Bimbi, D. S., Nanín, J. E., & Parsons, J. T. (2006). Race, ethnicity, gender, and generational factors associated with the coming-out process among gay, lesbian, and bisexual individuals. *Journal of Sex Research, 43*, 115–121.

GSA Network. (2013). Retrieved from http://www.gsanetwork.org.

Gurin, P., Dey, E. L., Hurtado, S., & Gurin, G. (2002). Diversity and higher education: Theory and impact on educational outcomes. *Harvard Educational Review, 72*, 330–367.

Hansen, A. L. (2007). School-based support for GLBT students: A review of three levels of research. *Psychology in the Schools, 44*, 839–848.

Hatzenbuehler, M. L., & Keyes, K. M. (2013). Inclusive anti-bullying policies and reduced risk of suicide attempts in lesbian and gay youth. *Journal of Adolescent Health, 53*, s21–s26.

Heinze, J. E., & Horn, S. S. (2009). Intergroup contact and beliefs about homosexuality in adolescence. *Journal of Youth and Adolescence, 38*, 937–951.

Hershberger, S. L., & D'Augelli, A. R. (1995). The impact of victimization on the mental health and suicidality of lesbian, gay, and bisexual youths. *Developmental Psychology, 31*, 65–74.

Himmelstein, K. E., & Brückner, H. (2011). Criminal-justice and school sanctions against nonheterosexual youth: A national longitudinal study. *Pediatrics, 127*, 49–57.

Horn, S. S. (2006). Heterosexual adolescents' attitudes and beliefs about homosexuality and gay and lesbian peers. *Cognitive Development, 21*, 420–440.

Horn, S. S., Szalacha, L. A., & Drill, K. (2008). Schooling, sexuality, and rights: An investigation of heterosexual students' social cognition regarding sexual orientation and the rights of gay and lesbian peers in school. *Journal of Social Issues, 64*, 791–813.

Huebner, D. M., Rebchook, G. M., & Kegeles, S. M. (2004). Experiences of harassment, discrimination, and physical violence among young gay and bisexual men. *American Journal of Public Health, 94*, 1200–1203.

Jacob, S. (2013). Creating safe and welcoming schools for LGBT students: Ethical and legal issues. *Journal of School Violence, 12*, 98–115.

Juvonen, J., Nishina, A., & Graham, S. (2000). Peer harassment, psychological adjustment, and school functioning in early adolescence. *Journal of Educational Psychology, 92*, 349–359.

Katz-Wise, S., & Hyde, J. S. (2012). Victimization experiences of lesbian, gay, and bisexual individuals: A meta-analysis. *Journal of Sex Research, 49*, 142–167.

Kochenderfer, B. J., & Ladd, G. W. (1996). Peer victimization: Cause or consequence of school maladjustment? *Child Development, 67*, 1305–1317.

Kosciw, J. G., Diaz, E. M., & Greytak, E. A. (2008). *2007 National school climate survey: The experiences of lesbian, gay, bisexual and transgender youth in our nation's schools.* New York: GLSEN.

Kosciw, J. G., Greytak, E. A., & Diaz, E. M. (2009). Who, what, where, when, and why: Demographic and ecological factors contributing to hostile school climates for lesbian, gay, bisexual, and transgender youth. *Journal of Youth and Adolescence, 38*, 976–988.

Ladson-Billings, G. (2006). From the achievement gap to the education debt: Understanding achievement in U.S. schools. *Educational Researcher, 35*, 3–12.

Larson, R. (2000). Toward a psychology of positive youth development. *American Psychologist, 55*, 170–183.

Larson, R. W., Hansen, D. M., & Moneta, G. (2006). Differing profiles of developmental experiences across types of organized youth activities. *Developmental Psychology, 42*, 849–863.

Lee, J. (2002). Racial and ethnic achievement gap trends: Reversing the progress toward equity? *Educational Researcher, 31*, 3–12.

Lee, O., & Buxton, C. (2008). Science curriculum and student diversity: A framework for equitable learning opportunities. *The Elementary School Journal, 109*, 123–137.

Lent, R. W., Brown, S. D., & Hackett, G. (1994). Toward a unifying social cognitive theory of career and academic interest, choice, and performance. *Journal of Vocational Behavior, 45*, 79–122.

Lent, R. W., Brown, S. D., & Hackett, G. (2000). Contextual supports and barriers to career choice: A social cognitive analysis. *Journal of Counseling Psychology, 47*, 36–49.

Libbey, H. P. (2004). Measuring student relationships to school: Attachment, bonding, connectedness, and engagement. *Journal of School Health, 74*, 274–283.

Lipkin, A. (1999). *Understanding homosexuality, changing schools: A text for teachers, counselors, and administrators.* Boulder, CO: Westview Press.

Mallon, G. P., & DeCrescenzo, T. (2006). Transgender children and youth: A child welfare practice perspective. *Child Welfare, 85*, 215–241.

Marsh, H. W., & Kleitman, S. (2002). Extracurricular school activities: The good, the bad, and the non-linear. *Harvard Educational Review, 72*, 464–514.

Marshal, M. P., Friedman, M. S., Stall, R., King, K. M., Miles, J., Gold, M. A., et al. (2008). Sexual orientation and adolescent substance use: A meta-analysis and methodological review. *Addiction, 103*, 546–556.

Martin, C. L., Fabes, R. A., & Hanish, L. D. (2014). Gendered-peer relationships in educational contexts. In L. S. Liben & R. S. Bigler (Vol. Eds.) *The role of gender in educational contexts and outcomes.* In J. B. Benson (Series Ed.), *Advances in child development and behavior: Vol. 47* (pp. 151–187). London: Elsevier.

Matthews, C. E., & Smith, W. S. (1994). Native American related materials in elementary science instruction. *Journal of Research in Science Teaching, 31*, 363–380.

McCormack, M. (2012). *The declining significance of homophobia: How teenage boys are redefining masculinity and heterosexuality.* New York: Oxford University Press.

McGuire, J., Anderson, C., Toomey, R. B., & Russell, S. T. (2010). School climate for transgender youth: A mixed method investigation of student experiences and school responses. *Journal of Youth and Adolescence, 39*, 1175–1188.

Messner, M. A. (1992). *Power at play: Sports and the problem of masculinity.* Boston: Beacon Press.

Meyer, I. H. (2003). Prejudice, social stress, and mental health in lesbian, gay, and bisexual populations: Conceptual issues and research evidence. *Psychological Bulletin, 129*, 674–697.

Meyer, I. H., Dietrich, J., & Schwartz, S. (2008). Lifetime prevalence of mental disorders and suicide attempts in diverse lesbian, gay, and bisexual populations. *American Journal of Public Health, 98*, 1004–1006.

Mishna, F., Newman, P. A., Daley, A., & Solomon, S. (2009). Bullying of lesbian and gay youth: A qualitative investigation. *The British Journal of Social Work, 39*, 1598–1614.

Murdock, T. B., & Bolch, M. B. (2005). Risk and protective factors for poor school adjustment in lesbian, gay, and bisexual (LGB) high school youth: Variable and person-centered analyses. *Psychology in the Schools, 42*, 159–172.

Nakamoto, J., & Schwartz, D. (2010). Is peer victimization associated with academic achievement? A meta-analytic review. *Social Development, 19*, 221–242.

Nishina, A., Juvonen, J., & Witkow, M. R. (2005). Sticks and stones may break my bones, but names will make me feel sick: The psychosocial, somatic, and scholastic consequences of peer harassment. *Journal of Clinical Child and Adolescent Psychology, 34*, 37–48.

O'Shaughnessy, M., Russell, S., Heck, K., Calhoun, C., & Laub, C. (2004). *Safe place to learn: Consequences of harassment based on actual or perceived sexual orientation and gender non-conformity and steps for making schools safer*. San Francisco, CA: California Safe Schools Coalition.

Pascoe, C. J. (2007). *Dude, you're a fag: Masculinity and sexuality in high school*. Los Angeles, CA: University of California Press.

Pearson, J., Muller, C., & Wilkinson, L. (2007). Adolescent same-sex attraction and academic outcomes: The role of school attachment and engagement. *Social Problems, 54*, 523–542.

Petersen, J., & Hyde, J. S. (2014). Gender-related academic and occupational interests and goals. In L. S. Liben & R. S. Bigler (Vol. Eds.) *The role of gender in educational contexts and outcomes*. In J. B. Benson (Series Ed.), *Advances in child development and behavior: Vol. 47* (pp. 43–76). London: Elsevier.

Phoenix, A., Frosh, S., & Pattman, R. (2003). Producing contradictory masculine subject positions: Narratives of threat, homophobia, and bullying in 11–14 year old boys. *Journal of Social Issues, 59*, 179–195.

Piquero, A. R. (2008). Disproportionate minority contact. *The Future of Children, 18*, 59–79.

Plummer, D. C. (2001). The quest for modern manhood: Masculine stereotypes, peer culture and the social significance of homophobia. *Journal of Adolescence, 24*, 15–23.

Poteat, V. P., & Anderson, C. J. (2012). Developmental changes in sexual prejudice from early to late adolescence: The effects of gender, race, and ideology on different patterns of change. *Developmental Psychology, 48*, 1403–1415.

Poteat, V. P., & Espelage, D. L. (2007). Predicting psychosocial consequences of homophobic victimization in middle school students. *Journal of Early Adolescence, 27*, 175–191.

Poteat, V. P., Espelage, D. L., & Koenig, B. W. (2009). Willingness to remain friends and attend school with lesbian and gay peers: Relational expressions of prejudice among heterosexual youth. *Journal of Youth and Adolescence, 38*, 952–962.

Poteat, V. P., Mereish, E. H., DiGiovanni, C. D., & Koenig, B. W. (2011). The effects of general and homophobic victimization on adolescents' psychosocial and educational concerns: The importance of intersecting identities and parental support. *Journal of Counseling Psychology, 58*, 597–609.

Poteat, V. P., Scheer, J. R., & Chong, E. S. K. (under review). Discipline disparities among lesbian, gay, bisexual, and questioning youth: Testing an empirical model of contributing factors and differential effects compared to heterosexuals.

Poteat, V. P., Scheer, J. R., DiGiovanni, C. D., & Mereish, E. H. (2014). Short-term prospective effects of homophobic victimization on the mental health of heterosexual adolescents. *Journal of Youth and Adolescence*, in press.

Poteat, V. P., Sinclair, K. O., DiGiovanni, C. D., Koenig, B. W., & Russell, S. T. (2013). Gay-Straight Alliances are associated with student health: A multi-school comparison of LGBTQ and heterosexual youth. *Journal of Research on Adolescence, 23*, 319–330.

Reijntjes, A., Kamphuis, J. H., Prinzie, P., & Telch, M. J. (2010). Peer victimization and internalizing problems in children: A meta-analysis of longitudinal studies. *Child Abuse & Neglect, 34*, 244–252.

Rivers, I. (2001). The bullying of sexual minorities at school: Its nature and long-term correlates. *Educational and Child Psychology, 18*, 32–46.

Rogers, R., & Mosley, M. (2006). Racial literacy in a second-grade classroom: Critical race theory, whiteness studies, and literacy research. *Reading Research Quarterly, 41*, 462–495.

Rosario, M., Schrimshaw, E. W., & Hunter, J. (2011). Cigarette smoking as a coping strategy: Negative implications for subsequent psychological distress among lesbian, gay, and bisexual youths. *Journal of Pediatric Psychology, 36*, 731–742.

Rosario, M., Schrimshaw, E. W., Hunter, J., & Gwadz, M. (2002). Gay-related stress and emotional distress among gay, lesbian and bisexual youths: A longitudinal examination. *Journal of Consulting and Clinical Psychology, 70*, 967–975.

Rosenberg, M. (2002). Children with gender identity issues and their parents in individual and group treatment. *Journal of the American Academy of Child and Adolescent Psychiatry, 41*, 618–621.

Rothstein, R. (2004). *Class and schools: Using social, economic, and educational reform to close the Black-White achievement gap*. New York: Teachers College Press.

Rowley, S. J., Ross, L., Lozada, F., Williams, A., Gale, A., & Kurtz-Costes, B. (2014). Framing black boys: Parent, teacher, and student narratives of the academic lives of black boys. In L. S. Liben & R. S. Bigler (Vol. Eds.) *The role of gender in educational contexts and outcomes*. In J. B. Benson (Series Ed.), *Advances in child development and behavior: Vol. 47* (pp. 301–332). London: Elsevier.

Russell, S. T., Kosciw, J., Horn, S., & Saewyc, E. (2010). Safe schools policy for LGBTQ students. *Society for Research in Child Development Social Policy Report, 24*, 3–17.

Russell, S. T., Kostroski, O., McGuire, J. K., Laub, C., & Manke, E. (2006). *LGBT issues in the curriculum promotes school safety*. California Safe Schools Coalition Research Brief No. 4. San Francisco, CA: California Safe Schools Coalition.

Russell, S. T., Muraco, A., Subramaniam, A., & Laub, C. (2009). Youth empowerment and high school gay-straight alliances. *Journal of Youth and Adolescence, 38*, 891–903.

Russell, S. T., Seif, H., & Truong, N. L. (2001). School outcomes of sexual minority youth in the United States: Evidence from a national study. *Journal of Adolescence, 24*, 111–127.

Russell, S. T., Sinclair, K. O., Poteat, V. P., & Koenig, B. W. (2012). Adolescent health and harassment based on discriminatory bias. *American Journal of Public Health, 102*, 493–495.

Ryan, C., Huebner, D., Diaz, R. M., & Sanchez, J. (2009). Family rejection as a predictor of negative health outcomes in White and Latino lesbian, gay, and bisexual young adults. *Pediatrics, 123*, 346–352.

Ryan, A. M., Patrick, H., & Shim, S. O. (2005). Differential profiles of students identified by their teacher as having avoidant, appropriate, or dependent help-seeking tendencies in the classroom. *Journal of Educational Psychology, 97*, 275–285.

Sandfort, T. G. M., Bakker, F., Schellevis, F., & Vanwesenbeeck, I. (2006). Sexual orientation and mental and physical health status: Findings from a Dutch population survey. *American Journal of Public Health, 96*, 1119–1125.

Savin-Williams, R. C. (2005). *The new gay teenager*. Cambridge, MA: Harvard University Press.

Schneider, M. S., & Dimito, A. (2010). Factors influence the career and academic choices of lesbian, gay, bisexual, and transgender people. *Journal of Homosexuality, 57*, 1355–1369.

Skiba, R. J., Michael, R. S., Nardo, A. C., & Peterson, R. L. (2002). The color of discipline: Sources of racial and gender disproportionality in school punishment. *Urban Review, 34*, 317–342.

Smith, S. J., Axelton, A. M., & Saucier, D. A. (2009). The effects of contact on sexual prejudice: A meta-analysis. *Sex Roles, 61*, 178–191.

Solmon, M. A. (2014). Physical education, sports, and gender in schools. In L. S. Liben & R. S. Bigler (Vol. Eds.) *The role of gender in educational contexts and outcomes.* In J. B. Benson (Series Ed.), *Advances in child development and behavior: Vol. 47* (pp. 117–150). London: Elsevier.

Stoelting, S. (2011). Disclosure as an interaction: Why lesbian athletes disclose their sexual identities in intercollegiate sport. *Journal of Homosexuality, 58*, 1187–1210.

Sweller, J. (1988). Cognitive load during problem solving: Effects on learning. *Cognitive Science, 12*, 257.

Szalacha, L. A. (2003). Safer sexual diversity climates: Lessons learned from an evaluation of Massachusetts safe schools program for gay and lesbian students. *American Journal of Education, 110*, 58–88.

Thurlow, C. (2001). Naming the 'outsider within': Homophobic pejoratives and the verbal abuse of lesbian, gay, and bisexual high-school pupils. *Journal of Adolescence, 24*, 25–38.

Toomey, R. B., McGuire, J. K., & Russell, S. T. (2012). Heteronormativity, school climates, and safety for gender nonconforming students. *Journal of Adolescence, 35*, 187–196.

Toomey, R. B., & Russell, S. T. (2013a). An initial investigation of sexual minority youth involvement in school-based extracurricular activities. *Journal of Research on Adolescence, 23*, 304–318.

Toomey, R. B., & Russell, S. T. (2013b). The role of sexual orientation in school-based victimization: A meta-analysis. *Youth & Society*, in press.

Toomey, R. B., Ryan, C., Diaz, R. M., Card, N. A., & Russell, S. T. (2010). Gender-nonconforming lesbian, gay, bisexual, and transgender youth: School victimization and young adult psychosocial adjustment. *Developmental Psychology, 46*, 1580–1589.

van Lier, P. A., Vitaro, F., Barker, E. D., Brendgen, M., Tremblay, R. E., & Boivin, M. (2012). Peer victimization, poor academic achievement, and the link between childhood externalizing and internalizing problems. *Child Development, 83*, 1775–1788.

van Merriënboer, J. J. G., & Sweller, J. (2005). Cognitive load theory and complex learning: Recent developments and future directions. *Educational Psychology Review, 17*, 147–177.

Wallace, J. M., Goodkind, S., Wallace, C. M., & Bachman, J. G. (2008). Racial, ethnic, and gender differences in school discipline among U.S. high school students: 1991–2005. *The Negro Educational Review, 59*, 47–62.

Walls, N. E., Kane. S. B., & Wisneski, H. (2010). Gay–straight alliances and school experiences of sexual minority youth. *Youth & Society, 41*, 307–332.

Wills, J. S. (2001). Missing in interaction: Diversity, narrative, and critical multicultural social studies. *Theory and Research in Social Education, 29*, 43–64.

Young, R., & Sweeting, H. (2004). Adolescent bullying, relationships, psychological well-being, and gender atypical behavior: A gender diagnosticity approach. *Sex Roles, 50*, 525–537.

CHAPTER NINE

Framing Black Boys: Parent, Teacher, and Student Narratives of the Academic Lives of Black Boys

Stephanie J. Rowley*,[1], Latisha Ross*, Fantasy T. Lozada*, Amber Williams*, Adrian Gale*, Beth Kurtz-Costes[†]

*Department of Psychology, University of Michigan, Ann Arbor, Michigan, USA
[†]Department of Psychology, University of North Carolina, Chapel Hill, North Carolina, USA
[1]Corresponding author: e-mail address: srowley@umich.edu

Contents

1. Introduction — 302
2. The Peril and Promise of Black Boys — 303
    2.1 Parent Narratives — 306
    2.2 Teacher Narratives — 310
3. Black Boys: A Social Problem — 311
4. Black Boys: Aggressive and Scary, Never Victims, Never Scared — 314
5. Black Boys: Unteachable and Undeserving — 315
    5.1 Black Boy Narratives — 317
6. Academic Identification — 317
7. Cool-Pose Theory — 318
    7.1 Black Boy Counter-Narratives — 320
8. Conclusions — 323
References — 327

Abstract

The discourse on Black boys tends to suggest that Black boys are in complete peril. We begin with evidence that Black boys are excelling in certain contexts (i.e., in certain states, in certain schools, and in certain courses). We then discuss the ways in which the narratives used by parents, teachers, and Black boys themselves may serve to further reinforce views that Black boys are beyond hope. Research on Black parents suggests that they tend to view their sons as vulnerable and have lower expectations for sons than for daughters. Studies of teachers show that they tend to view Black boys as unteachable, as social problems, and as scary. Research on Black boys shows that they are sometimes complicit in supporting these narratives by engaging in negative or stereotypical behavior. We also include recent research that includes counter-narratives of Black boys. We end with suggestions for future research.

1. INTRODUCTION

It seems that over the past decade academic journals have been flooded with discussions on the problems of Black boys. In his foreword to the recent Schott Foundation Report on the state of Black boys in America, Geoffrey Canada lamented the "nightmarish" statistics on the educational outcomes that were described within (Schott Foundation, 2010). Indeed, the Schott report suggests that high school completion rates for Black boys are extremely low when compared to those of other race/gender groups. We certainly agree that the poor educational outcomes for Black boys constitute a crisis and that the "urgency" suggested by the Schott Report is warranted. However, we also acknowledge the ways in which certain discourses regarding the lives of Black boys have far-reaching implications for their educational experiences.

Stereotypes of Black boys as criminal, lazy, rebellious, and anti-intellectual abound. Parents, teachers, peers, and sometimes the boys themselves have adopted "Black boy" narratives that may serve to reify and reinforce negative experiences. For example, parents tend to have lower educational attainment expectations for Black boys than for Black girls, even after controlling for their actual achievement (Wood, Kaplan, & McLoyd, 2007; Wood, Kurtz-Costes, Rowley, & Okeke-Adeyanju, 2010). In addition, Black parents' negative gender stereotypes are related to negatively biased perceptions of their own sons' academic abilities (Wood et al., 2010). These results show that parents are weighing forces beyond current performance as they set goals for Black boys. It appears that teachers also give in to negative Black boys' narratives by disproportionately referring Black boys for disciplinary action and special education without compelling evidence of more severe behavioral infractions or disability (Harry & Anderson, 1994; Skiba, Michael, Nardo, & Peterson, 2002). Moreover, there is some evidence that the boys themselves buy into the discourses engaged in by others around them by taking on behaviors that they know that teachers see as threatening (Noguera, 2003) and disengaging from school.

In this chapter, we aim to identify common educational narratives of Black boys and to consider the ways in which these narratives shape academic outcomes in these students. We begin by discussing data that hint at both very real race and gender disparities in educational outcomes and some areas of promise or irony that suggest that altering the narratives might improve the situation of Black boys. We end by suggesting ways to disrupt counterproductive or false narratives and to develop research that will identify ways to foster success in all youth.

2. THE PERIL AND PROMISE OF BLACK BOYS

A search of relevant scholarly search engines for the terms Black boys and school yielded titles such as, "The Trouble with Black Boys," "Students 'at risk': Stereotypes and the Schooling of Black Boys," "How Black Boys Survive Modern Schooling," and "No Place to Run, No Place to Hide: Comparative Status and Future Prospects of Black Boys." These titles suggest that Black boys are in peril, that mere survival should be their goal, and that their very futures are uncertain. Any number of studies has demonstrated that these concerns are warranted. Compared to Whites, Asians, and Black girls, Black boys tend to have the poorest academic outcomes in nearly every area (Rowley & Bowman, 2009). For example, Black boys are least likely to earn a high school diploma in 4 years (Schott Foundation, 2010), have the lowest standardized test scores (Aud, Fox, & KewalRamani, 2010), and are most likely to be in special education classes (Skiba, Simmons, Ritter, et al., 2008). In their chapter in this volume, Barbarin, Chinn, & Wright (2014) [Chapter 10 of this volume] provide a detailed overview of the school-related challenges facing African American boys.

We will argue in this chapter that these trends reflect complex processes that are explained, in part, by the ways that Black boys are framed by important others in their lives and even by themselves (Noguera, 2003). Rather than reiterate the long list of challenges faced by Black boys that can be reviewed elsewhere (Barbarin et al., 2014 [Chapter 10 of this volume]; Howard, 2013), we offer three examples that illustrate some of these complexities. Our goal is to begin to suggest that the picture for Black boys is not all bad, that solutions for Black boys lie in rethinking the risk narrative that we have applied to the case of Black boys, and to explore the ways in which social identities are shaped by complex interactions between internal processes and external pressures. We begin with three examples of ironic findings relative to Black boys' school performance.

First, of all race/gender groups, Black boys are least likely to take advanced placement (AP) courses *for which they are qualified* based on test scores (College Board, 2014). Only about one in four Black boys who are qualified to take an AP course actually enroll in the relevant course that is offered at their school. It is likely that Black boys who are capable of doing well in AP courses are not taking them for several reasons that are unrelated to their actual performance. Teachers are less likely to view them as capable (McCray, Neal, Webb-Johnson, & Bridgest, 2003) and may be less likely to refer them to rigorous courses in spite of grades and test scores. Parents may be less likely to encourage them to take more rigorous courses, and the boys themselves may not be willing to take the courses (Tyson, 2002). For example, Tyson found that many high performing Black boys opt for less challenging courses because they fear failing or because they want to preserve a good grade point average. This "AP course-taking gap" has significant implications for Black boys' futures. Compared to their matched peers who do not take AP courses, students who take AP courses (1) earn higher GPAs in college; (2) graduate from high school at higher rates; and (3) are more likely to graduate from college in 5 years (College Board, 2014). These College Board data suggest that the AP gap has long-term implications for Black boys and that reducing that gap would improve outcomes for Black boys in key areas. Effective intervention might be aimed at changing negative stereotypes held by teachers, parents, and students alike, as has been done for cultural stereotypes that undermine the performance of girls in math, science, and engineering (see Bigler, Hayes, & Liben, 2014 [Chapter 7 of this volume]; Liben & Coyle, 2014 [Chapter 3 of this volume]; Petersen & Hyde, 2014 [Chapter 2 of this volume]).

A related example is in the benefits that accrue to them from advanced course-taking in mathematics. Unlike other subjects, math progresses in a highly hierarchical fashion such that students must take courses in a relatively strict sequence. The completion of advanced mathematics courses, such as trigonometry and calculus, is a strong predictor of admission to college (Adelman, 2006). To reach these courses, it is important for youth to take Algebra 1 in or before ninth grade and to continue in this sequence of classes through graduation.

Riegle-Crumb (2006) studied race and gender differences in the effects of taking Algebra 1 at the start of high school on course-taking at the end of high school in a large, longitudinal study of American students. She confirmed the positive effect of advanced course-taking in ninth grade on outcomes, but found that this effect was significantly smaller for Black and Latino boys than for White boys or girls of any ethnicity. That is, Black boys who started out in advanced courses were more likely than others to move to a lower track mid-stream or to simply take fewer math courses in later years. There were no race/ethnicity differences in this effect among girls. Importantly, this effect remained significant even after taking family income, parental marital status, and student performance into account. Moreover, this effect was the same among boys receiving an A or B in their math courses. Thus, Black boys are more likely than others to fall off an advanced course-taking trajectory for reasons other than their performance.

Although Riegle-Crumb did not empirically explore explanations for these results, she speculated that bias on the part of teachers, misinterpretation of academic feedback on the part of the boys, or a rejection of the content of advanced math courses as possible explanations for the failure of Black boys to enroll in subsequent courses for which they were academically prepared. Broad discussions of the roles of these three factors in youths' academic trajectories are presented elsewhere in this volume (see Butler, 2014 [Chapter 1 of this volume]; Leaper & Brown, 2014 [Chapter 6 of this volume]; Petersen & Hyde, 2014 [Chapter 2 of this volume]). Furthermore, we add that parental expectations, which tend to be lower for Black boys than Black girls, despite actual academic performance, may also contribute to these results (Wood et al., 2007, 2010). Each of these possibilities suggests that our collective perceptions of Black boys may keep them from performing at the highest level.

A third example is found in evidence that Black boys are not underperforming in every context. The most recent report from the Schott Foundation (2010) noted that just over half of Black boys graduate from high school within 4 years of starting, in contrast to about three quarters of White boys. However, the report also highlights five states with negative disparities—states where Black boys are *more* likely to graduate from high school on time than their White counterparts. Interestingly, those states (e.g., Maine, Utah, and Vermont) tend to have very small numbers of Black male students. We suspect that Black boys in these relatively racially homogeneous locations have several advantages over those in other states. First, Black students in these contexts are less likely to attend high poverty schools (Orfield & Lee, 2006). Second, the lack of a critical mass of other Black boys may disrupt negative stereotypes held by teachers. Third, the boys themselves may feel less pressure to conform to others' stereotypes of their group (Noguera, 2012).

Similarly, Noguera (2012) identified a set of New York City public schools graduating over 80% of their low-income Black and Latino boys. He found that those successful schools tended to have strong administrative leaders who were not intimidating, teachers with high expectations for these boys, student-centered counseling, and effective mentoring structures (see also Barbarin et al., 2014 [Chapter 10 of this volume]). These data clearly demonstrate that given the right conditions, Black boys can thrive academically. The task is to learn more about what underlies these findings.

We do not offer these examples to suggest that all would be well with Black boys if they were only enrolled in more AP courses, taking more advanced math, or living in predominantly White states, or to minimize the very real challenges that Black males are facing. Rather, we share these examples with the hope that they might provide some alternative views of the group and to posit that the poor academic outcomes of Black boys reflect intrapsychic, interpersonal, and contextual factors that may prove to be malleable. We turn next to a discussion of research on parents' narratives of the vulnerability of Black boys.

2.1. Parent Narratives

Parents of Black boys are aware of the many challenges with which their children may have to contend not only in their academic lives, but also in their everyday experiences in today's society. This awareness can be a source of anxiety for many parents of Black boys. Reynolds (2010) asked a sample of middle class parents of Black boys to discuss their sons' school engagement. Many parents expressed their unease with the various barriers to success faced by their sons and the stigma they are confronted with in their schools and communities (Reynolds, 2010). Parents noted that teachers and community members of authority hold negative, essentialist views of Black boys. These parents worried that their boys would not be granted the benefit of the doubt in the event of trouble and would likely receive harsher punishment than children of other racial-gender subgroups suspected of similar offenses. Black parents recounted events of cultural misunderstanding in which the descriptively benign actions or casual behaviors of their Black sons were interpreted by teachers and school officials as acts of defiance. Indeed, parents' perceptions hold water. Research indicates that merely walking through school hallways in a manner that is consistent with stereotypes of Blackness is linked to teachers' perceptions of Black students as lower in achievement, higher in aggression, and in greater need of special education (McCray et al., 2003). Allen (2013) noted similar concerns expressed by Black fathers about their sons.

Research suggests that parents see these challenges as unique to their Black sons. Reynolds states that parents of Black boys "expressed a special challenge in managing their sons' educational processes as compared to their experiences with their daughters. All reported that navigating the educational terrain for their sons proved much more difficult" (Reynolds, 2010, p. 154). Sharp & Ispa (2009) found that Black mothers in their sample were more likely to express fatalism when discussing their goals and hopes for the future of their sons rather than their daughters. These mothers expressed deep concern for the future of both their sons and daughters, though they believed that their efforts to raise their sons to be "good" Black men may be in vain and that their sons would fall victim to one of two fates: "death or jail" (p. 664).

The narrative of vulnerability shows up in parents' expectations for Black boys relative to Black girls. Research has demonstrated that parents of Black children have lower expectations and aspirations for their sons than their daughters (Hill & Zimmerman, 1995; Sharp & Ispa, 2009; Wood et al., 2007, 2010). Parents of Black daughters also perceive them to be more academically competent than parents of Black sons, even controlling for actual performance (Wood et al., 2010). This line of work also demonstrates that these expectations and aspirations held by parents are related to lower expectations among the Black boys (Wood et al., 2007; Wood, Kurtz-Costes, & Copping, 2011) and lower expectations are negatively related to college preparatory behaviors, such as preparing for college entrance exams, applying to colleges, and visiting potential schools (Wood, Skinner, Kurtz-Costes, & Rowley, 2014). For example, in a sample of middle class Black families, Wood et al. (2011) found that parents' expectations of their sons' educational attainment were related to youths' own expectations both directly and indirectly through sons' perceptions of their mothers' expectations. Youths' expectations, in turn, predicted their on-time enrollment in college. Mothers seem to accept that their Black sons will inevitably fall victim to the challenges unique to Black males (Sharp & Ispa, 2009).

This narrative of Black boys' vulnerability may have significant consequences for parents' socialization strategies and for boys' outcomes. For example, Mandara, Varner, and Richman (2010) found that Black parents are more demanding of their daughters than of their sons. The authors suggested that these higher behavioral expectations for daughters are due to parents' assumptions that girls are more capable than boys. Interestingly, the gender difference was strongest when the authors accounted for birth order, comparing girls with later-born boys. Girls had more chores and more autonomous decision-making than later-born boys. It is not surprising, then, that later-born boys had significantly lower achievement than either first-born boys and girls or later-born girls. Even among first-born girls and boys, girls were higher achieving and exhibited less externalizing behavior (Mandara et al., 2010).

Another potential explanation for the differential expectations for Black boys and girls is that parents of Black boys are especially concerned that they will face racial discrimination (Allen, 2013; Reynolds, 2010). Varner and Mandara (2013) found that mothers of sons had more concerns about racial discrimination, whereas mothers of daughters had more concerns about gender discrimination. Mothers' concerns about racial discrimination were negatively related to academic and behavioral expectations (which included the probability of the child engaging in drug use, experiencing trouble with police, and being held back in school). Mothers' expectations for racial discrimination mediated the association between gender and academic and behavioral expectations. Thus, higher expectations of daughters than sons were due in part to mothers' higher expectations that sons would face racial discrimination. Additionally, mothers' expectations concerning both their children experiencing racial discrimination and their academic and behavioral outcomes mediated the association between gender and parenting behaviors (e.g., monitoring, rule enforcement, etc.). Allen (2013) similarly described Black fathers' acute awareness of the racism their sons face, particularly in the pursuit of their education. Allen's work details the concerns Black middle class fathers have for their sons, which are strikingly similar to the fears Black middle class mothers articulated in Reynolds' (2010) study.

Reynolds (2010) studied the connection between parent discrimination concerns and the socialization of their sons. He found that parents encouraged their sons to be vigilant in the immediate racial climate, to distance themselves from portrayals of stereotypical behavior by avoiding other Black children who may call unwanted attention to their child, and to engage in behavior and school performance that provided a counter-stereotypic example of Black maleness. In describing one such conversation with Black sons, one mother stated, "'They' think less of us and think…we're not smart. You know, they think you're lazy; they think you're going to be a slacker, and you got to show them that you're not" (Reynolds, 2010, p. 154). However, parents of Black boys who encourage such vigilance may inadvertently cause greater anxiety in their sons along with a distrust of individuals of authority—leading to greater alienation between Black boys and those authority figures. As Pipes McAdoo writes in the 2002 *Handbook of Parenting*, "This context of parenting is difficult and calls upon a full range of actions and messages from parents. They must protect their child from racism from outside the group and also from within their ethnic group. But parents cannot overprotect children, for children must be prepared to cope with racism their entire lives." (Pipes McAdoo, 2002, p. 48). This angst parents experience may influence the ways in which they differentially prepare their Black sons and daughters for adult life.

We have found similar themes in our study of Black mothers of children entering first grade. When the mothers were asked about the role that they expected race to play in their children's educational experiences, many expressed concerns that their sons would face significant racial discrimination at school. For example, one parent expressed concerns about her son being stereotyped by White teachers: "Um, I mean most of our teachers are White women and a lot of times they have preconceived notions about young Black males no matter how young they are...and that bothers me, you know...a lot of the time they don't even give them a chance." Mothers of boys also tended to have lower expectations for their sons' autonomy at school and reported expecting to be more involved at school to protect their sons. Additionally, such parenting practices may start a cycle by which lowered expectations lead to parenting practices such as fewer responsibilities for the child, which may lead to lower academic outcomes, further justifying lower academic expectations.

These concerns then appear in the discussions that mothers have with their sons about race. This issue was recently thrust into the public discourse with the death of Trayvon Martin, an unarmed Black teenager shot and killed by George Zimmerman, a White man who thought that Martin appeared threatening. Zimmerman was acquitted of first-degree murder charges, leading some parents of Black boys to worry that the law would not protect their sons. Corey Dade wrote, "For other boys coming of age, parents may end 'The Talk' after a lecture about sex, drugs, alcohol or Internet porn. The rite for Black boys often is more rigorous: We're also drilled on a set of rules designed to protect us against suspicions too often associated with the color of our skin" (Dade, 2012). Indeed, there is some indication that parents of Black boys spend more time talking with their sons about racial discrimination than parents of girls (Bowman & Howard, 1985).

While these messages about discrimination are not, in and of themselves, harmful, they may lead to worse outcomes if they are not accompanied by more positive racial socialization messages (Hughes et al., 2006), positive racial identity of the child, and information about effective coping. Smalls and Cooper (2012) found that discussions of racial discrimination were negatively associated with grades when sons had low private regard (i.e., had a less positive view of the Black community). This relationship was not significant for girls. Conversely, socialization that focuses on positive aspects of coping has the potential to benefit young Black men: Black boys who received more socialization around the importance of coping positively with racial barriers through means such as spirituality were less likely to have fears of falling prey to certain negative life experiences such as dying young or experiencing violence (Stevenson, Herrero-Taylor, Cameron, & Davis, 2002). Again, girls did not experience the same effect.

Although an over-emphasis on racial discrimination in parents' socialization may have negative consequences for Black boys, there may also be costs associated with the lower levels of positive racial socialization messages such as those regarding cultural pride. Neblett, Smalls, Ford, Nguyen, and Sellers (2009) utilized latent class analysis to examine the relation between parent racial socialization and youths' racial identity. Data supported a three-cluster model, including a high positive, a moderate positive, and a low-frequency cluster. Girls were more likely to receive high and moderately positive racial socialization messages than boys, whereas boys were more likely than girls to be in the low-frequency cluster (Neblett, Smalls, et al., 2009). In a separate study including only Black boys (thus providing no comparison to Black girls), boys who received more positive racial socialization messages had higher academic persistence than boys who received more negative or less frequent racial socialization messages (Neblett, Chavous, Nguyen, & Sellers, 2009). Thus, although positive racial socialization has significant benefits for boys, parents may be more likely to share those messages with girls.

To summarize, the literature suggests that Black parents tend to have to have lower academic and behavioral expectations for their sons than their daughters. There is some evidence that these differential expectations result from parents' desire to protect their sons in the face of racial discrimination from others. In addition, Black parents may engage in less adaptive racial socialization with boys than girls even though there is some indication that Black boys benefit more from healthy racial socialization than Black girls. Thus, it seems that the narrative of Black boy vulnerability is prevalent among parents with significant implications for the academic and socio-emotional development of these boys.

2.2. Teacher Narratives

Although it is clear that the explanation for the state of Black males' education is multi-faceted, teacher–student relations are often examined as one of the most proximal predictors of students' educational success and well-being (Gregory & Ripski, 2008). However, it seems that Black males are misunderstood by their primarily White, female teachers in every aspect of their demeanor including their classroom behaviors (Pigott & Cowen, 2000), academic ability (Ferguson, 2005), classroom emotional expression (Thomas, Coard, Stevenson, Bentley, & Zamel, 2009), and even their style of walk (McCray et al., 2003), speech (Harry & Anderson, 1994; Kunjufu, 1985), and acts of masculinity (Ferguson, 2000). Below we discuss teachers' narratives of Black males in terms of their beliefs, perceptions, and responses to Black males in the classroom (see also Barbarin et al., 2014 [Chapter 10 of this volume]). These narratives tell the story of Black boys being a social problem that needs to be solved (Noguera, 2003), of Black boys being viewed as aggressive and scary but never as being victims or being scared, and Black boys being considered unteachable. Although we know that not all teachers advance or perpetuate these ideas, we describe three common teacher narratives of Black boys to illustrate how teachers' perceptions of Black boys impact their school experiences.

3. BLACK BOYS: A SOCIAL PROBLEM

Across the nation, Black students have the highest rates of suspension in almost every state (Losen & Gillespie, 2012). Black boys make up, on average, 20% of the school population, yet are disproportionally represented in school suspensions and expulsions (Holzman, 2006; Losen & Martinez, 2013). For instance, in Boston, Black boys make up 25% of the school enrollment population but 44% of school suspensions and 56% of school expulsions. In Los Angeles where the Black male student population is only 6%, Black males make up 18% of the suspensions and 19% of the expulsions (Holzman, 2006). In fact, one in three Black middle school males were suspended between 2009 and 2010 (Losen & Martinez, 2013) and 25% of all Black male high school students were suspended at least one time over a 4-year period (Schiraldi & Ziedenberg, 2001). Similar trends are found in the rates of Black boys recommended for emotional support services (Irving & Hudley, 2008), and being labeled as having serious emotional disturbance (SED; Holzman, 2006) with Black males being the most likely of any student group to be labeled with SED (Coutinho, Oswald & Best, 2002). Moreover, 70% of Black males identified as having a disability have been suspended (Losen & Gillespie, 2012).

This scenario of high rates of suspension, expulsion, and special education instruction has serious implications for Black boys' abilities to take advantage of classroom instruction and educational opportunities. Black boys' increased out-of-class time ensures that they experience less classroom engagement, more strained relationships with their teachers, and ultimately lower classroom performance and academic success (Arcia, 2006). Arcia found that among students matched on sex, race, grade, and poverty status, those who were suspended at least once were three grade levels behind their unsuspended counterparts after 1 year and five grade levels behind after 2 years. Students who have been suspended are also three times more likely than those who have never been suspended to drop out of school by tenth grade (Losen & Gillespie, 2012). Furthermore, these numbers reinforce stereotypes of Black boys as being highly disobedient, aggressive, socio-emotionally incompetent, and most of all a disruption in the social and academic classroom environment. It seems that the Black boy is a social problem that many schools are desperate to fix.

The reason for the overrepresentation of Black males in exclusionary disciplinary action is unclear. Two of the predominant hypotheses are (1) disproportionate rates of misbehavior among Black males and (2) the presence of discrimination and bias in school discipline practices which target Black males (Skiba et al., 2002). These hypotheses reflect two paradigms of classroom management found within urban classrooms (Weiner, 2003). The first hypothesis reflects a *cultural deficit* paradigm in which the behavioral problems and academic underachievement of Black males is attributed to parenting, cultural norms, and Black communities (Collier & Bush, 2012; Weiner, 2003). According to this perspective, Black boys are lacking in the skills and experiences needed to be academically successful (Stinson, 2006). The *cultural deficit* paradigm allows teachers to take little responsibility for the behavioral problems and underachievement of Black boys in their classrooms, believing that any of the techniques or approaches they use will be ineffective in the face of a culture that does not encourage them to be successful in school. The second hypothesis reflects a *contextual analysis* paradigm that focuses on the deficiencies of educational institutions, administrators, and teachers, and their ability to meet the needs of Black males (Collier & Bush, 2012; Weiner, 2003). The *contextual analysis* paradigm calls for an examination of the policies and procedures put forth in schools around discipline and referral practices and the beliefs, perceptions, and biases school administrators and teachers have about Black boys. In this chapter, we follow a *contextual analysis* to identify teachers' *cultural deficit* beliefs which likely contribute to teachers' treatment of Black boys as a social problem in their classrooms.

There is often a cultural disconnect between Black boys and the White women who dominate the teaching staff of schools. It is likely that the negative media images of Black males as lazy, angry, disrespectful, and unintelligent (Carby, 1998) permeate teachers' beliefs about Black boys and allow them to blame poverty, broken homes, too much television, and hip hop culture for the difficulties Black boys experience in schools (Collier & Bush, 2012). A recent qualitative study of elementary school teachers found that when teachers had negative perceptions and beliefs about Black boys, there were frequent instances of differential treatment of Black boys (Collier & Bush, 2012). For instance, one teacher in the study described her Black male students as "lazy, loud, having attitude problems, and not taking responsibility for their actions" and their parents as being uncaring or having low expectations for their Black children (p. 87, Collier & Bush, 2012). Not surprisingly, teachers with these beliefs used Black boys as a classroom management strategy, in which in an attempt to control an entire class that was off task, a teacher would target a Black male student who was talking or misbehaving and call his name or punish him for his behavior even though other students were engaging in the same behavior (Collier & Bush, 2012). Another study described teachers as labeling elementary school-aged Black boys as "troublemakers" and being destined for jail cells (Ferguson, 2000). Observations of prekindergarten and kindergarten classes found that Black boys were separated from the class and placed in a desk near the teacher more often than their classmates. The teachers labeled these students as "difficult and disruptive" (Barbarin & Crawford, 2006). Black female students also experience a cultural disconnect with White teachers and are often viewed as loud or assertive (Morris, 2007). However, these stereotypes often position Black girls as "helpers" and "enforcers" in the classroom (Grant, 1984) and may be less associated with teachers' propensity to use classroom management strategies that isolate Black girls from the learning environment. In contrast, teachers' views of Black boys as "troublemakers" or "difficult" often put Black boys in the position of being policed and punished to maintain a successful classroom.

When teachers view Black boys as classroom problems, they tend to provide more surveillance and punishment to Black males over other children in the classroom. Such attitudes may also contribute to the elevated rates of problematic behaviors that teachers report for Black boys in comparison to other students. If Black boys are being watched more as a means of classroom management as suggested by Collier and Bush (2012), then it makes sense that Black boys will be called out for problematic behavior more often than other students. Elevated rates of punishment toward Black boys likely contributes to their early disengagement from the school context (Davis, 2003), as boys who may have started off being eager and enthusiastic to attend school (Tyson, 2002) begin to feel unwanted and out of place in the academic context because of early experiences of punishment and classroom isolation (Barbarin & Crawford, 2006; Davis, 2003). This disengagement may be apparent in the sudden decline in Black boys' test scores by fourth grade, with a steady decline in representation of Black boys among high test scores and reading levels throughout high school (see Davis, 2003 for a review). Next, we describe how teachers' beliefs about aggression and Black boys contribute to Black boys' school experiences.

4. BLACK BOYS: AGGRESSIVE AND SCARY, NEVER VICTIMS, NEVER SCARED

Black boys are depicted as violent and aggressive in a variety of media outlets (Carby, 1998) and thus, in many arenas are viewed as a group to be feared. This perception of aggression and resulting fear is reflected in the increasing number of young Black males who have been murdered because they were perceived as threats, without actually being threatening (e.g., Trayvon Martin, Jonathan Ferrell, Jordan Davis). Within the context of schools, researchers report that teachers perceive aggression in Black boys' language patterns and conversational styles of "verbal volleying" and "talking junk" (Harry & Anderson, 1994; Kunjufu, 1985), in Black boys' "verve" or preference for physicality, movement, and simultaneous action or activity (Tyler, Boykin, & Walton, 2006), and even their "stroll" or style of walk (McCray et al., 2003). Teachers' perceptions of aggression are also paired with feelings of fear and discomfort around Black male students. Teachers are even encouraged to "not be afraid of Black male students" in training sessions (e.g., Kendrick & Prioleau, 2011). Morgan (1995) suggests that there is an underlying fear in the interactions between Black boys and their White teachers and even sometimes with their Black teachers. The fear can be triggered even by the smallest classroom defiance by a Black boy because of the fear that his defiance will escalate into aggression.

The interpretation of Black boys as aggressive and scary within schools impacts Black boys' educational experiences. Thomas et al. (2009) found that Black boys' anger displays were related to teachers' reports of problematic behavior in the classroom. Specifically, when Black boys experienced anger yet held this anger in, teachers reported these students as engaging in less aggressive and over-reactive behaviors in the classroom. However, if Black boys experienced anger but engaged in outward anger expression, teachers perceived those boys as being aggressive and over-reactive. Additionally, expressing anger was a stronger predictor of teachers' perceptions of problematic behavior than well-managed anger expressions of holding anger in and controlling anger (Thomas et al., 2009). These findings suggest that Black males' effective emotion regulation and coping behaviors are less impactful on teachers' impressions of them than their moments of dysregulation. This is not surprising given the fact that individuals tend to remember and incorporate information that is consistent with their stereotypes and schemas (Fiske, 1998) and thus, teachers may be focusing more on Black boys' anger displays because they are consistent with their stereotype of Black males as aggressive.

Finally, teachers' and administrators' interpretation of Black boys as aggressive and scary, even as early as elementary school, implies that Black boys are not seen as naturally innocent as other children, and thus are never victims of wrongdoing and are never scared. Instead, their acts of disobedience are assumed to be indicative of an inherent deviant personality or propensity to do wrong (Ferguson, 2000) and that their defiance is associated with a lack of fear or an apathetic attitude toward punishment. Black boys are not given the same "boys will be boys" benefit of the doubt that White boys are given by schools. Instead, their early behaviors of disobedience in schools are thought to presage future trajectories of violence and prison sentences (Ferguson, 2000). This "adultification" of child behaviors is also present in views of Black girls, yet their misbehavior in the educational context is seen as being in contrast to their expected roles in being the strength, support, and representation of the Black community; a role that Black boys cannot be expected to fill because of their destiny with drugs, jail, and death (Ferguson, 2000). These fatalistic views of Black males, especially in juxtaposition to Black females, are particularly damaging as they are often expressed early within a Black boy's educational trajectory in response to misbehavior and may therefore have long-lasting impact on not only Black boys' place in the educational system, but also in the larger societal context. Such a narrative leads to the discouragement of teachers effectively engaging with their Black male students, but also in the prevention of teachers from seeing the potential of Black boys to grow and develop. Additionally, these beliefs may lead to self-fulfilling prophesies, in which Black boys internalize views of aggression, criminality, and community disappointment and contribute to poor school attendance, lack of classroom engagement, and overall low classroom performance and achievement. Ultimately, these beliefs suggest that Black boys are unteachable and undeserving of opportunity.

5. BLACK BOYS: UNTEACHABLE AND UNDESERVING

Similar to the suspension and expulsion trends of Black boys across schools in the United States, Black boys are also over represented in special education recommendations completed by teachers and underrepresented in gifted education programs (Ford, 2006). Black boys appear to be the most susceptible to the special education categories of educable mental retardation, trainable mental retardation, specific learning disability, and speech impairments (see Blanchett, 2009; Gardner & Miranda, 2001; Harry & Anderson, 1994 for a review). These recommendations and classifications perpetuate the view that many Black boys are unteachable and beyond help in standard or "normal" classroom settings, and that only teachers with special training can make a difference in the academic outcomes of these children. Once these boys are labeled with a special education classification, they sometimes have to attend special day classes that isolate them from the general school population and from general class instruction (Collier & Bush, 2012). Furthermore, these labels come with a stigma that follows Black boys throughout the remainder of their academic years.

Black youth are less likely to be referred for gifted programs than White youth, even when they meet the qualifications (Grantham, 2013; Winsler, Gupta Karkhanis, Kim, & Levitt, 2013). In addition, Black boys tend to be more underrepresented in gifted programs than Black girls (Ford & Whiting, 2010; Grantham, 2004). One potential reason for this under-representation is the over-reliance on standardized test scores to determine eligibility for gifted programs (Winsler et al., 2013). This under-representation in gifted programs has significant implications for the achievement of Black boys; Black boys identified as gifted have an increased likelihood of earning a bachelor's degree within 8 years of completion of high school (Rose, 2013).

That teachers hold negative stereotypes of Black boys is not lost on the students. Noguera (2003) noted that less than 25% of Black boys in his sample believe that their teachers support them. Black boys also report high levels of mistrust of teachers and school personnel (Honora, 2003).

Teachers' negative views of Black boys may be overcome by fostering understanding and empathy. McAllister and Irvine (2002) and Milner (2007) suggested that when teachers are empathetic *with* their students (not pitying of them), they take on student perspectives and begin to think of students' problems as situations that should be solved together. Teachers' classroom practices are enhanced and improved by empathetic attitudes toward students (McAllister & Irvine, 2002). However, it is also important that teachers know about themselves in relation to their students and examine their own histories, perspectives, beliefs, and narratives critically, particularly with regard to Black boys. Teachers must check their narratives about Black boys at the classroom door and arm themselves with knowledge about the biases that exist in our current educational system that put Black boys in the precarious position of punishment and failure. Teachers should recognize that Black boys may be at risk from the moment that they enter preschool in an educational structure that was not initially made to serve them. However, teachers should also be charged with "speaking possibility" (Milner, 2007) for Black boys into their classroom environments so that they may contribute to and change the educational narratives and images of Black boys as a social problem, as aggressive and scary, and as unteachable. Such a change in teachers' perspectives and beliefs about Black boys will undoubtedly contribute to Black boys' own narratives in education and allow them to feel a sense of belonging within educational contexts.

5.1. Black Boy Narratives

So far in this chapter, we have discussed narratives of adults who play pivotal roles in Black boys' schooling. While these narratives offer some insight into factors that influence Black boys in school, other literature suggests that in some ways Black boys are complicit in their own school struggles. Indeed, several theorists suggest that Black boys are active participants in their school experiences and must therefore take some of the blame for their own struggles (Davis, 2009; Noguera, 2003). When trying to cope with the reality of unpleasant school environments, Black boys sometimes engage in academically counterproductive behaviors (Ferguson, 2005). Researchers have found that Black boys may disidentify with school as a way of protecting their self-esteem, create an identity opposed to practices associated with dominant culture such as obtaining good grades or they may engage in a set of "cool pose" behaviors that may be interpreted as disrespectful or as demonstrating academic apathy. In this section, we present theoretical and empirical evidence that coping strategies make Black boys involved in their own academic difficulties.

6. ACADEMIC IDENTIFICATION

One indication of Black boys' "buying in" to the negative narratives that surround them is their level of identification with school. Steele (1997) suggested that repeated experiences with unfair treatment in school may lead some students to disidentify or remove school performance from their overall sense of self. This strategy may reduce motivation and engagement, but it may also protect the self-esteem in a domain in which Black boys do not feel valued or validated. "Disidentification" has been assessed by correlating students' achievement scores or school grades with measures of self-esteem (e.g., Osborne, 1995, 1997, 1999). Osborne (1997) found that by twelfth grade, the correlation between general self-esteem and grades was nonsignificant for Black boys, but remained significant for Black girls, White boys and girls, and Latino boys and girls. In support of Steele's (1997) theory, this process of disidentification occurred over time. That is, the positive correlation between self-esteem and grades was significant in middle school (eighth grade) and declined as students transitioned to high school (Osborne, 1997). This decline occurred for all students but remained significant for all groups except Black boys.

Other research indicates that as Black boys move into adolescence their value for high achievement may decline. Taylor and Graham (2007) measured the importance of academic achievement in the lives of Black and Latino youth by asking them to nominate peers they admired, respected, and/or wanted to be like. They found that in elementary school, all youth nominated high-achieving peers; however, Black boys in middle school did not show a preference for any achievement group and they nominated low achieving peers to a greater degree than did their second and fourth grade counterparts. They also found that for middle school Black boys (and no other group), nomination of low achieving peers related to their perceptions of academic and occupational barriers (Taylor & Graham, 2007). This may indicate a cycle by which Black boys perceive barriers to academic and occupational success and thus devalue traditional means of attaining success. As Steele has argued, negative stereotypes discourage their identification with school. Importantly, this process appears to be somewhat unique to Black boys and to intensify as they transition into adolescence.

7. COOL-POSE THEORY

In addition to academic disidentification, Black boys may use their own behavior to cope with feelings of discrimination and marginalization at school. There is some suggestion that Black boys may actually adopt stereotypic behaviors to defy teachers whom they see as unsupportive. Majors coined the term "cool pose" to reflect a set of "scripts, physical posturing, impression management, and carefully crafted performances that deliver a single, critical message: pride, strength, and control" (Majors & Billson, 1993, p. 4). Maintaining a cool pose is a way for Black males to assert their masculinity, boost their self-esteem, and maintain respect as men in the face of perceived societal challenges to their manhood. Harris, Palmer, & Struve (2011) suggested that Black males take on these behaviors because of dominant cultural themes of masculinity and white male dominance. Sewell

(1997) suggests that the end goal of cool behaviors is to promote their own efficacy and gain social credibility among peers (Sewell, 1997). For Black boys in schools, maintaining a cool pose means combating feelings of inadequacy in academic tasks as well as discrimination.

Just as cool pose behaviors allow Black boys to maintain self-respect and peer admiration, teachers often view Black boys' deportment as indicative of an oppositional stance toward school. Cool-pose behaviors may become especially problematic for Black boys when they escalate from benign and nonthreatening behaviors such as walking styles and grooming to self-damaging behaviors such as gang activity, violence, thrill seeking, and sexual promiscuity (Hall, 2009).

The complexity of Black male identity is found in the fact that even high-achieving Black boys engage in cool behaviors as a way of avoiding peer rejection and teasing (Stinson, 2008). Stinson (2008) used participative inquiry to examine strategies used by four academically successful Black males. He found that the young men were able to use cool behaviors to connect with other Black male peers and to maintain social credibility outside the classroom, but that they did not enact these behaviors in classroom, where teachers might interpret them as oppositional.

Sports participation is an interesting case. Majors, Wilkinson, & Gulam (2001) argued that sports has become a significant institutional context for the expression of cool pose. The sports arena is one where Black males can receive personal affirmation, high visibility, and a sense of connection at school (see Solmon, 2014 [Chapter 4 of this volume]). Research shows that Black boys tend to embrace the Black-boy-as-athlete narrative. They tend to feel more positively about their sports abilities than Black girls, White girls, and White boys (Hare & Castenell, 1985) and Black boys are more likely than all other race/ethnic and gender groups to be active in sports (Ewing & Seafeld, 1996; Fredricks & Eccles, 2006; Linver, Roth, & Brooks-Gunn, 2009). This, combined with other data showing positive effects of sports participation on achievement and well-being (Fredricks & Eccles, 2006), seems like good news. However, studies have also shown that whereas stereotypes of White male athletes tend to be positive, people tend to view Black male athletes as unintelligent (Devine & Baker, 1991; Sailes, 1991). In addition, stereotypes that Black males are "naturally athletic"(Sailes, 1991; Stone, Perry, & Darley, 1997) may undermine perceptions that they can also be naturally intelligent. Thus, the positive effects of sports participation may be reduced by its reinforcement of potentially damaging narratives of Black boys as unintelligent. Moreover, the provision of sports as a nonacademic context for the celebration of Black boys may further distance them from the classroom. Within a limited structure of opportunity, sports is one possible avenue to success, but for many Black men, "sports can lock them into their low-status positions in society" (Majors et al., 2001, p. 210). An additional conundrum related to Black boys' sports participation is the issue that arises for Black male nonathletes. Black boys without athletic skills or interest may experience distress over potential exclusion from Black boy peer groups (Schwing, Wong, & Fann, 2013). Ironically, nonathlete Black boys may suffer from missing out on positive effects of sports participation and the camaraderie with other boys.

In summary, Black boys appear to embrace some of the negative narratives associated with their group. Perhaps in efforts to protect their self-concepts and to comply with certain definitions of masculinity, Black boys sometimes behave in ways that undermine their academic values and beliefs. Although endorsement of these narratives by Black boys seems to be fairly common, it is also the case that some Black boys develop counter-narratives that reflect feelings of academic competence and strong academic value.

7.1. Black Boy Counter-Narratives

Thus far, we have tried to demonstrate how the various narratives that are used to frame the experiences of Black boys in schools may undermine their performance and participation. We have shown that parents tend to view Black boys as vulnerable, leading to lower expectations and fewer demands for maturity. We demonstrated that teachers tend to imagine Black boys as dangerous and unteachable, leading to frequent discipline referrals, placement in special education, and infrequent recommendations for advanced courses. Finally, we discussed studies that suggest that Black boys sometimes buy into others' negative views of them by embracing behaviors that may lead others to see them as scary or unintelligent. While these discourses on Black boys are prevalent and have serious implications for the behavior of important others toward Black boys, it is clear that they do not fully describe the experiences of Black boys. As noted, there are contexts in which Black boys are thriving, others have high expectations for them, and the boys themselves feel confident and capable (Noguera, 2003, 2012). Although the voices of Black boys and narratives that run counter to those that we have outlined have been rare historically, the literature has experienced a recent increase in the presentation of counter-stereotypic portrayals of Black boys (e.g., Berry, 2008; Harper, 2010). Moreover, the counter-narratives that are available touch on resistance to each of the traditional narratives presented above.

Our review demonstrated that parents often have lowered expectations for Black boys and that these expectations reflect their concern that their sons will face challenges. Thus, the lowered expectations of parents of Black boys represent love and concern on the part of the parents. Unfortunately, this concern may reduce boys' sense of efficacy and autonomy. The narratives of successful Black boys suggest that their parents tend to have high expectations for them, to actively seek out academic opportunities for their sons, and tell their sons about the value of a good education (Berry, 2008; Stinson, 2008). In addition, research finds that some Black parents provide their sons with specific strategies for negotiating negative stereotypes and discrimination at school and that these strategies allow them to avoid negative outcomes (Stinson, 2011). Very little literature including parents' counter-narratives of Black boys exists.

Teacher narratives of Black boys that are most prominent in the literature tend to emphasize teachers' negative stereotypes and biased behavior. However, there is considerable evidence in the literature on successful Black boys of educators playing a prominent role in their success (Ladson-Billings, 1995). The young Black men in Stinson's (2008) study noted the importance of having caring and committed teachers who established meaningful relationships with students and who had high expectations for the boys. In fact, he found that "within the schools, there was no other single factor" that was identified by the participants as being more important than teachers. Teachers of all races have the opportunity to positively shape the lives of Black boys, but research often emphasizes the shortcomings of teachers' efforts with them.

Traditional parent and teacher narratives of Black boys sometimes downplay the critical consciousness of Black boys. Parent narratives that emphasize Black boys' vulnerability and need for protection imply that Black boys are not aware of the forces that are affecting their academic experiences. Implied in parents' reports of greater protection of Black boys and increased vigilant involvement at school for these students is a lack of agency on the part of the boys. Teacher narratives often downplay the social intelligence of the boys and rarely reflect the complex identity negotiations in which Black boys engage. However, a number of studies note that Black boys are well aware of their position in the school and the multiple ways in which they negotiate the context. For instance, Black undergraduate males

(Harper & Davis, 2012) and high school drop-outs (Caton, 2012) reflecting on their later K–12 years articulated that as young boys they were aware that they were attending schools that "sucked," heavily policed and harshly punished Black boys for minor infractions, maintained general policies and practices that alienated Black boys, and systematically failed Black boys, in particular. Black young men expressed their familiarity with school and neighborhood factors that could render them vulnerable to underachievement, the criminal justice system, and violence. Even Black middle school boys demonstrate this awareness (Henfield, 2011). These middle school boys, similar to those discussed in Ferguson's *Bad Boys* (2000), recounted events in which insignificant transgressions were assumed to be intentional acts of deviance worthy of immediate and harsh punishment (e.g., being yelled at or chastised for tossing a pencil).

Counter-narratives of Black boys also describe their desire to achieve academic success. Contrary to the disidentification narrative discussed previously, many studies show that Black boys report identifying with academics and wanting to do well (Berry, Thunder, & McClain, 2011; Caton, 2012; Harper & Davis, 2012; Rose, 2013). Black boys also express complex emotions of sadness, disappointment, anger, regret, and indignation when considering their educational shortcomings (Caton, 2012). These reports paint a very different picture than studies emphasizing academic apathy or oppositional behaviors.

These alternate Black boy self-narratives also describe agency on the part of the boys. Many Black boys hold strong beliefs in the power of education to uplift and liberate Black people from the injustice of societal inequality and provide them access to individual opportunities (Harper & Davis, 2012; Stinson, 2008). Black boys and young men believe themselves to have the agency needed to persist through their educational systems and find success and have done so (Harper & Davis, 2012; McGee, 2013). They also report identifying and maintaining relationships with Black peers who similarly value education (Stinson, 2011). Contrary to portrayals of Black boys as victims of school systems, these narratives demonstrate their value for achievement and their engagement in their schooling.

In sum, these counter-narratives tell us that Black boys have the will, potential, and resilience required to thrive. It is up to scholars, educators, parents, and policy makers to acknowledge and foster these strengths in Black males. If we allow our schools to continue in their "failure to meet their unique needs...[of Black boys we] decrease the likelihood that educators will maximize Black males' academic potential which, ultimately, contributes to their disproportionate academic underachievement levels in comparison to their peers." (Henfield, 2013, p. 397). We must continue to expose and replicate these counter-narratives.

8. CONCLUSIONS

This chapter aimed to describe prominent narratives that are used by parents and teachers of Black boys to frame their academic lives. We also considered the narratives by which Black boys seem to be guided. We showed that each of these groups tend to hold views that are damaging to the academic development of Black boys. Parents tend to view Black boys as vulnerable and in need of protection, sometimes to the point that they undermine their autonomy and self-efficacy. Teachers tend to view Black boys as social problems and unteachable, often over-policing their behavior and holding low expectations for their academic achievement. Black boys are more likely than others to disidentify with school and to engage in the very stereotypical behaviors that teachers view as oppositional and indicative of their poor achievement motivation. We also noted, though, that many Black boys have considerable academic success and feel well supported by parents, teachers, and peers. In this final section, we offer suggestions for future directions in this field. We suggest that some of these negative narratives may result from a biased literature base, that too much of the research on parents' perspectives comes from mothers, that there is a danger in not recognizing the challenges of Black girls, and that more needs to be done to include the voices of Black boys in the research.

The prevalence of these negative narratives suggests that the Black boy research agenda may also be supporting the damaging discourses. Research on Black boys tends to take a deficit approach, describing the problems of Black boys. Relatively less research covers positive or normative outcomes. We propose that a paradigm shift in the research on the academic lives of Black boys can fill gaps in our understanding of not only what is going wrong, but also what is going right with Black boys. A research program with these goals is a vital step in developing a more complete and accurate picture of the academic lives of Black boys.

In addition to this limited focus on negative outcomes, nearly all of the research on parenting of Black boys includes only the perspectives of mothers. Much of the work contributing to the body of literature on differential socialization in Black families utilizes mother-reported data. Black fathers' parenting practices and perceptions of their sons and daughters as they relate to notions of risk/vulnerability and self-reliance are understudied. Research informs us that Black fathers make a strong contribution to the adopted gender ideologies and roles of their sons and daughters (Mandara, Murry, & Joyner, 2005; White, 2006) and are as likely to endorse an equitable gender ideology as Black mothers (Hill, 2002; White, 2006). However, there is little research explaining the gender-specific challenges Black fathers anticipate for their sons and daughters. The work that is available suggests that Black fathers may be more effective than mothers in supporting their sons' ability to navigate the unique challenges they face because Black fathers are equipped with the experiential capital of being Black and male. Brown, Linver, Evans, & DeGennaro (2009) found that while Black girls did not benefit from their fathers' messages about African American heritage, boys did, with more African American heritage messages being associated with higher grades. Additionally, maternal messages around African American heritage were not related to boys' grades at all. Other family members (e.g., siblings, grandparents, aunts, uncles) may be important in the academic lives of Black boys, particularly given the prevalence and importance of fictive kinship relations in Black families (Chatters, Taylor, & Jayakody, 2014). Understanding the roles of these important others may give new insight into sources of resilience for Black boys.

Research on Black boys has also been limited in its emphasis on their relationships with White women teachers. This makes sense in that most American teachers are White women. However, it is also important to study the perspectives of Black teachers and coaches. It is possible that these adults play important roles in the lives Black boys, but they are rarely represented in the research literature. Moreover, studies of White women teachers may be biased in their presentation. Researchers rarely ask teachers to recount effective strategies for working with Black male students, helpful training experiences, or positive outcomes; that is, we do not ask teachers to provide their own counter-narratives. By failing to ask the question, we imply that White teachers are always biased and ineffective. In his article on what schools can do to support the academic achievement of Black and Latino boys, Noguera (2012) noted that positive teacher–student relationships that resemble comfortable and relaxed mentoring relationships were part of the reason schools with high graduation rates of Black and Latino boys succeeded. More research on the methods by which teachers may benefit Black boys as role models, mentors, and educators is needed.

In addition to limiting the scope and source of the narratives that are sought, researchers of Black boys tend to examine Black boy narratives separately by focusing only on parents, teachers, or the boys. Little literature has considered the ways in which these narratives work in concert. Most of the work considering the intersection of Black boy narratives juxtaposes the teacher narrative of the aggressive and unteachable Black boy against the cool pose narrative of the boys themselves. In this scenario, negative teacher behavior leads the boys to embody those characteristics that the teacher, and sometimes their peers, expects of them (Noguera, 2003). Almost no research examines the interplay of parent and teacher narratives. What might it mean that Black parents view their sons as vulnerable to racial discrimination and biased treatment while the teachers of these boys view them as oppositional or disengaged? Parents may want to protect their sons' self-concepts by lowering demands for maturity and performance. This may be manifest in poorer self-regulation at school and reinforcement of teacher views of Black boys as disruptive. Likewise, biased disciplinary actions on the part of teachers may lead parents to adopt an adversarial stance in the parent–teacher relationship. In our own research with African American mothers of first graders, we found that some mothers of boys reported that they expected to be highly involved in their sons' classrooms so that they could protect their children from negative teacher treatment (as opposed to being involved to partner with the teacher or because of their learning goals for their sons). Mothers of girls in the same study often reported that the girls could "handle themselves" in the classroom (even in first grade). Ironically, this type of vigilant parent school involvement may lead teachers to have strained relationships with the students (Lareau & Horvat, 1999). Worse yet, biased discipline by teachers may lead parents to further lower expectations for their sons or to begin to view them as problems.

We also have some methodological concerns about the research on Black boys. Most studies have used cross-sectional research designs. The lack of longitudinal research on Black boys has several implications. First, it is difficult to assess the direction of effects. For example, it may be the case that Black parents are responding to Black boys' actual school performance with lowered expectations rather than the reverse. This seems unlikely given our work shows gendered concerns of Black parents even before their children begin formal schooling, this seems unlikely. Additionally, as mentioned above, Wood et al. (2007) found that parents had higher expectations for their daughters than sons, even after controlling for actual academic achievement. However, it is important that research begin to model the transactional nature of socialization that underlies these findings. Second, the developmental story of Black boys is lacking. There is some indication that academic deficits of Black boys are present very early in school (Matthews, Kizzie, Rowley, & Cortina, 2010), but there are few data to speak to a developmental progression in parent or teacher views of Black boys. It is important to determine whether the challenges of Black boys intensify with major school transitions, for example. Building this developmental story may aid in raising teacher and parent awareness of critical periods for Black boys. Longitudinal research is critical to this endeavor.

Finally, the research on the voices of Black boys themselves has been lacking. Much of the work on Black boys has involved understanding how the attitudes and actions of important others, specifically adults, in their lives relate to their academic outcomes. However, such a perspective ignores the boys' co-construction and processing of their own experiences. More qualitative work is needed in order to understand the specific ways in which Black boys interpret their place in American society. How might feeling valued for one's sports abilities compare to being valued for academic ability? How do Black boys deal with the intersections of being male (a position of relative privilege) with that of being Black (a position of relatively less privilege)? What are the coping mechanisms they use and how might this change over time? Research might also consider the perspectives of Black boys who are struggling. Most often, the experiences of Black boys who are not doing well are left to others (e.g., teachers) to describe. The experiences of Black boys who are also sexual minorities or gender variant also need more research attention (see Poteat, Scheer, & Mereish, 2014 [Chapter 8 of this volume]). The voices of Black boys may provide important insights in all of these cases.

In conclusion, the research on Black boys' academic outcomes has often been grim. However, it is just as important to focus on the positive aspects of Black boys' lives, of which there are plenty to celebrate. For example, as of 2013, Urban Prep in Chicago has graduated all of their high school students and all of them are college-bound for the fourth consecutive year (Wright & Lutz, 2013). Such a picture of positivity is in sharp contrast with the pictures of Black males engaged in violence and crime. The stories of young Black men who have been highly successful demonstrates that being Black, male, and poor does not automatically equate to a life of failure. It is a matter of shifting our paradigm to enhancing and developing the strengths of Black boys. Instead of focusing on avoiding failure, we must focus more on ways in which we can support thriving.

REFERENCES

Adelman, C. (2006). *The toolbox revisited: Paths to degree completion from high school through college.* Washington, DC: Government Printing Office; US Department of Education, Institute for Education Sciences.

Allen, Q. (2013). They think minority means lesser than: Black middle-class sons and fathers resisting microaggressions in the school. *Urban Education, 48*(2), 171.

Arcia, E. (2006). Achievement and enrollment status of suspended students outcomes in a large, multicultural school district. *Education and Urban Society, 38*(3), 359–369.

Aud, S., Fox, M. A., & KewalRamani, A. (2010). *Status and trends in the education of racial and ethnic groups (NCES 2010–015).* Washington, DC: National Center for Education Statistics.

Barbarin, O. A., Chinn, L., & Wright, Y. F. (2014). Creating developmentally auspicious school environments for African American boys. In L. S. Liben & R. S. Bigler (Vol. Eds.), *The role of gender in educational contexts and outcomes.* In J. B. Benson (Series Ed.), *Advances in child development and behavior: Vol. 47* (pp. 333–365). London: Elsevier.

Barbarin, O., & Crawford, G. (2006). Acknowledging and reducing stigmatization of African American boys. *Young Children, 66*(6), 79–86.

Berry, R. Q., III. (2008). Access to upper-level mathematics: The stories of successful African American middle school boys. *Journal for Research in Mathematics Education, 39*(5), 464–488.

Berry, R. Q., III, Thunder, K., & McClain, O. L. (2011). Counter narratives: Examining the mathematics and racial identities of black boys who are successful with school mathematics. *Journal of Black Males in Education, 2*(1), 10–23.

Bigler, R. S., Hayes, A. R., & Liben, L. S. (2014). Analysis and evaluation of the rationales for single-sex schooling. In L. S. Liben & R. S. Bigler (Vol. Eds.), *The role of gender in educational contexts and outcomes.* In J. B. Benson (Series Ed.), *Advances in child development and behavior: Vol. 47* (pp. 225–260). London: Elsevier.

Blanchett, W. J. (2009). A retrospective examination of urban education: From Brown to the resegregation of African Americans in special education—It is time to "go for broke". *Urban Education, 44*, 370–388.

Bowman, P. J., & Howard, C. (1985). Race-related socialization, motivation, and academic achievement: A study of Black youths in three-generation families. *Journal of the American Academy of Child Psychiatry, 24*(2), 134–141.

Brown, T. L., Linver, M. R., Evans, M., & DeGennaro, D. (2009). African-American parents' racial and ethnic socialization and adolescent academic grades: Teasing out the role of gender. *Journal of Youth and Adolescence, 38*(2), 214–227.

Butler, R. (2014). Motivation in educational contexts: Does gender matter? In L. S. Liben & R. S. Bigler (Vol. Eds.), *The role of gender in educational contexts and outcomes.* In J. B. Benson (Series Ed.), *Advances in child development and behavior: Vol. 47* (pp. 1–41). London: Elsevier.

Carby, H. V. (1998). *Race men.* Cambridge, MA: Harvard University Press.

Caton, M. T. (2012). Black male perspectives on their educational experiences in high school. *Urban Education, 47*(6), 1055–1085.

Chatters, L. M., Taylor, R. J., & Jayakody, R. (1994). Fictive kinship relations in black extended families. *Journal of Comparative Family Studies*, 297–312.

College Board. (2014). *10 years of advanced placement exam data show significant gains in access and success; Areas for improvement.* Retrieved from https://www.collegeboard.org/releases/2014/class-2013-advanced-placement-results-announced.

Collier, D., & Bush, V. L. (2012). Who am I? I am who you say I am: Black male identity and teacher perceptions. In T. E. Dancy II, & M. C. Brown II, (Eds.), *African American males and education: Researching the convergence of race and identity* (pp. 75–100). Charlotte, NC, USA: IAP Information Age Publishing.

Coutinho, M. J., Oswald, D. P., & Best, A. M. (2002). The influence of sociodemographics and gender on the disproportionate identification of minority students as having learning disabilities. *Remedial and Special Education, 23*, 49–59.

Dade, C. (2012). Florida teen's killing: A parent's greatest fear [Web log post]. http://www.npr.org/2012/03/21/149060167/florida-teens-killing-a-parents-greatest-fear.

Davis, J. E. (2003). Early schooling and academic achievement of African American males. *Urban Education, 38*(5), 515–537.

Davis, J. (2009). Toward an understanding of African American males and k-12 education. *The Sage Handbook of African American Education*, 85–88. Thousand Oaks, CA: SAGE Publications.

Devine, P. G., & Baker, S. M. (1991). Measurement of racial stereotype subtyping. *Personality and Social Psychology Bulletin, 17*(1), 44–50.

Ewing, M. E., & Seefeldt, V. (1996). Patterns of participation and attrition in American agency-sponsored youth sports. In *Children and youth in sport: A biopsychosocial perspective* (pp. 31–45).

Ferguson, A. A. (2000). Bad boys: Public schools in the making of Black masculinity. In *Public schools in the making of black masculinity*. Ann Arbor: University of Michigan Press.

Ferguson, R. F. (2005). Teachers' perceptions and expectations and the Black-White test score gap. In O. S. Fashola (Ed.), *Educating African American males: Voices from the field* (pp. 79–128). Thousand Oaks, CA US: Corwin Press.

Fiske, S. T. (1998). Stereotyping, prejudice, and discrimination. In D. T. Gilbert, S. T. Fiske, & G. Lindzey (Eds.), *The handbook of social psychology* (Vols. 1 and 2, 4th ed., pp. 357–411). New York, NY US: McGraw-Hill.

Ford, D. Y. (2006). Identification of young culturally diverse students for gifted education programs. *Gifted Education Press Quarterly, 20*, 2–4.

Ford, D. Y., & Whiting, G. W. (2010). Beyond testing: Social and psychological considerations in recruiting and retaining gifted black students. *Journal for the Education of the Gifted, 34*(1), 131.

Fredricks, J. A., & Eccles, J. S. (2006). Is extracurricular participation associated with beneficial outcomes? Concurrent and longitudinal relations. *Developmental Psychology, 42*(4), 698–713.

Gardner, R., III., & Miranda, A. H. (2001). Improving outcomes for urban African American students. *The Journal of Negro Education, 70*, 255–263.

Grant, L. (1984). Black females "place" in desegregated classrooms. *Sociology of Education, 57*(2), 98.

Grantham, T. C. (2004). Multicultural mentoring to increase Black male representation in gifted programs. *Gifted Child Quarterly, 48*(3), 232.

Grantham, T. C. (2013). Creativity and equity: The legacy of E. Paul Torrance as an upstander for gifted Black males. *The Urban Review, 45*(4), 518–538.

Gregory, A., & Ripski, M. B. (2008). Adolescent trust in teachers: Implications for behavior in the high school classroom. *School Psychology Review, 37*, 337–353.

Hall, R. E. (2009). Cool pose, Black manhood, and juvenile delinquency. *Journal of Human Behavior in the Social Environment, 19*(5), 531–539.

Hare, B. R., & Castenell, L. A. (1985). No place to run, no place to hide: Comparative status and future prospects of Black boys. In M. B. Spencer, G. K. Brookins, & W. R. Allen (Eds.), *Beginnings: The social and affective development of Black children* (pp. 201–214). Hillsdale, NJ: Lawrence Erlbaum.

Harper, S. R. (2010). In his name: Rigor and relevance in research on African American males in education. *Journal of African American Males in Education, 1*(1), 1.

Harper, S. R., & Davis, C. H. F., III. (2012). They (don't) care about education: A counternarrative on black male students' responses to inequitable schooling. *Educational Foundations, 26*(1–2), 103.

Harris, F., Palmer, R. T., & Struve, L. E. (2011). "Cool Posing" on campus : A qualitative study of masculinities and gender expression among Black men at a private research institution. *The Journal of Negro Education, 80*(1), 47–62.

Harry, B., & Anderson, M. G. (1994). The disproportionate placement of African American males in special education programs: A critique of the process. *The Journal of Negro Education, 63*, 602–619.

Henfield, M. S. (2011). Black male adolescents navigating microaggressions in a traditionally white middle school: A qualitative study. *Journal of Multicultural Counseling and Development, 39*(2), 141.

Henfield, M. S. (2013). Special issue: Meeting the needs of gifted and high-achieving black males in urban schools. *The Urban Review, 45*(4), 395.

Hill, M. (2002). Skin color and the perception of attractiveness among African Americans: Does gender make a difference? *Social Psychology Quarterly, 65*, 77–91.

Hill, S. A., & Zimmerman, M. K. (1995). Valiant girls and vulnerable boys: The impact of gender and race on mothers' caregiving for chronically ill children. *Journal of Marriage & the Family, 57*, 43–53.

Holzman, M. (2006). *Public education and Black male students: The 2006 state report card.* Cambridge, MA.

Honora, D. (2003). Urban African American adolescents and school identification. *Urban Education, 38*, 58–76.

Howard, T. C. (2013). How does it feel to be a problem? Black male students, schools, and learning in enhancing the knowledge base to disrupt deficit frameworks. *Review of Research in Education, 37*(1), 54.

Hughes, D., Rodriguez, J., Smith, E. P., Johnson, D. J., Stevenson, H. C., & Spicer, P. (2006). Parents' ethnic-racial socialization practices: A review of research and directions for future study. *Developmental Psychology, 42*(5), 747.

Irving, M. A., & Hudley, C. (2008). Cultural identification and academic achievement among African American males. *Journal of Advanced Academics, 19*, 676–698.

Kendrick, M. H., & Prioleau, M. (2011). *African American male youth: Community focus group input.*

Kunjufu, J. (1985). *Countering the conspiracy to destroy black boys* (African Am.). Chicago, IL: Afro-American Publishing Co.

Ladson-Billings, G. (1995). But that's just good teaching! The case for culturally relevant pedagogy. *Theory into Practice, 34*(3), 159–165.

Lareau, A., & Horvat, E. M. (1999). Moments of social inclusion and exclusion: Race, class, and cultural capital in family-school relationships. *Sociology of Education, 72*, 37–53.

Leaper, C., & Brown, C. S. (2014). Sexism in schools. In L. S. Liben & R. S. Bigler (Vol. Eds.), *The role of gender in educational contexts and outcomes.* In J. B. Benson (Series Ed.), *Advances in child development and behavior: Vol. 47* (pp.189–223). London: Elsevier.

Liben, L. S., & Coyle, E. F. (2014). Developmental interventions to address the STEM gender gap: Exploring intended and unintended consequences. In L. S. Liben & R. S. Bigler (Vol. Eds.), *The role of gender in educational contexts and outcomes.* In J. B. Benson (Series Ed.), *Advances in child development and behavior: Vol. 47* (pp. 77–116). London: Elsevier.

Linver, M. R., Roth, J. L., & Brooks-Gunn, J. (2009). Patterns of adolescents' participation in organized activities: Are sports best when combined with other activities? *Developmental Psychology, 45*(2), 354–367.

Losen, D. J., & Gillespie, J. (2012). *Opportunities suspended: The disparate impact of disciplinary exclusion from school.* Los Angeles, CA: The Civil Rights Project.

Losen, D. J., & Martinez, T. E. (2013). *Out of school & off track: The overuse of suspensions in American middle and high schools* (pp. 1–105). Los Angeles.

Majors, R., & Billson, J. M. (1993). *Cool pose: The dilemmas of black manhood in America.* New York: Lexington Books.

Majors, R., Wilkinson, V., & Gulam, W. (2001). Mentoring Black males: Responding to the crisis in education and social alienation. In R. Majors (Ed.), *Educating our Black children: New directions and radical approaches* (pp. 205–213). London: Routledge/Falme.

Mandara, J., Murray, C. B., & Joyner, T. N. (2005). The impact of fathers' absence on African American adolescents' gender role development. *Sex Roles, 53*(3–4), 207–220.

Mandara, J., Varner, F., & Richman, S. (2010). Do African American mothers really "love" their sons and "raise" their daughters? *Journal of Family Psychology, 24*(1), 41–50.

Matthews, J. S., Kizzie, K. T., Rowley, S. J., & Cortina, K. (2010). African Americans and boys: Understanding the literacy gap, tracing academic trajectories, and evaluating the role of learning-related skills. *Journal of Educational Psychology, 102*(3), 757–771.

McAllister, G., & Irvine, J. J. (2002). The role of empathy in teaching culturally diverse students. *Journal of Teacher Education, 53*, 433–443.

McCray, A. D., Neal, L. V. I., Webb-Johnson, G., & Bridgest, S. T. (2003). The effects of African American movement styles on teachers' perceptions and reactions. *Journal of Special Education, 37*, 49–57.

McGee, E. (2013). Young, Black, mathematically gifted, and stereotyped. *The High School Journal, 96*(3), 253–263.

Milner, H. R. (2007). African American males in urban schools: No excuses: Teach and empower. *Theory Into Practice, 46*(3), 239–246.

Morgan, H. (1995). *Historical perspectives on the education of Black children.* Westport, CT: Praeger.

Morris, E. W. (2007). "Ladies" or "Loudies"?: Perceptions and experiences of Black girls in classrooms. *Youth & Society, 38*, 490–515.

Neblett, E. W., Chavous, T. M., Nguyen, H. X., & Sellers, R. M. (2009). Say it loud—I'm black and I'm proud": Parents' messages about race, racial discrimination, and academic achievement in African American boys. *The Journal of Negro Education, 78*, 276–363.

Neblett, E. W., Smalls, C. P., Ford, K. R., Nguyen, H. X., & Sellers, R. M. (2009). Racial socialization and racial identity: African American parents' messages about race as precursors to identity. *Journal of Youth and Adolescence, 38*, 189–203.

Noguera, P. A. (2003). The trouble with Black boys: The role and influence of environmental and cultural factors on the academic performance of African American males. *Urban Education, 38*(4), 431–459.

Noguera, P. A. (2012). Saving black and Latino boys: What schools can do to make a difference. *Phi Delta Kappan, 93*(5), 8–12.

Orfield, G., & Lee, C. (2006). *Racial transformation and the changing nature of segregation.* Cambridge, MA: The Civil Rights Project at Harvard University.

Osborne, J. W. (1995). Academics, self-esteem, and race. A look at the underlying assumptions of the disidentification hypothesis. *Personality and Social Psychology Bulletin, 21*, 449–455.

Osborne, J. W. (1997). Race and academic disidentification. *Journal of Educational Psychology, 89*, 728–735.

Osborne, J. (1999). Unraveling underachievement among African American boys from an identification with academics perspective. *Journal of Negro Education, 68*(4), 555–565.

Petersen, J., & Hyde, J. S. (2014). Gender-related academic and occupational interests and goals. In L. S. Liben & R. S. Bigler (Vol. Eds.), *The role of gender in educational contexts and outcomes.* In J. B. Benson (Series Ed.), *Advances in child development and behavior: Vol. 47* (pp. 43–76). London: Elsevier.

Pigott, R. L., & Cowen, E. L. (2000). Teacher race, child race, racial congruence, and teacher ratings of children's school adjustment. *Journal of School Psychology, 38*, 177–196.

Pipes McAdoo, H. (2002). Diverse children of color: Research and policy implications. In H. Pipes McAdoo (Ed.), *Black children: Social, educational, and parental environments* (2nd ed., pp. 13–26). Beverly Hills, CA: Sage.

Poteat, V. P., Scheer, J. R., & Mereish, E. H. (2014). Factors affecting academic achievement among sexual minority and gender-variant youth. In L. S. Liben & R. S. Bigler (Vol. Eds.),

The role of gender in educational contexts and outcomes. In J. B. Benson (Series Ed.), *Advances in child development and behavior: Vol. 47* (pp. 261–300). London: Elsevier.

Reynolds, R. (2010). They think you're lazy, and other messages black parents send their black sons: An exploration of critical race theory in the examination of educational outcomes for black males. *Journal of African American Males in Education, 1*, 144–163.

Riegle-Crumb, C. (2006). The path through math: Course sequences and academic performance at the intersection of race-ethnicity and gender. *American Journal of Education, 113*(1), 101–122.

Rose, V. C. (2013). School context, precollege educational opportunities, and college degree attainment among high-achieving black males. *The Urban Review, 45*, 472–489.

Sailes, G. A. (1991). The myth of Black sports supremacy. *Journal of Black Studies, 21*, 480–487.

Schiraldi, V., & Ziedenberg, J. (2001). *Schools and suspensions: Self-reported crime and the growing use of suspensions*. Justice Policy Institute Policy Brief.

Schott Foundation for Public Education. (2010). *Yes we can: The 2010 State report on public education for black males*. Cambridge, MA: The Schott Foundation for Public Education. Retrieved from http://www.schottfoundation.org.

Schwing, A. E., Wong, Y. J., & Fann, M. D. (2013). Development and validation of the African American Men's Gendered Racism Stress Inventory. *Psychology of Men & Masculinity, 14*(1), 16–24.

Sewell, T. (1997). *Black masculinities and schooling: How Black boys survive modern schooling*. London: Trentham.

Sharp, E. A., & Ispa, J. M. (2009). Inner-city single black mothers' gender-related childrearing expectations and goals. *Sex Roles, 60*(9–10), 656–668.

Skiba, R. J., Michael, R. S., Nardo, A. C., & Peterson, R. L. (2002). The color of discipline: Sources of racial and gender disproportionality in school punishment. *The Urban Review, 34*(4), 317–342.

Skiba, R. J., Simmons, A. B., Ritter, S., et al. (2008). Achieving equity in special education: History, status, and current challenges. *Exceptional Children, 74*, 264–288.

Smalls, C., & Cooper, S. (2012). Racial group regard, barrier socialization, and African American adolescents' engagement: Patterns and processes by gender. *Journal of Adolescence, 35*, 887–897.

Solmon, M. A. (2014). Physical education, sports, and gender in schools. In L. S. Liben & R. S. Bigler (Vol. Eds.), *The role of gender in educational contexts and outcomes*. In J. B. Benson (Series Ed.), *Advances in child development and behavior: Vol. 47* (pp. 117–150). London: Elsevier.

Steele, C. M. (1997). A threat in the air: How stereotypes shape intellectual identity and performance. *American Psychologist, 52*(6), 613–629.

Stevenson, H., Herrero-Taylor, T., Cameron, R., & Davis, G. Y. (2002). Mitigating instigation: Cultural phenomenological influences of anger and fighting among "big-boned" and "baby-faced" African American youth. *Journal of Youth and Adolescence, 31*, 473–485.

Stinson, D. W. (2006). African American male adolescents, schooling (and mathematics): Deficiency, rejection, and achievement. *Review of Educational Research, 76*, 477–506.

Stinson, D. W. (2008). Negotiating sociocultural discourses: The counter-storytelling of academically (and mathematically) successful African American male students. *American Educational Research Journal, 45*, 975–1010.

Stinson, D. W. (2011). When the "burden of acting white" is not a burden: School success and African American male students. *The Urban Review, 43*(1), 43–65.

Stone, J., Perry, W., & Darley, J. M. (1997). "White Men Can't Jump": Evidence for the perceptual confirmation of racial stereotypes following a basketball game. *Basic and Applied Social Psychology, 19*(3), 291–306.

Taylor, A. Z., & Graham, S. (2007). An examination of the relationship between achievement values and perceptions of barriers among low-SES African American and Latino students. *Journal of Educational Psychology, 99*, 52–64.

Thomas, D. E., Coard, S. I., Stevenson, H. C., Bentley, K., & Zamel, P. (2009). Racial and emotional factors predicting teachers' perceptions of classroom behavioral maladjustment for urban African American male youth. *Psychology in the Schools, 46*, 184–196.

Tyler, K. M., Boykin, A. W., & Walton, T. R. (2006). Cultural considerations in teachers' perceptions of student classroom behavior and achievement. *Teaching and Teacher Education, 22*, 998–1005.

Tyson, K. (2002). Weighing in: Elementary-age students and the debate on attitudes toward school among Black students. *Social Forces, 80*(4), 1157–1189.

Varner, F., & Mandara, J. (2013). Discrimination concerns and expectations as explanations for gendered socialization in African American families. *Child Development, 84*, 875–890.

Weiner, L. (2003). Why is classroom management so vexing to urban teachers? *Theory into Practice, 42*, 305.

White, A. M. (2006). African American feminist fathers' narratives of parenting. *Journal of Black Psychology, 32*(43), 43–71.

Winsler, A., Gupta Karkhanis, D., Kim, Y. K., & Levitt, J. (2013). Being Black, male, and gifted in Miami: Prevalence and predictors of placement in elementary school gifted education programs. *The Urban Review, 45*, 416–447.

Wood, D., Kaplan, R., & McLoyd, V. C. (2007). Gender differences in the educational expectations of urban, low-income African American youth: The role of parents and the school. *Journal of Youth and Adolescence, 36*, 417–427.

Wood, D. A., Kurtz-Costes, B., & Copping, K. E. (2011). Motivational pathways to college for African American youth: A test of expectancy-value theory. *Developmental Psychology, 47*, 961–968.

Wood, D. A., Kurtz-Costes, B., Rowley, S. J., & Okeke-Adeyanju, N. A. (2010). Mothers' academic gender stereotypes and education-related beliefs about sons and daughters in African-American families. *Journal of Educational Psychology, 102*, 521–530.

Wood, D. A., Skinner, O. D., Kurtz-Costes, B., & Rowley, S. J. (2014). *Influences of parents' expectations on African American adolescents college preparatory behaviors: Greater sensitivity among boys.* Paper presented at the Biennial Meetings of the Society for Research on Adolescence, Austin, TX.

Wright, S., & Lutz, B. J. (2013, March). 100 percent of urban prep seniors college-bound. *5 NBC Chicago.* Retrieved from http://www.nbcchicago.com/news/local/urban-prep-academy-englewood-college-200485671.html.

CHAPTER TEN

Creating Developmentally Auspicious School Environments for African American Boys

Oscar A. Barbarin[*,1], Lisa Chinn[*], Yamanda F. Wright[†]

[*]Department of Psychology, Tulane University, New Orleans, Louisiana, USA
[†]Department of Psychology, University of Texas at Austin, Austin, Texas, USA
[1]Corresponding author: e-mail address: barbarin@tulane.edu

Contents

1. Overview	334
2. Challenges in Educating African American Boys	334
2.1 PJ: A Case Study	335
2.2 Factors Affecting African American Boys' Underachievement	336
3. Practices to Create Developmentally Auspicious School Environments	345
3.1 Foster Effective Classroom Management	345
3.2 Build Positive Teacher–Student Relationships	346
3.3 Improve Instructional Quality	347
3.4 Transform Peer Culture	348
3.5 Provide Ingroup Mentoring	348
3.6 Develop Respectful Collaborations with Families	349
3.7 Scaffold Socio-Emotional Development	350
3.8 Create Safe Spaces for Children in Low-Income Neighborhoods	351
3.9 Promote Counter-Stereotypic Narratives About African American Men and Boys	351
4. Single-Sex Schools: A Means of Rescuing African American Boys?	353
4.1 Possible Model: The Eagle Academy for Young Men in New York City	354
4.2 Empirical Evidence for the Efficacy of Single-Sex Education Among African American Boys	355
5. Conclusions and Future Directions	356
References	359

Abstract

African American (AA) boys face serious barriers to academic success, many of which are uncommon—or absent—in the lives of AA girls, other children of color, and European American children. In this chapter, we identify nine critical challenges to the successful education of AA boys and review possible solutions. In addition, we evaluate one particular reform, public single-sex schooling, as a possible solution to the challenges facing AA boys. Considering the evidence, we argue that recent efforts to expand the existence of public single-sex schools are rarely grounded in empirical findings. Given the lack of compelling evidence and the high stakes for AA boys, we call for more rigorous evaluations of the outcomes of sex-segregated programs that specifically target AA boys.

1. OVERVIEW

African American (AA) children remain at the lowest end of persistent achievement gaps between children of color (i.e., AA, Latino, and Native American children) and European American (EA) children in the United States (Vanneman, Hamilton, Anderson, & Rahman, 2009; Hemphill & Vanneman, 2011). Many AA children start preschool with moderate deficits in language skills compared to their EA peers (Jencks & Phillips, 1998). From prekindergarten through the 12th grade, gaps between AA and EA children's scores in reading and mathematics widen rather than narrow (Fryer & Levitt, 2004; Phillips, 2000). Although this pattern holds for AA children as a group, AA boys tend to fare even worse than AA girls, and the gender gap is broader among AA children than it is among EA children (Barbarin, 2002). AA boys face serious barriers to academic success, many of which are uncommon—or absent—in the lives of AA girls, other children of color, and EA children.

In this chapter, we identify critical challenges to the successful education of AA boys and promising solutions to these challenges, an overview of which appears in Table 1. Section 2 describes nine significant challenges in the education of AA boys. Section 3 suggests empirically supported solutions to these particular challenges. Section 4 provides an in-depth discussion of single-sex education, which has been embraced by some school districts and communities as a pedagogical strategy for supporting AA boys' academic achievement. We describe one such school, the Eagle Academy for Young Men in New York City, to illustrate many of the pedagogical strategies common to public single-sex schools serving students of color and review evidence concerning the efficacy of sex-segregated programs that specifically target AA boys. We end with Section 5, in which we present conclusions and make suggestions for future research.

2. CHALLENGES IN EDUCATING AFRICAN AMERICAN BOYS

To highlight the complexity of the social, emotional, and academic challenges that many AA boys face, we begin with the hypothetical case of "PJ," a 15-year-old AA boy. His personal characteristics and school

Table 1 Challenges to AA Boys' Academic Achievement and Possible Solutions

Challenge	Proposed Solution
1. Harsh, disparate school discipline	Foster effective classroom management
2. Poor teacher–student relationships	Build positive teacher–student relationships
3. Low-quality instruction	Improve instructional quality
4. Anti-academic peer culture	Transform peer culture
5. Father absence	Provide ingroup mentoring
6. Weak home–school alliances	Develop respectful collaborations with families
7. Socio-emotional adjustment difficulties	Scaffold socio-emotional development
8. Trauma and other sequelae of poverty	Create safe spaces for children in low-income neighborhoods
9. Cultural stereotypes	Promote counter-stereotypic narratives about AA men and boys

situation reflect a common narrative encountered by the first author in his work with at-risk youth of color.

2.1. PJ: A Case Study

PJ is in the 9th grade at a large, urban high school serving predominately AA, low-income students. The school emphasizes strict discipline as a gateway to academic excellence, with a severe dress code and rules that dictate every aspect of student life from posture and dress to movement through the school's crowded halls. PJ regularly feels invisible, voiceless, and disrespected by the adults at his school. He feels that, although there are a few nice teachers who show concern for their students, "Most of them don't really care whether [he learns] or not." He and his friends also observe that the school's strict rules are not enforced fairly. They feel that they are monitored more stringently and disciplined more harshly for small infractions than other students (mostly girls and the few EA students at the school). As a result, many of PJ's friends think school is a joke, and they do not take adults or schoolwork seriously.

Mid-way through the school year, PJ was referred by the assistant principal to the school's behavioral intervention team because of chronic rule violations. His teachers reported that he often resists tucking his shirt inside his pants, refuses to stay on the side of the hall designated for 9th graders, has trouble focusing in class, and occasionally talks back to adults. As a result, he receives in-school suspensions nearly once per month. In addition to compliance problems, his academic difficulties have grown worse over the years. He is of average intelligence, but he is performing below grade level in reading and mathematics. The school counselor, who was assigned by the assistant principal to evaluate PJ for emotional difficulties, is not having much success connecting with him. With resignation, she recently remarked to a colleague, "I think we are losing him."

As part of the behavioral intervention, a male social worker interviewed PJ. During the interview, the social worker observed that PJ appeared friendly and candid, displayed a warm sense of humor, and seemed to take care of himself, at one point refusing an offer of potato chips. PJ admitted to the social worker, however, that he had been feeling sad and hopeless since the accidental shooting of his 15-year-old cousin. He and his cousin were best friends. They attended the same school, belonged to same peer group, and spent most of their free time together. They tried hard to stay out of trouble, calling their group of friends the "A-Team," and would do things like pool their allowances to rent out the hall at their neighborhood community center for a party. Since his cousin's death, PJ spends most of his time alone "just watching the world go by." He also reported to the social worker that he gets agitated when he remembers his cousin, often disengaging or acting out in class to cope with the sadness.

PJ lives with his mother and older sister in a neighborhood just a few subway stops from school. The neighborhood is dangerous and thus PJ and his sister walk home as fast as they can after exiting the subway station each day. Their father left the family before PJ began schooling, so their mother must work two jobs to support the family. This means that PJ and his sister do not see her much and spend most of their free time home alone. PJ would like to work part-time to help his mother financially, but finding a job in their neighborhood seems impossible. PJ would like to believe that school is important, as his mother is constantly telling him, but he just cannot see its value. He is not sure what the future holds for him after high school. PJ's story illustrates real and persistent barriers to the academic success of legions of low-income, AA boys in the United States.

2.2. Factors Affecting African American Boys' Underachievement

Where do racial and gender gaps in academic achievement—which disproportionally affect AA boys' lives—originate? In the remainder of this section, we review nine commonly hypothesized causes of lower achievement outcomes among AA boys compared to AA girls and EA children.

2.2.1 Harsh, Disparate School Discipline

Across racial groups, boys tend to be more restless, hyperactive, and impulsive than girls (Else-Quest, Hyde, Goldsmith, & Van Hulle, 2006; McClowry et al., 2013), which may explain why they are more likely to be labeled "problem children" or "troublemakers" (Swanson, Cunningham, & Spencer, 2003). Boys of color—especially those in urban schools—bring additional layers of complexity. As noted above, AA boys are typically the lowest group with respect to academic performance and the highest group with respect to adjustment problems and discipline referrals (Davis, 2001, 2003). However, the evidence for racial differences in classroom misbehavior is mixed. Some studies show that AA children are slightly more likely to commit minor infractions in the classroom (e.g., skipping class or carving one's desk; McCarthy & Hoge, 1987), whereas others show no differences at all—neither according to students' self-reports nor school records (e.g., Bauer, Guerino, Nolle, & Tang, 2008; Skiba, Michael, Nardo, & Peterson, 2002; Wehlage & Rutter, 1986). AA boys are, nonetheless, more harshly disciplined than EA boys for offenses of equal severity (Skiba et al., 2008; Wallace, Goodkind, Wallace, & Bachman, 2008).

In many cases, racial discrepancies in discipline arise from teachers' differential responses to normal behavioral issues. Inexperienced teachers, for example, are more prone to respond to children's misbehavior by either overreacting or underreacting than veteran teachers (Fuller & Brown, 1975) and comprise a greater proportion of teaching faculty in schools serving children of color than in predominately EA schools (Clotfelter, Ladd, & Vigdor, 2005). Overreacting teachers may misinterpret AA boys' behavior as aggressive, hostile, or challenging when it is not (Davis, 2003; Swanson et al., 2003), even treating their misbehavior as adult aggression when it is within the normal range of childhood misbehavior (Welch & Payne, 2010). Other teachers may underrespond at first, trying to be flexible and sensitive (Ballenger, 1999). When over- and underreacting teachers' strategies are not met with quick success, they may either distance themselves emotionally or respond in anger to AA boys. Through these interactions with inexperienced teachers, AA boys' minor misconduct can lead to excessively harsh discipline with severe long-term consequences.

Moreover, in schools serving predominately students of color, children are perceived as more aggressive, and harsh punishment is more frequently confused with effective classroom management, than in predominately EA schools (Welch & Payne, 2010). Acting out, moodiness, and irritability—which may be signs of stress or an underlying mental health problem—are transformed into criminal justice issues, sometimes resulting in children being arrested at school (Poe-Yamagata & Jones, 2007). Furthermore, even when harsh discipline is appropriate (e.g., for physical violence), administration of such discipline is rarely systematic, consistent, or preventative. Starting as early as prekindergarten and extending through high school, AA boys are subjected to suspensions and expulsions more frequently than other groups of children and are affected disproportionately by such "zero-tolerance" policies (Gilliam, 2005; Shollenberger, 2013). In their daily operation, low-performing schools often fail to balance sanctions for undesirable behavior with rewards for desired behavior. Over time, these experiences may lead AA boys to become demoralized and lose interest in school, as evidenced by disproportionately high rates of disciplinary actions, grade retention, and dropout (Davis, 2001, 2003; Slaughter-Defoe & Rubin, 2001; Swanson et al., 2003).

2.2.2 Poor Teacher–Student Relationships

Strong teacher–student relationships are absolutely crucial to children's socio-emotional and cognitive development. Teachers may serve as alternate attachment figures, providing an additional base for the development of interpersonal trust, especially when children's ties to family members are weak, discordant, or marred by conflict (Bergin & Bergin, 2009). In addition, among students who already show behavioral issues, quality teacher–student relationships can mitigate aggressive or disruptive behavior in the classroom (Meehan, Hughes, & Cauel, 2003). Ming-Te, Brinkworth, and Eccles (2013) found that warm, trusting teacher–student relationships moderate the relation between adverse family environments and behavioral or emotional problems (Ming-Te et al., 2013).

Racial group differences in children's feelings of trust toward outgroup teachers may play a role in sustaining both gender and racial achievement gaps (Cohen & Steele, 2002; Yeager et al., 2014). Nearly 84% of public school teachers are EA, and 85% of public school teachers are female (Coopersmith, 2009). Thus, unlike their peers, the majority of AA boys are assigned to classrooms with teachers who are neither their same race nor their same gender. Importantly, children as young as 4 or 5 are aware of ingroup biases (Rhodes, 2012) and can presumably project such knowledge onto adults at school, which may undermine the development of warm, close relationships with outgroup teachers.

2.2.3 Low-Quality Instruction

AA boys disproportionately attend low-resource, low-performing schools that are unable to fully address the academic needs of their students. Racial group differences in access to high-quality instruction are present as early as preschool (Pianta et al., 2005). It has been noted that teachers employed in low-performing schools tend to use greater numbers of ineffective strategies (e.g., extended large-group instruction), and fewer numbers of effective strategies (e.g., instruction in small groups and one-on-one interaction), than their colleagues in high-performing schools. Rich language interactions between teachers and children are critical for the development of early reading and mathematical skills, yet these they are in short supply in many school programs serving children of color and those who are poor (Pianta et al., 2005). AA boys are especially susceptible to these deficiencies because they enter school with more limited language skills than AA girls, other children of color, and EA children.

Another possible reason that schools do not meet the needs of AA boys is that too often children of color are viewed as passive recipients of information rather than active participants in knowledge formation (Anyon, 1981; McAllister & Irvine, 2000). Pedagogical approaches that promote higher order thinking, such as those encouraging student exploration and discovery, creative expression, and learning through problem solving and reflection, are less common in low-performing schools than in high-performing schools (Anyon, 1981). Instruction in low-performing schools is less varied, relies too exclusively on whole group interactions, is excessively teacher-directed, and includes less frequent individualized feedback than instruction in high-performing schools (Delpit, 2006). Together, these qualities contribute to poor academic achievement among AA boys, who are more likely to attend low-performing schools than EA children, and who receive more negative attention in the classroom than AA girls and EA children.

Finally, some researchers have speculated that differences in temperament and interests coupled with a largely female teaching force leads to boys' social, emotional, and behavioral disengagement from school (e.g., Gurian, 2001). Boys and girls' interests tend to diverge very early in development. Young boys tend to have more male-stereotyped preferences, showing greater interest in active play and male-stereotyped toys such as trucks and building blocks, whereas girls show more female-stereotyped preferences (Fagot, 1974; Lobel & Menashri, 1993; Maccoby & Jacklin, 1974). To the extent that schools are structured around female-stereotyped preferences—an argument that has been put forth by several scholars in recent years (Gurian, 2001; Sax, 2009; Sommers, 2000)—boys may be at a cultural disadvantage in school environments, but empirical evidence for such a connection is scant (see Bigler, Hayes, & Liben, 2014 [Chapter 7 of this volume]; Eliot, 2009).

2.2.4 Anti-academic Peer Culture

Group norms exert a powerful influence on children's behavior. Children are more positive toward and accepting of peers who conform to group norms and share their attitudes and social behaviors (Nipedal, Nesdale, & Killen, 2010). Martin, Fabes, & Hanish (2014) [Chapter 5 of this volume] provide illustrations of these phenomena within the realm of gender. Among boys of color, such norms may reinforce maladaptive behavior such as physical aggression, rule breaking, and rejection of academic domains. Several researchers have even suggested that the peer culture among AA boys is decidedly anti-academic (e.g., Fordham & Ogbu, 1986; Xie, Dawes, Wurster, & Shi, 2013). Xie et al. (2013) found that anti-academic attitudes are especially present among AA and Latino boys in the years leading up to middle school, when peer acceptance becomes a more prominent concern for children and interest in school declines. In primary school, rule breaking and aggression afford higher reputational value among AA boys than among other groups, although EA and Latino boys rise to the level of AA boys by middle school.

These patterns of social interaction are especially evident in urban neighborhoods with high levels of community and domestic violence, which are disproportionately inhabited by AA children and other children of color. This is perhaps because violence is modeled as a means of resolving interpersonal conflict among family members, acquaintances, and strangers. In addition, aggression may become a means of asserting social dominance as AA males make the transition from elementary to middle school (Xie et al., 2013). Popularity and social acceptance of males within this group are more strongly associated with rule breaking and aggression than with behaviors associated with academic success. Being a good student who works hard and follows rules is devalued and at times ridiculed by peers, sometimes referred to as "acting White" (Fordham & Ogbu, 1986). Given that peer acceptance is especially important in middle childhood and adolescence, the charge of acting White is hypothesized to have powerful effects on AA boys' academic engagement and success (Fordham & Ogbu, 1986), but empirical studies of the effects of acting White on peer networks and academic achievement has largely been inconsistent (Ainsworth-Darnell & Downey, 1998; Cook & Ludwig, 1998; Fryer & Torelli, 2010).

2.2.5 Father Absence

In 1965, Daniel Patrick Moynihan, Assistant Secretary of Labor, published a report titled, "The Negro Family: The Case for National Action" (U.S. Department of Labor, 1965). In the report, Moynihan sounded an alarm about the rise in single-parent, female-headed households within AA communities. Moynihan described a "tangle of pathologies" that would unravel AA families, the most damaging of which, in his opinion, was the progression toward a matriarchal society that would result in harmful emasculation of AA men. The report also outlined in detail his predictions about the implications of such a shift for AA children's social and cognitive development.

From a contemporary vantage point, Moynihan's predictions might seem remarkably prescient. At the time of the report, single-parent, female-headed households comprised about one fourth of AA families; today, almost two thirds of AA households are headed by single mothers (Vespa, Lewis, & Kreider, 2013). In addition, many of the outcomes that Moynihan predicted have come to play (e.g., higher incarceration rates among AA men and boys; Alexander, 2012)—but in the years since the report, there has been much debate about his hypotheses regarding AA male emasculation (e.g., Acs, Braswell, Sorensen, & Turner, 2013). Cunningham, Swanson, and Hayes (2013) have noted a trend among AA boys toward development of *pseudo-masculine identity*, characterized by excessive toughness, callous indifference, and an exaggerated masculinity.

Alternatively, other societal and parent-related factors may explain the relation between an increase in single-parent households and AA boys' underachievement, such as a racially biased justice system, which contributes to higher rates of incarceration among AA men and poorer AA families (Acs et al., 2013; Alexander, 2012), or parents' gender attitudes (Graves, 2008; Wood, Kurtz-Costes, Rowley, & Okeke-Adeyanju, 2010). Graves (2008), for example, found that both AA mothers and AA fathers are more involved with, and have higher expectations for, AA girls than AA boys. By the time children start 1st grade, AA parents' expectations of AA boys start to become more pessimistic, whereas their expectations of AA girls remain relatively consistent over time. These gender differences in parental involvement and expectations account for a significant amount of the gender gap in AA children's reading and mathematics performance (Graves, 2008).

2.2.6 Weak Home–School Alliances

Strong working alliances between schools and families can facilitate AA boys' psychological adjustment to the school setting and, ultimately, improve their academic outcomes. Such working alliances are made easier when there is congruence between home and school in values, practices, goals, language, and discourse style. Unfortunately, incongruences between home and school are more common among AA families than EA or Latino families, placing greater demands on AA children to adapt to educational settings with unfamiliar rules, expectations, and practices (Barbarin, Downer, Odom, & Head, 2010). In general, American schools mirror the beliefs and practices of middle class EA homes, thus conferring an advantage to EA children when they enter school. For example, Rogoff (2003) found that EA teachers use language and styles of discourse that are dissimilar to those AA children encounter in their homes. Similar incongruences are noted with respect to support and discipline styles (Barbarin & Jean-Baptiste, 2013). Discrepancies between parents' and teachers' values, practices, goals, language, and discourse style may contribute to AA boys' difficulties in school.

Another impediment to close home–school relations is the psychological "baggage" that parents may bring from their own experiences in school. Parents have been shown to communicate mistrust of racial outgroup members and institutions, for example, through their conversations about race with their children. Hughes and Chen (1997) showed that some—but not most—AA parents' racial socialization practices promote cultural mistrust among AA children. Similarly, AA parents who themselves experienced difficulty in school or were subjected to frequent disciplinary actions may communicate unpleasant feelings about school to their children. Furthermore, for these parents, an action as simple as visiting the school might reawaken the pain of their own failures or frustrations with school. Parents may respond with avoidance, failing to show up for appointments or losing interest in the school's Parent Teacher Association. In turn, school staff may interpret these behaviors as indifference or lack of concern about the child.

The consequence of weak home–school alliances is that teachers and parents are unable to work together to meet the needs of many AA boys and other children of color. When parents and teachers work in concert, AA boys are likely to experience greater success at school compared to situations in which home and school are not aligned.

2.2.7 Trauma and Other Sequelae of Poverty
AA individuals are more likely to experience poverty than any other racial group (Macartney, Bishaw, & Fontenot, 2013). In fact, the poverty rate for AA children is more than double that of EA children (Macartney, 2011).

A host of ills, including poor physical health, low social capital, and a higher incidence of psychological trauma, are associated with poverty (Brooks-Gunn & Duncan, 1997; Maholmes & King, 2012). These factors, in turn, place AA children at greater risk for a variety of problems than other children, including academic underperformance. Importantly, AA children are exposed more frequently to trauma in the form of domestic and neighborhood violence than any other group, which may affect their performance and behavior in school. However, although boys are typically more aggressive than girls, they are actually less likely than girls to encounter neighborhood violence during the first few years of schooling (Guerra, Rowell Huesmann, & Spindler, 2003). Guerra et al. also found that boys and girls experience no differences in negative emotional outcomes following exposure to violence (e.g., becoming more aggressive themselves), with the exception of slightly more frequent fantasies about violence among girls. Still, AA boys witness and are victimized by neighborhood violence more frequently than other boys of color and EA children.

2.2.8 Socio-Emotional Adjustment Difficulties

Academic development is not the only domain in which AA boys struggle at school. Data from a longitudinal study of boys of color (Barbarin, 2013) show racial group differences in socio-emotional functioning as early as primary school. Compared to EA and Latino children, AA boys experience the steepest decline in attention and emotion regulation from preschool to 2nd grade.

AA boys also experience higher rates of internalizing symptoms than AA girls and EA boys. Although EA girls typically exhibit more internalizing difficulties than EA boys, this pattern is reversed among young AA children (Barbarin & Soler, 1993; Kistner, David, & White, 2003; Kistner, David-Ferdon, Lewis, & Dunkel, 2007). By the end of kindergarten, racial group differences in internalizing symptoms and problems with self-regulation arise. Latent group analysis of data from the Early Childhood Longitudinal Study (ECLS-K) show that early childhood (e.g., between kindergarten and the 1st grade) may be an important inflection point for mental health interventions for AA boys. In addition, when emotional functioning is defined as hopelessness about the future, AA boys attain lower scores with respect to emotional functioning than AA girls (Stoddard, Henly, Sieving, & Bolland, 2011). Developmental changes in hopelessness scores also vary by gender. Twice as many boys (i.e., 20% of boys vs. 10% of girls) report increasing hopelessness from ages 13 to 16.

Attention problems, relatively high rates of internalizing symptoms, and a sense of hopelessness may translate into academic disengagement or a "devil may care" attitude with respect to rules, which may ultimately push AA boys into schools' disciplinary systems at higher rates than AA girls and EA boys.

2.2.9 Cultural Stereotypes

Among the most serious obstacles to the academic success of AA boys are pervasive cultural stereotypes about AA boys and men, including widely held beliefs about their intellectual aptitude, academic motivation, and scholastic achievement (Bobo, 2001; Steele, 1997). Leaper and Brown (2014) [Chapter 6 of this volume] review the ways in which gender stereotypes, prejudice, and discrimination affect boys' educational experiences and outcomes, and note the importance of considering the intersections of gender and race for understanding these processes. AA males are viewed as lower in basic abilities and intelligence compared to EA and Asian American individuals, as well as less capable than AA girls in language and literacy domains (Lupart, Cannon, & Telfer, 2004). AA boys are also perceived as older, less innocent, more culpable for transgressions, and more physically menacing than EA boys (Goff, Eberhardt, Williams, & Jackson, 2008; Goff et al., 2014). As a consequence of these stereotypes, AA males are often held in low esteem, disparaged, and even feared by authority figures (Goff et al., 2014).

AA boys and their families are very aware of stereotypes associated with their ethnicity and gender and appear to be influenced by them (Rowley, Kurtz-Costes, Mistry, & Feagans, 2007). Rowley et al. (2007) found that AA youth frequently internalize the belief that AA individuals are less capable than EA individuals. Moreover, Evans, Copping, Rowley, and Kurtz-Costes (2011) found that internalization of negative racial stereotypes is more pronounced among AA male 7th and 8th graders than among AA girls in those grades. Even AA mothers have been shown to endorse negative stereotypes about AA boys' academic abilities, showing less optimism and more concern about academic prospects with sons than with daughters (Wood et al., 2010).

Negative racial stereotypes are of concern not only because of the potentially demoralizing impact they have on AA boys' self-concept but also because they may act as self-fulfilling prophecies, undermining AA boys' academic performance (Jussim & Harber, 2005). For these boys, the sense that prejudiced beliefs are held by school staff, as well as the internalization of such stereotypes, may contribute to academic underachievement.

3. PRACTICES TO CREATE DEVELOPMENTALLY AUSPICIOUS SCHOOL ENVIRONMENTS

Developmentally auspicious school environments for AA boys require careful consideration of each of the challenges reviewed in Section 2.2. Next, we discuss practices that hold the promise of mediating the effects of these challenges on AA boys' academic achievement. These solutions draw, in part, from best practices outlined by the Coalition of Schools Educating Boys of Color (COSEBOC, 2013) and Rimm-Kaufman and Chiu's (2007) findings about the effectiveness of the Responsive Classroom Approach for managing culturally diverse classroom environments.

3.1. Foster Effective Classroom Management

As reviewed earlier, AA males are subject to more punitive responses and lower expectations from adults than AA girls and children from other racial groups. Conversely, effective responses to behavior problems involve a combination of: (1) clear, realistic expectations, (2) firm but even-handed control, (3) close emotional contact, and (4) interpersonal warmth (COSEBOC, 2013; Rimm-Kaufman & Chiu, 2007). Although it is true that this prescription works for all children, the recommendations are especially important to remember in the case of AA boys for whom there is less room for error. In the end, teachers and schools are more likely to be effective if they resist the impulse to punish AA boys harshly to control behavioral issues—and instead focus on encouraging positive behavior.

Skilled teachers have several classroom habits that can be learned through culturally sensitive teacher training. They learn to anticipate problems by understanding the chain of events that leads to conflict and intervene before it erupts (e.g., by redirecting children away from confrontations). Even when correcting children, they are caring and open. They try to provide feedback while minimizing embarrassment and frustration. They teach students skills for understanding their feelings and coping with problems that arise, sometimes employing scripted programs integrated into the curriculum (e.g., Second Step; Sprague et al., 2001) to strengthen children's problem-solving and conflict management skills. In other words, they correct problematic behaviors in ways that leave children feeling respected.

Children's conduct is also strengthened by involving them in the development of rules. Letting children manage some of their own difficulties may be much more effective than constant monitoring (Rimm-Kaufman & Chiu, 2007). Serious problems can be exacerbated by teachers who erroneously assess the situation and punish or blame the wrong child. If children's sense of justice is violated, the classroom climate suffers. This may be the case when teachers use strategies such as punishing an entire group for the behavior of a single child, or when a child's behavior is misconstrued aggressive or threatening. This is particularly likely in the case of children who the teacher has already labled "troublemakers" (Delpit, 2006). AA boys are especially likely to be used as scapegoats in absence of sufficient information (McAllister & Irvine, 2000; Swanson et al., 2003).

Improvement may require, for instance, greater tolerance of the kind of rough and tumble play that is more common among boys' interactions than girls' interactions (Blakemore, Berenbaum, & Liben, 2009)—across groups. In addition, when AA boys and other children do commit serious offenses, teachers can use short-term punishments such as restorative justice practices in place of long-term solutions like suspension, which is almost always counterproductive (Reynolds et al., 2008). Finally, teachers should establish a mutually agreed upon and enforced contracts around acceptable behavior and collaborate with students on fashioning the type of environment they want the school to be (e.g., by agreeing on specific consequences for breaking things to foster a sense of community and ownership; Rimm-Kaufman & Chiu, 2007). Fair and effective disciplinary practices are also important for supporting sexuality minority and gender-variant youth (see Poteat, Scheer, & Mereish, 2014 [Chapter 8 of this volume]).

3.2. Build Positive Teacher–Student Relationships

It is often easier to describe warm, supportive relationships than to provide a road map of how to get there. Generally, warm, supportive relationships are characterized by positive regard, a preponderance of approval and affirmation over criticism and disapproval, palpable emotional investment in students' well-being, and an appreciation for students' strengths. To develop positive relationships like these, teachers and administrators should look beyond the superficial postures that boys adopt and try to conceptualize what is beneath the surface—the goals, longings, and struggles behind the posturing.

Research on culturally responsive classrooms (Au, 1993; Gay, 2000, 2002; Rimm-Kaufman & Chiu, 2007) has identified fairly simple ways to facilitate warm, supportive teacher–student relationships. For example, gathering as a whole class at the beginning of the school day to greet one another, share news, and set goals for the coming day has been shown to ground students and strengthen their relationships at school (Rimm-Kaufman & Chiu, 2007). These social gatherings may also afford children opportunities to talk about and gain support for distressing feelings. Similarly, Villegas and Lucas (2002) suggest incorporating honest, frank discussion about race and class into curricula, a strategy which has been adopted by many school districts struggling to meet the needs of low-income students of color (e.g., North Carolina; Schwartz, 2014). The positive effects of these strategies are likely twofold: they may make students more comfortable with engaging with racial outgroup teachers and make teachers more aware of the fact that race and gender differences are perceived by students as barriers to close relationships with them.

3.3. Improve Instructional Quality

Tailoring instruction to boys' needs requires attention both to curricula and pedagogical practices. Although wide individual differences exist, boys are often more restless in class, have relatively weaker language skills, and are more competitive and assertive than girls (Barbarin & Soler, 1993; Barbarin, 2002). Instruction should take advantage of these qualities rather than treat them as a nuisance. It should offer more action-tolerant instruction, such as the use of projects and concrete materials, for all students. Research suggests that teachers should vary settings and presentation methods, emphasizing discussions, problem-solving activities, and group projects as well as corrective comments and individual instruction (e.g., Slavin, 1987). In doing so, teachers can make the classroom more lively and involve boys more in their own education.

In selecting materials and projects, teachers should strive for a balance of topics that appeal to boys' and girls' interests: cars, cooking kits, machines, maps, babydolls, and dinosaurs, for example. Of course, each individual child's interests vary widely across time and setting, but teachers can clue into these interests by listening to what boys and girls talk about when they are free to be themselves. If the boys in one class seem particularly attracted to opportunities to compete with one another, then teachers might try to offer more frequent opportunities for academic competition (e.g., on word puzzles or mathematics problems). If the boys in a class seem drawn toward collaborative activities, then teachers should promote learning through cooperative assignments and play. Pedagogical approaches should be flexible and should consider the needs of all students, including both girls and boys (Rimm-Kaufman & Chiu, 2007). Additionally strategies for increasing students' willingness to engage in gender counter-stereotypic activities are reviewed by Liben and Coyle (2014) [Chapter 3 of this volume].

3.4. Transform Peer Culture

By middle school and later, the peer environment plays a critical role in education. Peer relationships can promote either positive, prosocial behavior or aggressive, antisocial behavior (Vaillancourt & Hymel, 2006). AA boys' involvement in antisocial behavior, teasing, and victimization increase in the years leading up to and during the middle school (Farmer, Laying, Lee, Hamm, & Lambert, 2012) and those boys who engage in such antisocial behaviors are not necessarily shunned or rejected by peers (Fryer & Torelli, 2010).

Schools can influence peer culture through greater adult involvement and by forming alliances with prosocial students who are connected with their school. Increased surveillance, a discernible presence, and more active engagement by adults have the potential to shift peer norms in a positive direction (Banerjee, 2002). Conversely, influencing peer norms through exhortations from authority figures, or institutionally sanctioned discourse, are unlikely to be effective—unless they are informally endorsed by persons who are widely known and respected across multiple subgroups within the setting. An effective strategy for influencing and altering group norms is to transmit desired attitudes and behaviors through key "opinion leaders," or students who are highly connected with both teachers and students and can therefore serve as liasons. Influencing students' collective norms is achieved more often through informal than formal channels (Paluck & Shepherd, 2012). To be successful, these methods require enormous, continuous attention and effort on the part of school staff.

3.5. Provide Ingroup Mentoring

The most obvious solution to a dearth of AA men in the lives of AA boys is to expose them to AA male teachers. In an ideal society, every AA child would grow up with nurturing relationships with AA men at home and at school. That is something we can strive for in the future. Today, however, only 16% of AA men graduate from college and only 2% of those men go on to become teachers (Lewis & Toldson, 2013). More could be done to recruit AA males into the teaching profession through scholarships, special certification programs, and improved compensation.

But even with Herculean efforts, the underrepresentation of AA males in the teaching profession is not likely to change any time soon. Moreover, even if it were possible to have an entirely AA male staff in a school, this is not an optimal solution because it would reduce opportunities for other groups of children to develop warm, close relationships with teachers from their racial backgrounds. The key is for AA boys to have access to AA male role models *either* inside or outside of school settings. If efforts to recruit AA male teachers fail at one particular school, then that school should try to recruit AA males from the community to serve as mentors. If not fathers, this strategy may involve enlisting students' adult relatives (e.g., grandfathers, uncles, and cousins) or formal mentoring organizations (e.g., Big Brothers) to take an active role in the boys' lives. Schools around the nation have developed mentoring programs such as these, carried out with local families, businesses, and fraternities.

Recruitment of AA male mentors is not easy and keeping them involved can be challenging. Success is more likely if there is clarity from the beginning about the school's expectations regarding contact and the duration of their commitment to the mentoring relationships. Mentors also need some training and support. They may not know what to do or may be unprepared to handle some of the social, personal, and behavioral problems of the most challenging students. These are issues that mentoring organizations in communities of color have dealt with for decades, but most schools and organizations eventually develop ways of handling them so that there is a greater likelihood that the mentoring relationship will be effective as well as sustained over time.

3.6. Develop Respectful Collaborations with Families

Improving home–school relations requires continuous, extended effort. Beginning in kindergarten, relationships between AA families and schools become increasingly distant, so that by high school many parents are virtually invisible to, and uninvolved with, teachers. Improving home–school relations requires continuous, extended effort.

Good relationships are built on knowledge, trust, and mutual respect. Teachers should use a variety of strategies to get to know their students' families, such as home visits, telephone calls, and brief chats when parents come to pick up or drop off their children. Respect derives from a combination of knowledge and humility. Knowledge pertains to an understanding of their students' families and lives, the history of AA people, and cultural differences between racial groups. Humility pertains to the need for EA teachers, female teachers, and other outgroup teachers to surrender their sense of cultural superiority and appreciate that the worldviews, values, practices, and preferences inherent in one's own culture are not necessarily better than those of other racial groups. This sort of cultural stance enables teachers to approach AA boys and their families with an open mind, which leads to mutual trust and respect—and ultimately a positive home–school alliance.

Frequent communication is also essential to maintaining relationships with AA boys' families. Letters and memos sent home are a first step in developing open communication with parents, but too often this is where schools' communication efforts end. Instead, teachers might use strategies such as a telephone "calling tree" to notify parents of activities and important events (e.g., parent-teacher conferences and student performances). School events should also be scheduled during nonworking hours to make them more accessible, offering childcare and refreshments to reduce obstacles to attending. Home visits also offer an effective way for school staff to reach out and get to know families in nonschool contexts. Some schools even provide van service for teachers to visit their students' neighborhoods, especially when families live in dangerous neighborhoods. These are just some examples of inventive ways for educators to break the barriers between home and school. Respect and perseverance are key to developing strong home–school alliances.

3.7. Scaffold Socio-Emotional Development

Schools can begin to address the socio-emotional needs of boys though multilevel mental health services that include universal mental health screening, socio-emotional curricula, and services designed for boys. Alongside the benchmark testing done for reading and math, schools should provide mental health screenings several times a year to track the emotional status of boys of color. They should provide the traditional Response to Intervention services but also make available nontraditional mental health interventions, such as the "Playing with Anger" program developed for AA boys by Howard Stevenson at the University of Pennsylvania (Stevenson, 2003). Schools should use social emotional learning programs that promote individual agency and self-regulation. They can employ nontraditional approaches to mental health outreach and service delivery in the school. Given that talk therapy will not be readily accepted by some boys and may not be a natural approach for most boys, other mental health models (e.g., "Playing with Anger") may be more successful.

Access to supplemental psychosocial services is important for school effectiveness. School discipline policies and effective behavior management at the classroom level may not offer a remedy that is effective for all children. Some children may need supplemental help at the individual or family level to cope with the demands of school. In these cases, schools should have resources such as social workers and school psychologists available to complement the educational staff's classroom activities and teaching efforts. Effective schools are likely to have a well-coordinated system of service delivery that integrates psychosocial interventions with educational ones.

3.8. Create Safe Spaces for Children in Low-Income Neighborhoods

Low-income, inner-city environments have fewer safe, recreational areas (e.g., outdoor parks and playgrounds) than middle class or high-income areas, and those that do exist are usually poorly maintained (Moore, Diez Roux, Evenson, McGinn, & Brines, 2008). Given that AA children, across gender, are overrepresented in low-income communities, it is imperative that parents and educators within these communities designate safe spaces for children to learn and play. Designated safe spaces may serve to reduce or prevent many of the physical threats facing AA children in low-income neighborhoods, thereby bolstering AA boys' (and other low-income children's) physical well-being and academic success. One particularly creative and successful example of this kind of initiative is the organization KaBOOM!, which builds and maintains safe playgrounds in some of the country's lowest-income neighborhoods (Bornstein, 2011). KaBOOM! has been shown to improve the quality and frequency of children's recreational activities in low-income neighborhoods (KaBOOM!, 2009) as well as provide mentoring opportunities for parents and educators in the communities that it serves (Knight Foundation, 2011).

3.9. Promote Counter-Stereotypic Narratives About African American Men and Boys

Racism and negative stereotypes can have severely damaging effects on AA boys' academic motivation. One possible solution is to resist the dominant narrative about AA boys by offering counter-narratives to widely endorsed stereotypes regarding AA male inferiority (Barbarin & Crawford, 2006; Rowley et al., 2014) [Chapter 9 of this volume]. Celebrating these models shows that achievement and success are attainable for AA boys and men. To be successful, these counter-narratives must begin with recognizing the absence of incentives for AA boys to learn. For example, Perry (2003) argued that low motivation to perform in school is to be expected when it is not clear that effort and resulting accomplishments will be recognized, valued, or transformative for economic prospects or social status. There is a disconnect between individual effort and rewards attained.

Promoting counter-stereotypical narratives about AA males may help AA boys develop a broader sense of purpose related to academic achievement, perhaps based on the philosophy that liberation is the purpose of education. One such narrative focuses on the idea that education is a way of asserting oneself as a free person, defending one's humanity, and working to uplift one's race—in other words, "freedom for literacy and literacy for freedom" (phrase attributed to Robert Stepto in Perry, 2003, p. 12). The AA community's historical narrative around the value of education extends from slavery when people of African descent were not permitted to learn to read, to the post-slavery era when they were not allowed to attend schools, to the era of Jim Crow when they were confined to separate and unequal schools, up to the current day when many AA children still disproportionately attend low-performing schools. Discussing these historical moments provide AA boys with a counter-stereotypic narrative about themselves and the personal value education. The narrative involves reframing what is possible for AA males to achieve and extending it to include notions of academic competence and the development of specific skills. This approach strengthens group identity and a sense of responsibility to do well and break the negative racial stereotypes.

Although there are many potential benefits of this approach, one potential downside is that it may make boys vulnerable to *stereotype threat*—or the process by which an individual's performance is impaired because he or she is worried about being judged as confirming of a stereotype (Steele, 1997). There is some evidence suggesting that children who learn about historical instances of racism and sexism may be at heightened risk for experiencing stereotype threat effect (e.g., Hartley & Sutton, 2013), but other, related research suggests that these effects can be easily reversed by simple interventions (see Bigler & Wright, 2014).

It is perhaps also important to note that some strategies are ineffectual, or even counterproductive, for countering the effects of cultural racial stereotypes on AA boys. For example, many adults reflexively attempt to bolster AA boys' self-esteem. However, a nonspecific focus on self-esteem, particularly in the absence of concrete performance data, may be ineffective because it appears deceptive or insincere (Yeager et al., 2014). The goal is not to help boys feel good about themselves every hour of every day so much as to reassure them that the system for evaluating their work and behavior is navigable.

4. SINGLE-SEX SCHOOLS: A MEANS OF RESCUING AFRICAN AMERICAN BOYS?

Although numerous researchers have put forth suggestions for how to best serve racially diverse classrooms and schools, AA children continue to lag behind their peers on educational and socio-emotional outcomes (Davis, 2003; Ladson-Billings, 2006). In the face of continuing failure to decrease racial achievement gaps, single-sex education is increasingly being adopted as a strategy for addressing the challenges facing AA boys, particularly within low-income areas (Klein, 2012; Datnow, Hubbard, & Conchas, 2001; Hubbard & Datnow, 2005). Single-sex schools have garnered support in many different quarters of the country, including Florida, Pennsylvania, Texas, and Wisconsin.

Single-sex schools are perhaps an attractive option because they offer new opportunities for devoting resources to previously underserved schools, thereby enabling schools to address many of the challenges facing low-income AA boys. Moreover, such specialized attention and additional resources are often viewed within the schools' surrounding communities as beneficial not only to boys of color, but also indirectly to girls of color and the community at large. This model garners resources to provide more auspicious environments for boys and increases the likelihood of success, while at the same time decreasing the likelihood that AA women will bear the responsibility for raising children alone. In light of these potential benefits, some AA communities may consider the potentially negative effects of single-sex schooling (detailed below and reviewed by Bigler et al., 2014 [Chapter 7 of this volume]) to be more tolerable than the continued failure of their AA boys.

In the absence of much empirical data in support of single-sex education as a solution to the challenges facing AA boys, it is perhaps useful to look anecdotally at extraordinary single-sex schools and their methods.

4.1. Possible Model: The Eagle Academy for Young Men in New York City

The Eagle Academy for Young Men in the Bronx, NY is an all-male public school that predominately serves boys of color (grades 6–12). After Eagle Academy's first location in the Bronx proved to be successful—with impressive statistics such as a graduation rate for AA boys that was more than double the graduation rates of AA boys in the rest of the city—the school opened additional locations in Queens, Brooklyn, Newark, and Harlem (Eagle Academy Foundation, 2014a). Today it is heralded as a model school uniquely meeting the needs of inner-city AA boys (e.g., Foderaro, 2008).

What does schooling at the academy look like? Starting in the 6th grade, Eagle Academy students receive a rigorous curriculum and high-quality instruction from 8 a.m. to 5 p.m. each week day (Eagle Academy Foundation, 2014b). The school offers a combination of high expectations (e.g., college and career readiness courses) and high social support (e.g., mentoring, life-skills training) for students from racially diverse, and often socioeconomically disadvantaged, backgrounds. Other key features of the schools' model include: a strict uniform policy, a competitive athletics program, extended-day and Saturday programs, and high parent involvement (Eagle Academy Foundation, 2014b). Whereas other schools might lower their expectations for struggling racial minority students, thereby unintentionally perpetuating racial achievement gaps, the Eagle Academy model maintains the expectation that its students will succeed, and that all students deserve to attend college if they so desire.

Importantly, most Eagle Academy mentors are men of color. This is no small feat, considering that AA male mentors are often more difficult to find. To do so, the school partners with professional mentoring organizations, such as 100 Black Men of America, Inc., (2014) and makes use of social media such as Twitter and Facebook, making it easier for prospective mentors to identify and get involved with student causes. As discussed earlier, research indeed shows that children best model themselves after people of the same sex (Bussey & Bandura, 1984). Students benefit most from mentors with whom they feel they can relate, and they find it is easier to relate to individuals who seem similar to themselves (e.g., same-race and same-gender individuals). Eagle Academy mentors of color act as role models and challenge negative stereotypes against AA males and other minorities.

For Eagle Academy, this model has produced a unique school environment in which boys of color attending a public school in the heart of

New York—boys who would usually be identified as "at-risk"—are thriving academically. According to the Eagle Academy Foundation's website, Eagle Academy schools have successfully improved educational outcomes among AA boys in several domains, including:
- A 95% attendance rate at the Queens location
- An improvement from 17% of new students at the Brooklyn location in the 6th grade reading at grade level to 84% of students reading at grade level by the 8th grade
- A 85% graduation rate at the Bronx location in 2010
- Four-year college attendance by 90% of Eagle Academy graduates

Eagle Academy graduates remain on-track for success after graduation as well as during their time at Eagle Academy. Within 3 years after graduation, 83% of the 2008 class was still enrolled in college (Eagle Academy Foundation, 2014d). More recent classes have achieved similar college attendance rates. These outcomes are inspiring because they demonstrate that inner-city boys of color, who often enter the 6th grade behind grade-level standards, are able to catch up to grade level and are fully capable of excelling in middle school, high school, and beyond. Furthermore, graduates of such rigorous, culturally sensitive schools go on to further break stereotypes specific to their race and gender. Through their own successes and their contributions back to their communities later in life, successful Eagle Academy alumni can steadily reduce racial disparities and segregation in the workforce and schools. Eagle Academy facilitates long-term transformations through their Professional Development Institute (Eagle Academy Foundation, 2014c), in which teachers, administrators, and community members learn how to use the Eagle Model (e.g., to emotional intelligence in student).

However, what the Eagle Academy model does not show is strong empirical evidence in support of sex segregation in its schools. Indeed, recent educational and developmental research has revealed very little justification for this aspect of the Eagle Academy model.

4.2. Empirical Evidence for the Efficacy of Single-Sex Education Among African American Boys

Before expanding the presence of single-sex schools in underserved communities, it is crucially important to raise the question of whether single-sex education is effective. That is, although there have been some successful single-sex schools, it is not yet clear how *sex segregation* per se addresses the problems facing AA boys. In fact, some researchers have found negative effects of single-sex education on children's gender role development (Halpern et al., 2011) and stereotypes regarding hypersexuality of AA individuals (Goodkind, Schelbe, Joseph, Beers, & Pinsky, 2013). Children also report diminished satisfaction with their experiences in school after switching from coeducational to single-sex school environments (Goodkind et al., 2013). Other studies have found positive effects of single-sex schooling, but those studies have focused on private-schools students whose higher performance relative to students attending coeducational schools is confounded by their higher socioeconomic status and stronger academic backgrounds (Mael, Alonso, Gibson, Rogers, & Smith, 2005).

Moreover, it is unclear how fully most single-sex schools are designed to specifically address the problems undermining the education of AA boys, such as those identified here. Accounts of the efficacy of single-sex schools with AA children rest largely on anecdotal reports (Goodkind et al., 2013). Few existing schools are based in theory or findings about the critical factors that promote positive development among AA boys or the best intervention methods. The effectiveness of the designs of current single-sex schools is unclear. The community must consider and take advantage of developmental science findings on the sources of the problems boys face and the best times at which to intervene.

The absence of rigorous and well-controlled evaluations means that answers to questions about efficacy remain ambiguous. To advance the possibility of conducting rigorous evaluations, this chapter identifies a set of practices currently available to address the issues faced by AA boys. These best practices might find value as a checklist against which to evaluate school quality and gauge the potential of single-sex schools to create more auspicious environments for AA boys.

5. CONCLUSIONS AND FUTURE DIRECTIONS

Despite decades of attention to the serious educational challenges facing boys of color, AA boys—in particular—have shown little improvement in their academic achievement relative to girls and EA children. Advancing AA boys' educational outcomes stands as one of the most formidable social and moral challenges of our day. AA boys face myriad obstacles to academic success, including individual, school-level, and institutional factors. Crucially, these obstacles originate in, and are continually nurtured by, longstanding prejudice and discrimination against people of color in the

United States and widely endorsed stereotypes about boys' needs and abilities. That is, AA boys are unfortunately situated at the intersection of powerful social forces—racism, sexism, and poverty—which undermine their academic achievement from the moment they begin formal schooling.

The list of mechanisms by which racism, sexism, and poverty undermine AA boys' educational attainment is long and varied. AA boys are overrepresented in principal's offices, correctional facilities, low-performing schools, low-income households, and dangerous neighborhoods, as well as misrepresented (i.e., negatively stereotyped and devalued) in the American psyche. AA boys remain in dire need of our attention as educators, researchers, community activists, and parents.

Fortunately, there is also ample evidence of resilience among AA boys. We should not ignore the fact that most AA boys are competent students, and many are excelling academically (see Rowley et al., 2014 [Chapter 9 of this volume]). This is perhaps because some school districts and communities have already begun to adopt the strategies that we propose above for creating developmentally auspicious school environments for AA boys. The remedies that we propose do, in all likelihood, help girls and children from other racial backgrounds as well, but implementing them with a particular focus on AA boys may be more efficient as it allows us to focus on the group that is struggling the most as a result of their positioning at the intersection of race, gender, and class-related inequalities.

The introduction of public single-sex schooling for low-income boys of color has been celebrated as the embodiment of this sort of efficiency. For many, public single-sex schools seem to address the unique needs of AA boys as a distinct social group; for others, public single-sex schools simply provide hope that something is being done to stem the tide of oppression experienced by AA boys. In either case, single-sex schools continue to fuel optimism that significant improvements will occur in the form of better academic and socio-emotional outcomes for AA boys. Some communities that have welcomed public single-sex schools have experienced the benefits that can arise from additional financial resources, special attention, and structural modifications in schools. Other communities have ended their experiments with single-sex schooling, often after encountering difficulties with respect to implementation and the legality of their programs (e.g., in Alabama, North Carolina, Massachusetts, Wisconsin, and Pennsylvania; Bohn, 2013; Rose, 2011).

Regardless of the apparent success of some existing single-sex schools, it must be conceded that most studies purported to support the effectiveness of single-sex education are actually either inconclusive or flawed, with shortcomings such as biased selection of students (e.g., districts "cherry-picking" the best available students for single-sex schooling; Halpern et al., 2011) or a failure to employ proper comparison groups (e.g., Hayes, Pahlke, & Bigler, 2011).

There are likely to be several reasons for the failure of single-sex schooling to produce outcomes that are superior to those of coeducational schooling, the most important of which is that existing public single-sex schools lack clear and precise thinking about how single-sex education should be linked to improved outcomes for AA boys and boys from other racial backgrounds. For example, how should single-sex classrooms and curricula be designed? What pedagogical and structural elements maximize their effectiveness? Many existing programs are guided by specious claims about endogenous or neuropsychological differences between boys and girls promulgated by claims of questionable scientific merit. Most of these claims are based on gross exaggerations of small differences in cognition and behavior that do not hold up to empirical scrutiny. The bottom line is: we are not yet certain that properly structured, theory-driven single-sex schooling even works, because there have been no rigorous tests of existing single-sex schools. It is possible that the single-sex school structure might be responsible for providing benefits to AA boys that are distinct from benefits that could be delivered in coeducational settings. Likewise, it is possible that such benefits, if documented, outweigh the costs, but as yet there is no empirical evidence in support of either of these possibilities. Questions about the efficacy of single-sex schooling for AA boys are important enough, and the debates over them are heated enough, that they deserve more rigorous testing than has been conducted to date.

Several steps are necessary for progress on these issues. First, funders of educational research must step into the breach to support empirical research that can provide greater clarity regarding single-sex schooling and other sex-segregated programs as solutions to the educational challenges facing AA boys. Second, we cannot assume that single-sex schooling is the panacea of gender and racial discrepancies in academic achievement because it is correlated with improvements in AA boys' grades. Instead the research we propose must isolate the exact factors responsible for improved outcomes among AA boys (e.g., at schools like the Eagle Academy for Young Men) and identify the contextual elements that actually matter. Finally, we must establish ethical standards around which single-sex schools should be organized so that they meet AA boys' needs without reinforcing or establishing gender and racial stereotypes. The benefits of supporting and implementing empirically derived solutions will far outweigh the costs associated with haphazard implementation of public single-sex education in communities of color. It is critical that sound and effective solutions are identified and implemented so that they can meet the significant and disturbing challenges that AA boys continue to face in our educational system.

REFERENCES

100 Black Men of America, Inc. (2014). *Education.* http://www.100blackmen.org/education.aspx.
Acs, G., Braswell, K., Sorensen, E., & Turner, M. A. (2013). *The Moynihan Report revisited.* Washington, DC: The Urban Institute.
Ainsworth-Darnell, J., & Downey, D. (1998). Assessing the oppositional culture explanation for racial/ethnic differences in school performance. *American Sociological Review, 63*, 536–553.
Alexander, M. (2012). *The New Jim Crow: Mass incarceration in the age of colorblindness.* New York: The New Press.
Anyon, J. (1981). Social class and school knowledge. *Curriculum Inquiry, 11*(1), 3–42.
Au, K. H. (1993). *Literacy instruction in multicultural settings.* New York: Harcourt-Brace.
Ballenger, C. (1999). *Teaching other people's children: Literacy and learning in a bilingual classroom.* New York, NY: Teachers College Press.
Banerjee, R. (2002). Audience effects on self-presentation in childhood. *Social Development, 11*, 487–507.
Barbarin, O. (2002). African American males in kindergarten. In J. U. Gordon (Ed.), *The African-American male in American life and thought* (pp. 1–12). New York: Nova Science Publishers.
Barbarin, O. (2013). A longitudinal examination of socio-emotional learning in African American and Latino boys across the transition from pre-k to kindergarten. *American Journal of Orthopsychiatry, 83*, 156–164.
Barbarin, O., & Crawford, G. (2006). Acknowledging and reducing stigmatization of African American boys. *Young Children, 61*(6), 79–86.
Barbarin, O., Downer, J., Odom, E., & Head, D. (2010). Home-school differences in beliefs, support, control and their relations to the competence of children in publicly sponsored pre-k programs. *Early Childhood Research Quarterly, 25*, 368–372.
Barbarin, O., & Jean-Baptiste, E. (2013). The relation of dialogic, control, and racial socialization practices to early academic and social competence: Effects of gender, ethnicity, and family SES. *American Journal of Orthopsychiatry, 83*, 207–217.
Barbarin, O., & Soler, R. (1993). Behavioral, emotional and academic adjustment in a national probability sample of African American children: Effects of age, gender and family structure. *Journal of Black Psychology, 19*(4), 423–446.
Bauer, L., Guerino, P., Nolle, K. L., & Tang, S. W. (2008). *Student victimization in U.S. schools: Results from the 2005 school crime supplement to the national crime victimization survey (NCES 2009-306).* Washington, DC: U.S. Department of Education.
Bergin, C., & Bergin, D. (2009). Attachment in the classroom. *Educational Psychology Review, 21*(2), 141–170.
Bigler, R. S., & Wright, Y. F. (2014). Reading, writing, arithmetic, and racism? Risks and benefits to teaching children about intergroup biases. *Child Development Perspectives, 8*, 18–23.
Bigler, R. S., Hayes, A. R., & Liben, L. S. (2014). Analysis and evaluation of the rationales for single-sex schooling. In L. S. Liben, & R. S. Bigler (Vol. Eds.), *The role of gender in educational contexts and outcomes.* In J. B. Benson (Series Ed.), *Advances in child development and behavior: Vol. 47* (pp. 225–260). London: Elsevier.

Blakemore, J. E. O., Berenbaum, S. A., & Liben, L. S. (2009). *Gender development.* New York: Psychology Press.

Bobo, L. (2001). Racial attitudes and relations at the close of the twentieth century. In N. J. Smelser, W. J. Wilson, & F. Mitchell (Eds.), *America becoming: Racial trends and their consequences* (pp. 264–301). Washington, DC: National Academy Press.

Bohn, A. (2013). Back to school minus the sex stereotypes. In *ACLU blog of rights.* https://www.aclu.org/blog/womens-rights/back-school-minus-sex-stereotypes.

Bornstein, D. (2011). Mobilizing the playground movement. In *The New York Times.* http://opinionator.blogs.nytimes.com/2011/06/13/mobilizing-the-playground-movement/.

Brooks-Gunn, J., & Duncan, G. J. (1997). The effects of poverty on children. *The Future of Children, 7*(2), 55–71.

Bussey, K., & Bandura, A. (1984). Influence of gender constancy and social power on sex-linked modeling. *Journal of Personality and Social Psychology, 47*(6), 1292–1302.

Clotfelter, C. T., Ladd, H. F., & Vigdor, J. (2005). Who teaches whom? Race and the distribution of novice teachers. *Economics of Education Review, 24*(4), 377–392.

Cohen, G. L., & Steele, C. M. (2002). A barrier of mistrust: How negative stereotypes affect cross-race mentoring. In J. Aronson (Ed.), *Improving academic achievement: Impact of psychological factors on education* (pp. 303–327). San Diego, CA: Academic Press.

Cook, P., & Ludwig, J. (1998). The burden of 'acting White': Are there race differences in attitudes toward education? In C. Jencks, & M. Phillips (Eds.), *The Black-White test score gap* (pp. 375–400). Washington, DC: Brookings Institution.

Coopersmith, J. (2009). *Characteristics of public, private, and Bureau of Indian Education elementary and secondary school teachers in the United States: Results from the 2007–08 schools and staffing survey (NCES 2009–324).* Washington, DC: U.S. Department of Education.

COSEBOC. (2013). *Standards & promising practices for schools educating boys of color: Executive summary.* Boston, MA: Coalition of Schools Educating Boys of Color. http://www.coseboc.org/sites/coseboc.org/files/assets/Executive.

Cunningham, M., Swanson, D. P., & Hayes, D. M. (2013). School- and community-based associations to hypermasculine attitudes in African American adolescent males. *American Journal of Orthopsychiatry, 83*(2–3), 244–251.

Datnow, A., Hubbard, L., & Conchas, G. Q. (2001). How context mediates policy: The implementation of single gender public schooling in California. *Teachers College Record, 103*(2), 184–206.

Davis, J. E. (2001). Transgressing the masculine: African American boys and the failure of schools. In W. Martino & B. Meyenn (Eds.), *What about the boys?: Issues of masculinity in schools* (pp. 140–153). Maidenhead, BRK, England: Open University Press.

Davis, J. E. (2003). Early schooling and academic achievement of African American males. *Urban Education, 38*, 515–537.

Delpit, L. (2006). *Other people's children: Cultural conflict in the classroom.* New York, NY: The New Press.

Eagle Academy Foundation. (2014a). *Our schools.* http://eagleacademyfoundation.com/schools.htm.

Eagle Academy Foundation. (2014b). *The Eagle Academy Model.* http://eagleacademyfoundation.com/model.htm.

Eagle Academy Foundation. (2014c). *Professional Development Institute.* http://eagleacademyfoundation.com/pdi.htm.

Eagle Academy Foundation. (2014d). *Results: The Eagle Academy Model works.* http://eagleacademyfoundation.com/results.htm.

Eliot, L. (2009). *Pink brain, blue brain: How small differences grow into troublesome gaps—And what we can do about it.* New York: Houghton Mifflin Harcourt Publishing Company.

Else-Quest, N. M., Hyde, J. S., Goldsmith, H. H., & Van Hulle, C. A. (2006). Gender differences in temperament: A meta-analysis. *Psychological Bulletin, 132*, 33–72.

Evans, A. B., Copping, K. E., Rowley, S. J., & Kurtz-Costes, B. (2011). Academic self-concept in Black adolescents: Do race and gender stereotypes matter? *Self and Identity*, *10*, 263–277.

Fagot, B. I. (1974). Sex differences in toddlers' behavior and parental reaction. *Developmental Psychology*, *10*, 554–558.

Farmer, T. W., Laying, K. L., Lee, D. L., Hamm, J. V., & Lambert, K. (2012). The social functions of antisocial behavior: Considerations for school violence prevention strategies for students with disabilities. *Behavioral Disorders*, *37*, 149–162.

Foderaro, L. (2008). For striving 6th graders, history is now and their future just changed. *The New York Times*, p. P7.

Fordham, S., & Ogbu, J. U. (1986). Black students' school success: Coping with the burden of acting White.'. *Urban Review*, *18*, 176–206.

Fryer, R. G., & Levitt, S. D. (2004). Understanding the Black-White test score gap in the first two years of school. *The Review of Economics and Statistics*, *86*, 447–464.

Fryer, R. G., & Torelli, P. (2010). An empirical analysis of 'acting White. *Journal of Public Economics*, *94*, 380–396.

Fuller, F., & Brown, O. (1975). Becoming a teacher. In K. Ryan (Ed.), *Teacher education: Seventy-fourth yearbook of the National Society for the Study of Education* (pp. 25–52). Chicago, IL: University of Chicago Press.

Gay, G. (2000). *Culturally responsive teaching: Theory, research, and practice*. New York: Teachers College Press.

Gay, G. (2002). Preparing for culturally responsive teaching. *Journal of Teacher Education*, *53*, 106–116.

Gilliam, W. S. (2005). *Prekindergarteners left behind: Expulsion rates in state prekindergarten systems*. New Haven, CT: Yale University Child Study Center.

Goff, P. A., Eberhardt, J. L., Williams, M., & Jackson, M. C. (2008). Not yet human: Implicit knowledge, historical dehumanization, and contemporary consequences. *Journal of Personality and Social Psychology*, *94*, 292–306.

Goff, P. A., Jackson, M. C., Allison, B., Di Leone, L., Culotta, C. M., & DiTomasso, N. A. (2014). The essence of innocence: Consequences of dehumanizing Black children. *Journal of Personality and Social Psychology*, *106*, 526–545.

Goodkind, S., Schelbe, L., Joseph, A. A., Beers, D. E., & Pinsky, S. L. (2013). Providing new opportunities or reinforcing old stereotypes? Perceptions and experiences of single-sex public education. *Children and Youth Services Review*, *35*, 1174–1181.

Graves, S. (2008). Are we neglecting African American males: Parental involvement differences between African American males and females during elementary school? *Journal of African American Studies*, *14*(2), 263–276.

Guerra, N. G., Rowell Huesmann, L., & Spindler, A. (2003). Community violence exposure, social cognition, and aggression among urban elementary school children. *Child Development*, *74*(5), 1561–1576.

Gurian, M. (2001). *Boys and girls learn differently!: A guide for teachers and parents*. San Francisco, CA: Jossey-Bass.

Halpern, D. F., Eliot, L., Bigler, R. S., Fabes, R. A., Hanish, L. D., Hyde, J., et al. (2011). The pseudoscience of single-sex schooling. *Science*, *333*(6050), 1706–1707.

Hartley, B. L., & Sutton, R. M. (2013). A stereotype threat account of boys' academic underachievement. *Child Development*, *84*(5), 1716–1733.

Hayes, A. R., Pahlke, E., & Bigler, R. S. (2011). The efficacy of single-sex education: Testing for selection and peer quality effects. *Sex Roles: A Journal of Research*, *65*, 693–703.

Hemphill, F. C., & Vanneman, A. (2011). *Achievement gaps: How Hispanic and White students in public schools perform in mathematics and reading on the national assessment of educational progress (NCES 2011–459)*. Washington, DC: U.S. Department of Education.

Hubbard, L., & Datnow, A. (2005). Do single-sex schools improve the education of low-income and minority students? An investigation of California's public single-gender academies. *Anthropology & Education Quarterly, 35*, 115–131.

Hughes, D., & Chen, L. (1997). When and what parents tell children about race: An examination of race-related socialization among African American families. *Applied Developmental Science, 1*(4), 200–214.

Jencks, C., & Phillips, M. (1998). *The Black-White test score gap (pp. 103–145)*. Washington, DC: Brookings Institution Press.

Jussim, L., & Harber, K. D. (2005). Teacher expectations and self-fulfilling prophecies: Knowns and unknowns, resolved and unresolved controversies. *Personality and Social Psychology Review, 9*, 131–155.

KaBOOM! (2009). *Play matters: A study of best practices to inform local policy and process in support of children's play*. Washington, DC: KaBOOM!, Inc.

Kistner, J. A., David-Ferdon, C. F., Lopez, C. M., & Dunkel, S. B. (2007). Ethnic and sex differences in children's depressive symptoms. *Journal of Clinical Child and Adolescent Psychology, 36*(2), 171–181.

Kistner, J. A., David, C. F., & White, B. A. (2003). Ethnic and sex differences in children's depressive symptoms: Mediating effects of perceived and actual competence. *Journal of Clinical Child and Adolescent Psychology, 32*(3), 341–350.

Klein, S. (2012). *State of public school sex segregation in the United States 2007–2010*. Washington, DC: Feminist Majority Foundation.

Knight Foundation. (2011). *Playgrounds that build communities: An evaluation of KaBOOM! In eight cities*. Miami, FL: The John S. and James L. Knight Foundation.

Ladson-Billings, G. (2006). From the achievement gap to the education debt: Understanding achievement in U.S. schools. *Educational Researcher, 35*, 3–12.

Leaper, C., & Brown, C. S. (2014). Sexism in schools. In L. S. Liben, & R. S. Bigler (Vol. Eds.), *The role of gender in educational contexts and outcomes*. In J. B. Benson (Series Ed.), *Advances in child development and behavior: Vol. 47* (pp. 189–223). London: Elsevier.

Lewis, C. W., & Toldson, I. (Eds.). (2013). *Black Male Teachers: Diversifying the United States' Teacher Workforce*. Bingley, UK: Emerald Group Publishing Limited.

Liben, L. S., & Coyle, E. F. (2014). Developmental interventions to address the STEM gender gap: Exploring intended and unintended consequences. In L. S. Liben, & R. S. Bigler (Vol. Eds.), *The role of gender in educational contexts and outcomes*. In J. B. Benson (Series Ed.), *Advances in child development and behavior: Vol. 47* (pp. 77–116). London: Elsevier.

Lobel, T. E., & Menashri, J. (1993). Relations of conceptions of gender-role transgressions and gender constancy to gender-typed toy preferences. *Developmental Psychology, 29*(1), 150–155.

Lupart, J. L., Cannon, E., & Telfer, J. A. (2004). Gender differences in adolescent academic achievement, interests, values, and life-role expectations. *High Ability Studies, 15*, 25–42.

Macartney, S. (2011). *Child poverty in the United States 2009 and 2010: Selected racegroups and Hispanic origin*. Washington, DC: U.S. Census Bureau.

Macartney, S., Bishaw, A., & Fontenot, K. (2013). *Poverty rates for selected detailed race and Hispanic groups by state and place: 2007–2011*. Washington, DC: U.S. Census Bureau.

Maccoby, E. E., & Jacklin, C. N. (1974). *The psychology of sex differences*. Stanford, CA: Stanford University Press.

Mael, F., Alonso, A., Gibson, D., Rogers, K., & Smith, M. (2005). *Single-sex versus coeducational schooling: A systematic review*. Washington, DC: American Institutes for Research.

Maholmes, V., & King, R. B. (Eds.). (2012). *The Oxford handbook of poverty and child development*. New York: Oxford University Press.

Martin, C. L., Fabes, R. A., & Hanish, L. D. (2014). Gendered-peer relationships in educational contexts. In L. S. Liben, & R. S. Bigler (Vol. Eds.), *The role of gender in educational contexts and outcomes*. In J. B. Benson (Series Ed.), *Advances in child development and behavior: Vol. 47* (pp. 151–187). London: Elsevier.

McAllister, G., & Irvine, J. J. (2000). Cross cultural competency and multicultural teacher education. *Review of Educational Research, 70*(1), 3–24.

McCarthy, J. D., & Hoge, D. R. (1987). Social construction of school punishment. *Social Forces, 65*, 1101–1120.

McClowry, S. G., Rodriguez, E. T., Tamis-LeMonda, C. S., Spellmann, M. E., Carlson, A., & Snow, D. L. (2013). Teacher/student interactions and classroom behavior: The role of student temperament and gender. *Journal of Research in Childhood Education, 27*(3), 283–301.

Meehan, B. T., Hughes, J. N., & Cavell, T. A. (2003). Teacher-student relationships as compensatory resources for aggressive children. *Child Development, 74*(4), 1145–1157.

Ming-Te, M., Brinkworth, M., & Eccles, J. (2013). Moderating effects of teacher–student relationship in adolescent trajectories of emotional and behavioral adjustment. *Developmental Psychology, 49*, 690–705.

Moore, L., Diez Roux, A., Evenson, K., McGinn, A., & Brines, S. (2008). Availability of recreational resources in minority and low socioeconomic status areas. *American Journal of Preventative Medicine, 34*(1), 16–22.

Moynihan, D. P. (1965). *The Negro family: A case for national action*. Washington, DC: U.S. Department of Labor.

Nipedal, C., Nesdale, D., & Killen, M. (2010). Social group norms, school norms, and children's aggressive intentions. *Aggressive Behavior, 36*, 195–204.

Paluck, E. L., & Shepherd, H. (2012). The salience of social referents: A field experiment on collective norms and harassment behavior in a school social network. *Journal of Personality and Social Psychology, 103*, 899–915.

Perry, T. (2003). *Young, gifted, and black: Promoting high achievement among African-American students*. Boston, MA: Beacon Press.

Phillips, M. (2000). Understanding ethnic differences in academic achievement: Empirical lessons from national data. In D. Grissmer, & M. Ross (Eds.), *Analytic issues in the assessment of student achievement* (pp. 103–132). Washington, DC: U.S. Department of Education, National Center for Education Statistics.

Pianta, R., Howes, C., Burchinal, M., Bryant, D., Clifford, R. M., Early, D. M., et al. (2005). Features of pre-kindergarten programs, classrooms, and teachers: Prediction of observed classroom quality and teacher-child interactions. *Applied Developmental Science, 9*, 144–159.

Poe-Yamagata, E., & Jones, M. A. (2007). *And justice for some: Differential treatment of youth of color in the justice system*. Washington, DC: National Council on Crime and Delinquency. http://www.nccdglobal.org/sites/default/files/publication_pdf/justice-for-some.pdf.

Poteat, V. P., Scheer, J. R., & Mereish, E. H. (2014). Factors affecting academic achievement among sexual minority and gender-variant youth. In L. S. Liben, & R. S. Bigler (Vol. Eds.), *The role of gender in educational contexts and outcomes*. In J. B. Benson (Series Ed.), *Advances in child development and behavior: Vol. 47* (pp. 261–300). London: Elsevier.

Reynolds, C. R., Skiba, R. J., Graham, S., Sheras, P., Conoley, J. C., & Garcia-Vazquez, E. (2008). Are zero tolerance policies effective in the schools?: An evidentiary review and recommendations. *The American Psychologist, 63*(9), 852–862.

Rhodes, M. (2012). Naive theories of social groups. *Child Development, 83*(6), 1900–1916.

Rimm-Kaufman, S. E., & Chiu, Y.-J. I. (2007). Promoting social and academic competence in the classroom: An intervention study examining the contribution of the Responsive Classroom Approach. *Psychology in the Schools, 44*(4), 397–413.

Rogoff, B. (2003). *The cultural nature of human development*. New York: Oxford University Press.

Rose, S. (2011). Following ACLU demands Pittsburgh ditches single-sex schools. In *ACLU blog of rights*. https://www.aclu.org/blog/womens-rights/following-aclu-demands-pittsburgh-ditches-single-sex-school-plans.

Rowley, S. J., Kurtz-Costes, B., Mistry, R., & Feagans, L. (2007). Social status as a predictor of race and gender stereotypes in late childhood and early adolescence. *Social Development, 16*(1), 150–168.

Rowley, S. J., Ross, L., Lozada, F., Williams, A., Gale, A., & Kurtz-Costes, B. (2014). Framing black boys: Parent, teacher, and student narratives of the academic lives of black boys. In L. S. Liben, & R. S. Bigler (Vol. Eds.), *The role of gender in educational contexts and outcomes*. In J. B. Benson (Series Ed.), *Advances in child development and behavior: Vol. 47* (pp. 301–332). London: Elsevier.

Sax, L. (2009). *Boys adrift: The five factors driving the growing epidemic of unmotivated boys and underachieving young men*. New York: Basic Books.

Schwartz, K. (2014). Facing race issues in the classroom: How to connect with students. Mind/Shift. http://blogs.kqed.org/mindshift/2014/04/how-can-teachers-address-race-issues-in-class-ask-students/.

Shollenberger, T. L. (2013). *Racial disparities in school suspension and subsequent outcomes: Evidence from the National Longitudinal Survey of Youth 1997*. Paper prepared for the Center for Civil Rights Remedies and the Research-to-Practice Collaborative. Los Angeles, CA: National Conference on Race and Gender Disparities in Discipline.

Skiba, R. J., Michael, R. S., Nardo, A. C., & Peterson, R. L. (2002). The color of discipline: Sources of racial and gender disproportionality in school punishment. *Urban Review, 34*, 317–342.

Skiba, R. J., Simmons, A. B., Ritter, S., Gibb, A. C., Rausch, M. K., & Cuadrado, J. (2008). Achieving equity in special education: History, status, and current challenges. *Exceptional Children, 74*, 264–288.

Slaughter-Defoe, D. T., & Rubin, H. H. (2001). A longitudinal case study of Head Start eligible children: Implications for urban education. *Educational Psychologist, 36*(1), 31–44.

Slavin, R. E. (1987). Developmental and motivational perspectives on cooperative learning: A reconciliation. *Child Development, 58*(5), 1161–1167.

Sommers, C. H. (2000). *The war against boys: How misguided policies are harming our young men*. New York: Simon & Schuster.

Sprague, J., Walker, H., Golly, A., White, K., Myers, D. R., & Shannon, T. (2001). Translating research into effective practice: The effects of a universal staff and student intervention on indictors of discipline and school safety. *Education and Treatment of Children, 24*(4), 495–511.

Steele, C. M. (1997). A threat in the air: How stereotypes shape intellectual identity and performance. *American Psychologist, 52*(6), 613–629.

Stevenson, H. C., Jr. (2003). *Playing with anger: Teaching coping skills to African American boys through athletics and culture*. Westport, CT: Greenwood Publishing, Praeger.

Stoddard, S. A., Henly, S. J., Sieving, R. E., & Bolland, J. (2011). Social connections, trajectories of hopelessness, and serious violence in impoverished urban youth. *Journal of Youth and Adolescence, 40*(3), 278–295.

Swanson, D. P., Cunningham, M., & Spencer, M. B. (2003). Black males' structural conditions, achievement patterns, normative needs, and "opportunities". *Urban Education, 38*(5), 608–633.

Vaillancourt, T., & Hymel, S. (2006). Aggression and social status: The moderating roles of sex and peer-valued characteristics. *Aggressive Behavior, 32*, 396–408.

Vanneman, A., Hamilton, L., Anderson, J. B., & Rahman, T. (2009). *Achievement gaps: How Black and White students in public schools perform in mathematics and reading on the national assessment of educational progress (NCES 2009–455)*. Washington, DC: U. S. Department of Education.

Vespa, J., Lewis, J. M., & Kreider, R. M. (2013). *America's families and living arrangements: 2012. Current Population Reports (pp. 20–570).* Washington, DC: U.S. Census Bureau.

Villegas, A. M., & Lucas, T. (2002). Preparing culturally responsive teachers: Rethinking the curriculum. *Journal of Teacher Education, 53*(1), 20–32.

Wallace, J. M., Jr., Goodkind, S., Wallace, C. M., & Bachman, J. G. (2008). Racial, ethnic, and gender differences in school discipline among U.S. high school students: 1991–2005. *Negro Educational Review, 59,* 47–62.

Wehlage, G. G., & Rutter, R. A. (1986). Dropping out: How much do schools contribute to the problem? *Teachers College Record, 87,* 374–393.

Welch, K., & Payne, A. A. (2010). Racial threat and punitive school discipline. *Social Problems, 57*(1), 25–48.

Wood, D., Kurtz-Costes, B., Rowley, S. J., & Okeke-Adeyanju, N. (2010). Mothers' academic gender stereotypes and education-related beliefs about sons and daughters in African American families. *Journal of Educational Psychology, 102,* 521–530.

Xie, H., Dawes, M., Wurster, T. J., & Shi, B. (2013). Aggression, academic behaviors, and popularity perceptions among boys of color during the transition to middle school. *The American Journal of Orthopsychiatry, 83*(2 Pt 3), 265–277.

Yeager, D. S., Purdie-Vaughns, V., Garcia, J., Apfel, N., Brzustoski, P., Master, A., et al. (2014). Breaking the cycle of mistrust: Wise interventions to provide critical feedback across the racial divide. *Journal of Experimental Psychology: General, 143*(2), 804–824.

AUTHOR INDEX

Note: Page numbers followed by "*f*" indicate figures.

A

Abrams, D., 155, 171, 194–195
Acosta, R.V., 144–145
Acs, G., 341
Adams-Curtis, L.E., 201
Adelman, C., 304
Adler, T.F., 6, 45–46, 45*f*, 58–59, 61, 91
Agnoli, F., 198
Ahn, A., 24–25
Ainsworth-Darnell, J., 340
Alabi, B.O., 191–192, 206, 207–208
Alatupa, S., 31
Alden, A.R., 69, 94
Alegria, M., 273
Alexander, J.M., 27
Alexander, M., 341
Alfeld, C.J., 66
Allen, A.B., 235
Allen, C., 98–99
Allen, E., 196
Allen, Q., 306, 307–308
Allison, B., 344
Allison, C.M., 110, 211, 212, 229–230, 233–234, 237, 240
Alonso, A., 229–230, 233–234, 355–356
Alper, J., 68–69, 82
Altermatt, E.R., 14
Amazeen, P.G., 175, 178–179
Ambady, N., 199
Anders, Mary C., 165
Anderson, C.J., 269, 276–277, 279–280
Anderson, D.M., 196–197, 200
Anderson, J.B., 334
Anderson, K.J., 246–247
Anderson, L., 193
Anderson, M.G., 302, 310–311, 314, 315–316
Andre, T., 195, 198
Andrews, D.W., 159–160
Andrews, N.C.Z., 173, 177
Angold, A., 273
Anyon, J., 339

Apfel, N., 70, 267, 338, 352–353
Aragon, S.R., 263–264, 268–269
Arbreton, A.J.A., 27
Arcia, E., 311–312
Arias, D.M., 209
Armstead, P., 21
Armstrong, P.I., 27, 44, 56
Aronson, J., 46, 47, 70
Arthur, A.E., 156–157, 205–206
Aspenlieder, L., 263, 270
Aspray, W., 50
Atkinson, J.W., 4–5, 7–8, 20–21
Attar-Schwartz, S., 213
Au, K.H., 201–202
Aubrey, J., 196
Aud, S., 303
Axelton, A.M., 291
Ayala, A., 198
Ayres, M.M., 198, 209
Azmitia, A., 192
Azzarito, L., 121, 127–128, 130, 138–141, 143–144, 146

B

Baartmans, B.J., 69–70, 94–95
Bachman, J.G., 274–275, 337
Baer, D.M., 87
Baines, E., 155–156
Bakeman, R., 276–277
Baker, S.M., 319–320
Bakker, F., 273
Ballenger, C., 337
Banaji, M.R., 9–10, 191
Bandura, A., 9, 49, 57, 63, 87–88, 89, 265, 354
Banerjee, R., 348
Barbaranelli, C., 49, 57, 63
Barbarin, O.A., 29, 34, 169–170, 191–192, 202, 210, 234–235, 269, 278, 292–293, 303, 305, 310–311, 312–313, 334, 341–342, 343, 347, 351–352
Barber, B.L., 58, 66, 285

Barber, N., 102
Barbu, S., 156–157
Barron, B., 198
Barron, K.E., 7–8
Barron, M., 280, 285–287
Bartkiewicz, M.J., 204
Bashe, E., 194–195
Basow, S.A., 191–192, 236, 239–240
Bates, C., 24–25
Bauer, L., 337
Baumert, J., 9–10, 11
Baumgartner, T.A., 135–136
Beam, M., 231–232
Beaman, R., 26–27, 31, 242, 243
Beers, D.E., 355–356
Beilock, S.L., 63–64, 193–194, 195–196
Belcher, D., 132, 133
Bell, L.A., 24–25
Bem, S.L., 67–68
Bempechat, J., 194–195
Benbow, C.P., 82–83, 94
Benenson, J.F., 250–251
Benner, A.D., 206
Bennett, L., 194
Bentley, K., 310–311, 314–315
Berenbaum, S.A., 23–24, 27–28, 85–86, 89–90, 241, 346
Berger, C., 175–176
Bergin, C., 338
Bergin, D., 338
Berndt, T.J., 159–160
Berry, R.Q. III., 320–321, 322
Besag, V.E., 250–251
Best, A.M., 311
Betts, L.R., 152
Beyer, C., 283, 284–285
Beyer, S., 12–13
Bhanot, R., 199–200
Bigler, R.S., 9, 28, 34, 44, 53–54, 56, 59, 60, 64–66, 68–69, 85–86, 90–91, 100–102, 103–105, 109, 121–122, 155, 156–157, 166, 167–169, 205–206, 207–208, 210–211, 212–213, 226, 229–230, 232, 245, 248, 251–252, 283, 303–304, 339–340, 352, 353, 355–356, 357–358
Bijou, S.W., 87
Biklen, S.K., 242–243
Billson, J.M., 318–319

Bimbi, D.S., 276–277
Bishaw, A., 342–343
Bjork, R., 237–238
Bjorklund, D.F., 86, 155
Black, W.W., 290–291
Blanchett, W.J., 315–316
Blair-Loy, M., 66
Blakemore, J.E.O., 85–86, 89–90, 98–99, 241, 346
Blatchford, P., 155–156
Bleeker, M.M., 29, 62, 63, 195–196, 199–200
Blessing, J.S., 68–69
Blomfield, C.J., 285
Bobo, L., 344
Bochenek, M., 267
Boekaerts, M., 240
Bohn, A., 357
Bohn, C.M., 175
Bolch, M.B., 267, 281–282
Bolen, R.M., 204
Bolland, J., 343
Bontempo, D.E., 274–275
Borders, A., 169–170
Borker, R.A., 24
Bornstein, D., 351
Boulton, M., 273
Bowen, N.K., 192
Bowman, P.J., 309
Boykin, A.W., 314
Boysen, G.A., 212
Braddock, J.H., 124, 144, 236–237
Bradford, J., 263–264
Bradford, S., 280, 285–287
Bradley, R.H., 231
Braswell, K., 341
Bray, S.R., 118, 131, 133–134
Brechwald, W.A., 159–160
Brescoll, V.L., 44, 63, 65
Bridgest, S.T., 303–304, 306, 310–311
Brines, S., 351
Brinkworth, M., 338
Broaddus, M., 196–197
Brody, C., 251–252
Brody, G.H., 206
Bronfenbrenner, U., 24, 83–84
Brooks-Gunn, J., 319–320, 342–343
Brophy, J., 25–26, 238–239

Brown, A.W., 267
Brown, B.B., 194
Brown, C.S., 6, 29–30, 31, 46–47, 48,
    63, 80–81, 85–86, 141–142, 169,
    191–192, 194–195, 196, 198, 199,
    200, 201–202, 203–204, 205, 206,
    207–208, 209, 234, 240, 244, 245,
    246, 304–305, 344
Brown, E., 53–54, 68–69
Brown, H., 24–25
Brown, J.R., 192
Brown, O., 337
Brown, R.P., 46–47, 171
Brown, S.D., 264–265, 266, 277, 292–293
Brown, T.L., 323–324
Bruce, N.W., 249
Brückner, H., 278
Bryant, A.L., 274–275
Bryant, D., 339
Bryden, M.P., 51, 82–83, 94
Brzustoski, P., 338, 352–353
Buchanan, C.M., 263, 270
Buchanan, N.T., 64–65
Buhs, E.S., 273
Bukowski, W.M., 159–160, 172
Burchinal, M., 339
Burg, S., 9
Burk-Braxton, C., 205, 207–208
Burr, J.E., 175
Bush, V.L., 312–313, 315–316
Bussey, K., 87–88, 354
Buswell, B.N., 9, 55
Butler, R., 8, 15, 16–19, 20, 21, 22–23,
    45–46, 62, 85–86, 94, 128, 130, 174,
    233–234, 240, 243, 266, 274, 304–305
Buxton, C., 292–293
Byrd, J.E., 66–67
Byrd, T., 231, 242, 243–244,
    251–252
Byrd-Craven, J., 176

C

Cahill, S., 273–274
Cairney, J., 118, 131, 133–134
Caldwell, K., 152
Cale, L., 134
Calhoun, C., 287, 288
Callanan, M.A., 196

Callina, K.S., 83–84
Cameron, L., 155, 171, 194–195
Cameron, R., 309
Campbell, W.K., 12, 21
Cannon, E., 344
Caprara, G.V., 49, 57, 63
Carby, H.V., 312–313, 314
Card, N.A., 176
Cark, E., 53–54, 68–69
Carlson, A., 337
Carpenter, L.J., 144–145
Carpenter, T.P., 193, 244
Carrington, B.B., 193, 241
Carter, D.B., 154
Carter, J.A., 141–142
Casey, B., 98–99
Caspersen, C.J., 118
Castenell, L.A., 319–320
Caton, M.T., 321–322
Cavalier, D., 102–103
Cavell, T.A., 338
Ceci, S.J., 27–28, 44, 64–65
Centers, R.E., 98–99
Chadwell, D.W., 168–169, 226, 229,
    233–234, 237, 241
Chambers, S., 195, 198
Chang, A., 98–99, 196
Chavous, T.M., 309–310
Chen, A., 129
Chen, L., 342
Chen, J., 203–204
Chen, Y.F., 206
Chesir-Teran, D., 287, 290–291
Chhin, C.S., 29, 62, 63, 195–196
Chinn, L., 29, 34, 169–170, 191–192, 202,
    210, 234–235, 269, 278, 292–293, 303,
    305, 310–311
Chiodo, D., 203–204
Chiu, Y.-J.I., 345–348
Chomitz, V.R., 119
Chong, E.S.K., 278–279
Chow, A., 198–199
Christensen, A.E., 82–83
Chronaki, A., 195–196
Chu, H., 205, 207–208
Cianciotto, J., 273–274
Clance, P., 14
Clark, R.A., 4–5, 7–8, 66–67

Clarke, G., 200
Clasen, L.S., 236
Clear, E.R., 212
Cleveland, N., 132, 133
Clifford, R.M., 339
Clifton, R., 132
Clotfelter, C.T., 337
Coard, S.I., 310–311, 314–315
Cochran, S.D., 273
Cockburn, C., 200
Cohen, G.L., 70, 267, 338
Cohen, J., 49–50
Coker, A.L., 212
Colburne, K.A., 154, 155–156
Coleman, C.C., 152, 250
Collier, D., 312–313, 315–316
Collins, K.E., 285–286
Collinsworth, L.L., 213, 246
Compas, B.E., 208–209
Conchas, G.Q., 353
Conn, S., 145
Connolly, J.A., 203–204, 245, 246, 250–251
Connor-Smith, J.K., 208–209
Conoley, J.C., 346
Conroy, D.E., 201
Conway, J.K., 227
Cook, C.R., 262
Cook, J.M., 156–157
Cook, P., 340
Cook-Craig, P.G., 212
Cooper, B.S., 227
Cooper, C.E., 168, 205–206, 229–230, 233–234, 237, 238–239, 240
Cooper, H., 6, 235
Cooper, S., 309
Coopersmith, J., 338
Copping, K.E., 307, 344
Corbett, C., 82, 94–95, 197–198
Corno, L., 240
Cornwell, C., 82
Corrigall, E., 59–60, 68
Cortina, K.S., 30, 325–326
Cortina, L.M., 64–65, 209
Corwyn, R.F., 231
Costello, E.J., 273
Cothran, D.J., 126–127, 129–130, 137–138, 140–142
Coutinho, M.J., 311

Covatto, A.M., 250
Covington, M.V., 13
Cowen, E.L., 310–311
Coyle, E.F., 6, 9, 28, 98, 103, 109, 110, 174, 240, 241, 303–304, 347–348
Coyle, E.J., 69–70
Craig, W.M., 203–204, 245, 246, 250–251
Cramer, J., 12–13
Craske, M.L., 14
Craven, R., 20–21
Craver, C.B., 9
Crawford, G., 312–313, 351–352
Crick, N.R., 175
Crisp, R.J., 291
Crocker, J., 15, 21
Crocker, P.R.E., 131
Croosk, C., 203–204
Crosby, F., 206
Croson, R., 22
Cross, S., 130–131, 132
Crowley, K., 196
Crowley, M., 53
Cuadrado, J., 337
Cullerton-Sen, C., 175
Culotta, C.M., 344
Cundiff, J., 110
Cunningham, M., 337, 341, 345–346
Cureton, K.J., 118, 134
Cvencek, A., 9–10
Cvencek, D., 198
Czopp, A.M., 212

D

Dade, C., 309
Daley, A., 285
Daly, P., 231
Damon, W., 280–281, 293
Daniels, E.A., 138
Darley, J.M., 319–320
Darling, N., 285
Datnow, A., 253, 353
Daubman, K.A., 24–25
D'Augelli, A.R., 262, 263, 269–270, 274–275, 279–280, 281–282
David, C.F., 343
David-Ferdon, C.F., 343
Davidson, W., 13, 30–31, 243
Davies, K., 196–197

Davis, C.H.F. III., 321–322
Davis, G.Y., 309
Davis, J.E., 313, 317, 337–338, 353
Davis-Kean, P.E., 199–200, 246–247
Dawes, M., 340
Dawkins, M.P., 124, 144
Dawson, G.F., 119
Dawson, J.D., 117–118
De Munter, A., 202
de Vries, B., 263–264
De Winter, A.F., 175–176
DeBare, I., 227–228
Debus, R.L., 20–21
DeCrescenzo, T., 269, 279–280
DeGennaro, D., 323–324
Del Río, M.F., 198
Deleon, J., 279–280
Delpit, L., 339, 345–346
Denault, A.S., 285
DeRosier, M.E., 263–264
Devine, P.G., 319–320
Devos, T., 198
Dey, E.L., 290
Di Leone, L., 344
Diaz, E.M., 204, 269–270, 276, 288, 290, 291
Diaz, R.M., 273, 281–282
DiBiase, R., 231–232
Dickhäuser, O., 198–199
DiDonato, M.D., 175, 176, 178–179
Diekman, A.B., 53–54, 68–69, 196–197
Diesendruck, G., 155
Dietrich, J., 269
Diez Roux, A., 351
DiGiovanni, C.D., 262, 263–264, 267–268, 271, 272–274, 281–284
Dill, K.E., 196
Dillow, S.A., 2–3
Dimito, A., 266
Dinella, L., 60–61, 67, 68, 157–158
DiPrete, T.A., 202
Dishion, T.J., 159–160
DiTomasso, N.A., 344
Doan, S.N., 202
Dolan-Pascoe, B., 55
Doll, M., 279–280
Domangue, E.A., 135, 136–138

Domene, J.F., 57
Donnelly, J.E., 119
Doty, N.D., 281–282
Dovidio, J.F., 44, 63, 65
Downer, J., 341–342
Downey, D.B., 238–239, 340
Drill, K., 287–288
DuBois, D.L., 6, 205, 207–208
Duckworth, A.L., 13–14, 31
Dunbar, M.D., 201
Duncan, A., 244
Duncan, G.J., 342–343
Dunkel, S.B., 343
Dupeyrat, C., 9–10, 20–21
Durik, A.M., 58
Duveen, G., 166–167
Dweck, C.S., 7–8, 13–14, 30–31, 130–131, 142, 243
Dyer, G., 249

E

Eagly, A.H., 48, 52, 53, 54, 84–85
Early, D.M., 339
Eberhardt, J.L., 344
Eccles, J.S., 6, 9–11, 27, 28, 29, 30–31, 45–46, 45*f*, 49, 50, 57, 58–59, 61–62, 66, 71, 82, 91, 119, 128–129, 130–131, 192, 195–196, 198–200, 201, 233–234, 246–247, 262, 285, 319–320, 338
Egan, S.K., 194–195, 234
Egger, H.L., 273
Ehri, L.C., 238
Eisenberg, M.E., 267, 281–282
Eisenberg, R., 17–18
Ekstrom, R.B., 278
Eliot, L., 167–169, 210–211, 339–340, 353, 355–356, 357–358
Elliot, A.J., 7–8, 130–131, 142
Elliot, L., 226
Ellis, A., 50, 57
Else-Quest, N.M., 48, 57, 63, 84–85, 198–199, 238–239, 337
Elze, D.E., 273–274, 288–289
Engel, M., 242
England, D.E., 171–172, 173
Enna, B., 13, 30–31, 243
Ennis, C.D., 122–123, 126–128, 129–130, 140–141

Ericson, B., 80–81, 80f
Escribe, C., 9–10, 20–21
Espelage, D.L., 263–264, 268–269, 271, 276, 290, 292
Essex, M.J., 66–67
Evans, A.B., 344
Evans, L., 196–197
Evans, M., 323–324
Evans, S.M., 155
Evenson, K., 351
Ewing, M.E., 319–320

F

Fabes, R.A., 23–24, 85–86, 154–156, 157–158, 159–160, 163–164, 165, 167–170, 175, 176, 177, 178–180, 202, 210–211, 226, 229–230, 233–234, 237, 238–239, 240, 241, 250–251, 291, 340, 355–356, 357–358
Faddis, B.J., 231–232
Fagot, B.I., 339–340
Fagrell, G., 127
Fann, M.D., 319–320
Farago, F., 166–167
Farfield, H., 84–85
Faris, R., 177
Farkas, G., 198–199
Farmer, T.W., 348
Farnham, S.D., 191
Faught, B.E., 118, 131, 133–134
Favreau, O.E., 202
Feagans, L., 200, 202, 344
Fedewa, A.L., 290–291
Feldman, A.F., 285
Felmee, D., 177
Feng, J., 69
Fennema, E., 193, 244
Ferguson, A.A., 310–311, 312–313, 315
Ferguson, R.F., 310–311, 312–313, 315, 317, 321–322
Ferrara, M.M., 249
Ferrell, J., 171, 194–195
Ferrer-Caja, E., 129
Field, R.D., 173
Field, T., 250
Filipowicz, A.T., 98–99
Fineran, S., 194, 204, 246
Finkelstein, N.D., 70

Finnie, L., 199
Fisher, B.S., 212
Fiske, S.T., 190–191, 314–315
Floyd, F.J., 276–277
Foderaro, L., 354
Foehr, U.G., 69
Folkman, S., 208–209
Fontenot, K., 342–343
Forbes, C., 46–47
Forbes, G.B., 201
Ford, D.Y., 315–316
Ford, K.R., 309–310
Fordham, S., 340
Fox, M.A., 303
Francis, B.B., 193
Franklin-Stokes, A., 21
Fredenburg, K., 132, 133
Fredricks, J.A., 201, 285, 319–320
Freedman-Doan, C., 27, 61–62, 82, 195
Freedson, P.S., 118, 134
Freeman, P., 50
French, J., 242
French, K., 131
French, P., 242
Frenzel, A.C., 27
Frey, K.S., 10, 17–19
Friedel, J.M., 30
Friedman, C. K., 209
Friedman, M.S., 262, 263, 270, 274–275
Frome, P., 61–62, 82, 192, 195
Frome, P.M., 29, 66
Frosh, S., 263, 271, 290, 292
Fryer, R.G., 334, 340, 348
Fulcher, M., 57, 60–61, 62–63, 67, 68
Fuller, F., 337
Fuller, K., 251–252
Fuller-Rowell, T.E., 202
Funderburk, J.R., 209
Futterman, R., 6, 45–46, 45f, 58–59, 91

G

Gaertner, B.M., 171–172, 177, 179–180
Gaertner, L., 16–17
Gale, A., 29, 191–192, 202, 248–249, 269, 278, 292–293, 351–352, 357
Galligan, K.M., 168–170, 202
Ganley, C.M., 47
Garcia Coll, C., 110

Garcia, D.M., 229
Garcia, J., 70, 267, 338, 352–353
Garcia, L.S., 212
García-Cuesta, S., 195
Garcia-Vazquez, E., 346
Garn, A.C., 124–125, 135
Garofalo, R., 263–264, 279–280
Gardner, R., III., 315–316
Garrahy, D.A., 193
Gauthier, R., 155–156
Gauze, C., 172
Gay, G., 346–347
Ge, X., 206
Geary, D.C., 86, 155, 176
Gelman, S.A., 155, 156–157
Gentile, B., 55
Gerson, H., 69–70
Gewirtz, J.C., 156–157, 194–195
Gheen, M.H., 21
Gibb, A.C., 337
Gibbons, A., 68–69
Gibbons, F.X., 206
Gibson, D., 229–230, 233–234, 355–356
Gill, D.L., 132, 285–286
Gillespie, J., 311–312
Gilliam, W.S., 337–338
Gini, G., 262, 273
Ginton, R., 156–157
Glaser, H.M., 243–244
Glick, G.C., 194–195
Glick, P., 190–191
Glienke, B.B., 9
Gneezy, U., 22
Goble, P.M., 155–156, 163–164, 178–179
Godes, O., 58
Goertz, M.E., 278
Goetz, T., 9, 27
Goff, P.A., 344
Goff, S.B., 6, 45–46, 45f, 58–59, 91
Gogtay, N., 236
Gold, M.A., 274–275
Goldberg, W.A., 62–63
Goldfein-Elbaz, R., 155
Goldsmith, H.H., 238–239, 337
Goldstein, S.E., 246–247
Golinkoff, R.M., 98–99
Golly, A., 345
Gonzalez, K.A., 290–291

Good, C., 47, 70
Good, T., 238–239
Goodenow, C., 273–274, 278–279, 283–284
Goodkind, S., 235, 337, 355–356
Gootman, J.A., 285
Gordeeva, T., 9
Gosetti, P., 251–252
Goudreau, J., 234–235
Grabe, S., 55, 204
Graham, M.J., 44, 63, 65
Graham, R., 263–264
Graham, S., 206, 263–264, 272–273, 282–283, 318, 346
Gralinski, J.H., 12–13
Granger, K.L., 166–167
Grant, L., 312–313
Grantham, T.C., 316
Grasshof, M., 9
Graves, R., 250
Graves, S., 341
Gray, V., 227
Green, V.A., 65–66, 205, 212–213, 245, 251–252
Greene, M.L., 206
Greenstein, D.K., 236
Greenwald, A.G., 9–10, 191, 198
Gregory, A., 278, 310–311
Greytak, E.A., 204, 269–270, 276, 288, 290, 291
Griffin, P., 283, 284–286
Grodsky, E., 107–108
Grossman, A.H., 263, 269, 270, 279–280
Grov, C., 276–277
Guan, J., 133–134
Guerino, P., 337
Guerra, N.G., 262, 342–343
Gulam, W., 319–320
Gulko, J., 154, 155–156
Gunderson, E.A., 63–64, 193–194, 195–196
Gupta Karkhanis, D., 316
Gurian, M., 86, 167–168, 210, 236, 237, 239, 249, 339–340
Gurin, G., 290
Gurin, P., 290
Gwadz, M., 269–270

H

Hacker, K.A., 119
Hackett, G., 264–265, 266, 277, 292–293
Halim, M.L., 205–206
Hall, I.I., 193
Hall, R.E., 318–319
Hallinan, M.T., 248–249
Halpern, D.F., 86, 95–96, 167–169, 210–211, 226, 355–356, 357–358
Halverson, C.F., 90–91, 156–157
Hamilton, L., 334
Hamilton, M.C., 196–197
Hamm, J.V., 348
Hand, J.Z., 246
Hand, L.L., 69, 94
Handelsman, J., 44, 63, 65
Hanish, L.D., 23–24, 85–86, 155–156, 157–158, 159–160, 163–164, 165, 167–170, 175, 176, 177, 178–180, 210–211, 226, 241, 250, 291, 340, 355–356, 357–358
Hannover, B., 247–248
Hansen, A.L., 288
Hansen, D.M., 262
Hansot, E., 226–227
Harackiewicz, J.M., 7–8, 29–30, 58, 62
Harber, K.D., 193, 344
Hardesty, J.L., 205, 207–208
Hare, B.R., 319–320
Harker, R., 231
Harold, R.D., 6, 9–10, 27, 29
Harper, G.W., 279–280
Harper, S.R., 320–322
Harradine, C., 343
Harris, F., 318–319
Harris, J.R., 134, 154, 160
Harrison, K., 196
Harrison, L., 127, 130, 138–139, 140–141, 143
Harry, B., 302, 310–311, 314, 315–316
Hartley, B.L., 202
Hatzenbuehler, M.L., 287, 288
Hawley, P.H., 176
Hayes, A.R., 9, 34, 64–65, 68–69, 85–86, 109, 110, 121–122, 167–168, 169, 210, 211, 230, 231, 232, 252, 283, 303–304, 339–340, 341, 353, 357–358
Hayes, D.M., 341

Hayes, J., 97–98
Head, D., 341–342
Heath, G.W., 118, 134
Heatherington, L., 24–25
Heatherton, T.F., 199
Hebblethwaite, C., 248
Heck, K., 287, 288
Hedges, L.V., 49–50, 52
Hegarty, M., 82–83, 94
Heinze, J.E., 291
Helwig, R., 193
Hemphill, F.C., 334
Henderson, K., 245, 250–251
Hendricks, B.L., 58
Hendrickson, A., 195, 198
Henfield, M.S., 321–323
Henley, P., 86, 167–168
Henly, S.J., 343
Herbert, J., 192, 193
Herrero-Taylor, T., 309
Hershberger, S.L., 262, 269–270, 281–282
Herzog, M., 159–160
Hessler, E.E., 175, 178–179
Heyman, G.D., 10–11, 171
Hidi, S., 27–28, 237–238
Higgins, E.T., 17–18
Hill, C., 82, 197–198
Hill, J.P., 11
Hill, M., 323–324
Hill, S.A., 307
Hilliard, L.J., 109, 154, 166, 170–171, 248
Hills, L.A., 138, 143
Himmelstein, K.E., 278
Himsel, A., 62–63
Hines, M., 85–86
Hinkley, J.W., 20–21
Hintsanen, M., 31
Hirsch, L.M., 62
Hirsh-Pasek, K., 98–99
Hirt, E.R., 13–14
Hoard, M.K., 176
Hoffman, L.W., 5–6
Hoffman, M.L., 155–156
Hoge, D.R., 337
Hogg, M.A., 156–157
Holahan, C.J., 209
Holt, K., 20–21
Holzman, M., 311

Honora, D., 316
Horn, S.S., 194–195, 276–277, 287–289, 291
Horner, M.S., 5–6
Horvat, E.M., 325
Howard, C., 309
Howard, T.C., 303
Howes, C., 177, 339
Hoza, B., 172
Hubbard, L., 253, 353
Hudley, C., 311
Huebner, D.M., 262, 273, 281–282
Huet, N., 9–10, 20–21
Hughes, D., 287, 290–291, 309, 342
Hughes, J.M., 65, 205–206
Hughes, J.N., 338
Hughes, R., 203–204
Hulette, E., 239–240, 250
Hulleman, C.S., 29–30, 58, 62
Humphries, M., 244
Hunter, J., 269–270, 274–275, 278–279
Hurtado, A., 192
Hurtado, S., 290
Hutchings, M.M., 193
Hutchison, K.B., 233
Huynh, V.W., 191–192, 206, 207–208
Hyde, J.S., 3–4, 6, 9, 27, 28, 29–30, 48–50, 51, 52, 55, 57, 62, 63, 66–67, 69, 80–81, 82–83, 84–86, 91, 96–97, 100, 110, 128–129, 167–169, 174, 193–194, 197–199, 203–204, 210–211, 212, 226, 229–230, 233–234, 237–239, 240, 253, 262, 266, 270, 271–272, 273, 303–305, 337, 355–356, 357–358
Hyde, W.D., 86
Hymel, S., 348

I

Imes, S.A., 14
Inzlicht, M., 46–47
Iruka, I.U., 343
Irvine, J.J., 316–317, 339, 345–346
Irving, M.A., 311
Ispa, J.M., 306–307
Ito, T.A., 70

J

Jacklin, C.N., 154, 163, 339–340
Jackson, A.S., 135–136
Jackson, C., 26
Jackson, C.D., 193
Jackson, C.K., 168
Jackson, M.C., 344
Jacob, S., 287–288
Jacobs, J.E., 6, 9–11, 29, 61–62, 63, 82, 195–196, 199–200
Jaffe, P., 203–204
James, A.N., 168–169
Jansen-Yeh, E., 175
Janz, K.F., 117–118
Jay, J., 118, 131, 133–134
Jean-Baptiste, E., 341–342
Jelenec, P., 198
Jencks, C., 334
Jewell, J.A., 194–195, 201–202
Jiang, D., 203–204
Jodl, K., 61
Johannesen-Schmidt, M.C., 54
Johns, M., 46–47, 70
Johnson, D.J., 309
Johnson, K.E., 27
Johnson, M.S., 201
Johnson, S.P., 82–83
Johnson, W., 58
Johnston, A., 53–54, 68–69
Johnston, L.D., 274–275
Jokela, M., 31
Jones, E., 237–238
Jones, I., 98–99
Jones, M.A., 337–338
Jones, S., 193, 202
Joseph, A.A., 355–356
Josephs, R.A., 46–47
Jouanjean, A., 156–157
Jovanovic, J., 199–200, 239–240
Joyner, T.N., 323–324
Jussim, L., 30–31, 193, 344
Juvonen, J., 263–264, 272–273, 282–283

K

Kaczala, C.M., 6, 30–31, 45–46, 45f, 58–59, 61, 91
Kafer, K., 167–168
Kaiser, C.R., 209
Kaminer, W., 231
Kamphuis, J.H., 262
Kane, E., 191–192

Kanitkar, K., 245
Kaplan, H.B., 233–234
Kaplan, R., 193, 302, 304–305, 307, 325–326
Karau, S., 54
Karimpour, R., 179–180
Karkkainen, R., 62
Kasanen, K., 62
Kastens, K.A., 82–83
Katzew, A., 143–144, 146
Katz-Wise, S., 262, 270, 271–272, 273
Kaukiainen, A., 213
Keating, C.F., 175
Keating, D.P., 57, 58
Keefe, K., 159–160
Keener, E., 169
Kegeles, S.M., 262
Keiper, S., 30–31
Kelleher, C., 97
Keller, B.K., 195–196
Keller, C., 193
Kelley, K., 27
Kelley, W.M., 199
Kemp, C., 26–27, 31, 242, 243
Kendrick, M.H., 314
Kennedy, C.L., 123–124
Kenney-Benson, G.A., 24–25, 30
Kenny, S., 28
Kersh, J.E., 98–99
Kerstetter, D.L., 200
Kessels, U., 25, 198–199, 202, 247–248
Kessler-Harris, A., 70–71
KewalRamani, A., 303
Keyes, K.M., 287, 288
Khmelkov, V.T., 248–249
Kiefer, S. M., 202
Kiesler, S., 97
Killen, M., 248–249, 340
Kim, A., 199
Kim, T.E., 262
Kim, Y.K., 316
Kindermann, T.A., 159–160
King, B., 107–108
King, K.M., 274–275
King, R.B., 342–343
King, S.S., 239–240
Kirk, D., 138
Kistner, J.A., 343
Kitayama, S., 11–12

Kizzie, K.T., 325–326
Klein, M.H., 66–67
Klein, S., 167–168, 210, 226, 227–228, 353
Kleine, M., 9
Kleitman, S., 285
Kling, K.C., 9, 55
Kochenderfer, B.J., 152, 250, 263–264
Koenig, B.W., 262, 263–264, 267–268, 271–274, 276, 281–284
Koeske, G.F., 262, 263, 270
Koestner, J., 13–14
Koestner, R., 13–14
Kohlberg, L., 87, 89–90
Konrad, A.M., 59–60, 68
Kornienko, O., 155–156, 163–164, 166–167
Korr, W.S., 262, 263, 270
Kosciw, J.G., 194–195, 204, 269–270, 276, 287–289, 290, 291
Kostroski, O., 290, 291
Kost-Smith, L.E., 70
Koul, R., 22
Kowalski, K., 245
Kreider, R.M., 341
Krendl, A.C., 199
Krogh, H.R., 205–206
Kunjufu, J., 310–311, 314
Kurita, J.A., 156–157
Kurland, B., 199–200
Kurman, J., 9–10
Kurtz-Costes, B., 29, 191–192, 200, 202, 248–249, 269, 278, 292–293, 302, 304–305, 307, 341, 344, 351–352, 357
Kusku, F., 71
Kwan, M.Y., 118, 131, 133–134

L

La Freniere, P., 155–156
Lacasse, A., 203–204
Ladd, G.W., 152, 250, 263–264, 273
Ladd, H.F., 337
Ladson-Billings, G., 267, 269, 321, 353
Lalonde, R.N., 206
Lamb, L.M., 212, 245, 251–252
Lambert, K., 348
Lambourne, K., 119
Lane, K.A., 193–194
Lanza, S., 9, 10–11

Lareau, A., 325
Largie, S., 250
Larson, J., 194
Larson, R.W., 262, 280–281
Larsson, H., 127
Laub, C., 283, 287, 288, 290, 291
Lavy, V., 26–27, 193, 238–239, 242
Laying, K.L., 348
Lazarus, R.S., 208–209
Lazear, E.P., 242–243
Leaper, C., 6, 28, 29–30, 31, 46–47, 48, 52, 53, 61–62, 63, 80–81, 85–86, 141–142, 154, 160–161, 169, 192, 194–195, 196, 198, 199–200, 203–204, 207–208, 209, 234, 240, 244, 245, 246–247, 304–305, 344
Lee, A.M., 119, 130–132, 133
Lee, C., 283, 284–285, 305
Lee, D.L., 348
Lee, E., 195
Lee, J.S., 192, 267, 269
Lee, O., 292–293
Lee, V.E., 66, 231, 242, 243–244, 251–252
Leffingwell, R.J., 193
Legare, C.H., 10–11
Legewie, J., 202
Leibham, M.E., 27
Leinhardt, G., 242
Le-Maner-Idrissi, G., 156–157
Lenney, E., 15
Lenroot, R.K., 236
Lent, R.W., 264–265, 266, 277, 292–293
Leonard, S., 157–158, 159–160
Lerdpornkulrat, T., 22
Lerner, R.M., 83–84
Levine, S.C., 63–64, 193–194, 195–196
Levitt, J., 316
Levitt, S.D., 334
Lewis, C.W., 348
Lewis, J.M., 341
Lezin, G., 97–98
Li, Q., 193
Li, Y., 110, 211, 230, 231
Libbey, H.P., 285
Liben, L.S., 6, 9, 28, 34, 44, 56, 59, 60, 68, 69–70, 82–83, 85–86, 89–92, 96, 98, 100, 103, 109, 110, 121–122, 154, 155, 156–157, 166, 167–168, 169, 170–171, 174, 205–206, 210, 211, 212, 226–227, 229–230, 237, 238–239, 240, 241, 245, 248, 250–252, 283, 303–304, 339–340, 346, 347–348, 353
Lieb, P., 59–60, 68
Lindahl, K.M., 281–282
Lindberg, S.M., 50, 51, 57, 62, 80–81, 197–198, 204
Lindenberg, S., 175–176
Lindner, N.M., 198
Linn, M.C., 48, 50, 51, 52, 57, 63, 80–81, 82–83, 84–85, 197–199
Linver, M.R., 319–320, 323–324
Lipkin, A., 289
Lipsanen, J., 31
Little, T.D., 9, 176
Liu, X., 233–234
Lloyd, B., 166–167
Lobel, T.E., 156–157, 194–195, 339–340
Loftus, S.J., 126–127, 137–138, 140–142
Long, J.D., 175–176
Lopez, C.M., 343
Losen, D.J., 202, 311–312
Lowell, E.L., 4–5, 7–8
Lozada, F., 29, 191–192, 202, 248–249, 269, 278, 292–293, 351–352, 357
Lubienski, S.T., 192
Lubinski, C.A., 193, 244
Lubinski, D., 82–83, 94
Lucas, T., 346–347
Lucas-Thompson, R., 62–63
Lucey, A.B., 285–286
Lüdtke, O., 9–10, 11
Ludwig, J., 340
Lundeberg, M.A., 242–243
Lundy, B., 250
Lupart, J.L., 344
Lutz, B.J., 326
Lynch, M.E., 11
Lytton, H., 27–28

M

Ma, X., 58
Macartney, S., 342–343
Maccoby, E.E., 23–24, 34–35, 152, 154, 160–161, 162–163, 168–169, 171, 339–340
Madden-Derdich, Debra A., 165

Madon, S., 30–31
Maeda, Y., 51
Mael, F.A., 229–230, 231, 233–234, 355–356
Magley, V.J., 208–209
Mahar, M.T., 135–136
Maholmes, V., 342–343
Mahoney, L.T., 117–118
Maitino, A., 55
Major, B., 208–209
Majors, R., 318–320
Makhijani, M., 54
Malanchuk, O., 61, 246–247
Malik, N.M., 281–282
Mallon, G.P., 269, 279–280
Maltz, D.N., 24
Manago, A., 192
Mandara, J., 307–308, 323–324
Mandel, O., 16
Manke, E., 290, 291
Margie, N.G., 248–249
Mark, A.Y, 212
Markovits, H., 250–251
Marks, H.M., 231, 242, 243–244, 251–252
Markus, H.R., 11–12, 33–34, 130–131, 132
Marques, J.M., 155
Marsh, H.W., 11, 20–21, 229, 231, 241, 285
Marshal, M.P., 274–275
Martens, A., 70
Martin, A., 241
Martin, C.L., 23–24, 27–28, 85–86, 88, 89–91, 154–158, 159–160, 163–164, 165, 166–167, 168–170, 171–172, 173, 175, 176, 177, 178–180, 205, 210–211, 241, 250–251, 291, 340
Masten, C.L., 191–192, 206, 207–208
Master, A., 70, 267, 338, 352–353
Mathason, L., 69
Martinez, T.E., 311
Matjasko, J.L., 285
Matsumoto, H., 11–12
Matthews, C.E., 292–293
Matthews, J.S., 238–239, 325–326
Mayes, T.A., 246
Mays, V.M., 273
McAllister, G., 316–317, 339, 345–346
McBride, C., 250
McBride, R., 133–134

McCarthy, J.D., 337
McClain, O.L., 322
McClelland, D.C., 4–5, 7–8
McCloskey, L.A., 24
McClowry, S.G., 337
McCormack, M., 270–271
McCray, A.D., 303–304, 306, 310–311
McCrea, S.M., 13–14
McDaniel, M., 237–238
McDermott, C., 191–192
McDougall, P., 263, 270
McGee, E., 322
McGinn, A., 351
McGowan, R.J., 119
McGraw, R., 192
McGuire, J.K., 263, 267, 269, 270, 279–280, 290, 291
McKinney, M.K., 343
McLean, A., 84–85
McLoyd, V.C., 193, 302, 304–305, 307, 325–326
McMaster, L.E., 203–204, 246
McPherson, M., 156–157
Meadow, N.G., 69, 94
Meece, J.L., 6, 9, 20–21, 30–31, 45–46, 45f, 58–59, 91
Meehan, B.T., 338
Meegan, S.P., 250
Mehta, C.M., 154, 155, 169
Mellott, D.S., 191
Meltzoff, A.N., 9–10, 198
Menashri, J., 339–340
Mendelson, M.J., 203–204
Mensinger, J.L., 251–252
Mercer, S.H., 263–264
Mercier, E.M., 198
Mereish, E.H., 195, 204, 245, 262, 263–264, 267–268, 271, 272–274, 281–283, 326, 346
Merrell, C., 241
Mertz, J.E., 168
Messner, M.A., 201, 285–286
Meyer, I.H., 264–265, 269–270, 275, 278–279, 293
Michael, A., 61
Michael, R.S., 278, 312, 337
Midgley, C., 13–14, 21, 30
Mikulski, B., 233

Miles, J., 274–275
Miller, C.T., 171–172, 177, 179–180, 208–209
Miller, D.I., 95–96
Miller, P.H., 68–69
Milner, H.R., 316–317
Miner, K.N., 64–65
Mingle, L.A., 47
Ming-Te, M., 338
Minton, S., 213
Miranda, A.H., 315–316
Mischel, W., 87
Mishna, F., 285
Mistry, R., 200, 202, 344
Mitchell, S.E., 119
Miyake, A., 70
Mliner, S., 175
Moghaddam, F.M., 206
Moller, L.C., 154, 155–156
Monaghan, E.J., 226–227
Moneta, G., 262
Monteith, M.J., 212
Moore, D.S., 82–83
Moore, L., 351
Moos, R.H., 209
Moradi, B., 209
Morgan, H., 314
Morris, E.W., 312–313
Morris, Z.E., 58
Morrison, F.J., 238–239
Morrow, R.G., 285–286
Morse, S., 229
Moscato, S., 251–252
Mosley, M., 289
Moss, A., 159–160
Moss-Racusin, C.A., 44, 63, 65
Moynihan, D.P., 341
Muller, C., 107–108, 198–199, 263–264, 267–268, 269, 272, 276, 277
Muller Mirza, N., 34–35
Mullola, S., 31
Munro, P., 121
Muraco, A., 283
Murdock, T.B., 267, 281–282
Murnen, S.K., 196–197
Murray, C.B., 323–324
Murray, L., 273
Murry, V.M., 206

Mustard, D.B., 82
Muzzatti, B., 198
Myers, D.R., 345
Myhill, D., 193, 202

N

Nagel, N., 251–252
Nagy, G., 9–10, 11
Nakamoto, J., 262
Nanín, J.E., 276–277
Nardo, A.C., 278, 302, 312, 337
Nash, R., 231
Neal, L.V.I., 303–304, 306, 310–311
Neblett, E.W., 309–310
Neff, K.D., 205–206
Nelson, D., 97–98
Nelson, S., 13, 30–31, 243
Nesdale, D., 340
Neumark, N., 155
Newcomb, A.F., 172
Newcomb, T., 98
Newcombe, N.S., 69, 98–99
Newcomer, R.R., 201
Newman, P.A., 285
Newstead, S.E., 21
Nguyen, H.X., 309–310
Nicholls, J.G., 7–8, 12
Nimmo, J., 237–238
Nipedal, C., 340
Nishina, A., 263–264, 272–273, 282–283
Noack, P., 198
Noguera, P.A., 278, 302, 303, 305, 310–311, 316, 317, 320–321, 324, 325
Nolen, S.B., 22
Nolen-Hoeksema, S., 15
Noll, R.B., 172
Nolle, K.L., 337
Norasakkunkit, V., 11–12
Nosek, B.A., 9–10, 191, 198
Nowell, A., 49–50, 52
Numtee, C., 176
Nunes, S.R., 238

O

Oakes, P.J., 156–157
O'Brien, C., 245
O'Brien, K.M., 58
O'Connor, K.M., 198

Odom, E., 341–342
Oettingen, G., 9
Ogbu, J.U., 340
Okeke-Adeyanju, N.A., 302, 304–305, 307, 341, 344
Olson, J.M., 206
Olweus, D., 175–176
O'Malley, P.M., 274–275
Omelich, C.L., 13
O'Moore, A., 213
Orfield, G., 305
Ormel, J., 175–176
Ormerod, A.J., 213, 246
Ortega, A.N., 273
Osborne, J.W., 317–318
Osgood, D.W., 9, 10–11
O'Shaughnessy, M., 287, 288
Oshima, T.C., 12–13
Osmer, E., 279–280
Ostrov, J.M., 175
Oswald, D.P., 311
Ozbilgin, M.F., 71

P

Pace, G., 251–252
Pahl, K., 206
Pahlke, E.E., 65–66, 110, 168, 169–170, 202, 205, 210–211, 212–213, 229–230, 231, 232, 233–234, 237, 238–239, 240, 250, 252, 357–358
Pajares, F., 10, 16
Pakalka, A.H., 201
Pálmen, R., 195
Palmer, R.T., 318–319
Paluck, E.L., 348
Palumbo, P., 30–31
Park, L.E., 15
Parker, J.G., 159–160
Parsons, J.E., 30–31
Parsons, J.T., 276–277
Pascoe, C.J., 195, 263, 270, 271, 290, 292
Pashler, H., 237–238
Pastoreli, C., 49, 57, 63
Patal, E.A., 235
Patrick, H., 24–25, 30, 274
Patterson, C.J., 62–63
Patterson, G.R., 159–160
Patterson, M.M., 205–206, 231, 250

Pattman, R., 263, 271, 290, 292
Pausch, R., 97
Payne, A.A., 337–338
Pearson, J., 263–264, 267–268, 269, 272, 276, 277
Peckham, P., 12–13
Peden, B., 318–319
Pekrun, R., 9, 27
Pellegrini, A.D., 155, 175–176
Pennington, G.L., 206
Pepler, D.J., 203–204, 245, 246, 250–251
Perret-Clermont, A., 34–35
Perry, D., 194–195
Perry, D.G., 234
Perry, L.A., 213, 246
Perry, M., 47
Perry, T., 351–352
Perry, W., 319–320
Petersen, A.C., 51, 82–83
Petersen, J., 3–4, 6, 9, 27, 28, 51, 80–81, 82–83, 84–86, 91, 100, 110, 128–129, 174, 193–194, 197–198, 237–238, 240, 266, 303–305
Petersen, J.L., 80–81, 197–198, 203–204
Petersen, J.S., 80–81, 82–83, 84–86, 91, 100, 110
Peterson, P.L., 193, 244
Peterson, R.L., 278, 302, 312, 337
Pettigrew, T.F., 169
Phillips, M.G., 121–122, 144, 334
Phoenix, A., 263, 271, 290, 292
Pianta, R., 339
Picho, K., 199
Pickett, M.W., 124, 144
Pigott, R.L., 310–311
Pilkington, N.W., 281–282
Pinsky, S.L., 355–356
Pintrich, P.K., 7–8
Pipes McAdoo, H., 308
Piquero, A.R., 278
Pittinksy, T.L., 199
Plante, I., 202
Plummer, D.C., 271, 276, 290, 292
Poe-Yamagata, E., 337–338
Pollack, J.M., 278
Pollard, D., 242–243
Pollock, S.J., 70
Pomerantz, E.M., 14, 24–25, 30

Ponitz, C.C., 238–239
Pornpitakpan, C., 212
Poteat, V.P., 195, 204, 245, 262, 263–264, 267–269, 271–274, 276–277, 278–279, 281–284, 290, 292, 326, 346
Poulin, F., 285
Powlishta, K.K., 152, 154, 155–156, 171
Pozzoli, T., 262, 273
Pras, R., 156–157
Prause, J., 62–63
Preckel, F., 9
Preston, C., 24–25
Prinstein, M.J., 159–160
Prinzie, P., 262
Prioleau, M., 314
Pronin, E., 248
Purdie-Vaughns, V., 338, 352–353
Purdy, K.T., 203–204
Pustjens, H., 202

Q
Qin, H., 97–98
Quinn, D.M., 46–47
Quinn, K.A., 206
Quinn, P.C., 82–83

R
Ralston, P., 175
Rahman, T., 334
Ramirez, G., 63–64, 193–194, 195–196
Rao, A., 210
Rasinski, H.M., 212
Raty, H., 62
Rausch, M.K., 337
Ravaja, N., 31
Read, B.B., 193
Rebchook, G.M., 262
Redelius, K., 127
Reesing, A., 159–160
Regner, I., 9–10, 20–21
Reicher, S.D., 156–157
Reijntjes, A., 262
Reilly, D., 52
Renninger, K.A., 27–28, 237–238
Renold, E., 24–26
Resnick, M.D., 267, 281–282
Reyna, A. III., 124
Reynolds, C.R., 346

Reynolds, R., 306–308
Rhodes, M., 155, 338
Richeson, J.A., 199
Richman, S., 307
Rideout, V.J., 69
Ridgeway, C.L., 44, 71
Riegle-Crumb, C., 107–108, 198–199, 244, 304–305
Rimm-Kaufman, S.E., 345–348
Riordan, C., 231–232
Ripski, M.B., 310–311
Risser, W., 233–234
Ritchie, E., 59–60, 68
Ritter, S., 303, 337
Rivers, I., 269–270
Roach, K.A., 199–200
Roberts, D.F., 69
Roberts, G.C., 128
Roberts, T.A., 15
Robinson, P., 231
Robnett, R.D., 52, 53, 203, 204
Rock, D.A., 278
Rodger, S.H., 97–98
Rodkin, P.C., 175–176, 179–180
Rodriguez, A., 199
Rodriguez, E.T., 337
Rodriguez, J., 309
Roese, N.J., 206
Roeser, R.W., 262
Rogers, K., 229–230, 233–234, 355–356
Rogers, R., 289
Rogoff, B., 341–342
Rohrer, D., 237–238
Rolland, R.G., 21–22
Romney, D.M., 27–28
Ronholt, H., 141–142
Roper, A.P., 121–122, 144
Rosario, M., 269–270, 274–275, 278–279
Rose, A.J., 23–24, 160–161, 194–195
Rose, S., 357
Rose, V.C., 316, 322
Rosenberg, M., 279–280
Roseth, C.J., 175
Ross, L., 29, 191–192, 202, 248–249, 269, 278, 292–293, 351–352, 357
Rotenberg, K.J., 152
Roth, J.L., 319–320
Rothstein, R., 267

Rotter, J.B., 7
Rounds, J., 27, 44, 56
Rowe, D.A., 135–136
Rowell Huesmann, L., 342–343
Rowley, S.J., 29, 191–192, 200, 202, 248–249, 269, 278, 292–293, 302, 304–305, 307, 325–326, 341, 344, 351–352, 357
Roy, L., 22
Rozek, C.S., 29–30, 62
Rubel-Lifschitz, T., 27–28
Rubin, H.H., 337–338
Rubin, K.H., 159–160
Rubin, L., 191–192
Ruble, D.N., 10, 17–19, 23–24, 27–28, 85–86, 88, 89–90, 156–157, 171–172, 205–206
Rudman, L.A., 191
Rudolph, K.D., 23–24, 160–161
Russell, S.T., 194–195, 262, 263–264, 267–268, 269, 270, 271–272, 273, 279–280, 283–284, 287–289, 290, 291
Rutland, A., 155, 171, 194–195
Rutter, R.A., 337
Ryan, A.M., 21, 24–25, 30, 47, 152, 202, 274
Ryan, C., 273, 281–282
Ryan, K., 47
Ryckman, D.B., 12–13

S

Sabiston, C., 131
Sabo, D., 201
Sadek, S., 262
Sadker, D., 242, 243–244, 246, 251–252
Sadker, M., 242, 243–244, 246, 251–252
Saewyc, E., 194–195, 287–289
Sailes, G.A., 319–320
Sáinz, M., 195
Sallquist, J., 175, 176
Salmela-Aro, K., 198–199
Salmivalli, C., 213
Salomone, R.C., 210, 233–234, 239–240, 245, 251–252
Saltzman, H., 208–209
Sameroff, A., 61
Sanchez, J., 273, 281–282
Sanchez, L., 246

Sanders, K.A., 249
Sandfort, T.G.M., 273
Sandhofer, C.M., 196
Santos, C.E., 166–167, 202
Satina, B., 126–127, 137–138, 140–142
Saucier, D.A., 291
Savin-Williams, R.C., 270–271
Sax, L., 86, 167–168, 210, 226, 233–234, 236, 237, 239, 241, 249, 339–340
Saxon, J.L., 14
Schaefer, B., 238–239
Schaefer, D.R., 155–156, 163–164
Scheer, J.R., 195, 204, 245, 271, 278–279, 326, 346
Schelbe, L., 355–356
Schellevis, F., 273
Schiraldi, V., 311
Schlosser, A., 26–27, 238–239, 242
Schmader, T., 46–47, 70
Schmalz, D.L., 200
Schmidt, A., 244
Schneider, M.S., 266
Schoeshine-Rokach, M., 156–157
Schrimshaw, E.W., 269–270, 274–275, 278–279
Schulenberg, J.E., 274–275
Schultz, A.M., 285–286
Schutz, R.W., 131
Schwartz, D., 262
Schwartz, K., 346–347
Schwartz, S.H., 27–28, 68–69, 269
Schwing, A.E., 319–320
Seager, A., 231–232
Seaton, M., 210
Sedikides, C., 12, 16–17, 21
Seefeldt, V., 319–320
Seewald, A.M., 242
Seif, H., 263–264, 267–268, 269
Seligman, M.E.P., 13–14, 31
Sellers, R.M., 309–310
Sells, L.W., 57, 58
Serbin, L.A., 154, 155–156, 166
Sesma, E., 210, 226, 227–228
Settles, I.H., 64–65
Sewell, T., 318–319
Shakib, S., 200, 201
Shannon, T., 345
Shapiro, J.R., 199

Author Index

Shapka, J.D., 57, 58
Sharp, E.A., 306–307
Shaver, K., 195–196
Shea, D.L., 82–83
Sheldon, A., 24
Shepherd, H., 348
Sheras, P., 346
Sherriff, N., 202
Shi, B., 340
Shih, M., 199
Shim, S.O., 274
Shoken-Topaz, T., 194–195
Shollenberger, T.L., 337–338
Showers, C.J., 9, 55
Shuttleworth, I., 231
Siedentop, D., 125
Sieving, R.E., 343
Signorella, M.L., 96, 110, 211, 226, 229–230, 231, 245
Signorielli, N., 192
Silva, J.M., 201
Silvestre, A.J., 262, 263, 270
Simmons, A.B., 303, 337
Simons, R.L., 206
Simpkins, S.D., 199–200
Sinclair, K.O., 262, 271–272, 273, 283–284
Sinno, S., 248–249
Sippola, L.K., 172, 263, 270
Sites, E.W., 262, 263, 270
Skelton, C.C., 193
Skiba, R.J., 278, 302, 303, 312, 337, 346
Skinner, O.D., 307
Slaughter-Defoe, D.T., 337–338
Slavin, R.E., 236–237, 347
Slining, M.M., 119
Smalls, C.P., 309–310
Smith, A., 30–31
Smith, E.P., 309
Smith, M., 229–230, 233–234, 355–356
Smith, R.L., 194–195
Smith, S.J., 291
Smith, T.E., 194–195, 234
Smith, W.S., 292–293
Smithers, A., 231
Smith-Lovin, L., 156–157
Smoll, F.L., 131
Smyth, F.L., 198
Snijders, T.A.B., 158

Snow, C.E., 199–200
Snow, D.L., 337
Snyder, T.D., 2–3
Soler, R., 343, 347
Solmon, M.A., 21–22, 119, 121, 124–125, 126–128, 129–132, 133–134, 135, 136–142, 143, 197, 286, 319–320
Solomon, S., 285
Sommers, C.H., 339–340
Sorby, S.A., 69–70, 94–95, 96
Sorensen, E., 341
Spellman, B.A., 110
Spellmann, M.E., 337
Spencer, M.B., 337, 345–346
Spencer, S.J., 46–47
Spicer, P., 309
Spielhagen, F.R., 226–227
Spiess, C.K., 66–67
Spinath, B., 9–10, 11–12, 29
Spindler, A., 342–343
Spracklen, K.M., 159–160
Sprague, J., 345
Sriram, N., 198
St. Rose, A., 82, 197–198
Stahl, S.A., 238
Stall, R., 274–275
Stannard, L., 98–99
Starks, M.T., 263, 270
Steele, C.M., 46–47, 248, 317–318, 338, 344, 352
Steffens, M.C., 198
Steglich, C.E.G., 158
Steinmayr, R., 9–10, 11–12, 29, 202
Stern, A., 156–157
Sternglanz, S.H., 166
Stetsenko, A., 9
Stevenson, H.C. Jr., 309, 310–311, 314–315, 350
Stevenson, R.L., 241
Stewart, A., 191–192
Stiensmeier-Pelster, J., 198–199
Stiller, J., 152
Stinson, D.W., 312, 319, 321, 322
Stipek, D.J., 12–13, 192, 193
Stockin-Davidson, K., 126–127, 137–138, 140–142
Stoddard, S.A., 343
Stoeger, H., 14

Stoelting, S., 286
Stone, J., 319–320
Strasser, K., 198
Strayer, F.F., 155–156
Strough, J., 154, 155, 169, 250
Strutchens, M.E., 192
Struve, L.E., 318–319
Su, R., 27, 44, 56
Subramaniam, A., 283
Susskind, J.E., 68
Sutfin, E.L., 62–63
Sutton, R.M., 202
Svoboda, R.C., 29–30
Swanson, D.P., 337–338, 341, 345–346
Sweeting, H., 194–195, 270
Sweller, J., 275
Swenson, L.P., 205, 207–208
Swim, J.K., 208–209
Szalacha, L.A., 273–274, 278–279, 283–284, 287–288, 290, 291
Szkrybalo, J., 88

T

Tajfel, H., 156–157
Takeuchi, D., 273
Tamis-LeMonda, C.S., 337
Tang, S.W., 337
Tannen, D., 52
Tanney, A., 231–232
Tatli, A., 71
Taylor, A.Z., 318
Taylor, D.M., 206
Taylor, L.C., 343
Taylor, M.G., 156–157
Teig, S., 68
Telch, M.J., 262
Telfer, J.A., 344
Tenenbaum, H.R., 61–62, 196, 199–200
Terlecki, M., 69
Tevendale, H.D., 205, 207–208
Théorêt, M., 202
Thill, K.P., 196
Thomas, D.E., 310–311, 314–315
Thomas, J.R., 131
Thomas, M.A., 208–209
Thompson, M.E., 250–251
Thompson, T., 228
Thomsen, A.H., 208–209

Thrush, T.M., 7–8
Thunder, K., 322
Thurlow, C., 271
Tiedemann, J., 192, 193
Tiggemann, M., 249, 251–252
Timmerman, G., 194, 246
Tindal, G., 193
Tinker, I., 69
Tipton, E., 69, 94
Toguchi, Y., 16–17
Toldson, I., 348
Tonick, I.J., 166
Toomey, R.B., 262, 263, 267, 269, 270, 271–272, 279–280, 287
Torelli, P., 340, 348
Trautwein, U., 9–10, 11
Troop-Gordon, W., 195
Tropp, L.R., 169
Trueman, M., 152, 273
Trueman, T., 86, 167–168
Truong, N.L., 263–264, 267–268, 269
Tucker, R., 97–98
Turner, J.C., 30, 156–157
Turner, K.L., 191–192
Turner, M.A., 341
Turner, R.N., 291
Twenge, J.M., 55, 59–60
Tyack, D., 226–227
Tyler, K.M., 314
Tyler, R., 318–319
Tymss, P., 241
Tyson, K., 303–304, 313

U

Umaña-Taylor, A.J., 209
Underleider, C., 228
Updegraff, K.A., 58, 177, 179–180, 209
Urdan, T., 13–14, 21
Usher, E.L., 16
Uttal, D.H., 69, 94

V

Vaillancourt, T., 348
Valentine, J.C., 6
Valentiner, D.P., 209
Valiante, G., 10
Valla, J., 27–28
Van Damme, J., 202

van de Bunt, G., 158
Van de Gaer, E., 202
van Engen, M.L., 54
Van Hulle, C.A., 238–239, 337
van Lier, P.A., 262
van Merriënboer, J.J.G., 275
Van Parys, J., 82
Van Ryzin, M., 175
Van, S.R., 28
Vance, N., 175
Vanneman, A., 334
Vanska, J., 62
Vanwesenbeeck, I., 273
Varner, F., 307–308
Vasilyeva, M., 47
Veenstra, R., 175–176
Vekiri, I., 195–196
Veliz, P., 201
Velizen, S., 118, 131, 133–134
Verdine, B.N., 98–99
Verhulst, F.C., 175–176
Veroff, J., 5
Vespa, J., 341
Veurink, N.L., 94–95
Vigdor, J., 337
Vigil, J., 176
Villegas, A.M., 346–347
Voeten, M., 213
Vogt Yuan, A.S., 238–239
Voyer, D., 51, 82–83, 94, 110, 240
Voyer, S.D., 51, 82–83, 94, 110, 240
Vygotsky, L.S., 131–132

W

Wadsworth, M.E., 208–209
Wai, J., 82–83, 94
Walker, B.W., 201
Walker, H., 345
Walkerdine, V., 24–25
Wallace, C.M., 337
Wallace, G.L., 236
Wallace, J.M. Jr., 278, 337
Walls, N.E., 283–284
Walton, T.R., 314
Wang, M.T., 28
Ward, P., 125
Ware, N.C., 66
Warren, C., 94

Wartena, H., 138
Wasti, S.A., 209
Watt, H.M.G., 9–10, 11, 27, 58–59
Waugh, J., 283, 284–285
Way, N., 206
Webb-Johnson, G., 303–304, 306, 310–311
Wehlage, G.G., 337
Wei, H., 203–204
Weil, E., 86, 210, 238–239, 240–241
Weiner, B., 7, 12
Weiner, L., 312
Weisgram, E.S., 28, 44, 53–54, 56, 59, 60–61, 67, 68, 100–102, 103–104, 212–213
Weiss, M.R., 129
Welch, K., 337–338
Wells, B.E., 55
Wells, E.M., 236
Wentzel, K.R., 152
Westheimer, K., 273–274, 278–279, 283–284
Wetherell, M.S., 156–157
Wheldall, K., 26–27, 31, 242, 243
Whigham, M., 195, 198
Whiston, S.C., 195–196
White, A.M., 323–324
White, B.A., 343
White, K.B., 201, 343, 345
Whiting, G.W., 316
Whitmire, R., 210
Wigfield, A., 9, 10–11, 27, 58, 119, 128–129, 130–131, 198–199, 233–234
Wiggin, K.D., 241
Wilcox, S., 5
Wilkins, J.L.M., 9
Wilkinson, L., 263–264, 267–268, 269, 272, 276, 277
Wilkinson, V., 319–320
Williams, A.M., 29, 191–192, 199, 202, 248–249, 269, 278, 292–293, 351–352, 357
Williams, C.M., 50, 57, 212
Williams, K.R., 262
Williams, M., 344
Williams, T., 203–204
Williams, W.M., 44, 64–65
Willoughby, B.L.B., 281–282
Willows, D.M., 238
Wills, J.S., 289

Wilson, T., 179–180
Wilson-Smith, D.N., 156–157
Winn, D.C., 343
Winsler, A., 316
Witkow, M.R., 273
Wolfe, D.A., 203–204
Wolfgang, C., 98–99
Wong, Y.J., 319–320
Wood, D.A., 193, 302, 304–305, 307, 325–326, 341, 344
Wood, W., 48, 52, 84–85
Woodruff, A.L., 205–206
Wrangham, R.W., 250–251
Wright, S.C., 206, 326
Wright, Y.F., 29, 34, 169–170, 191–192, 202, 210, 234–235, 269, 278, 292–293, 303, 305, 310–311, 352
Wrohlick, K., 66–67
Wurf, E. Jr., 130–131, 132
Wurster, T.J., 340
Wyman, H., 155
Wysocki, A., 69–70

X

Xiang, P., 133–134
Xie, H., 340

Y

Yeager, D.S., 338, 352–353
Yee, D.K., 62, 195–196
Yee, M., 171
Yeung, A.S., 11
Yoon, K.S., 27, 195
Yoon, S.Y., 51
Yoons, K.S., 61–62, 82
Young, J.M., 98–99
Young, K., 196–197
Young, R., 194–195, 270
Yuile, A., 203–204

Z

Zakaria, F., 197
Zamel, P., 310–311, 314–315
Ziedenberg, J., 311
Ziegler, A., 14
Zijlstra, B.J.H., 175–176
Zimmerman, M.K., 307
Zittleman, K.R., 242, 243, 246, 251–252
Zosuls, K.M., 171–172, 173
Zucker, K.J., 156–157
Zuckerman, M., 13–14

SUBJECT INDEX

Note: Page numbers followed by "*f*" indicate figures and "*t*" indicate tables.

A

AA boys. *See* African American boys
AA children. *See* African American children
AA fathers. *See* African American fathers
AA girls. *See* African American girls
AA men. *See* African American men
AA mothers. *See* African American mothers
AA parents. *See* African American parents
AAU. *See* American Athletic Union
AAUW. *See* American Association of University Women
Abilities
  boys responding to cues of, 14
  effort influencing, 13
  females rating, 13
  gender differences in, 14
  gender segregation and, 49–55
  girls responding to cues of, 14
  maladaptive consequences, 13
  males' orientation to, 3
  males rating, 13
  parents emphasizing, 30
  praise for, 14
  self-perceived, job success and, 49
Ability beliefs. *See* Competence
Academic abilities. *See* Abilities
Academic disparities, 264–272
Academic identification of AA boys, 317–318, 322
Academic motivation, 32–35, 231–232
Academic outcomes
  anti-discrimination policies influencing, 289
  attributions sex similarities, 12
  causes influencing, 7
  exclusionary discipline influencing, 279
  gender as linked to, 78
  physical education and, 119
  sport and, 119
  substance use's implications for, 275
  support influencing, 282–283
Academic performance, 24–27

AA boys' ironic findings about, 303–306
  inclusive curricula promoting, 290–293
  physical education influencing, 119
  sports influencing, 119
  support as tied to, 282–283
  victimization influencing, 266, 272–280
Academic resilience, 280–293
Academic self-concepts, 6, 9–12
Academic self-efficacy, 9, 16
Academics, achievement in, 25, 318, 322
Achievement. *See also* Attributions
  academic, 25, 318, 322
  achievement goals influencing, 21
  females providing themes of, 5
  gender biases in school, 197–202
  gender segregation in, 201
  girls increasing, 26–27
  interests and, 23–28
  males providing themes of, 5
  men's writings on, 5, 6
  motivation and, 8, 23–28
  need, 4–5
  SES predicting, 231
  social goals and, 23–28
  values and, 23–28
  women's writings on, 5–6
Achievement goal theory, 7–8
Achievement goals, 20–23
Achievement motivation. *See* Motivation
Action video game, 69
Administrators, 125, 144
Adolescents. *See also* Discrimination; Sexism; Single-sex schools
  aggression of, 175–176
  discrimination perceived by, 206, 207, 208
  English, 26
  German, 25
  occupational goals of, 68
  sexism in, 169
  STEM enrollment of, 29–30
  values consolidated by, 28

387

Adultification, 315
Adults, resilience supported by, 281–283
Advanced Placement (AP), 80–81, 80f, 198, 249, 303–304, 305–306
Affective attitudes, 171–172
Affiliation, motivation influenced by, 3
African American (AA) boys. *See also* Discrimination; Narratives
  AA fathers influencing, 323–324
  academic identification of, 317–318, 322
  adultification of, 315
  agency of, 322
  aggression and, 314–315, 337–338, 340
  anger expressed by, 314–315
  AP courses taken by, 303–304, 305–306
  as athletes, 319–320
  case study, 334, 335–336
  classroom management, 312–313
  college attended by, 355
  in cool-pose theory, 318–320
  coping strategies influencing, 317–320
  disidentification of, 317–318
  education challenges, 334–344, 335t
  emasculation of, 341
  exclusionary discipline of, 311–315, 338
  in gifted programs, 316
  group norms influencing, 340
  high school graduated by, 305, 326, 355
  hopelessness scores of, 343
  internalization of, 343, 344
  masculinity preserved by, 318, 320
  methodological concerns, 325–326
  overview of, 302, 323–326, 334, 356–359
  parental expectations for, 307–310, 321, 325–326, 341
  as passive information recipients, 339
  peers nominated by, 318
  positive aspects of lives of, 326
  research focus on, 323–326
  resilience among, 357
  school awareness of, 321–322
  school disengagement of, 313, 317–318, 339–340, 343
  school environments for, 345–356
  school performance ironic findings, 303–306
  self-esteem bolstering of, 352–353
  as social problem, 311–313, 337
  socialization of, 308–310
  in special education, 315–316
  sports participated in by, 319–320
  SS schools rescuing, 353–356
  STEM courses taken by, 304–306
  stereotype threat vulnerability of, 352
  stereotypes of, 302, 314–317, 337–338, 340, 344, 351–353
  teachers benefiting, 324, 345–346
  teachers differentially responding to, 312–317, 337–338
  teachers' relationships with, 338, 346–347
  underachievement factors influencing, 336–344, 356–357
  as underperforming, 305–306
  as victims, 315
  vigilance of, 308–310
  violence influencing, 343
African American (AA) children, 192. *See also* Black students
  discrimination influencing, 65
  gender segregation, 341
  high-status jobs pursued by, 65
  overview of, 334
  race noticed by, 248–249
  reading performance of, 341
  socialization of, 342
  SS schools geared to, 234–235
  STEM performance of, 341
  trauma exposure of, 343
African American (AA) fathers, 323–324, 341. *See also* African American parents
African American (AA) girls
  adultification of, 315
  discrimination against, 307–308, 309
  as enforcers, 313
  as helpers, 313
  parental expectations for, 307–308, 310, 325–326, 341
  socialization of, 309, 310
African American (AA) men, 341, 348–349, 354
African American (AA) mothers, 307–309, 323–324, 325. *See also* African American parents
African American (AA) parents, 306–310, 323–324, 325, 342, 349–350. *See also* Parental expectations

African Americans, sport strides of, 124
Agency, of AA boys, 322
Aggressive behaviors, 174–179, 201, 314–315, 337–338, 340
Alice software, 97–98
Altruism, 101–102
Ambivalent sexism model, 190–191
American Association of University Women (AAUW), 203, 229
American Athletic Union (AAU), 123
American Institutes for Research, 229
Anger, AA boys expressing, 314–315
Anti-discrimination policies, 287–289
AP. *See* Advanced Placement
Approach strategies, 208–209
Aptitudes, 231–232, 235, 237–238
Argonne National Laboratory, 103
Art contest, 207
Athletes, 138, 145, 319–320
Athletic directors, 144
Athletic programs, 144, 145
At-risk girls, 233–234
At-risk students of color. *See* Students of color
Attainment value, 129
Attitudinal pathway, 91
Attribution theory, 7, 12–15
Attributions
  academic outcomes, sex similarities in, 12
  bias, 12
  expectancy influenced by, 7
  retraining, 14
Australian students, 58
Avoidance strategies, 208
Awards, motivation influenced by, 136–137

B

Bachelor's degrees, 79–80, 79f, 197, 201
Bad bodies narratives, 140
Bad Boys (Ferguson), 322
Barbie, 103, 109
Basketball, gender differences in, 123
Behavioral similarity, 157–158, 157f
Bem sex-role inventory, 59–60
Benevolent sexism, 190–191
Bias-resistance training, 65
Binary view of socialization, 161–165, 164f
Black boys. *See* African American boys

Black students in stereotype threat experiment, 46
Bodily meanings, 138–140, 146
Borderland bodies, 140
Boys, 8, 9, 11–12, 14, 20–21, 24–27, 30. *See also* African American boys; Coeducational schools; Gender biases; Gender differences; Gender segregation; Gender similarities; Gender socialization; High-achieving boys; Low-achieving boys; Physical education; Same-sex peer groups; Sex differences; Sexes; Sexism; Single-sex schools; Sports
Bright boys. *See* High-achieving boys
Buddy-Up program, 177
Bullying, 213, 250. *See also* Victimization
Butterfly Beauty Shop, 99

C

Canadian students, 58, 204
Career aspirations. *See* Occupational goals
Career values, 100–105
Careers. *See* Jobs
CE schools. *See* Coeducational schools
Chad, 78
Cheating, 21
Children. *See also* African American children; Elementary school children; European American children; Gender segregation; Interventions; Latino children; Preschool children; Sexism; Single-sex schools
  affective attitudes of, 171–172
  competence perceptions of, 130–131
  discrimination perceived by, 205–208
  GBRE of, 173–174
  gender atypical, 234
  gender schema formed by, 67–69
  gendered-peer environment selection role of, 170–174
  parental role models influencing, 62–63
  parents socializing, 23
  peer interactions influencing, 160
  physical activity of, 118

Children (*Continued*)
  rules developed by, 345–346
  same-sex peer groups and, 160–161, 162*f*
  violence influencing, 343
Chronic vigilance, 275–276
Classroom outcomes. *See* Academic outcomes
Classrooms
  AA mothers' involvement in, 325
  boys dominating, 26–27, 234–237, 239–240, 242–244
  coeducational, 34–35
  comfort in, 178–179
  community, 178
  culturally responsive, 346–347
  gender differences in, 23–24
  girls as benefit to, 26–27, 168, 238
  management, 312–313, 345–346
  single-sex, 226–252
  as social arenas, 23–24
  social gatherings in, 346–347
Coaches, 144, 201, 324
Coalition of Schools Educating Boys of Color (COSEBOC), 345
Coeducational classes, 34–35
Coeducational (CE) schools, 226. *See also* Single-sex schools
  financial rationale for, 227
  history of, 227
  sexism reduced by, 209, 210, 211
  sexual distraction in, 249
  SS schools' methods transported to, 253
  Title IX rationale for, 227–228
Cognitions, 7–8
Cognitive maturation, 236–237
"Cognitive–Behavioral Similarity Model," 157–159, 157*f*, 159*f*
College students. *See also* Bachelor's degrees; Gender differences; Sexism
  female, 5, 47, 66
  on jobs, 68
  male, 5, 47
  sex differences, 12, 16
  spatial performance improvement of, 94–96
  stereotype threat influencing, 46
Colleges, 122, 144, 268, 355
Comfort, 139–140, 178–179

Communal goals, 53–54
Communication, 52–53, 350
Comparison groups, 106–107
Compatibility, 155–156
Competence, 8–12, 17*f*–18*f*, 27–28, 130–134, 142. *See also* Improving; Proving
Competent behaviors, 177–179
Competition, 3, 5–6
Computer game, preschool girls playing, 103, 109
Computer science (CS) intervention, 97–98
Confidence, 8–15. *See also* Self-confidence
Confrontation, 212
Conscious stereotyped attitudes, 191
Consideration, motivation influenced by, 3
Constructed environments, 88
Construction worker, 105
Contextual analysis paradigm, 312
Cool-pose theory, 318–320
Cooperative behaviors, 174–180
Coping, 204, 205, 208–209, 274–275, 317–320
COSEBOC. *See* Coalition of Schools Educating Boys of Color
Counter-narratives, 320–323, 351–353
Creative intelligence, 16
Critical mass hypothesis, 71
Crocker, Arnette, 239
Cultural deficit paradigm, 312
Cultural differences, gender differences shaped by, 70–71
Cultural inventory, 143
Cultural stereotypes. *See* Stereotypes
Culturally responsive classrooms, 346–347
Culturally sensitive teacher training, 345–346
Curricula
  class in, 347
  hidden, 141, 251–252
  inclusive, 289–293
  interests influencing, 241
  physical education
    issues, 125–128
    multi-activity model, 126–127, 140–141, 143

transformation, 127–128, 134, 140–141, 143, 146
race in, 347
resilience promoted by, 289–293

D

Department of Education, U.S. (DOE), 210, 211
Development. *See also* Gender development
gendered-peer relationships influencing, 159–165
physical activity influencing, 121
same-sex peer groups influencing, 154
school environments auspicious for, 345–353
socio-emotional, 343–344, 350–351
Developmental interventions, *See* Interventions
Discipline disparities, 278–279, 337–338
Discrimination. *See also* Sexism
against AA girls, 307–308, 309
AA mothers' concerns of, 307–309
AA parents over-emphasizing, 307–310
adolescents perceiving, 206, 207, 208
African American children influenced by, 65
children perceiving, 205–208
coping with, 209
definition of, 190
elementary school children facing, 308–309
in intervention, 103–104
job, 56, 63
in physical education, 126–127
programming, 103–104
sex, 56, 64–65
in sports, 124, 126–127
in STEM, 63, 64, 65, 212–213
stereotypes and, 63–66
students perceiving, 65–66
Disidentification, 317–318
Dispositions, gender segregation and, 49–55
Disruptive behavior, 235, 238–239
Distal stressors, 265, 266, 275
Diversity within sexual minority youth community, 269
DOE. *See* Department of Education, U.S.

Dominance, 176
Dual-pathway models (DPM), 90–91

E

EA children. *See* European American children
Eagle Academy for Young Men, 234–235, 354–355
Early Childhood Longitudinal Study (ECLS-K), 343
Earth Microbiome Project, 103
ECLS-K. *See* Early Childhood Longitudinal Study
Education. *See also* Academic outcomes; Physical education
E-V model on choices in, 6
liberation as purpose of, 352
low-quality, 339–340
motivation's implications for, 34–35
peer environment playing critical role in, 348
quality improvement, 347–348
special, 315–316
sport and, 144–145
Education Amendments. *See* Title IX
Educational outcomes. *See* Academic outcomes
Effect size, 50
Effort, 12, 13–14, 26, 30
Effortful control, 31
Egalitarian occupational beliefs, 65–66
Ego goals. *See* Performance goals
Elementary school, physical education in, 126
Elementary school children, 325. *See also* Gender differences; Sex differences; Sexism; Single-sex schools
competence perceptions of, 130–131
discrimination faced by, 308–309
female elementary teachers, 65
homophobic victimization, 276
in intervention, 104–105
PCPFS completed by, 137
physical competence, 119
skill development, 126
Elementary teachers, STEM anxiety of, 63–64

Emasculation, 341
English. *See* Reading and language arts
English adolescents, 26
Environments, 88, 89. *See also* Gender environmentalism; Gendered-peer environments
Equitable climates, 140–144
Ethnic discrimination. *See* Discrimination
Ethnicity, 191–192
European American (EA) children, 191–192, 248–249
European American (EA) students, 46, 249
European Commission, 100
E-V Theory. *See* Expectancy-value theory
Evaluation, 15–20, 106–109
Exclusionary discipline, 278–279, 311–315, 338
Expanding Your Horizons (EYH), 100–102, 104
Expectancies, 4–5, 6, 7, 45–46, 57–58. *See also* Parental expectations
Expectancy-value (E-V) theory, 6, 45–46, 91, 128–134
Explicit stereotyped attitudes, 191
Expulsion. *See* Exclusionary discipline
Extracurricular activities, resilience promoted by, 285–287
EYH. *See Expanding Your Horizons*

F

Faculty, men as, 3
Failure, 8, 12–13
Families. *See* Home-school alliances
Family devotion, 66–67
Family Leave policy, 66–67
Fathers. *See* African American fathers; Parents
Fear of success, 5–6
Females. *See also* Girls; Improving; Sex differences; Sexes; Sexism; Sexual minority youth; Women
  ability rated by, 13
  administrators, 144
  athletes, sexualized images of, 138
  athletic directors, 144
  college students, 5, 47, 66
  deficiencies orientation of, 3
  doubts expressed by, 9
  effort rated by, 13
  high school students, achievement themes provided by, 5
  homemakers, 59
  imposter phenomenon vulnerability of, 14
  motivation of, second-wave feminism coinciding with interest in, 5
  successful, 9
  teacher STEM anxiety, 63–64
Femininity. *See* Gender stereotypes
Feminism, 2, 5, 227
Feminist standpoint theory, 191–192
Fitness testing, 134–138
FITNESSGRAM®, 135, 136
Freedom for literacy, 352

G

Gay, Lesbian, and Straight Education Network (GLSEN), 288–290
Gay-Straight Alliances (GSAs), 283–285
GBRE. *See* Gender-based relationship efficacy
Gender. *See also* Gender segregation; Sex differences; Sexes
  academic motivation importance of, 32–35
  academic outcomes' link to, 78
  achievement goals and, 20–23
  ethnicity interacting with, 191–192
  motivation influenced by, 2–4
  as neglected topic, 2
  performing, 24–27
  race interacting with, 191–192
  relationships and, 23–24
  similarities, 4
  social cognitions about, 156–157
Gender attention, SS schools reducing, 247–252
Gender atypical children. *See* Gender-variant youth
Gender biases, 191, 197–202, 212, 244, 245. *See also* Sexism
Gender constructivism, 88–91
Gender convergence hypothesis, 11
Gender development, 49, 67–69, 85–91

Gender differences. *See also* Gender biases; Gender segregation; Gender stereotypes; Interventions; Sex differences
  in ability, 14
  in AP exams, 80–81, 80f, 198
  in basketball, 123
  in classrooms, 23–24
  in communication, 52–53
  contexts increasing, 251
  cultural differences shaping, 70–71
  in effort, 13–14
  exaggeration, 4
  explanations, 83–84
  in fitness testing, 135–137
  gender segregation and, 49–55
  gender similarities and, 49–55
  in helping behavior, 53
  in jobs, 59–61, 68
  in leadership, 54
  in mastery goal structure, 22–23
  in occupational goals, 55–71
  in occupational interests, 55–61
  overview of, 71
  in parental expectations, 307–308
  in performance goal structure, 22–23
  in physical activity, 118, 120–125, 131–134
  in physical education, 122–123, 128–134
  in practice, 69
  in self-concept, 55
  in self-esteem, 55
  in self-handicapping, 13–14, 21
  in spatial performance, 51, 69–70, 82–83
  in sports, 121–125, 144
  as SS schools' rationale, 235–241
  in STEM, 48, 51, 56, 57, 58–59, 61–62, 63–64, 65, 66, 67, 68–70, 79–81, 79f, 80f, 82–84, 197–198
  in teacher attention, 242–243
  teacher reinforcing, 141–142
  in training, 69–70
  in U.S., 57
  in utility values, 58–59
  in verbal skills, 51–52
Gender discrimination. *See* Discrimination
Gender environmentalism, 87–88
Gender equality, 70–71, 141–143

Gender essentialism, 86–87
Gender gap. *See* Gender segregation; Interventions
Gender inequities. *See* Gender differences
Gender integrated interactions. *See* Peer interactions
Gender intensification theory, 11
Gender labeling, 248
Gender salience filters, 90–91
Gender salience in SS schools, 247–249, 253–254
Gender schema theory (GST), 67–68, 90–91
Gender segregation. *See also* Gender equality; Gendered-peer environments; Interventions; Same-sex peer groups; Sexism, Single-sex (SS) schools
  in AA children's STEM and reading performance, 341
  ability and, 49–55
  in achievement, 201
  aggressive behavior implications, 174–179
  in bachelor's degrees, 201
  children's
    binary view of, 161–165, 164f
    compatibility influencing, 155–156
    expanded explanation for, 157–158, 157f
    gradient view of, 163–165, 164f
    overview of, 154–159, 180–181
    reasons for, 155–159, 159f
    shared interests influencing, 155–156
    similarity influencing, 157–159, 157f, 159f
    social cognitions about gender influencing, 156–157
    social networks analyses exploration of, 158–159, 159f
  cooperative behavior implications, 174–179
  dispositions and, 49–55
  factors contributing to, 45
  gender differences and, 49–55
  gender similarities and, 48–55
  gender stereotypes as related to, 169–170, 211
  interventions, 70, 177

Gender segregation (*Continued*)
  jobs influencing, 60–61
  overview of, 45, 71
  in pay, 71
  in physical education, 122–123
  in public schools, 167–170
  in school environments, 165–170
  sex differences increased by, 168–169
  sexism as related to, 169–170
  STEM, 79–85, 79*f*, 80*f*, 81*f*, 197
  theoretical frameworks, 45–49
  in U.S., 44, 71, 78, 197, 201
Gender similarities, 48–55
Gender socialization, gender-differentiated activities as arenas of, 24
Gender stability hypothesis, 11
Gender stereotypes, 143–144. *See also* Stereotype threat
  bodily meanings influenced by, 138–140
  developmental interventions addressing, 103–105
  fitness testing reinforcing, 138
  gender segregation as related to, 169–170, 211
  junior high school students' beliefs in, 169–170
  parental expectations and, 61–62, 201
  parents' views on, 199–200
  peers endorsing, 242, 245
  physical activity influenced by, 131–132
  physical education influenced by, 132–133
  self-schemata, 132
  sports influenced by, 133–134
  STEM, 198–200
  in video games, 196
Gender theories, 156–159
Gender-based relationship efficacy (GBRE), 173–174
Gender-differentiated activities, 24
Gendered-peer environments, child's role in selecting, 170–174
Gendered-peer interactions, 153
Gendered-peer relationships, 153, 159–165
Gender-segregation cycle, 161, 162*f*
Gender-variant youth, 234. *See also* Resilience; Victimization
  academic disparities faced by, 267–269
  exclusionary discipline influencing, 278–279
  grades of, 277
  minority stress model and, 264–265
  overview of, 262–264, 293–294
  peers teasing, 194–195, 212
  in SCCT model, 265–267, 277
  STEM courses taken by, 276
  teachers as allies to, 274
Generic Alice software, 97–98
German adolescents, 25
Germany, 67
Gifted programs, 316
Girl Scouts, 97–98
Girls. *See also* African American (AA) girls; Bullying; Coeducational schools; Discrimination; Gender biases; Gender differences; Gender equality; Gender salience; Gender segregation; Gender similarities; Gender socialization; Gender stereotypes; High-achieving girls; Interventions; Physical education; Same-sex peer groups; Sex differences; Sexes; Sexism; Single-sex schools; Sports
  ability cues responded to by, 14
  academic achievement costs paid by, 25
  achievement increased by, 26–27
  at-risk, 233–234
  in Chad, 78
  as classroom benefit, 26–27, 168, 238
  educational achievement of, 3
  effort cues responded to by, 14
  in EYH, 100–102, 104
  as good, 24–27
  hidden curriculum detected by, 251–252
  as ideal student, 24–25
  mastery goals tended to by, 8, 20–21
  music excellence of, 25
  parents orienting, 30
  physics excellence of, 25
  possible selves of, 132
  self-stereotyping of, 251–252
  stereotype threat among, 47
  teachers' STEM anxiety influencing, 63–64
  toys and, 98–99

Subject Index

GLSEN. *See* Gay, Lesbian, and Straight Education Network
Goals, 7–8, 91–93, 93f, 93t. *See also* Achievement goals; Mastery goals; Occupational goals; Performance goals; Social goals
GoldieBlox, 98, 99
Grades, 267, 268, 271, 277, 317–318, 324
Gradient view of socialization, 163–165, 164f
Group norms, 340
GSAs. *See* Gay-Straight Alliances
GST. *See* Gender schema theory

H

Handbook of Parenting (Pipes McAdoo), 308
Help avoidance, 274
Helping behavior, 53–54
Heterosexism, 190
Heterosexual youth, victimization of, 270–271
Hidden curriculum, 141, 251–252
High school. *See also* Secondary school
  AA boys graduating, 305, 326, 355
  physical education in, 122, 126, 127
  sexual minority youth completing, 268–269
High school students, 5, 57, 80–81, 80f, 127, 139–140, 143. *See also* Bullying; Gender differences; Junior high school students
High-achieving boys, 23, 25–26, 29–30
High-achieving girls, STEM courses taken by, 29–30
Homemakers, 59
Home-school alliances, 341–342, 349–350
Homophobic victimization. *See* Victimization
Hopelessness scores, 343
Hostile sexism, 190–191

I

Identities, 27–29, 143, 209, 341
Implicit stereotyped attitudes, 191
Imposter phenomenon, 14
Improving, 3, 7, 8, 15–20, 24, 32–35
Inclusive curriculum, 289–293
In-group, 171

Ingroup mentoring, 348–349
Instruction. *See* Education
Interests, 6, 23–29, 155–156, 235, 240–241. *See also* Occupational interests
Interpersonal dominance, 176
Interscholastic sports, 145
Interventions, 350–351
  assessing, 96
  building on, 109–110
  characterizing, 109–110
  comparison groups, 106–107
  CS, 97–98
  discrimination in, 103–104
  elementary school children in, 104–105
  evaluation of, 106–109
  extensions, 110
  gender development theories, 85–91
  gender segregation, 70, 177
  gender stereotypes addressed by, 103–105
  goals taxonomy, 91–93, 93f, 93t
  illustrations of, 94–105
  mechanisms, 85–91
  meta-analysis of, 110
  overview of, 78–79, 105–111
  recategorizing in, 92, 93t, 99–105
  recommendations, 106–111
  refocusing in, 92, 93t, 99–105
  relational perspective revisiting, 110–111
  remediation in, 92, 93t, 94–96
  replications, 110
  resisting in, 92, 93f, 93t, 99–105
  revising in, 92, 93f, 93t, 96–99
  sexism reduced by, 209, 211–213
  social role theory approaches for, 84–85
  spatial skills, 94–96
  STEM-relevant outcome measures, 107–108
  STEM-relevant strategies
    recategorize individuals, 92, 93t, 99–105
    refocus attention, 92, 93t, 99–105
    remediate girls, 92, 93t, 94–96
    resist stereotypes, 92, 93f, 93t, 99–105
    revise STEM, 92, 93f, 93t, 96–99
  stereotype threat dealt with by, 70
  teacher attention, 242–243
  theoretical foundations articulated by, 106
  unintended outcomes measurement, 108–109

Intrinsic value, 129
Israel, 23

J

Jim Crow era, 352
Jobs. *See also* Gender segregation;
    Occupational goals; Occupational
    interests
  African American children pursuing
    high-status, 65
  attribute preferences, 59–61, 68
  college students on, 68
  communication's importance to, 52, 53
  discrimination, 56, 63
  egalitarian beliefs about, 65–66
  E-V model on choices in, 6
  gender differences in, 59–61, 68
  gender segregation influenced by, 60–61
  self-confidence's importance in, 53
  self-efficacy influencing choice of, 63
  self-perceived ability for success in, 49
  sex differences in, 28
  STEM importance in choosing, 50
  verbal skills importance to, 51
  women's underrepresentation in STEM,
    50, 52, 53–54, 55, 78, 81, 82, 100,
    101
  work-family balance influencing choice
    of, 66–67
Junior high school students, gender
    stereotype beliefs of, 169–170.
    See also Gender differences
Justice system, 341

K

KaBOOM!, 351
Kraus-Weber minimum fitness test, 135

L

Language arts. *See* Reading and language arts
Latino boys, 305
Latino children, SS schools geared to, 192,
    234–235
Leadership, 54
Leaky pipeline, 68–69, 82
Learning, victimization influencing,
    272–280
Learning goals. *See* Mastery goals

LEGO, 98–99
Lesbian, gay, bisexual, transgender (LGBT).
    See Sexual minority youth
Liberation, 352
Literacy for freedom, 352
Locus of control, 7
Low-achieving boys, 23, 29–30
Low-income neighborhoods, 351
Low-quality instruction, 339–340

M

Males. *See also* Boys; Men; Proving; Sex
    differences; Sexes; Sexism; Sexual
    minority youth
  abilities orientation of, 3
  ability rated by, 13
  beneficial results obtained by, 9
  coaches, 145
  college students, 5, 47
  effort construed by, 13
  high school students providing
    achievement themes, 5
  psychologists, 5
  psychology bias, 5
  successful, 9
Martin, Trayvon, 309
Masculinity, 201–202, 318, 320. *See also*
    Gender stereotypes
Mastery goals
  in achievement goal theory, 7–8
  definition of, 7
  girls tending to, 8, 20–21
  motivation maintained by, 8
  in physical education, 142
  structure of, 8, 21, 22–23, 34–35
Mathematics, 46–52, 54, 56–59, 61–64, 66,
    68–70, 79–81, 87, 197–199
Maturation, 235–237
Mean level of construct, 4
Media, sexism perpetrated by, 192,
    196–197
Men. *See also* Gender differences; Gender
    segregation; Gender similarities;
    Sex differences; Sexes; Sexism
  AA, 341
  on ability, 14
  achievement writings of, 5, 6
  books written by, 3

Subject Index

as breadwinner, 67
competitive settings influencing, 5, 6
confidence conveyed by, 8
as faculty, 3
families thought of by, 67
motivation research based on, 5
in sociocultural theory, 48
success feared by, 5, 6
work achievement of, 3
"Men and Things, Women and People" (Su), 56
Mental health, 272–273, 282, 350–351
Mental rotation, 51, 69–70
Mentoring, 348–349, 354
Meta-analyses, 49–55, 68
  of cognitive maturation, 237
  of interventions, 110
  of SS schools literature, 229–230, 237, 240
  of stereotype threat, 199
  of victimization, 270
Middle school, 126, 231. See also Secondary school; Single-sex schools
Middle school students
  in EYH, 100–102, 104
  in interventions, 96, 97, 100
  in Israel, 23
  on mastery goal structure, 23
  peers nominated by, 318
  on performance goal structure, 23
  programming learned by, 97–98
  school awareness of, 322
  spatial performance improved by, 96
Mile run, 136
Military personnel, 135
Minorities, 191–192. See also African American boys; African American children; Latino children; Sexual minority youth; Students of color
Minority stress model, 264–265, 275–276, 278–279
Mixed-sex play, 177, 178–179
Mothers. See Parents
Motivation. See also Academic motivation
  achievement and, 8, 23–28
  achievement goals and, 20–23
  affiliation influencing, 3

approaches, 4–8
awards influencing, 136–137
cognitions in, 7
competence influencing, 130–134, 142–144
competition influencing, 3
confidence and, 8–15
consideration influencing, 3
as construct, 128
contemporary approaches, 4–8
definition of, 128
early approaches, 4–8
educational implications, 34–35
evaluation and, 15–20
expectancies role, 6
of failure avoidance, 8
female, 5
fitness testing influencing, 134–137
focus, 3–4
frameworks, 128–134
gender differences in physical education, 128–134
gender influencing, 2–4
interests and, 23–28
intrinsic, 129
locus of control influencing, 7
mastery goals maintaining, 8
men basis of research on, 5
men's success, 5, 6
overview of, 2–4, 32–35
for physical activity, 128–134, 141–142
as process, 128
research implications, 33–34
self-promotion influencing, 3
sex differences and, 4
social goals and, 23–28
social influences and, 29–31
success and, 5–6
theoretical frameworks, 4–8, 12–15, 33–34
values and, 6, 23–28
variables yielding styles of, 4
women's success, 5–6
Multi-activity model, 126–127, 140–141
Music, 25

N

NACE. *See* National Association for Choice in Education
Narratives, 302
  counter-, 320–323, 351–353
  interplay of, 325
  parent, 306–310, 323–324, 325
  research influencing, 323–326
  teacher, 310–317, 321, 324–325
NASPE. *See* National Association for Physical Education and Sport
NASSPE. *See* National Association for the Advancement of Single-Sex Public Education
National Assessment of Educational Progress, 50
National Association for Choice in Education (NACE), 252–253
National Association for Physical Education and Sport (NASPE), 119–120, 125
National Association for the Advancement of Single-Sex Public Education (NASSPE), 252–253
National award. *See* President's Challenge Physical Fitness Awards Program
National Basketball Association (NBA), 102–103
National Football League (NFL), 102–103
National Geographic Bee, 83
National Science Foundation (NSF), 79*f*, 81*f*
Nature, 65
NBA. *See* National Basketball Association
NCLBA. *See* No Child Left Behind Act
Need to achieve, 4–5
Negative bias, 9–10
Negative feedback, 15–16, 17
"The Negro Family: The Case for National Action" (Moynihan), 341
New York City, New York, 305, 354–355
New York Review of Books, 3
NFL. *See* National Football League
No Child Left Behind Act (NCLBA), 167–168, 210, 228
Novel job, 60
NSF. *See* National Science Foundation

O

Occupational goals, 55–71
Occupational interests, gender differences in, 55–61
Occupations. *See* Jobs
Oregon, 288
Other-sex peers. *See* Gender segregation; Gendered-peer environments; Peer interactions
Out-group, 171, 172

P

Parental expectations
  for AA boys, 307–310, 321, 325–326, 341
  for AA girls, 307–308, 310, 325–326, 341
  about daughters' math abilities, 29–30, 61–62
  gender differences in, 307–308
  gender stereotypes and, 61–62, 201
  occupational goals shaped by, 61–63
  sex differences in, 29–30
  in sports, 201
  in STEM, 61–62
Parents. *See also* African American parents
  abilities emphasized by, 30
  boys oriented by, 30
  children influenced by role model, 62–63
  children socialized by, 23
  effort emphasized by, 30
  gender-stereotypical views of, 199–200
  girls oriented by, 30
  resilience supported by, 281–283
  sexism perpetrated by, 192, 195–196, 199–200
  sex-typed beliefs of, 29–30
  as social influence, 29–30
Participatory style, 235, 239–240
Part-time employment of women, 67
Pay, 71
PCPFAP. *See* President's Challenge Physical Fitness Awards Program
PCPFS. *See* President's Council for Physical Fitness and Sport
Peer interactions, 152–153, 159–160, 177–181. *See also* Gendered-peer environments; Gendered-peer interactions; Gendered-peer relationships

Subject Index

Peers. *See also* Gender-variant youth
  anti-academic culture of, 340
  culture transformation of, 348
  educational role played by, 348
  gender stereotyping, 242, 245
  gender-atypical peers teased by, 194–195, 212
  homophily, 250–251
  rejection, 250–251
  resilience supported by, 281–283
  schools influencing norms of, 348
  sexism perpetrated by, 192, 194–195, 245
  sexual harassment perpetrated by, 194, 242, 246–247
Perceived cost, 129
Perceptions, 8–15, 129–131
Performance, stereotype threat impairing, 46–47
Performance goals
  in achievement goal theory, 7–8
  boys tending to, 8, 20–21
  competence demonstration, 7
  definition of, 7
  mastery goal demonstration, 7
  self-serving bias increased by, 21
  structure of, 8, 21–23, 31, 35
Performance-approach goals, 8, 20–21
Performance-avoidance goals, 8
Performing bodies, 143–144
Performing identities, 143–144
Personal pathway, 91
Philadelphia 76ers, 103
Phonics instruction, 238
Physical activity. *See also* Physical education; Sports
  benefits of, 117–118
  of children, 118
  competence in, 130–134
  definition of, 118
  development influenced by, 121
  gender differences in, 118, 120–122, 124–125
  gender stereotypes influencing, 131–132
  of high school students, 139–140
  history of, 121–125
  motivation for, 128–134, 141–142
  overview of, 117–125
  physical education promoting, 118

  sports promoting, 118
  in U.S., 117–118
Physical education
  academic outcomes and, 119
  academic performance influenced by, 119
  administrative support for, 125
  bodily meanings influenced by, 138–140
  in colleges, 122
  curricula
    issues, 125–128
    multi-activity model, 126–127, 140–141, 143
    transformation, 127–128, 134, 140–141, 143, 146
  decline of, 124–125
  discrimination in, 126–127
  in elementary school, 126
  equitable climates in, 140–144
  E-V theory in, 128–134
  fitness testing in, 134–138
  gender differences in, 122–123, 126, 127
  gender equality in, 141–143
  gender segregation in, 122–123
  gender stereotypes influencing, 132–133
  in high school, 122, 126, 127
  high school students in, 127, 139–140
  intrinsic value of, 129
  mastery climate in, 142
  in middle school, 126
  perceptions of value in, 129–130
  performing identities in, 143–144
  physical activity promoted by, 118
  purpose of, 119–120
  in school districts, 122–123
  single-sex, 122–123
  socialization influenced by, 119
  sport as distinct from, 119–120
  supervision for, 125
  teachers, 122–123, 141–142
  in universities, 122
Physical fitness testing, 134–138
Physical health, victimization's association with, 273
Physics, 25, 247–248
Piagetan theory, 89
PISA. *See* Programme for International Student Assessment
Playing with Anger program, 350

Playmobil character, 103, 109
Positive bias, 9
Positive feedback, sex differences in, 17
Possible selves, 132–133
Post-slavery era, 352
Poverty, 342–343, 356–357
Practice, gender differences in, 69
Praise, 14
Prejudice, 190
Preschool children. *See also* Peers
  aggression of, 175, 176
  computer game played by, 103, 109
  occupational goals of, 68
  in same-sex peer groups, 158–159, 159f, 161–165, 164f, 166
Prescriptive attitude, 190
President's Challenge Physical Fitness Awards Program (PCPFAP), 135–137
President's Council for Physical Fitness and Sport (PCPFS), 135
Principals, 125
Professionalization, 145
Programme for International Student Assessment (PISA), 48, 52
Programming, 97–98, 103–104
Proscriptive attitude, 190
Proving, 3, 7, 8, 15–20, 24, 26, 32–35
Proximal stressors, 265, 266
Pseudo-masculine identity, 341
Psychologists, male, 5
Public schools, 167–170, 305. *See also* Single-sex schools

R

Race, 191–192, 235, 248–249, 347. *See also* Ethnicity
Racial discrimination. *See* Discrimination
Racial socialization. *See* Socialization
Racial stereotypes. *See* Stereotypes
Racism, 356–357
Reading and language arts, 9, 10–11, 29, 341
Recategorizing, 92, 93t, 99–105
Refocusing, 92, 93t, 99–105
Relationships, 23–24, 179–180, 349–350. *See also* Gendered-peer relationships
Religious institutions, 227
Remediation, 92, 93t, 94–96

Resilience, 280–293, 357
Resisting, 92, 93f, 93t, 99–105
Revising, 92, 93f, 93t, 96–99
Role models, 62–63
Rules, children developing, 345–346
Running, 135–136, 141–142

S

Safe spaces, 351
Same-sex aggression, 175–176
Same-sex peer groups, 34. *See also* Gendered-peer environments
  children learning from, 160–161, 162f
  development influenced by, 154
  improving in, 24
  physical education, 122–123
  preschool children in, 158–159, 159f, 161–165, 164f, 166
  proving in, 24
  socialization influenced by, 154–155, 161–166, 164f
Same-sex romantic attractions, 250
Same-sex sexual harassment, 246
Same-sex similarity expectancy, 157–159, 157f, 159f
Sanford Harmony Program, 177, 179–180
SCCT. *See* Social cognitive career theory
Scholastic aptitude. *See* Aptitude
School achievement. *See* Achievement
School administrators, 125
School performance. *See* Academic performance
Schools. *See also* Bullying; Coeducational schools; Public schools; Single-sex schools; Teachers
  AA boys' awareness of, 321–322
  AA boys disengaging from, 313, 317–318, 339–340, 343
  developmentally auspicious environments of, 345–353
  enhancing gender integrated interactions at, 179–180
  female-stereotyped preference structure of, 339–340
  as feminine arena, 25–26
  gender segregation in, 165–170
  homes' alliances with, 341–342

Subject Index

inclusive curriculum associated with safety of, 290, 291
low-performing, 339
middle students' awareness of, 322
peer norms influenced by, 348
physical education in, 122–123
resilience promoted by, 287–293
sexism reduced by, 209–213
sexual harassment in, 202–204
sexual minority youth belonging to, 267
socialization influenced by, 119
socio-emotional needs addressed by, 350–351
teachers promoting gender segregation in, 166–167
Title IX influencing, 122–123
transgender youth marginalized by, 286–287
victimization causing avoidance of, 273–274
Schott Foundation, 302, 305
Science, Technology, Engineering, and Mathematics (STEM). *See also* Interventions
　AA boys taking courses in, 304–306
　AA children's performance in, 341
　adolescents' enrollment in, 29–30
　AP exams, 80–81, 80*f*, 198
　bachelor's degrees in, 79–80, 79*f*, 197
　communal goals in, 53–54
　competitions related to, 83
　discrimination in, 63, 64, 65, 212–213
　elementary teachers' anxiety in, 63–64
　gender biases in, 197–200, 244, 245
　gender differences in, 48, 51, 56, 57, 58–59, 61–62, 63–64, 65, 66, 67, 68–70, 79–81, 79*f*, 80*f*, 82–84, 197–198
　gender segregation in, 79–85, 79*f*, 80*f*, 81*f*, 197
　gender similarities in, 50–51
　gender stereotypes, 198–200
　gender-variant youth taking courses in, 275, 276
　high school student importance of, 57
　high-achieving boys taking courses in, 29–30
　high-achieving girls taking courses in, 29–30
　intervention program, 29–30, 44, 45, 47–59, 61, 63, 64, 68–71, 79–82, 84–87, 94–105
　job choice importance of, 50
　jobs, 78, 101, 103, 105, 109
　low-achieving boys taking courses in, 29–30
　outcome measures relevant to, 107–108
　parental expectations in, 61–62
　parents' beliefs on sex differences in, 29, 44, 45, 47–61, 63, 64, 68–71, 79–87, 89, 94, 110
　sex differences, 9–11, 12–13. *See also* gender differences in
　sexism in, 193–194, 195–196, 197–200
　sexual minority youth taking courses in, 268, 275, 276
　spatial performance's importance to, 51, 82–83, 94–95, 107
　standardized tests, 198
　stereotype threat, 47, 199
　utility value of, 58–59, 62
　women's underrepresentation in jobs in, 50, 52, 53–54, 55
　workforce, 81*f*
Science Cheerleaders program, 102–103, 109
Science: It's a Girl Thing! (European Commission), 100
Scripps National Spelling Bee, 83
SCT. *See* Social cognitive theory
Secondary schools, 126, 127
Second-wave feminism, 5, 227
Selected environments, 88
Self-aggrandizement, 11–12
Self-appraisal. *See* Self-evaluation
Self-concepts, 6, 9–12, 55
Self-confidence, 52–53
Self-denigrating biases, 12
Self-efficacy, 9, 16, 88
　definition of, 265
　as function of parental behavior, 195–196
　job choice influenced by, 63
　in SCCT, 265–267
　of sexual minority youth, 268
Self-enhancement, 15–16
Self-esteem, 55, 317–318, 352–353
Self-evaluation, 16–20
Self-evaluative bias, 9–11

Self-handicapping, 13–14, 21, 26
Self-improvement, 15
Self-perceived ability for job success, 49
Self-promotion, motivation influenced by, 3
Self-schemata, 132
Self-serving bias, 12, 21
Self-stereotyping, 251–252
Self-views. *See* Self-concepts
SES. *See* Students' socioeconomic background
Sex differences, 4. *See also* Gender differences
   in academic motivation, 32–35
   in academic self-concepts, 9
   in academic self-efficacy, 16
   in achievement goals, 20–21
   in aptitudes, 235, 237–238
   in attribution retraining, 14
   in cheating, 21
   in disruptive behavior, 235, 238–239
   in effortful control, 31
   in failure, 12–13
   gender segregation increase, 168–169
   in help, 21
   innate, 210, 227
   in interests, 27–28, 235, 240–241
   in jobs, 28
   mathematics, 46–52, 54, 56–59, 61–64, 66, 68–70
   in maturation, 235–237
   in negative feedback, 15–16, 17
   in parental expectations, 29–30
   in parents' perceptions, 29–30
   in participatory style, 235, 239–240
   in perceived competence, 8–12
   in positive feedback, 17
   in reading and language arts, 9, 10–11, 29
   in self-evaluative bias, 9–11
   in social comparison, 16–19
   in social feedback, 17
   in spatial skills, 51, 69, 82, 83, 94–96, 107
   in STEM, 9–11, 12–13, 29, 79–87, 89, 94, 110
   in success, 12–13
   in teacher communication, 30–31
   in teacher control, 31
   in values, 28
Sexes. *See also* Coeducational schools; Same-sex peer groups; Single-sex schools
   age influencing, 11–12
   boys as detriment to, 26–27
   as control, 4
   discrimination, 56, 64–65
   motivation and differences between, 4
   similarities, 12, 227
   tests for, 4
   variance within, 4
Sexism, 356–357. *See also* Gender stereotypes; Sexual harassment
   in adolescents, 169
   awareness of, 204–208, 212–213
   in books, 196–197
   confrontation reducing, 212
   coping with, 204, 205, 208–209
   ethnicity influencing, 191–192
   gender segregation as related to, 169–170
   identity's importance to, 209
   masculinity and, 201–202
   overview of, 190–192, 213–214
   perpetrators of, 192–197, 199–200, 202, 207, 212
   race influencing, 191–192
   schools reducing, 209–213, 241–247
   in STEM, 193–194, 195–196, 197–200
   types of, 190–192
Sexual distraction, 249–250
Sexual harassment, 191
   consequences of, 204
   peers perpetrating, 194, 242, 246–247
   prevalence of, 203–204
   same-sex, 246
   in school, 202–204
   video games justifying, 196
Sexual minority youth. *See also* Gender-variant youth; Resilience; Victimization
   academic disparities faced by, 267–269
   college gone to by, 268–269
   coming out process of, 276–277
   diversity within community of, 269
   exclusionary discipline influencing, 278–279
   grades of, 267–268, 277
   help avoided by, 274
   high school completed by, 268–269
   in minority stress model, 264–265
   overview of, 262–264, 293

Subject Index

in SCCT model, 265–267, 268, 277
school belonging of, 267
schools marginalizing, 286–287
self-efficacy of, 268
in sports, 285–287
STEM courses taken by, 268, 276
teachers as allies to, 274
unique stressors among, 279–280
Sexual violence, 201
Sexualized images of female athletes, 138
SIENA. *See* Simulation Investigation for Empirical Network Analysis
Similarity, 157–159, 157*f*, 159*f*.
    See also Gender similarities
Simulation Investigation for Empirical Network Analysis (SIENA), 158–159, 159*f*
Single-sex (SS) schools
  AA boys and, 234–235, 353–356, 357–359
  academic motivation and, 231–232
  aptitudes and, 231–232, 235, 237–238
  at-risk girls thriving in, 233–234
  CE schools methods transportation of, 253
  confounds, 230
  disruptive behavior and, 235, 238–239
  gender atypical children in, 234
  gender labeling in, 248
  gender salience in, 247–249, 253–254
  history of, 226–228
  interests and, 235, 240–241
  Latino youth and, 234–235
  maturation and, 235–237
  meta-analyses of literature on, 229–230, 237, 240
  NCLBA easing restrictions on, 228
  overview of, 226, 252–254
  participatory style and, 235, 239–240
  peer gender stereotyping in, 242, 245
  peer rejection in, 250–251
  peer sexual harassment in, 242, 246–247
  race emphasized by, 235
  rationales for
    analysis of, 228–252
    contemporary, 228–252
    evaluation of, 228–252
    gender attention reduction, 247–252
    gender differences, 235–241
    historical, 226–228
    sexism reduction, 241–247
  works for all students, 229–232
  works for some students, 233–235, 252–253
  recommendations, 252–254
  religious institutions pressing for, 227
  same-sex romantic attractions in, 250
  selection effects, 230, 231–232
  self-stereotyping in, 251–252
  SES and, 230–231
  sexism reduced by, 209, 210–211, 241–247
  sexual distraction in, 249–250
  students of color thriving in, 234–235
  teachers in, 241, 242–245
  in U.S., 226–227
Slavery, 352
SLT. *See* Social learning theory
Social cognitions about gender, 156–157
Social cognitive career theory (SCCT), 264–268, 277, 292–293
Social cognitive theory (SCT), 87–88, 89
Social comparison, 16–19, 19*f*
Social construction of bodily meanings, 138–140
Social development. *See* Socialization
Social dominance, 176
Social dosage, 154–155, 163
Social feedback, sex differences in, 17
Social gatherings, 346–347
Social goals, 23–28
Social influences, 29–31
Social learning, students influenced by, 6
Social learning theory (SLT), 87. *See also* Social cognitive theory
Social networks analyses, 158–159, 159*f*
Social role theory. *See* Sociocultural theory
Socialization. *See also* Gender socialization
  of AA boys, 308–310
  of AA girls, 309, 310
  AA parent, 307, 308–310
  binary view of, 162–165, 164*f*
  definition of, 119
  gradient view of, 163–165, 164*f*
  physical education influencing, 119
  same-sex peer groups influencing, 154–155, 161–165, 164*f*
  schools influencing, 119
  sports influencing, 119

Sociocultural theory, 48, 84–85
Socio-emotional development, 343–344, 350–351
Spatial performance, 51, 69–70, 82–83, 94–96
Special education, 315–316
Sports. *See also* Physical activity; Physical education
  AA boys participating in, 319–320
  academic outcomes and, 119
  academic performance influenced by, 119
  African Americans making strides in, 124
  aggression in, 201
  bodily meanings influenced by, 138–139
  in cool-pose theory, 319–320
  discrimination in, 124, 126–127
  education and, 144–145
  gender biases in, 200–201
  gender differences in, 121–122, 144–145
    changes reducing, 134, 146
    Title IX influencing, 123–125, 200
  gender stereotypes influencing, 133–134
  in history, 121–122, 144
  interscholastic, 145
  parental expectations in, 201
  physical activity promoted by, 118
  physical education as distinct from, 119–120
  as required, 120
  in secondary schools, 145
  sexual minority youth in, 285–287
  socialization influenced by, 119
  transgender youth in, 286–287
  victimization in, 285
SS schools. *See* Single-sex schools
Stable causes, 7, 13
Standardized tests, 198
STEM. *See* Science, Technology, Engineering, and Mathematics (STEM)
STEM interventions. *See* Interventions, STEM-relevant strategies
Stereotype threat, 46–47, 70, 199, 352
Stereotypes. *See also* Gender stereotypes
  of AA boys, 302, 344, 351–353
  attitudes, 191
  definition of, 190
  discrimination and, 63–66
  self-, 251–252
Storytelling Alice software, 97–98, 99
Students. *See also* Black students; Bullying; Coeducational schools; College students; European American students; High school students; Middle school students; Physical education; Schools; Sexism; Single-sex schools; Sports; Teachers
  in achievement goal theory, 7–8
  Australian, 58
  Canadian, 58, 204
  cheating, 21
  discrimination perceived by, 65–66
  in E-V theory, 6
  girls as ideal, 24–25
  goals constructed by, 8
  help asked for by, 21
  historical lesson taught to, 65–66
  interest of, 6
  as interested, 27–28
  mastery goals orienting, 8, 21
  performance goals orienting, 8, 21
  self-concepts formed by, 6, 9–12
  social learning influencing, 6
  success views of, 6
  U.S., STEM performance of, 50–51
Students of color in SS schools, 234–235. *See also* African American children; Latino children
Students' socioeconomic background (SES), 230–231
Subjective task value, 45, 46
Substance use, as coping strategy, 274–275
Success
  expectancy for, 45–46, 57–58
  fear of, 5–6
  females with, 9
  job, self-perceived ability for, 49
  males with, 9
  men fearing, 5, 6
  motivation and, 5–6
  praise for, 14
  sex differences in, 12–13
  students' views of, 6

women avoiding, 5–6
women with, 9
Support, 281–285
Suspension. *See* Exclusionary discipline

T

Task values. *See* Values
Teachers. *See also* Elementary school teachers
  AA boys benefiting from, 324, 345–346
  AA boys differential responses, 337–338
  AA boys' relationships with, 338, 346–347
  AA men as, 348–349
  AA parents knowing, 349–350
  as allies, 274
  attention, 242–243
  communications, sex differences in, 30–31
  control, 31
  culturally sensitive training for, 345–346
  expectations, 242, 244–245
  fitness testing influencing, 135
  gender differences reinforced by, 141–142
  girls influenced by STEM anxiety of, 63–64
  interaction, 242, 243–244
  in low-performing schools, 339
  mastery goal structure created by, 21, 22, 34–35
  narratives, 310–317, 321, 324–325
  performance goal structure created by, 21–22, 31
  physical education, 122–123, 141–142
  racial biases of, 305, 306, 308, 325, 336–344
  schools' gender segregation promoted by, 166–167
  sexism perpetrated by, 192, 193–194, 202, 207, 212
  as social influence, 30–31
  in SS schools, 241, 242–245
  STEM anxiety of female, 63–64
  student interaction, 243–244
  Title IX influencing, 122–123
Teasing, 171, 172
Teens. *See* Adolescents

Temporal comparison, developmental trends in, 18–20, 19f
Tentative speech, 52–53
Test anxiety, 4, 21
Title IX, 144–145
  CE schools' and, 227–228
  physical activity influenced by, 122–125
  physical education influenced by, 122–123, 126, 127
  school districts influenced by, 122–123
  sports influenced by, 122–125, 200
  teachers influenced by, 122–123
Toys, girl friendly versions of, 98–99
Tracing task, 17–20
Tracking, 252
Training, gender differences in, 69–70
Transactional leader, 54
Transformational leader, 54
Transgender youth. *See* Sexual minority youth
Trauma, 343
Trends in International Mathematics and Science Study, 48
Truck, 90
Turkey, 71

U

Unconscious stereotyped attitudes, 191
Unintended outcomes, 108–109
United States (U.S.). *See also* Interventions
  anti-discrimination policies in, 288
  family devotion beliefs in, 66–67
  gender segregation in, 44, 71, 78, 197, 201
  high school students, 57, 80–81, 80f
  pay gap in, 71
  physical activity in, 117–118
  SS schools in, 226–227
  students' STEM performance, 50–51
  tracking in, 252
United States Family and Medical Leave Act, 66–67
Universities, physical education in, 122
Unstable causes, 7, 13
Urban neighborhoods, 340, 351
Urban Prep, 326
Utility values, 46, 58–59, 62, 129

V

Values, 4–5. *See also* Utility values
  achievement and, 23–28
  adolescents consolidating, 28
  attainment, 129
  career, 100–105
  expanding your horizons (EYH), 100
  identity and, 27–29
  interests and, 27–29
  intrinsic, 129
  locus of control influencing, 7
  motivation and, 6, 23–28
  perceptions of, 129–130
  sex differences in, 28
  and sex-role concepts, 89
Values-affirmation technique, 70
Variables, 4
Verbal skills, 51–52
Victimization. *See also* Resilience
  academic disparities and, 269–272
  academic performance influenced by, 266, 272–280
  academic resilience promoted in face of, 280–293
  chronic and prolonged, 269–270
  discipline disparities contributed to by, 278–279
  grades and, 271–272
  of heterosexual youth, 270–271
  homophobic, 262, 265, 269–277, 282, 290, 292
  of LGBT youth, 262
  learning influenced by, 272–280
  mental health diminishment predicted by, 272–273, 282
  meta-analyses on, 270
  in minority stress model, 275–276, 278–279
  onset of, 276–277
  overview of, 262–264
  physical health's association with, 273
  research, 269–272
  as risk factor, 276–277
  school avoidance caused by, 273–274
  in sports, 285–286
  substance use as coping strategy for, 274–275
  timing of, 276–277
  of transgender youth, 279–280
  vigilance caused by, 275–276
Victims, AA boys as, 315
Video games, 69, 196
Vigilance, 275–276, 308–310
Violence, 201, 340, 343
Vocational interests. *See* Occupational interests

W

Weiner's attribution theory of achievement motivation, 7, 12–15
White European American children. *See* European American children
White students. *See* European American students
Women. *See also* Discrimination; Gender differences; Gender equality; Gender salience; Gender segregation; Gender similarities; Sex differences; Sexes; Sexism; Stereotype threat
  achievement writings of, 5–6
  competitive settings influencing, 5–6
  educational achievement of, 3
  on effort, 13–14
  family devotion of, 66–67
  part-time employment of, 67
  psychology's aberrant results with, 5
  in sociocultural theory, 48
  STEM jobs underrepresentation of, 50, 52, 53–54, 55
  stereotype threat for college, 47
  success avoided by, 5–6
  successful, 9
  tentative speech used by, 52–53
  as unprepared, 8
  work-family balance influencing, 66–67
Work-family balance, 66–67
Workplace discrimination. *See* Discrimination
World War I (WWI), 70
World War II (WWII), 70–71

Z

Zimmerman, George, 309

CONTENTS OF PREVIOUS VOLUMES

VOLUME 1

Responses of Infants and Children to Complex and Novel Stimulation
Gordon N. Cantor

Word Associations and Children's Verbal Behavior
David S. Palermo

Change in the Stature and Body Weight of North American Boys during the Last 80 Years
Howard V. Meredith

Discrimination Learning Set in Children
Hayne W. Reese

Learning in the First Year of Life
Lewis P. Lipsitt

Some Methodological Contributions from a Functional Analysis of Child Development
Sidney W. Bijou and Donald M. Baer

The Hypothesis of Stimulus Interaction and an Explanation of Stimulus Compounding
Charles C. Spiker

The Development of "Overconstancy" in Space Perception
Joachim F. Wohlwill

Miniature Experiments in the Discrimination Learning of Retardates
Betty J. House and David Zeaman

Author Index–Subject Index

VOLUME 2

The Paired-Associates Method in the Study of Conflict
Alfred Castaneda

Transfer of Stimulus Pretraining to Motor Paired-Associate and Discrimination Learning Tasks
Joan H. Cantor

The Role of the Distance Receptors in the Development of Social Responsiveness
Richard H. Walters and Ross D. Parke

Social Reinforcement of Children's Behavior
Harold W. Stevenson

Delayed Reinforcement Effects
Glenn Terrell

A Developmental Approach to Learning and Cognition
Eugene S. Gollin

Evidence for a Hierarchical Arrangement of Learning Processes
Sheldon H. White

Selected Anatomic Variables Analyzed for Interage Relationships of the Size-Size, Size-Gain, and Gain-Gain Varieties
Howard V. Meredith

Author Index–Subject Index

VOLUME 3

Infant Sucking Behavior and Its Modification
Herbert Kaye

The Study of Brain Electrical Activity in Infants
Robert J. Ellingson

Selective Auditory Attention in Children
Eleanor E. Maccoby

Stimulus Definition and Choice
Michael D. Zeiler

Experimental Analysis of Inferential Behavior in Children
Tracy S. Kendler and Howard H. Kendler

Perceptual Integration in Children
Herbert L. Pick, Jr., Anne D. Pick, and Robert E. Klein

Component Process Latencies in Reaction Times of Children and Adults
Raymond H. Hohle

Author Index–Subject Index

VOLUME 4

Developmental Studies of Figurative Perception
David Elkind

The Relations of Short-Term Memory to
Development and Intelligence
John M. Belmont and Earl C. Butterfield

Learning, Developmental Research, and
Individual Differences
Frances Degen Horowitz

Psychophysiological Studies in Newborn
Infants
S.J. Hutt, H.G. Lenard, and H.F.R. Prechtl

Development of the Sensory Analyzers during
Infancy
Yvonne Brackbill and Hiram E. Fitzgerald

The Problem of Imitation
Justin Aronfreed

Author Index–Subject Index

VOLUME 5

The Development of Human Fetal Activity
and Its Relation to Postnatal Behavior
Tryphena Humphrey

Arousal Systems and Infant Heart Rate
Responses
Frances K. Graham and Jan C. Jackson

Specific and Diversive Exploration
Corinne Hutt

Developmental Studies of Mediated Memory
John H. Flavell

Development and Choice Behavior in
Probabilistic and Problem-Solving Tasks
L.R. Goulet and Kathryn S. Goodwin

Author Index–Subject Index

VOLUME 6

Incentives and Learning in Children
Sam L. Witryol

Habituation in the Human Infant
Wendell E. Jeffrey and Leslie B. Cohen

Application of Hulle Spence Theory to the
Discrimination Learning of Children
Charles C. Spiker

Growth in Body Size: A Compendium of
Findings on Contemporary Children
Living in Different Parts of the World
Howard V. Meredith

Imitation and Language Development
James A. Sherman

Conditional Responding as a Paradigm for
Observational, Imitative Learning and
Vicarious-Reinforcement
Jacob L. Gewirtz

Author Index–Subject Index

VOLUME 7

Superstitious Behavior in Children: An
Experimental Analysis
Michael D. Zeiler

Learning Strategies in Children from Different
Socioeconomic Levels
Jean L. Bresnahan and Martin M. Shapiro

Time and Change in the Development of the
Individual and Society
Klaus F. Riegel

The Nature and Development of Early
Number Concepts
Rochel Gelman

Learning and Adaptation in Infancy:
A Comparison of Models
Arnold J. Sameroff

Author Index–Subject Index

VOLUME 8

Elaboration and Learning in Childhood and
Adolescence
William D. Rohwer, Jr.

Exploratory Behavior and Human
Development
Jum C. Nunnally and L. Charles Lemond

Operant Conditioning of Infant Behavior: A
Review
Robert C. Hulsebus

Birth Order and Parental Experience in
Monkeys and Man
G. Mitchell and L. Schroers

Fear of the Stranger: A Critical
Examination
*Harriet L. Rheingold and
Carol O. Eckerman*

Applications of Hulle Spence Theory to the Transfer of Discrimination Learning in Children
Charles C. Spiker and Joan H. Cantor

Author Index–Subject Index

VOLUME 9

Children's Discrimination Learning Based on Identity or Difference
Betty J. House, Ann L. Brown, and Marcia S. Scott

Two Aspects of Experience in Ontogeny: Development and Learning
Hans G. Furth

The Effects of Contextual Changes and Degree of Component Mastery on Transfer of Training
Joseph C. Campione and Ann L. Brown

Psychophysiological Functioning, Arousal, Attention, and Learning during the First Year of Life
Richard Hirschman and Edward S. Katkin

Self-Reinforcement Processes in Children
John C. Masters and Janice R. Mokros

Author Index–Subject Index

VOLUME 10

Current Trends in Developmental Psychology
Boyd R. McCandless and Mary Fulcher Geis

The Development of Spatial Representations of Large-Scale Environments
Alexander W. Siegel and Sheldon H. White

Cognitive Perspectives on the Development of Memory
John W. Hagen, Robert H. Jongeward, Jr., and Robert V. Kail, Jr.

The Development of Memory: Knowing, Knowing About Knowing, and Knowing How to Know
Ann L. Brown

Developmental Trends in Visual Scanning
Mary Carol Day

The Development of Selective Attention: From Perceptual Exploration to Logical Search
John C. Wright and Alice G. Vlietstra

Author Index–Subject Index

VOLUME 11

The Hyperactive Child: Characteristics, Treatment, and Evaluation of Research Design
Gladys B. Baxley and Judith M. LeBlanc

Peripheral and Neurochemical Parallels of Psychopathology: A Psychophysiological Model Relating Autonomic Imbalance to Hyperactivity, Psychopathy, and Autism
Stephen W. Porges

Constructing Cognitive Operations Linguistically
Harry Beilin

Operant Acquisition of Social Behaviors in Infancy: Basic Problems and Constraints
W. Stuart Millar

Mother–Infant Interaction and Its Study
Jacob L. Gewirtz and Elizabeth F. Boyd

Symposium on Implications of Life-Span Developmental Psychology for Child Development: Introductory Remarks
Paul B. Baltes

Theory and Method in Life-Span Developmental Psychology: Implications for Child Development
Aletha Huston-Stein and Paul B. Baltes

The Development of Memory: Life-Span Perspectives
Hayne W. Reese

Cognitive Changes during the Adult Years: Implications for Developmental Theory and Research
Nancy W. Denney and John C. Wright

Social Cognition and Life-Span Approaches to the Study of Child Development
Michael J. Chandler

Life-Span Development of the Theory of Oneself: Implications for Child Development
Orville G. Brim, Jr.

Implication of Life-Span Developmental
Psychology for Childhood Education
Leo Montada and Sigrun-Heide Filipp

Author Index–Subject Index

VOLUME 12

Research between 1960 and 1970 on the
Standing Height of Young Children in
Different Parts of the World
Howard V. Meredith

The Representation of Children's Knowledge
David Klahr and Robert S. Siegler

Chromatic Vision in Infancy
Marc H. Bornstein

Developmental Memory Theories: Baldwin
and Piaget
Bruce M. Ross and Stephen M. Kerst

Child Discipline and the Pursuit of Self: An
Historical Interpretation
Howard Gadlin

Development of Time Concepts in Children
William J. Friedman

Author Index–Subject Index

VOLUME 13

Coding of Spatial and Temporal Information in
Episodic Memory
Daniel B. Berch

A Developmental Model of Human Learning
Barry Gholson and Harry Beilin

The Development of Discrimination Learning:
A Levels-of-Functioning Explanation
Tracy S. Kendler

The Kendler Levels-of-Functioning Theory:
Comments and an Alternative Schema
Charles C. Spiker and Joan H. Cantor

Commentary on Kendler's Paper: An
Alternative Perspective
Barry Gholson and Therese Schuepfer

Reply to Commentaries
Tracy S. Kendler

On the Development of Speech Perception:
Mechanisms and Analogies
Peter D. Eimas and Vivien C. Tartter

The Economics of Infancy: A Review of
Conjugate Reinforcement
Carolyn Kent Rovee-Collier and Marcy J. Gekoski

Human Facial Expressions in Response to
Taste and Smell Stimulation
Jacob E. Steiner

Author Index–Subject Index

VOLUME 14

Development of Visual Memory in
Infants
John S. Werner and Marion Perlmutter

Sibship-Constellation Effects on Psychosocial
Development, Creativity,
and Health
Mazie Earle Wagner, Herman J.P. Schubert, and Daniel S.P. Schubert

The Development of Understanding of the
Spatial Terms Front and Back
Lauren Julius Harris and Ellen A. Strommen

The Organization and Control of Infant
Sucking
C.K. Crook

Neurological Plasticity, Recovery from Brain
Insult, and Child Development
Ian St. James-Roberts

Author Index–Subject Index

VOLUME 15

Visual Development in Ontogenesis: Some
Reevaluations
Jüri Allik and Jaan Valsiner

Binocular Vision in Infants: A Review and a
Theoretical Framework
Richard N. Aslin and Susan T. Dumais

Validating Theories of Intelligence
Earl C. Butterfield, Dennis Siladi, and John M. Belmont

Cognitive Differentiation and Developmental
Learning
William Fowler

Children's Clinical Syndromes and
  Generalized Expectations of Control
  Fred Rothbaum

Author Index–Subject Index

VOLUME 16

The History of the Boyd R. McCandless
  Young Scientist Awards: The First
  Recipients
  David S. Palermo

Social Bases of Language Development: A
  Reassessment
  *Elizabeth Bates, Inge Bretherton, Marjorie
  Beeghly-Smith, and Sandra McNew*

Perceptual Anisotropies in Infancy:
  Ontogenetic Origins and Implications of
  Inequalities in Spatial Vision
  Marc H. Bornstein

Concept Development
  Martha J. Farah and Stephen M. Kosslyn

Production and Perception of Facial
  Expressions in Infancy and Early
  Childhood
  Tiffany M. Field and Tedra A. Walden

Individual Differences in Infant Sociability:
  Their Origins and Implications for
  Cognitive Development
  Michael E. Lamb

The Development of Numerical
  Understandings
  Robert S. Siegler and Mitchell Robinson

Author Index–Subject Index

VOLUME 17

The Development of Problem-Solving
  Strategies
  Deanna Kuhn and Erin Phelps

Information Processing and Cognitive
  Development
  Robert Kail and Jeffrey Bisanz

Research between 1950 and 1980 on
  UrbaneRural Differences in Body Size and
  Growth Rate of Children and Youths
  Howard V. Meredith

Word Meaning Acquisition in Young
  Children: A Review of Theory and
  Research
  Pamela Blewitt

Language Play and Language Acquisition
  Stan A. Kuczaj II

The Child Study Movement: Early Growth
  and Development of the Symbolized
  Child
  Alexander W. Siegel and Sheldon H. White

Author Index–Subject Index

VOLUME 18

The Development of Verbal Communicative
  Skills in Children
  Constance R. Schmidt and Scott G. Paris

Auditory Feedback and Speech Development
  *Gerald M. Siegel, Herbert L. Pick, Jr., and
  Sharon R. Garber*

Body Size of Infants and Children around the
  World in Relation to Socioeconomic
  Status
  Howard V. Meredith

Human Sexual Dimorphism: Its Cost and
  Benefit
  James L. Mosley and Eileen A. Stan

Symposium on Research Programs:
  Rational Alternatives to Kuhn's Analysis
  of Scientific Progress–Introductory
  Remarks
  Hayne W. Reese, Chairman

World Views and Their Influence on
  Psychological Theory and Research:
  Kuhn-Lakatos-Laudan
  Willis F. Overton

The History of the Psychology of Learning as a
  Rational Process: Lakatos versus Kuhn
  Peter Barker and Barry Gholson

Functionalist and Structuralist Research
  Programs in Developmental Psychology:
  Incommensurability or Synthesis?
  Harry Beilin

In Defense of Kuhn: A Discussion of His
  Detractors
  David S. Palermo

Comments on Beilin's Epistemology and Palermo's Defense of Kuhn
Willis F. Overton

From Kuhn to Lakatos to Laudan
Peter Barker and Barry Gholson

Overton's and Palermo's Relativism: One Step Forward, Two Steps Back
Harry Beilin

Author Index–Subject Index

VOLUME 19

Response to Novelty: Continuity versus Discontinuity in the Developmental Course of Intelligence
Cynthia A. Berg and Robert J. Sternberg

Metaphoric Competence in Cognitive and Language Development
Marc Marschark and Lynn Nall

The Concept of Dimensions in Developmental Research
Stuart I. Offenbach and Francine C. Blumberg

Effects of the Knowledge Base on Children's Memory Strategies
Peter A. Ornstein and Mary J. Naus

Effects of Sibling Spacing on Intelligence, Interfamilial Relations, Psychosocial Characteristics, and Mental and Physical Health
Mazie Earle Wagner, Herman J.P. Schubert, and Daniel S.P. Schubert

Infant Visual Preferences: A Review and New Theoretical Treatment
Martin S. Banks and Arthur P. Ginsburg

Author Index–Subject Index

VOLUME 20

Variation in Body Stockiness among and within Ethnic Groups at Ages from Birth to Adulthood
Howard V. Meredith

The Development of Conditional Reasoning: An Iffy Proposition
David P. O'Brien

Content Knowledge: Its Role, Representation, and Restructuring in Memory Development
Michelene T.H. Chi and Stephen J. Ceci

Descriptions: A Model of Nonstrategic Memory Development
Brian P. Ackerman

Reactivation of Infant Memory: Implications for Cognitive Development
Carolyn Rovee-Collier and Harlene Hayne

Gender Segregation in Childhood
Eleanor E. Maccoby and Carol Nagy Jacklin

Piaget, Attentional Capacity, and the Functional Implications of Formal Structure
Michael Chapman

Index

VOLUME 21

Social Development in Infancy: A 25-Year Perspective
Ross D. Parke

On the Uses of the Concept of Normality in Developmental Biology and Psychology
Eugene S. Gollin, Gary Stahl, and Elyse Morgan

Cognitive Psychology: Mentalistic or Behavioristic?
Charles C. Spiker

Some Current Issues in Children's Selective Attention
Betty J. House

Children's Learning Revisited: The Contemporary Scope of the Modified Spence Discrimination Theory
Joan H. Cantor and Charles C. Spiker

Discrimination Learning Set in Children
Hayne W. Reese

A Developmental Analysis of Rule-Following
Henry C. Riegler and Donald M. Baer

Psychological Linguistics: Implications for a Theory of Initial Development and a Method for Research
Sidney W. Bijou

Psychic Conflict and Moral Development
Gordon N. Cantor and David A. Parton

Knowledge and the Child's Developing Theory of the World
David S. Palermo

Childhood Events Recalled by Children and Adults
David B. Pillemer and Sheldon H. White

Index

VOLUME 22

The Development of Representation in Young Children
Judy S. DeLoache

Children's Understanding of Mental Phenomena
David Estes, Henry M. Wellman, and Jacqueline D. Woolley

Social Influences on Children's Cognition: State of the Art and Future Directions
Margarita Azmitia and Marion Perlmutter

Understanding Maps as Symbols: The Development of Map Concepts
Lynn S. Liben and Roger M. Downs

The Development of Spatial Perspective Taking
Nora Newcombe

Developmental Studies of Alertness and Encoding Effects of Stimulus Repetition
Daniel W. Smothergill and Alan G. Kraut

Imitation in Infancy: A Critical Review
Claire L. Poulson, Leila Regina de Paula Nunes, and Steven F. Warren

Author Index–Subject Index

VOLUME 23

The Structure of Developmental Theory
Willis F. Overton

Questions a Satisfying Developmental Theory Would Answer: The Scope of a Complete Explanation of Development Phenomena
Frank B. Murray

The Development of World Views: Toward Future Synthesis?
Ellin Kofsky Scholnick

Metaphor, Recursive Systems, and Paradox in Science and Developmental Theory
Willis F. Overton

Children's Iconic Realism: Object versus Property Realism
Harry Beilin and Elise G. Pearlman

The Role of Cognition in Understanding Gender Effects
Carol Lynn Martin

Development of Processing Speed in Childhood and Adolescence
Robert Kail

Contextualism and Developmental Psychology
Hayne W. Reese

Horizontality of Water Level: A Neo-Piagetian Developmental Review
Juan Pascual-Leone and Sergio Morra

Author Index–Subject Index

VOLUME 24

Music and Speech Processing in the First Year of Life
Sandra E. Trehub, Laurel J. Trainor, and Anna M. Unyk

Effects of Feeding Method on Infant Temperament
John Worobey

The Development of Reading
Linda S. Siegel

Learning to Read: A Theoretical Synthesis
John P. Rack, Charles Hulme, and Margaret J. Snowling

Does Reading Make You Smarter? Literacy and the Development of Verbal Intelligence
Keith E. Stanovich

Sex-of-Sibling Effects: Part I. Gender Role, Intelligence, Achievement, and Creativity
Mazie Earle Wagner, Herman J.P. Schubert, and Daniel S.P. Schubert

The Concept of Same
Linda B. Smith

Planning as Developmental Process
Jacquelyn Baker-Sennett, Eugene Matusov, and Barbara Rogoff

Author Index–Subject Index

VOLUME 25

In Memoriam: Charles C. Spiker (1925–1993)
Lewis P. Lipsitt

Developmental Differences in Associative Memory: Strategy Use, Mental Effort, and Knowledge Access Interactions
Daniel W. Kee

A Unifying Framework for the Development of Children's Activity Memory
Hilary Horn Ratner and Mary Ann Foley

Strategy Utilization Deficiencies in Children: When, Where, and Why
Patricia H. Miller and Wendy L. Seier

The Development of Children's Ability to Use Spatial Representations
Mark Blades and Christopher Spencer

Fostering Metacognitive Development
Linda Baker

The HOME Inventory: Review and Reflections
Robert H. Bradley

Social Reasoning and the Varieties of Social Experiences in Cultural Contexts
Elliot Turiel and Cecilia Wainryb

Mechanisms in the Explanation of Developmental Change
Harry Beilin

Author Index–Subject Index

VOLUME 26

Preparing to Read: The Foundations of Literacy
Ellen Bialystok

The Role of Schemata in Children's Memory
Denise Davidson

The Interaction of Knowledge, Aptitude, and Strategies in Children's Memory Performance
David F. Bjorklund and Wolfgang Schneider

Analogical Reasoning and Cognitive Development
Usha Goswami

Sex-of-Sibling Effects: A Review Part II. Personality and Mental and Physical Health
Mazie Earle Wagner, Herman J.P. Schubert, and Daniel S.P. Schubert

Input and Learning Processes in First Language Acquisition
Ernst L. Moerk

Author Index–Subject Index

VOLUME 27

From Form to Meaning: A Role for Structural Alignment in the Acquisition of Language
Cynthia Fisher

The Role of Essentialism in Children's Concepts
Susan A. Gelman

Infants' Use of Prior Experiences with Objects in Object Segregation: Implications for Object Recognition in Infancy
Amy Needham and Avani Modi

Perseveration and Problem Solving in Infancy
Andréa Aguiar and Renée Baillargeon

Temperament and Attachment: One Construct or Two?
Sarah C. Mangelsdrof and Cynthia A. Frosch

The Foundation of Piaget's Theories: Mental and Physical Action
Harry Beilin and Gary Fireman

Author Index–Subject Index

VOLUME 28

Variability in Children's Reasoning
Karl S. Rosengren and Gregory S. Braswell

Fuzzy-Trace Theory: Dual Processes in Memory, Reasoning, and Cognitive Neuroscience
C.J. Brainerd and V.F. Reyna

Relational Frame Theory: A Post-Skinnerian
  Account of Human Language and
  Cognition
  *Yvonne Barnes-Holmes, Steven C. Hayes,
  Dermot Barnes-Holmes, and
  Bryan Roche*

The Continuity of Depression across the
  Adolescent Transition
  Shelli Avenevoli and Laurence Steinberg

The Time of Our Lives: Self-Continuity in
  Native and Non-Native Youth
  Michael J. Chandler

Author Index–Subject Index

VOLUME 29

The Search for What is Fundamental in the
  Development of Working Memory
  *Nelson Cowan, J. Scott Saults,
  and Emily M. Elliott*

Culture, Autonomy, and Personal Jurisdiction
  in Adolescent–Parent Relationships
  Judith G. Smetana

Maternal Responsiveness and Early Language
  Acquisition
  *Catherine S. Tamis-Lemonda and Marc H.
  Bornstein*

Schooling as Cultural Process: Working
  Together and Guidance by Children
  from Schools Differing in Collaborative
  Practices
  *Eugene Matusov, Nancy Bell, and Barbara
  Rogoff*

Beyond Prototypes: Asymmetries in Infant
  Categorization and What They Teach Us
  about the Mechanisms Guiding Early
  Knowledge Acquisition
  Paul C. Quinn

Peer Relations in the Transition to
  Adolescence
  Carollee Howes and Julie Wargo Aikins

Author Index–Subject Index

VOLUME 30

Learning to Keep Balance
  Karen Adolph

Sexual Selection and Human Life History
  David C. Geary

Developments in Early Recall Memory:
  Normative Trends and Individual
  Differences
  *Patricia J. Bauer, Melissa M. Burch, and Erica E.
  Kleinknecht*

Intersensory Redundancy Guides Early
  Perceptual and Cognitive Development
  Lorraine E. Bahrick and Robert Lickliter

Children's Emotion-Related Regulation
  Nancy Eisenberg and Amanda Sheffield Morris

Maternal Sensitivity and Attachment in
  Atypical Groups
  L. Beckwith, A. Rozga, and M. Sigman

Influences of Friends and Friendships:
  Myths, Truths, and Research
  Recommendations
  Thomas J. Berndt and Lonna M. Murphy

Author Index–Subject Index

VOLUME 31

Beyond Point And Shoot: Children's
  Developing Understanding of
  Photographs as Spatial and Expressive
  Representations
  Lynn S. Liben

Probing the Adaptive Significance of
  Children's Behavior and Relationships in
  the School Context: A Child by
  Environment Perspective
  Gary W. Ladd

The Role of Letter Names in the Acquisition of
  Literacy
  Rebecca Treiman and Brett Kessler

Early Understandings of Emotion, Morality,
  and Self: Developing a Working Model
  *Ross A. Thompson, Deborah J. Laible, and
  Lenna L. Ontai*

Working Memory in Infancy
  Kevin A. Pelphrey and J. Steven Reznick

The Development of a Differentiated
  Sense of the Past and the Future
  William J. Friedman

The Development of Cognitive Flexibility and Language Abilities
Gedeon O. Deák

A Bio-Social-Cognitive Approach to Understanding and Promoting the Outcomes of Children with Medical and Physical Disorders
Daphne Blunt Bugental and David A. Beaulieu

Expanding Our View of Context: The Bio-ecological Environment and Development
Theodore D. Wachs

Pathways to Early Literacy: The Complex Interplay of Child, Family, and Sociocultural Factors
Megan M. McClelland, Maureen Kessenich, and Frederick J. Morrison

Author Index–Subject Index

VOLUME 32

From the Innocent to the Intelligent Eye: The Early Development of Pictorial Competence
Georgene L. Troseth, Sophia L. Pierroutsakos, and Judy S. DeLoache

Bringing Culture into Relief: Cultural Contributions to the Development of Children's Planning Skills
Mary Gauvain

A Dual-Process Model of Adolescent Development: Implications for Decision Making, Reasoning, and Identity
Paul A. Klaczynski

The High Price of Affluence
Suniya S. Luthar and Chris C. Sexton

Attentional Inertia in Children's Extended Looking at Television
John E. Richards and Daniel R. Anderson

Understanding Classroom Competence: The Role of Social-Motivational and Self-Processes
Kathryn R. Wentzel

Continuities and Discontinuities in Infants' Representation of Objects and Events
Rachel E. Keen and Neil E. Berthier

The Mechanisms of Early Categorization and Induction: Smart or Dumb Infants?
David H. Rakison and Erin R. Hahn

Author Index–Subject Index

VOLUME 33

A Computational Model of Conscious and Unconscious Strategy Discovery
Robert Siegler and Roberto Araya

Out-of-School Settings as a Developmental Context for Children and Youth
Deborah Lowe Vandell, Kim M. Pierce, and Kimberly Dadisman

Mechanisms of Change in the Development of Mathematical Reasoning
Martha W. Alibali

A Social Identity Approach to Ethnic Differences in Family Relationships during Adolescence
Andrew J. Fuligni and Lisa Flook

What Develops in Language Development?
LouAnn Gerken

The Role of Children's Competence Experiences in the Socialization Process: A Dynamic Process Framework for the Academic Arena
Eva M. Pomerantz, Qian Wang, and Florrie Ng

The Infant Origins of Intentional Understanding
Amanda L. Woodward

Analyzing Comorbidity
Bruce F. Pennington, Erik Willcutt, and Soo Hyun Rhee

Number Words and Number Concepts: The Interplay of Verbal and Nonverbal Quantification in Early Childhood
Kelly S. Mix, Catherine M. Sandhofer, and Arthur J. Baroody

Author Index–Subject Index

VOLUME 34

Mapping Sound to Meaning: Connections Between Learning About Sounds and Learning About Words
Jenny R. Saffran and Katharine Graf Estes

A Developmental Intergroup Theory of Social
Stereotypes and Prejudice
Rebecca S. Bigler and Lynn S. Liben

Income Poverty, Poverty Co-Factors, and the
Adjustment of Children in Elementary
School
Brian P. Ackerman and Eleanor D. Brown

I Thought She Knew That Would Hurt My
Feelings: Developing Psychological
Knowledge and Moral Thinking
Cecilia Wainryb and Beverely A. Brehl

Home Range and The Development of
Children's Way Finding
Edward H. Cornel and C. Donald Heth

The Development and Neural Bases of Facial
Emotion Recognition
Jukka M. Leppänen and Charles A. Nelson

Children's Suggestibility: Characteristics and
Mechanisms
Stephen J. Ceci and Maggie Bruck

The Emergence and Basis of Endogenous
Attention in Infancy and Early Childhood
John Colombo and Carol L. Cheatham

The Probabilistic Epigenesis of Knowledge
James A. Dixon and Elizabeth Kelley

Author Index–Subject Index

VOLUME 35

Evolved Probabilistic Cognitive Mechanisms:
An Evolutionary Approach to Gene ×
Environment × Development Interactions
David F. Bjorklund, Bruce J. Ellis, and Justin S. Rosenberg

Development of Episodic and
Autobiographical Memory: A Cognitive
Neuroscience Perspective
Nora S. Newcombe, Marianne E. Lloyd and Kristin R. Ratliff

Advances in the Formulation of Emotional
Security Theory: An Ethologically Based
Perspective
Patrick T. Davies and Melissa L. Sturge-Apple

Processing Limitations and the Grammatical
Profile of Children with Specific Language
Impairment
Laurence B. Leonard

Children's Experiences and Judgments about
Group Exclusion and Inclusion
Melanie Killen, Stefanie Sinno, and Nancy Geyelin Margie

Working Memory as the Interface between
Processing and Retention: A
Developmental Perspective
John N. Towse, Graham J. Hitch, and Neil Horton

Developmental Science and Education:
The NICHD Study of Early Child Care
and Youth Development Findings from
Elementary School
Robert C. Pianta

The Role of Morphology in Reading and
Spelling
Monique Sénéchal and Kyle Kearnan

The Interactive Development of Social Smiling
Daniel Messinger and Alan Fogel

Author Index–Subject Index

VOLUME 36

King Solomon's Take on Word Learning: An
Integrative Account from the Radical
Middle
Kathy Hirsh-Pasek and Roberta Micnnick Golinkoff

Orthographic Learning, Phonological
Recoding, and Self-Teaching
David L. Share

Developmental Perspectives on Links between
Attachment and Affect Regulation Over
the Lifespan
Lisa M. Diamond and Christopher P. Fagundes

Function Revisited: How Infants Construe
Functional Features in their
Representation of Objects
Lisa M. Oakes and Kelly L. Madole

Transactional Family Dynamics: A New
Framework for Conceptualizing Family
Influence Processes
Alice C. Schermerhorn and E. Mark Cummings

The Development of Rational Thought:
A Taxonomy of Heuristics and Biases
Keith E. Stanovich, Maggie E. Toplak, and Richard F. West

Lessons Learned: Recent Advances in Understanding and Preventing Childhood Aggression
Nancy G. Guerra and Melinda S. Leidy

The Social Cognitive Neuroscience of Infancy: Illuminating the Early Development of Social Brain Functions
Mark H. Johnson, Tobias Grossmann, and Teresa Farroni

Children's Thinking is Not Just about What is in the Head: Understanding the Organism and Environment as a Unified System
Jodie M. Plumert

Remote Transfer of Scientific-Reasoning and Problem-Solving Strategies in Children
Zhe Chen and David Klahr

Author Index–Subject Index

VOLUME 37

The Role of Dyadic Communication in Social Cognitive Development
Maria Legerstee

The Developmental Origins of Naïve Psychology in Infancy
Diane Poulin-Dubois, Ivy Brooker, and Virginia Chow

Children's Reasoning About Traits
Gail D. Heyman

The Development of Autobiographical Memory: Origins and Consequences
Elaine Reese

The Development of Temperament from a Behavioral Genetics Perspective
Kimberly J. Saudino

Developmental Changes in Cognitive control Through Adolescence
Beatriz Luna

Author Index–Subject Index

VOLUME 38

Declarative Memory In Infancy: An Introduction to Typical and Atypical Development
Patricia J. Bauer

Finding the Right Fit: Examining Developmentally Appropriate Levels of Challenge in Elicited-imitation Studies
Melissa M. Burch, Jennifer A. Schwade, and Patricia J. Bauer

Hearing the Signal Through the Noise: Assessing the Stability of Individual Differences in Declarative Memory in the Second and Third Years of Life
Patricia J. Bauer, Melissa M. Burch, and Jennifer A. Schwade

Declarative Memory Performance in Infants of Diabetic Mothers
Tracy Riggins, Patricia J. Bauer, Michael K. Georgieff, and Charles A. Nelson

The Development of Declarative Memory in Infants Born Preterm
Carol L. Cheatham, Heather Whitney Sesma, Patricia J. Bauer, and Michael K. Georgieff

Institutional Care as a Risk for Declarative Memory Development
Maria G. Kroupina, Patricia J. Bauer, Megan R. Gunnar, and Dana E. Johnson

Declarative Memory in Abused and Neglected Infants
Carol L. Cheatham, Marina Larkina, Patricia J. Bauer, Sheree L. Toth, and Dante Cicchetti

Declarative Memory in Infancy: Lessons Learned from Typical and Atypical Development
Patricia J. Bauer

Author Index–Subject Index

VOLUME 39

Poor Working Memory: Impact and Interventions
Joni Holmes, Susan E. Gathercole, and Darren L. Dunning

Mathematical Learning Disabilities
David C. Geary

The Poor Comprehender Profile: Understanding and Supporting Individuals Who Have Difficulties Extracting Meaning from Text
Paula J. Clarke, Lisa M. Henderson, and Emma Truelove

Reading as an Intervention for Vocabulary, Short-term Memory and Speech Development of School-Aged Children with Down Syndrome: A Review of the Evidence
Glynis Laws

Williams Syndrome
Deborah M. Riby and Melanie A. Porter

Fragile X Syndrome and Associated Disorders
Kim M. Cornish, Kylie M. Gray, and Nicole J. Rinehart

Author Index–Subject Index

VOLUME 40

Autobiographical Memory Development From an Attachment Perspective: The Special Role of Negative Events
Yoojin Chae, Gail S. Goodman, and Robin S. Edelstein

Links Between Attachment and Social Information Processing: Examination of Intergenerational Processes
Matthew J. Dykas, Katherine B. Ehrlich, and Jude Cassidy

The Development of Episodic Foresight: Emerging Concepts and Methods
Judith A. Hudson, Estelle M.Y. Mayhew, and Janani Prabhakar

From Little White Lies to Filthy Liars: The Evolution of Honesty and Deception in Young Children
Victoria Talwar and Angela Crossman

A Model of Moral Identity: Applications for Education
M. Kyle Matsuba, Theresa Murzyn, and Daniel Hart

Cultural Patterns in Children's Learning Through Keen Observation and Participation in their Communities
Maricela Correa-Chávez, Amy L.D. Roberts, and Margarita Martínez Pérez

Family Relationships and Children's Stress Responses
Rachel G. Lucas-Thompson and Wendy A. Goldberg

Developmental Perspectives on Vulnerability to Nonsuicidal Self-Injury in Youth
Andrea L. Barrocas, Jessica L. Jenness, Tchikima S. Davis, Caroline W. Oppenheimer, Jessica R. Technow, Lauren D. Gulley, Lisa S. Badanes, and Benjamin L. Hankin

More Similarities Than Differences in Contemporary Theories of Social Development?: A Plea for Theory Bridging
Campbell Leaper

Monitoring, Metacognition, and Executive Function: Elucidating The Role of Self-Reflection in the Development of Self-Regulation
Kristen E. Lyons and Philip David Zelazo

Author Index–Subject Index

VOLUME 41

Positive Youth Development: Research and Applications for Promoting Thriving in Adolescence
Richard M. Lerner, Jacqueline V. Lerner, and Janette B. Benson

The Development of Intentional Self-Regulation in Adolescence: Describing, Explaining, and Optimizing its Link to Positive Youth Development
Christopher M. Napolitano, Edmond P. Bowers, Steinunn Gestsdóttir, and Paul A. Chase

Youth Purpose and Positive Youth Development
Jenni Menon Mariano and Julie Going

Positive Pathways to Adulthood: The Role of Hope in Adolescents' Constructions of Their Futures
Kristina L. Schmid and Shane J. Lopez

Intrinsic Motivation and Positive Development
Reed W. Larson and Natalie Rusk

School Engagement: What it is and Why it is Important for Positive Youth Development
Yibing Li

Religion, Spirituality, Positive Youth Development, and Thriving
Pamela Ebstyne King, Drew Carr, and Ciprian Boitor

The Contribution of the Developmental Assets Framework to Positive Youth Development Theory and Practice
Peter L. Benson, Peter C. Scales, and Amy K. Syvertsen

Youth Activity Involvement and Positive Youth Development
Megan Kiely Mueller, Selva Lewin-bizan, and Jennifer Brown Urban

Media Literacy and Positive Youth Development
Michelle J. Boyd and Julie Dobrow

Advances in Civic Engagement Research: Issues of Civic Measures and Civic Context
Jonathan F. Zaff, Kei Kawashima-Ginsberg, and Emily S. Lin

Shortridge Academy: Positive Youth Development in Action within a Therapeutic Community
Kristine M. Baber and Adam Rainer

Integrating Theory and Method in the Study of Positive Youth Development: The Sample Case of Gender-specificity and Longitudinal Stability of the Dimensions of Intention Self-regulation (Selection, Optimization, and Compensation)
Alexander Von Eye, Michelle M. Martel, Richard M. Lerner, Jacqueline V. Lerner, and Edmond P. Bowers

Author Index–Subject Index

VOLUME 42

Loneliness in Childhood: Toward the Next Generation of Assessment and Research
Molly Stroud Weeks and Steven R. Asher

Cognitive and Linguistic Correlates of Early Exposure to More than One Language
Nameera Akhtar and Jennifer A. Menjivar

The Legacy of Early Interpersonal Experience
Glenn I. Roisman and R. Chris Fraley

Some (But Not Much) Progress Toward Understanding Teenage Childbearing: A Review of Research from the Past Decade
Claire A. Coyne and Brian M. D'onofrio

Social-Emotional Development Through a Behavior Genetics Lens: Infancy Through Preschool
Lisabeth Fisher Dilalla, Paula Y. Mullineaux, and Sara J.W. Biebl

The Relation Between Space and Math: Developmental and Educational Implications
Kelly S. Mix and Yi-Ling Cheng

Testing Models of Children's Self-regulation Within Educational Contexts: Implications for Measurement
C. Cybele Raver, Jocelyn Smith Carter, Dana Charles Mccoy, Amanda roy, Alexandra Ursache, and Allison Friedman

Producing and Understanding Prosocial Actions in Early Childhood
Markus Paulus and Chris Moore

Food and Family: A Socio-Ecological Perspective for Child Development
Barbara h. Fiese and Blake L. Jones

Author Index
Subject Index

VOLUME 43

The Probable and the Possible at 12 Months: Intuitive Reasoning about the Uncertain Future
Nicolò Cesana-Arlotti, Erno Téglás and Luca L. Bonatti

Probabilistic Inference in Human Infants
Stephanie Denison and Fei Xu

Reasoning about Instrumental and Communicative Agency in Human Infancy
György Gergely and Pierre Jacob

Can Rational Models Be Good Accounts of Developmental Change? The Case of Language Development at Two Time Scales
Colin R. Dawson and LouAnn Gerken

Learning about Causes from People and about People as Causes: Probabilistic Models and Social Causal Reasoning
Daphna Buchsbaum, Elizabeth Seiver, Sophie Bridgers, and Alison Gopnik

Rational Randomness: The Role of Sampling in an Algorithmic Account of Preschooler's Causal Learning
E. Bonawitz, A. Gopnik, S. Denison, and T.L. Griffiths

Developing a Concept of Choice
Tamar Kushnir

When Children Ignore Evidence in Category-Based Induction
Marjorie Rhodes

A Number of Options: Rationalist, Constructivist, and Bayesian Insights into the Development of Exact-Number Concepts
Barbara W. Sarnecka and James Negen

Finding New Facts; Thinking New Thoughts
Laura Schulz

Unifying Pedagogical Reasoning and Epistemic Trust
Baxter S. Eaves Jr. and Patrick Shafto

The Influence of Social Information on Children's Statistical and Causal Inferences
David M. Sobel and Natasha Z. Kirkham

The Nature of Goal-Directed Action Representations in Infancy
Jessica A. Sommerville, Michaela B. Upshaw, and Jeff Loucks

Subject Index
Author Index

VOLUME 44

Relationism and Relational Developmental Systems: A Paradigm for Developmental Science in the Post-Cartesian Era
Willis F. Overton

Developmental Systems Theory: What Does It Explain, and How Does It Explain It?
Paul E. Griffiths and James Tabery

Emergence, Self-Organization and Developmental Science
Gary Greenberg, Kristina Schmid, and Megan Kiely Mueller

The Evolution of Intelligent Developmental Systems
Ken Richardson

Embodiment and Agency: Toward a Holistic Synthesis for Developmental Science
David C. Witherington and Shirley Heying

The Origins of Variation: Evolutionary Insights from Developmental Science
Robert Lickliter

Cytoplasmic Inheritance Redux
Evan Charney

Evolutionary Psychology: a House Built on Sand
Peter T. Saunders

A Contemporary View of Genes and Behavior: Complex Systems and Interactions
Douglas Wahlsten

Genetic Causation: A Cross Disciplinary Inquiry
Sheldon Krimsky

Pathways by which the Interplay of Organismic and Environmental Factors Lead to Phenotypic Variation within and across Generations
Lawrence V. Harper

Subject Index
Author Index

VOLUME 45

Introduction: Embodiment and Epigenesis: A View of the Issues
Richard M. Lerner and Janette B. Benson

Dynamic Models of Biological Pattern Formation Have Some Surprising Implications for Understanding the Epigenetics of Development
Peter C.M. Molenaar and Lawrence Lo

A Developmental Systems Approach to Executive Function
Ulrich Müller, Lesley Baker, and Emanuela Yeung

No Genes for Intelligence in the Fluid Genome
Mae-Wan Ho

The Lost Study: A 1998 Adoption Study of Personality That Found No Genetic Relationship between Birthparents and Their 240 Adopted-Away Biological Offspring
Jay Joseph

A Relational Developmental Systems
  Approach to Moral Development
  Jeremy I.M. Carpendale, Stuart I. Hammond, and Sherrie Atwood

Adolescent Rationality
  David Moshman

Developing through Relationships: An
  Embodied Coactive Systems Framework
  Michael F. Mascolo

Multiple Trajectories in the Developmental
  Psychobiology of Human Handedness
  George F. Michel, Eliza L. Nelson, Iryna Babik, Julie M. Campbell, and Emily C. Marcinowski

Positive Movement Experiences: Approaching
  the Study of Athletic Participation,
  Exercise, and Leisure Activity through
  Relational Developmental Systems
  Theory and the Concept of
  Embodiment
  Jennifer P. Agans, Reidar Säfvenbom, Jacqueline L. Davis, Edmond P. Bowers, and Richard M. Lerner

Integration of Culture and Biology in Human
  Development
  Jayanthi Mistry

Author Index
Subject Index

VOLUME 46

Demystifying Internalization and Socialization:
  Linking Conceptions of How
  Development Happens to Organismic-
  Developmental Theory
  Catherine Raeff

Adolescents' Theories of the Commons
  Constance Flanagan and Erin Gallay

LGB-Parent Families: The Current State of the
  Research and Directions for the Future
  Abbie E. Goldberg and Nanette K. Gartrell

The Impact of Parental Deployment to War on
  Children: The Crucial Role of Parenting
  Abigail H. Gewirtz and Osnat Zamir

Shining Light on Infants' Discovery of
  Structure
  Jennifer K. Mendoza and Dare Baldwin

Development of Adaptive Tool-Use in Early
  Childhood: Sensorimotor, Social, and
  Conceptual Factors
  Gedeon O. Deák

Edge Replacement and Minimality as Models
  of Causal Inference in Children
  David W. Buchanan and David M. Sobel

Applying Risk and Resilience Models to
  Predicting the Effects of Media Violence
  on Development
  Sara Prot and Douglas A. Gentile

Bringing a Developmental Perspective to Early
  Childhood and Family Interventionists:
  Where to Begin
  Anne E. Hogan and Herbert C. Quay

Vocabulary Development and Intervention for
  English Learners in the Early Grades
  Doris Luft Baker, Stephanie Al Otaiba, Miriam Ortiz, Vivian Correa, and Ron Cole

Author Index
Subject Index

Edwards Brothers Malloy
Ann Arbor MI. USA
August 28, 2014